SELF-INJURIOUS BEHAVIOUR

To the memory of Bernie Spain,
who believed in allowing everyone
access to knowledge

SELF-INJURIOUS BEHAVIOUR

a collection of published papers
on prevalence, causes, and treatment
in people who are mentally handicapped or autistic

Editors
GLYNIS MURPHY
BARBARA WILSON

First published 1985

© **British Institute of Mental Handicap**
(Registered Charity 264786)
Wolverhampton Road,
Kidderminster, Worcs. DY10 3PP

The publishers have made every attempt to produce accurately the content of all papers originally published elsewhere. Apologies are extended for any errors or omissions which have occurred. As good copies of some of the original works are no longer available it is regretted that the quality of some of the figures and photographs is not as clear as might be thought desirable.

(Hbk.) ISBN 0 906054 55 9

(Pbk.) ISBN 0 906054 49 4

Typeset and Printed by Birmingham Printers (1982) Ltd.
Stratford Street North
Birmingham B11 1BY.

Contents

Acknowledgements

We would like to thank the many authors of the papers included in this book, and their respective publishers, for permission to reproduce their work.

We particularly acknowledge the role of many children and staff from Hilda Lewis House in the formation of our views on self-injurious behaviour.

We are also most grateful to Mrs. S. J. Newbould and Miss A. Whelpton from BIMH for their untiring assistance in the production of this book.

GLYNIS MURPHY
BARBARA WILSON

Foreword

Self-injurious and self-destructive behaviour in people who are mentally handicapped or autistic is characterised by its chronicity and repetitive nature. It presents, perhaps, the most difficult problem of all in the management of people with these disabilities and, as the late Professor Alistair Forrest pointed out:

"Doctors, nurses, psychologists and parents have certain role expectations which are quite disrupted by a patient (allegedly under their care) who injures himself. This anxiety makes staff demand more intervention, whether by drugs, restraints or aversion therapy, and the increased (social) reinforcement this entails exacerbates the self-injury. This draws attention away from patients with less dramatic problems and leads to greater difficulty in staffing residential institutions".

A similar situation occurs in schools and in families with a self-injuring member, whose behaviour often leads to intolerable stress among other members of the family and conflict over management of the self-injury.

Older texts on mental handicap and autism offer little help or advice, but over the past few years there has been an explosion of interest in the management of self-injurious behaviour, which has arisen mainly as a result of advances in behavioural treatment and a recognition of specific forms of self-injury, such as those occurring in the Lesch-Nyhan syndrome.

A number of reviews of the literature relating to self-injurious behaviour and its treatment have appeared, but these are not easily accessible to the general reader, nor do they give sufficient detail of individual studies to enable readers to make a critical evaluation of the importance of their findings.

This book fills an important gap. It brings together in one volume a selection of previously published key papers in their orginal form, which are linked by the editors' commentaries on prevalence and aetiology, the development and maintenance of the problem, and its treatment.

The causes of self-injury are largely unknown and treatment procedures meet with varying degrees of success. It is, therefore, appropriate and helpful that our accumulated knowledge should be brought together in a form which can enable readers to make independent judgement of possible causes and treatments and which will encourage further research into this particularly problematic topic.

JOHN CORBETT

Introduction

Bringing up a child is a difficult task for any parent, the more so when the child happens to have a mental handicap or suffers from autism. Some of the extra problems arise from the longer period of dependency that mental handicap and autism usually entail. In addition, children who are mentally handicapped or autistic have a much higher chance of developing behaviour problems than children who are not handicapped (Corbett, 1977), thus putting an added strain on their parents.

All parents want their children eventually to lead an independent life, and promotion of a child's development is one of the most important parenting skills. With non-handicapped children, development is largely a matter of exposure to the necessary variety of experiences, since they learn readily by observation and modelling (Bandura, 1969). Children who are handicapped, however, need more structured teaching and training to acquire everyday skills (Carr, 1980a).

Most parents also feel that they need to protect their children from the vicissitudes of life until such a time as the children are able to live independently. This is especially important for children with handicaps, who are not only less quick at learning the necessary skills but are also more at risk of suffering (from bullying and teasing, for example) in a potentially hostile environment. Added to this are the parents' aspirations for their children to feel secure and happy whatever their handicaps may be.

When a child who is mentally handicapped or autistic begins to injure himself,* the people who care for him will naturally feel distressed. Self-injury is worrying, not merely because it may produce open wounds which need medical attention but also because its appearance suggests to those who are caring for the child that they are failing him. It may seem to them, because he is injuring himself, as though they are failing to make the child happy especially as self-injury is frequently accompanied by visible signs of misery in the child, including a dismal howling. Secondly, they may feel that they are failing to protect the child from adverse events in his environment, since they cannot protect him from himself. Thirdly, it may seem to them to be impossible to teach the child any of the skills he needs for independent living when he persists in self-injury.

Consequently, eradication of the self-injurious behaviour becomes the most important goal. Most people will go to enormous lengths to stop a child from injuring himself, whether they are parents or professionals. The methods tried will usually include physical protection of the child by

*For convenience we will refer to "him", "his", and "himself", but what is said applies equally to both sexes unless explicitly stated otherwise.

constant cuddling, protective clothing (such as helmets or arm restraints), and padding of hard objects in the environment on which the child might otherwise harm himself. Also, most people will wonder whether they are handling the child correctly and will attempt to alter their responses to him, both when he self-injures and at other times, in an attempt to alleviate the self-injury.

It is not uncommon for a bewildering variety of potential solutions to be tried, sometimes with different people in the child's environment trying different strategies during the same period of time. In this situation it is not easy to keep track of the effect of each person's actions on the child's self-injury and, all too soon, bitter disagreements may arise between those caring for him as to whose methods of handling are "right", and who is making him "worse".

The main aim of this book is to provide a source of information about self-injury to which parents and professionals can turn when faced with a child who self-injures. Although its occurrence is not very common, self-injury has been widely researched because it is an extraordinarily upsetting and difficult problem with which to deal. It is not possible to provide *definitive* answers to questions concerning the reasons why self-injury arises. Neither is it possible to be certain about effective methods of treatment. It is possible, though, to provide an insight into some of the potential causes and some of the treatments which others have used successfully.

Up until now this kind of information has resided in academic journals and books, to which most people caring for children who are mentally handicapped or autistic have no access. This book contains a selection of the published research, together with a series of introductory sections designed to guide readers through the research papers.

It has not, of course, been possible to include all of the published papers. Those which have been included are listed in the Contents pages at the beginning of the book under the appropriate Section. They have been selected for a variety of reasons: they may be the only published work on a particular topic; or they may be classic and much-quoted studies; or they may be modest reports which happen to illustrate a particular point well. All of them have been reproduced word for word from their original published sources. Details of these sources and the addresses of the respective authors most recently known to us are given at the end of each paper.

The reviews and references listed at the end of the book will provide further reading for those who are interested, and will give readers a wider view of the problem of self-injury.

As far as possible we have tried to be open-minded about the approaches to self-injury which others have adopted. We have, therefore, included some research papers which we feel are not necessarily useful contributions to the problem, but which are the best examples we can find of a particular approach. In this way, we hope that we can leave readers relatively free to make their own decisions regarding the most likely causes of self-injurious behaviour and the treatments that are likely to be most effective for individual children.

Definitions of self-injurious behaviour

Self-injurious behaviour is notoriously difficult to define unequivocally. Up until now we have assumed that we are all agreed about what constitutes self-injury but it is important, before we discuss its prevalence, causes, and treatment, for readers to be quite clear what we mean by the term. For the purposes of this book self-injury will be defined as: any behaviour, initiated by the individual, which directly results in physical harm to that individual. Physical harm will be considered to include bruising, lacerations, bleeding (internal or external), bone fractures and breakages, and other tissue damage. Most commonly, self-injury takes the form of hand-to-head banging and head-to-object banging. Other behaviours include: face and finger gouging or picking, where this produces open wounds; self-biting, where this produces bruising, bleeding, or even amputation; and self-pinching, where this produces physical damage.

Self-injury can be very variable in degree, sometimes only occasionally producing tissue damage, sometimes resulting in such a level of laceration that the child needs to be permanently restrained. The following extracts from published papers illustrate two severe cases of self-injury:

"Phil was a 4-year-old child, physically small for his age, who was confined to a crib in an institution for the mentally retarded. He attracted the attention of visitors, when he was not restrained, by the forcefulness with which he slapped and punched himself on his cheeks and mouth, banged his head and scratched his body. These behaviors, which left visible injuries, were part of his almost ceaseless motor and tactual activity during most of his waking hours." (Meyerson, Kerr, and Michael, 1967). See also Bailey and Meyerson, 1970.

(A patient with Lesch-Nyhan syndrome, who began biting himself before the age of three years and whose biting escalated:) "Eventually, extensive restraints were required to prevent self-injury. He was confined to a wheel-chair with his arms restrained in extension by splints, wore a helmet and shoulder pads, and at night was restrained in bed by a jacket and safety straps. In addition to biting, other maladaptive behaviors developed, including breath-holding, removing finger and toe nails, throwing himself from chairs and bed, screaming, spitting, neck snapping, projectile vomiting, banging his head and limbs. . ." (Bull and La Vecchio, 1978). See also p. 307.

Some classes of behaviour exhibited by individuals who are mentally handicapped or autistic are hard to differentiate from self-injurious behaviour. This applies particularly to stereotyped behaviour which has been defined by Baumeister (1978) as: "highly consistent and repetitious motor or posturing responses which are excessive with respect to rate, frequency, and/or amplitude and which do not appear to possess any adaptive significance". Such behaviour includes repetitive body rocking, hand flapping, finger twining, head weaving, eye-poking, and so on.

It seems clear from this definition that stereotyped and self-injurious behaviours are different. In practice, however, it can be extremely difficult to distinguish the one from the other. For example, repeated poking of the eye is usually considered to be stereotyped behavior; but if it is severe enough such behaviour can cause injury to the eye and so it could be termed self-injurious. In some ways, of course, these distinctions are unimportant and, as will be seen later, many of the treatment techniques which have been effective in reducing self-injurious behaviour have also been effective in reducing stereotypies. Indeed, it is likely that at least some self-injurious behaviour is a form of stereotyped behaviour which has acquired a different function for the individual because of the social consequences of self-injury (see Section II — Self stimulation and learned behaviour hypotheses).

Other kinds of behaviour which are considered by some to constitute self-injurious behaviour are less directly injurious than the responses described under "Definitions" on page 15 and in the examples of Meyerson, Kerr, and Michael (1967), and Bull and La Vecchio (1978), but can, nevertheless, be life-threatening. For instance, a child may repeatedly ruminate and vomit food to such a degree that his life is in danger (for example, the child described by Lang and Melamed, 1969); or he may climb so uncontrollably that repeated falls are likely and are considered by those who care for him to endanger his life (for example, the boy described by Risley, 1968). Again, some of the same treatment techniques which have been successful for more classical self-injurious behaviour have been effective in reducing these kinds of life-threatening behaviours, so that, although the behaviours may have arisen in different ways from other self-injurious behaviours, it would be unhelpful to exclude them from consideration within the field of self-injury.

Finally, a word is necessary about the range of individuals who self-injure who are covered in this book. The majority of individuals who injure themselves severely are children with mental handicap, but the problem is by no means unknown in adults who are mentally handicapped (Schroeder, Schroeder, Smith, and Dalldorf, 1978). Moreover, although self-injury is most common amongst people who are very severely and profoundly mentally handicapped (see Section I), it also occurs amongst brighter children. Some children with Lesch-Nyhan syndrome who have self-injured have apparently been of normal intelligence (Christie, Bay, Kaufman, Bakay, Borden, and Nyhan, 1982. See p. 123).*

Individuals who self-injure fall into a number of different diagnostic categories, including Down's syndrome, autism, rubella embryopathy, Lesch-Nyhan syndrome, and de Lange's syndrome, to name just a few. In general, though, there is little evidence to suggest that self-injurious behaviour is very different in form or function for handicapped individuals of different ages, abilities, or diagnostic categories. It is certainly true that some of the individuals described in the research reports have very few self-help or self-occupational skills (that is, they may not feed themselves, may not be toilet trained, may be uninterested in toys), while

---

*We will not be covering the deliberate self-mutilation seen in adult psychiatric patients (typically in young, depressed women). Further information on this topic is given by Morgan (1979).

others have considerable skills and sometimes even extensive expressive language. The types of treatment for self-injury contained in this book, however, can be applied across a wide spectrum of individuals (with minor adjustments in some cases). Where particular forms of treatment are thought not to be effective for certain individuals this will be explicitly stated.

Contents of the book

The main part of the book is divided into three sections. The first deals with the prevalence and incidence of self-injurious behaviour in people who are mentally handicapped or autistic, in normal children, and in animal populations. The papers in this section are concerned with the following questions. How often does self-injury occur in this population? What kind of self-injury is it? How long does it persist? And (sometimes), in what situation did it arise?

The second section deals with the hypotheses which have been generated to explain the appearance and the persistence of self-injurious behaviour. The papers provide evidence which has a bearing on questions such as: Why does this person self-injure? What makes him go on doing it? How did he start?

The third section is concerned with the question of treatment: How do we stop this person from self-injuring? It is arranged so that different approaches are covered separately (as is Section II) and some of the treatments proposed can be clearly linked to hypotheses covered in Section II regarding how the self-injury may have arisen in the first place.

Each section of the book begins with an introductory passage to guide readers through the collection of papers. It has not, unfortunately, been possible to eliminate the use of technical terms, particularly in the treatment section. However, references are provided to introductory texts which will explain the terms in greater detail for readers who require such information. Alternatively, of course, local experts may be able to help with explanations.

We hope that the book will not be used by isolated people, struggling with individuals who self-injure. We would prefer it to be used, as a reference book and a source of ideas, by groups of people, including parents and professionals, who cooperate with each other in an attempt to reduce self-injury in individuals who are handicapped and to provide those individuals with a more rewarding existence.

SECTION I

The prevalence of self-injurious behaviour in animals, normal infants, and individuals who are mentally handicapped or autistic

Introduction

Behaviour commonly labelled as "self-injurious" in individuals who are mentally handicapped or autistic can be very varied, both in form and in intensity, as we have already seen. Behaviours as different as face picking and head banging can be classified as self-injurious, using the definition given on p. 15, if they are severe enough to produce some kind of tissue damage. Some individuals may spend the majority of their waking hours engaged in intense self-injurious behaviour (SIB), while others may show only very occasional bouts of SIB. Consequently, the apparently simple question of how many individuals who are mentally handicapped or autistic show self-injurious behaviour is actually quite complex. Clearly, the percentage of a handicapped population regarded as showing such behaviour depends on the definition of SIB employed. Equally, the answers to questions regarding the appearance of self-injurious behaviour in other kinds of populations, for example in animal species or in normal human infants, are also dependent on the precise definition of SIB adopted.

SIB in animals

The study of animals can be instructive for the study of man, as has been shown in the field of operant learning theory, although direct extrapolations from one species to another are dangerous. A search for reports of self-injurious behaviour in animals will, however, be remarkably unproductive: it seems to be very rare for animals to deliberately and repeatedly injure themselves in such a way and to such an extent that tissue damage results.*

It is, however, not uncommon for animals, particularly primates, to engage in repetitive behaviours which closely resemble the stereotyped behaviours of people who are mentally handicapped or autistic, given certain rearing conditions. Such behaviours reliably appear in primates

---

*We are excluding here self-scratching resulting from dermatological irritation, such as that due to allergies, flea bites, infectious diseases, and so on. We are also excluding self-injury resulting from nerve damage, where an animal no longer recognises a limb as his own.

which have been reared in isolation and, during the 1960's, a number of workers in America studied small groups of isolation-reared monkeys and chimpanzees to learn more about the appearance and function of their stereotyped behaviours (Mason and Green, 1962; Davenport and Menzel, 1963).

Mason and Sponholz (1963) observed four rhesus monkeys, two of whom had been brought up in total isolation (the isolate pair) and two of whom had been within sight and sound of other monkeys but not in contact with them (the restricted pair). It is clear from the report that when these four monkeys were tested in pairs they all showed the highly disordered social behaviour typical of isolation-reared primates, spending much of their time in stereotyped crouching, rocking, and thumb-sucking, quite unlike normal wild-born monkeys. One of the pair of isolate monkeys developed a behaviour which could be termed self-injurious: the female (no. 19) crouched in a corner repeatedly rocking and head banging. It is unclear whether the male isolate monkey also head banged. Secondly, it is reported that the male restricted monkey bit himself repeatedly, usually prior to attacking the female.

Levison (1970), in the second paper, describes a rather similar rhesus monkey who was also isolation-reared but who did not develop the usual stereotyped rocking and self-clasping behaviour (perhaps because of extra handling). This monkey was accidently injured by a knock on the head from a cage door during part of an experimental training procedure. When the experimenter wanted to repeat the training procedure subsequently, the monkey exhibited head banging. The training procedure was later abandoned, but the monkey was observed to head bang in other situations, mainly when his feeding was delayed but also when alterations in routine occurred (such as strangers visiting the laboratory, or equipment being fixed to his cage).

Precisely why these monkeys head banged is unclear. It does seem likely that their disordered behaviour was connected with the lack of maternal contact during early rearing. Several investigators have suggested that, in the absence of the mother, the isolation-reared primate develops behaviour related to itself which would have normally been related to the mother; so that it clasps itself instead of clasping the mother, rocks itself instead of being moved by the mother, and sucks its own digits instead of sucking the mother's nipples (Mason, 1968; Berkson, 1967). There is some evidence from studies which have provided surrogate mothers that this is indeed the case for stereotyped behaviour (Harlow and Harlow, 1971) but precisely why some of the animals head banged is uncertain. The relationship between isolation-reared primate head banging and self-injurious behaviour in children who are mentally handicapped or autistic is further discussed in Section II (on the development and maintenance of SIB).

Reports of self-injurious behaviour in animals below the primate on the evolutionary scale are rare. The administration of large doses of caffeine and theophylline to rats and rabbits, however, has been found to produce self-biting (Boyd, Dolman, Knight, and Sheppard, 1965; Morgan, Schneiderman, and Nyhan, 1970). This has been studied as a possible animal model for self-injurious behaviour in a small sub-group of handicapped children, those with Lesch-Nyhan syndrome (see p. 112).

The third paper in the section on SIB in animals is a report by Morgan, Schneiderman, and Nyhan (1970), of self-biting in rabbits given large doses of theophylline. The connection between self-injury in these animals and that in children with Lesch-Nyhan syndrome is very tentative: it is quite possible that similar behaviour appears in the two populations for quite different reasons (see also Section II on the development and maintenance of SIB).

SIB in normal infants

Normal infants very rarely show repeated self-injury of the kind seen in people who are mentally handicapped or autistic. They do, however, often engage in repetitive behaviours, like rocking, which closely resemble the stereotypies of people who are handicapped. Sometimes, one of these repetitive behaviours is head banging, which is usually of a rhythmic nature and which occurs only at bedtime (often accompanied by rocking). It seems to differ from the kind of head banging seen in handicapped children who self-injure, in that tissue damage, bruising, and bleeding rarely occurs and, when it does, is relatively mild; even though much of the head banging is apparently on hard objects like bed headboards and walls (see Kravitz, Rosenthal, Teplitz, Murphy, and Lesser, 1960, p. 146).

The three papers in this section report studies of head banging and other "rhythmic habit patterns" in infants. Lourie's paper of 1949 contains a brief report of the incidence of rocking and head banging in clinical populations, followed by a long consideration of possible causes, interspersed with interesting, but tantalisingly brief, descriptions of particular cases. Lourie is, incidentally, one of the few to comment that head banging in normal infants can produce bruises and callouses (see also Kravitz, Rosenthal,, Teplitz, Murphy, and Lesser, 1960, p. 146). de Lissovoy (1961) reports the results of a questionnaire survey of several hundred normal infants up to two-and-a-half years old born in a New York hospital. The infants' mothers were asked about their children's present and past rocking and head banging. Finally Kravitz and Boehm (1971) investigated a number of "rhythmic habit patterns"; including head rolling, rocking, and head banging, in a series of normal infants and in a few children with handicaps. Most of their data was collected by questionnaire (apart from the hand sucking figures which arose from direct observation of the infants).

The three surveys seem to agree that only a minority of normal infants engage in head banging, that they tend to begin at about eight or nine months of age, frequently rock as well, and usually stop the habit when about three or four years old. There is some disagreement about the exact percentage of children who head bang: Lourie (1949) and de Lissovoy (1961) found about 15 per cent of normal infants engaged in the behaviour; Kravitz and Boehm (1971) found only seven per cent. A more recent survey, by Sallustro and Atwell (1978), reported a figure of five per cent. This difference is probably mainly due to the younger age-group surveyed by the latter two surveys (some of their infants may have started head banging after one year of age and thus were not included in their figures).

The function of infant head banging is uncertain. The three papers included in this section provide some suggestions; for example, that the behaviour is tension-reducing or stimulus-producing, but the suggestions are largely speculative. In Section II, on the development and maintenance of SIB, the function of infantile head banging will be considered further, along with the relationship of this "rhythmic habit pattern" to self-injurious behaviour in children who are mentally handicapped or autistic.

SIB in individuals who are mentally handicapped or autistic

There have been a number of surveys of self-injurious behaviour in children and adults who are mentally handicapped or autistic, both here and in America. Most studies are of people who are mentally handicapped and, of these, some have autistic features and a few are classified primarily as autistic. A few studies concern children who are autistic only. The first two papers in this section are of this type (Green, 1967; Bartak and Rutter, 1976). The second two papers (Ballinger, 1971; Schroeder, Schroeder, Smith, and Dalldorf, 1978) report investigations of self-injury in hospitalised children and adults who are mentally handicapped.

Where surveys have commented on the relationship of diagnosis to SIB among people who are mentally handicapped, it has appeared that SIB is by no means confined to particular diagnostic categories. Maisto, Baumeister, and Maisto (1978) found, for example, that the most common diagnosis for self-injuring individuals was encephalopathy (disease of the brain) due to uncertin cause (18 per cent of self-injurers), but numerous other diagnoses were also represented.

Surveys of the kind reported in the four papers included in this section, and in other similar surveys not included here because of the limitations of space (McCoull. 1971; Maisto, Baumeister, and Maisto, 1978), do provide some indication of how common self-injury is in mentally handicapped and autistic populations. In general it appears that between five and 15 per cent show some self-injury, although occasional surveys (like Green's (1967)) produce far higher figures. It also seems to be agreed that SIB is more common among the most profoundly handicapped (Ballinger, 1971; Bartak and Rutter, 1976; Maisto, Baumeister, and Maisto, 1978; Schroeder, Schroeder, Smith, and Dalldorf, 1978), only one study finding no relationship between SIB and intelligence quotient (Green, 1967).

Of course studies are not in *exact* agreement about the percentage of individuals who engage in self-injury, but this is hardly surprising in view of the way the figures were collected. Firstly, none of the surveys employed direct observational measures of individuals' behaviour, so that the data are based on retrospective reports of whether self-injury occurred. Such retrospective evidence may be unreliable: for example, if it is based on case notes, these may contain omissions; if it is based on the memories of staff or parents, then these may be inaccurate, particularly if long periods of time have elapsed. Secondly, it is rare for precise definitions of what constitutes self-injurious behaviour to be given in survey reports, so that those producing lower figures may have counted only the more severe forms of self-injury, while those producing higher figures may have included more minor self-injury.

Thirdly, the investigators have not usually described the length of time which they were surveying. Clearly, where survey questions concern the appearance of SIB in a whole year, or even several years of an individual's life, a higher rate of self-injury will be recorded than if the questions concern the appearance of self-injury within one month. Finally, the surveys have not usually included whole populations of handicapped individuals: most commonly hospital populations have been surveyed, so that differences in prevalence may reflect differences in hospital admission policies (for example, a hospital with patients who are more profoundly handicapped is likely to have a higher rate of self-injury than one whose patients are less profoundly handicapped).

Surveys which have examined the age of people who are handicapped and who exhibit self-injurious behaviour have tended to find that SIB is more common in the younger age-groups (Ballinger, 1971; Maisto, Baumeister, and Maisto 1978; Schroeder, Schroeder, Smith, and Dalldorf, 1978). However, the behaviour does not totally disappear with increasing age, and Ballinger (1971) reported a particularly high prevalence between 60 and 69 years, following a declining prevalence from 30 years onwards. Some studies have found that as many male individuals show self-injurious behaviour as females (Schroeder, Schroeder, Smith, and Dalldorf, 1978); but others have found higher rates in females (Ballinger, 1971; Green, 1967). Maisto, Baumeister, and Maisto (1978) reported that the female patients in their hospital survey were more likely to show milder self-injury than the male patients, and were also more likely to have multiple forms of self-injurious behaviour.

Some surveys have contained reports of a positive correlation between the length of hospitalisation and the appearance of self-injury (Maisto, Baumeister, and Maisto, 1978). This may be the product of a number of processes which retrospective surveys cannot tease out: hospitalisation might provoke SIB in some way; or alternatively, the appearance of SIB may result in earlier hospitalisation than would otherwise have occurred.

Either way, it would be expected that the prevalence of self-injurious behaviour within whole populations of individuals who are handicapped would be lower than the prevalence in hospital populations alone. Few surveys of whole populations exist, but those which do actually report prevalence figures of the same order as hospital surveys. Corbett (1975), for example, found 13 per cent of people with mental handicaps living in Camberwell, all of whom were on the Camberwell Register, showed self-injurious behaviour. Bartak and Rutter (1976) found that 70 per cent of the retarded autistic children in their community-based group had shown SIB at some time in their lives.

Quite how many of the individuals who self-injure detected in the surveys provide major management problems is another rather unclear issue. According to Ballinger's study (1971) only 14 of the 93 patients who were found to self-injure in the mental handicap hospital produced management difficulties (that is, less than 0.5 per cent of the total hospital population). Corbett (1975), though, found 1.3 per cent of his total survey showed SIB of sufficient severity to have warranted physical restraint or protection over long periods of time. Schroeder, Schroeder, Smith, and Dalldorf (1978) reported that a quarter of individuals in their survey, about two per cent of the total hospital population, were injuring themselves sufficiently to cause tissue damage which required medical intervention. Precisely what kinds of intervention were effective will be considered at length in Section III (the treatment of SIB). However, it is interesting to note that Ballinger (1971), Maisto, Beaumeister, and Maisto (1978), and Schroeder, Schroeder, Smith, and Dalldorf (1978) all comment that, although drugs were frequently prescribed for self-injurious behaviour, medication appeared to be an ineffective form of treatment.

Finally, there is the issue of the long-term prognosis for individuals who self-injure. Many of the reports in the treatment section (Section III) give the impression that self-injurious behaviour is a persistent and intransigent form of behaviour if untreated. This is undoubtedly true for people who self-injure very severely (see, for example, Murphy and Wilson, 1981, p. 403). Little is known, however, about the prognosis for less severe self-injury, and very few of the surveys of prevalence include a long-term follow-up. The most informative data is provided by Schroeder, Schroeder, Smith, and Dalldorf (1978), who found that 90 per cent of the individuals in their surveys who self-injured were judged to have changed their behaviour, for better or worse, in subsequent surveys. 21 per cent actually ceased self-injury without any formal treatment. Singh, Gregory, and Pulman (1980) also discovered that the individuals in their study, who were treated by behavioural techniques, remained substantially free from SIB after three years, suggesting that at least some instances of self-injurious behaviour can be reduced with relative ease.

BEHAVIOR OF RHESUS MONKEYS RAISED IN ISOLATION*

William A. Mason, R. R. Sponholzt

Yerkes Regional Primate Research Center of Emory University

Summary

1. Two rhesus monkeys (isolates) were raised in enclosed isolation cages from birth until early adolescence (16 months). Two additional monkeys of the same age, raised routinely in wire mesh cages, were used as a comparison group (restricted monkeys).

2. Isolates were paired with each other and with restricted monkeys in various phases of the experiment and in all received more than 1000 hours of exposure to the test situations.

3. The isolates appeared to be traumatized by the extra-cage environment. Crouching was their characteristic posture throughout the experiment. Few responses were directed toward other animals or the physical environment and the most common reactions to social contact were submission or flight.

Introduction

A large number of animal studies have demonstrated the important influence of experience acquired during infancy and childhood on later behavior. (For reviews see Beach and Jaynes[1], and Denenberg[2].) In his discussion of parameters relevant to studies concerning the effects of early experience on adult behavior patterns, King[3] recognizes seven variables as particularly significant. Among these are included (a) the duration or quantity of the experience; (b) the type or quality of the experience, and (c) the type of performance measure obtained.

This report is primarily concerned with the effects of the second of these factors, the type or quality of the experience, on the social and manipulatory responsiveness of young rhesus monkeys. In previous studies the social behavior of adolescent monkeys raised from infancy in individual wire mesh cages was compared with the behavior of wild-born animals the same age. Laboratory-reared monkeys fought more than feral animals, groomed less and were deficient in their sexual performance[4]. In the present experiment the behaviour of pubescent monkeys reared in the ordinary laboratory environment, as were the restricted subjects of the earlier experiment, is compared with the behavior of monkeys exposed from infancy to a more severe form of environmental restriction.

Method

Subjects

The subjects were 4 pubescent rhesus monkeys. There was one male and one female in each group. All animals were between 15 and 16 months old when the present experiment began and between 21 and 22 months old when they were permanently removed from their regular living cages for the final phase of testing. None of them had had previous exposure to any of the test situations.

Rearing conditions

All animals were separated from their mothers at birth and housed individually in cages providing a living space 24 in. × 18 in. × 15 in. Two monkeys (restricted monkeys) were maintained in wire mesh cages in a room where they could see and hear other monkeys. They had no direct contact with other animals, however, and their contacts with human

*This research was conducted at the University of Wisconsin Primate Laboratory. The authors are grateful to Dr. HARRY F. HARLOW for his co-operation and support. The research was supported through funds received from the Graduate School of the University of Wisconsin, and from Grant M-722, National Institutes of Health.
†Primate Laboratory, University of Wisconsin.

beings were limited to routine testing and caretaking activities.

The two remaining monkeys (isolates) were housed alone from birth in enclosed cages which minimized all contact with the extra-cage environment. A schematic view of an isolation cage is shown in Fig. 1. The cage included a living space and two stimulus presentation compartments, one at each end of the living space. The ceilings of these compartments were constructed of translucent white plexiglas and illumination of the interior of the compartments and of the living space was provided by two 25-W bulbs, one placed above each compartment. Access to the stimulus presentation compartment from the living space was through horizontal bars and sliding opaque screens could be lowered between the living space and the presentation compartments, thus permitting the animals to be maintained and tested in complete social isolation[5]. Ventilation was provided by a blower which also served as a partial masking noise. The isolation cages were placed in a room which was separate from the nursery proper. The isolates were tested for manipulatory responsiveness during the first 90 days of life[5] and one of them was tested on various discrimination learning tasks starting when it was about 5 months old[6]. Performance in these situations compared favorably with data for non-isolated monkeys of similar age.

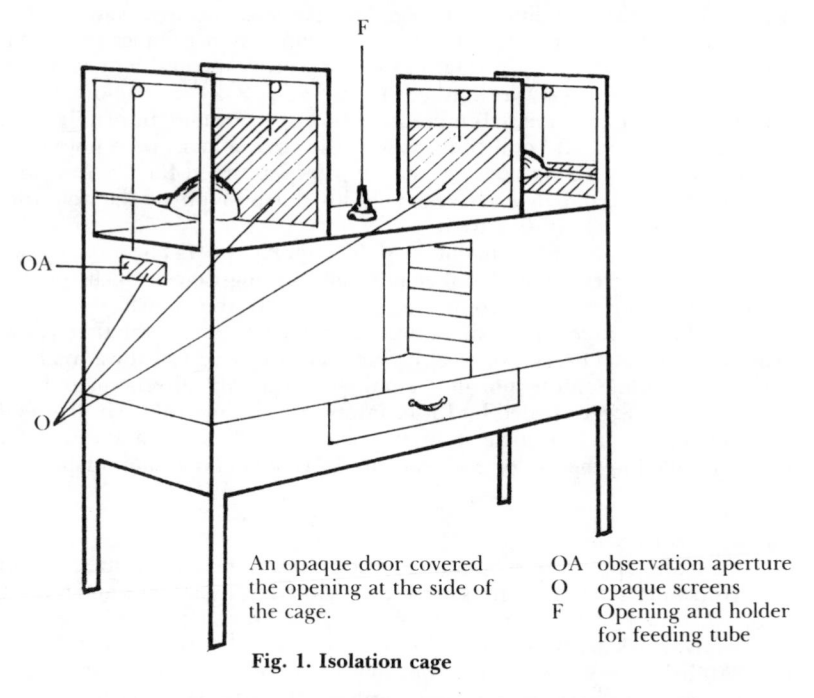

An opaque door covered the opening at the side of the cage.	OA	observation aperture
	O	opaque screens
	F	Opening and holder for feeding tube

Fig. 1. Isolation cage

Apparatus

Until the final phase of testing the monkeys were observed in a chamber 6ft long, 2ft wide and 30 in. high. It was framed in angle iron and had a front of clear plastic. A sliding opaque door could be lowered to divide the cage into two sections, each 3ft long. For competitive food-getting tests a short length of tubing with a cup formed at one end was inserted at each end of the chamber. For the last phase of testing the monkeys were placed in pairs in expanded metal cages (30 in. × 30 in. × 30 in.) within a colony room. The cages were shielded to prevent visual contact with other animals. One-way vision screens were used throughout to prevent the subjects from seeing the observer.

Procedure

The experiment was conducted in four phases, shown in Table 1. In Phase I (homogeneous pairs) isolates and restricted monkeys were paired only with each other. One pair was tested a day for a total of 15 sessions a pair. The animals were introduced at

Table I. Experimental Schedule

Date	Phase	Original housing	
6/17 to 7/26	I	Homogeneous pairings	Fifteen 45-min. sessions/pr.
7/30 to 9/27	II	All pairings	Fifteen 45-min. sessions/pr.
10/2 to 11/27	III	Competitive food-getting	Five 20-trial sessions/pr.
		Caged in Pairs	
12/9 to 12/22	IV	Homogeneous pairings	Twenty 5-min. sessions/pr.
12/23 to 1/19		Mixed pairings	Twenty 5-min. sessions/pr.

opposite ends of the chamber with the center door lowered. After 5 min the door was raised and the subjects were observed for 45 min. Social interactions were recorded on a continuous ink-writer according to a method described elsewhere[4]. Procedures in Phase II (all pairs) were identical to those for Phase I, except that pairings were made across as well as within the rearing condition variable. Two pairs were tested daily until each of the six possible pairs had been observed on fifteen 50-min sessions. On sessions 3 to 15 of Phase II a count was obtained of individual locomotor activity during the testing period. For this purpose the cage floor was marked off in 18 in. × 24 in. sections and a counter was advanced each time an animal entered a section up to the midline of its body. On the last five sessions all manual and oral contacts with the environment were noted. Phase III tested competitive food-getting. Each of the six pairs was tested for five sessions. A total of 20 grapes was delivered in each session, with the position of the rewarded food chute alternating by blocks of five trials.

The original housing was maintained through Phase III. The monkeys were brought to and from the observation chamber in small carrying cages, which for the isolates were completely enclosed. Upon completion of Phase III, the animals were housed in pairs in expanded metal cages. The pairs were homogeneous during the first two weeks and new pairs were formed every two weeks. Each pair was observed for a total of twenty 5-min sessions, five times in the morning, ten times in the early afternoon and five times after 9 p.m. Behavior was recorded by 15-sec intervals on a time-ruled check sheet[10]. During the first (homogeneous) pairing a 13-in. furnace chain with a ring at the end was attached to a counter bolted to the top of each cage to provide data on manipulatory activity.

Results
Homogeneous pairings
The isolates appeared to be traumatized by the situation and spent the majority of the time crouching at opposite ends of the cage, clutching themselves and rocking. The female (No. 19) usually sat in the corner facing away from her partner. As she rocked she frequently struck her head against the wall with enough force to shake the cage. The male's (No. 20) behavior was similar except that he more often looked about and occasionally lipsmacked, drew back his ears and vocalized. The formal criterion of a social approach (within 6 in. of the partner) was met on only 25 occasions (five sessions). In almost every instance approach appeared to be adventitious. For example, on session 9 when the first approach was scored both animals were sitting next to the center door before the session started and fell together as it was raised. They broke apart at once. On a few other occasions approach occurred during a burst of activity in which one or both monkeys would dash frantically across the cage, sometimes colliding in passing. The cause of these episodes is unknown. They lasted only a few seconds and the animals quickly returned to their usual crouching postures. The only clear instance of a response directed specifically toward the partner occurred on session 12. Following a burst of activity both animals came to rest on the same side of the cage. During the remainder of the session the male advanced a few inches at a time toward the female until they were about a foot apart. He then leaned toward her several times and gently touched her head. She made no response to contact initially, then withdrew.

The behavior of the restricted monkeys contrasts sharply with this picture. Locomotor and manipulatory activity were high throughout. Although the restricted monkeys also displayed the syndrome of crouching, self-clasping and rocking, this comprised a much smaller portion of their total behavior than it did for the isolates. Their social behavior conformed in most respects to the general pattern described for restricted monkeys[4]. They were scored with 527 approaches and both animals exhibited play, grooming and aggression. On a few occasions the male (No. 23) attempted unsuccessfully to mount the female (No. 22), but he more often engaged in autoerotic behavior, usually by thrusting against his leg. He frequently became highly excited and danced about the cage, biting himself and pulling at his hair. These displays usually culminated in an attack on the female. At first aggression was shown by both animals, but by session 3 it was apparent that the male was dominant and thenceforth he initiated most of the approaches and all of the aggression, while the female generally withdrew from contact. Social facilitation of environmental manipulation[4] occurred on 91 occasions and was displayed by both animals. The female, however, usually waited until the male ceased to manipulate and had moved away before approaching the scene of his activity and engaging in similar behavior.

All pairings

When tested together in Phase II the restricted monkeys showed no important change from the pattern already described. The male continued to be the aggressor and made 502 approaches, compared to 33 for the female. Both animals received high scores for locomotion (No. 22 = 6910; No. 23 = 4900) and for manipulation of the environment (No. 22 = 279; No. 23 = 617). The isolates also behaved together much as they had during the previous phase. They were scored with 12 approaches (on five sessions), all apparently adventitious. As would be expected, locomotor activity was low (No. 19 = 8; No. 20 = 89), and manipulation of the environment was infrequent (No. 19 = 22; No. 20 = 14). In mixed pairings the behavior of the isolates reflected the activities of their partners. With the active and aggressive restricted male the isolates were initially passive and either submitted to rough treatment or made ineffectual attempts to push him away. They showed no counter-aggression. Within a few sessions both isolates adopted a pattern of withdrawing whenever the restricted male approached. This resulted in high activity scores and in rank-order correlations greater than 0·90 between their withdrawal responses and his approaches. Because the restricted female made few approaches, the locomotor scores of the isolates when paired with her were only slightly higher than when they were paired with each other. Table 2 presents data for locomotion and environmental manipulation for each isolate-restricted pair.

Table 2. Total frequency of responses for mixed pairs. Phase II

	Pairs							
	A		B		C		D	
	19(I)	22(R)	19(I)	23(R)	20(I)	22(R)	20(I)	23(R)
Locomotion	56	662	2453	3906	101	912	3025	3096
Manipulation	36	58	47	493	8	105	10	430

Competitive food-getting tests

Little new information was yielded by competitive testing. In mixed pairings the restricted monkeys obtained 81 per cent of the food. The male entered both sides of the cage freely with all partners and clearly dominated the situation. The restricted female was more cautious. When paired with the restricted male she took food only when he was away from the food chute and always withdrew when he approached. She took all of the food delivered to her side of the cage when she was with the isolate male and she made hesitant approaches toward his side of the cage which caused him to vocalize, deterring her from going further. She entered both sides of the cage when paired with the female isolate and received all of the food. Both isolates tended to remain at one end of the cage unless approached by another animal and the primary difference between them was that the male

Table 3. Total frequency of response for homogeneous pairs. Phase IV

	Isolate	Restricted
Locomotion	175	512
Crouch	344	202
Initiates contact	4	64
Manipulates environment	141	251
Manipulates chain	218	5248

Table 4. Total frequency of responses for mixed pairs. Phase IV

	Pairs							
	A		B		C		D	
	19(I)	22(R)	19(I)	23(R)	20(I)	22(R)	20(I)	23(R)
Locomotion	77	257**	209	365**	178	275*	80	262**
Crouch	275	177**	109	50*	211	104**	304	167
Initiates contact	1	3	0	162**	0	69**	0	111**
Aggression	0	0	0	113**	0	43**	0	69**
Passive	3	0	77	0**	24	0**	32	0
Withdrawal	37	0**	203	0**	92	6**	73	0**
Grimace	3	0	110	0**	56	0**	69	0**
Manipulation	86	94	16	172**	75	112*	20	114**

* p<0·05
** p<0·01

took food when it was uncontested, while the female remained crouching almost continuously and took food only once.

Observations in living cages

During the entire period in which they were together the isolates generally avoided each other and were much less active than the restricted monkeys. Table 3 presents totals for homogeneous pairs for measures of crouching, locomotor activity, initiation of social contacts and manipulation of the environment and chain. Table 4 presents similar data on each animal for mixed pairings. Data are also included for aggression, withdrawal from social contact, passive acceptance of social contact and grimaces (believed to indicate fear or submission[7]). To provide some indication of the consistency of differences between members of a pair, sign tests were performed comparing responses over twenty sessions. The restricted monkeys received higher scores for locomotor activity, manipulation of the environment, and all social responses except withdrawal. The isolates were consistently higher in withdrawal, passive acceptance of social contact, crouching and grimaces.

Following the final series of observations the animals were separated and housed individually in expanded metal cages in a room with other monkeys. Non-systemic observations of the isolates made over a period of months gave no evidence of any important change in their behaviour. One of us (R. R. Sponholz) had an opportunity to observe the isolates in social pairings after they had been exposed to the normal laboratory environment for about two years. Their behaviour was essentially similar to the patterns already described.

Discussion

While the number of animals used in this experiment is small, the results suggest that monkeys kept in isolation until early adolescence are severely and persistently handicapped in their ability to cope with other monkeys and with novel situations. The isolates' behaviour can perhaps best be described as a form of traumatic withdrawal. Crouching was their characteristic posture during more than 1000 hr of exposure to the test situations. Few responses were directed toward other animals or the physical environment and the most common reactions to social contact were submission or flight.

It should be emphasized that the behaviour of neither group was normal, compared to wild-born monkeys. All animals displayed the syndrome of crouching, self-clasping, thumb-sucking and stereotyped rocking which is characteristic of socially deprived monkeys and apes, particularly in stressful situations[8]–[11]. Thus, the important contrast between groups is not in the presence or form of these behaviors, but rather in the lack of other responses in the isolates. This is especially interesting because the isolates gave no indication of unusual behavioral constriction when they were observed and tested while living in their original isolation cages.

The persistent failure of the isolates to adapt to the extra-cage environment is probably related to two factors: One of these is the age of animals when they were first removed from isolation (early adolescence) and the other is the contrast between the rearing environment and the test situations. While the specific test conditions used in this experiment were new to both groups, the restricted monkeys had experienced from birth a more complex and changing environment, including some exposure to situations other than the living cage, and they had had almost continuous visual contact with other monkeys. This experience was presumably a major factor facilitating their adjustment to the test situations.

References

1. Beach, F. A., Jaynes, J. Effects of early experience upon the behaviour of animals. *Psychol. Bull.*, 1954; **51**, 239-263.
2. Denenberg, V. H. The effects of early experience. *In* Hafez, E. S. E. (Ed.) The Behavior of Domestic Animals. (pp. 108-138.) Baltimore: Williams and Wilkins, 1962.
3. King, J. A. Parameters relevant to determining the effect of early experience upon adult behavior of animals. *Psychol. Bull.*, 1958; **55**, 46-58.
4. Mason, W. A. The effects of social restriction on the behavior of rhesus monkeys. I. Free social behavior. *J. Comp. Physiol. Psychol.*, 1960; **53**, 582-589.
5. Mason, W. A. Effects of age and stimulus characteristics on manipulatory responsiveness of monkeys raised in a restricted environment. *J. Genet. Psychol.*, 1961; **99**, 301-308.
6. Mason, W. A., Fitz-Gerald, F. L. Intellectual performance of an isolation-reared rhesus monkey. *Percept. Mot. Skills,* 1962; **15**, 594.
7. Bernstein, S., Mason, W. A. The effects of age and stimulus conditions on the emotional responses of rhesus monkeys: Responses to complex stimuli. *J. Genet. Psychol.*, 1962; **101**, 279-298.
8. Berkson, G., Mason, W. A., Saxon, S. Situation and stimulus effects on stereotyped behaviors of chimpanzees. *J. Comp. Physiol. Psychol.*, 1963 (in press).
9. Mason, W. A. Socially mediated reduction in emotional responses of young rhesus monkeys. *J. Abnorm. (Soc.) Psychol.*, 1960; **60**, 100-104.
10. Mason, W. A., Green, P. C. The effects of social restriction on the behavior of rhesus monkeys. IV. Responses to a novel environment and to an alien species. *J. Comp. Physiol. Psychol.*, 1962, **55**, 363-368.
11. Menzel, E. W., Jr., Davenport, R. K., Jr., Rogers, C. M. The effects of environmental restriction upon the chimpanzee's responsiveness in novel situations. *J. Comp. Physiol. Psychol.*, 1963 (in press).

Reprinted from *J. Psychiat. Res.*, 1963; **1**, 299-306 by kind permission of the publishers Pergamon Press Ltd., Oxford OX3 0BN.

THE DEVELOPMENT OF HEAD BANGING IN A YOUNG RHESUS MONKEY[1]

Cathryn A. Levison

Department of Psychiatry, University of Chicago, 950 East 59th Street, Chicago, Illinois 60637.

Summary

This report describes the development of head banging in a rhesus monkey which had been reared under conditions of early social and visual deprivation, but which had, after release from deprivation, exhibited no stereotyped behaviors. Head banging developed as a consequence of a particular set of interactions with the experimenter and subsequently generalized to other related areas of behavior.

Head banging has been observed in several diverse clinic populations: mentally deficient children, psychotic children, and blind children. The head banging pattern typically includes repeated and rhythmic blows of the head against a surface. There is little agreement among clinicians or experimentalists on the questions of origin of this behavior or its treatment.

Monkeys and apes separated from their mothers at birth show stereotyped behaviors similar to the stereotyped behaviors exhibited by abnormal humans (c.f. Davenport & Menzel, 1963; Berkson, 1968; Mason, 1968). These stereotypes include non-nutritive sucking, crouching, self-clasping, body rocking, and head banging. The same behaviors are also seen in animals raised with their mothers, but are not present to any significant degree (Berkson, 1968).

Observational studies of head banging in humans have been conducted by deLissovoy (1962) and Kravitz, Rosenthal, Teplitz, Murphy, and Lesser (1960) describing the behavior in noninstitutionalized infants. Onset is generally in the last half of the first year (Kravitz et al., 1960). In the majority of the cases, the head banging occurred at bedtime. In the 28 cases of the Kravitz et al. study in which electroencephalograms (EEGs) were given, the EEGs were normal. In the total population which they studied ($N = 123$), there were no cases of brain injury or other severe trauma as a result of head banging. A higher incidence of head banging was noted in males than in females. Rocking often preceded the onset of head banging and continued after head banging had ceased.

Very little head banging is reported in the animal literature, in contrast to the child literature. As opposed to such behaviors as sucking, crouching, and self-clasping, an activity such as head banging appears to be less general and more individual in its expression (Berkson, 1968). Berkson (1968) reports that head banging may occur incidental to rocking. Davenport and Menzel (1963) found that head banging was very infrequent in their animals, occurring in only 1 percent of the minutes of their test condition (this consisted of being placed in an unfamiliar test cubicle). None of the other five animals in our laboratory who were similarly reared exhibited head banging.

Since very little information is available in the clinical literature about the specific development of particular types of stereotyped behavior, the observations made on the animal in this report are considered to be relevant in the development of increased understanding about the onset of such behaviors. Although human behavior related to stereotyped acts is more complex and variable than that of nonhuman primates, observations and experiments with nonhuman primates may provide fresh perspectives into the problems of stereotyped behaviors found in institutions, inadequate homes, and problem families. In the monkey which is the subject of this report, the experimenter was

[1]This work was supported by a General Research Support Grant from the University of Chicago and PHS Grant No. HD 02477-01 from the Department of Health, Education, and Welfare. With special thanks to Peter K. Levison and Linda Crnic for their contributions to this work.

able to observe the development of head banging and, subsequently, to manipulate conditions in the environment which appeared related to the incidence of head banging.

Development of head banging in a rhesus monkey

Early rearing conditions and previous experimental history

The subject, a male rhesus monkey (Macaca Mulatta), was born in an established breeding colony on March 11, 1968, and was immediately separated from the mother. He was a subject in an experimental sequence investigating the effects of differential early rearing conditions on early stimulation-seeking, or curiosity-motivated behavior. All rhesus monkeys in the experiment were separated from their mothers at birth and installed in a surrogate rearing apparatus on the first day of life. The mother-surrogate chair functionally approximates many of the features of the natural mother monkey (Held & Bauer, 1967) — the infant is held in an upright position, is firmly supported around its trunk by a padded cylinder, has a furry substance attached to a sturdy frame for its hands and feet to grasp, and has continuous access to milk from a nipple. The chair was enclosed in an air-filtered and heated plexiglass cubicle. One group of subjects was restricted from access to patterned visual stimulation for the first 60 days. Restriction was accomplished by a translucent plexiglass chamber which enclosed the monkey's head. A second group was reared in identical conditions in the mother-surrogate chair, except that these monkeys had unrestricted visual access to the laboratory. All monkeys were removed from the chairs once daily for cleaning, an operation requiring from 5 to 10 minutes. The head of the restricted subject was covered with a porous bag during this operation to prevent patterned vision. The subject was reared in the total restriction condition. (For a fuller description of similar rearing conditions used for an earlier group of animals, see Levison, Levison, & Norton, 1968.)

Testing began on the first day of life. For 1 hour daily, the subject had the opportunity to supply patterned visual stimulation for himself. In the test session, a lever was fastened onto the surrogate structure at hand-level; the visual pattern deprivation box was converted to a test chamber with a projection screen facing the animal. Lever presses resulted in the projection of patterned stimuli onto the screen from the rear. The stimuli were: (a)unpatterned white light, (b)a black cross on a white background, (c)a set of six black lines randomly placed in a white background, and (d)a colored, abstract modern painting. On Days 60 through 75, restriction of pattern vision was terminated and the deprivation chamber was absent except during testing. Deprivation conditions were then resumed until Day 100. On Day 100, the animal was removed from the surrogate rearing apparatus and placed alone in a cage. The subject's stimulation-seeking behavior during this experiment did not differ from that of the other animals in the restricted group. A relevant aspect of the subject's early experience, in addition to the experimental conditions, was that on his fourteenth day of life, his arm was injured accidentally when it became jammed in the padded cylinder which enclosed the midsection of his body. The injury became infected and gangrene eventually developed, despite medication. His fingers self-amputated on Day 54. During this time, because of the additional medical treatment required, he was removed from the chair two to three times daily (rather than once daily as were the other animals), thus receiving 10 to 30 minutes of additional handling each day. His behavior at this time was not observably different from that of the other animals in the restricted group.

After he was removed from the experimental situation and placed in a cage, the subject's behavior was noticeably different from that of the other pattern-deprivation animals in the same situation. He did not exhibit any of the usual deprivation stereotypes. He did not rock, crouch, bite himself, or clasp himself. Restricted monkeys tended to be excitable and fearful in the post experiment cage compared with the visually nonrestricted subjects. However, the subject's emotional behavior resembled that of the latter animals. At least one other study (Harlow, Dodsworth, & Harlow, 1965) has reported an absence of stereotyped behaviors following rearing under conditions of total social isolation, but the animals were highly fearful. In this instance, the extra handling which the subject received as a consequence of his injury may have affected the subsequent lack of stereotypes and the relatively less fearful behavior. No interaction occurred between subject and caretaker except for the routine care given to all of the animals, which consisted of twice-daily feeding and watering, and cage cleaning and changing of bedding every other day. All of the animals were isolated from other human contact.

Development of head banging

When the subject was 1 year old, the experimenter began training him to enter a transfer cage, in preparation for daily removal to an experimental chamber for a new experiment. The subject quickly learned the following sequences for food rewards: (a)to run into the cage for food, (b)to sit, and (c)to let the door close. The cage training took about 10 minutes each day. However, on 2 subsequent days, the door of the transfer cage accidentally dropped on the subject, glancing off his head and shoulders. This was apparently very frightening to him; his response was to race away from the transfer cage and crouch in the left rear corner of the cage where he sat huddled in the corner. After this, the introduction of the transfer cage into his home cage was correlated with very emotional behavior: refusal to enter the transfer cage, even when very hungry; biting of the cage door; racing out of the cage; crouching, rocking, and head banging. He would sit in the left rear corner of the cage and rhythmically bang his head against the plastic wall of the cage. The subject was never observed to rock without also head banging. He would also bang his head when the experimenter was transfer-cage training other animals. An attempt was made to desensitize him to the transfer cage by extended, benign, and careful handling by a second experimenter, with little success.

At this point, for various reasons, it was decided to test the animals in their home cages and transfer-cage training stopped. The subject was occasionally seen to be head banging in the early part of the next 2-month period; toward the end, head banging was not observed at all.

After this 2-month period, the experimenter introduced some variations into the handling of the subject's feeding routine to determine the conditions under which head banging might reoccur, if at all. All observed instances of head banging are reported. The following observations were made, starting in his fourteenth month of age:

> *14 months, 20 days:* The subject was fed last, rather than in his usual position in the feeding sequence. Before he was fed he drank half his water, then, crouched and started head banging. The experimenter gave him a few pieces of monkey chow (considerably less than the regular portion) and left the animal room. The subject resumed head banging after eating the small portion of food.
>
> *14 months, 21 days:* The subject was fed last. When the experimenter began feeding the other animals, he immediately began banging his head. Head banging occurred earlier in the feeding sequence than on the previous day.
>
> *14 months, 22 days:* The subject began head banging when the experimenter entered the animal room and opened the food canister, preparatory to feeding the animals. Then he stopped, but resumed head banging when the experimenter fed the animals on either side of him.

On the next three days, the subject was fed in his previous position in the sequence; on the fourth day, delay in feeding was again introduced.

> *14 months, 26 days:* The subject did not head bang until the experimenter fed animals on either side of him.
>
> *14 months, 27 days:* Banged head briefly when the experimenter put in new bedding in an adjacent cage, but did not resume head banging until the experimenter left the room without feeding him, having fed the other animals.
>
> *14 months, 28 days:* Same sequence and behavior as previous day.
>
> *14 months, 29 days:* The subject head banged until the experimenter passed out sugar cubes (which contained their daily dose of isoniazid); this was usually done before feeding the animals. The subject was then fed first and he stopped head banging.

On the following 5 days, he was given his food in his usual sequence; no head banging was observed. On the sixth day following, delay in feeding was again introduced, and the training cage was reintroduced into his home cage.

15 months, 4 days: The other animals were fed first; after they were fed, he head banged. The transfer cage was placed in his home cage to retest his reactions to it. He became upset when the transfer cage was inserted, and sat in his usual head banging posture, as if to head bang, but did not. He turned his head and became interested in exploring the cage and finally entered it. He allowed the experimenter to partially close the door of the transfer cage before running out, which was unusual because, in previous cage training subsequent to his being hit by the door, he had run out as soon as he saw the experimenter's hand approaching the door of the transfer cage. After running out, he returned into the transfer cage, but would not eat there.

15 months, 5 days: Banged head when not fed in the usual sequence. When the training cage was put in, he was more apprehensive than on the previous day, made unusual vocalizations, and sat in the rear left corner of the cage (the usual place) and banged his head. He did enter the transfer cage to obtain his food, but was very upset and remained upset throughout the feeding routine.

Following this, the subject was always fed in the usual sequence and head banging was observed in the following instances:

16 months, 11 days: When holes were being drilled in his cage front.
16 months, 12 days: When a stranger was in the doorway of the animal room.
16 months, 18 days: When animal on left was fed.

A second set of experiments with the entire group of animals was begun at this time. In this sequence, testing was conducted in the home cage. Every lever response produced a visual stimulus on a screen immediately in front of the cage.

Following the beginning of the new experiment, head banging was noted in the following instances:

16 months, 23 days: When the door to his cage was closed (i.e., when the experimenter finished cleaning cage and he no longer could grab at sponge, etc.).
16 months, 30 days: As the experimenter cleaned adjacent animal's bedding (usually done by animal caretaker).
17 months, 2 days: As the experimenter repaired lever box on front of cage to the left of subject's cage.
17 months, 3 days: When the experimenter stopped washing the subject's cage (signalling end of opportunity to snatch at sponge, etc.).
17 months, 7 days: When the experimenter withdrew glove and sponge from the subject's cage (The subject had been attacking them). When the experimenter worked on apparatus on cage on left.
17 months, 9 days: Head banging on this day occurred in a different location: on the top of the cage. He also ran into the wall of the cage and hit his head.
17 months, 10 days: As equipment was moved into place in front of cage.
17 months, 22 days: When the experimenter fixed equipment on cage to left of the subject's cage.

Head banging was not observed to occur when a person was not in the room except under the conditions noted previously, i.e., when he had not been fed.

Discussion

In this monkey, head banging appeared as a response to a negative situation (cage door glancing off his head and shoulders) and subsequently was exhibited in other negative situations. The first three observations indicate that when the regular feeding schedule was disrupted, the subject very quickly began to anticipate not being fed, and head banging appeared progressively earlier in the feeding sequence, finally starting with the first act of the sequence: the experimenter opening the food container. However, after he was fed in the usual sequence, head banging did not occur. When delay in feeding was again introduced, he appeared to learn quickly that he eventually would be fed, and would then head bang only after all the others had been fed or after the experimenter left the room without feeding him. However, after the delay in feeding procedure was terminated, head banging continued to be observed in the following three general kinds of situations: (a) disruption of the customary environment; (b) in response to strangers; (c) at the termination of his interactions with the experimenter at cage cleaning time. All three might globally be described as negative situations, the third being the termination of an apparently positive sequence.

Although the number and variety of stereotyped behaviors increase with the complexity of the organism (c.f. Davenport, Menzel, & Rogers, 1966), head banging does occur in both human and nonhuman primates, although apparently at lower frequencies in the nonhuman primate. Even in humans the incidence is, however, variable depending on the population. In what proportion of the population head banging occurs is indeterminate, but Escalona (1968) found a very low incidence in the population of intellectually-average children whom she studied. Incidence is high among mental retardates, and low in the institution children described by Province and Lipson (1962).

Two relatively well-established and related ideas about the development of stereotyped behavior in nonhuman primates do not seem to apply to head banging. The first is that the frequency of particular patterns are related to the length of time of isolation. Berkson (1968) separated groups of crab-eating macaques from their mothers at 0, 1, 2, 4, or 6 months of age. Abnormal stereotyped behaviors developed in all groups, but the frequencies of different patterns were related to the length of time of isolation. Stereotyped behaviors developed more rapidly and to a higher frequency in animals separated in the first 2 months. However, frequency of head banging was not systematically related to length of time of isolation.

The stereotyped behaviors present in animals have also been described in terms of substitute behavior (e.g., Foley, 1935). The development of the stereotyped behavior is believed to be related to the lack of stimulation usually provided by the mother during normal maternal care. Care of the infant by the mother during a critical early period seems permanently to meet certain of the infant's needs so that stereotyped behaviors do not develop later in life, even under conditions of extreme monotony and social deprivation (Davenport et al., 1966, p. 137).

Mason (1968) suggests that behaviors such as digit-sucking and self-clasping have their counterparts in the contact-seeking behavior which is present in the normal relation of mother to infant. Berkson (1968) describes non-nutritive sucking, self-grasping, crouching and the stereotypy of location as homologous respectively to sucking, grasping the mother's fur and skin, maintaining contact and remaining with the mother either for sleeping or for safety when there is a disturbance in the environment.

In an experimental analysis of the relationship between early experience and later development of stereotyped behavior, Mason and Berkson (c.f. Mason, 1968) manipulated the early environment of the rhesus and showed a relationship between self-rocking and the quality of "maternal" stimulation. Two groups of animals were reared on a cloth-covered surrogate. One group was reared with a surrogate that moved freely about the cage on an irregular schedule; the other with an identical but stationary surrogate. Animals reared with the stationary surrogate developed stereotyped rocking, while those with the moving surrogate did not.

Headbanging in animals does not appear to be related either to length of deprivation experience or to characteristics of the early maternal stimulation provided. Similarities in form to early behaviors are not obvious in the case of head banging, nor are homologous behaviors readily identified. The head banging in the animal described in this report was clearly related to immediate antecedent environmental events. It may well be that head banging can appear in normal human infants or in mental defectives as a result of a specific set of events.

The suggestion that head banging may be situation-specific is supported by reports in the literature on human infants. Two of the mothers in the study by deLissovoy (1962) noted that if their children started head banging during the night, it was a signal that they needed changing; after the diaper change, head banging ceased in both of these cases. deLissovoy (1963) found a higher incidence of otitis media in a group of head bangers as compared to a control group of subjects. He also noted that in four of six cases where head banging was associated with otitis media, head banging appeared after the onset of otitis. The most severe cases of otitis media also showed the most severe head banging. In several cases studied by Kravitz et al. (1960), head banging had stopped, but started again with the eruption of a new set of teeth. Levy (1944) reports a case of a child head banging in an orphanage; the head banging stopped when the child's favorite toys were restored to him. The observation by Kravitz et al. (1960) that head banging also occurred in siblings in 20 percent of the observed cases also suggests that particular patterns of interaction present in the relationship between either mother and child, or mentally deficient child and caretaker, are of relevance.

Head banging, a low frequency behavior in nonhuman primates, developed in a rhesus monkey with no previous stereotyped behaviors as a consequence of a particular set of interactions with the experimeter. It is suggested that onset of head banging in infants and mental retardates may similarly be a consequence of specific relatively immediate antecedent conditions.

References

Berkson, G. Development of abnormal stereotyped behavior. *Dev. Psychobiol.*, 1968; **1**:2, 118-132.

Davenport, R. K., Menzel, E. W. Stereotyped behavior in the infant chimpanzee. *Arch. Gen. Psychiat.*, 1963; **8**, 99-104.

Davenport, R. K., Menzel, E. W., Rogers, C. M. Effects of severe isolation on "normal" juvenile chimpanzees. *Arch. Gen. Psychiat.*, 1966; **14**, 134-138.

deLissovoy, V. Headbanging in early childhood. *Child Dev.*, 1962; **33**, 43-56.

deLissovoy, V. Headbanging in early childhood: a suggested cause. *J. Gen. Psychol.*, 1963; **102**, 109-114.

Escalona, S. K. *The roots of individuality.* Chicago: Aldine Publ. Co., 1968.

Foley, J. B., Jr. Second year development of a rhesus monkey (Macaca Mulatta) reared in isolation during the first 18 months. *J. Gen. Psychol.*, 1935; **47**, 73-97.

Harlow, H. F., Dodsworth, R. O., Harlow, M. K. Total social isolation in monkeys. *Proceed. Nat. Acad. Sci.*, 1965; **54**, 90-97.

Held, R., Bauer, J. A., Jr. Visually guided reaching in infant monkeys after restricted rearing. *Science*, 1967; **155**, 718-720.

Kravitz, H., Rosenthal, V., Teplitz, Z., Murphy, J. B., Lesser, R. E. A study of head banging in infants and children. *Dis. Nerv. Syst.*, 1960; **21**, 203-208.

Levison, C. A., Levison, P. K., Norton, H. P. Effects of early visual conditions on stimulation-seeking behavior in infant rhesus monkeys. *Psychon. Sci.*, 1968; **11**, 101—102.

Levy, D. M. On the problem of movement restraint: Tics, stereotyped movements, hyperactivity. *Am. J. Orthopsychiat.*, 1944: **14**, 644-671.

Mason, W. A. Early social deprivation in the non-human primates: implications for human behavior. *In* Glass, D. C. (Ed.). *Environmental influences.* New York: The Rockefeller University Press and Russell Sage Foundation, 1968.

Province, S., Lipton, R. *Infants in institutions.* New York: International Universities Press, 1962.

Reprinted from *Am. J. Ment. Defic.*, 1970; **75**:3, 323-328 by kind permission of the publishers American Association on Mental Deficiency, Washington DC 20009.

THEOPHYLLINE: INDUCTION OF SELF-BITING IN RABBITS[1]

Laura L. Morgan, Neil Schneiderman, William L. Nyhan[2]

University of California, San Diego, La Jolla, Calif. 92037, and University of Miami, Coral Gables, Fla. 33124

A tentative animal model is presented for studying the self-mutilating behavior seen in children with an abnormality of purine metabolism. Each of four groups of rabbits was given a quarter-normal diet and daily injections of saline or 46.0, 61.5, or 92.0 mg/kg of anhydrous theophylline (1,3-dimethylxanthine). The major findings were that (1) the greatest number of self-biters were found in the 61.5 mg/kg group, (2) mortality was directly related to drug dosage, and (3) the onset of biting occurred earliest with the highest dosage.

The Lesch-Nyhan syndrome is a familial disorder of uric acid metabolism and nervous system function (Lesch & Nyhan, 1964). The most striking aspect of the disease is self-destructive biting of the lips and fingers. Clinical symptoms also include cerebral palsy with chorea, athetosis, hypertonia, and mental retardation. The severity of the mental retardation and other behavioral effects of the Lesch-Nyhan syndrome are difficult to assess, not only because of the patient's disability, but also because of the need to keep the patient in restraints. Furthermore, ethical consideration involved with studying human patients requires the exploration of animal models for the examination of relationships between purine metabolism and behavior.

While studying the effects of caffeine toxicity in starved rats, Peters (1966) observed incidental evidence that rats receiving a reduced diet and high doses of the methylpurine caffeine show self-mutilative behavior. In studying the biochemical structure activity relationships in rats receiving another methylpurine, theophylline, McDonald, Morgan, Sage, Sweetman, & Nyhan (in preparation) have also observed self-biting behavior. The purpose of the present experiment was to determine systematically whether or not the administration of theophylline would induce self-mutilation in the rabbit, an animal that, unlike the rat, does not use its teeth in aggressive behavior.

Methods

Forty-two New Zealand male albino rabbits, weighing 1.6 to 2.9kg, were housed individually in wire cages and maintained ad lib on water. They were offered a quarter normal daily diet of Purina Rabbit Chow. After receiving the diet for 2 days, four groups of 10 rabbits each were given daily intraperitoneal injections of 0.15N saline or 46.0, 61.5, or 92.0 mg/kg anhydrous theophylline (1,3-dimethylxanthine) in saline for 25 days. Two additional rabbits received 107 mg/kg of theophylline. Dosages were adjusted daily to compensate for weight changes. Theophylline was obtained from Mann Research Laboratories and Nutritional Biochemicals Corporation; it was added to the saline and heated until dissolved, and then cooled to body temperature before injection. Assessments of self-biting behavior were made by two independent Os.

Results

Percentages of rabbits showing self-biting in the saline control and theophylline groups may be seen in Fig. 1. Self-biting was observed in each of the treated groups but not in the

1. Supported by National Science Foundation Grant GB7944 and USPHS Grant HD 04608 and Training Grant HD 01187 from the National Institute of Child Health and Human Development. National Institutes of Health.

2. Requests for reprints should be sent to Neil Schneiderman, Department of Psychology, University of Miami, Coral Gables, Fla. 33124.

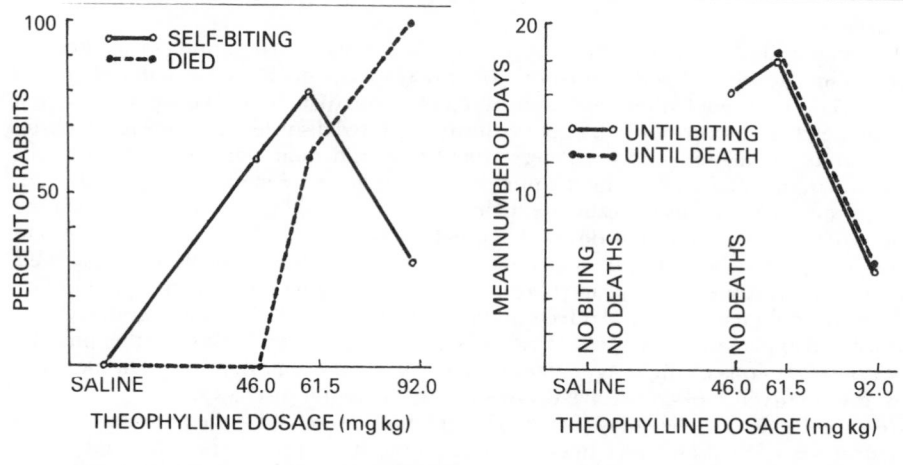

Fig. 1. Incidence of self-mutilation and incidence of deaths in rabbits treated intraperitoneally with theophylline while receiving reduced rations of food.

Fig. 2. Number of days from the start of the experiment until the onset of biting, and until death.

control group. The greatest number of self-biters, eight, occurred in the group receiving 61.5 mg/kg of theophylline. The number of rabbits dying during the experiment increased monotonically as a function of drug dosage. Analyses of x^2 indicated the presence of reliable (p <.01) differences among groups in the number of rabbits showing self-biting and in the number of rabbits dying during the course of the experiment.

The mean number of days until self-biting occurred may be seen in Fig. 2. No self-biting occurred in the control group. The mean numbers of days until biting occurred were 16.1, 18.0, and 5.8 days, respectively, in the 46.0-, 61.5-, and 91.0-mg/kg theophylline groups. An analysis of variance in conjunction with Duncan range posttests indicated reliable (p < .05) differences between the control and each of the drug groups and between the 46.0- and 61.5-mg/kg vs the 92.0-mg/kg theophylline groups.

During the 25 days of the experiment, no deaths occurred in the saline or in the 46.0-mg/kg theophylline groups. In contrast (Fig. 2), the mean number of days until death occurred was 18.2 in the 61.5-mg/kg and 6.0 in the 92.0-mg/kg drug group. An analysis of variance in conjunction with Duncan range posttests indicated the presence of reliable (p<.01) differences between (a) the two highest drug-dosage groups, (b) the saline control group and each of the two highest drug-dosage groups, and (c) the 46.0-mg/kg drug group and each of the two highest drug-dosage groups.

Although 80% of the rabbits revealed self-biting in the 61.5-mg/kg drug group, the mean number of days until self-biting began was 18. In contrast, the three rabbits showing self-biting in the 92-mg/kg drug group began after 3.0, 6.0, and 9.0 days. All three rabbits in the 92.0-mg/kg theophylline group revealed severe self-biting, whereas self-biting in the 61.5-mg/kg drug group ranged from mild to severe. Of course, others in the group might have bitten later had they survived. The relatively smaller incidence of self-biting in this group is probably attributable to the high incidence of mortality before self-biting would be expected to develop. In the 61.5-mg/kg group, the mean number of days of injection until biting began was 18, whereas in the 92.0-mg/kg group, no animal lived more than 13 days after injection and the mean was 6 days. Two animals given theophylline dosages of 107 mg/kg had convulsions and died within 24 h.

When self-biting occurred in this experiment, it generally followed a particular sequence that began with mutilation of the forepaws and progressed proximally towards the foreleg socket and abdomen. Death in the experimental animals was preceded by a marked diminution of respiratory rate and convulsions. Postmortem examination typically revealed evidence of hemmorrhage in the heart and lungs. In animals maintained on the drug for more than 2 weeks, hemmorrhages were sometimes also observed in the kidneys.

Discussion

The major finding of this experiment was that rabbits given appropriate doses of theophylline developed self-mutilation. In this respect, the behavior induced by the administration of theophylline bears some resemblance to that observed in human children with the Lesch-Nyhan syndrome, a genetically transmitted disorder of purine metabolism.

In a study of caffeine toxicity, Peters (1966) observed tonic-clonic seizures and self-mutilation in rats. Caffeine is a methylpurine in which there are methyl groups in the 1, 3, and 7 positions. Since rats typically use their teeth in aggression, it is conceivable that the biting represents a form of self-directed aggression. However, rabbits, now found also to show self-mutilative behavior, are much less aggressive animals and usually do not use their teeth in this fashion. It appears therefore, that this behavior is complicated. The mechanism could induce central effects in the brain or irritation of sensory nerve endings. A peripheral explanation is suggested by the findings of Luduena (1942) that theophylline causes puresthesions of the tongue, mouth, face, and upper limbs in man. On the other hand, the occurrence of convulsive death supports a central mechanism.

Gross similarities in behavior of rats, rabbits, and humans receiving methylpurine, as well as the features of the Lesch-Nyhan syndrome suggest that continued research in this area may provide insight into relationships between purine metabolism and behavior.

References

Lesch, M., Nyhan, W. L. A familial disorder of uric acid metabolism and nervous system function. *Am. J. Med.,* 1964; **36**, 501-570.

Luduena, F. P. Bronchial antispasmodic actions of theophylline derivatives including effects of continued administration. *J. Pharmacol. & Exp. Thera.,* 1942; **75**, 316-327.

Peters, J. M. Caffeine toxicity in starved rats. *Toxicol. & Appl. Pharmacol.,* 1966; **9**, 390-397.

Reprinted from *Psychonomic Sci.,* 1970; **19**:1, 37-38 by kind permission of the authors, and the publishers The Psychonomic Society, Inc., Austin, Texas 78705.

THE ROLE OF RHYTHMIC PATTERNS IN CHILDHOOD[1]

Reginald S. Lourie

Director, Department of Psychiatry, Children's Hospital, Washington, D.C.

Summary

Rhythmic motor patterns are presented as a normal phenomenon in the infant, appearing to serve the purpose of satisfying an instinctual need and facilitating motor and ego growths and development. Clinically, in the course of the child's use of such motor patterns, secondary values are often found to become prominent, and the repetitive movements then seem to serve other needs in addition to their organizing and mobilizing effects. Such secondary uses take the form of expression of pleasure, expression and relief of tension and anxiety, and provision of a form of compensatory satisfaction. In childhood schizophrenia they seem to represent also a regressive phenomenon. Such secondary values and uses of the stereotyped motor activity may cause the persistence of such patterns past the infantile period.

Investigations into the nature and sources of the rhythmic movements reveal that auditory, kinesthetic, tactile, and visual stimuli are their important components and that the auditory component is probably the most significant one in the head banger. The rate of the rhythmic movements seems to have a definite relationship to one of the time beats in the body, with usually the heart or breathing rate acting as the pacemaker.

The neurophysiological basis and the uses of the rhythmic movement are considered. Observations are offered as to the handling and treatment of such patterns where they have acquired psychopathological or nuisance value. Speculations are offered as to the possible use of rhythmic motor activities in therapy.

We have come to think of rhythmic activity as an integral part of almost all processes in the living organism. Rhythmicity is demonstrated not only in such things as the chemical and electrical aspects of physiological functioning, but also in the breathing, feeding, sucking, and peristalsis of infants. Crying is a more or less rhythmic expression. It was long ago found that the infant is comforted by rocking in its uncomfortable periods or times of distress. The rocking cradle was standard equipment for the child. Rocking chairs for nursing mothers are no longer fashionable, but it is reported that they too were a great comfort to young infants.

If we follow the maturational process in the asynergic, incoordinated newborns as they develop cephalocaudad motor control, we see a certain number of them, usually healthy in every discernible way, supplying their own rhythmic patterns. By the time they are 2 to 3 months of age, a few of them are rocking their own heads, the only part of their bodies over which they have some voluntary control. By the time they are 6 to 10 months of age, more of them are rocking their heads and a few others have gone into more dramatic forms of rhythmic activity such as banging their heads actively against their crib headboards or getting up on their hands and knees and rocking rhythmically back and forth.

This study reports the observations in 130 such children. The youngest child encountered in this type of activity began it at 1 month of age — the latest onset was at 2 years. About 5% more boys are involved than girls. In all these children these movements were definitely voluntary and without nystagmus, appearing to be thus differentiated from spasmus nutans and similar involuntary head movements.

With some of the children these rhythmic movements are transitory. In others they remain for months, or even years. In an unselected pediatric clinic population 15%-20% of

[1] Read at the 104th annual meeting of The American Psychiatric Association, Washington, D.C., May 17-20, 1948.

From Rochester Guidance Center, and the Departments of Psychiatry and Pediatrics, University of Rochester School of Medicine and Dentistry, and the Strong Memorial Hospital, Rochester, New York.

the children had rocked, banged, or swayed in one form or another for a longer or shorter time. In private practice the figure is smaller, 10%. In the 5% of children in which these patterns last longer they go on usually until the child is 2½ to 3 years old. Occasionally, however, we see it prolonged much past this point. We have seen it persisting in pure form in children up to 12 years of age. In the older children this rocking or swaying behavior is in some cases continuous from infancy, while others return to it under varying conditions. But in the vast majority, as the children have gotten older, these larger rhythmic patterns have changed in form instead of being dropped completely.

Sooner or later the children appear to realize that the adults around them are concerned about these motor activities. The adults want to do something about the hair that's rubbed off by the head roller and the bruises and callouses of the head banger. The noise made by the crib as it is rocked across the floor has had considerable nuisance value such as broken leases and irritable neighbors. Many pressures are put on these children to modify these activities. Many ingenious contrivances have been devised to harness the disturbing and supposedly aimless movement, sometimes justifiably, to allow the rest of the family a night's sleep. In spite of the ineffectiveness of such restraints and devices the prognosis is better than it is for snoring. The children either eventually decide to conform to the wishes of their elders, no longer need the larger rhythmic patterns, or else they substitute other patterns for them. We see a variety of partializations of the original rhythmic forms or isolation of the movement to one part of the body. Examples are rhythmic toe curling, tooth grinding, ear pulling, finger tapping, nose rubbing, and skin scratching, among many possible variations. Many of these substitutes can be carried into adult life, often acquiring other uses and values. Other repetitive activity forms which appear about the time of spontaneous disappearance of rocking and swaying are the stereotyped play patterns described by Bender and Schilder as impulsions(2).

Considerations on clinical varieties of childhood rhythmic patterns

When we examine these motor phenomena of a repetitive nature in early childhood we see them as apparently having a common denominator at their onset and for a varying period afterward. In origin they appear to represent an attempt to experience movement for the kinesthetic sensations that play an important rôle in the infant's development(8). In this connection Mahler(19) has observed that motor release is the most important and soundest device of the growing child to serve ego growth and obtain balance. These rhythmic activities seem at this point to provide a means for helping the infant in its mobilization to achieve control. There are apparently wide variations in the constitutional needs of different children for such movement play and experience, and it seems to be more marked in children whose control over motility is less easily developed. In some cases there seems to be a familial tendency to this type of movement. For example, one mother, who together with her 2 sisters had rocked their beds, now had 3 children who rocked their beds.

Clinically, the most common time for the onset and use of rhythmic motor patterns is when an infant is in the transition between one stage of growth and development and the next. A classical instance is the child who can only sit but is struggling with a drive to stand which it cannot carry through. At this point it may be found either beginning, or having an exacerbation of, rhythmic body movements. These often become diminished or drop out completely after maturation has proceeded far enough to allow it to stand. When this same child is ready to take its first step out on its own but keeps falling, then rocking, shaking, or head rolling may recur or again become more active. This phenomenon may occur too in the face of deprivation. At any point in its course a secondary value may become prominent, and the repetitive movement then seems to take on the nature of an additional need or satisfaction in addition to its organizing and mobilizing effect.

In some infants these rhythmic movements seem to have a predominantly pleasure value. The 6 month infant who sways, rocks, or shakes when music plays has been described as obtaining movement pleasure(16). This is seen in older children too in the face of lack of play outlets, monotony of interest and life, as in orphanages and institutions for mental defectives. In addition to the "pleasure from movement" factor there are a number of children who only rock when they are pleased with what they have accomplished, such as when they have had a particularly satisfying meal, are praised, are successful, admired, or having pleasant thoughts. It has been observed in this connection that in some children thumbsucking sometimes seems to represent more than a need for oral-sucking satisfaction. In such infants and children, it is usually found that they suck their thumbs particularly after their hunger appears to be completely satisfied. In such individuals it appears to be different from the drive to satisfy sucking needs. At such a stage, thumbsucking and its substitutes may be equated with the pleasure-expressing use of the other rhythmically repeated motor phenomena. Examples are the infant who didn't suck its thumb before feedings and when hungry, but sucked it for hours after apparent satiation of its hunger; the child of 6 who sat and rocked whenever he did anything pleasing to himself or was praised when he had the right answers in school; the 12-year-old girl who audibly and rhythmically sucked her tongue only when happy and when listening to musical selections she liked.

Probably in the over-all picture of their use the most widespread function of the rhythmic motor patterns in children is to express and relieve tension and anxiety. Kubie(15) feels that "manifestations even of normal repetitiveness arise from the recurrence of ungratified demands; in other words, when an instinctual demand encounters delay or ultimate frustration. To such an experience the child's inevitable reaction must be to try again, to restate its tension and need by whatever method of expression it has learned to use." Mahler(19) has observed that motor release forms an always available safety valve against anxiety. While the origins of the rocking and other rhythmic forms observed in this series usually are not in tension-producing situations, they are often used sooner or later to announce and/or try to relieve apprehension, dissatisfactions, anger, threats, boredom, pain, and frustration. Where this secondary value has become prominent, it is the chief cause of their persistence past one year of age. Their correlations with thumbsucking in this regard are striking. Indeed, thumbsucking at times is interchangeable with bed rocking, etc. The greatest use of these manifestations in relieving tension is as a prelude to sleep. If awakened, the infant who uses this "relaxational expedient"(10) must rock its body or roll its head to fall asleep again. One infant was encountered whose parents rocked it to sleep in a Taylor Tot every night and therefore it didn't have to rock itself. However, if it wakened, the parents would have to remove it from bed and rock it again. A 6-months-old infant may be mentioned who began rocking its head when the family was moving, stopped after a month, began again at 18 months when family moved again. There was also the 11-months-old boy who began rocking when his family was preparing to move and stopped when the parents were able to be more relaxed on arrival in a new home in another city.

This tension-relieving or expressing rôle seems to be closely related to another function served by these movements, that of supplying compensatory satisfaction. This is true in children whose movement is restricted, as Levy has shown in his studies on movement restraint. Many forms of stereotyped rocking or swaying movements are found in children confined by illness or in cribs, playpens, tied down in hospital beds, etc. Interesting correlations have been made between these patterns in children and the headshaking behavior of closely confined hens, the weaving tics of horses confined to their stalls, the upsweeping head movements of caged bears (18). Illness in particular may initiate rhythmic movement forms. Children with chronic limiting illnesses such as severe congenital heart disease are not unusually found to resort to this type of activity in the absence of any other. Acute illness may foster a return to previously present but long gone rocking or swaying.

This principle applies equally as well to children whose motility is constricted or disturbed on an intrinsic basis as it does to those with environmentally imposed movement restrictions. Thus some infants with organic brain damage resulting in considerable loss of motility will adopt rhythmic patterns to the limit of their ability to move. Then too, the child who is able to get around, but whose motility is awkward, distorted or frustrating, will seek compensatory motor satisfaction in stereotyped patterns of movement.

The same principle would seem to be applicable to children with "head-rolling rickets." The children presenting this symptom have, in addition to weakness, reportedly also shown bone changes which delay the acquisition of motor skills.

Similarly, children who are frustrated from achieving intellectual satisfactions have been seen to select this form of expression of dissatisfaciton and/or compensatory satisfaction.

Since mental defectives often have both inferior motility and ability to adjust it should not be surprising that many of them indulge in repetitive patterns of a motor nature, increasing in degree as they are increasingly unable to adapt successfully to the demands of their environments. Apparently in such defective children these manifestations can become very readily fixed and exaggerated as a form of satisfaction. In fact, it is so prominent in this group that some recent pediatric texts describe head rocking and banging as indicative of mental deficiency.

Characteristic of the entire group in which motility disturbances, confinement, frustration, and deprivation are prominent is the usual disappearance of the repetitive rocking or swaying and their substitutes, once the movement restraint is relieved, the disturbed motility is corrected, or better compensatory satisfactions are provided.

Another group in which these rhythmic body movements seem to serve a purpose includes older children with special problems limiting not only motility but also perception. A 7-year-old boy with 70%-80% loss of vision on a hereditary basis displayed a rhythmic swaying and whirling in preparation for carrying out requests or initiating any unfamiliar activity or game. Such whirling is reported to be not uncommon in blind children (21).

An 11-year old moderately severe cerebral spastic girl of normal intelligence, who had great speech difficulty, rhythmically rocked back and forth in situations where she particularly wanted to be clearly understood, and then she could come out with intelligible speech. One wonders whether in such cases the rhythmic movements do not supply a means of overflow of distracting and poorly directed motor impulses, providing a mobilizing factor much like the rhythmic patterns some stutterers use before they can get a word started.

Childhood schizophrenia provides still another opportunity to observe rhythmic forms of motility. Some schizophrenic children spend hours in rhythmic body play. An island of intact perception and contact with reality is often found in such children in their interest in, and response to, classical music, which can often quiet them in disturbed periods. In these cases the stereotyped, repetitive body movements appear to be in the nature of regressive phenomena, a return to infantile motility patterns, representing a return to a narcissistic level of movement satisfaction. These children can be thought of as being deprived of their usual motor outlets in the presence of the catastrophic process which has involved, among many other functions, their ability to use or obtain satisfactions from many of the motor skills they had developed before their illness.

One variety of rhythmic movement pattern which does not fit into any of the previous categories is the apparently normal infant who rocks only in its sleep. This form begins when the child is able to get up on its hands and knees or can sit up. It rarely persists beyond 2½ to 3 years of age. It is not a "relaxational expedient" in Gesell's terms, although some of these children do rock themselves to sleep in addition. The sleep rocking begins sometimes hours after the child has fallen asleep and may continue for hours. It will stop if the child is awakened. (It does not depend on darkness as does spasmus nutans, because it occurs during daytime naps too.) More striking possibly than the rocker is the infant who bangs its head while sound asleep, in some cases sitting up. Some of these children seem to be not completely asleep.

Five cases, 2 girls and 3 boys, have come to attention in whom bed rocking and body swaying are the presenting or prominent symptoms later in childhood. In each of these children, ranging in age from 7 to 12 years, the persistent symptom had its roots in early childhood, but in 2 of them it had dropped out of sight for 2 and 4 years respectively. An example of this group is a passive, repressed, anxious, unhappy, 9-year-old Italian-American girl of average intelligence who, from 1 to 3 years of age, had rocked from side to side in her sleep, lying on her back with her right arm tucked under her. At 7 she was exposed to a series of shifting environments because her promiscuous, alcoholic mother refused to care for her. In each foster home she began rocking in her sleep within a week of placement, persisting in it until she was returned home by sleepy-eyed, baffled foster parents. The rocking would then stop until her mother placed her again. This pattern continued for 2 years until the mother's asocial activities brought her a penitentiary sentence. After the girl was prepared for a placement with her maternal grandmother with her mother out of the picture, no further rocking was evident.

The nature and sources of the rhythmic movement

Explorations into the characteristics of rhythm, actively carried on from 1890 to 1920 (22), have been summarized by Elcanon Isaacs (13) as indicating that there is no rhythmic experience which is limited to one form of sensation. Rhythmic experience is a grouping of auditory, kinesthetic, tactual, and visual stimuli. These are interrelated and depend on each other.

Titchener's extensive observations (25) led to his feeling that the existence of the kinesthetic sensation is primarily linked to auditory stimulation, probably chiefly due to contraction of the tensor tympani of the middle ear. This thesis seems to be borne out by the head banger in whom the auditory sensation produced by its activity is not only an integral part of the rhythmic movement but appears to be its most important component, although the vestibular apparatus is also concerned. Following out this premise a series of preliminary experiments were attempted. A metronome was set in action at the bedsides of 2 diurnal, purposeful head bangers and 2 children who banged their heads in their sleep. The children ranged in age from 12 months to 26 months. When the metronome was set at the same tempo that the child was using in its head banging it invariably stopped the activity. The sleeping children remained asleep but quiet. When the metronome was stopped, only the daytime head bangers sooner or later (3 to 15 minutes) resumed the head banging. When the metronome beat was slowed, one of the awake and consciously aware children returned to its own preferred rhythmic tempo. One of the sleeping children woke up. When the metronome was speeded up, they all stopped their movement but resumed it within 15 minutes after the superimposed rhythm was stopped. These maneuvers were also tried with one sleep rocker but he did not stop his rocking.

The extremely small numbers involved in these uncontrolled experiments would in themselves make them unreliable. It must also be considered that the supposedly substitute auditory stimulus could have had a predominantly distracting value. They are, however, mentioned here as a basis for speculating on the rôle of the auditory experience in the head banger and to point a direction for further exploration.

Sherrington (23) felt that the ultimate basis of all rhythmic experience rests on a series of definite time units. Subjective time units or "mental time beats" have been postulated (13) and this is confirmed in the children studied here. In the great majority of the children who rock, roll, bang, or sway the pacemaker is the heart beat. Possibly this also has an auditory component since, as reported by Clausen, a great many individuals can distinctly hear their own pulses, with the sound localized to their ears. When the rhythmic movement is used for expression or relief of tension, anger, or any situation that will increase heart rate, the rate of rhythmic movement increases correspondingly but not always to the same extent as the rise in pulse. This is true not only for the body rocker or the head banger, but is also dramatically displayed by the older thumbsucker who, when disturbed, will suck its thumb furiously. The increased rate of the rhythmic activity seems not only to serve the purpose of stating and relieving the child's upset state, but also seems to serve a homeostatic function in that the rhythmic movement often has a retarding effect on the heart rate at such times.

In a minority of the children in this series the pacemaker is the breathing rate. The same acceleration with anger or stress and the secondary retarding action operates in these cases as is found where the pulse provides the subjective time unit. Possibly this phenomenon adds to the evidence of a physiological basis for Coleman's (5) clinical observation that rhythm of movement is the essential factor in development of endurance and postponement of fatigue.

Somewhat fragmentary but impressive evidence has been accumulated (summarized by Kubie (15)) which indicates that there is a basis in organic brain structure and physiology for repetitive behavior. Brickner's work in which stimulation of a certain brain area produces repetitive speech phenomena is indicative of such an organic function. In Kubie's own experimental work on ablation of certain cortical zones in monkeys, perseverating acts have sometimes resulted. Freeman and Watts (7) in their postoperative observations on prefrontal lobotomy patients report similar perseverative behavior. Clinically, in the epilepsies and some postencephalitics, repetitiveness in activity patterns is characteristic. Kubie concludes, "The brain is so organized as to offer a physiological substratum for automatic repetitiveness, both of fragments of behavior and of more complex patterns of behavior."

It is felt that such a concept of a neuro-physiological basis for repetitive, stereotyped activity may be needed to explain the sleeping bed rocker and head banger. One wonders if during sleep, with cortical inhibition diminished, reflex motor expression of rhythmic activity of the brain at rest is not permitted. Adrian (1) points out that "the physical source of an act may be thought of as a more or less stable pattern of electrical eddies forming itself in some part of the brain. The pattern, like a system of ripples, may expand and dominate the brain for the time being or it may remain in the larval form, ready to grow when the conditions are favorable to it. Since the rhythmic motor activities in some children are suspected of supplying a fundamental need by playing a part in the expression of instinctual drives and furthering ego growth, one wonders, when the use of the repetitive motility patterns is not compatible with the conditions and pressures in a child's environment, whether these patterns may not be suppressed but remain in larval form, in Adrian's terms, ready to be expressed when conditions are more favorable, as during sleep.

One cannot leave a discussion of the nature and sources of the need for rhythmic expression in the infant and child without being tempted to speculate on the role of prenatal factors. This has been mentioned but discarded, but the possibility of persistence of remnants or memory traces of intrauterine experience is not remote and cannot be discounted entirely (11). During its intrauterine existence the fœtus is constantly exposed to a variety of rhythmic experiences, the most prominent of which is the aortic pulse which can often be easily palpated through the pregnant uterus in the later stages of pregnancy. It is conceivable that during times of stress or tension the infant could be, through rhythmic body activity, attempting to recreate the conditions of the period of its life in which it had its greatest security.

The use of the rhythmic movement

We may possibly better understand the child's use of rhythmic movement if we scrutinize the rhythmic and movement components separately. First, considering the repetition of movement, Susan Isaacs (14) has summarized its most obvious uses in children as an impulse to growth, and as a means of developing movement skills by repeating movements, at the same time providing a form of pleasure. Children, like adults, freely use movement as one of the manifestations through which they express their dissatisfaction or discomposure. The anxiety-driven child may not infrequently be hyperactive. Conversely, anxiety or tension may be found in the child who becomes less active, easily fatigued, or lethargic.

Considering the rhythmic component of such stereotyped movement, it was accepted as far back as the Greek dance and expressed by Darwin that "emotional expression belongs to rhythmical forms" (6). Wundt felt from his studies (26) that rhythm has a large element of affective tone associated with it, that it arises from feelings of expectation and satisfaction, and that it depends on repetition of feelings of tension. In fact, rhythm is defined as movement in time characterized by alternation of tension and relaxation.

On the basis of this evidence it is suggested that rhythm and movement serve similar roles and complement each other in their association to further growth, express tension and pleasure, and achieve relaxation.

Howard Hanson, approaching the problem from the musician's viewpoint of the effects of rhythm, points out (12) that rhythm is the modality through which effects are largely obtained which are soothing or exhilarating, quieting or disturbing:

> Everything else being equal, the further the tempo is accelerated from the pulse rate — the greater becomes the emotional tension.
> If the rhythm is regular and the accents remain strictly in conformity with the basic pattern, the effect may be exhilarating, but will not be disturbing.
> Rhythmic tension is heightened by the extent to which the dynamic accent is misplaced in terms of metric accent.

It would seem that Hanson's postulates recognize the same basis for the use of rhythm in music as has been seen here in the child expressing or attempting to relieve its tension, expressing pleasure and anger. Looking further, we can suspect the latter purpose not only in popular music as Hanson had, but also in such mobilizing and tension-building activities as the war dances of primitives.

At some time or other in its course most parents and many doctors equate the child's bed rocking and some of the other repetitive movements with genital masturbation. There is no clear evidence for this equation in the younger children in terms of the rhythmic activity being a substitute for genital masturbation. We can confirm Langford's observations that erections do not occur as part of such activity in boys. However, a rare individual has been seen who was frustrated by parents in masturbation during the phallic stage and who then returned to rhythmic motor patterns. Under these circumstances the old rhythmic patterns seemed to be serving a new function in these older children, appearing to some extent to have acquired the same values as the denied form of masturbation.

Therapeutic considerations

It is only a relative minority of parents who become concerned about the varied rhythmic manifestations in their children, because if the rhythmic patterns do not get out of bounds or take on other values most parents seem to realize intuitively their normalcy. Where the repetitive movements have become more than annoying or reached symptom proportions, the problem of relieving them has been approached from 3 aspects. First, in those cases where it has been troublesome and appeared to have taken on values other than its normal ones in growth and development, an attempt has been made to replace the rhythmic movement with a rhythmic auditory stimulus (as described earlier) with the intent of interrupting the undesired activity. Results have been variable, but in a few cases it has been reported by parents that sometimes, once the movement pattern is replaced or substituted for by tapping or by using a metronome, the child does not resume the rocking that night. One parent bought a loud-ticking alarm clock, and reported that the bed rocking disappeared except for occasional recurrences.

A second and somewhat more fruitful approach has been to attempt to make the rhythmic movements purposeful. One mother put the swaying and rocking to music with reportedly good results in relieving the inconvenient rocking. Hobby horses, swings, see-saws, participation in rhythm bands, eurythmics, etc., have been prescribed for such children, but again with variable results. Of 10 children so approached parents reported definite decrease in frequency and intensity of the rhythmic activity in 2, and definite "cures" in 2 others. Since all 4 children were 18 to 28 months of age it must be considered (18) that they were possibly ready to give up the rhythmic patterns in any case. However, in blind children this approach was almost specific in relieving the need to precede activity with swaying or whirling.

Probably the most constructive approach when these repetitive patterns are found is to use them as an indication that one should scrutinize the emotional climate and environment in which the child is functioning, looking particularly for constrictions and tension-producing conditions, as Langford suggests (17). This is particularly true in children over 2½ years of age, including defective children.

Finally, after seeing how rhythmic motor patterns have been used by normal children in facilitating normal growth and development and also by handicapped children to help achieve better adaptation, the potentialities of the use of such rhythmic activities and therapeutic tools with disturbed children should be considered. The observations reported here on the blind and cerebral palsied children may indicate that similar approaches might be more extensively attempted with other handicapped children. Bender and Boas (3) have successfully used music and creative dance in the study, therapy, and training of deviate children. In some schizophrenic children, their rhythmic patterns offer one of the few means through which they can be approached by a therapist in establishing the relationships so necessary for treatment.

Bibliography

1. Adrian, E. C. The mental and the physical origins of behavior. *Int. J. Psychonal.,* 1946; **27,** 1.
2. Bender, L., Schilder, P. Impulsions. *Arch. Neurol. & Psychiat.,* 1940; **44,** 990.
3. Bender, L., Boas, F. Creative dance in therapy. *Am. J. Orthopsychiat.,* 1941; **11,** 235.
4. Brickner, R. M. A human cortical area producing repetitive phenomena when stimulated. *J. Neurophysiol.,* 1940; **3,** 128.
5. Coleman, W. M. Psychological significance of the bodily rhythms. *J. Comp. Psychol.,* 1921; **1,** 213.

6. Darwin. C. *The Expression of the Emotions.* London: J. Murray, 1872.
7. Freeman, W., Watts, J. W. An interpretation of the functions of the frontal lobe based upon observations in forty-eight cases of pre-frontal lobotomy. *Yale J. Biol. & Med.,* 1939; **11,** 527.
8. Freud, A., Burlingham, D. *Infants Without Families.* New York: Internat. Univ. Press, 1944.
9. Gee, S. Miscellanies. *St. Bartholomew's Hospital Rep.,* 1886; **22,** 96.
10. Gessel, A., Ilg, F. L. Infant and Child in the Culture of Today. New York: Harper & Bros., 1943.
11. Greenacre, P. The predisposition to anxiety. *Psychoanal. Quart.,* 1941; **10,** 66.
12. Hanson, H. Some objective studies of rhythm in music. *Am. J. Psychiat.,* 1944; **101,** 364.
13. Isaacs, Elcanon. The nature of the rhythmic experience. *Psychol. Rev.,* 1920; **27,** 270.
14. Issacs, Susan. *The Nursery Years.* New York: Vanguard Press, 1938.
15. Kubie, L. S. The repetitive core of neurosis. *Psychoanal. Quart.,* 1941; **10,** 23.
16. Landauer, K. Die kinderliche Bewegungsunruhe. *Internat. z-f. Psychoanal.,* 1926; **12,** 279.
17. Langford, W. S. *In* Holt and MacIntosh, *Holt's Diseases of Infancy and Childhood, (11th edn.)* New York: Appleton—Century, 1940.
18. Levy, D. M. On the problem of movement restraint. *Am. J. Orthopsychiat.,* 1944; **14,** 644.
19. Mahler, M. S. *Ego-psychology applied to behavior problems. In* Lewis & Pacella, *Modern Trends in Child Psychiatry.* New York: Internat. Univ. Press, 1945.
20. Mustafa, K. Die factatio bei kindern. *Monats. F. Psych.,* 1936; **93,** 185.
21. New York State Dept. of Welfare, Division of Pre-School Blind Children. Personal communication from M. Vanden Broek.
22. Ruckmich, C. A. Bibliography of rhythm. *Am. J. Psychol.,* 1924; **35,** 407.
23. Sherrington, C. S. *The Integrative Action of the Nervous System.* New Haven: Yale Univ. Press, 1906.
24. Sontag, L. W., Wallace, R. F. The response of the human foetus to sound stimuli. *Child Devel.,* 1935; **6,** 253.
25. Titchener, E. B. *Textbook of Psychology.* New York: Macmillan, 1919.
26. Wundt, W. *Vorlesungen über der menschen und thier-seele. (3rd edn.)* Hamburg & Leipzig: L. Voss, 1897.

HEAD BANGING IN EARLY CHILDHOOD
A STUDY OF INCIDENCE

Vladimir de Lissovoy

Associate Professor of Child Development and Family Relationships, College of Home Economics, The Pennsylvania State University, University Park, Pa.

Summary

On the basis of 75.5 per cent returns of questionnaires sent to mothers who gave birth to normal full-term babies in an upstate New York hospital during the year 1958, 57 children were identified by mothers as head bangers (15.2 per cent of the sample). Of these 44 were boys and 13 girls. In addition to the children who were head bangers 46 were crib rockers only.

Head banging is a curious behavior pattern sometimes seen in infancy and early childhood. This activity consists of repetitive movements marked by a definite rhythm and monotonous continuity. The head is struck rhythmically against the headboard, side railing of the crib, or other objects. This is not a tantrum type of behavior but is marked by an almost compulsive repetitiveness. A systematic description of this behavior based on observations of head bangers is to be found in other publications.[1, 2]

Most of the references dealing with head banging describe its frequency with such words as "often," "frequent," and "common." The lack of statistical reference in judging incidence suggests caution in the use of these words for such behavior.

Lourie[3] found that 15 to 20 per cent of children in "an unselected pediatric clinic population" had "rocked, banged or swayed in one form or another for a longer or shorter time." He suggests that 10 per cent of the children seen in private practice manifest rhythmic behavior patterns. By contrast Margaret Mead[6] stated, "I have never seen a case of rhythmic behavior which you describe."

Levy and Patrick[4] studied the relation of headaches and fainting in mothers to infantile convulsions, head banging, and breath holding. Of a total of 422 children, 14 were head bangers (3.32 per cent); of these 10 were boys and 4 were girls.

The incidence of Negro children with rhythmic behavior patterns has been estimated by Roland Scott[5] to be 10 per cent of a hospital population.

This study attempts to establish the incidence of head banging in a population of normal, not hospitalized infants and young children.

Sample and methodology

The sample consisted of 487 normal, full-term babies born in an upstate New York hospital during 1958. From the hospital records the date of birth, weight at birth, birth order, age of mother, and occupation of the father were obtained.

Mothers were contacted by mail. A letter explained the purpose of the study and a short questionnaire together with a return-addressed envelope was included. A total of 374 replies were received (76.8 per cent); of these 6 were not used. Two of the children had died since birth; 4 questionnaires left out most of the needed information. The data presented in this study are based upon a 75.5 per cent return of questionnaires. An examination of the sex distribution of the children whose mothers failed to return the questionnaire disclosed no bias in favor of either sex.

The questionnaire included two main questions:

1. Some children rock back and forth for a long period of time, either in their cribs or in bed. Usually children are on their hands and knees when they do this although other positions are commonly assumed. Did your child ever go through this stage?

2. In some cases a child will hit his head over and over against a pillow, the head-board, the side of the crib, or the back of the sofa. We do not mean bang his head on the floor in anger or in a tantrum, rather we mean a persistent, habitlike banging. Did your child ever go through this stage?

The mothers were also asked to indicate when rhythmic behavior was first noted and to indicate if the child at the present time rocked or banged his head.

The question regarding crib rocking was included because Lourie[3] had noted these two behavior patterns to be concomitant. Also, in a previous study[1, 2] this investigator noted that crib rocking or other rhythmic behavior consistently preceded the onset of head banging.

Results

It will be noted from the data in Table I that boys tend to exceed girls in the total sample and that 57 children, or 15.2 per cent, were or had been head bangers. The prevalence of boys among head bangers has been noted by Lourie,[3] Levy and Patrick,[4] Kravitz,[7] and de Lissovoy.[1]

Table I. Incidence of head banging in 374 normal, not hospitalized children aged 19 to 32 months

	Boys (N = 198)	Girls (N = 176)	Total (N = 374)
Number of head bangers	44	13	57
Per cent of head bangers	22.3	7.4	15.2

The average age of mothers of children who were head bangers was 26.22 years; mothers whose children did not follow this pattern of behavior averaged 27.40 years of age.

The occupation of fathers by Shartle's[8] classification:

Professional	5
Semiprofessional	2
Business, proprietors, and managers	6
Clerical	5
Crafts, operatives, and laborers	37
Students	2
Total	57

In addition to the 57 head bangers, 32 of whom were also identified by their mothers as crib rockers, 19 boys and 27 girls were crib rockers only. There was no difference in birth weight between boys who were rockers and those who were not. Girls who were "rockers only" were on the average 3 ounces lighter at birth than were nonrocking girls. An examination of birth weight of head bangers showed the differences noted in Table II.

Table II. Birth weight of head bangers and non-head bangers by sex (average birth weight in ounces)

	Head bangers	Non-head bangers
Boys	(N = 44) 119.25	(N = 134) 119.41
Girls	(N = 13) 109.23	(N = 136) 117.53

It will be seen from the data in Table II that girls who were head bangers were, on the average, 8 ounces lighter at birth than were non-head-banging girls. This difference did not prevail in boys.

Fifteen of the head bangers were first born while 42 were last born into families with other children (chi square = 12.3, p < .001). This finding is contrary to the opinion of Spock,[9] ". . . the first baby in a family is more likely to bang his head. . . ." In a series of 30 head bangers I[1] found that 6 were only children, 1 was a middle child, 2 were first-born, and 21 were last-born children. Although it is not the purpose of this report to suggest correlates of head banging, available data indicate a prevalence of head banging among last-born children.

It was noted in my previous study[1] that head banging was preceded in all instances by other forms of rhythmic activity such as body rolling, head rolling, or crib rocking. The data in this study are not so clear-cut. Rocking activity was noted in 32 cases prior to head banging, but in 25 cases mothers indicated that no rocking had been noted prior to the onset of head banging. Of the children who were "rockers only" 15 were first-born children and 31 were last born at the time of this study (chi square = 5.6, p < .02).

Table III. Months of age when head banging was first noted by mothers

Months	Girls	Boys
1-3	1	1
4-6	2	8
7-9	2	10
10-12	2	11
13-15	-	6
16-18	1	3
19 or over	5	5
Total	13	44

It can be seen from Table III that 37 children were noted by their mothers to be head bangers prior to their first birthday. The last half of the first year appears to have been the period of onset most often noted by mothers in this sample of children. This finding is in accordance with previous observations.[1, 3, 9]

References
1. de Lissovoy, V. *Head banging in early childhood: an exploratory study of an atypical behavior pattern.* (Unpublished thesis). Cornell University, 1959.
2. de Lissovoy, V. Head banging in early childhood. *Child Dev.,* (in press).
3. Lourie, R. S. The role of rhythmic patterns in childhood. *Am. J. Psychiat.,* 1949; **105**, 653.
4. Levy, D. M., Patrick, H. T. Relation of infantile convulsions, head banging and breath holding to fainting and headaches in the parents. *Arch. Neurol. & Psychiat.,* 1928; **19**, 865.
5. Scott, R. B. Personal communication.
6. Mead, M. Personal communication.
7. Kravitz, H., *et al.* Reported in the Chicago *Daily News,* May 3, 1960, p. 16.
8. Shartle, C. *Occupational Information,* New York: Prentice-Hall, Inc., 1952.
9. Spock, B. *Baby and Child Care* (p. 206). New York: Pocket Books, Inc., 1957.

RHYTHMIC HABIT PATTERNS IN INFANCY: THEIR SEQUENCE, AGE OF ONSET, AND FREQUENCY

Harvey Kravitz, John J. Boehm
Northwestern University School of Medicine

The onset of hand to mouth sucking was studied in 140 normal newborn infants, and in 79 newborn infants of normal and low birth weight with low Apgar scores and neonatal disease. Results indicated a significant delay in hand sucking in abnormal newborn infants. The sequence, age of onset, and the frequency of other common rhythmic habit patterns was also recorded in 200 older infants. There is a marked delay in the onset of the common rhythmic habit patterns in infants with Down's syndrome and cerebral palsy. Rhythmic habit patterns may be of value in the diagnosis of developmental retardation in infants.

The subject of rhythmic habit patterns is one that has long interested pediatricians, psychologists, and psychiatrists. Motor rhythms have been defined by Bakwin and Bakwin (1960) as head rolling, body rocking and head banging. We have expanded the definition to include thumb and finger sucking, foot kicking, lip biting, toe sucking and teeth grinding and have called the entire group rhythmic habit patterns. Although rhythmic habit patterns have been studied individually, no systematic study of their onset, frequency, and clinical significance has been undertaken. This is the subject of this paper.

There is no clear neurologic explanation of the rhythmic habit patterns. These patterns do not appear to be related to higher cerebral functions and may have their origin in the cerebellar or thalamic areas of the brain. But in experimental and clinical neuropathologic studies, Kubie (1941) has found evidence for anatomic and physiologic bases for repetitive behavior. He was able to produce perseverating acts in monkeys following experimental ablation of certain cortical zones of their brains. Freeman and Watts (1939) also have reported perseverating behavior in patients following prefrontal lobotomies. Perseverating behavior is also seen classically in epilepsy and postencephalitis. Rhythmic habit patterns may be important in the development of the infant's discovery of his body image. The concept of the body image was first reported by Schilder (1935), who concluded that infants develop body image by exploration of one's own body through cutaneous, visceral, kinesthetic and special sensory impulses. Hoffer (1949), Lourie (1949), Mittelman (1954), and Piaget (1942) have stated that rhythmic patterns are intimately associated with the maturation and development of motor skills and learning in the infants.

Mittelman (1954) noted that the intensity and patterning of motor activities is intimately connected with the maturation of the organism as well as with cultural customs. The evolution of the infant's image of himself and of his ability to differentiate between himself and objects around him are closely associated with the development of motility (rhythm). Hoffer (1949) states that, even in infants who engage in hand-mouth activities from the beginning, there is considerable involvement of newly developing skill and learning in mouth-hand coordinates during the latter months. Piaget (1942) concludes that rhythm is one of the three fundamental structures which govern psychic performance and enables the individual to assure an increasing measure of control over his actions.

Lourie (1949) states that rhythmic patterns in infancy and childhood appear to be a normal phenomenon satisfying instinctive needs and facilitating motor and personality development. He also states that rhythmic activities seem to serve the secondary functions of expression of pleasure and release of tension and give compensating satisfaction; these secondary values may be the cause of the persistence of these patterns into childhood.

We are indebted to Robert B. Lawson, M.D., Jerry Schulman, M.D., Herbert Grossman, M.D., and Gershon Berkson, Ph.D., for reviewing the manuscript. We are also indebted to the nurses of Lutheran General Hospital, Park Ridge, Illinois; Evanston Hospital, Evanston, Illinois; Saint Francis Hospital, Evanston, Illinois; Misericordia Hospital, Oregon, Illinois; and the Mark Lund Nursing Home, Bloomingdale, Illinois. We wish to thank Arthur Neyhus, Ph.D., for the statistical analysis of the data. Author Kravitz's address: Children's Memorial Hospital, 2300 Children's Plaza, Chicago, Illinois 60614.

Other theories regarding the etiology of rhythmic movements are based on the observations of psychiatrists. Freud (1938) and Spitz (1944) considered these activities to be autoerotic activities. Freud (1949) considered these rhythmic habit patterns to be due to self-directed aggression toward the child's own body. Bender and Yarnell (1941) and English and Pearson (1937) advanced the theory of a disturbed parent-child relationship as the cause for rhythmic habit patterns. In a study of motor rhythms in animals, including monkeys and apes, Harlow and Harlow (1962) noted rhythmic body-rocking movements in monkeys raised in isolation. DeLissovoy (1963) has pointed out that these theories are not supported by normative data and were based on observation of small numbers of disturbed children. None of these studies were carried out on large numbers of normal infants.

Method

Subjects

Group I consists of 140 randomly selected newborn infants above 2,500 grams, with Apgar scores of 8 or higher. These infants were normal vaginal deliveries seen in the nurseries of Evanston Hospital, Evanston, Illinois. All infants with gross congenital anomalies; respiratory, cardiac, cerebral, and orthopedic disease; or evidence of perinatal disease were excluded from this group. The infants were observed from the minute of birth by nurses who recorded the minute and hour each infant began to suck any part of the hand. Three sucks of any part of the hand were required for a successful try. All infants had their hands uncovered and kept free outside of blankets.

Group II consisted of 25 infants with weight over 2,500 grams, with Apgar scores of 6 or below, and evidence of perinatal disease. This group was studied from the minute and hour of onset of hand sucking.

Group III consisted of 22 infants of low birth weight, with Apgar scores below 6, and with evidence of perinatal disease and were similarly studied.

Group IV consisted of 32 infants of low birth weight, with Apgar scores above 7, with no evidence of perinatal disease. This group was similarly studied at the onset of hand sucking.

In addition, 200 normal infants were followed from 1 month to 1 year. All infants with gross congenital anomalies; respiratory, cardiac, cerebral, and orthopedic disease; or evidence of perinatal disease were excluded from the study. Starting with the first monthly visit, each mother was questioned about the onset of foot kicking, lip biting, body rocking, toe sucking, head banging, teeth grinding, and head rolling. Each rhythm was recorded as present if it occurred for more than 2 days.

A series of 12 infants with cerebral palsy was studied for the onset of the rhythmic habit patterns as previously described. Twenty-two cases of infants with Down's Syndrome were similarly observed.

The null hypothesis is that there is no significant difference in the median age of onset of the rhythmic habit patterns between normal infants and those classified as abnormal.

Results

Hand sucking

Hand sucking was observed in all of the 140 infants weighing more than 2,500 grams, with Apgar scores of 8 or higher, and free of perinatal disease. The median sucking time was 54 minutes. Sixty percent hand sucked within 1 hour; 85.8 percent, within 100 minutes; and 89.3 percent sucked within 2 hours (fig. 1).

The very early onset of handsucking is in marked contrast to that found in infants of the abnormal groups (Groups II, III, and IV) (table 1). The median sucking times of these groups were 1,834, 1,343, and 1,476 minutes respectively. The median sucking time of Groups II, III, and IV were significantly higher than those of Group I. (The median-test x^2s were all statistically significant beyond .001). The median time of onset was shortened by the 10 deaths in Groups II and III, which lowered the period of observation for hand sucking. The deaths were due to the respiratory-distress syndrome, to cerebral anoxia, or cerebral hemorrhage. No deaths occurred in the infants in Group I.

Since hand sucking has been observed in utero by Liley (1965) it is not surprising that it should be seen so early in the neonatal period. Bakwin (1948) and Brazelton (1956) have stated that finger and thumb sucking is a normal activity of infants. Gesell and Ilg (1937) believed that thumb and finger sucking was a sign of maturation of the nervous system. Our findings appear to confirm these statements.

The onset of hand sucking in the first hours of life in "normal" newborns is considerably earlier than those previously reported by Brazelton (1956), Klackenberg (1949), Levy (1928), and Traisman (1958), whose observations were carried out after the newborns were discharged from the newborn nurseries.

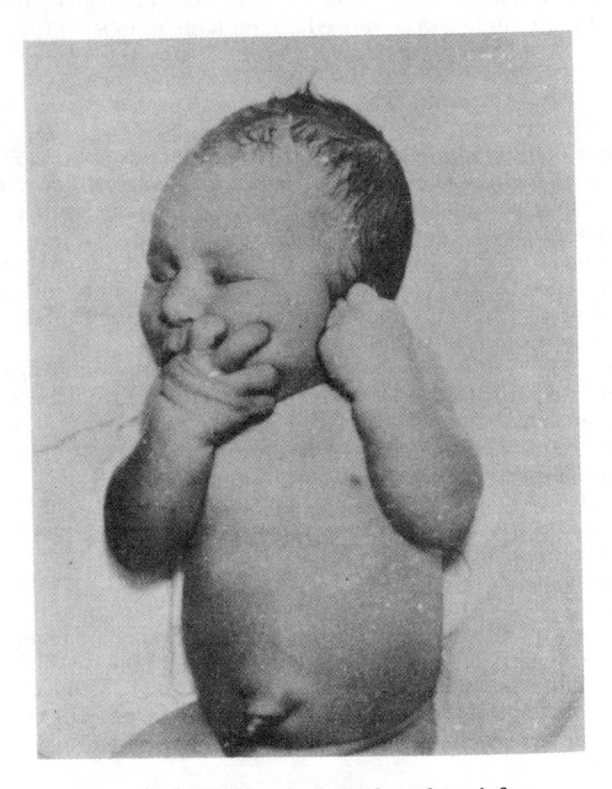

Fig. 1. Hand sucking in normal newborn infant.

Table 1. Hand-sucking times in newborn infants

Group and Type of Infant	N	Median (Minutes)	Range (Minutes)	Deaths (N)
I: Infant of normal birth weight: Apgar score above 7; no perinatal disease	140	54	7-310	0
II: Infant of normal birth weight; Apgar score below 6; with perinatal disease	25	1,835[a]	28-10,080	4
III: Infant of low birth weight; Apgar score below 6; and perinatal disease	22	1,343[b]	60-24,480	6
IV: Infant of low birth weight; Apgar above 7; and no perinatal disease	32	1,476[c]	7-31,680	0

[a]Observed difference between Groups I and II significant beyond .001 level; median-test $\chi^2 = 20.0$.
[b]Observed difference between Groups I and III significant beyond .001 level; median-test $\chi^2 = 22.1$.
[c]Observed difference between Groups I and IV significant beyond .001 level; median-test $\chi^2 = 31.7$.

53

Table 2. Age of onset and frequency of common rhythmic habit patterns in normal infants (from birth to 1 year)

Age of Onset (Months)	Rhythmic Habit Patterns							
	Hand Sucking (N = 140)	Foot Kicking (N = 200)	Lip Biting (N = 200)	Body Rocking (N = 200)	Toe Sucking (N = 200)	Head Rolling (N = 200)	Head Banging (N = 200)	Tooth Grinding (N = 200)
Birth–1......	140(100.0)	14(7.0)	...	...	...	...	...	...
2......	...	127(63.0)	...	...	...	...	...	...
3......	...	41(20.5)	26(13.0)	...	...	...	...	...
4......	...	8(4.0)	59(29.5)	33(16.5)	5(2.5)	3(1.5)	...	...
5......	...	6(3.0)	56(28.0)	65(32.5)	35(17.5)	2(1.0)	1(0.5)	...
6......	...	2(1.0)	23(11.5)	34(17.0)	44(22.0)	3(1.5)	2(1.0)	2(1.0)
7......	...	...	9(4.5)	26(13.0)	47(23.5)	3(1.5)	7(3.5)	16(8.0)
8......	...	...	9(4.5)	16(8.0)	32(16.0)	2(1.0)	1(0.5)	22(11.0)
9......	...	...	2(1.0)	4(2.0)	2(1.0)	1(0.5)	...	14(7.0)
10......	...	...	...	4(2.0)	2(1.0)	5(2.5)	2(1.0)	30(15.0)
11–12......	...	...	2(1.0)	...	...	1(0.5)	1(0.5)	28(14.0)
>12......	...	2(1.0)	14(7.0)	18(9.0)	33(16.5)	180(90.0)	186(93.0)	88(44.0)
Median	.004[a]	2.7	5.3	6.1	6.7	>12	>12	10.6
Range (mo.)	...	1–12+	3–12+	4–12+	4–12+	3–12+	5–12+	6–12+

[a] The median for hand sucking was 54 minutes; the range of hand sucking was 7-310 minutes.

Foot kicking

Foot kicking was observed in 198 (99 percent) infants. The median age of onset for foot kicking was 2.7 months (table 2).

This rhythmic activity was first reported by Washburn (1929). He described foot kicking as occurring commonly in infants at about 10 weeks of age. It is found in normal infants in the supine position during joyous excitement and is characterized by movements of the extremities often symmetrical with flapping of the hands and forearm up and down and flexion and extension of the legs and the knees. We have observed the rhythm with unilateral flexion and extension of one foot. In some of our cases, rhythmic thumping of one foot has been noted, often when the infant is going to sleep. Rhythmic flexion and extension of the lower extremities have been also observed by Ames (1941) when infants are crying.

Fig. 2. A classic example of lip biting (*David*, Borghese Museum, Rome).

Fig. 3. Lip biting in a 9-month-old infant.

Foot kicking may persist as foot swinging in children and adults when sitting with legs dangling on tables or atop benches or walls. This act is often observed during sporting events, especially during periods of waiting or anticipation of activities. Gesell (1956) mentions foot tapping and knee movements in his study of 10-16-year-olds, but no mention of this activity was found in infants and younger children.

Lip sucking and lip biting

Lip sucking or lip biting was noted in 186 of 200 (93.0 percent) infants. The median age of onset was 5.3 months (table 2).

The frequency of this phenomenon has been previously reported by Kravitz (1964) to be 166 in 177 infants studied (94.3 percent). Its association with the eruption of the lower medial incisors was emphasised. Lip biting decreases after the eruption of the lateral mandibular incisors. Massler (1955) has reported that children at 6 and 7 often exhibit this habit when they are cutting their permanent incisors. It is seen in later childhood and adult life during periods of acute emotional stresss or intensive concentration such as during school examinations or during extensive athletic exertion or difficult work. Gesell, Ilg, and Ames (1956) mention its occurrence in the age group between 10 and 16 years.

Massler (1955) describes lip biting in children as the mentalis habit. He described this phenomenon as the activity or passive thrusting of the lip between the upper and lower incisors. The lower lip is turned inward and grasped between the incisors, placing pressure anteriorly behind the upper incisors. The latter are then tipped labially. Figure 2 shows a classic example of the mentalis habit. Figure 3 shows a 9-month-old infant with lip biting.

Body rocking

Body rocking was noted in 182 infants in this series (91 percent). The median age of onset was 6.1 months. Body rocking occurred in 106 boys and 76 girls in this series. There was no significant difference in the age of onset of body rocking for the sexes (table 2).

The incidence of body rocking in our series is higher than the 35.6 percent reported by Spitz (1944) in a series of 196 infants seen in an institution setting. In a previous study of 135 head bangers by Kravitz, Rosenthal, Teplitz, Murphy, and Lesser (1960), it was shown that 67 percent of the cases had a history of body rocking prior to the onset of head banging. This finding was also noted by DeLissovoy (1962).

Berkson (1967) observed body rocking in monkeys only' when they are raised in an isolated environment. He states that rocking, sucking, and head banging are seen in normal infants. Berkson believes there is a phylogenetic progression of "stereotyped" behavior. A greater variety of rhythmic patterns would therefore be found in human infants than in infant monkeys. Berkson cautions against applying conclusions about rhythmic patterns of one species to another.

Toe sucking

Toe sucking is noted in about 83.4 percent of the cases in our series (see table 2 and fig. 4). The median age of onset was 6.7 months. No sex differences were noted as to frequency and age of onset.

Although a large number of reports have appeared on thumb and finger sucking, there is a scant mention of this activity in the pediatric literature. It is neurologically important because it represents the discovering of the distal end of the infant. It can be considered to be a form of extranutritional sucking satisfaction as described by Brazelton (1956). Gesell (1947) mentions the foot being placed in the infant's mouth at 28 weeks of age but does not mention its frequency.

Head rolling

Head rolling was observed in 20 (10 percent) of the infants. The median age of onset was greater than 12 months. No sex differences in the frequency or age of onset was noted (table 2).

Lourie (1949) described head rolling in infants beginning at 2 to 3 months and increasing up to 6 to 10 months. He found that head rolling, body rocking, and head banging were observed in 15-20 percent of the unselected, pediatric clinic population. These rhythmic patterns were only about one-half as frequent in private practice according to Lourie. He

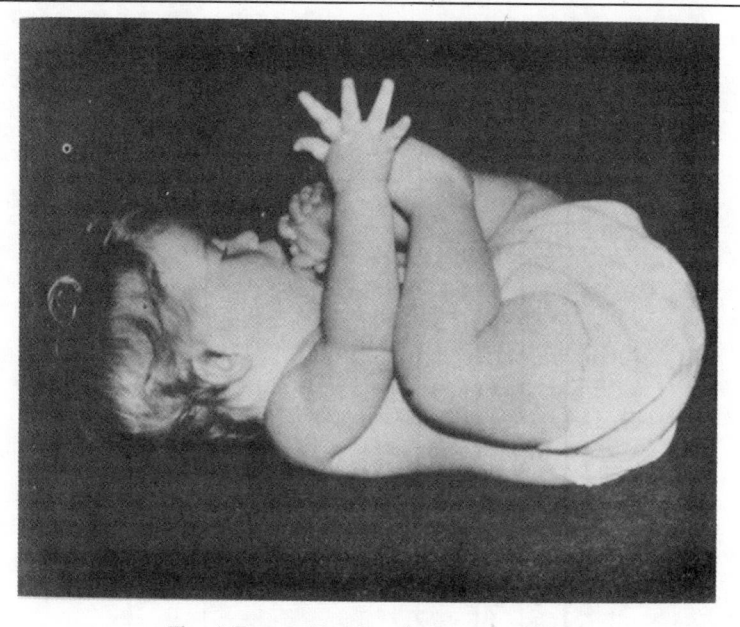

Fig. 4. Toe sucking in a 7-month-old infant.

presented no specific data on the actual number of infants who were head rollers, body rockers, or head bangers.

Gesell (1947) reported that head rolling occurred in institutionalized infants between 16 and 28 weeks of age. Nelson's *Textbook on Pediatrics* (1964) states that head rolling is often seen in young infants suffering from emotional deprivation and undernourished and chronically ill children. The infants in this series showed no evidence of retardation of development or emotional deprivation.

Head banging

Head banging occurred in 14 cases or 7 percent of our series. The median age of onset for both boys and girls was greater than 12 months in the 14 cases in this series (table 2).

Levy (1928) reported an incidence of 3.32 percent of head banging in a series of 422. DeLissovoy (1961) reported 15.2 percent of a small series were head bangers. In a previous paper on head banging, Kravitz et al. (1960) reported 3.6 percent of head banging in males and females. The age of onset agrees fairly well with a mean of 8 months reported in two previous studies. DeLissovoy (1961) reported that the age of onset of head banging in boys was 7.6 months, while the mean for girls was 9 months. Gesell (1943) reported head banging beginning at 40 weeks. A recalculation of the series of 135 head bangers, reported by Kravitz et al. (1960), showed a slight difference in the age of onset. The average age of onset was 8.6 months for boys and 8.9 months for girls. There were 3.5 boys who were head bangers to each girl, which was in close agreement with the 3.4 boys for every girl found by DeLissovoy (1961).

The cause of head banging has been considered to be due to autoeroticism (Freud 1938), a disturbed child-mother relationship (Bender & Yarnell 1941), motor release (Mittelman 1954), or self-directed aggression (Bender & Yarnell 1941; Gesell 1943). Kravitz (1960) noted that those infants with head banging are quiet, relaxed, and happy and find solace and comfort during this activity. These infants tolerate pain well and hardly cry. They show a great interest in music. This has previously been noted by Ilg and Ames (1955). DeLissovoy (1963) points out that most of the observations of head banging by psychiatrists were on very small numbers of children. DeLissovoy (1963) believes that head banging is a form of pain relief. He noted the onset of head banging in association with otitis media. We

Table 3. Age of onset and frequency of common rhythmic habit patterns in infants with Down's syndrome or cerebral palsy (from birth to 1 year)

Age of Onset (months)	Hand Sucking Down's (N = 22)	Hand Sucking C.P. (N = 12)	Foot Kicking Down's (N = 22)	Foot Kicking C.P. (N = 12)	Lip Biting Down's (N = 22)	Lip Biting C.P. (N = 12)	Body Rocking Down's (N = 22)	Body Rocking C.P. (N = 12)	Toe Sucking Down's (N = 22)	Toe Sucking C.P. (N = 12)	Head Rolling Down's (N = 22)	Head Rolling C.P. (N = 12)	Head Banging Down's (N = 22)	Head Banging C.P. (N = 12)	Tooth Grinding Down's (N = 22)	Tooth Grinding C.P. (N = 12)
Birth–1.	2															
2.	1	1	1		1											
3.																
4.	2	2	2													
5.	5		1	2												
6.	1															
7.	2						2				1					
8.																
9.				1		1	2	2	2	1	2	2	2	1		
10.											1	1	1	1		
11–12.																
>12.	9	9	17	11	21	10	18	12	20	11	19	7	20	10	22	12
Age																
Median	5	>12	>12	>12	>12	>12	>12	>12	>12	>12	>12	>12	>12	>12	>12	>12
Range	1–12+	3–12+	3–12+	10–12+	9–12+	10–12+	8–12+	12+	8–12+	9–12+	5–12+	5–12+	10–12+	9–12+	12+	12+

Rhythmic Habit Patterns

Table 4. Comparison of age of onset of common rhythmic habit patterns between normal infants and those with Down's syndrome

Rhythmic Habit Patterns	Median Age of Onset (Months)		χ^2
	Normals (N = 140)	Down's Syndrome (N = 22)	
Hand sucking..........................	0.001	5	153.8*
Foot kicking	2.7	>12[a]	39.8*
Lip biting................................	5.3	>12	37.5*
Body rocking..........................	6.1	>12	33.1*
Toe sucking............................	6.7	>12	25.4*
Head rolling...........................	>12.0	>12	...
Head banging	>12.0	>12	...
Tooth grinding	10.6	>12	24.6*

[a] Infants were observed only up to the twelfth month.
$* p < .001.$

Table 5. Comparison of age of onset of common rhythmic habit patterns between normal infants and those with cerebral palsy

Rhythmic Habit Patterns	Median Age of Onset in Months		χ^2
	Normals (N = 140)	Cerebral Palsy (N = 12)	
Hand sucking..........................	0.001	>12[a]	138.9*
Foot kicking	2.7	>12	22.2*
Lip biting................................	5.3	>12	27.4*
Body rocking..........................	6.1	>12	18.2*
Toe sucking............................	6.7	>12	13.3*
Head rolling...........................	>12.0	>12	...
Head banging	>12.0	>12	...
Tooth grinding	10.6	>12	12.8*

[a] Infants were observed only up to the twelfth month.
$* p < .001.$

have reported head banging to occur with teething episodes. DeLissovoy (1963) concludes that the folk expression "to rock with pain" illustrates the possibility that pain stimulus serves to release from the inhibitive control of the cortex normal, meaningless movements and that the reward of the lowering of the threshold of pain tended to foster repetitiveness.

Teeth grinding

A surprisingly large percentage of 112 (56 percent) infants were reported to be teeth grinders. The median age of onset was 10.5 months (table 2).

Allen (1964) believes that bruxism is probably a manifestation of the nervous, high-strung children. Bakwin and Bakwin (1960) states that it occurs in mental defectives but it is also seen in children of normal mentality. Bakwin and Bakwin (1960) mentions that teeth grinding was reported by the parents in 2 percent of the children brought to Kanner's Clinic. A search of the literature fails to mention the age of onset of bruxism in infancy.

Rhythmic habit patterns in retardates

A preliminary study of the onset of rhythmic habit patterns in two groups of retardates indicated a marked delay in this group compared with the normal infants (table 3). In the first group of 22 infants with Down's Syndrome. there was a marked delay in the onset of the rhythmic habit patterns. In a second group of 12 infants with a diagnosis of cerebral palsy retardation, there was very little rhythmic habit activity in the first year of life.

The differences are statistically significant for each of the rhythms with the exception of head rolling and head banging (tables 4 and 5). Using the median test, the x^2s were significant beyond .001 (Siegel 1956).

Although the number of cases of retardates is small, the marked delay and the number of cases without rhythmic habit activities in the first year of life illustrates the marked difference in rhythmic habits in retardates compared with those of the normal infants. Particularly significant is the marked delay in the onset of hand-to-mouth sucking in retardates and infants with neonatal distress, due to cerebral anoxia or cerebral hemorrhage of the respiratory distress syndrome. Wolf (1968) reported on the nutritive and nonnutritive sucking of neonates and noted that the nonnutritive sucking patterns of infants with anoxia differed from those of normals.

Discussion

The data describes the sequence, age of onset, and frequency of the common rhythmic habit patterns in normal infants from birth to 1 year. A preliminary study of retardates of similar age has demonstrated a considerable delay of the common rhythmic habit patterns. Infants of normal and low birth weights, with low Agpar scores, and neonatal distress due to the respiratory-distress syndrome, or cerebral hemorrhage, or anoxia have significantly prolonged hand-sucking times when compared with those of infants of normal weight with high Agpar scores. The findings suggest that the recording of the common rhythmic habit patterns may be of value in the early diagnosis of developmental retardation.

Human infants have many rhythmic habit patterns which are normal and are not seen in other primates. Comparing the rhythms of one species with those of another may not be valid. Rhythmic habit patterns may represent an overflow of excess energy in the normal infant, child, and adult. Rhythms may be the characteristic of the normal child in a state of well-being.

Much more work has to be done to determine the effects of infectious, metabolic, neurologic, and psychologic diseases on rhythmic habit patterns. The significance of the persistence of rhythmic habit patterns into childhood and adult life needs further study. Much more basic information is needed on rhythmic habit patterns in normal and retarded infants and children. The study of rhythmic habit patterns may enable us to gain more information of the maturation and development of motor skills and learning in infants.

References
Allen, K. R. Oral habits. *Pediat. Digest,* 1944; **6**, 75-88.
Ames, L. B. Motor correlates of infant crying behavior. *J. Psychol.,* 1941; **59**, 239-247.
Bakwin, H. Thumbsucking in children. *J. Pediat.,* 1948; **32**, 99-101.
Bakwin, H., Bakwin, R. M. *Clinical Management of Behavior Disorders in Children.* Philadelphia: Saunders, 1960.
Bender, L., Yarnell, H. Observation nursery: study of 250 children on psychiatric division of Bellevue Hospital. *Am. J. Psychiat.,* 1941; **97**, 1158-1174.
Berkson, G. Development of abnormal stereotyped behaviors. *Developmental Psychology* 1 (2), 1967, 118-132.
Brazelton, T. B. Sucking in infancy. *Pediatrics,* 1956; **17**, 400-404.
DeLissovoy, V. Head banging in early childhood. *Journal of Pediatrics,* 1961; **48**, 803-805.
DeLissovoy, V. Head banging in early childhood. *Child Development,* 1962; **33**, 43-56.
DeLissovoy, V. Head banging in early childhood. *Journal Genetic Psychology,* 1963; **102**,109-114.
English, O. S., & Pearson, G. H. *Common neuroses of children and adults.* New York: Norton, 1937.
Freeman, W., & Watts, J. W. An interpretation of the functions of the frontal lobe based upon observations in 48 cases of prefrontal lobotomy. *Yale Journal of Biology and Medicine,* 1939; **11**, 527-539.
Freud, A. Aggression in relation to emotional development: normal and pathological. *The psychoanalytic study of the child.* Vols. 3 and 4. New York: International Universities Press, 1949.
Freud, S. *Three contributions to the theory of sex: the basic writings of Sigmund Freud.* New York: Modern Library, 1938.
Gesell, A. *Developmental diagnosis.* New York: Hoeber, 1947.
Gesell, A. *The infant and child in the culture of today.* New York: Harper, 1943.
Gesell, A., Ilg, F. L., & Ames, L. B. *Youth — the years from ten to sixteen.* New York: Harper, 1956.
Gesell, A., & Ilg, F. L. *Feeding behavior of infants.* Philadelphia: Lippincott, 1937.

Harlow, H. F., & Harlow, M. Social deprivation in monkeys. *Scientific American*, 1962; **207**, 137-146.

Hoffer, N. Mouth, hand and ego-integration. *The psychoanalytic study of the child*. Vols. 3 and 4. New York: International Universities Press, 1949.

IIg, F. L., & Ames, L. B. *Child behavior*. New York: Harper, 1955.

Klackenberg, G. Thumbsucking: frequency and etiology. *Pediatrics*, 1949; **4**, 418-423.

Kravitz, H. Lip biting in infants. *Journal of Pediatrics*, 1964; **65**, 136-138.

Kravitz, H.; Rosenthal, V.; Teplitz, Z; Murphy, J. B.; & Lesser, R. F. A study of head banging in infants and children. *Diseases of the Nervous System*, 1960, **21**, 203-208.

Kubie, L. B. The repetitive core of neuroses. *Psychoanalytic Quarterly*, 1941, **10**, 23-43.

Levy, D. M. Finger-sucking and accessory movements in early infancy: etiologic study. *American Journal of Psychiatry*, 1928, **17**, 881-918.

Liley, A. W. *Studies in Physiology*. Berlin: Springer-Verlag, 1965.

Lourie, R. S. Role of rhythmic patterns in childhood. *American Journal of Psychiatry*, 1949; **105**, 653-660.

Massler, M. Oral habits. *Journal of Dentistry for Children*, 1955; **22**, 132-141.

Mittelman, B. Motility of infants, children and adults: patterning and psychodynamics. *In* Eisler, R. et al. (Ed.). *The psychoanalytic study of the child*. Vol. 9. New York: International Universities Press, 1954.

Nelson, W. E. *Textbook of pediatrics*. (8th ed.) Philadelphia and London: Saunders, 1964.

Piaget, J. Les trois structures fondamentales de la vic psychique: rhythme, regulation et groupement. *Revue Suisse Psychologic Pure Appliquee*, 1942; **1**, 9-21.

Schilder, P. *The image and appearance of the human body*. New York: International Universities Press, 1935.

Siegel, S. *Nonparametric statistics*. New York: McGraw-Hill, 1956.

Spitz, R., & Wolf, K. M. Autoeroticism: some empirical findings and hypotheses on three of its manifestations in the first year of life. *In* Eisler, R. et al. (Ed.). *The psychoanalytic study of the child*. Vols. 3 and 4. New York: International Universities Press, 1944.

Traisman, A. S., & Traisman, H. S. Thumb and finger-sucking: a study of 2,650 infants and children. *Journal of Pediatrics*, 1958; **5**, 566-571.

Washburn, R. N. A study of the smiling and laughing of infants during the first year of life. *Genetic Psychology Monograph*, 1929; **6**, 397.

Wolf, P. H. The serial organization of sucking in the young infant. *Pediatrics*, 1968; **42**, 943-956.

Reprinted from *Child Development*, 1962; **33**, 43-56 by kind permission of the publishers The Society for Research in Child Development Inc., Chicago, Illinois 60637.

SELF-MUTILATION IN SCHIZOPHRENIC CHILDREN

Arthur H. Green

Henry Ittleson Center for Child Research, 5050 Iselin Avenue, Bronx, NY 10471

Summary

The review of the literature has confirmed the presence of self-mutilation of various types in both animals and humans. In the latter, self-mutilation was observed under conditions of ego immaturity or ego impairment, often in the presence of sensory deprivation. The self-mutilation occurring in a group of 70 school age schizophrenic children at a residential treatment center was investigated. These children demonstrated a higher incidence of self-mutilative behavior than normal children do above the age of 5. Within the schizophrenic group, those children displaying self-mutilation differed from those who didn't. The incidence of self-mutilation was higher in the girls than in the boys. Of particular interest was the greater incidence of a history of infantile headbanging in the self-mutilative group. The infantile headbanging was visualized as a precursor to the self-mutilative behavior, and as a factor in the specific localization of self-mutilation to the head. The self-mutilators did not differ from the nonself-mutilators in the incidence of cerebral dysfunction or in the level of ego functioning. However, case analysis suggested that the ego level did influence the individual patterning and the psychodynamic content of the self-mutilation. In discussing the data, a hypothesis is offered to account for the stepwise development of self-mutilative behavior in these schizophrenic children from their precursor patterns in infancy. The hypothesis stresses the interplay between early precursor physiological patterns serving homeostasis, and the environmental responses which reinforced their persistence. The hypothesis notes the relatively later investment of the self-mutilation with psychodynamic significance. It also considers the effect of the widespread ego deficits, especially the disordered pain behavior, in facilitating the development of self-mutilative behavior in these children.

Self-mutilation has been observed as a frequent occurrence in a group of schizophrenic children living in a residential treatment center, and has stimulated many questions regarding its significance and etiology. The types of self-mutilation encountered most frequently were self-scratching, self-hitting, self-biting, self-pinching, headbanging, and hairpulling. These children did not respond to their self-inflicted injuries with appropriate concern and expression of distress. Typically, they failed to acknowledge the obviously painful quality of these acts, and at times even seemed to derive pleasure from them. Historically, the onset of the self-mutilation in most of these children dated back to early childhood. In addition, the parents often reported an antecedent history of infantile rocking and headbanging. These clinical observations raised questions concerning possible differences between the self-mutilators and nonself-mutilators in the schizophrenic group, which could account for the presence of this trait. It was also felt that information regarding self-mutilation would cast light on differences between schizophrenic and normal children in their response to pain. The schizophrenic children at the Ittleson Center for Child Research seemed especially suitable for investigation because of the opportunity for 24-hour observation and the extensive treatment and research data compiled for each child during his residence at the Center. The children all came from structurally-intact families, a circumstance which facilitated the collection of valid and reliable historical data. Well-documented, detailed case histories and treatment records of both child and family were available for all of the children studied.

Self-mutilation occurs in animals as well as humans. It has been observed in apes and monkeys reared in isolation, or separated from their mates.[1-5] It has also been produced by experimentally induced brain lesions. It has been observed in decerebrate cats when stimulated to sham rage,[6] and in monkeys whose temporal lobes had been removed bilaterally.[7] Self-mutilation has not been reported in animals under natural conditions.

Self-mutilation has been more frequently described in humans than in animals, in both normal and pathological situations. Shentoub and Soulairac observed self-mutilation to be a fairly frequent occurrence in a normal infant population studied longitudinally at a child care center.[8] Three hundred infants were followed from the ages of 9 months to 6 years (Table 1). Self-mutilation in the form of self-biting, pinching, scratching, hitting, hairpulling, and headbanging was frequently observed up to the age of 2. It occurred from 11% to 17% of the group at ages 9 to 18 months, and in about 9% of the group at the age of 2 years. The incidence decreased rapidly thereafter, and was completely absent among the children by the age of 5 years. The rapid decrease in the incidence of self-mutilation after 18 months was accompanied by a striking increase in the amount of heteroaggressive behavior, such as hitting, throwing objects, and temper tantrums. The authors concluded that the self-mutilation in these children represented primitive, misdirected expressions of aggressivity. The turning inwards of the aggression was facilitated by the presence of an immature body image, and was reversible with further maturation. Mittleman described a crying pattern in infants beginning as early as 3 months of age, in which windmill movements of the arms are coupled with extension and flexion of the legs.[9] The windmill movements were often observed to bring the hands and fingers towards the face, which resulted in the infant scratching himself. He also observed rhythmic slapping of the thighs beginning at 7 months of age, during crying. Mittleman felt that these early rhythmic patterns served as precursors to later aggression directed both outwardly and inwardly. He suggested that headbanging could be a later form of self-mutilation which might facilitate the development of masochistic behavior.

The association between early rhythmic activity and subsequent self-mutilation becomes even more apparent in studies of headbanging occurring in normal infant populations. DeLissovoy systematically described headbanging occurring in 33 normal children,ranging in age from 10 to 45 months.[10] He reported that in every case, the headbanging was preceded by rhythmic activity, as noted by the mothers. Varieties of rhythmic activity included head rolling, rocking, swaying, and body rolling. In another study, DeLissovoy reported the incidence of headbanging to be 15.2% in a normal population aged 19 to 32 months.[11] Of the boys, 22.3%, and 7.4% of the girls were affected. In a study of 1,168 normal infants, Kravitz et al[12] reported a lower incidence of headbanging than did DeLissovoy. They found 3.6% to be headbangers, with boys out-numbering girls by a ratio of 3.5 to 1. They found the average of onset to be 8 months, with an average duration of 17 months. They noted that 67% of the headbangers also indulged in body rocking. They viewed headbanging as a tension reducing device which could be associated with the eruption of the central and lateral incisors, and with the transition from sitting to crawling. Lourie reported the incidence of rocking, headbanging, or swaying in one form or another in 15% to 20% of a normal pediatric clinic population.[13] These patterns often persisted to the age of 2½ to 3 years, and were sometimes accompanied by ear pulling, finger tapping, teeth grinding, or skin scratching. Lourie hypothesized that these rhythmic patterns facilitated the child's control over early motility in addition to their usefulness in reducing tension.

Self-mutilation has been frequently described in abnormal situations, such as in children with aberrant care. Spitz and Wolfe reported frequent episodes of headbanging and other forms of self-mutilation in infants deprived of maternal care, as they lapsed into the state of anaclitic depression.[14] The infants recovered when the maternal object returned, and proceeded to bite, kick, and scratch others instead of themselves. Spitz and Wolfe explained this by postulating that the infant's aggressive and libidinal drives were turned inwards when no external object was available. Silberstein et al described autoerotic headbanging as a substitute for incomplete maternal stimulation, which could be reversed when the necessary stimulation was provided.[15] They recommended therapeutic involvement with the mothers to help them correct the deficit in maternal care. Anna Freud and Burlingham observed self-destructive behavior in institutionalized children.[16] Levy observed a disappearance of stereotyped movements in orphanage children when normal outlets for play and interests were provided.[17]

Self-mutilation has also been described in children with impaired brain function. Hoffer reported self-biting in a 6-month-old mentally defective girl following weaning.[18] Berkson and Davenport studied stereotyped movements including elements of self-mutilation, such as swaying, rocking, headbanging, eyepoking, self-biting, picking, and scratching in mentally defective male children and adults.[19] Two thirds of the mental defective group presented these stereotyped movements and postures; and a higher incidence of such movements was recorded in the blind defectives, and in those with lower intelligence quotients. The degree of stereotyped patterning, including self-mutilation, was correlated with the amount of self-manipulation present, and had an inverse relationshp with the amount of environmental manipulation. These findings were confirmed by further studies of Berkson and Mason, who found that a reduction in the amount of stereotyped behavior, including self-mutilation, accompanied the introduction of play objects to the group and an increase in performance of other activities.[20] The authors felt that the stereotyped behavior provided needed tactile, vestibular, and kinesthetic stimulation. In an experimental study with severely regressed 5-year-old schizophrenic twins, Lovaas et al demonstrated that painful electric shock was effective in eliminating autistic stereotyped patterns which included self-mutilation.[21] Affectionate and other social behaviors towards adults increased after adults had been associated with shock reduction. The authors explained their results by the theory of operant conditioning, and demonstrated that pain reduction can be used as a positive social reinforcer.

The stereotyped, frequently self-destructive rhythmic patterns described above, occurred under conditions of ego impairment (mental retardation, schizophrenia) or ego immaturity (infancy) which diminish the child's reception or integration of sensory stimuli. They also occurred in response to a reduction of environmental stimulation (institutionalization, isolation) irrespective of ego impairment. As these defects in the child are modified, resulting in the increased capacity of the ego for perception and interaction with the stimulus world, or when the environment is made richer, the rhythmic patterns lose their adaptive value and may disappear. The self-mutilative behavior accompanying these rhythmic patterns seems to be enmeshed in this primitive adaptive response without having conflictual significance.

This observation has been supported by the psychoanalytic literature, which has often distinguished between a primitive, pre-conflictual type of self-mutilation coinciding with immature ego development, and a later self-destructive activity which is psychologically motivated and related to guilt and conflict. Beres differentiated between an "attack upon the body" which accompanied immature ego development in the absence of guilt and a formed superego, and an "attack on the ego" which required a considerable amount of ego and superego development and was related to guilt and masochism.[22] Anna Freud similarly distinguished between the self-injury in children which is a remnant of maturational defect and the later turning of aggression against the self which serves as a defense mechanism used by the ego under the impact of conflict.[23] Mittleman postulated four stages in the development of aggression against the self; blind rage vented on the self, attacking a painful, rejected, hostile part of the self (as in body pain), self-injury out of conscience, and self-injury as expiation to avoid punishment.[9] The latter two stages implied the presence of guilt and superego mechanisms. He adds the notion of the child's tendency to externalize and dissociate from the self a painful body part, and then to attack it as an external object. He likened this to Rado's concept of riddance.[24] Greenacre viewed headbanging as an attempt to establish a body reality in the absence of kinesthetic stimulation.[25] Kulka et al stressed the importance of early kinesthetic stimulation in the infant's development.[26] They postulated a kinesthetic phase, preceding the stage of orality. If insufficiently satisfied, the kinesthetic needs led to rocking and headbanging. This concept is supported by Levy's description of tics, hyperactivity, and stereotyped movements, including rocking and headbanging, following movement restraint.[17] Geleerd observed that even the self-destructive acts and fantasies of three adults were revealed in analysis to be a product of a partial regression of the ego to the early phase preceding differentiation between the ego and the love object.[27]

Most of the theories concerning the later forms of self-mutilation which imply the presence of a mature ego and superego have been largely influenced by Freud's writings concerning the self-destructive components of melancholia, which he attributed to the attack by the superego on the ambivalently held love object which had been introjected and

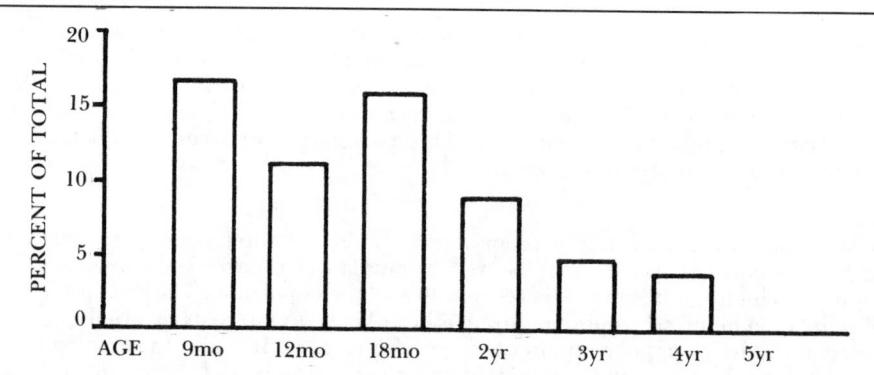

Fig. 1.—Incidence of self mutilative behavior in normal children up to 5 years of age (from Shentoub and Soulairac[8]).

incorporated in the ego.[28] Subsequent authors, for example, Klein[29] and Bychowski,[30] have described introjective and projective mechanisms and their relationship to masochism and self-mutilation, whereas others, such as Beres and Schaefer, have focused on the development of the superego and its role in the formation of self directed aggression.[22,31]

The many different theories and observations regarding the possible etiologies and significance of self-mutilation attest to its complexity. Most of the observations cited above were confined to descriptive accounts of self-mutilation in various populations, or of the associated rhythmic patterns acting as possible precursors. Many of the psychodynamic theories were speculations based on examination of individual cases. Up to the present, no attempts have been made to study this phenomenon systematically and to assess its relationship to early rhythmic patterns. The main purpose of the present study, therefore, has been to investigate the incidence and nature of self-mutilative behavior commonly seen in a group of schizophrenic children in a residential treatment center. The relationship of the self-mutilation to possible precursors and other variables has been studied, in an attempt to clarify the developmental stages of this disorder. In addition, the defensive and adaptive value of self-mutilation has been investigated.

Design of study

A review was made of all of the children treated at the Henry Ittleson Center for Child Research from its inception in 1953 through 1963. All those children who were diagnosed as schizophrenic, and who had been in residence for at least six months were selected for the study. Approximately one third of the children so selected were in residence at the time of the case review, while two thirds of the population have been discharged from the Center after having been treated and observed for an average of three years. A total of 70 children, including 52 boys and 18 girls, satisfied the above criteria. They ranged in ages from 5 to 12 during their residence at the Center.

The children were investigated as to the presence or absence of self-mutilative behavior during their period of residence. Special attention was focused on the quality and quantity of this behavior, its precipitating factors, and its natural course. The children were then divided into two groups; a self-mutilative group, and a nonself-mutilative group. These two groups were compared with one another as to prior history of headbanging, sex, cerebral dysfunction, and intellectual functioning. Cerebral dysfunction was defined as the presence of evidence of central nervous system pathology based on careful neurological examination designed to elicit the more obscure "soft signs" of neurological impairment. The full IQ in the Wechsler Intelligence Scale for Children (WISC) was employed as a measure of intellectual functioning. This was considered to be the best single measure of "ego strength." The IQ obtained on admission was used; where WISC scores were not available and Stanford-Binet IQ's were available, the latter were transformed into equivalent WISC IQ scores.

For purposes of this study, self-mutilation was defined as any overtly painful or destructive act committed by the child on his own body. Symbolic or ill-defined indicators of self-mutilation, such as destruction of one's clothing, expressions of self-mutilation in play and fantasy, masochistic provocativeness, and accident proneness were not included. The observations of self-mutilative behavior were made by one or several members of the professional staff psychiatrists, psychologists, social workers, child care workers, and teachers. Data regarding the children who had been discharged were culled from detailed clinical and research records of the Center.

Results

The incidence of self-mutilative behavior in schizophrenic children while in treatment at the Ittleson Center is noted in Table 1. Self-mutilation occurred in 28 of the 70 schizophrenic children while in residence, or in 40% of the population. The high incidence of self-mutilation in this schizophrenic group is in striking contrast to its reported absence in a normal children's population after the age of 5 (Fig. 1). It is also to be noted that self-mutilation was significantly more prevalent in the girl's group (61.1%) than in the boy's (32.7%) ($P<0.05$).

Table 1. Incidence of self-mutilative behavior in schizophrenic children at Ittleson Center

	Boys		Girls		Total	
	No.	%	No.	%	No.	%
SMB	17	32.7	11	61.1	28	40
NonSMB	35	67.3	7	38.9	42	60
Total	52	100	18	100	70	100

$$x^2=4.49 \quad P=<0.05$$

Table 2. Previous history of infantile headbanging in schizophrenic children

	Boys		Girls		Total	
	No.	%	No.	%	No.	%
Headbanging	13	25	8	44.4	21	30
No headbanging	39	75	10	55.6	49	70
Total	52	100	18	100	70	100

$$x^2=2.4 \quad P=>0.05$$

It was believed that self-mutilation recorded during residence at the Ittleson Center was related prior to headbanging, therefore, the incidence of a positive history of infantile headbanging in the schizophrenic children was determined. The presence of infantile headbanging was reported in 21 of the 70 schizophrenic children, or in 30% of the entire population, as shown in Table 2. This was a strikingly higher incidence of headbanging than that reported in studies of normal infants and young children by DeLissovoy and Kravitz et al. (The true incidence is probably even higher in our group, when we allow for the loss of positive findings as a result of history taking, in comparison with the observed data of the previous studies (Fig 2). As was the case with self-mutilation, the incidence of infantile headbanging was reported more frequently (44.4%) in the girls than in the boys (25%). This difference, while suggestive, was not statistically significant. In any case, the finding of more boys than girls in a normal group with headbanging was not noted in our schizophrenic group.

The relationship between infantile headbanging and the subsequent development of self-mutilation was further explored by investigating possible differences in the incidence of infantile headbanging between those schizophrenic children who manifested self-mutilation and those who did not. As was expected, there was a significantly higher incidence of infantile headbanging in both boys (52.9%) and girls (63.6%) manifesting self-mutilative behavior than in boys (11.4%) and girls (14.3%) with no self-mutilative

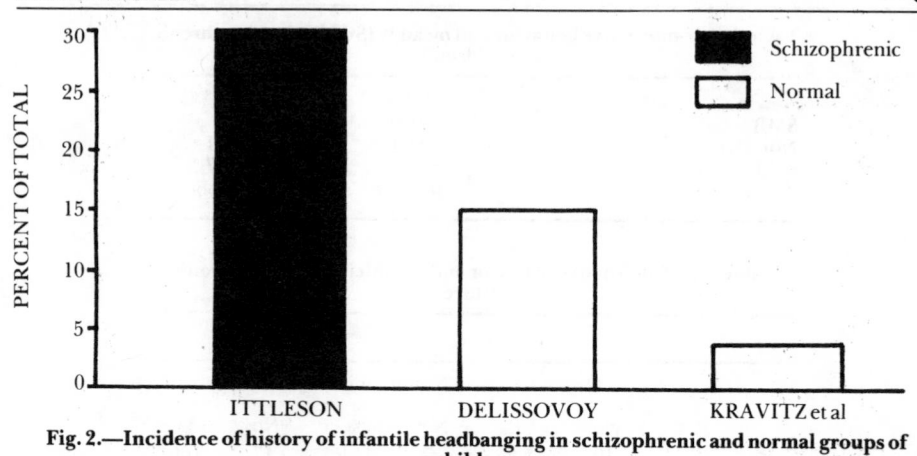

Fig. 2.—Incidence of history of infantile headbanging in schizophrenic and normal groups of children.

behavior (Table 3). This suggests that infantile headbanging acts as a precursor to the subsequent development of self-mutilative behavior.

The possibility that children with lower adaptive capacity would be more prone to the development of self-mutilative behavior than the higher functioning children was investigated by comparing differences in intelligence between the children manifesting self-mutilation and those who did not (Table 4). The WISC IQ obtained soon after admission to the Center was selected as the measure of adaptive capacity (ego strength). With both boys and girls, there was no significant difference in mean IQ between the self-mutilative and nonself-mutilative groups. Therefore, the level of adaptive capacity, as measured by the WISC IQ, was not related to the development of self-mutilative behavior.

It was also deemed important to assess the positive effect of cerebral dysfunction on the development of self-mutilative behavior. However, comparison of the incidence of cerebral dysfunction between the self-mutilative and the nonself-mutilative groups, as measured by careful neurological examination, failed to demonstrate significant differences in both the boys and girls ($P=<0.05$) (Table 5).

In summary, the results indicated that there was a higher incidence of self-mutilative behavior and infantile headbanging in a group of schizophrenic children at a residential

Table 3. Self-mutilative behavior and history of headbanging in schizophrenic children

Boys

| | Headbanging | | | | | |
| | Present | | Absent | | Total | |
	No.	%	No.	%	No.	%
SMB	9	52.9	8	47.1	17	100
NonSMB	4	11.4	31	88.6	35	100
Total	13	25	39	75	52	100

$x^2=10.5$ $P=<0.01$

Girls

| | Headbanging | | | | | |
| | Present | | Absent | | Total | |
	No.	%	No.	%	No.	%
SMB	7	63.6	4	36.4	11	100
NonSMB	1	14.3	6	85.7	7	100
Total	8	44.4	10	55.6	18	100

$x^2=5.7$ $P=<0.05$

Table 4. Self-mutilative behavior and mean WISC IQ of schizophrenic children

	Boys	Girls
SMB	71.9	71
NonSMB	81.1	72.1
o diff	7.5	8.7
	P=0.22	P=0.88

Table 5. Self-mutilative behavior and organicity in schizophrenic children

	Boys					
	Organic		Nonorganic		Total	
	No.	%	No.	%	No.	%
SMB	10	58.8	7	41.2	17	100
NonSMB	15	42.8	20	57.2	35	100
Total	25	48.1	27	51.9	52	100

$$x^2=1.16 \quad P=<0.05$$

	Girls					
	Organic		Nonorganic		Total	
	No.	%	No.	%	No.	%
SMB	3	27.3	8	72.7	11	100
NonSMB	3	42.8	4	57.2	7	100
Total	6	33.3	12	66.7	18	100

$$x^2=0.47 \quad P=<0.05$$

treatment center than in previously investigated groups of normal children. The self-mutilation was related to a prior history of infantile headbanging, and was unrelated to the level of intelligence or the presence of cerebral dysfunction.

Comment

The wide prevalence of self-mutilative behavior in our group of schizophrenic children as compared to its virtual absence in normal children of the same age is one aspect of the more global ego impairment encountered in childhood schizophrenia. The diagnosis of childhood schizophrenia, according to Goldfarb[32] implies the presence of ego lacunae at all levels; receptive, integrative, and executive, with a related impairment in self-awareness. The disordered body image, the impairment of differentiation of self from nonself, and the faulty perception and integration of painful stimuli, resulting in a disordered self-awareness, from the matrix in which self-mutilation develops.

The observed relationship between infantile headbanging and the subsequent development of self-mutilative behavior in these schizophrenic children supports the hypothesis that the headbanging is a precursor to the self-mutilation. This also suggests the hypothesis that headbanging represents an earlier and self-mutilation represents a later form of the same ego aberration.

This link between infantile headbanging and later self-mutilative behavior gains greater clarity when the longitudinal case histories of children manifesting self-mutilative behavior are studied. These children can be divided into three main categories. Some of the children maintained their infantile headbanging throughout childhood as the favored mode of self-mutilation. In this group minor modifications of headbanging occurred, for example one child who, as a baby, banged his head against his crib bangs his head against the wall at a later age. Another group of children acquired self-mutilative traits such as self-pinching, scratching, and biting in addition to the persisting headbanging. The final category included those children who gave up their infantile headbanging in favor of self-attack directed against the rest of their bodies. In the shift in the focus of self-mutilation from the head to the remainder of the body, the rhythmic, repetitive, stereotyped quality of the orginal headbanging was often maintained. In other cases, the self-mutilation was characterized by more explosive, nonrhythmic movements. Approximately two thirds (68.7%) of the self-mutilators who manifested infantile headbanging continued to utilize headbanging as a later form of self-mutilation, whereas only one child (8.3%) in this group developed later headbanging although there had been no previous history of infantile headbanging. Eleven out of 12 (91.6%) later headbangers had banged their heads in infancy. These longitudinal case studies confirm the importance of infantile headbanging not only as a general precursor to subsequent self-mutilative behavior, but also as a factor in the eventual localization of self-mutilation to the head.

Just as the infantile headbanging acts as a precursor to a subsequent disorder in pain behavior (self-mutilation), the associated rhythmic patterns in the form of body rocking and head rolling could act as precursors of the rhythmic disorders common to childhood schizophrenia, which include whirling, flapping, rocking, and other stereotyped movements.

Of course it is also true that some of the children with self-mutilative behavior gave no history of infantile headbanging. We have considered the possibility that other experiences could disturb the development of normal pain responses, resulting in self-mutilative behavior. For example, we have been impressed in our therapeutic work by the case histories of some of the children manifesting self-mutilative behavior which describe exposure to repeated and very severe physical violence at the hands of one or both parents. In these cases, the repeated external administration of painful stimuli could have a traumatic effect on the developing ego similar to self-inflicted headbanging, and might have facilitated the development of self-mutilative behavior. It should be stressed that this is merely a clinical observation which is being more completely investigated.

Although the data failed to reveal any significant relationship between WISC IQ scores as a measure of relative ego strength, and the incidence of self-mutilation, clinical observation of the mutilators yielded the impression that the level of ego functioning could influence the individual patterns of self-mutilation. For example, in the higher functioning schizophrenic children the self-mutilative episodes were often clearly provoked by a frustrating incident and could be explained by intrapsychic events. The children were usually aware of the painful nature of the self-attack, which was frequently used for the solution of an unconscious intrapsychic conflict.

CASE 1.—Carla became upset following her return from a traumatic Sunday visit with her parents and younger brother. She had succeeded in touching off a violent quarrel between her mother and father by provoking her volatile, psychotic mother. She assaulted herself verbally and physically. While tearing at her skin and ripping her clothes, she uttered the following: "Stupid Carla, ugly Carla, toilet bowl Carla, I'm no good, I hope I die soon. My brother is better because he can stay at home." The self-mutilation and the accompanying self-deprecation could be understood as a form of self-punishment which acted to assuage her guilty feelings concerning her provocativeness.

In the lower functioning schizophrenic children, the self-mutilation often seemed to be spontaneous and unprovoked, and without obvious conflictual significance. These children often manifested a diminished sensibility to pain and frequently displayed clear cut cerebral dysfunction.

CASE 2.—Paul, a lower-functioning, organically-impaired youngster reacted to minor frustrations with severe episodes of headbanding and face-slapping while showing no awareness of pain. Once he banged his forehead forcefully against concrete, completely macerating the skin and causing profuse bleeding, without showing discomfort.

One can speculate that the self-mutilation in these lower-functioning children satisfied more primitive physiological needs, such as tactile, kinesthetic, vestibular, and motility requirements, and helped to delineate their body boundaries from that of the outside world. In this sense, this type of self-mutilation might be described as essentially preconflictual in nature. Some children manifested both of these main categories of self-mutilative behavior; at times their self-mutilation was clearly motivated and aimed at conflict resolution, and at other times it appeared to be removed from conflict. Some children seemed to satisfy both physiological and conflictual needs in a single episode of self-mutilation.

CASE 3.—Muriel, a girl who was given to prominent rhythmic behavior, banged her head and hit her legs rhythmically on the bed before going to sleep. Just previously, she had been scolded for fighting.

In other children, the self-mutilative behavior which primarily satisfied primitive physiological needs developed a subsequent motivational significance through the process of secondary gain.

CASE 4.—Laura's quiet, rhythmic, headbanging which accompanied her withdrawn state became louder and more spectactular when another child received attention from her favorite counselor. She frequently chose the most resonant object for a banging surface during these instances, such as a blackboard or a hollow door.

Let us now consider the data concerning the variable of sex and its relationship to the presence of self-mutilative behavior. The girls demonstrated both a higher incidence of self-mutilative behavior and antecedent headbanging than the boys. This greater incidence of female headbanging shows a striking reversal of the typical male preference for headbanging described in normal child populations. One can speculate regarding the increased proneness of the schizophrenic girls towards self-mutilation. One factor might be the tendency of parents to discourage the expression of overt aggression in girls, which would be condoned or even encouraged among boys. Our schizophrenic boys were able to express more aggression in their play and fantasy than the girls. The blocking of the external direction of these impulses could promote their being turned inwards via self-mutilation. Another possible factor concerns the fact that the girls tended to come from more highly disturbed families than the schizophrenic boys, in accordance with the findings of Goldfarb and Meyers.[33] Thus, the more highly pathological responses of the parents of the schizophrenic girls may have been more conducive to both the original development of headbanging, and its reinforcement and transformation into the self-mutilative behavior of later childhood. The importance of intrafamilial and environmental factors in the genesis of headbanging in our schizophrenic girls is further emphasized by the usual rarity of headbanging in the normal female infant population. Another possible determinant in the predilection of the schizophrenic girls for self-mutilative behavior might be their unusual degree of body image distortion secondary to their more pronounced castration feeling, and to their more widespread bodily changes prior to puberty. The resulting diffusion of ego boundaries could facilitate the substitution of the self for the object during an aggressive outburst.

Any discussion of possible predisposing factors in the development of self-mutilation must ultimately be concerned with the deviant pain behavior which is implicit in the self-injury. Goldfarb described a high frequency of aberrant pain reactions in schizophrenic children and indicated both their difficulties in perceiving and communicating pain. He stressed the interference with learned aspects of pain by either organic or environmental factors. In many of our cases, the failure of the parents to intervene actively to interrupt the infantile headbanging or early self-mutilation, or their overt or covert encouragement of it, represented an avoidance of its painful implication. For example, one father casually accepted his daughter's severe headbanging without heeding its painful component. He limited his concern to the movement of the crib across the floor which he remedied by removing its wheels. Many of the parents made no attempt to divert the child from the headbanging by removing it from the crib, holding it, or restraining the banging movements. Many parents reacted similarly to their children's subsequent self-mutilative behavior. This passive acceptance of early self-mutilation may represent satisfaction of the parent's unconscious hostility towards the child. At any rate, these parental attitudes serve to impair the child's capacity to learn the significance of pain, and the appropriate patterns for coping with painful stimuli, and contribute to the development of self-mutilative behavior. Some of the parents also may have reinforced headbanging and self-mutilation by responding to the children almost exclusively when the children were hurting themselves, while ignoring them at other times. Under these circumstances, it is easy to imagine how the child might become motivated to seek the pleasurable components (rocking, rhythmic patterns, attention getting) of the headbanging and self-mutilation, while subordinating or denying their painful aspects. From whatever source, the impaired perception and understanding of painful stimuli may in turn complicate the task of ego differentiation, and the maintenance of ego boundaries.

At this point, we can hypothesize concerning the evolution of self-mutilative behavior in this group of schizophrenic children. However, the development of self-mutilation can be better understood when contrasted with the normal chain of events in early ego development. Normally, the process of separation and individuation leading to the establishment of ego boundaries and self-awareness is noted at the age of 8 months with beginning differentiation of strange from familiar objects. It is well towards completion by the age of 2 to 2½. This process is fostered by the appearance of locomotion at 8 to 9 months, which increases in the second year with walking, manipulation, hand-to-mouth movements, and tactile exploration of the body. Auditory, visual, and kinesthetic stimulation also seem to be necessary for the establishment of ego boundaries. In some cases where there exists a diminished sensory stimulation from the environment, the child may stimulate himself by rocking, headbanging, scratching, and hairpulling, etc. These self-stimulatory patterns of the immature ego are usually transitory, and.become superfluous and disappear with the establishment of ego boundaries, or when various sensory needs are satisfied by the environment. (It is noteworthy that the period from 8 months to 2½ years is the time in which the peak amount of rocking, headbanging, and transitory self-mutilative behavior occur in normal children.) Thus the rocking and headbanging frequently described in the "normal" children's population probably represents a temporary adaptive device for the fulfillment of basic sensory needs. These patterns are usually modified by appropriate parental handling, ie, substitution of appropriate external stimulation, and direct discouragement of the self-stimulatory pattern. When the basic sensory needs are fulfilled, the child will be freer to explore the environment with more effective sensory receptors (the distance receptors: sight and hearing) which will enable him to interact more effectively with external objects. Rocking, headbanging, and other rhythmic patterns become superfluous and are rarely encountered in the "normal" population after the age of 2½.

In our schizophrenic children, we can assume that the separation-individuation process proceeds less smoothly. Owing to the impaired ego capacity and maturational lag, the child manifests greater difficulty in the differentiation of himself from the external world. Infantile rhythmic patterns, including rocking and headbanging, are utilized more readily as adaptive tools in the establishment of ego boundaries. The schizophrenic child's proneness towards faulty perception and integration of painful stimuli tends to perpetuate these self-stimulatory patterns which are then subject to a greater amount of parental reinforcement than one would expect from families of nonschizophrenic children. These patterns frequently retain their adaptive value past the age of 2½ and may become transformed into more structured self-mutilative behavior, which may become a permanent part of the child's behavioural repertoire.

The particular sequence of events might be the following. Rocking becomes the first adaptive response to the need for increased sensory input and greater ego boundary delineation. The child eventually bangs his head in the course of rocking, and may repeat it because of its association with the pleasurable aspect of the rocking. The random headbanging may then develop into a persistent activity on the basis of conditioning (association with rocking pleasure). The headbanging may then become the precursor to subsequent self-mutilative behavior via reinforcement and conditioning based on parental responses. One may assume that this sequence of events could be interrupted at each level by appropriate corrective responses of the parents. For instance, the rocking child could be picked up and soothed by the parent, who would then be attending to the various sensory needs satisfied by the rocking. The headbanging could similarly be discouraged by a parental intervention which focused on the bizarre and painful nature of the act. However, the responses of some of the parents of our schizophrenic children tended to encourage and reinforce the rocking and banging. Once firmly established, the headbanging may be continued uninterruptedly into later childhood as an expression of self-mutilation, or it may act as a model for other varieties of self-injury displaced towards other parts of the body. As in the case with headbanging, the painful aspects of the self-mutilative behavior may become subordinated to the pleasurable components (environmental reward, component rhythmic pattern). Similarly, in the cases in which the self-mutilation could be traced to previous physical attacks by the parents, the pleasurable component of the attack (parental attention which was otherwise unattainable) sustained the painful component and provided the impetus for its transformation into self-mutilation. The foregoing hypothesis implies that self-mutilative behavior is basically a learned phenomenon largely shaped by environmental influences according to the principles of operant conditioning. It is derived from unlearned, adaptive precursors which serve to maintain homeostasis in the face of sensory deficits and ego impairment. The earliest self-mutilative behavior and its precursor patterns are devoid of fantasy and are without conflictual significance. As the pattern of self-mutilation becomes more firmly established, it may become secondarily invested with fantasy content and used for the solution of intrapsychic conflict. (The greater tendency of these schizophrenic children to utilize defenses of projection and introjection than normals, and their handicaps in ego differentiation facilitate the substitution of the self for the external object as a target for aggression. This is observed clinically when the angry child attacks himself instead of the frustrating adult. The self-attack serves both to spare the highly-valued adult from injury and as punishment to the child for his hostile impulses. At times, the child will project his self-mutilation onto the adult, and accuse him of the injury).

References
1 Yerkes, R. M. The mental life of monkeys and apes: a study of ideational behavior. *Behav. Monogr.*, 1916; **3**, 1-145.
2 Tinklepaugh, O. L. The self mutilation of a male macacus rhesus monkey. *J. Mammal.*, 1928; **9**, 293-300.
3 Finch, G. Chimpanzee frustration responses. *Psychosom. Med.*, 1942; **4**, 233-251.
4 Mason, W. A., Sponholz, R. R. Behavior of rhesus monkeys reared in isolation. *J. Psychiat. Res.*, 1963; **1**, 299-306.
5 Harlow, H. F. Love in infant monkeys. *Am. Psychol.*, 1962; **17**, 1-9.
6 Hendrick, I. *Facts and Theories of Psycho-analysis (edn. 2)*. New York: Alfred A. Knopf, Inc., 1950.
7 Kluver, H., Bucy, P.C. Preliminary analysis of functions of the temporal lobes in monkeys. *Arch. Neurol. Psychiat.*, 1939; **42**, 979-1000.
8 Shentoub, S. A., Soulairac, A. L'enfant automutilateur. *Psychiat. Enfant.*, 1961; **3**, 119.
9 Mittleman, B. *Motility in infants, children, and adults: patterning and psychodynamics. In* Eissler, R., *et al.* (eds.). *The Psychoanalytic Study of the Child.* (Vol 9, p. 142.). New York: International Universities Press, Inc., 1954.
10 deLissovoy, V. Headbanging in early childhood. *Child Develop.*, 1962; **33**, 43-56.
11 deLissovoy, V. Headbanging in early childhood: a study of incidence. *J. Pediat.*, 1961; **58**, 803-805.
12 Kravitz, H., *et al.* Headbanging in infants and children. *Dis. Nerv. Syst.*, 1960; **21**, 203.
13 Lourie, R. S. The role of rhythmic patterns in childhood. *Am. J. Psychiat.*, 1949; **105**, 653-660.
14 Spitz, R., Wolf, K. *Anaclitic depression. In* Eissler, R., *et al.* (eds.). *The Psychoanalytic Study of the Child.* (Vol. 2.). New York: International Universities Press, Inc., 1946.
15 Silberstein, R., Blackman, S., Mandell, W. Autoerotic headbanging: a reflection on the opportunism of infants. *J. Child. Psychiat.*, 1966; **5**, 235-243.
16 Freud, A., Burlingham, D. *Infants Without Families.* New York: International Universities Press, Inc., 1944.
17 Levy, D. M. On the problem of movement restraint. *Am. J. Orthopsychiat.*, 1944; **14**, 644-671.
18 Hoffer, W. Oral agressiveness and ego development. *Int. J. Psychoanal.*, 1950; **31**, 156-160.
19 Berkson, G., Davenport, R. K. Stereotyped movements of mental defectives: I—Initial survey. *Am. J. Ment. Defic.*, 1962; **66**, 849-852.
20 Berkson, G., Mason, W. Stereotyped movements of mental defectives: IV—Effects of toys and the character of the acts. *Am. J. Ment. Defic.*, 1964; **68**, 511-524.
21 Lovaas, O. I., *et al. Experimental studies in childhood schizophrenia: building social behavior using electric shock.* Read before the American Psychological Association meetings, Los Angeles, September, 1964.
22 Beres, D. *Clinical notes on aggression in children. In* Eissler, R., *et al.* (eds.). *The Psychoanalytic Study of the Child.* (Vol. 7.). New York: International Universities Press, Inc., 1952.
23 Freud, A. *The Ego and the Mechanisms of Defense.* New York: International Universities Press, Inc., 1946.

24 Rado, S. *Emergency behavior; with an introduction to the dynamics of conscience.* In *Psychoanalysis of Behavior, Collected Papers.* New York: Grune and Stratton, Inc., 1956.

25 Greenacre, P. In Problems of infantile neurosis: a discussion. Eissler, R., *et al.* (eds.). *The Psychonalytic Study of the Child.* (Vol. 11.). New York: International Universities Press, Inc., 1954.

26 Kulka, A., Fry, C., Goldstein, F. Kinesthetic needs in infancy. *Am. J. Orthopsychiat.,* 1960; **30**, 562-571.

27 Geleerd, E. *Clinical contribution to the problem of the early mother-child relationship: some discussion of its influence on self destructive tendencies and fugue states.* In Eissler, R. *et al.* (eds.). *The Psychoanalytic Study of the Child.* (Vol. 11.). New York: International Universities Press, Inc., 1956.

28 Freud, S. *Mourning and melancholia. In Collected Papers.* (Vol. 4, pp 152-170). London: Hogarth Press, Ltd., 1925.

29 Heimann, P. *A combination of defense mechanisms in paranoid states.* In Klein, M., *et al.* (eds.). *New Directions in Psychoanalysis.* London: Tavistock Publications, 1955.

30 Bychowski, G. Some aspects of masochistic involvement. *J. Am. Psychoanl. Assoc.,* 1959; **7**, 248-273.

31 Schaefer, R. *Loving and beloved superego.* In Eissler, R., *et al.* (eds.). *The Psychanalytic Study of the Child.* (Vol. 15.). New York: International Universities Press, Inc., 1960.

32 Goldfarb, W. *Childhood Schizophrenia.* Cambridge, Mass: Harvard University Press, 1961.

33 Meyers, D., Goldfarb, W. Psychiatric appraisal of parents and siblings of schizophrenic children. *Am. J. Psychiat.,* 1962; **118**, 902-915.

34 Goldfarb, W. Pain reactions in a group of institutionalized schizophrenic children. *Am. J. Orthopsychiat.,* 1958; **28**, 777-785.

Reprinted from *Arch. Gen. Psychiat.,* 1967; **17**, 233-244 by kind permission of the publishers American Medical Association, Chicago, Illinois 60610. Copyright AMA, 1969.

DIFFERENCES BETWEEN MENTALLY RETARDED AND NORMALLY INTELLIGENT AUTISTIC CHILDREN

Lawrence Bartak, Michael Rutter[1]
Institute of Psychiatry, London

Autistic children with an IQ below 70 and with an IQ above 70 were systematically compared. The two groups differed somewhat in the pattern of symptoms, but were closely similar in terms of the main phenomena specifically associated with autism. However, the low IQ and high IQ autistic children differed more substantially in terms of other symptoms such as self-injury and stereotypies and there were major differences in outcome. The possibility that the nature of the autistic disorder may differ according to the presence or absence of associated mental retardation needs to be taken into account in planning studies of etiology.

When he first described the syndrome of infantile autism, Kanner (1943) suggested that autistic children were all of basically normal intelligence. This idea was based on the children's usually good rote memory and manipulation of objects and on the absence of the physical stigmata associated with mental defect. The low scores obtained on IQ tests by many autistic children were thought to be a consequence of social withdrawal and hence a misleading indicator of cognitive skills. However, subsequent investigations have shown this view to be mistaken. In the first place, both clinical and experimental studies have demonstrated that austistic children perform some cognitive tasks much better than others, and that there is a characteristic pattern of cognitive performance which is associated with autism (Lockyer & Rutter, 1970; Hermelin & O'Connor, 1970; Bartak, Rutter & Cox, 1975). In the second place, several follow-up studies have shown that IQ scores obtained by autistic children function in much the same way and have the same predictive power as in any other group of children (Lockyer & Rutter, 1969; Rutter, 1970; Rutter & Bartak, 1973; De Myer, Barton, Alpern, Kimberlin, Allen, Yang, & Steele, 1974; Goldfarb, 1974). It has become clear that the behavioral syndrome of infantile autism can occur at all levels of intelligence and that the syndrome is frequently (but by no means always) associated with some degree of general intellectual impairment.

These findings raise the question of whether autism is the same condition when it occurs in the presence of mental retardation as when it is associated with normal levels of nonverbal intelligence. Various studies have indicated differences associated with IQ level. Thus, mentally retarded autistic children seem more likely to show difficulties in sequencing and in feature extraction (Hermelin & O'Connor, 1970), more likely to exhibit neurological dysfunction (Goldfarb, 1961; Rutter, 1970), less likely to make educational progress (Rutter & Bartak, 1973; De Myer et al., 1974) and less likely to make a good social adjustment in adult life (Rutter, 1970). However, these studies do not satisfactorily show the degree of overlap between the retarded autistic children and the normally intelligent autistic children, nor have they examined behavioral differences between the groups. The present study was planned to provide further information on both these points.

Design of study

Sample

The data derive from two studies of autistic children: a comparison of children's progress in three rather different units (Bartak & Rutter, 1973; Rutter & Bartak, 1973) and a comparison between autistic and "dysphasic" children (Bartak et al., 1975; Cox, Rutter, Newman, & Bartak, 1975). All the children attended special or ordinary schools in the community, so that the sample excluded the more severely retarded and handicapped

[1]Requests for reprints should be sent to Prof. Michael Rutter, Department of Child and Adolescent Psychiatry, Institute of Psychiatry, De Crespigny Park, Denmark Hill, London SE5 8AF, England.

autistic children found in long-stay hospitals. In both studies the same methods of assessment were used, and autism was defined as a disorder evident before 30 months of age in which there was a profound and general failure to develop normal social relationships together with delayed and deviant language development and the presence of ritualistic or compulsive phenomena.

The two samples were pooled and attention was restricted to boys aged less than eleven years. The population was then divided into two sub-groups on the basis of nonverbal IQ scores. The mentally retarded (A-MR) group ($N = 17$) consisted of boys with a nonverbal IQ of 69 or less and the normally intelligent (A-NI) group ($N = 19$) consisted of boys with a nonverbal IQ of 70 or more. Because the data were gathered for other purposes without any view to IQ comparisons there is no likelihood of any observer bias relevant to this study.

Methods

Intelligence was assessed on nonverbal tests consisting of either the Merrill-Palmer Scales of Mental Tests (Stutsman, 1948) or the WISC Performance Scale (Wechsler, 1949).

Information about the child's symptoms and behavior was obtained both from an interview with the mother and from direct observation of the child in a structured play situation with an adult. The parent interview was designed to yield standardized information about the child's early development and present behavior, including motor and speech development, toilet training, social development, occurrence of ritualistic and stereotyped behaviors, and current social behavior. The father's occupational status was also obtained. Further information was obtained from a structured play situation. The child was shown toys and pictures by the tester and encouraged to talk freely and to play. At the end of the play period, the child was immediately rated on a checklist of social behaviors including items of *social responsiveness* such as lack of eye-to-eye gaze and lack of variation in facial expression or affect, and items of *deviant behaviors* such as self-injury and hand or finger stereotypies (Rutter & Bartak, 1973).

Results

The mean nonverbal IQ in the A-MR group was 45.7 ($SD = 14.63$). In the A-NI group, the mean IQ was 92.6 with a SD of 14.05 ($t = 9.78$; $df = 34$; $p < .001$). The groups did not differ in age, mean ages in the two groups being 8 years 7 months and 8 years 5 months, respectively ($t = .36$; $df = 34$; n.s.).

Phenomena most characteristic of autism

Social relationships

All the autistic children in both groups showed a serious impairment in the development of social relationships which was especially marked with other children. Thus, none of the children had made personal friendships and all functioned poorly in a group play situation. Furthermore, almost all had shown lack of eye-to-eye gaze in early childhood, although this was present in fewer children by the time they were examined (see Table I). On the other

Table I. Social development

	A-MR N	Group (N = 17) %	A-NI N	Group (N = 19) %	χ^{2a}	p
Lack of eye-to-eye gaze (ever)	17	(100)	17	(90)	.42	n.s.
Lack of-eye-to-eye gaze in test situation	7	(41)	2	(11)	3.01	n.s.
Lack of emotional expression (ever)	13	(76)	7	(37)	4.21	.05
Lack of emotional expression in test situation	12	(71)	8	(42)	1.91	n.s.
No cooperative play with examiner	13	(77)	4	(21)	8.94	.01
Nondifferentiation of parents	10	(59)	2	(10)	7.37	.01
Not cuddly as baby	12	(71)	5	(26)	5.39	.05

[a]Each comparison in this and all succeeding tables has Yates's correction.

Table II. Deviant social responses (as observed in test situation)

	A-MR N	Group (N = 17) %	A-NI N	Group (N = 19) %	χ^2	p
Smelling adult	11	(65)	2	(11)	9.19	.01
Touching adult	7	(41)	1	(5)	4.78	.05
Withdrawal from adult	5	(29)	3	(16)	.66	n.s.
One or more of the above	14	(82)	5	(26)	9.17	.01

hand, the normally intelligent autistic children (A-NI) were less likely to show impaired physical responsiveness in infancy (as indicated by a failure to cuddle) and the deficits in their social behavior with adults were less severe. Whereas three-fifths of the mentally retarded autistic children (A-MR) failed to differentiate their parents from other adults, this was so with only 10% of the A-NI children. Similarly, a lack of emotional expression was twice as common in the A-MR group and three times as many A-MR children were unable to engage in simple cooperative play with the psychologists in the test situation. Deviant social responses (such as smelling the psychologist or touching his body during testing) were also much commoner in the A-MR group (Table II).

Language

All the austistic children in both groups were late in speaking and all showed a marked impairment in imaginative or pretend play in early childhood (suggesting a defect in "inner language," Rutter, 1972). However, although both groups were delayed in speech the A-MR group displayed more severe retardation. The mean age of first use of single words was 4 years 7 months for the A-MR group and 2 years 6 months for the A-NI group ($t = 2.78$; $df = 33$; $p < .01$). The mean age of first use of phrases to communicate was 6 years 5 months in the A-MR group and 4 years 8 months in the A-NI group ($t = 2.68$; $df = 32$; $p < .05$).

In both groups echolalia had occurred in virtually all children who could speak. Most of the speaking children had also shown pronominal reversal, using *you* for *I*. This occurred in over four-fifths (85%) of the children of normal IQ compared with half (45%) of the retarded group, although the difference fell short of significant ($\bar{\chi}^2 = 2.54$). There was a greater tendency for the normally intelligent children to have shown undue sensitivity to noise; 90% had displayed this compared with 53% of the retarded children ($\bar{\chi}^2 = 4.29$; $df = 1$; $p < .05$). However, there were no differences between the groups in the number of children who had been thought to be deaf at some time (about 80% of each group).

Ritualistic or compulsive behaviors

All the children in both groups had shown some form of stereotyped, ritualistic, or compulsive behavior but the pattern of such behavior differed somewhat between the groups (see Table III). Resistance to environmental change and attachments to odd objects were both twice as common in the A-MR group. Over half the retarded autistic children

Table III. Ritualistic or compulsive behaviors (as reported by parents)

	A-MR N	Group (N = 17) %	A-NI N	Group (N = 19) %	χ^2	p
Resistance to change	14	(82)	8	(42)	4.54	.05
Attachment to odd objects	11	(65)	6	(32)	2.73	n.s.
Both of above	9	(53)	2	(11)	5.74	.025
Rituals	5	(29)	13	(68)	4.01	.05
Difficult adaptation to new situations	9	(53)	14	(74)	.90	n.s.
Quasi-obsessive behaviors	12	(71)	16	(84)	.34	n.s.

Table IV. Stereotyped movements and self-injury

	A-MR N	Group (N = 17) %	A-NI N	Group (N = 19) %	χ^2	p
Self-injury (ever)[a]	12	(71)	6	(32)	4.01	.05
Self-injury in test situation	1	(6)	0	(0)	.00	n.s.
Hand stereotypies (ever)[a]	13	(77)	8	(42)	3.06	n.s. (= .06)
Hand stereotypies in test situation	8	(47)	2	(11)	4.29	.05
Other stereotyped movements in test situation	8	(47)	9	(47)	.10	n.s.
Facial grimacing in test situation	5	(29)	3	(16)	.34	n.s.
At least 4 of above	7	(41)	1	(5)	4.78	.05

[a]The two "ever" items are based on parental reports.

Table V. Disturbance in public (as reported by parents)

Disturbance	A-MR N	Group (N = 17) %	A-NI N	Group (N = 19) %	χ^2	p
Visiting relatives	9	(64)	6	(35)	1.55	n.s.
In restaurants	8	(53)	5	(26)	1.57	n.s.
In hotels and guest houses	11	(85)	10	(62)	.82	n.s.
In 2 or 3 of above	10	(83)	5	(36)	4.21	.05
Relatives visiting	5	(33)	4	(22)	.10	n.s.
Friends visiting	6	(40)	6	(33)	.49	n.s.
Visiting friends	10	(71)	12	(75)	.04	n.s.
At theatre, circus, etc.	9	(60)	11	(58)	.05	n.s.
In shops	15	(94)	11	(58)	4.12	.05
On buses and trains	7	(44)	1	(6)	4.91	.05

showed both symptoms compared with only one in nine of those in the normally intelligent group. On the other hand, rituals were twice as common in the A-NI group and problems in adapting to new situations were slightly (but not significantly) commoner in the intelligent children.

Other phenomena

Stereotyped movements and self-injury

Three-fifths of the A-MR children were reported to have shown self-injurious behavior such as head banging or wrist biting but this had occurred in only a third of the A-NI group (see Table IV). Also, hand and finger stereotypies were considerably more frequent in the retarded autistic children than in those of normal intelligence. Other stereotyped movements (such as rocking) did not differ between the groups.

The A-MR children differed markedly from the A-NI children in the number of these features shown. Each child was given a score 0 to 6 according to the number of features listed in Table IV which were present. Four-fifths of the retarded autistic children displayed at least one and two-fifths showed four or more. In contrast, only some half of the intelligent children showed any of the features and only one out of the 19 A-NI children had four or more ($t = 2.79$; $df = 34$; $p < .01$).

Social disturbance

The great majority of the autistic children in both groups showed disruptive or socially embarrassing behavior in public situations or in the company of other people (see Table V). Thus, three-quarters of the children in both groups showed disturbance when visiting the houses of family friends and a similar proportion did so when taken to hotels or guest houses. In both groups autistic children showed less disturbance when people visited their home than when taken to other people's houses or to public buildings. However, in most situations the A-MR children were somewhat more likely than the A-NI children to show disturbance and in several instances the difference reached statistical significance. Nearly all the A-MR children (94%) showed disturbance in shops compared with 58% of A-NI children, and more than two-fifths of the A-MR group (44%) showed disturbance in buses or trains in contrast to only one child (6%) in the A-NI group.

Developmental milestones

More A-MR children than A-NI children were delayed in their motor development (see Table VI). Only two A-MR children (13%) were able to sit without support on a flat surface by age 7 months, whereas over half of the A-NI children could do so. Similar but less marked trends (falling short of statistical significance) were present with the ages of standing without support and of walking unaided. For the group as a whole about a third of the children were delayed in their gross motor development as shown by the 90% level on the Denver scales (Frankenburg & Dodds, 1967).

Autistic children were also delayed in their acquisition of bowel and bladder control (Table VII) but the two groups did not differ in this respect. A third were still soiling at age 4 years and half were not yet dry at night by 5 years of age.

Social class

In both groups the great majority of the fathers held nonmanual jobs. There was a nonsignificant tendency ($p = .07$ on two-tail exact test) for more of the A-NI children to come from professional or managerial families (Table VIII).

Table VI. Motor development (as reported by parents)

	A-MR N	Group (N = 16)[a] %	A-NI N	Group (N = 19) %	χ^2	p
Sitting up unaided by 7 months	2	(13)	10	(53)	4.57	.05
Standing holding support by 10 months	3	(19)	7	(37)	.65	n.s.
Walking unaided by 14 months	4	(25)	7	(37)	.15	n.s.

[a] 1 not known.

Table VII. Toilet training (as reported by parents)

	A-MR N	Group (N = 17) %	A-NI N	Group (N = 19) %	$\bar{\chi}^2$	p
Not clean by 4 years	4	(24)	9	(47)	1.30	n.s.
Not dry during day by 4 years	9	(53)	11	(58)	.00	n.s.
Not dry at night by 5 years	10	(59)	9	(47)	.13	n.s.

Table VIII. Social class

Social class	A-MR N	Group (N = 17) %	A-NI N	Group (N = 19) %
Professional/managerial	9	(53)	14	(74)
Clerical	7	(41)	2	(11)
Manual	1	(6)	3	(16)

Follow-up findings

Findings on differences in the course of autistic children's development according to IQ level are available from two studies; the three units study already mentioned (Bartak & Rutter, 1973; Rutter & Bartak, 1973) and the long-term follow-up of children who had attended the Maudsley Hospital (Rutter, 1970).[2] The first shows the level of educational attainments in autistic children, all of whom attended special units and who had reached at least 10 years of age (see Tables IX and X). Although some of the mentally retarded autistic children had made worthwhile scholastic progress, the attainments in both arithmetic and reading were considerably greater in children of normal intelligence. This is; of course, what would be found in any group of nonautistic children.

Table IX. Reading accuracy according to IQ level (three units study — children aged at least 10 years at follow-up)[a]

	IQ (at start of Study)		
Neale reading age	69 or less	70 or more	Total
Below floor of test	21	1	22
R.A. below 8 years	4	6	10
R.A. 8 years or higher	6	7	13
Total	31	14	45

[a]$\chi^2 = 10.88$; $df = 2$; $p < .01$.

Table X. Arithmetical skills according to IQ level (three units study — children aged at least 10 years at follow-up)[a]

	IQ (at start of study)		
Arithmetical skills	69 or less	70 or more	Total
No skills	13	0	13
Single skills only (e.g., counting)	12	4	16
All four basic skills (with double-figure numbers)	6	10	16
Total	31	14	45

[a]$\chi^2 = 10.54$; $df = 2$; $p < .01$.

Table XI. Follow-up findings by IQ level (Maudsley Hospital follow-up)

	Initial IQ		Follow-up IQ	
	< 70 (N = 45)	70 + (N = 19)	< 70 (N = 47)	70 + (N = 17)
Epileptic seizures	35.6%	.0%a	31.9%	5.9%b
Work/higher education	6.7%	36.8%c	.0%	58.8%d

[a]$\chi^2 = 7.21$; $p < .01$.
[b]$\chi^2 = 3.23$; $p < .10$.
[c]$\chi^2 = 7.08$; $p < .01$.
[d]$\chi^2 = 28.46$; $p < .001$.

[2]The figures from both studies have been reanalyzed in order to enable the results to be expressed in terms of the same IQ split used in the rest of this paper.

The Maudsley Hospital study shows the outcome in 64 youngsters, all of whom had been followed until at least 17 years of age. The findings are given separately according to the IQ at the time of initial assessment and at the time of follow-up. Only 10 of the 64 children were in a different IQ group on the two occasions and the results of the two comparisons are closely similar (see Table XI). A third of the children with an IQ below 70 developed epileptic seizures during adolescence, whereas scarcely any of those of normal intelligence did so. In contrast, very few of the mentally retarded autistic children obtained paid employment but roughly half of those with an IQ of 70 or above got jobs on the open market.

Discussion

Previous studies (Rutter, 1966; Bartak et al., 1975) have shown the main features which characterize autistic children and which differentiate them from children with other psychiatric disorders or with a serious developmental language disorder. These features (impaired development of social relationships, delayed and deviant language development, ritualistic behaviors, and social disturbances) are present in autistic children of both low and high intelligence. In some respects the mentally retarded autistic children showed a more severely autistic picture in that their language delay was greater, their personal relationships were more severely disturbed, and they exhibited more socially disruptive behavior in more situations. However, some autistic features were more frequent in autistic children of higher intelligence. This was the case, for example, with pronominal reversal, undue sensitivity to noise, and rituals. It appears that, to some extent, the pattern of autistic symptoms differs according to the child's nonverbal IQ level, although the similarities between the A-MR and A-NI groups outweigh the dissimilarities.

The differences according to IQ level are greater with respect to phenomena less centrally associated with autism and are greatest in terms of prognosis. Mentally retarded autistic children more often show self-injury, hand and finger stereotypies, deviant social responses, and delayed social development. Also, as already noted, other studies have indicated that they more often show a wider range of perceptual deficits and of neurodevelopmental abnormalities. The present findings demonstrate that mentally retarded autistic children are much more likely to develop epileptic siezures during adolescence and to have a worse outcome in terms of educational attainments and employment. In all these respects, mentally retarded autistic children behave similarly to nonautistic children of low IQ, although the presence of autism is associated with additional social problems.

In terms of scholastic progress, social competence, and work opportunities, the child's IQ level is as influential as is the presence of autism. It is necessary to appreciate this in the clinical care of autistic children. It is also important to recognize that a lack of cognitive skills may increase the likelihood to certain types of abnormal behavior, as suggested both by this report and by experimental studies (Churchill, 1971; Koegel & Covert, 1972). What still remains uncertain is how far differences in IQ level in autistic children are associated with differences in etiology or in the nature of the disorder. Whereas, at least in early childhood, the behavior of mentally retarded and intelligent autistic children is fairly similar, there are some differences in pattern of symptoms and there is a very large difference in the frequency of epilepsy. These findings suggest the possibility that there may be differences in the origin of autism according to the presence or absence of mental retardation. This possibility should be taken into account when undertaking biological, genetic, social, psychological, or developmental studies which aim to assess possible etiological factors in autism.

References

Bartak, L., Rutter, M. Special educational treatment of autistic children: a comparative study. I. Design of study and characteristics of units. *J. Child. Psychol. & Psychiat.*, 1973; **14**, 161-179.

Bartak, L., Rutter, M., Cox, A. A comparative study of infantile autism and specific developmental receptive language disorder. I. The children. *Br. J. Psychiat.*, 1975; **126**, 127-145.

Churchill, D. W. Effects of success and failure in psychotic children. *Arch. Gen. Psychiat.*, 1971; **25**, 208-214.

Cox, A., Rutter, M., Newman, S., Bartak, L. A comparative study of infantile autism and specific developmental receptive language disorder. II. Parental characteristics. *Br. J. Psychiat.*, 1975; **126**, 146-159.

DeMyer, M. K., Barton, S., Alpern, G. D., Kimberlin, C., Allen, J., Yang, E., Steele, R. The measured intelligence of autistic children. *J. Autism & Child. Schiz.*, 1974; **4**, 42-60.

Frankenburg, W. K., Dodds, J. B. The Denver developmental screening test. *J. Pediat.*, 1967; **71** 181-191.

Goldfarb, W. *Childhood Schizophrenia.* Cambridge, Massachusetts: Harvard University Press, 1961.

Goldfarb, W. *Growth and change of schizophrenic children: a longitudinal study.* New York: John Wiley, 1974.

Hermelin, B., O'Connor, N. *Psychological experiments with autistic children.* Oxford: Pergamon Press, 1970.

Kanner, L. Autistic disturbances of affective contact. *Nerv. Child,* 1943; **2**, 217-250.

Koegel, R. L., Covert, A. The relationship of self-stimulation to learning in autistic children. *J. Appl. Behav. Anal.*, 1972; **5**, 381-387.

Lockyer, L., Rutter, M. A five to fifteen-year follow-up study of infantile psychosis—III. Psychological aspects. *Br. J. Psychiat.*, 1969; **115**, 865-882.

Lockyer, L., Rutter, M. A five to fifteen-year follow-up study of infantile psychosis—IV. Patterns of cognitive ability. *Br. J. Soc. & Clin. Psychol.*, 1970; **9**, 152-163.

Rutter, M. Behavioural and cognitive characteristics of a series of psychotic children. *In* Wing, J. K. (Ed.), *Early Childhood Autism: clinical, educational and social aspects.* London: Pergamon Press, 1966.

Rutter, M. Autistic children: Infancy to adulthood. *Seminars in Psychiat.*, 1970; **2**, 435-450.

Rutter, M. The effects of language delay on development. *In* Rutter, M., Martin, J. A. M., (Eds.), *The child with delayed speech.* (Clinics in Developmental Medicine No. 43.) London: SIMP/Heinemann, 1972.

Rutter, M., Bartak, L. Special educational treatment of autistic children: a comparative study— II. Follow-up findings and implications for services. *J. Child. Psychol. & Psychiat.*, 1973; **14**, 241-270.

Stutsman, R. *Guide for Administering the Merrill-Palmer Scale of Mental Tests.* New York: Harcourt, Brace and World, 1948.

Wechsler, D. *Wechsler Intelligence Scale for Children.* New York: Psychological Corporation, 1949.

Reprinted from *J. Autism & Child. Schiz.*, 1976; **6**:2, 109-120 by kind permission of Dr. Lawrence Bartak, Monash University, Clayton, Victoria, Australia 3168, Professor M. Rutter, Institute of Psychiatry, London SE5 8AF and the publishers Plenum Publishing Corp., New York, NY 10013.

MINOR SELF-INJURY

Brian R. Ballinger

Senior Registrar, Dundee Psychiatric Service: Royal Dundee Liff Hospital, Liff, By Dundee.

Summary

A survey was made of self-injury in patients in a mental subnormality hospital and a psychiatric hospital. Ninety-three out of 626 subnormals (14·9 per cent) and 20 out of 584 psychiatric patients (3·4 per cent) had injured themselves in the previous month. The relationship of self-injury to other characteristics of the patients is considered. It is suggested that individual attention, recreation and constructive occupations may be more important than drug treatment in the alleviation of these symptoms.

Introduction

Self-injury is a frequent occurrence in both mentally subnormal and mentally ill patients. The aim of this study was to determine its prevalence and nature in hospital populations of such individuals.

Self-injury is common during normal early development: many infants scratch, hit or bite themselves, bang their heads or pull their hair. Self-injury is also found in children deprived of maternal care or in institutions and in the psychoses of childhood (Green, 1967).

Berkson and Davenport (1962) reported stereotyped movements in two-thirds of a group of severely subnormal individuals, and some of these resulted in self-injury. They found a negative correlation with intelligence.

Self-injury is seen in neurotic conditions, and in both functional and organic psychoses (Battle and Pollitt, 1964). Groups of incidents of self-injury may occur among the inmates of institutions. Offer and Barglow (1960) have described an outbreak of wrist scratching and cutting in patients aged 14 to 22 years in a small psychiatric unit.

Menninger (1938) suggested that self-mutilation may be a form of attenuated suicide, a compromise which averts total annihilation.

Method

For the purpose of this study, self-injury was defined as any painful or destructive act, committed by the patient against his own body. Accidents, tearing clothes, window-breaking, swallowing dirt and refusal of food were excluded. Nail-biting was the subject of a separate study (Ballinger, 1970). Rubbing and scratching were only included when persistent and causing visible injury.

The study was limited to examples of self-injury occurring within the previous month and whilst the patient was in hospital. All patients were examined by the writer, and the further details were obtained from the ward nursing staff.

All the patients in Strathmartine Hospital, Dundee on 1 February 1969 (N 631) were studied, except for 5 who were discharged before they could be examined. Strathmartine Hospital is the only hospital for the mentally subnormal in the Eastern Region, Scotland. The intelligence quotients were taken as noted in the case records.

All the patients in the Royal Dundee Liff Hospital (N 598) on 1 November 1969 were studied, except for 14 who were discharged before they could be examined. The Royal Dundee Liff Hospital is a psychiatric hospital serving Dundee and the surrounding districts. The diagnoses were taken as recorded in the case notes.

Results

In the subnormality hospital, 93 out of 626 patients (15 per cent) had injured themselves in the previous month: 46 out of 343 males (13 per cent) and 47 out of 283 females (17 per cent). In the psychiatric hospital 20 patients out of 584 (3 per cent) had injured themselves in the previous month: 6 out of 226 males (3 per cent) and 14 out of 358 females (4 per cent). The distribution according to age is shown in Table I.

Table I. Self-injury and age

Age range	Mentally subnormal			Mentally ill		
	Total	Self-injury	% Self-injury	Total	Self-injury	% Self injury
0-9	40	7	17·5	0	0	0·0
10-19	102	18	17·9	4	2	50·0
20-29	151	27	17·9	34	0	0·0
30-39	117	13	11·1	41	1	2·4
40-49	109	14	12·8	38	1	1·1
50-59	66	6	9·1	96	3	3·1
60-69	33	7	21·2	142	7	4·9
70 and over	8	1	12·5	179	6	3·3
Total	626	93	14·9	584	20	3.4

There did not seem to be any clear relationship between self-injury and length of stay in hospital in either group, but the patients admitted to the subnormality hospital before 1940 had a rather lower prevalence than the remainder of the patients in that hospital (7 out of 114 or 6 per cent).

The distribution of self-injury according to intelligence quotient in the subnormality hospital is shown in Table II. In this hospital self-injury was significantly more prevalent amongst the 161 patients who were non-ambulant or who walked with difficulty, occurring in 36 (22 per cent) of them ($\chi^2 = 9·7$, p<0·01).

Table II. Self-injury and IQ in subnormals

IQ	Total	Self-injury	% Self-injury
0–19	143	42	29·4
20–35	146	26	17·8
36–51	144	15	10·4
52–67	142	8	5·6
68 and over	51	2	3·9

In the psychiatric hospital population, more than half the instances of self-injury occurred in schizophrenics, but instances were also found in patients with organic psychosis, depressive psychosis, paranoid psychosis, personality disorder and epilepsy (see Table III).

Table III. Self-injury and diagnosis in psychiatric hospital patients

Diagnosis	Total	Self-injury	% Self-injury
Organic psychosis	141	4	2·8
Schizophrenia	170	11	6·5
Depressive psychosis	108	2	1·8
Mania and hypomania	15	0	—
Paranoid psychosis	63	1	1·6
Personality disorder and neurosis	56	1	1·6
Other	31	1	3·2

Thirty out of 93 (32 per cent) subnormals and 9 out of 20 (45 per cent) psychiatric patients who injured themselves were regularly engaged in some form of occupational or industrial therapy off the ward. In each case this was lower than the overall rate for the hospital.

Only 42 out of 93 subnormals (45 per cent) had been visited by relatives or friends during the preceding three months, and this was significantly less than the rate of visitation for the rest of the hospital population, which was 59 per cent ($\bar{X}^2 = 5.8$, p<0.02).

In the subnormality hospital the types of self-injury were picking, striking, scratching, banging, biting, pulling hair out and rubbing (see Table IV). Some patients injured themselves in more than one manner. In this sample self-biting and pulling hair out did not occur in any patients with IQs over 35. Some forms of self-injury tended to occur particularly at one site, and biting was usually confined to the upper limb, whereas self-striking mainly involved the face and head. Picking the skin caused large ulcers in a few instances, sometimes even with destruction of cartilage.

In the psychiatric hospital population the forms of self-injury were scratching, picking, striking, rubbing, cutting and tying string round fingers (see Table IV).

Table IV. Type of self-injury, number of instances

	Mentally subnormal	Mentally ill
Picking	35	7
Striking	20	4
Scratching	19	8
Banging	17	—
Biting	14	—
Pulling out hair	6	—
Rubbing	6	1
Cutting	—	1
Tying string round arm	—	1
Total instances	117	22
Total patients involved	93	20

The nursing staff were asked about the factors that appeared to provoke self-injury. In the subnormality hospital these were given as annoyance (19 instances), frustration (6), excitement (4), boredom (2), attention seeking (1), depression (1), constipation (1), involuntary movements (1) and no apparent cause (58). In the psychiatric patients the causes were given as agitation (3), delusions (2), anger (2), hallucinations (1), depression (1), boredom (1) and no apparent cause (10).

In 14 of the mentally subnormal and 4 of the psychiatric patients self-injury was said by the nursing staff to produce major difficulties in management. This was usually because of fears that the patients might injure themselves severely.

Of the subnormals 57 and of the psychiatric patients 10 were receiving psychotropic drugs, in some instances partly to control the tendency to self-injury. According to the ward staff, medication may have reduced the incidence of self-injury of 14 of the subnormals, and one psychiatric patient, the drugs concerned being phenothiazines (7), antidepressants (3), benzodiazepines (2), barbiturates (2) and lithium (1).

In a few instances restraint was used.

Discussion

The definition of self-injury adopted was inevitably somewhat arbitrary, and some of the acts excluded may have sometimes involved an element of self-injury, e.g. window-breaking and eating dirt. The restriction of the study to recent in-patient behaviour led to the exclusion of all instances of attempted suicide.

Self-injury was common in the mental sub-normality hospital, and some of the less severe instances may have been missed. It was commoner in patients in the lower IQ ranges; which supports the concept that it may be regarded as an aspect of constitutional failure of development. However, as the more severely subnormal patient was less likely to be involved in activities and occupations, environmental factors were also involved.

The staff could suggest possible precipitating factors in only a minority of the subnormal patients. A few had features suggesting the presence of a superadded mental illness, but these could not be clearly related to the self-injury.

In the psychiatric hospital population only 3 per cent of the patients injured themselves, as opposed to 15 per cent of the subnormals. Most psychiatric patients did not give any explanation of their self-injury. A 69-year-old paranoid psychotic patient who picked her face said that she had wire coming out through her skin. A schizophrenic girl of 17 years said that her self-inflicted scratches were caused by cats.

In both hospitals self-injury occurred over a wide range of ages. In the subnormals there was a fall in the prevalence of self-injury after the age of 30, apart from a peak in the seventh decade.

It was my impression that environmental restriction, boredom and frustration played a part in worsening self-injury in many patients. The majority of patients who injured themselves did not take part in any regular activity off the ward, and most of them spent the greater part of their time lying or sitting in the ward without any occupation. In some instances the severity of the mental subnormality or illness made it difficult or impossible to provide any constructive occupation, and staff shortages limited the amount of individual attention that could be given.

In both hospitals self-injury was said to be a major management problem in only a minority of patients, and sometimes this was because of fears of severe injury which may not always have been realistic. The staff appeared to have more difficulty in dealing with self-injury in patients with personality disorders or less severe mental subnormality than in those with gross psychosis, dementia or severe mental subnormality. Some staff members thought that such behaviour, sometimes described as being 'attention seeking', should be dealt with by ignoring it. Others thought that this made matters worse, and that self-injury could best be avoided by forming a good relationship with the patient.

Drugs appear to be of benefit in only a few patients and then not always clearly so. In most instances it is probably more important to provide individual attention, occupation and diversity of surroundings, at a level appropriate to the individual.

Acknowledgements

I wish to thank the Consultant Psychiatrists at Royal Dundee Liff Hospital and Strathmartine Hospital for their helpful suggestions and for permission to study patients under their care. I am grateful to Professor I. R. C. Batchelor for his advice during the preparation of this paper.

References

Ballinger, B. R. The prevalence of nail-biting in normal and abnormal populations. *Br. J. of Psychiat.,* 1970; **117**, 445-6.

Battle, R. J. V., Pollitt, J. D. Self inflicted injuries. *Br. J. of Plastic Surgery,* 1964; **17**, 400-12.

Berkson, G., Davenport, R. K. Stereotyped movements of mental defectives. *Am. J. of Ment. Defic., 1962;* **66**, 849-52.

Green, A. H. Self-mutilation in schizophrenic children. *Arch. Gen. Psychiat.,* 1967; **17**, 234-44.

Menninger, K. (1938). *Man Against Himself.* London: George C. Harrap, 1938.

Offer, D., Barglow, P. Adolescent and young adult self-mutilation incidents in a general psychiatric hospital. *Arch. Gen. Psychiat.* 1960; **3**, 194-204.

PREVALENCE OF SELF-INJURIOUS BEHAVIORS IN A LARGE STATE FACILITY FOR THE RETARDED: A THREE-YEAR FOLLOW-UP STUDY[1]

Stephen R. Schroeder, Carolyn S. Shroeder, Becky Smith, Joanna Dalldorf
The University of North Carolina at Chapel Hill

A combined informant questionnaire and interview survey of self-injurious behavior (SIB) at a large state facility for the retarded was conducted independently three times over a 3-year period. Prevalence consistently was about 10% of the population. SIB cases tended to be younger and institutionalized longer than the rest of the population. Severe cases had a longer history of chronic SIB. SIB cases had more seizure disorders, severe language handicaps, visual impairments, and severe or profound retardation than the rest of the population. They appeared to fulfil most of the Rutter (1966) criteria for autism. But unlike the severely autistic, there was little relation of sex to incidence of SIB. Over 90% of SIB cases changed status over 3 years, suggesting that SIB was amenable to behavior modification in most cases (94%). Psychotropic behavior control medications helped in some intervention programs (32%). SIB remitted spontaneously in 21% of SIB cases where there had been no behavioral or drug intervention.

Introduction

Self-injurious behavior (SIB) is defined as repetitive acts by individuals directed toward themselves which result in physical harm or tissue damage (Tate & Baroff, 1966). The most commonly noted topographies are head banging, self-biting, and self-scratching. The prevalence of such bizarre behaviors has been studied mostly among residential populations, yet the estimates vary for different clinical populations. Green (1967) and Shodell and Reiter (1968) found that up to 40% of schizophrenic children in residential centers engaged in SIB. An extensive review by Baumeister and Rollings [1976] reported prevalence of 10-17% among the institutionalized retarded.

Analytic prevalence studies of SIB in clinical populations may give some hints as to how these behaviors developed, how they cluster, why they persist, and what their prognosis for remission is. A good example is a factor-analytic study of SIB recently performed by Maisto, Baumeister, and Maisto (in press) on a questionnaire survey of an entire institution of 1,300 retarded persons. Measures were taken on the severity and type of SIB, other maladaptive behaviors, length of institutionalization, medical diagnosis, IQ, organic pathology, sex, and several environmental variables. Their main conclusions were that SIB was more prevalent among the profoundly retarded, neurologically impaired, younger female residents but was more severe among males. SIB cases also exhibited high rates of stereotypy and aggressive behavior.

In the only study of prevalence of SIB in autistic children Bartak and Rutter (1976) reported on stereotyped movements and self-injury in a group of 36 autistic children in outpatient settings. Self-injurious behavior was found to be present significantly more often in autistic children whose performance IQ was in the retarded range ($IQ < 70$) as compared to those with performance IQs in the nonretarded range ($IQ \geq 70$). In this respect mentally retarded autistic children appear to behave similarly to mentally retarded nonautistic children (Ross, 1972).

[1]This research was supported by USPHS Grant #HD-03-110 to the Child Development Research Institute of the University of North Carolina at Chapel Hill and DDSA H.I.P. Grant #51-P-20521 to Murdoch Center, Stephen R. Schroeder, project director. Thanks are due to Carolyn Westcot and Patricia Wesley for assistance in collection of the data.

Prevalence estimates of SIB among schizophrenic children in residential centers (Green, 1967; Shodell & Reiter, 1968) have been considerably higher (30-40%) than those for the institutionalized retarded. These differences may be due simply to different survey techniques used. In the Green (1967) study hospital records only were searched. In the Shodell and Reiter (1968) study staff were instructed to look for SIB among their patients for a 10-day period. In both studies no distinction was made as to whether prevalence included history and/or current performance of SIB. Bartak and Rutter (1976) found in their outpatient population of autistic boys that 71% of those who were retarded were reported by parents to have performed SIB at one time or another, whereas only 6% of the same population currently exhibited SIB when observed directly in a test situation. A more thorough study of SIB prevalence among the autistic should be conducted since it is often taken as a sign of severe handicap and poor prognosis (Rutter, 1966).

The focus of the study to be reported involved repeated independent surveys of SIB over a period of 3 years in the entire population (1,150) of a residential facility for the retarded. This longitudinal approach allowed a review of the incidence of new cases reported as well as a follow-up of previously reported cases.

Method

The survey was conducted at Murdoch Center, a state facility for retarded persons who ranged in age from 5 to 85 years. Fifty-five percent of the population was female.

Procedure and survey questionnaire

Three independent surveys were performed, one in the fall of 1973, one in the spring of 1975, and one in the fall of 1976. Each survey proceeded in a stepwise fashion: (1) All social workers of the institution were asked to refer the SIB cases in their residential units to a special federally funded program for SIB residents. (2) Next, each social worker was interviewed by a pediatrician or a psychologist or an educator to establish reliable definitions and severity of SIB for each referral. The SIB was classified as severe if it occurred at least once a day and caused in the client at some time bleeding, bruises, broken bones, or other tissue damage that required intervention by the medical staff. All other referrals were considered mild cases. (3) Using a checklist, the interviewers searched the medical and programming file of each referral for pertinent developmental history. (4) This same checklist served as a questionnaire in a group interview with the ward staff where each resident lived. This procedure allowed an interlocking check involving the program file, the medical file, and the residential care staff. Any discrepancies between staff interviewed had to be resolved before data were used. Less than 1% of the disagreements could not be resolved.

The checklist/questionnaire consisted of 15 major categories. These were (1) background information including name, date of birth, sex, birthweight, number of siblings, birth order, admitting date, diagnosis, history of institutional placement, and level of retardation; (2) history of self-stimulatory behaviors or rhythmic movements including types, dates of onset, current behavior, and siblings with self-stimulatory behavior or rhythmic movements; (3) history of self-injurious behavior (i.e., headbanging, biting, scratching, gouging, pinching, pica, coprophagy, ruminative vomiting, aerophagia, and polydipsia), including descriptions, date of onset, current behavior, provoking events (if known), and treatment; (4) history of other deviant behaviors (i.e., aggression, destruction, stereotypy, hyperactivity, screaming, tantrums, stripping in public, and psychotic behaviors); (5) history of injuries including type and date; (6) history of seizure and other organic disorders (i.e., cerebral palsy, hydrocephalus, poliomyelitis, tuberous sclerosis, hypoxia, anoxia, congenital anomalies, birth trauma, and meningitis), including onset date, type, frequency, medication history, and family history; (7) history of ear infections; (8) visual, hearing, and other sensory deficits; (9) history of physical punishment; (10) history of migraine headaches; (11) drug history; (12) nutritional problems; (13) communication skills, including dates of first words, sentences, gestures, unintelligible sounds, and present verbal behavior; (14) responses to auditory stimuli, including likes and dislikes; and (15) responses to other stimuli such as olfactory or kinesthetic.

Results

Prevalence of SIB

A total of 208 different SIB cases was identified over a 3 year period. For each individual survey the number of referrals was relatively constant (100, 119, 114) at about 10% of the institutional population. Of the 208 clients 70 were referred on two of the surveys and only 31 were referred on all three surveys. Out of 163 cases referred in the first two surveys in 1973 or 1975, referral of 62 was not renewed in 1975 or 1976.

Table I. Relative prevalence of sex and severity of SIB as a function of level of retardation, chronological age, chronicity, and length of institutionalization

Variables	Mild SIB			Severe SIB			Total non-SIB institutional population
	Male	Female	Total mild	Male	Female	Total severe	
Mean percentage of Cases	51	49	100	53	47	100	100
Mildly retarded	0	1	1	0	0	0	4
Moderately retarded	4	4	8	4	2	6	11
Severely or profoundly retarded	47	44	91	49	45	94	85
Average age (years)	23.5	21.1	22.3	18.0	25.9	22.2	25.6
Average chronicity of SIB (years)	7.5	6.1	6.8	12.2	11.1	11.6	–
Average length of institutionalization (years)	10.1	8.5	9.3	11.4	12.3	11.8	6.7

Table 1 gives a breakdown of the total sample of 208 SIB cases according to sex, severity, level of retardation, chronological age, chronicity, and length of institutionalization. SIB occurred more frequently among the more severely retarded residents ($\bar{x}^2 = 8.72$, $df = 2$, $p < .02$). SIB was reported among 2% of the total mildly retarded institutional population, among 9% of the moderately retarded, and among 14% of the severely and profoundly retarded. Average age of SIB clients was slightly but significantly younger than that of a random sample chosen from the non-SIB institutional population ($t = 1.98$, $df = 414$, $p < .025$). Average length of institutionalization of the SIB cases was significantly longer than that of the non-SIB institutional sample ($t = 2.78$, $df = 414$, $p < .005$).

Of the 208 different cases of SIB reported, 47 (23%) were considered severe in at least one of the surveys and 161 cases were reported as mild. However, comparisons of severe and mild SIB cases in Table 1 yielded no significant differences except for chronicity. Average chronicity of severe SIB cases was nearly twice as long (11.6 vs. 6.8 years) as that of mild SIB cases ($t = 3.02$, $df = 26$, $p < .01$). However, chronicity data could only be obtained in 27% of all SIB cases, so this finding must be interpreted with caution.

Comparisons of sex differences on the variables in Table 1 yielded essentially no statistically significant differences except for average age of severe male versus female SIB cases ($t = 2.93$, $df = 22$, $p < .01$).

Other problems of SIB clients

Table II shows the other behavior problems of SIB cases as a function of severity of SIB. Again there were no significant differences as a function of sex or severity, the only exception being that there were more seizure disorders among severe than among mild SIB cases ($\bar{x}^2 = 7.22$, $df = 1$, $p < .01$). However, there were significantly more impairments among SIB cases than in the institutional sample in vision ($\bar{x}^2 = 18.72$, $df = 1$, $p < .001$), receptive language ($\bar{x}^2 = 25.16$, $df = 1$, $p < .001$), and expressive language ($\bar{x}^2 = 99.60$, $df = 1$, $p < .001$). No differences in hearing impairments or "other organic disorders" were noted.

Changes in status of SIB children

During the period of the three surveys, a federally funded Hospital Improvement

Program dealing with SIB existed at the institution. The three surveys were checked to see if those referred in the 1973 and/or 1975 had changed status in 1975 and/or 1976. Results showed that over 90% of the referrals had changed status. Of particular interest were those clients reported in 1973 or 1975 but not reported again in 1975 or 1976. An interviewer reinterviewed all relevant ward staff to ask them specifically what had happened to these clients. The changes in status of all clients referred in 1973 and 1975 for whom complete records could be obtained are shown in Table III.

Table II. Percentages of SIB and non-SIB cases with other behavior problems

Associated problems	SIB population		Total non-SIB institutional population
	Severe	Mild	
Stereotyped behaviors	37	35	_[a]
Other misbehaviors	25	30	_[a]
Seizure disorders	41	20	22
Other organic disorders	22	21	20
Severe visual impairment	22	23	7
Severe hearing impairment	8	8	5
No receptive language	40	33	13
No expressive language	63	72	20

[a]Information not available.

Table III. Frequency of changes in status of SIB clients over a 3-year period as a function of behavior management and medication contingencies

Medication	Behavior management			
	No program		Program	
	Improved	Worse or no change	Improved	Worse or no change
Seizure only	0	5	2	0
Neuroleptic only	2	5	8	0
Combination	10	20	9	1
No medication	6	22	10	1
Total	18	52	29	2

Table III reveals some very interesting results. Of 31 clients, all of whom were severe chronic SIB cases and who were in behavior modification programs designed to control SIB, 29 (94%) were judged by the direct care staff to have improved whether or not they were receiving behavior-control medication. Statistical analysis showed the effect of being in a behavior modification program versus not being in one to be significant ($x^2 = 42.50$, $df = 1$, $p < .001$). Of those 70 cases not in a behavior modification program 37 were receiving neuroleptic medication, e.g., Melleril, Thorazine, Haldol, or some combination of drugs. A typical combination would be Phenobarbitol, Thorazine, Artane, and Tofranil. Thirty-three cases were receiving seizure medication only or no medication. Neuroleptic medication was judged by direct care residential staff to have a positive effect in 32% of cases, whereas 18% of cases on no medication or seizure drugs alone improved. The difference between those receiving neuroleptic medication and those receiving no neuroleptic medication or only seizure-control medication was not significant.

Discussion

SIB prevalence among the retarded and the autistic

SIB occurred consistently in about 10% of the institutionalized population at Murdoch Center. Table I suggests that it was more prevalent among the younger, more severely retarded residents who had been institutionalized longer. Severe cases tended to have a longer history of SIB than mild cases. These findings support similar results found in previous studies of the institutionalized retarded (Maisto et al., in press; Smeets, 1971; Soule & O'Brien, 1974).

There does appear to be considerable overlap in the SIB of the autistic and the retarded. Certainly most of the clients in the present survey appeared to meet the Rutter (1966) criteria for autism, i.e., social unrelatedness, language disorders, ritualistic behaviors, and social disturbance. Even though the populations of schizophrenic children surveyed by Green (1967) and Shodell and Reiter (1968) contained the typical 4:1 ratio of boys to girls, the percentage of girls performing SIB was higher than the percentage of boys who performed SIB. A slightly higher percentage of female SIB cases also among the institutionalized retarded was found by Maisto et al. (in press) and Soule and O'Brien (1974), but not by Smeets (1971) or by the present study. The relation of sex to prevalence of SIB is unclear.

Bartak and Rutter (1976) raised the question of whether autism is the same condition when it occurs in the presence of mental retardation as when it is associated with normal levels of nonverbal intelligence. Their survey, which compared 19 nonretarded (IQ > 70) autistic boys younger than 11 years with 17 retarded autistic boys (IQ $\leq$ 70), revealed that the latter performed more self-injury, hand and finger stereotypies, and deviant social responses, and were more delayed in social development. This agrees with the results of the present survey and Maisto et al. (in press) that frequency of SIB is negatively related to IQ.

Although it is probably not a fruitful exercise to try to partial out behaviors resulting from autism and mental retardation, both populations exhibit behaviors that, when combined, may put the child at risk for developing SIB. Both the severely autistic and the severely retarded show more neurological dysfunctions, language and communicative disorders, and antisocial behaviours than the less severely handicapped (Bartak & Rutter, 1976; Goldfarb, 1961; Ross, 1972; Rutter, 1970). That these deficits are correlated with high incidence of SIB is shown for the retarded (see Table II) and for schizophrenic children (Shodell & Reiter, 1968).

The high incidence of visual and language disorders lends support to the view that SIB clients may use their SIB as a discrimative stimulus for reward (Bachman, 1972). In this view SIB is considered a primitive form of communication, a generalized conditioned response that a client uses to establish control and countercontrol of his or her environment. Thus SIB has been noted to increase in rate when, according to ward personnel, the client "gets upset" or "wants something." If the communicative repertoire of a client is restricted by organic handicaps, SIB is a response that can easily become reinforced inadvertently by caretakers.

Acute versus chronic SIB

In the present study 90% of all referrals changed status from one survey to the next, i.e., they were judged by the direct care staff as improved, worse, or no longer a problem. This result is contrary to the pessimistic view (Romanczyk & Goren, 1975) that SIB is always an intransigent problem resistant to intervention. This may be true for some cases but probably not for the majority, as is shown in Table III. Over 94% of cases in behavior modification programs were judged improved. In fact, 6 out of 28 cases (21%) on no medication or formal program remitted their SIB spontaneously. However, it must be noted that, while all clients on behavior modification programs were severe cases, 77% of those on no program were listed as mild cases by the direct care staff.

Behavioral versus pharmacological intervention for SIB

The final point to be made from the data in Table III is that more careful study of the long-term effect of behavioral and pharmacological intervention with SIB seems indicated.

At the facility currently surveyed 63% of severe SIB cases and 51% of mild SIB cases were receiving behavior-control medication, primarily neuroleptics. This is not an unusual practice (Cohen & Sprague, Note 1). Yet the direct care staff reported little evidence of positive therapeutic effects on SIB. The serious side effects of the neuroleptics, e.g., tardive dyskinesia, lenticular opacities (McAndrew, Case, & Treffert, 1972; Polizos, Engelhardt, Hoffman, & Waizer, 1973), suggest cautious use only in cases where therapeutic benefits make the risks worth taking. Just what the therapeutic effects of the neuroleptics are would require a more sophisticated methodology than the single-blind, non-randomized-sample, questionnaire-type design used in the present study and most of the other studies to date on this problem (Sprague & Baxley, in press).

Reference note

1 Cohen, M. N., & Sprague, R. L. *Survey of drug usage in two midwestern institutions for the retarded.* Paper presented at the Gatlingburg Conference on Research in Mental Retardation, Gatlingburg, Tennessee, March 1977.

References

Bachman, J. A. Self-injurious behavior: a behavioral analysis. *J. Abnorm. Psychol.*, 1972; **80**, 211-224.
Bartak, L., Rutter, M. Differences between mentally retarded and normally intelligent autistic children. *J. Aut. & Child. Schiz.*, 1976; **6**, 109-120.
Baumeister, A. A., Rollings, J. P. *Self-injurious behavior. In* Ellis, N. (Ed.). *International review of research in mental retardation.* (Vol. 8). New York: Academic Press, 1976.
Goldfarb, W. *Childhood Schizophrenia.* Cambridge: Harvard University Press, 1961.
Green, A. H. Self-mutilation in schizophrenic children. *Arch. Gen. Psychiat.*, 1967; **17**, 234-244.
Maisto, C. R., Baumeister, A. A., Maisto, A. A. An analysis of variables related to self-injurious behavior among institutionalized retarded persons. *J. Ment. Defic. Res.* (In press).
McAndrew, J. B., Case, Q., Treffert, D. A. Effects of prolonged phenothiazine intake on psychotic and other hospitalized children. *J. Aut. & Child. Schiz.*, 1972; **2**, 79-91.
Polizos, P., Engelhardt, D. M., Hoffman, S. P., Waizer, J. Neurological consequences of psychotropic drug withdrawal in schizophrenic children. *J. Aut. & Child. Schiz.*, 1973; **3**, 247-253.
Romancyzk, R., Goren, E. Severe self-injurious behavior: the problem of clinical control. *J. Clin. Psychol.*, 1975; **43**, 730-739.
Ross, R. T. Behavioral correlates of levels of intelligence.. *Am. J. Ment. Defic.*, 1972; **76**, 545-549.
Rutter, M. *Behavioural and cognitive characteristics of a series of psychotic children. In* Wing, J. K. (Ed.). *Early Childhood Autism: clinical, educational and social aspects.* London: Pergamon Press, 1966.
Rutter, M. Autistic children: infancy to adulthood. *Seminars in Psychiat.*, 1970; **2**, 435-450.
Shodell, M., Reiter, H. Self-mutilative behavior in verbal and non-verbal schizophrenic children. *Arch. Gen. Psychiat.*, 1968; **19**, 453-455.
Smeets, P. M. Some characteristics of mental defectives displaying self-mutilative behavior. *Train. Sch. Bull.*, 1971; **68**, 131-135.
Soule, D., O'Brien, D. Self-injurious behavior in a state center for the retarded: incidence. *Res. & the Retard.*, 1974; **1**, 1-8.
Sprague, R. L., Baxley, G. *Drugs used for the management of behavior in mental retardation. In* Ellis, N. R. (Ed.). *Handbook of mental deficiency.* (2nd edn.). New York: Erlbaum Associates, in press.
Tate, B. G., Baroff, G. S. Aversive control of self-injurious behavior in a psychotic boy. *Behav. Res. & Ther.*, 1966; **4**, 281-287.

Reprinted from *J. Autism & Child. Schiz.*, 1978; **8**:3, 261-269 by kind permission of the authors and the publishers Plenum Publishing Corp., New York, NY 10013.

SECTION II

The development and maintenance
of self-injurious behaviour in individuals
who are mentally handicapped or autistic

Introduction

The appearance of self-injurious behaviour in children or adults (whether in hostels, hospitals, or in their own homes) is a distressing experience for those who care for them. It is rare for parents or staff to record precisely how the self-injury arises. It is likely that the exact moment when an apparently innocuous behaviour (such as face rubbing) becomes injurious (face gouging) will be hard to define, even if extensive observations are being made. Consequently, the original point at which self-injury first occurs is almost always uncertain in any individual, as is the reason for the emergence of that behaviour. However, a number of hypotheses have been put forward as to the causes of SIB and these are discussed in this section.

Once self-injurious behaviour has appeared, for whatever reason, it may or may not continue, as we have already seen (Schroeder, Schroeder, Smith, and Dalldorf, 1978). For some individuals self-injury becomes the preponderant form of behaviour; for others it remains an occasional event; and for still others it disappears altogether. Precisely why self-injurious behaviour takes different courses in different individuals is uncertain. Again, a number of hypotheses have been proposed which are described in this section.

It is rare for any differentiation to be made between the original emergence of self-injurious behaviour and its continued occurrence. Consequently, the hypotheses pertaining to the emergence and maintenance of SIB are all considered together. However, it is quite possible that self-injury may originate in one manner (for example, as a side effect of a minor illness) and continue for other reasons (for example, because of the social consequences of the behaviour).

It is often difficult, as we have said, to be certain exactly how and why any individual's self-injurious behaviour arose. This is largely because of the retrospective nature of the information available. In the papers which follow, some procedures are described which may allow people caring for an individual who self-injures to deduce the function (or functions) of SIB for that individual. This functional analysis may lead to the devising of an effective treatment for SIB in that individual.

Sometimes, however, the procedures necessary for such a functional analysis may be impossible to carry out, for practical or ethical reasons (for example, Lovaas and Simmons' (1969) extinction technique, see pp. 195-209). In this situation it may be advisable, instead, to adopt a "best guess" as to the function of the individual's self-injury and to use this strategy to devise a series of possible treatment programmes which can be tried sequentially (see Section III for a further discussion of the importance of functional analysis).

In this section, six different hypotheses regarding the causes of self-injury are discussed. Some papers describe direct testing of the hypothesis by experiment (for example, Lovaas and Simmons, 1969); in others, the hypothesis has arisen retrospectively from observations of self-injury (for example, de Lissovoy, 1963): yet others are largely "armchair" hypotheses, valuable perhaps, but in need of direct experimental evidence to back them up (for example, the psychodynamic hypotheses and th' psychopharmacological hypotheses).

Psychodynamic hypotheses

Several hypotheses have been generated in the psychodynamic literature to explain the appearance of self-injury in children who are handicapped or autistic. The papers included in this section are a selection of them. None of the authors provides direct experimental evidence for his theories because the explanations put forward are untestable.

Firstly, there are extracts from the proceedings of a conference held in New York in 1954, with Anna Freud as the main guest speaker (Freud, Greenacre, and Bychowski, 1954).* The conference was entitled "Psychoanalysis and education" and the speakers concentrated on children's early experience and the development of infantile neurosis. As can be seen from the extracts, a number of speakers touched on the subject of rocking and head banging, largely in relation to non-handicapped children. Even in this brief conference, a number of different hypotheses were advanced in relation to the function of head banging, some speakers putting forward several views. Greenacre (1954) suggested that head banging was essentially an auto-erotic behaviour, but later considered that it might have to do with establishing "body reality". Freud, on the other hand, thought head banging and other self-mutilative behaviours were auto-aggressive, rather than auto-erotic (Freud, 1954). Bychowski hypothesised, from his experiences with adult patients, that the function of head banging was to trace ego-boundaries (Bychowski, 1954).

Secondly, there is a brief paper by Zuk (1960). Interestingly, Zuk differentiates between the self-injury of children with psychosis (presumably autistic), which he considers to reflect aggressive impulses against the self, and that of children who are mentally handicapped, which he sees as aggression directed against an object (the child's own body), not perceived as the self because of "regression of the ego to an infantile level".

* Unfortunately we were unable to obtain permission to reprint these extracts. Readers are, therefore, referred to the full conference proceedings.

Finally, Richmond, Eddy, and Green (1958) describe persistent rumination in several infants (in the absence of any medical disorder), something which many would classify as self-injurious behaviour. Such behaviour is by no means unknown in paediatric populations (Russo, Carr, and Lovaas, 1980) and Richmond asserts that the behaviour arises because of a disordered mother-baby relationship. The babies tended to show other unusual behaviours as well, such as body rocking and head rolling, behaviours probably best classified as stereotypies. It is interesting that some of Richmond's theories about the origins of such behaviours in his infants are reminiscent of the theories put forward to explain the stereotypies of primates subjected to isolate rearing (see p. 29). Richmond, however, does not provide much beyond his clinical impressions to support his theory. He takes no direct observational measures and many of his interpretations are very open to question.

Organic and psychopharmacological hypotheses

We have already seen in Section I, the section on the prevalence of self-injurious behaviour, that individuals showing self-injury do not all come from the same diagnostic category. There are, however, two rare conditions in which self-injury very often occurs: Lesch-Nyhan syndrome (Lesch and Nyhan, 1964) and de Lange syndrome (Bryson, Sakati, Nyhan, and Fish, 1971). The existence of these two syndromes, both of which are congenital, provides some evidence in support of hypotheses which maintain that self-injury is organic in nature: that is, that it arises not from any events in the individual's life, but from his biological constitution.

Precisely what part of his biological constitution is to blame is not clear: certainly, a considerable amount is now known about the biochemical origins and consequences of Lesch-Nyhan syndrome (Christie *et al.*, 1982, p. 123), and yet it is still not possible to delineate precisely what has produced the self-injury. Some of the consequences of the inherited absence of the HGRPT enzyme in Lesch-Nyhan syndrome, such as the rise in uric acid, can now be treated but this has no effect on the self-injurious behaviour (Christie *et al.*, 1982, p. 131). It seems possible that the explanation may relate to the distribution of neuro-transmitters in the brain (see Mizuno and Yugari, 1974, in Section III; and Lloyd *et al.*, 1981) but it is at present too early to be more precise. As we have already seen in the section on SIB in animals, it is possible to make animals self-injure by pharmacological interventions; but precisely why they do so, and how this relates to self-injury in children with Lesch-Nyhan syndrome or others who are mentally handicapped or autistic, is unclear.

Even less is known about de Lange syndrome than about Lesch-Nyhan syndrome. Children with de Lange's syndrome have several common features, as described by Bryson, Sakati, Nyhan, and Fish (1971) on p. 134, yet no causal agents have been described and it is still uncertain whether the syndrome is of genetic origin, though this seems likely. Again, it appears probable that the cause of the self-injury is neurological, although the precise nature of the organic dysfunction is uncertain. It seems unlikely, as Bryson, Sakati, Nyhan, and Fish (1971) comment, to be simply the result of sensory neuropathy since self-injury in this case ought to be accidental (as it is usually in other sensory neuropathies) rather than compulsive, as it is in de Lange's syndrome.

Self-injurious behaviour has also been described in connection with a small number of other congenital disorders, such as the 47XYY syndrome, the 49XXXXY syndrome, spina bifida, and the Riley-Day or familial dysautonomia syndrome (Singh, 1981; Axelrod, Nachtigal, and Dancis, 1974; Altman, Haavik, and Higgins, 1983). In the former two cases, it is unclear whether the self-injury can be specifically linked to the syndromes; in the latter two cases the self-injurious behaviour is almost certainly a function of reduced sensitivity to pain.

Finally, Corbett and Campbell (1981) have proposed that self-injurious behaviour is explicable in terms of the neurological and biochemical events in various parts of the brain, particularly the limbic system. Their hypothesis represents one attempt to link the action of various neurotransmitters to the appearance of SIB in people who are mentally handicapped. Of necessity, their paper draws on much of the animal neuropharmacological literature, since there have been no definite demonstrations of altered neurotransmitter distribution or function in mentally handicapped individuals who self-injure, except for a report of altered dopamine distribution in patients with Lesch-Nyhan syndrome (Lloyd *et al.*, 1981) and a case study of the effectiveness of naloxone, a morphine antagonist, in reducing self-injurious behaviour in one patient (Richardson and Zaleski, 1983 — see p. 290).

Certainly, the close association between self-injury and the extreme levels of organic dysfunction which must be presumed to occur in profound mental handicap, is seen by some professionals to suggest that it will eventually be possible to delineate causal organic or biochemical features in children and adults who self-injure.

Developmental hypotheses

The appearance of head banging in normal infants (see Section I) has led to the suggestion that self-injurious behaviour in individuals who are mentally handicapped or autistic is developmentally appropriate behaviour which persists and becomes problematic because the individuals do not grow beyond it in the way that normal children do. Some of the evidence pertaining to head banging in normal infants has already been described (see Section II); in this section two further papers on the subject are included which provide a more detailed picture of the phenomenon.

Both Kravitz, Rosenthal, Teplitz, Murphy, and Lesser (1960) and de Lissovoy (1962) describe head banging in infancy as appearing at around eight months and disappearing mostly by four years of age. Their descriptions of the behaviour are remarkably consistent and it is clear that little physical damage usually occurs to the child's head. It would be interesting to compare the mental ages of individuals who are mentally handicapped or autistic and who self-injure to those of the normal infants who head bang. Unfortunately, most of the surveys of SIB amongst handicapped children discuss intelligence quotient rather than mental age, so the comparison is rather difficult.

It seems likely, though, that since self-injury occurs most often amongst people who are profoundly mentally handicapped, the mental age of individuals who head bang in the two populations is roughly equivalent in most cases (that is, between eight months and four years of age). Even so, it should be noted that the kind of head banging shown by normal infants is different from that shown by children who are handicapped. In normal infants, head banging almost invariably occurs in only one situation, the bed (de Lissovoy, 1962, p. 153), rarely produces major injuries, and does not become an all engrossing activity as it does in some individuals who are handicapped. Moreover, normal infants between eight months and four years of age do not usually indulge in other forms of self-injury (like self-biting, face gouging, and so on), which also distinguishes them from people with mental handicap who self-injure.

Even supposing that head banging in normal infants and self-injury in handicapped individuals could be supposed to be equivalent (which seems unlikely, for the reasons noted above), there would still remain the problem of the exact function of the behaviour. Certainly, the behaviour may have a develomental or developmentally-linked function, but discerning this is not an easy matter. The repetitive and invariant nature of the behaviour makes it seem unlikely to be of educational value to the child (compared, for example, with constructive play).

Suggestions have been made, though, that the behaviour is tension-reducing and/or stimulus-producing. Both of these hypotheses have been put forward as explanations of stereotyped behaviour in individuals who are handicapped and they will be discussed later under the self-stimulation hypothesis (pp. 95-96). Finally, it is possible that, in individuals who are mentally handicapped, head banging is a primitive attempt to communicate by a person developmentally unable to use language. This possibility is discussed further under learned behaviour hypotheses (pp. 97-98).

Side effect of minor illness hypothesis

We have already discussed the possibility that self-injurious behaviour may start for one reason and continue for another. Here we will consider one of the possible ways in which self-injury may originate.

It is possible that a person who is mentally handicapped or autistic may begin to self-injure as a side effect of a minor illness, his self-injury being at first merely a way of relieving an irritation or an internal pain. Thus, for example, a child might start scratching a rash because it itches and only later develop this into face or flesh gouging (perhaps as a result of the social consequences, which will be discussed below under learned behaviour hypothesis). Alternatively, he might begin head banging to relieve earache resulting from an ear infection, and then continue head banging for other reasons.

There is actually no direct evidence for this hypothesis from the mental handicap literature. However, de Lissovoy, 1963 (see p. 163) did find that a larger proportion of his group of normal infants who head banged had experienced otitis media (middle ear infections) than his normal infant control group who did not head bang. The phenomenon of head banging has also been reported in mice with otitis media (Harkness and Wagner, 1975).

Carr and McDowell (1980) reported a case of a boy, with an intelligence quotient within the normal range, who developed self-injurious behaviour as a consequence of a minor physical ailment. The boy had begun scratching after contact with poison oak had produced dermatitis. Medical treatment cleared the dermatitis within a week, but the boy continued to scratch for a further three years, producing multiple scars and lesions. Carr and McDowell considered that, although the scratching had begun because of the dermatitis, it had continued because of social reinforcement. A successful treatment procedure was subseqently developed. (See Section III for further discussion of the types of treatment used.)

Self-stimulation hypothesis

The similarity of self-injurious behaviour to the stereotyped behaviour of individuals who are mentally handicapped or autistic was referred to in the Introduction. One of the hypotheses which has been put forward to explain SIB developed in relation to stereotyped behaviour, and it involves the assumption that self-injury is merely another form of stereotypy. This is not an altogether unwarranted assumption: as mentioned in the Introduction, the two classes of behaviour look very similar at times and, moreover, individuals who tend to indulge in one frequently indulge in the other. (This is also true of normal infants who head bang, since they tend to rock too.) The social consequences of the two kinds of behaviour are probably very different, however, and this will be further discussed under the learned behaviour hypothesis.

Supposing for the moment that self-injurious behaviour is merely another form of stereotyped behaviour, like rocking or hand flapping, let us consider what implications this has for the question of causality.

It has been proposed by numerous workers that the function of stereotyped behaviour in individuals who are mentally handicapped or autistic is to provide sensory stimulation which they find rewarding. The evidence to support this proposition comes from a variety of sources. Firstly, individuals who have sensory deficits, like blindness, frequently engage in stereotyped behaviour. Moreover, handicapped individuals in the unstimulating environment of an understaffed hospital ward often show high stereotypy rates. Secondly, it is well established that the stereotypy levels of a person who is mentally handicapped decrease when the person is distracted by an object or toy, even when it is physically possible for the individual to engage in both behaviours at once (Davenport and Berkson, 1963; Berkson and Mason, 1964; Murphy, Carr, and Callias, 1985). Presumably, the toys or objects are providing some sensory input which obviates the need for the stereotypy (Murphy, 1983). Thirdly, there is considerable evidence from studies which deliberately provide an external source of stimulation — such as lights, sounds, or vibration — contingent on simple responses such as lever presses, that stereotypies reduce in approximate proportion to the level of this alternative stimulation (Williams, 1978; Goodall and Corbett, 1982; Murphy, 1982). Indeed, Rincover's research suggests that very close links can be seen between the stimuli produced by an individual's stereotypies and his preferred external stimuli (Rincover, 1978; Rincover, Cook, Peoples, and Packard, 1979).

It must be said, however, that other theories of stereotypies exist, one of which claims that stereotyped behaviour serves to reduce an individual's level of tension or arousal (see the review of stereotypies by Baumeister and Forehand, 1973). There is, however, little direct evidence for this view since independent measures of arousal are rarely taken (Murphy, 1983).

Williams and Surtees have attempted to combine the two hypotheses by proposing that a U-shaped relationship exists between arousal, or stimulus level, and stereotypies, such that stereotypies would occur at both low and high stimulus levels, but would disappear or reduce at medium stimulus levels (Williams and Surtees, 1975, see p. 391). They suggested that individuals who were mentally handicapped could be set at the low arousal end of the curve (so that their stereotypies would be essentially stimulus-producing), while individuals who were autistic could be set at the high arousal end (so that their stereotypies would be essentially arousal-reducing). The hypothesis is attractive but it remains rather speculative, particularly at the high arousal end, given Rincover's recent evidence that at least some of the stereotypies of children who are autistic disappear when alternative stimuli are available.

Both the papers in this section provide convincing evidence that stereotyped behaviour (and, by implication, SIB) is essentially stimulus-producing. The first one is a report by Bailey and Meyerson (1970) of a child with profound mental handicap and high levels of stereotyped and self-injurious behaviour. It appeared that the provision of a vibratory stimulus greatly reduced the SIB, whether or not the child was required to make a response to obtain the vibration. The second paper is a report by Rincover of the disappearance of stereotypies in children who are autistic when the sensory consequences of those stereotypies are eliminated. The implicaton of the study is that the function of the stereotyped behaviour was the production of sensory consequences.* More recently, several papers have reported a reduction in self-injury with the provision of sensory stimulation or the elimination of the sensory consequences of SIB (Wells and Smith, 1983; Rincover and DeVaney, 1982; Favell, McGimsey and Schell, 1982).

*Interestingly, Lourie (1949) (see p. 45) and de Lissovoy (1962) (see p. 153) report some success in reducing head banging in normal infants by the provision of an alternative source of rhythmic sound.

Learned behaviour hypothesis

Most parents, when their child has learned a new skill, will react with enthusiasm, praising, applauding, and/or cuddling the child every time he displays the new behaviour. In doing so, the operant learning theorist would say that they are probably reinforcing the behaviour, making it more likely to reappear in the future (which is, of course, entirely appropriate). Equally, most parents will have experienced the difficulty of persuading their child, particularly around the 1½-2 year old stage, to do something he does not wish to do, whether it be sitting on his potty or leaving his friends to go home after an exciting afternoon's play. Many parents will have felt themselves forced to give in to their child's wishes in these situations, particularly if the child has responded to their first requests with tantrums. In allowing the child his own way, they may be reinforcing tantrum behaviour, making it more likely to occur again in similar situations (a rather undesirable outcome).

The same kinds of events may occur in the life of the child who is mentally handicapped, and if the behaviour reinforced is a self-injurious one, then this behaviour is likely to increase. This is the essence of the learned behaviour hypothesis, one of the most influential "explanations" of self-injury and the basis of the most widely-used set of treatment procedures for self-injury (see Section III, p. 237).

A proper understanding of this hypothesis depends on a certain amount of knowledge of operant learning theory, which was originally developed in relation to lower animals, and which can be pursued in a number of relatively simple texts (Blackman, 1974; Yule and Carr, 1980; Carr, 1980(b)). Alternatively, a brief account of the major propositions can be seen in the extract from Baumeister and Rollings' excellent review of self-injurious behaviour (Baumeister and Rollings, 1976, p. 184).

Briefly, the learned behaviour hypothesis involves the proposal that self-injurious behaviour may, at first, occur for any one of a variety of reasons (such as an accidental response, or as a side effect of minor illness), the behaviour then continuing because it is reinforced or rewarded in some way, usually by social events. The kinds of social events envisaged are cuddling, extra attention, the provision of a favourite toy, or cessation of an activity the child wishes to avoid. These are, of course, all too likely to occur when a child starts to self-injure, since all the people around him will want to persuade him to cease the behaviour. Social events of this kind do, initially, appear to solve the problem of reducing a child's self-injury: immediately the child is given the cuddle or toy, or is removed from his potty, for example, the self-injury will stop.

However, the short-term solution leads to long-term problems, since rewarding the child for his self-injurious behaviour (which is in effect what has happened) will make the behaviour more likely to occur on future occasions. In a sense, the individual is being trained to self-injure, since the provision of rewarding social events contingent on the SIB are precisely equivalent to the provision of enthusiastic applause and praise following displays of good behaviour. Indeed, for an individual who is handicapped or autistic, and who cannot speak, self-injurious behaviour may become a very effective, though maladaptive, manner of "getting his own way". It can almost obviate the need for speech, since the child will quickly learn that, immediately he self-injures, adults in his environment will rapidly provide him with whatever he wants.

The first paper in this section is an extract from the review of self-injurious behaviour by Baumeister and Rollings (1976) which has already been mentioned. It provides a clear account of the two major ways in which SIB may be learned (as an avoidance response, and as a response to positive reinforcement). The next two papers give experimental evidence of what Baumeister and Rollings refer to as the "discriminative stimulus hypothesis" (Schaeffer, 1970; Lovaas and Simmons, 1969). The next paper, by Carr, Newsom, and Binkoff (1976) is one of the few in the literature to illustrate the other major way to learn self-injurious behaviour. It demonstrates that SIB can act as an escape response, reinforcement for the response being the termination of the aversive situation (in this case, the demand condition).

The paper by Schaeffer (1970), describes an attempt to teach two rhesus monkeys to self-injure, using standard operant learning theory techniques (Blackman, 1974). The animals were reinforced (or rewarded) for SIB with food, and were kept somewhat hungry so that the food would be effective. The monkeys' initial self-injuring responses were trained by successive approximation or shaping; that is, reinforcement at first followed responses only somewhat like the target behaviour (for example, lifting the arm towards the head), but gradually the responses were required to be more and more like the target behaviour (hitting the head with the hand) in order to be reinforced. Other operant techniques were also used, such as establishing a discriminative stimulus, in the presence of which the SIB was to occur. In the absence of this stimulus the self-injury was not to occur (see Blackman, 1974, for a description of these procedures). By the end of 14 days the two monkeys had been trained to bang their heads with their hands in the presence of the experimenter (particularly when he said certain phrases such as, "Poor boy. Don't do that. You'll hurt yourself"), provided they were hungry. When the monkeys were not hungry the behaviour did not appear. Interestingly, Schaeffer was unable to teach the monkeys to bang their heads onto objects (as opposed to banging their hands to their heads). However Schaeffer had demonstrated that rhesus monkeys, who do not usually self-injure (see Section I), could be taught to hit themselves in certain situations, given an effective reinforcer.

For a child who is mentally handicapped or autistic the process of learning to self-injure may be very similar, although the reinforcers are more likely to be social than edible. The fact that Schaeffer's monkeys did not self-injure when they were not hungry suggests that continuous provision of reinforcers will prevent the appearance of self-injury, and this is indeed what is often found. For example, continuous cuddling of a child who self-injures frequently eradicates the SIB for as long as the cuddling lasts, but in doing so, it traps the parents or professionals who are caring for the child in an impossible situation.

The paper by Lovaas and Simmons (1969) is probably one of the most important papers in the literature. Lovaas and Simmons argued that SIB in children who are mentally handicapped might be produced by the kinds of procedures described above; that is, by the provision of reinforcement (social attention) contingent on the self-injurious responses. Moreover, they deduced that *not* providing the contingent attention should result in the eventual elimination of the self-injurious behaviour (this is termed extinction in operant learning theory). They reported the result of such an extinction procedure with two children with mental handicap who showed severe levels of self-injury. Both children's self-injurious behaviour dropped, from very high levels, to zero or near-zero when it was ignored, but only after a very large number of un-reinforced responses. Furthermore, the third section* of the paper (p. 205) described how one child's self-injury worsened when he was provided with kindly, compassionate social attention and playthings whenever he did self-injure. Favell, McGimsey, Jones, and Cannon, 1981 (see Section III, p. 417) have reported similar findings with the provision of certain kinds of restraint contingent on self-injurious behaviour.

The third paper, by Carr, Newsom, and Binkoff (1976), provides a clear description of a child in whom SIB had become an effective means of escaping from aversive situations. In sessions where the boy was asked to carry out simple tasks (such as, "Point to the door") SIB was very frequent, ranging up to 100 hits per minute. In other sessions, where no demands were made on him, the SIB occurred at extremely low rates. Presumably, in the past the boy had learned that if he self-injured when demands were made they would then cease.

Carr, Newsom, and Binkoff (1980) demonstrated that aggressive behaviour (such as hitting others) can also develop as a means of escaping demand situations, much like SIB. Furthermore, they showed that the aggressive behaviour could be reduced in several different ways (by reinforcing alternative behaviours, by teaching a different escape response, and by refusing to allow aggressive behaviour to terminate the demand condition). This may also be true for self-injurious behaviour when it is functioning as an escape response (for further discussion, see Section III).

Conclusions

There is, then, a rather bewildering variety of hypotheses about the causes of self-injurious behaviour. Some of the hypotheses are largely speculative, while others have a considerable weight of experimental evidence behind them.

The psychodynamic "explanations" of self-injury are, as we have already said, largely untestable. Many people who have had extensive contact with handicapped individuals who self-injure are likely to find these

*The second part of the paper describes the use of contingent shock, a treatment technique which will be discussed in Section III.

psychodynamic hypotheses implausible, dealing as they do in abstract concepts of which the individuals in question could probably not even conceive. Richmond's (1958) suggestion, however, that a disordered mother-baby relationship leads to rumination of a life-threatening kind in infants is more easily testable, and might be applicable to other kinds of self-injurious behaviour as well. So far, no direct experimental evidence has been published in support of this hypothesis.

The organic hypotheses, on the other hand, appear to be appropriate explanations for the self-injurious behaviour of certain individuals, such as those with Lesch-Nyhan syndrome and de Lange's syndrome. However, the fact that individuals with these syndromes can respond positively to treatment techniques based on learning theory (Bull and La Vecchio, 1978; Singh and Pulman, 1979; Altman, Haavik, and Higgins, 1983) suggests that the interactions between organic conditions and environmentally mediated learning are complex and not to be underestimated, as workers in other fields have also maintained (Blakemore, 1978; Davies and Katz, 1983).

Developmental hypotheses alone, as we have seen, are also insufficient explanations for the appearance and persistence of self-injurious behaviour in individuals who are mentally handicapped or autistic. Perhaps both organic and developmental factors are best seen as providing an individual with a propensity for showing SIB, rather than as total explanations of the phenomenon. Similarly, minor illnesses can be visualised as possible starting points for self-injurious behaviour, other factors then accounting for its continued maintenance. Thus an individual may begin self-injuring because of minor illnesses, or because of developmental or organic predisposing factors, but he may continue self-injuring for other reasons.

The two remaining major theories propose that self-injurious behaviour is self-stimulatory and that it is a learned behaviour. At first sight these two hypotheses may appear irreconcilable. However, it is possible to view them both as part of a wider form of operant hypothesis, in which both sensory stimuli (produced by the SIB) and social (or other) external events can act as reinforcers for the self-injurious behaviour. It is not, in fact, new to view sensory stimuli as potential reinforcers, as Kish made just such a suggestion in the 1960's (Kish, 1966). Moreover, there is ample evidence to suggest that the kinds of sensory stimuli which stereotyped behaviours produce can act like any other reinforcers when presented externally (Murphy, 1982).

It is perhaps harder to envisage the types of sensory stimuli produced by SIB as potential reinforcers, since the responses involved would be expected to be painful. It may be, though, that the few individuals for whom the sensation produced by the SIB is reinforcing have an altered sensitivity to pain (Goldfarb, 1958). Thus it is proposed that a child (or adult) may begin self-injuring for a variety of reasons, as described above. He may then continue self-injuring because he finds the sensations produced by the self-injurious responses rewarding or, alternatively,

TABLE I. A screening sequence to determine the motivation of self-injurious behaviour

	Result positive	Result negative
Step 1 Screen for genetic abnormalities (e.g. Lesch-Nyhan and de Lange syndromes), particularly if lip, finger, or tongue biting is present. Screen for non-genetic abnormalities (e.g. otitis media), particularly if head banging is present.	Motivation may be organic	Proceed to Step 2
Step 2 Does self-injurious behaviour increase under one or more of the following circumstances: (a) When the behaviour is attended to? (b) When reinforcers are withdrawn for behaviours other than SIB? (c) When the child is in the company of adults, rather than alone?	Motivation may be positive reinforcement	Proceed to Step 3
Does self-injurious behaviour occur primarily when demands or other aversive stimuli are presented?	Motivation may be negative reinforcement	
Step 3 Does self-injurious behaviour occur primarily when there are no activities available and/or the environment is barren?	Motivation may be self-stimulation	

This information is reproduced from Carr, E. G. The motivation of self-injurious behaviour: a review of some hypotheses. *Psychol. Bull.,* 1977; **84,** 800-816.

because rewarding social events consistently follow his self-injurious responses (cuddles, social attention, the provision of favourite toys, or the removal of unpleasant tasks or demands). For some individuals both the sensations from and the social consequences of self-injury may be reinforcing; for others only one of these may be effective in maintaining the behaviour. Furthermore, it may be that, for individuals who engage in several forms of SIB, different consequences (sensory and social) may maintain the different forms of self-injury, as Durand (1982(b)) has shown.

Carr (1977) reasoned along rather similar lines and proposed a sequence of steps which could be followed to determine the factors maintaining an individual's self-injurious behaviour (see Table I), with which we would substantially agree. Such an analysis has clear implications for treatment of any individual, and many of the treatment techniques described in Section III can be clearly linked to factors presumed to be maintaining individuals' self-injurious behaviour. It seems likely that future advances in the behavioural treatment of SIB will arise largely from this kind of functional analysis and the final paper in this section, by Iwata and colleagues, demonstrates one method of formally analysing the function of an individual's SIB.

Iwata, Dorsey, Slifer, Bauman, and Richman (1982) recorded the SIB of nine children, with varying degrees of handicap, in four different settings. In one setting, "academic" demands were made, that is, the children were required to engage in educational tasks, appropriate to their developmental level. In a second setting, the social disapproval condition, they were allowed free play with toys but, after each incident of SIB, the trainer made a concerned or disapproving statement. The third setting was a barren environment devoid of toys. The fourth was a comparison condition. The results Iwata describes show that some children reacted with increased SIB in certain conditions and not in others, so that the function of their SIB appeared clear-cut. For others, however, mixed results were obtained. Iwata discusses the implications in some detail.

Certainly, one of the most important research tasks now is to examine the extent to which linking treatment plans to functional analysis will improve treatment success (Murphy, 1985). A number of research projects have begun to investigate precisely this, using both Iwata's method of analysis and other methods (Durand, 1984; Iwata, Pace, Cataldo, Kalsher, and Edwards, 1984). Indeed, recent reports indicate that Carr's ideas can be directly employed in designing treatment plans for individuals who self-injure (Iwata, Dorsey, Slifer, Bauman, and Richman, 1982).

PSYCHODYNAMIC IMPLICATIONS OF SELF-INJURY IN DEFECTIVE CHILDREN AND ADULTS

G. H. Zuk[1]

St. Christopher's Hospital for Children, Philadelphia

Summary

There seems reason not to equate self-injury with self-mutilation, although they may be overlapping in a single individual. Self-injury as described in this paper involves none of the ritual that is often associated with self-mutilation. In self-mutilation, it is often the object of the victim, either consciously or subconsciously, to punish himself for certain transgressions. Self-injury represents a distortion of the impulse to punish someone else. These pathological behaviors are felt to have quite different diagnostic significance.

This report will describe and interpret self-injury in defective children and adults.[2] Self-injury is a rather unique pathological behavior about which remarkably little has been written. As used here, it refers to an individual hitting, banging, biting or otherwise bruising his own body. It differs from psychotic self-mutilation, such as has been described by Dobrowski[1], in that the aggressive impulse is apparently *not* directed against the self — as it often appears to be in self-mutilation — but rather against some frustrating event, object or person. Common to both behaviors, on the other hand, would seem to be the "frustration-anger-hostility" trinity that Thorne[6] implicated in the arousal of many abnormal mental states. Support for the view that the aggressive impulse in self-injury is directed against an external frustrating agent is offered in the following case presentations.

Case materials

The following were more or less chance observations of self-injury as it happened. In each of these it was possible to reconstruct the circumstances that led up to the behavior.

CASE 1.—A young adult male in a state institution for mental defectives. This young man was observed walking along and muttering to himself loudly. Suddenly he was seen to strike himself in the eye with his fist. He continued to mutter angrily about something and struck himself several times. Seemingly more stirred up with every blow, he broke into a run after another boy who was standing nearby. However, he was easily outdistanced in the footrace. He stopped, muttered again, and then again struck himself in the eye. The writer, having observed all this, approached the young man and asked what the trouble was. Excitedly, he pointed after the boy who had escaped him and shouted: "He's been picking on me!" The young man was reassured that he would no longer be bothered. This appeared to calm him and after a minute or so he walked away.

CASE 2.—A girl of perhaps 8 years in a state institution for mental defectives. This child was observed in a play area screaming, moaning and pulling violently at her own hair. She yanked so hard that she actually pulled herself down to the ground. The writer's attention was drawn to a little boy standing near the girl who appeared to enjoy her antics and made "faces" which only further enraged her. Finally, an attendant was called and removed the girl from the area. The attendant later reported that the girl indulged in such behavior whenever teased or provoked.

CASE 3.—A negro boy of about 7 years in a nursery school for retarded children. This boy was observed, while seated on a chair, to strike himself on the side of his face with his fist. The teacher of the class went to the boy and restrained him playfully by holding his hands and then clapping them together as if in a game. This appeared to calm the boy and he

[1]Psychologist with the mental retardation clinic, John Bartram, M.D., director, which is sponsored by the Children's Bureau, Department of Health, Education and Welfare and the Pennsylvania State Department of Health, Division of Maternal and Child Health.
[2]A version of this paper was read at the scientific session of the Department of Psychiatry, Temple University Medical School, November, 1958.

stopped his self-injury. As the writer reconstructed it from the teacher, she had apparently provoked the boy by insisting that he remained seated. He had gotten up from his seat previously to roam about the room. Her restraint set off the behavior which began immediately after she had returned him to his seat.

In the following two cases, direct observation of the self-injury was not made but was reported by the victims' mothers. They are of interest because they shed some further light on the type of defective child who may commit self-injury and the circumstances that favor its appearance.

CASE 4.—L., a 6 year old girl, was seen by the writer for psychological examination. She was quite typically defective in appearance: her mouth dropped open, her eyes had a dullish cast and there were signs of self-injury in the form of bitten wrists and bruised ears. She showed mental abilities not much beyond the 18 month level. On the Cattell Infant Intelligence Scale, she earned an MA of 1-6, IQ 26. On the Vineland Scale, she earned an SA of 1-11, SQ 33. Her behavior was generally that of a cranky 18 month to 2 year old child. She displayed considerable resistive and negativistic behavior. She ran to the door of the office and grabbed the knob in an effort to get out. At one point, her mother pulled L. from the door with the explanation: "Sometimes she needs this. You've got to watch her all the time. The older she gets, the worse off she is." There was much evidence of her mother's rejection of L. She showed little warmth toward the child. She talked about her as an object rather than as a child of her own.

CASE 5.—R., a 5 year old negro girl, seen by the writer for psychological examination. She was ambulatory but babbled meagerly and was not toilet trained. On the Kuhlmann-Binet Scale she earned an MA of 1-3, IQ 25. On the Vineland Scale she earned an SA of 1-7, SQ 32. R's mother faced the overwhelming task of caring for 11 children on a meager income. She was poorly educated but made a sincere effort to care for the children despite the great problem of how to support them. Her only complaint about R was that because all the other children in the family "waited on her", she refused to do things for herself and was easily upset when things weren't done for her. When upset she would scream, bang her head against the floor and bite her hands.

Discussion

The writer can conceptualize the psychodynamics of self-injury only by postulating a regression of the ego to an infantile level with a consequent breakdown of the identification of the ego and the body. The body is no longer perceived as an extension of the self but as an *object* in the environment. When for some reason, perhaps fear of reprisal or lack of availability, aggression cannot be directed against its true object, it is conceivable that it is expended against the most immediate or the nearest object. Since the victim obviously has easy access to his own body, it tends frequently to get selected as the object of the aggression.

Theoretical support for this interpretation comes from some of the psychoanalytic writers as well as the developmental psychologist, Piaget. Freud himself remarked that "before its cleavage into an ego and an id, the mental apparatus makes use of different methods of defense from those which it employs after" [3, p. 157]. Anna Freud[2] has vividly described how the young infant does not differentiate between himself and the outside world. Under the influence of the pleasure principle the infant perceives that what is pleasant is part of himself, what is unpleasant is not. She has noted that even in the second year, children will occasionally behave with their mothers as if their bodies were one. A child who likes to suck his thumb will suddenly take the mother's thumb rather than his own; or while feeding, he will put the spoon into his mother's mouth. Hoffer[4] has pointed out that through touching himself the infant comes to experience his self as different from the outside world. Piaget[5] has stated that with maturation actions become meaningful. Thus the infant moves its hand to grasp an object and the sensation of effort and achievement as well as those of impatience and waiting are among the first emotional experiences of the self as differentiated from the outside environment.

References
1. Dobrowski, C. Psychological bases of self-mutilation. *Genet. Psychol. Monogr.*, 1937; **19**, 1-104.

2. Freud, Anna. Some remarks on infant observation. *In Psychanalytic Study of the Child.* (Vol. VIII.) New York: International Universities Press, 1953.

3. Freud, S. *The Problem of Anxiety.* New York: Norton, 1935.

4. Hoffer, W. Development of the body ego. *In Psychoanalytic Study of the Child.* (Vol. V.) New York: International Universities Press, 1950.

5. Piaget, J. *The Construction of Reality in the child.* New York: Basic Books, 1954.

6. Thorne, F.C. The frustration-anger-hostility states: a new diagnostic classification. *J. Clin. Psychol.*, 1953; **9**, 334-339.

Reprinted from *J. Clin. Psychol.*, 1960; **16**, 58-60 by kind permission of Vladimir Pishkin, Editor-in-Chief for Clinical Psychology Publishing Co. Inc., Brandon, Vermont 05733.

RUMINATION: A PSYCHOSOMATIC SYNDROME OF INFANCY

Julius B. Richmond, Evelyn Eddy, and Morris Green

Department of Pediatrics, State University of New York Upstate Medical Center at Syracuse (J.R. and E.E.), and Department of Pediatrics, School of Medicine, Indiana University (M.G.).

Summary. This study has been concerned with observations of four infants manifesting the syndrome of rumination and the mothers of these infants. The findings suggest that the syndrome develops in response to a disordered relationship between parents and baby. Some formulations concerning the pathogenesis of rumination are presented. It is hoped that further studies of this and other syndromes reflecting disturbances in the development of object relationships in infants will provide a better understanding of healthy as well as disordered growth in early life.

Rumination may be defined as the regurgitation of previously swallowed food and the rechewing and reswallowing of the food. In ruminating animals this process is, of course, physiologic. Because of the withdrawal of the ruminating animal from the herd and the air of introspection and contemplation which seems to be associated with the process, rumination has also come to mean deliberate meditation or reflection.

When rumination occurs in infants — in contrast to animals — it is not a physiologic process. Upon regurgitation, the infant undertakes some rechewing and reswallowing movements which are not complete. The considerable food and fluid loss resulting is self-destructive inasmuch as inanition, fluid and electrolyte disturbances, and loss of life, may result if the process is uninterrupted.

The pediatric literature of the early decades of this century abounds in reports on rumination. A comprehensive historic review has been presented by Kanner.[1] It is of interest to note that with the exception of a publication by Lourie[2] the subject has received little attention in the American pediatric literature of the past decade. This may be a reflection of the decline in incidence of this disorder. It is the impression of many pediatricians that rumination is considerably less prevalent than it was in the early decades of this century and that this is a result of the over-all improvement in infant care as a consequence of improving social and economic conditions.

The literature reflects the confusion which has prevailed concerning this syndrome. Speculations concerning anatomic and physiologic abnormalities are abundant. Numerous feeding techniques and a large variety of mechanical devices — particularly "ruminator caps" — were designed in an effort to prevent rumination. A thread runs through all the literature: that there probably are psychologic factors related to the development of the disorder. The emphasis generally was on the "neuropathic traits" of the infant. Very little attention was given to parent-infant interaction. Our study has therefore been concerned with such observations.

Because it so effectively describes the syndrome, the following is quoted from an article by Cameron[3] published in 1925: "All my cases have been in artificially fed infants. After taking the meal quite in the ordinary way, the baby, as a rule, lies quiet for a time. Then begin certain purposive movements, by which the abdominal muscles are thrown into a series of violent contractions — the head is held back, the mouth is opened, while the tongue projects a little and is curved from side to side so as to form a spoon-shaped concavity on its dorsal surface. After a varying time of persistent effort, sometimes punctuated by grunting or whimpering sounds, expressive of irritation at the failure to achieve the expected result, with each contraction of the abdominal muscles milk appears momentarily in the pharynx at the back of the mouth. . . . Finally a successful contraction ejects a great quantity of milk forwards into the mouth. The infant lies with an expression of supreme satisfaction upon its face, sensing the regurgitated milk and subjecting it to innumerable sucking and chewing movements. . . . It is very evident that achievement of his purpose produces a sense of beatitude, while failure results in nervous unrest and irritation. . . . The power to ruminate successfully is not suddenly acquired. In the earliest stages, before dexterity has been achieved, the act differs relatively little from that of vomiting. . . . In its earlier development, therefore, rumination is very apt to be mistaken for habitual vomiting due to other causes, and it may require careful observation to make the distinction evident. Nor are such babies easy to observe. It is characteristic of the ruminating child that it sins its sin only in secret. To watch it openly is to put a stop to the whole procedure. . . . Only when the child is alone and in a drowsy, vacant state, while nothing distracts attention or excites curiosity, does the act take place."

Observations

Our study includes observations of four infants and their mothers. There is relatively limited data on the fathers. Although the nature of the problems encountered in these families placed significant limitations on the observations which could be obtained, the information which is available does provide some basis for furthering our understanding of this disorder.

The data which has been obtained are summarized in Table I. We may note that although some gastrointestinal disturbances might have been present earlier, the youngest age of onset of rumination was 3½ months. All of the babies in this study were males, although this has not been true of all reported cases. The degree of underweight was rather considerable as estimated from accepted standards. None of the infants in this series was breast-fed.

The diagnoses which had been considered prior to the recognition of the syndrome of rumination are of interest. In the first patient, the constant loss of food and the relatively low concentration of chloride in the serum, associated with constant loss of gastric juice,

Table I. Summary of clinical manifestations

Patient	Age (mo) On-set	Age (mo) Re-fer-ral	Sex	Weight (kg) Birth	Weight (kg) Ad-mis-sion	Ap-prox. % Un-derwt.	Prior Diagnoses	Associated Neurotic Traits	Maternal Characteristics
R.C.	3½	6	M	3.2	5.1	31	Adrenal in-sufficiency	Autistic posturing	Striking immaturity. Fear that baby would die. Severely compulsive; fearful regurgitation would soil furniture or clothes. Did not voluntarily come to visit baby in hospital.
T.B.	8	20	M	2.5	8.18	25	Pyloric stenosis Possible adrenal insufficiency	Genital and fecal play Body rocking Head rolling and banging Autistic play with hair	Mother's early care in an institution and multiple foster homes. An unwanted pregnancy; religious conflict. Fear fetus would die. Continued preoccupation about death of child. Conscious attempts at compensation for the above; strong tendency for projection of problems onto organic disorders.
D.E.	5	7½	M	3.05	4.83	44	Severe feeding problem	Head rolling	Psychiatric diagnosis of psychopathic personality. No additional information available.
R.M.	4	10	M	2.6	6.0	31	Severe feeding problem Food allergy pylorospasm Celiac syndrome Esophageal chalasia Duodenal ulcer	Finger and thumb sucking	Extremely compulsive; fearful regurgitation would soil furniture. Fear that baby would die of cancer (her father died of cancer 2 years previously with vomiting as a major symptom). Depressed. Provided very little physical contact with baby (stated he preferred to be left alone). Fearful that baby would love father more. Marital discord over care of baby.

suggested the diagnosis of adrenal insufficiency, for which this infant had been treated without success for a number of weeks. Other diagnoses considered were pyloric stenosis, food allergies, duodenal ulcer, esophageal abnormalities and severe feeding problems of unspecified origin. These mistaken diagnoses have particular significance for the pediatrician since physical deterioration of the child and loss of life may occur if the true nature of the problem continues to be unrecognized. Thus, although the syndrome is not common, it is important for the pediatrician to keep it in mind in differential diagnosis of gastrointestinal disorders of infants.

The nature of the underlying disorder in this syndrome is suggested by the presence of associated neurotic traits. In the first patient, autistic posturing was prominent; in the second patient, there was excessive genital and fecal play, body rocking, head rolling and banging, and autistic play with his hair. In the third patient, head rolling was prominent, and in the fourth patient there was excessive finger and thumb sucking.

We were struck by the apparent preoccupation of the infant with himself when left alone or in the process of ruminating. The act of rumination would not occur when there was significant stimulation in the immediate environment. Although these infants were described as having somewhat flattened affect, their response to stimulation was prompt. Most significant perhaps was the widely opened and searching appearance of the eyes, which was designated by some of the staff as "radar-like."

The observations of the mothers revealed considerable incapacity to relate adequately to the baby. In one case we had relatively little data concerning the mother beyond that a diagnosis of psychopathic personality had been made by a psychiatrist. The baby was born out of wedlock, and the mother had all but abandoned him. He was cared for largely by a relatively ineffective foster mother until the time we saw him.

Although there is considerable detail concerning the individual mothers in this study which it might be interesting to present, the following problems seemed common to each:

1. A striking inability to fulfill an adult psychosexual role which reflects itself as an incapacity to want, accept, and give to the baby. In one case this was sufficiently striking as to suggest the diagnosis of pre-psychotic behavior; in one mother, as already indicated, the diagnosis of psychopathic personality was made.

2. Marital conflict. This is undoubtedly in part a reflection of the immaturity observed in the mothers. We may speculate that their husbands also had significant psychopathology. There seemed to be very little evidence of any mature love relationship in the family. Ultimately, the conflict extended to the management of the symptoms which the baby manifested.

3. The fear that the baby would die. This would also seem related to the inability of these women to mother their infants and probably is a reflection of death wishes which these mothers may harbor.

There were other observations which were not common to all of the mothers. Marked compulsivity and fear that regurgitation would soil furniture and clothes were observed in two of the mothers; one mother was considerably depressed and was fearful that the baby would have greater love for the father.

As an illustration of the case material, the following brief summary of one case is presented.

Case report

History

T.B., a 20-month-old white male, was admitted to the hospital for vomiting, electrolyte imbalance and malnutrition.

He was the third and youngest of three children of a 36-year-old mother and 37-year-old father. The siblings were 4 and 7 years of age, respectively. The pregnancy was unwanted; religious background intensified the mother's conflict regarding these feelings. The mother's blood type was Rh negative; this necessitated more than the usual number of visits to the obstetrician. A rising Rh antibody titer during the latter months of pregnancy added to the earlier feeling that there would be something wrong with the infant and that it would die.

The patient weighed 2,460 gm at birth, after a precipitous delivery. An exchange transfusion was done, and apparently the infant improved rapidly and was discharged from the hospital at 6 days of age.

The patient was bottle-fed; the bottle was never propped, though the mother stated she had done so with the other chidren. He seemed eager to feed, but fussed continually through the feeding. No difficulty was encountered with the addition of solid foods.

The mother reported that the patient refused the bottle entirely at 8 months of age, and took little fluid for more than 1 week. He then began to accept cup feedings, and within a few days began "vomiting."

He sat at 9 months of age and walked at 1 year. At 20 months he spoke relatively little and communicated mainly by signs. He had been noted to roll the head and body, and to bang the head. The mother stated he did not respond to pain like other children and that he would obey only when vigorously spanked. He frequently played with feces and the mother stated that she had rubbed feces in his mouth in an attempt to make him as disgusted as she, since she was very disturbed by the habit.

Physical findings and course

The patient was thin, dehydrated, pale, listless, and ruminating. Physical examination was otherwise not contributory. It soon became apparent after admission to the hospital that the patient was ruminating rather than vomiting. At the time of admission, this occurred about 20 times a day. When alone the patient was observed to engage in a number of rhythmic bodily activities such as head rolling, head banging, and body rocking. He would also play with the genitalia and feces. Rumination could be interrupted by diverting his attention. For example, it was not possible to record rumination on motion picture film because of his interest in the activities going on about him.

Although the appearance was that of a small lonely boy with flattened affect, he would smile when given close attention by nursing staff and would cry when left by the nurse. He ceased ruminating while in the hospital, as the nursing staff provided stimulating tender and intimate care, and he gained 1,800 gm in a period of 2 months.

Family and social background

Interviews with the mother revealed continued fear that the child would die and insistence that there must be some organic cause for the difficulty. Her continued rejection of him was evident from the statement that when she took him home from the hospital, he would not get very much of her time and attention, since he had already had a disproportionate amount at the expense of the other children. During the interview, emotional instability was evidenced by frequent crying, nail-biting, and fidgeting. She had considerable concern about her own health; she gave no indication of concern over the needs of her husband.

The maternal grandmother was 17 years old when the mother was born. She was said to be of limited intellect as a result of an attack of meningitis as a child. The grandfather deserted the grandmother 5 months after the mother was born. She was then placed in an institution for infants and spent her childhood in numerous foster homes.

The father is a salesman who is away from home 2 or 3 days a week. He was superficially congenial and seemed interested in keeping the family together. He indicated that he was able to absorb the emotional swings manifested by his wife, although her displays of wrath and crying were quite frequent.

Discussion

To borrow a biochemical model, we may now consider the interaction between the reagents (parental care) and the biologic substrate (the baby). The dynamic understanding of babies with this disorder lies in an evaluation of parental care and the physiologic responsiveness of the infant. The data presented offer an opportunity to formulate some thoughts concerning the pathogenesis of rumination.

The inability of these mothers to fulfill an adult psychosexual role reflected itself in marital inadequacy in our series. In addition, the need to satisfy their own dependent needs was prominent and undoubtedly contributed to the marital difficulties. In the process of attempting to meet their own needs, the women seemed quite incapable of providing warm, comfortable, and intimate physical care for the infants. The mother of the patient we presented in more detail illustrated a not uncommon background for highly dependent women who exerience difficulty in mothering. The institutional background and care in multiple foster homes would suggest that dependent needs had not been adequately met since she experienced inadequate mothering during early life. It has often been suggested that the best preparation for motherhood is to have had adequate mothering.

We can only speculate concerning the preoccupation which three of the mothers had concerning the potential death of the infants. Once the rumination had become an established pattern there was some realistic basis for the fear. There was no question that the fear preceded the development of symptoms and was pervasive. Because of the general immaturity of the women, one may reasonably speculate that this preoccupation with death was a manifestation of unconscious death wishes. We would further suggest that, in the conscious efforts to deal with these wishes, the mothers tended to be relatively distant from the babies. They probably engaged in relatively little of the ordinary play which goes on between parents and baby after vision has developed to the point of recognition of the love object.

We may now direct our attention to the reactions of the infant to the "mothering" provided by these women. Inasmuch as the infant's communication with the outside world is largely through feeding and fondling, we may speculate that lack of comfort and gratification which ordinarily comes from *without* (outside) causes him to seek and re-create such gratification from *within*. Particularly during the period of growing differentiation of psychologic from physiologic processes, it would seem that the lack of stimulation and gratification from the environment would tend to enhance the exploration of substitution for these experiences. Perhaps the best evidence for the searching for gratification from the environment is the alert, wide-eyed appearance of the babies which we have previously referred to as "radar-like."

In any psychosomatic syndrome, curiosity concerning the choice of symptoms and the timing of onset of symptoms is justified. Although we have been interested in constitutional differences in autonomic function in infants, we have no evidence that this is a predisposing factor. We would speculate that other factors are of greater consequence, as follows:

1. These are not completely deprived infants in that perhaps their greatest source of gratification — even though incomplete — has been through feeding. Substitution for this process in the form of rumination therefore may be interpreted as an effort to re-create the feeding process.

2. The infants seemed to have an unusual capacity to explore substitute visceral gratification as well as other forms of bodily manipulation such as head rolling and banging, body rocking, hair pulling, and fecal and genital play.

3. We would suggest that the onset of the disorder follows the development of visual maturation to the point of recognition of love objects (parents). Lacking the opportunity for sufficient gratification in the form of visual — and probably auditory — stimulation, the infant seeks substitution from within.

It is important to emphasize that we are not suggesting that specific maternal psychopathology results in rumination in the infant. Rather, we suggest that any factors which deprive the infant of intimate, stimulating relationships may predispose to the disorder. In the early part of the century, poor environmental circumstances probably accounted for such deprivation most commonly. Currently, maternal psychopathology which prevents the mother from developing a close and comfortable relationship with the baby is probably a more common cause.

In the light of the severity of the psychopathology of these mothers, one might speculate that the prognosis would be rather dismal. Although our follow-up is not sufficiently long to make any long-term predictions, the reversal of symptoms during treatment has been striking. With an interruption of the mother-infant relationship by hospitalization of the baby and the provision of a stimulating, warm environment with a substitute mother figure, the infants have dramatically ceased to ruminate. During hospitalization of the baby, the mother has some relief from the anxiety concerning the physical care of the baby and, through her relationship with the staff, develops a greater feeling of confidence concerning her ability to care for the infant. On returning home these babies have not resumed ruminating.

For really effective help, deeper and more long-term therapy for the mothers would seem indicated. This is an objective toward which we are striving for both research and therapeutic purposes. The immaturity of these mothers may minimize the possibility of engaging them more fully in formal psychiatric treatment and investigation. We should not minimize the effect of supportive therapy in the pediatric setting, however, since more intensive psychotherapy is often not available. Particularly for mothers with the degree of immaturity which these women manifest, continuing contact with a pediatrician with insight may provide just enough ego support to permit the mother to carry on with some degree of adequacy and, perhaps, to permit growth to a more adequate level.

References
1 Kanner, L. Historical notes on rumination in man. *M. Life.*, 1936; **43**, 27.
2 Lourie, R. S. Experience with therapy of psychosomatic problems in infants. *In* Hock, P., Zubin, J., (eds.). *Psychopathology of Children.* (p. 254). New York: Grune, 1955.
3 Cameron, H. C. Forms of vomiting in infancy. *Br. Med. J.*, 1925; **1**, 872.

Reprinted from *Pediatrics*, 1958; **12**:1, 49-55 by kind permission of Julius B. Richmond, Harvard University Medical School, Boston, MA 02215, Morris Green, and the publishers American Academy of Pediatrics, Evanston, Illinois 60204.

A FAMILIAL DISORDER OF URIC ACID METABOLISM AND CENTRAL NERVOUS SYSTEM FUNCTION*

Michael Lesch†
Baltimore, Maryland

William L. Nyhan
Miami, Florida

Summary

A syndrome consisting of hyperuricemia, mental retardation, choreoathetosis and self-destructive biting has been described in two brothers aged five and eight years. The uric acid pools in these patients were found to be similar in size to those reported for gouty adult subjects; their rates of turnover were greater than any previously reported. The daily excretion of uric acid in the urine was considerably higher than those of control patients and approximated total values found in gouty adult "hyperexcretors." The formation of uric acid from glycine in these patients exceeded that of control patients by 200 times. These data suggest that the patients described represent a distinct clinical and metabolic syndrome.

Primary gout is a metabolic disease which occurs predominantly in the adult man in whom it usually does not become manifest until after the third decade of life. It has been described in children [1], but hyperuricemia in children less than ten years of age is extremely rare. It is the purpose of this report to describe two brothers, aged five and eight years, in whom hyperuricemia, choreoathetosis and mental retardation appear to constitute a syndrome.

Case reports

Patient M. W. (*JHH 857202*). At the age of four and a half years this boy was admitted to the Harriet Lane Home because of hematuria. He had been born after uneventful gestation and delivery, but by three months of age it was apparent that his development was slow. He was first seen in this clinic at the age of eight months at which time he was found to have marked spasticity, a double hemiparesis and choreoathetosis. His subsequent development was markedly retarded, and at the age of four and half years he could not sit unassisted.

His first episode of hematuria was accompanied by fever and occurred five months prior to admission. A diagnosis of hemorrhagic cystitis was made and antibiotic treatment initiated. Fever and hematuria subsided within three days on this regimen. Thereafter he was well until two days prior to admission when fever and vomiting developed. Fluid intake and urinary output were decreased. On the day prior to admission he experienced hematuria. When examined in the outpatient department, he was found to have marked crystalluria and was admitted with a diagnosis of cystinuria. It soon became apparent that there was no cystine in the urine and that the crystals were of uric acid.

Both the mother and the father were twenty-five years old and well. Each had had febrile convulsions as children. An older brother is described as Patient E. W. The family history was negative for gout and disease of the central nervous system. Past and family history were otherwise negative.

The patient was a well developed, rather thin white boy with advanced cerebral palsy. (Fig. 1) Temperature was 39.3°c., pulse 140 beats per minute, respirations 40 per minute

*From the Departments of Pediatrics, The Johns Hopkins University School of Medicine, Baltimore, Maryland, and the University of Miami School of Medicine, Miami, Florida. This work was aided by Grant AM-07929 from the U. S. Public Health Service. Manuscript received June 25, 1963.
†Work carried out during the tenure of a Medical Student Research Fellowship (U. S. Public Health Service Experimental Training Grants 2-R-9(C4) and 2T5-GM9-06).

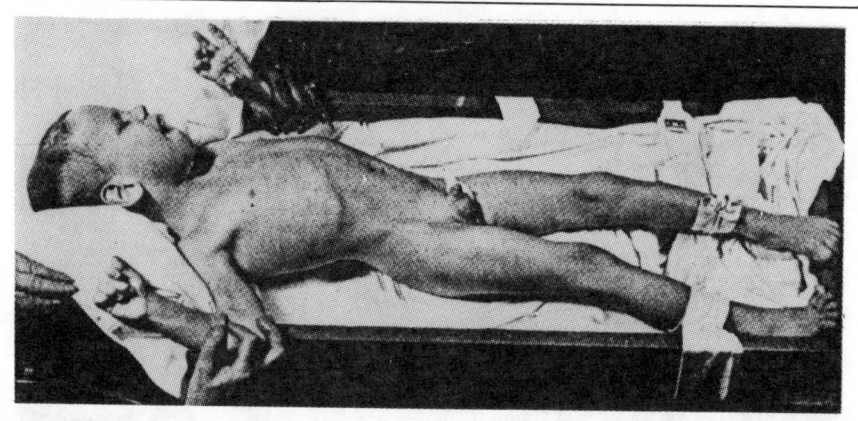

Fig. 1. Patient M. W. at four and a half years of age. The legs are in the characteristic position.

and blood pressure 110/70 mm. Hg. His weight was 14.3 kg. Choreoathetosis was marked. Muscle tone was greatly increased; the legs were kept in a scissor position with the feet and toes plantar flexed. Deep tendon reflexes were increased throughout , and sustained ankle clonus was elicited. Plantar reflexes were flexor. Developmentally he appeared retarded, although the severity of the motor defect precluded adequate evaluation. He could not walk, stand or sit without assistance. He spoke little, although he appeared to comprehend better than communicate. His most striking behavioral characteristic was destructive biting of the fingers and lips. His behavior clearly indicated that there was no sensory anesthesia; he appeared terrified and screamed as if in pain during the process and appeared happy only when restrained securely. There was no evidence of joint disease or tophi. The remainder of the physical examination was within normal limits.

The hemotocrit was 40 per cent, the erythrocyte sedimentation rate 15mm., corrected, and the leukocyte count 17,200 per cu. mm. with 85 per cent neutrophils,11 per cent lymphocytes and 4 per cent monocytes. Urinalysis showed gross hematuria, 1 plus proteinuria and many hexagonal crystals that dissolved in alkali. Chemical analysis of the serum revealed sodium 146, potassium 3.9, chloride 104 and carbon dioxide 21.6 mEq. per L.,calcium 10.6, phosphorus 4.0 and serum urea nitrogen 31 mg. per 100 ml. On the fifth hospital day the uric acid concentration of the serum was found to be 16.8 mg. per 100 ml., when the serum urea nitrogen was 30 mg. per 100 ml. An intravenous pyelogram demonstrated slightly decreased function bilaterally and a nephrogram effect suggesting distal obstruction. On cystoscopy the bladder was coated with fine yellow crystals. Roentgenographic survey of the chest, abdomen and bones was normal except for bilateral coxa valga deformities of the hip.

With the diagnosis of hyperuricemia, alkali therapy was initiated using Polycitra.® Within three days the serum urea nitrogen was 13 mg. per 100 ml.; four days later it was 5mg. per 100 ml., at which level it remained. Phenolsulfonphthalein excretion was 60 per cent in eighty minutes. Repeat cystoscopy and intravenous pyelography yielded normal findings. The concentraation of uric acid in the serum varied from 8.9 to 10.3mg. per 100 ml. The concentrations of sugar and cholesterol were 86 and 160 mg. per 100 ml., respectively. The serum total lipids were 0.74, total proteins 7.4, albumin 4.5 and globulin 2.9 gm. per 100 ml. The concentration of glycine in the plasma was 1.7 mg. per 100 ml.; the concentration of uric acid in the cerebrospinal fluid was 0.4 mg. per 100 ml. Studies of the chromosomes revealed no abnormality in number or structure.

The patient was discharged and maintained on alkali therapy until he could be admitted to the Pediatric Clinical Research Unit for the studies to be described. On completion of the studies treatment was initiated with probenecid. He was given 15 mg. per kg. per day for four weeks and then 25 mg. per kg. per day; Polycitra therapy was resumed as well. In four months his serum uric acid level decreased to 4.8 mg. per 100 ml. During this period his

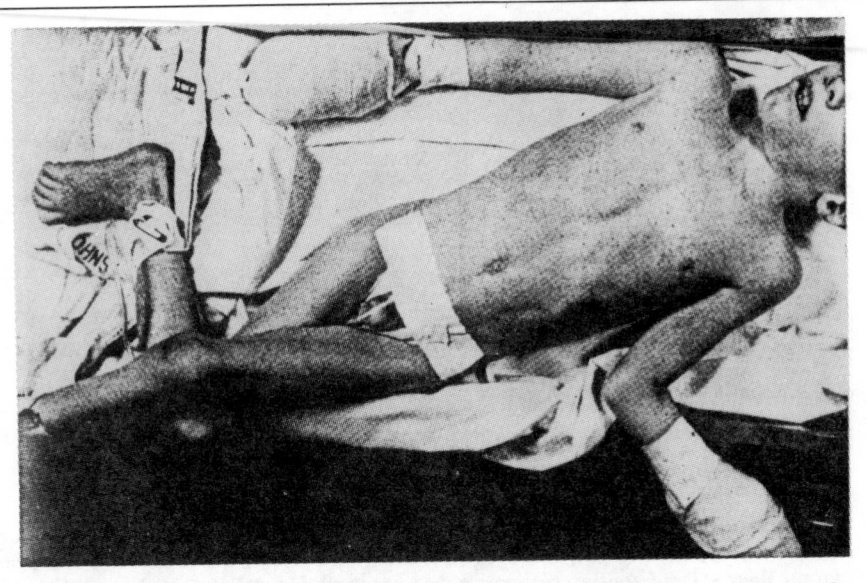

Fig. 2. Patient E. W. at the age of eight years. The mittens on the hands are to protect the child from biting his fingers. The lower lip has been chewed away and is no longer accessible to the central incisors. The marked hypertonia is suggested by the position of the legs.

weight increased 1.5 kg., and his behavior appeared to improve. The primary incisors and canines have been extracted in order to inhibit the biting of lips and fingers. No attacks of acute arthritis or of renal colic occurred throughout the course.

Patient E. W. (*JHH 857203*). The eight year old brother of Patient M. W. was found to have increased levels of uric acid in his serum and was admitted for studies of uric acid metabolism. The patient was first noted to be retarded at five months of age when he did not grasp or sit. He was first seen at the Harriet Lane Home at seventeen months of age, at which time he could not sit without support. Deep tendon reflexes were hyperactive, and plantar reflexes were extensor. At the age of five years he was admitted for diagnostic studies. At this time double hemiparesis with marked hypertonicity and athetoid movements were noted. The patient appeared mentally retarded. He had begun to bite his hands and lips at four years of age. Investigation during this admission included negative ferric chloride test results and a normal cerebrospinal fluid with glutamic oxaloacetic transaminase of 15 units, glutamic pyruvate transaminase 0 and protein 14 mg. per 100 ml. An electroencephalogram appeared to be disorganized, but there was no seizure discharges. A pneumoencephalogram revealed minimal cerebral atrophy bilaterally as indicated by somewhat dilated lateral ventricles. Shortly after discharge the patient was institutionalized. One month prior to admission he had an episode of severe pain in the right knee. The joint was described as hot, tender, somewhat violaceous and with limited active and passive motion. Roentgenograms of the knees were negative. No history of renal colic was elicited.

On admission, the patient was a fairly well developed and wellnourished white boy with cerebral palsy. (Fig. 2) The weight was 16.3 kg. and the height 110 cm. He was active in bed but could not sit or crawl. There was marked hypertonia with scissoring of the legs. The arms were usually extended and abducted. There was, however, no limitation to active motion, and the patient could make purposeful movements well. The severity of the motor defect precluded precise evaluation of his mental function. However, it was apparent that he was severely retarded. Biting of the hands and lips followed the pattern described in the younger brother. This patient had partially amputated the distal phalanx of one finger and had completely chewed away his lower lip, so that it was no longer accessible to his teeth. Deep tendon reflexes were symmetrically hyperactive. There were bilateral Babinski responses. Careful examination revealed no evidence of tophi. The remainder of the examination was negative.

The hematocrit was 36 per cent, the leukocyte count 11,000 per cu. mm. with 66 per cent neutrophils, 25 per cent lymphocytes, 2 per cent eosinophils and 8 per cent monocytes. Urinalysis was negative. Examination of the blood revealed concentrations of uric acid of 9.9 to 11.2 mg. per 100 ml. The serum urea nitrogen was 12, glucose 58 and cholesterol 210 mg. per 100 ml., carbon dioxide 22.5, sodium 157, potassium 4.4 and chloride 111 mEq. per L. Serum total lipids were 0.82 gm. per 100 ml., total protein 7.4, albumin 4.7 and globulin 2.7 gm. per 100 ml. The serum lactic acid was 8.5 and the pyruvic acid 1.0 mg. per 100 ml. The plasma concentration of glycine was 0.7 mg. per 100 ml. Inulin clearance was 118 ml. per minute per 1.72 M^2. The uric acid concentration of the cerebrospinal fluid was 0.9 mg. per 100 ml. Roentgenograms of the skeleton revealed coxa valga deformities of both hips, and the right femoral head was displaced laterally, changes which appeared to be secondary to the cerebral palsy. On the left hand there was an abnormality of the distal phlanax of the fourth finger with truncation of the distal ungual tuft and irregularity of soft tissues, which appeared to be a traumatic amputation. Otherwise, examination of the bones was normal.

Materials and methods

The two children described (M. W. and E. W.) and three control patients (B. S., E. S. and W. H.) were admitted to the Pediatric Research Unit of the Harriet Lane Home for the duration of study. Two of the control patients (B. S. and E. S.) were brothers aged five and eight years, respectively, with non-specific mental retardation. Their IQ's were estimated at less than 50. The third control patient (W. H.) was a five year old boy with mongolism of the 21 trisomy type. The control patients weighed 17.5, 37.2 and 17.9kg., respectively. All had normal motor function. Concentrations of uric acid in their serum were 4.0, 2.7 and 4.0 mg. per 100 ml. and in their cerebrospinal fluid 0, 0 and 0.4 mg. per 100 ml., respectively. The concentrations of electrolytes, glucose, cholesterol, lipid and protein were within normal limits in the plasma of all control patients. Concentrations of glycine in the plasma ranged from 0.6 to 1.7 mg. per 100 ml.

All patients were given a "purine free" diet containing 110 calories per kg. per day and 3.5 gm. protein per kg. per day three to four days prior to the initiation of study. The diet contained no meats or leguminous vegetables. The excretion of uric acid was constant throughout the period of study. In both patients with hyperuricemia (M. W. and E. W.) the sizes of the uric acid pools and their rates of turnover were determined after the intravenous injection of uric acid -2-C^{14}. In these patients and in the control patients the formation of uric acid was studied by determination of the rate of incorporation of isotope into the urinary uric acid following the intravenous injection of glycine-U-C^{14}. Following the injection of each isotope, serial twelve hour urine collections were initiated, and the uric acid from an aliquot of each collection period was isolated, purified and its specific activity determined as counts per minute per milligram uric acid.

In experiments with uric acid-2-C^{14}, urine was collected until isotope could no longer be found in the urinary uric acid. The natural logarithm of the specific activities of the urinary uric acid were plotted against time. In view of the virtual linearity obtained, the best straight

Table I. Miscible pool of uric acid and turnover rate

Patient	Body Weight (kg.)	Dose Injected (mg.)	Antilog Intercept (c.p.m./mg.)	Miscible Pool (mg.)	Slope (day^{-1})	Turnover (mg./day)	Turnover/ Kilogram (mg./kg./day)16
M. W.	14.3	0.250	1.82×10^4	530	2.06	1,090	76.2
E. W.	16.3	0.288	1.26×10^4	787	1.61	1,270	77.9

Note: Pool sizes were calculated from the equation $A = a \left(\dfrac{I_i}{I_o} - 1 \right)$ in which A is pool size; a, milligrams of uric acid injected; I_o, antilog of the intercept; and I_i, specific activity of the isotope administered (3.44×10^7 c.p.m. per mg.) [3,4].

line was drawn to describe the points and extrapolated to the intercept to give the specific activity of a miscible uric acid pool. The size of the pool was calculated by a standard isotope dilution formula [2,3]. (Table I.) Turnover rates were calculated from the slopes of the lines and multiplied by pool size to obtain total daily turnover in milligrams of uric acid. These lines were also calculated by the method of least squares, but since the slopes and intercepts found did not differ from those obtained graphically, the graphic method has been illustrated.

In experiments on the formation of uric acid from glycine-U-C[14], the specific activity of the uric acid isolated from the urine in each collection period was determined and plotted as a function of time. From these data, the total volumes of urine and their uric acid concentrations and the total isotope (c.p.m.) excreted per day in uric acid were calculated. The per cent conversion was calculated as

$$\frac{\text{total c.p.m. excreted in twenty-four hours as uric acid}}{\text{total c.p.m. injected in glycine}} \times 100,$$

and this was plotted cumulatively for seven days [4,5].

Uric acid-2-C[14]* had a specific activity of 0.65 μc. per mg. It was dissolved in 0.73 per cent lithium carbonate, sterilized by filtration through a sterile sintered glass funnel and diluted with isotonic saline solution. The concentration of isotope and uric acid were determined in an aliquot prior to injection. It was injected intravenously in a dose of 1μc. per kg. in a volume of 5 ml. Glycine uniformly labeled with C[14] (glycine-U-C[14]†) was obtained in 0.01 N hydrochloric acid in a specific activity of 82 mc. per mM. It was neutralized with sodium hydroxide, diluted and assayed for isotope content. It was assayed for radiochemical purity on Moore-Stein columns [6]. Aliquots for injection were made isotonic with saline solution and sterilized by autoclaving. They were injected intravenously in a dose of 2μc. per kg. in a volume of 5 ml.

Assay for uric acid concentration was carried out by the enzymatic spectrophotometric method as described by Liddle et al. [7] on each twelve hour specimen of urine and on lithium carbonate solutions of the purified uric acid isolated from these urine samples. Serum concentrations of uric acid were routinely determined by the method of Archibald [8] with which the values for normal persons vary from 2 to 6 mg. per 100ml. in this laboratory, but similar values were obtained on the serum using the enzymatic method. Plasma glycine concentrations were determined chromatographically [6]. Two methods were employed for the isolation of uric acid from the urine. The high concentrations of uric acid (> 1.0 mg. per ml.) present in the urine specimens of the patients with hyperuricemia permitted isolation directly by acidification and cooling. Glacial acetic acid was added in the amount of 2 ml. to 50 ml. of urine. The amount of urine used varied from 100 to 400 ml. depending on the quantity available. The acidified urine was allowed to stand at 4°c. for twelve to eighteen hours. The precipitate was collected by centrifugation and washed with cold distilled water. The precipitate was then dissolved in 30 ml. of 0.73 per cent lithium carbonate. Small amounts of charcoal (Norit A®**) were added in sufficient quantity to produce a colorless supernatant fluid after centrifugation. The solution was filtered by gravity, and 1.0 ml. glacial acetic acid was added to the filtrate and the solution stirred vigorously. The precipitate obtained immediately or after one to two hours at 4°c. was collected by centrifugation. After the precipitate was washed with 40 ml. cold distilled water and collected by centrifugation it was dissolved in 6 to 10 ml. of 0.73 per cent lithium carbonate and filtered through a sintered glass funnel. The purified uric acid was precipitated by dropwise acidification with 2.0 M acetic acid to pH 5.5 and cooled. The precipitate was collected by centrifugation. Recrystallization from lithium carbonate by this procedure was repeated three times.

*Nuclear Chicago Corp., Des Plaines, Illinois.
†New England Nuclear Corp., Boston,, Massachusetts.
**The Pfanstiehl Laboratories, Inc., Waukegan, Illinois.

Table II. Twenty-four hour urinary excretion of uric acid*

Patient	No. of Samples	Mean (mg.)	Range (mg.)	Corrected for Body Weight (mg./kg.)
M. W.	7	669	487–792	46.8
E. W.	7	712	518–918	43.7
B. S.	7	176	56–265	10.1
E. S.	7	289	198–364	7.8
W. H.	7	233	201–268	13.0

* Urinary excretions of uric acid in patients (M. W. and E. W.) and control patients (B. S., E. S. and W. H.) on a low purine diet.

This procedure was not applicable to the isolation of uric acid from the urine of control patients in whom this concentration was less than 1.0 mg. per ml. For this purpose an isolation method was developed which represents a modification of the analytic method of Carr and Pressman [9]. A 300 to 400 ml aliquot of urine was adjusted to pH 7.5 and passed through a Dowex-2-X10®* acetate form column (7 cm. by 2 cm.) with suction. The neutral effluent and that obtained on washing with 50 to 100 ml. distilled water contained no uric acid and were discarded. The column was eluted with 350 ml. of a solution made by mixing equal volumes of 0.04 M hydrochloric acid and 1.0 M sodium chloride. This effluent which contained the uric acid was evaporated *in vacuo* in a flash evaporator to approximately 5 ml. The moist uric acid-sodium chloride mixture was transferred with a minimum of cold 2.0 M acetic acid to a small Erlenmeyer flask and placed in the cold for thirty-six hours. The uric acid was collected by centrifugation, extracted with cold dilute acetic acid to remove any remaining salt and dissolved in 15 to 25 ml. lithium carbonate solution. The solution was decolorized, centrifuged, filtered and precipitated as described previously. Recrystallization from lithium carbonate was repeated once. When aliquots of the same urine were subjected to both methods of isolation the specific activity of the uric acid obtained was identical.

To determine specific activity the isolated uric acid was dissolved in 4 to 8 ml. of lithium carbonate solution. An aliquot was diluted 1:500 and its uric acid concentration determined. Undiluted aliquots (0.2 ml.) were plated directly on stainless steel planchets, dried and assayed for radioactivity. The apparatus used for the determination of radioactivity (D-47†) records 1 μc. as 5.71 × 10^5 c.p.m.

Results

Urinary Excretion of Uric Acid. The ranges of twenty-four hour urinary excretion of uric acid in these patients and the three control patients are shown in Table II. It is clear that there was no overlap between the two groups. In the patients the mean rate of excretion was 690 mg. per day, which is in the range of adult patients with gout who have been classified as "hyperexcretors" on the basis of excreting more than 600 to 628 mg. per day [10,11]. In contrast, control children excreted a mean of 233 mg. per day. When the data were adjusted for differences in body weight, the patients were found to excrete 45 mg. per kg. per day, a value that was four and a half times that of the control patients.

The pH of the urine in these patients varied from 5.5 to 6.5. In one patient (M. W.) the urinary excretion of uric acid was 487 mg. per twenty-four hours when the urinary pH was between 5.5 and 6.5 and 461 mg. per twenty-four hours after a period of alkali therapy which raised the urinary pH to 7.5.

Miscible Pool of Uric Acid and Its Rate of Turnover. Following injection of uric acid-2-C^{14} the specific activity of the uric acid isolated from the urine of these patients fell relatively rapidly over a period of three days. (Fig. 3) Isotope was not detectable after five days. The

*Dow Chemical Co., Midland, Michigan.
†Nuclear Chicago Corp., Des Plaines, Illinois.

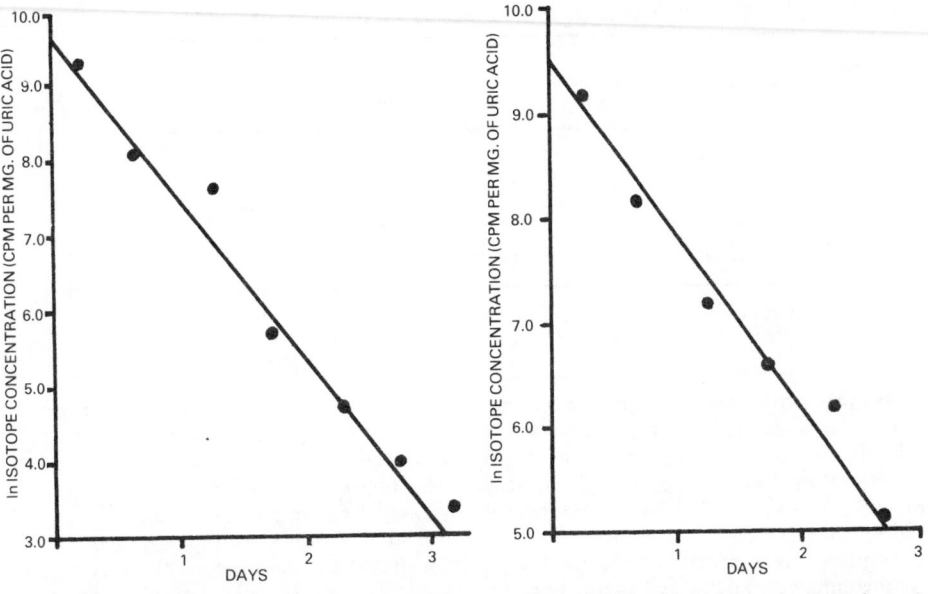

Fig. 3A. Semilogarithmic plot of the isotope concentration in urinary uric acid following intravenous injection of uric acid-2-C^{14} in Patient M. W., age five years, weight 14.3 kg., slope — 0.086 hours^{-1}, miscible pool 530 mg., daily turnover 1.090 gm. and turnover time 0.49 days.

Fig. 3B. Semilogarithmic plot of the isotope concentration in urinary uric acid following intravenous injection of uric acid-2-C^{14} in Patient E. W., age eight, weight 16.3 kg., slope — 0.0673 hours^{-1}, miscible pool 787 mg., daily turnover 1.272 gm. and turnover time 0.62 days.

decline in the natural logarithm of the specific activity was linear over the three day period in both patients. These data indicate that the slopes of the lines are functions of endogenous production of uric acid and are consistent with clinical observations that there were no tophi. In the presence of tophi, slow equilibration of solid urate with miscible urate has been demonstrated [*12*], and the semilogarithmic plot of the isotope concentration against time does not yield a straight line [*13*]. Calculation of the sizes of the miscible pools after extrapolation of the lines to the intercept is given in Table I.

In the first patient (M. W.) the miscible pool of uric acid was 530 mg. In his brother it was 787 mg. When these data were corrected for body weight, a mean pool size of 43 mg. per kg. was obtained, a value similar to that observed in adults with nontophaceous gout [*3*].

The theoretic concentration that would result if the uric acid of the total pool were uniformly distributed throughout the total body water, estimated at 70 per cent of the body weight, was calculated [*2*]. Uric acid concentrations of 5.3 and 6.7 mg. per 100 ml. were obtained, which approximated half the plasma concentrations. This was the relation observed in normal adult subjects [*12*] and in adult subjects with nontophaceous gout [*3*]. These data are confirmatory of the absence of tophi and indicate that all the uric acid in the measured pool was present in soluble form. In this situation values obtained for the size of the pool and its rate of turnover would be expected to have considerably greater validity than when these criteria are not met.

The turnover rates obtained in both patients described (M. W. and E. W.) were 2.06 and 1.61 pools per day, respectively. These are extremely high rates of turnover for uric acid. Multiplication of these data by the number of milligrams of uric acid in the pool gave values of 1.09 and 1.27 gm. of uric acid per day. Adjustment for the body weight gave values of 76.2 and 77.9 mg. per kg. per day. The amounts of uric acid excreted in the urine represented 58 per cent of the total amount formed each day as indicated by the turnover rate. This relationship is consistent with the observation of others on adult subjects [*3*].

Incorporation of Isotopically Labeled Glycine into Uric Acid. The concentration of isotope in urinary uric acid during the seven days following the injection of glycine-U-C^{14} is

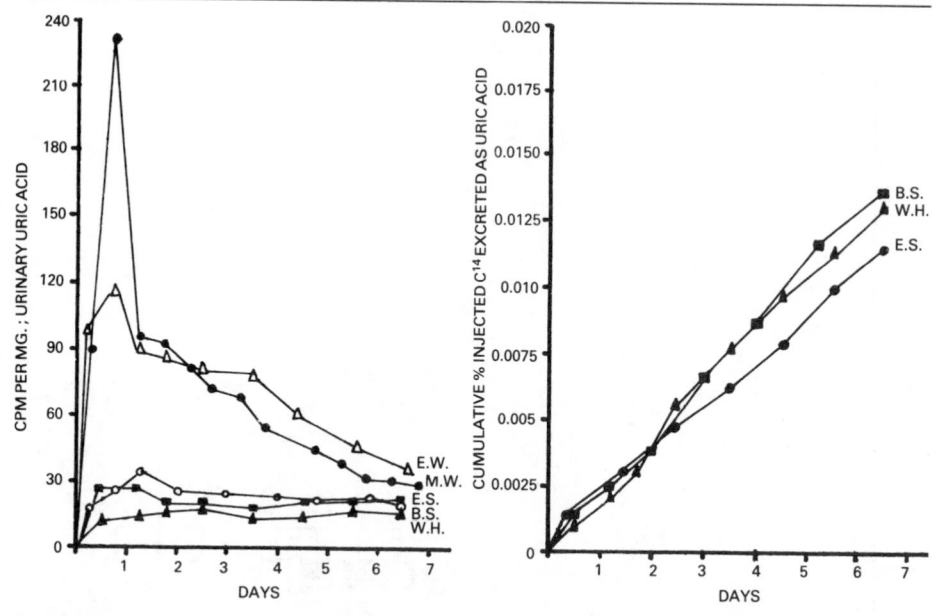

Fig. 4. Specific activities of urinary uric acid following intravenous administration of glycine-U-C¹⁴.

Fig. 5. The cumulative excretion of C¹⁴ in urinary uric acid in three control patients following the intravenous administration of glycine-U-C¹⁴.

indicated in Figure 4. In the patients, maximal specific activity was observed in the first twenty-four hours. After thirty-six hours there was a gradual decline in specific activity. In the control patients, peaks in the curves were not prominent, but the highest specific activities were found in the first thirty-six hours; a low level of activity was observed throughout the period of study. The patients described differed clearly from the control patients, and there was no overlap between the two groups. At their peaks, the specific activities of the patients described were four to eight times those observed in the control patients.

When experiments of this sort have been carried out in adult subjects with gout and in adult control subjects, it has not been possible to distinguish the two populations regularly on the basis of the specific activity of the urinary uric acid [5,11]. Thus the cumulative recovery of isotope in urinary uric acid over a seven day period after the administration of glycine has been employed to characterize those in whom gout is associated with overproduction of uric acid from glycine. The similarity observed when this analysis was performed in the three control children is documented in Figure 5. These patients converted only 0.012 per cent of the injected isotope to urinary uric acid in seven days. The data obtained in the patients described is compared with those of the control patients in Figure 6. On this scale the curve representing the control patients is adjacent to the abscissa. In the patients described a mean of 2.25 per cent of the isotope of glycine injected was recovered in urinary uric acid in seven days. This represents 200 times greater utilization of glycine for production of uric acid than in the control patients.

Genetic Studies. A survey of the family for the levels of uric acid in the blood was carried out. (Fig. 7.) Both parents were found to have normal levels of uric acid. Asymptomatic hyperuricemia was found in two paternal uncles and the paternal grandfather.

Comments

The striking clinical manifestations observed in the two patients described in this report, as well as its familial nature, suggest a distinct syndrome. The cardinal features of the disorder are mental retardation, cerebral palsy, choreoathetosis, self-destructive biting and hyperuricemia. A review of the literature on cases of gout occurring in patients less than ten

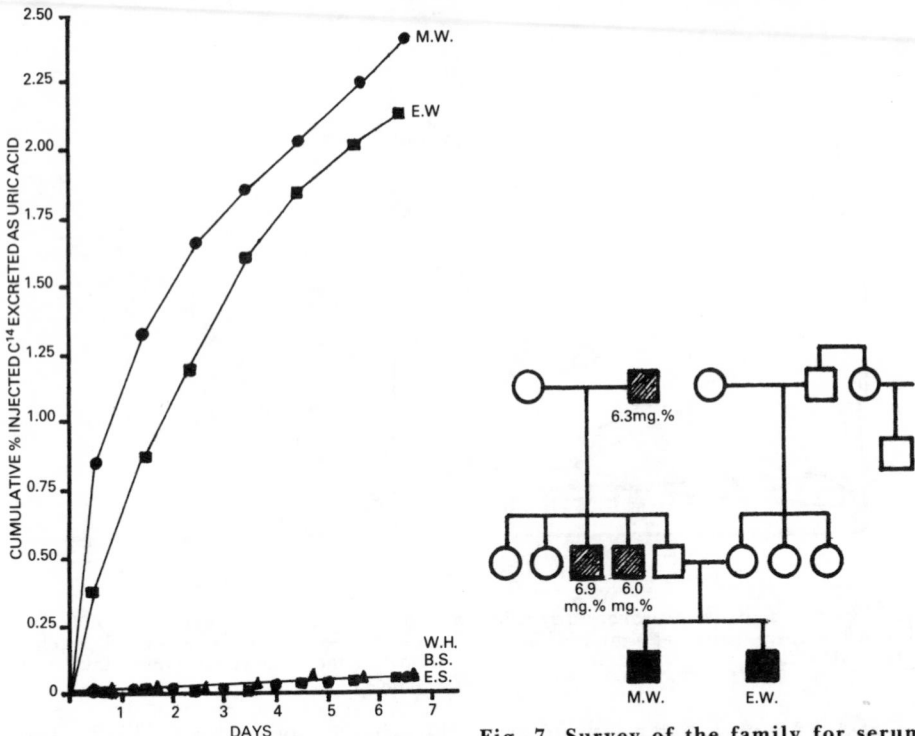

Fig. 6. The cumulative excretion of C¹⁴ in urinary uric acid in three control patients (B. S., E. S. and W. H.) and patients with cerebral palsy and hyperuricemia (M. W. and E. W.) following the administration of glycine-U-C¹⁴.

Fig. 7. Survey of the family for serum concentrations of uric acid. The open figures represent normal serum uric acid levels; the cross-hatched figures represent asymptomatic hyperuricemia found in two paternal uncles and the paternal grandfather. The patients are indicated in black.

years of age has revealed fifteen cases reported since 1823 [*14-26*]. (Table III.) In two of these [*21,22*] choreoathetosis and mental retardation were also present, and in one [*22*] a

Table III. Hyperuricemia in children less than ten years of age

Investigator	Sex and Age of Onset	Mental Condition	Remarks
Scudamore [*14*]	F, 8 yr.	...	
Garrod [*15*]	M, 9 yr.	Probably intact	
	F, 7 yr.	Probably intact	Psoriasis, anemia, general poor health
	M, 8 yr.	...	
Still [*16*]	F, 3½ yr.	...	Gout in father and grandfather
von Schopf [*17*]	M, 5 wk.	Neurologic intact	Severe tophi on fingers, white blood cell count 34,000 per cu. mm. with shift to left, died five days later with bronchopneumonia
Rauch [*18*]	F, 3½ yr.	Intact	Insidious onset, hands affected first
Recht [*19*]	F, 5 yr.	Intact	Severely deformed by age 27
Talbott [*20*]	M, 6 yr.	Intact	At 6 yr. diagnosis of tuberculous arthritis of hip, at 12 yr. diagnosis of rheumatic fever, gout diagnosis at age 15, severe tophaceous gout
Catel, Schmidt [*21*]	M, 2½ yr.	Choreoathetosis, mental retardation	Family history of mental retardation, gout, and renal disease; elevated uric acid level, no nitrogen retention
Riley [*22*]	M, 3 yr.	Choreoathetosis, mental retardation, lip biting	Severe tophi by 8 yr.
Trousseau [*23*]	..., 6 yr.	...	...
Decker [*24*]	M, 6 yr.	Intact	Renal calculi preceding gouty arthritis, obstructive renal disease 6 yr., first arthritis at 13 yr., diagnosis of gout and hyperuricemia at 16 yr.
Smythe, Cutchin [*25*]	M, 6 mo. or 16 yr.	Neurologic intact, somewhat slow mentally	Failure to thrive and abdominal enlargement at 6 mo., obvious dwarfism 6 yr., tophi 16 yr., arthritis 17 yr., died in renal failure 23 yr.
Rosenthal et al. [*26*]	M, 3 mo.	Intact	History of gout in both maternal and paternal families

photograph clearly illustrates a severely bitten lip. Metabolic studies have not previously been carried out. With a total of four patients with similar manifestations, it appears that 24 per cent of patients reported to have essential hyperuricemia before the age of ten years have had this disorder. It seems likely that the total incidence of this condition may be considerably higher, for in populations of children with mental retardation or cerebral palsy serum concentrations of uric acid are rarely determined.

Studies of uric acid metabolism have further indicated that these patients have an unusual disorder. The uric acid pool sizes and its rate of turnover has been determined by Sorenson [3] using uric acid-2-C^{14} in adult control subjects and adult patients with gout, with results similar to those of earlier studies with uric acid-N^{15} [2]. Correction for body weight of the pool sizes reported by Sorenson yielded a figure of 36 mg. per kg. in two adults with nontophaceous gouty, which approximated three times the mean obtained in nongouty control subjects. Pool sizes of 37 and 49 mg. per kg. obtained in the patients described in this report appear to be similar to those of the adults with nontophaceous gout. On the other hand, the turnover rates observed in these patients were considerably greater than those of adults with or without gout [2,3,12,13,27]. Turnover rates of 1.61 and 2.06 pools per day constitute turnover rates higher than any previously reported. Adults even in the presence of gouty tophi, have usually been found to turn over about half of the uric acid pool each day. The highest turnover rate previously reported in a patient with gout was 0.96 pools per day [27], a figure which can be considered too high for the person studied, since he was overtly tophaceous. The net turnover of over 1 gm. of uric acid a day in these children, weighing 14 and 16 kg., is in the same range observed in adults weighing approximately 70 kg. Expressed in terms of body weight, the amounts of uric acid turned over by these patients per kilogram of body weight was approximately six times that of gouty adult subjects. Consideration of the excretion of uric acid in the urine leads to similar conclusions as to the magnitude of the metabolic defect in these patients. The total amounts of uric acid found in the urine each day were in the range observed in the relatively small proportion of gouty adults who have been classified as "hyperexcretors." Adjustment of the excretion data for patient weight markedly accentuates the hyperexcretion of uric acid that characterizes these patients.

Studies of the formation of uric acid from glycine in these patients have differed from those previously reported in that the intravenous route was employed. In addition, with the idea that it might permit more versatility in the ultimate search for other metabolic products of glycine, the tracer was uniformly labeled with C^{14}. In the studies of Gutman and colleagues [10], the ranges obtained for the cumulative excretion of isotope of glycine-1-C^{14} in the urinary uric acid of control subjects were similar to those obtained with glycine-2-C^{14} when the isotope was given in trace amounts. In studies utilizing orally administered glycine-1-C^{14} control adult subjects have been reported to convert a mean of 0.17 per cent in seven days [5,10,28]. The value in many gouty adult subjects does not differ significantly from this mean [5,10,28]. In gouty adults in whom over-production has been designated and in whom increased quantities of uric acid are usually found in the urine, a greater conversion, averaging 0.5 per cent, has been reported [5,10,28]. The low rates of conversion of glycine to uric acid observed in the pediatric control patients could reflect differences in methodology or the diversion of glycine which enters the pathways of uric acid biosynthesis preferentially into the nucleic acids of growing subjects. However, Balis and Samarth [29] found that the incorporation of glycine into the ribonucleic acid adenine of young hamsters was significantly lower than in adult hamsters. The normal levels of glycine in the plasma of the patients described and the control patients suggest that significant differences in glycine pool size were not present. The children with hyperuricemia and cerebral palsy converted over 2 per cent of the glycine administered to urinary uric acid. Thus, whereas the gouty adult in whom overproduction can be demonstrated converts two to three times as much isotope-labeled glycine to urinary uric acid as do adult control subjects, these patients converted 200 times the amount found in control children.

The occurrence of such a marked metabolic defect in patients with unusual neurologic and behavioral characteristics suggests the possibility that the two may be related. A relationship between uric acid and central nervous system function has been considered for many years, because of the high incidence of gout among those who have been important in the intellectual development of western civilization. In view of the mental retardation of the patients described in this report, it seems possible that an excess of uric acid, or one of its products or precursors, could produce marked toxicity under the conditions of permeability and of development of neural structures that obtain in early infancy.

Acknowledgment: We gratefully acknowledge the assistance of Dr. Floyd M. Kregenow, physician of Patient M. W., and of the staff of the Rosewood State Training School for permission to study Patient E. W.

References
1. Bernstein, S. S. Gout in early life. *J. Mt. Sinai Hosp.*, 1974; **14**, 747.
2. Benedict, J. D., Forsham, P. H., Stetten D., Jr. The metabolism of uric acid in the normal and gouty human studied with the aid of isotopic uric acid. *J. Biol. Chem.*, 1949; **181**, 183.
3. Sorenson, L. B. The elimination of uric acid in man. *Scandinav. J. Clin. & Lab. Invest.*, 1960; **12**, (supp.), 54.
4. Benedict, J. D., Roche, M., Yü, T. F., Bien, E. J., Gutman, A. B., Stetten, D., Jr. Incorporation of glycine nitrogen into uric acid in normal and gouty man. *Metabolism.*, 1952; **1**, 3.
5. Wyngaarden, J. B. Overproduction of uric acid as the cause of hyperuricemia in primary gout. *J. Clin. Invest.*, 1957; **36**, 1508.
6. Spackman, D. H., Stein, W. H., Moore, S. Automatic recording apparatus for use in the chromatography of amino acids. *Anal. Chem.*, 1958; **30**, 1190.
7. Liddle, L., Seegmiller, J. E., Laster, L. The enzymatic spectrophotometric method for determination of uric acid. *J. Lab. & Clin. Med.*, 1959; **54**, 903.
8. Archibald, R. M. Colorimetric measurement of uric acid. *Clin. Chem.*, 1957; **3**, 102.
9. Carr, M. H., Pressman, B. C. An improved method for determination of uric acid in serum. *Anal. Biochem.*, 1962; **4**, 24.
10. Gutman, A. B., Yü, T. F., Black, H., Yalow, R. S., Berson, S. A. Incorporation of glycine-1-C[14], glycine-2-C[14], and glycine-N[15] into uric acid in normal and gouty subjects. *Am. J. Med.*, 1958; **25**, 917.
11. Seegmiller, J. E., Grayzell, A. I., Laster, L., Liddle, L. Uric acid production in gout. *J. Clin. Invest.*, 1961; **40**, 1304.
12. Benedict, J. D., Forsham, P. H., Roche, M., Soloway, S., Stetten, D., Jr. The effect of salicylates and adrenocorticotropic hormone upon the miscible pool of uric acid in gout. *J. Clin. Invest.*, 1950; **29**, 1104.
13. Sorenson, L. B. The pathogenesis of gout. *Arch. Int. Med.*, 1962; **109**, 379.
14. Scudamore, C. *A Treatise on the Nature and Cure of Gout and Gravel.* (4th edn.) London: Longmans, Green & Co., 1823.
15. Garrod, A. B. *A Treatise on Gout and Rheumatic Gout.* (3rd edn.) London: Longmans, Green & Co., 1876.
16. Still, G. F. *Common Disorders and Diseases of Childhood.* (5th edn., p. 570.) London: Oxford University Press, 1927.
17. von Schopfe, E. M. Gicht bei einem 5 Wochen alten Säugling. *Klin. Wchnschr.*, 1930; **9**, 2148.
18. Rauch, H. W. M. Gicht bei einem 3½ jährigen Mädchen. *Med. Monatsschr.*, 1950; **4**, 931.
19. Recht, L. A case of severe gout in a woman aged 27. *Acta Med. Scandinav.*, 1954; **150**, 189.
20. Talbott, J. H. *Gout.* New York: Grune & Stratton, Inc., 1957.
21. Catel, W., Schmidt, J. Über familiäre gichtische Diathese in Verbindung mit zerebralen und renalen Symptomen bei einem Kleinkind. *Deutsche Med. Wchnschr.*, 1959; **84**, 2145.
22. Riley, I. D. Gout and cerebral palsy in a three year old boy. *Arch. Dis. Child.*, 1960; **35**, 293.
23. Spanopoulos, G. A case of gout in a teenager. *Practitioner*, 1960; **185**, 674.
24. Decker, J. L., Vandeman, P. R. Renal calculi preceding gouty arthritis in a child. *Am. J. Med.*, 1962; **32**, 805.
25. Smythe, C. M., Cutchin, J. H. Primary juvenile gout. *Am. J. Med.*, 1962; **32**, 799.
26. Rosenthal, I. M., Gaballah, S. and Rafelson, M. Metabolic studies in a young child with elevated serum uric acid levels. *Am. J. Dis. Child.*, 1961; **102**, 631.
27. Bishop, C., Garner, W., Talbott, J. H. Pool size, turnover rate, and rapidity of equilibration of injected isotopic uric acid in normal and pathological subjects. *J. Clin. Invest.*, 1951; **30**, 879.
28. Seegmiller, J. E., Laster, L., Liddle, L. V. Failure to detect consistent overincorporation of glycine-1-C[14] into uric acid in primary gout. *Metabolism*, 1958; **7**, 376.
29. Balis, M. E., Samarth, K. Influence of age on glycine and purine metabolism. *Arch. Biochem.*, 1962; **99**, 517.

Reprinted from *Am. J. Med.*, 1964; **36**, 561-570 by kind permission of the publishers Technical Publishing, 875 Third Avenue, New York, NY 10022.

LESCH-NYHAN DISEASE: CLINICAL EXPERIENCE WITH NINETEEN PATIENTS

Richard Christie, Carolyn Bay, Irvin A. Kaufman, Bohdan Bakay,
Margaret Borden, William L. Nyhan

Summary

The clinical phenotype in Lesch-Nyhan disease has been analyzed in 19 patients studied in hospital. In each case the diagnosis was made on the basis of inactivity of the enzyme hypoxanthine guanine phosphoribosyltransferase in erythrocyte lysates. All had hyperuricemia, and the presence of 'orange sand' in the diaper was a prominent early complaint. All had self-mutilative behavior, of which the most characteristic form was biting the fingers or lips. All had the neurological syndrome of spasticity and choreoathetoid involuntary movements. All but one had less-than-normal intelligence.

Introduction

Lesch-Nyhan disease is an inborn error of the metabolism of purines, which is determined by an abnormal gene on the X chromosome. Its expression, which is fully recessive, is in the virtually complete absence of activity of the enzyme hypoxanthine guanine phosphoribosyltransferase (HGRPT) (Seegmiller *et al.* 1967), which normally catalyzes the conversion of hypoxanthine to inosinic acid and of guanine to guanylic acid. Children with this disorder (exclusively males) have the highest rates of purine synthesis observed in man (Lesch and Nyhan 1964, Nyhan 1968). They also have hyperuricemia and markedly increased excretion of uric acid in the urine.

In addition to the consequences of hyperuricemia, the disease is characterized clinically by a neurological syndrome of spasticity, choreoathetosis and mental retardation. A unique feature is the regular occurrence of abnormal, compulsive, aggressive behavior, the main component of which is self-mutilation by biting.

The disease was first reported in two brothers by Lesch and Nyhan (1964). Since then a number of individual case reports have documented that the disease occurs in many races throughout the world (Nyhan *et al.* 1965, 1967; Sass *et al.* 1965; Jeune *et al.* 1966; Michel 1966; Manzke 1967; Labrune *et al.* 1968; Rosenberg *et al.* 1968; Seegmiller 1968; VanDerZee *et al.* 1968; Mizuno *et al.* 1970; Wood *et al.* 1972; Kaiser *et al.* 1973; Müller and Stermberger 1974; Allison *et al.* 1975; Beyer *et al.* 1975; Rivard *et al.* 1975; Nyhan 1980).

A number of review articles have been published (Crawhall *et al.* 1972; Nyhan 1973, 1978, 1979; Seegmiller 1976; Kelly and Wyngaarden 1978), but there has been no systematic assembly of clinical information from a series of patients studied closely by a single team. The present report describes a series of 19 patients observed in hospital.

Patient and methods (Table I)

For all 19 patients, the diagnosis was established by documenting that the activity of HGRPT in erythrocyte lysates was almost nil (Bakay *et al.* 1969, Sweetman and Nyhan

Acknowledgements: This study was aided by U.S. Public Health Service Research Grants No. HDO4608 from the National Institute of Child and Human Development, GM 17702 from the National Institute of General Medical Sciences, and General Clinical Research Center No. RR00827 from the Division of Research Resources, National Institutes of Health, Bethesda, Maryland; and NF 1–377 from the March of Dimes-Birth Defects Foundation.

AUTHORS' APPOINTMENTS
Richard Christie, Research Associate;
Carolyn Bay, Clinical Instructor;
Bohdan Bakay, Research Biochemist;
Margaret Borden, Specialist;
William L. Nyhan, M.D. Ph.D., Professor and Chairman; Department of Pediatrics, University of California, San Diego, La Jolla, Ca. 92093.
Irvin A. Kaufman, M.D., Assistant Clinical Professor (UCSD), Children's Health Center, 8001 Frost Street, San Diego, Ca. 92123.

Table I. Patients with Lesch-Nyhan disease

Patient	Age at time of observation (yrs)	Age at onset (yrs:mths)	Self-mutilation Type	Serum uric acid before treatment (mg/dl)	Other abnormalities
M.P.	17	2:0	Biting lips and tips of fingers	10·4	Undescended testes
C.W.	17	2:6	Biting lips, tongue and fingers	NA	Renal calculi
L.S.	16	2:6	Biting tongue and fingers, poking eyes and nose	15·4	Convulsions at 5 yrs; tophi on external ears
G.C.	16	4:0	Biting lips and fingers, head-banging	NA	
J.R.	15	0:8	Opisthotonic movements	8·9	
R.S.	15	2:0	Biting fingers	12·9	Imperforate anus
J.J.	15	0:6	Biting lips and hands	12·0	Tophus on external ear
D.D.	14	2:0	Biting inside of mouth and fingers	NA	
M.J.	13	2:6	Biting lips and fingers	NA	Megaloblastic anemia
T.G.	9	NA	NA	NA	
E.W.	8	4:0	Biting lips and hands	11·2	
B.W.	7	2:0	Biting lips and fingers	NA	
D.M.	7	2:6	Biting fingers	8·8	
O.K.	7	2:0	Biting lips and fingers	NA	
A.W.	6	2:0	Biting fingers	NA	
M.M.	5	NA	Biting lower lip	NA	
P.B.	5	NA	NA	NA	
M.W.	4½	NA	Biting lips and fingers	16·8	
S.S.	3	1:6	Biting hands	NA	Herniorrhaphy at 4 mths; seizures

NA = not available

1972). This is the way we have defined Lesch-Nyhan disease, but the clinical phenotype or Lesch-Nyhan syndrome may be caused by other variants of the HGPRT enzyme (McDonald and Kelley 1971). Each patient was examined by one of us after admission to one of three general clinical research centers. Over the years a number of other cases have been seen as outpatients, but this study was restricted to patients actually admitted to hospital under our observation.

Hospital records were reviewed and questionnaires were sent to the patients' families to obtain additional information about symptomatology, age at onset of the disease, the type of self-mutilation (both past and present), complications secondary to the syndrome, the patient's present abilities, and attendance and performance at school. Of the 15 families that could be contacted, 13 returned the questionnaire. Individual schools were also contacted to obtain the results of intelligence tests and of academic and psychological evaluations: these details were obtained for eight children.

The patients' ages ranged from eight to 24 years at the time the data were compiled for this paper. Some had been followed for as long as 16 years: one had been followed from birth, but most were first seen considerably later and details of their early life were obtained from the mothers' histories.

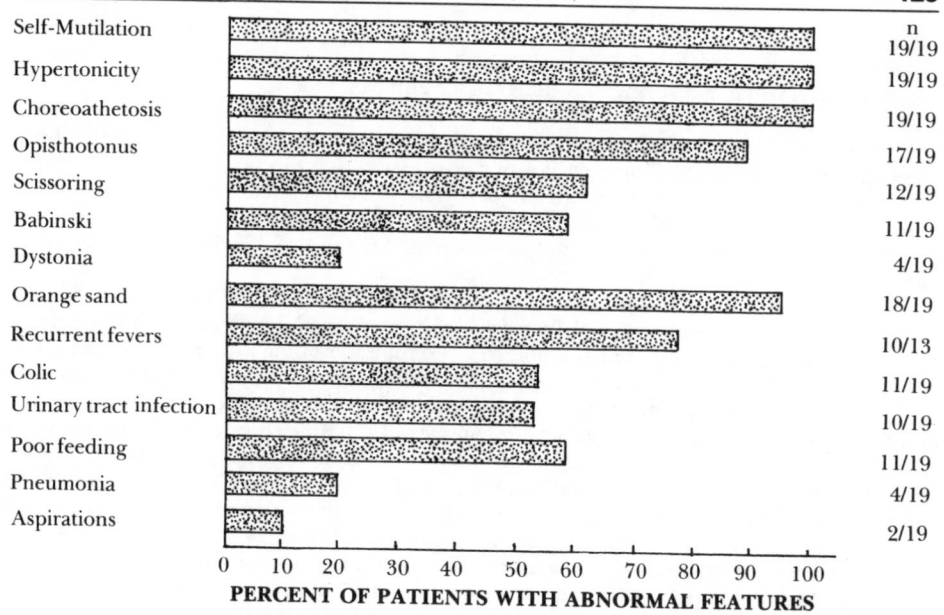

Fig. 1. Clinical manifestations among 19 patients with Lesch-Nyhan disease

Results

Behavioral and neurological features were prominent clinical manifestations among the 19 patients (Table I, Fig.1).

Pregnancies were described as normal in all cases. One child had been a breech presentation and his Apgar score was 4 at three minutes and 8 at 15 minutes: he required suctioning after birth and was sent home after four days. Another was born by caesarean section *(vide infra)*. Two other children had congenital anomalies: one an imperforate anus and the other a dysmorphic external left-ear. A third child had undescended testes.

Generally the neonatal period had been unremarkable, but in three cases feeding was poor during the first days of life: one of these had been admitted to hospital for gavage feeding. Orange sand or crystals had been noted in the diapers of 18 patients (Fig. 1), but in most cases this was reported retrospectively in response to direct questioning. Some mothers remembered mentioning this finding to a physician, but in no case was hyperuricemia diagnosed as a consequence. Some parents had observed this orange sand soon after birth, but others had not noticed it until the child was three years old.

The complaints most commonly first noticed were poor motor development, abnormal muscle tone or spasticity, generally between the ages of three and five months. One infant underwent a herniorrhaphy at four months, after which his development was noted to be delayed and athetoid cerebral palsy was diagnosed. However, it had been noted that although delivery had been by caesarean section, there was no history of perinatal anoxia or kernicterus.

For 15 of the 19 patients the initial diagnosis was something other than the Lesch-Nyhan syndrome (Table II), the most common diagnosis being cerebral palsy. One patient was initially diagnosed as having gout, although he also had neurological abnormalities.

Among the earliest findings in these patients were alterations in muscle tone, all recorded as hypertonic. One boy had been noted earlier to by hypotonic, and it is likely that this sequence would also have been observed in others had serial observations of muscle tone been made. Similarly, it is our impression that hyperactive deep-tendon reflexes occur in all patients at some time, but these were recorded in only nine cases. Hypoactive deep-tendon reflexes were noted in one patient. Often reflexes are difficult to elicit in these patients because of their involuntary movements, which invariably accelerate when they are being physically examined. Also, many patients become very thin (especially if they are in institutions), and deep-tendon reflexes diminish as muscle mass decreases. Positive Babinski responses were elicited in 11 patients, in one of whom the plantar response reverted to normal. Scissoring was noted in 12 children.

Choreoathetosis was observed in all the patients, four of whom were described as dystonic. Opisthotonic spasms or episodic arching of the back were characteristic, being recorded for 17 patients. However, it is our impression that this occurs at some time in all patients with the Lesch-Nyhan syndrome. Possibly as a consequence of spasticity, seven of the 18 patients for whom the information was available had dislocated hips, many of which were bilateral. In two cases roentgenograms revealed coxa valga. Tophi on the external ear were noted in two patients.

The degree of motor disability was severe in all cases. None was able to walk or sit without support, but all could sit in a wheelchair if correctly restrained. However, most were unable to keep the head erect. One child was able to stand for a short time with braces on his legs. At least two could move their wheelchairs by themselves. One had been toilet-trained.

Mental ability varied widely: IQ scores were available for only nine of the children, and ranged from 25 to 101. The mean was 58, and six of the nine children had scores greater than 50. 14 out of 17 children were able to talk (there was no information in the records for two children), seven of whom used sentences and seven only single words. Speech was always dysarthric and difficult to understand. Two of the 19 children could read, and another five were able to distinguish letters, numbers and pictures. Information on school attendance was available for 15 patients, of whom 11 were attending schools for the physically and mentally handicapped and one a regular public school, with a special room and teacher, but also attending a few regular classes in a mainstream program. At the time of this study his age was 15 years 3 months and his performance was at the eight-grade level, though he was achieving mostly As and Bs. He read with great difficulty, and required large print at a distance out of arm's reach. His IQ was 101 on the Peabody Picture Vocabulary Test and the Wechsler Intelligence Scale for Children.

The average age at onset of any symptoms was four months, but the average age at which self-mutilating behavior began was 26 months (range six months to four years). All 19

Table II. Initial diagnoses and ages at Lesch-Nyhan diagnosis

Patient	Age (mths)	Onset of symptoms Type	Initial diagnosis	Age at diagnoses (yrs:mths) Initial	Lesch-Nyhan
M.P.	8	Slow development	Cerebral palsy	0:8	7:0
C.W.	3	Slow development	Cerebral palsy	2:0	2:6
G.C.	1	Unable to push up without falling over	Cerebral palsy	0:3	10:0
L.S.	5	Unable to hold up head, spasticity	Psychiatric disorder		
J.R.	6	Unable to hold up head	Spasticity	0:6	2:6
R.S	1	Low-grade fevers	Gout	0:4	5:0
J.J.	1	Opisthotonic spasms	Cerebral palsy	0:6	11:0
D.D.	1	Poor feeding, lethargy	Brain damage	0:3	1:0
M.J.	5	Slow development and weight loss	Mental retardation, cerebral palsy	0:9	4:6
T.G.	4	Abnormal muscle tone	Cerebral palsy	1:0	4:6
E.W.	5	Unable to grasp or sit	Cerebral palsy	1:0	8:0
B.W.	7	Unable to sit	Lesch-Nyhan disease	0:7	0:7
D.M.	½	Hypertonicity	Cerebral palsy	0:6	2:6
O.K.	3	Abnormal muscle tone	Lesch-Nyhan disease	0:9	0:9
A.W.	5	Unable to roll over	Microcephalic retardation	0:8	1:3
M.M.	8	Unable to lift head	Lesch-Nyhan disease	0:10	0:10
P.B.	8	Colic abdominal pain	Lesch-Nyhan disease	1:6	1:6
M.W.	3	Slow development	Cerebral palsy	1:0	4:6
S.S.	2	Slow development	Athetoid cerebral palsy	0:6	1:6

Table III. Characteristics of biting behavior

Characteristic biting pattern	No.*
Frequent	11/16
Infrequent	5/16
Upper lip	8/18
Lower lip	15/18
Shoulders	3/15
One finger	2/15
Two fingers	3/15
More than two fingers	10/15
Resulting in amputations	3/15

*Numbers vary because information was not available for all patients.

children exhibited this behavior, and all on whom we had specific information bit their hands (Table III). Self-mutilation was described as frequent in 11 out of 16 patients, and infrequent in the other five. Two children bit only one finger and three bit only two, the index fingers and thumbs being most commonly attacked. Four children showed a preference for either the right or the left hand. In most cases the biting activity broke the skin. The majority of patients bit their lips. Three children bit their shoulders.

The diagnosis of Lesch-Nyhan syndrome had not been made in 12 cases until after self-mutilation had begun. Permanent loss of tissue was a regular consequence of biting. One child had amputated the distal phalanx of the fifth finger on the left hand, as well as mutilating the other fifth finger and both thumbs. Another child had also amputated the distal phalanx of a finger, and a third had amputated the anterior portion of the tongue. 18 of the 19 patients had extensive loss of lip-tissue, and nine had had some teeth extracted to prevent mutilation of the lips.

Head-banging was common among nine patients, but voluntary head-banging can be difficult to distinguish from accidental injury to the head during opisthotonic movements, so this figure may be too high. In one well-documented case, deliberate head-banging has become the major form of self-mutilation. This teen-age boy throws his head forward vigorously while seated in a wheelchair, producing bruises and lacerations, particularly of the chin. Most patients throw their heads backward, but this patient's chair was well-padded behind his head, so he has learned to throw his head forward. His parents now arrange a stack of pillows in his lap above his restrained hands, reaching to his chin, so if he throws his head forward he strikes only the soft surface.

Fourteen patients frequently attempted to hit other people, and 11 attempted to bite others. Other aggressive actions were spitting at others and vomiting on them; the latter occurred often among 10 patients, but the frequency could be diminished by operant conditioning in the classroom.

In the day-to-day management of the syndrome, restraints are required to prevent self-mutilation. Of 14 patients for whom specific information was available, 12 required restraints both day and night. Of the other two, one needed to be restrained only at night and one only infrequently needed restraint either during the day or the night.

Generally these children become very agitated when their restraints are removed, and in most cases the hand immediately moves towards the mouth. However, with age, most children appear to develop some degree of control over their behavior. Some place their hands behind their back, for example, or sit on them. One 18-year-old asked to have his restraints removed at various times, and when this was done he would talk to his hand, saying 'be good, right hand'.

These children are very aware of their disability and of their aggressive behavior. During a physical examination, one child repeatedly tried to kick the physician in the head. The physician asked whether he hit other people and the mother said 'No', but the child reminded her that recently he had bitten his dentist. His mother said 'But you didn't really mean that', and he said 'Yes, I did!'. Since they are aware of their handicaps, they must also learn to deal with constantly being restrained and fully cared for. One child spoke to his psychologist about these concerns, particularly his relationship with his siblings. He became frustrated to the point of tears when these normal children went out of the house, leaving him at home. While he recognized that crying was not a 'permissible' response to frustration or anger, he thought it was acceptable in two situations, when he was homesick (he lived most of the time in an institution, returning home for a week every three or four weeks), and 'when I bite my fingers'.

Most of the children for whom records were available were retarded in growth and development (Table IV). Generally height and weight were well below the third percentile: height-age was within normal limits for only two children, and weight for only one. Low height-ages ranged from 28 to 92 per cent of chronological age, with a median of 60 per cent. In most cases weight was reduced even further: the ratio of weight-age to height-age usually was less than 1, ranging to as low as 0·45 (median, 0·75).

Of the 13 boys examined roentgenographically, all showed some retardation of bone age. However, among those for whom results of both assessments were available, skeletal retardation was either less severe than or equal to linear growth retardation, except among the very youngest children. Six children were also described as microcephalic: comment about head size was made in 16 cases, but actual head-circumference measurements were available for only half the patients.

By the time of this study, when the patients' ages ranged from eight to 24 years, 12 had had a total of 33 admissions to hospital for non-elective reasons (mode three admissions, range one to 11). Of the admissions, 17 were because of renal complications, including renal stones, urinary-tract infections and hematuria. After an intercurrent illness associated with diminished fluid intake, one child developed an acute obstruction of both ureters, uric acid sludge causing complete anuria. This was treated successfully by bilateral nephrostomy and manually washing out the ureters. Four other admissions were because of respiratory infection and four because of pneumonia. Two patients developed pulmonary aspiration and two had had seizures.

Among the eight patients for whom the information was available, concentrations of uric acid in serum before treatment ranged from 8·8 to 16·8mg/dl. Treatment with allopurinol, which is highly effective in reducing concentrations of uric acid in body fluids, has become the rule in this disorder. Dosages for the patients in this study ranged from 6·67 to 38·1

Table IV. Indices of physical growth

Patient	Chron. age (yrs:mths)	Height Inches (cm)	Height age (yrs:mths)	Weight Lbs (kg)	Weight age (yrs:mths)	Weight age: height age	Bone age (yrs:mths)
M.P.	16:9	54 (137)	10	46 (21)	6	·60	11:6
L.S.	16	53 (135)	9:6	62 (28)	10	1·05	10
R.S.	14:6	54½ (138)	10:2	60 (27)	8:9	·86	11:6
J.J.	14:6	44½ (112)	6:9	46 (21)	5	·74	7
D.D.	13:11	48½ (124)	6:3	52 (23)	7:6	1·2	10:6
T.G.	8:9	43½ (109)	5	33½ (15)	3:4	·67	8
E.W.	8	—	5	36 (16)	3:9	·75	—
D.M.	7:5	—	—	—	—	—	6
O.K.	6:10	46 (117)	6:3	49½ (22)	6:7	1·05	—
B.W.	6:9	39 (99)	3:6	33 (15)	3:2	·90	4:6
A.W.	6:1	39 (99)	3:6	27 (12)	2:3	·64	3:6
M.J.	6	33 (84)	1:8	19 (9)	0:9	·45	2
M.M.	5:5	40½ (103)	4	33 (15)	3:2	·79	5
P.B.	5	—	—	—	—	—	4:6
M.W.	4:6	—	—	31 (14)	2:9	—	—
S.S.	2:11	34½ (88)	2:3	23½ (11)	1:3	·56	1:9

Height age and weight age calculated as 50th percentile for given height and weight from National Center for Health Statistics Growth Charts (1976). (*Monthly Vital Statistics Report*, 25, No.3 Supp. (HRA) 76-1120.)
For some patients, data in this Table were obtained at different ages from those in Table 1.

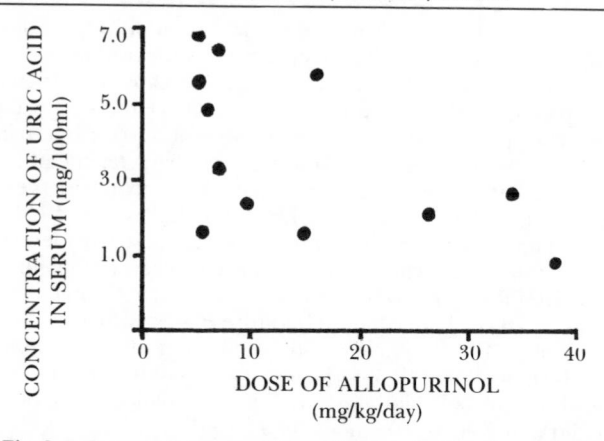

Fig. 2. Relationship between dose of allopurinol and concentration of uric acid in serum of 12 patients with Lesch-Nyhan disease

mg/kg bodyweight; absolute doses ranged from 100 to 800mg/day. The relationship between dosage of allopurinol and level of uric acid in the blood is illustrated in Figure 2. It can be seen that in some cases concentrations of uric acid in serum of 3mg/dl or less were achieved on doses of 10mg or less. However, in many cases doses of 20mg/kg or more were required to maintain the concentration of uric acid in serum at an acceptable level.

Discussion

The clinical phenotype of Lesch-Nyhan disease was remarkably similar in the 19 patients in this study. The disease occurs exclusively in males: unlike other X-linked disorders, there appears to be selection against expression in the heterozygous female (Nyhan *et al.* 1970). Furthermore, reproductive capacity in affected males seems to be nil, so the occurrence of the disease in a female would require an XO karyotype, or a mutation in a second X chromosome, along with inheritance of the abnormal gene on the other X chromosome, events which would be expected to occur very infrequently.

Self-mutilation was a prominent feature among all 19 patients. They were not chosen for study because of this or any other clinical feature, but because HGPRT activity could not be distinguished from zero. Over the years during which these patients have been observed we have also studied a number of cases with HGPRT variants (Kogut *et al.* 1970), in whom there were varying degrees of partial activity of the enzyme, and in recent years the number of such cases has increased as we actively sought to study variation at the HGPRT locus (Nyhan and Bakay 1974; Nyhan 1977, 1980).

In general, it appears that self-mutilation is characteristic of the Lesch-Nyhan variant, but not of other variants, and patients who do not mutilate themselves are turning out to have other variants of the enzyme (Bakay *et al.* 1979). Self-mutilation is also seen in children with non-specific mental retardation, but it is unusual for there to be the extensive loss of tissue seen in the Lesch-Nyhan syndrome. Children with the De Lange syndrome engage in aversive, self-stimulatory behavior, and sometimes produce deformities of the lips similar to those of Lesch-Nyhan children (Bryson *et al.* 1971, Shear *et al.* 1971). However, their behavior is relatively easily managed with operant conditioning techniques, especially aversive therapy, whereas Lesch-Nyhan patients tend to become worse with aversive measures (Anderson *et al.* 1977).

The etiology of the self-mutilation remains unknown, but increased concentrations of uric acid itself have been ruled out because infants treated to prevent hyperuricemia from the time of birth have also manifested the same behavior (Marks *et al.* 1968). There is increasing evidence that the balance of biogenic amines in the central nervous system may be involved (Nyhan *et al.* 1980).

The neurological syndrome observed in these patients clearly is also a uniform feature. All 19 displayed hypertonicity and choreoathetosis, and there was poor motor control and inability to maintain the head or trunk in the vertical position. Opisthotonic extensor spasms of the trunk are characteristic, but deep-tendon reflexes may not appear to be increased because of inanition and loss of muscle mass, or because of difficulty in eliciting them in a writhing patient with involuntary movements. However, usually they are increased. The Babinski response may or may not be present: it was present in one patient but was then observed to disappear. Convulsions are not characteristic of the syndrome.

It has become apparent that the neurological syndrome of patients with the classic disease also may be seen in patients with other variants of HGPRT (Bakay *et al.* 1979), for example among those who do not mutilate themselves and whose enzyme activity level can be shown to be different from that of the Lesch-Nyhan variant. However, the majority of patients with partial defects of HGPRT have no cerebral or behavioral abnormalities (Kogut *et al.* 1970, Sweetman *et al.* 1978, Nyhan 1980). Therefore it seems that in the spectrum of clinical manifestations of HGPRT deficiency, the neurological syndrome is a little less specific for the Lesch-Nyhan variant than is the behavioral syndrome, which occurs in 100 per cent of cases. However, the behavior also occurs in a few patients with other variants of the enzyme (McDonald and Kelley 1971, Page *et al.* 1981).

The effect of HGPRT deficiency on intelligence varies, even within the Lesch-Nyhan syndrome. Six of nine patients in our series had IQs greater than 50, but it is difficult to test IQ among children with the syndrome because of their physical disabilities and the restraints necessary to prevent self-mutilation. Performance is difficult to assess accurately when the child is restrained, and impossible to evaluate if the restraints are removed, when most patients can attend to nothing except biting or its avoidance. Generally, only verbal estimates can be used. It is possible, therefore, that measurement of IQ may underestimate the actual ability of these patients and result in a less than vigorous attempt at education. One of our patients who is now learning in a formal education program was not placed in any type of school until the age of 15 years. On the other hand, the measurement of IQ in this study was not systematic and the values were obtained by different psychologists, so there may have been a bias if the most severely retarded children were not tested.

There have been a few reports of patients with normal intelligence (Scherzer and Ilson 1969, Bull and LaVecchio 1978), but details of the assessment of HGPRT were not given, and in general the children in other reports have been similar to ours. Bull and LaVecchio suggested that their patient might soon walk, but so far that has not happened (Ampola 1979). None of our patients has walked. One had a normal IQ, and he had not been exposed to behavior modification. The most frequently cited patient with a normal IQ and considered to have this syndrome (Catel and Schmidt 1959, Manzke *et al.* 1979) has now been shown to have a different defect from the Lesch-Nyhan variant (Bakay *et al.* 1979). It would be interesting to have a systematic correlation between the various facets of intelligence and enzyme activity.

In almost all cases the physical growth and development of these children were considerably retarded, generally linear growth, increase in mass and osseous development, but usually the retardation was not symmetrical. Usually the least affected measurement was bone age, then height, and the most affected was weight. These findings suggest that the problem has a nutritional basis. These children are difficult to feed because of athetosis, and they vomit frequently. Furthermore, the metabolic defect must require considerable synthetic energy, the products of which are lost in the urine, along with the amounts of carbon and nitrogen tied up in uric acid. Thus their requirements for nutrients probably are greater than normal. Extensive endocrine studies of these patients, to account for their short stature, have produced negative results (Skyler *et al.* 1974).

Increased concentrations of uric acid in body fluids are a regular feature of the syndrome. Virtually all patients have hyperuricemia, as did all the patients in our series. An occasional patient may sometimes have a normal concentration of uric acid in the blood, but uric acid in urine is always increased. The most convenient method of assessment is to determine the uric acid: creatinine ratio (Kaufman *et al.* 1968).

Orange sand in the diaper is usually the first clinical sign of the disease, and virtually all our patients had such a history. On the other hand, no patient has yet been diagnosed on the basis of this striking presentation. The greatest value of early diagnosis may be the measures of genetic control, through heterozygote detection, counseling and prenatal diagnosis, that can be set in motion for the entire family at risk. It is also important, of course, to prevent nephropathy, nephrolithiasis, infection and obstructive uropathy. These may be of even greater importance in patients with other HGPRT defects, in whom intelligence and behavior may be normal. Urinary-tract consequences of hyperuricemia were the major complications among our patients; they are a major source of morbidity and can be largely prevented, especially before stones occur, by treatment with allopurinol and a generous intake of fluid.

Allopurinol is an effective inhibitor of xanthine oxidase, so is highly effective in controlling the accumulation of uric acid in body fluids. This was evident from the data obtained in the present series. At the same time, it must be said that a number of different physicians were managing these patients, and we ourselves prescribed only some of the doses. In general it is our experience that, even when very young, these patients require considerably greater doses than do adults with gout. We usually start treatment with a dose of 15 to 20mg/kg and assess the concentration of uric acid in blood until we have ascertained that it is 3mg/dl or less. We then determine the levels of the three oxypurines — uric acid, xanthine and hypoxanthine — in the urine in order to obtain an optimal balance that will avoid the formation of stones composed of uric acid and xanthine.

Effective management of hyperuricemia with allopurinal does not alter the neurological or behavioral effects of the disease. A number of infants have now been diagnosed at birth and managed continuously with allopurinol, and it is clear that this treatment does not prevent the full manifestation of the neurological and behavioral syndromes.

A variety of other pharmacological approaches also have been unsuccessful in treating the abnormal behavior. Among the most promising were attempts to alter the balance of biogenic amines in the central nervous system by increasing the content of serotonin, using 5-hydroxytryptophan and the peripheral decarboxylase-inhibitor carbidopa (Nyhan *et al.* 1980). However, while these agents, usually in conjunction with imipramine, dramatically altered the self-mutilating behavior, the patients rapidly became tolerant and the effect disappeared completely. Tolerance could still be demonstrated a year later. While these observations may well be relevant to the mechanism generating the behavior, they are not useful for management.

Management of the behavior depends on physical restraint. Usually it is useful to remove some or even all primary teeth to prevent severe self-mutilation, but it is not usually necessary to remove all permanent teeth. Lip-biting tends to lessen with age, which leads us to believe that these patients do develop some control over their behavior. The development of language helps too, as the child can then call for assistance if the restraints come undone. Also, as mentioned earlier, some patients learn to inhibit biting their hands by sitting on them or putting them under seat-belts. While it seems probable that a measure of control does develop with time, this has never been studied systematically and in our experience the self-mutilation never stops completely.

A variety of types of restraint have been developed (Nyhan 1976) which permit the use of the hands or arms, and alternative methods should be used for each individual patient. Restraint is essential during sleep. All hard surfaces with which the child may come into contact should be padded.

These patients enjoy being in the upright position, and a narrow wheelchair in which the patient is tied securely about the waist and chest permits maximum benefit from his environment and attendance at school. Educational management must be considered on an individual basis, but there is an enormous range of possibilities because of the wide variation in intelligence. Very few of our patients have been sufficiently intelligent to enter normal classes at school, and their performance has had to be judged by oral examinations because their movement disorder does not permit writing. However, some special-school experience should be possible for all these patients. Imaginative use of operant conditioning can successfully modify socially objectionable behavior such as spitting at or vomiting on other people.

References

Allison, A. C., Watts, R. W. E., Hovi, T., Webster, A. D. B. Immunological observations on patients with

Lesch-Nyhan syndrome, and on the role of de novo purine synthesis in lymphocyte transformation. *Lancet*, 1975; **2**, 1179-1183.

Ampola, M. *Personal commuication.* 1979.

Anderson, L. T., Dancis, J., Herrman, L., Alpert, M. Punishment learning and self-mutilation in Lesch-Nyhan disease. *Nature*, 1977; **265**, 461-463.

Bakay, B., Telfer, M. A., Nyhan, W. L. Assay of hypoxanthineguanine and adenine phosphoribosyl transferases. A simple screening test of the Lesch-Nyhan syndrome and related disorders of purine metabolism. *Biochem. Med.*, 1969; **3**, 230-243.

— Nissinen, E., Sweetman, L., Francke, U., Nyhan, W. L. Utilization of purines by an HPRT variant in an intelligent, nonmutilative patient with features of the Lesch-Nyhan syndrome. *Pediat. Res.*, 1979; **13**, 1365-1370.

Beyer, P., Bieth, R., Lutz, D., Boilletot, A., Chemouny, J. Detection of heterozygous forms of Lesch-Nyhan syndrome. Enzyme estimation in the hair follicles. *Annales de Pédiatrie.*, 1975; **22**, 285-288.

Bryson, Y., Sakati, N., Nyhan, W. L., Fish, D. H. Self-mutilative behavior in the Cornelia de Lange syndrome. *Am. J. Ment. Defic.*, 1971; **76**, 319-324.

Bull, M., LaVecchio, F. Behavior therapy for a child with Lesch-Nyhan syndrome. *Dev. Med. & Child Neurol.*, 1978; **20**, 368-375.

Catel, W., Schmidt. J. Uber familiare gichtische Diathese in Verdundung mit zerebralen und renalen Symptomen bei einem Kleinkind. *Deutsche Medizinische Wochenschrift.*, 1959; **84**, 2145-2147.

Crawhall, J. C., Henderson, J. F., Kelley, W. N. Diagnosis and treatment of the Lesch-Nyhan syndrome. *Pediat. Res.*, 1972; **6**, 504-513.

Jeune, M., Hermier, M., Rosenberg, D. Encephalopathie familiale avec hyperuricemie. A propos d'une observation. *Pédiatrie.*, 1966; **21**, 663-675.

Kaiser, W. P., Stremberger, H., Müller, M. M. Der Nachweis von Enzymprotein der Hypoxanthin-guanin-phosphoribosyltransferase bei Lesch-Nyhan syndrome. *Klinische Wochenschrift.*, 1973; **51**, 88-89.

Kaufman, J. M., Greene, M. L., Seegmiller, J. E. Urine uric acid to creatinine ratio: Screening test for disorders of purine metabolism. *J. Pediat.*, 1968; **73**, 583-592.

Kelley, W. N., Wyngaarden, J. B. *In*: Stanbury, J. B., Wyngaarden, J. B., Fredrickson, D. S. (Eds.). *The Metabolic Basis of Inherited Disease, 4th Edn.* (pp. 1011-1036). New York: McGraw-Hill, 1978.

Kogut, M. D., Donnell, G. N., Nyhan, W. L., Sweetman, L. Disorder of purine metabolism due to partial deficiency of hypoxanthine-guanine phosphoribosyltransferase. *Am. J. Med.*, 1970; **48**, 148-161.

Labrune, B., Cartier, M., Hamet, M. M., Bonnenfant, F., Velin, J., Ribierre, M., Mallet, R. Encephalopathie familiale avec hyperuricemie. *Presse Medicale.*, 1968; **76**, 2337-2340.

Lesch, M., Nyhan, W. L. A familial disorder of uric acid metabolism and central nervous system function. *Am. J. Med.*, 1964; **36**, 561-570.

Manzke, H. Hyperuricamie mit cerebralparese Syndrom eines hereditaren Purenstoffwechselleidens. *Helvetica Paediat. Acta.*, 1967; **22**, 258-270.

— Harms, D., Dormer, K. Zur Problematik der Behandlung der Kongenitalen Hyperuikämie. *Monatsschrift für Kinderheilkunde.*, 1971; **119**, 424-428.

McDonald, J. A., Kelley, W. N. Lesch-Nyhan syndrome: altered kinetic properties of mutant enzymes. *Science.*, 1971; **171**, 689-691.

Marks, J. F., Baum, J., Keele, D. K., Kay, J. L., MacFarlen, A. Lesch-Nyhan syndrome treated from the early neonatal period. *Pediatrics.*, 1968; **42**, 357-359.

Michel, M. *L'encephalopathie Familiale avec Hyperuricemie.* Lyon: Thèse de Doctorate. Imprimerie F. Clouzet, 1966.

Mizuno, T., Segawa, M., Kurumada, T., Maruyama, H., Onisawa J. Clinical and therapeutic aspects of the Lesch-Nyhan syndrome in Japanese children. *Neuropädiatrie*, 1970; **2**, 38-52.

Müller, M. M., Stermberger, H. Biochemische und immunologische Untersuchungen der Hypoxanthin-Guanin-Phosphoribosyltransferase in den Erythrozyten von Lesch-Nyhan patienten. *Weiner Klinische Wochenschrift.*, 1974; **86**, 127-131.

Nyhan, W. L. Clinical features of the Lesch-Nyhan syndrome: introduction, clinical and genetic features. *Federation Proceedings.*, 1968; **27**, 1027-1033.

— The Lesch-Nyhan syndrome. *Ann. Rev. Med.*, 1973; **24**, 41-60.

— Behavior in the Lesch-Nyhan syndrome. *J. Autism & Child. Schiz.*, 1976; **6**, 235-252.

— Genetic heterogeneity at the locus for hypoxanthineguanin-phosphoribosyltransferase. *In: Purine and Pyrimidine Metabolism, Ciba Foundation Symposium 48.* (pp. 65-81). Amsterdam: Elsevier/Medica/North Holland, 1977.

— *In*: Edelmann, Jr., C. M. (Ed.)., *Pediatric Kidney Disease.* (Vol. II, pp. 894-906). Boston, Mass.: Little, Brown, 1978.

— In: Kelley, V. C. (Ed.). *Practice of Pediatrics* (Chapter 70.). Hagerstown, Md.: Harper & Row, 1979.

— Inborn errors of purine metabolism. *In: Proceedings of the International Symposium on Inborn Errors of Metabolism, Interlaken, September 2-5, 1980. (In press,* 1980).

— Bakay, B. (1974) Mutiple molecular forms of the purine phosphoribosyl transferases. *In*: Markert, C. L. (Ed.) *Isozymes II. Physiological Function. (Proceedings of the Third International Conference of Isozymes, Yale Univ., 1974* (pp. 385-394). New York: Academic Press. 1974.

— — Connor, J. D., Marks, J. F., Keele, D. L. Hemizygous expression of glucose-6-phosphate dehydrogenase in erythrocytes of heterozygotes for the Lesch-Nyhan syndrome. *Proceed Nat. Acad. Sci.*, 1970; **65**, 214-218.

— Johnson, H. G., Kaufman, I. A., Jones, K. L. Serotonergic approaches to the modification of behavior in the Lesch-Nyhan syndrome. *Appl. Res. Ment. Retard.*, 1980; **1**, 25-40.

— Oliver, W. J., Lesch, M. A familial disorder of uric acid metabolism and central nervous system function II. *J. Pediat.*, 1965; **67**, 257-263.

— Pesek, J., Sweetman, L., Carpenter, D. G., Carter, C. H. Genetics of an X-linked disorder of uric acid metabolism and cerebral function. *Pediat. Res.*, 1967; **1**, 5-13.

Page, T., Bakay, B., Nissinen, E., Nyhan, W. L. Hypoxanthine guanine phosphoribosyl transferase variants: correlation of clinical phenotype with enzyme activity. *J. Inherit. Metabol. Disord.*, 1981; **4**, 203-206.

Rivard, G. E. Izadi, P., Lazerson, J., McLaren, J. D., Parker, C., Fish, C. H. Functional and metabolic studies of platelets from patients with Lesch-Nyhan syndrome. *Bri. J. Haematol.*, 1975; **31**, 245-253.

Rosenberg, D., Monnet, P., Mamelle, J. L., Columbel, M., Salle, B., Bovier-Lapierre, M. Encephalopathie avec troubles du metabolisme des purines. *Presse Medicale.*, 1968;; **76**, 2333-2336.

Sass, J. K., Itabashi, H. H., Dexter, R. A. Juvenile gout with brain involvement. *Arch. Neurol.*, 1965; **13**, 639-655.

Scherzer, A. L., Ilson, J. B. Normal intelligence in the Lesch-Nyhan syndrome. *Pediatrics.*, 1969; **44**, 116-120.

Seegmiller, J. E. Lesch-Nyhan syndrome — management and treatment. *Federation Proceed.*, 1968; **27**, 1097-1104.

— Inherited deficiency of hypoxanthine-guanine phosphoribosyltransferase in X-linked uric aciduria (the Lesch-Nyhan syndrome and its variants). *Adv. in Human Genet.*, 1976; **6**, 75-163.

— Rosenbloom, F. M., Kelley, W. N. Enzyme defect associated with a sex-linked human neurological disorder and excessive purine syntheses. *Science.*, 1967; **155**, 1682-1684.

Shear, C. S., Nyhan, W. L., Kirman, B. H., Stern, J. Self-mutilative behavior as a feature of the de Lange syndrome. *J. Pediat..*, 1971; **78**, 506-509.

Skyler, J. S., Neelon, F. A., Arnold, W. J., Kelley, W. N., Lebovitz, H. E. Growth retardation in the Lesch-Nyhan syndrome. *Acta Endocrinologica*, 1974; **75**, 3-10.

Sweetman, L., Hoch, M. A., Bakay, B., Borden, M., Lesh, P., Nyhan, W. L. A distinct human variant of hypoxanthine-guanine phosphoribosyl transferase. *J. Pediat.*, 1978; **92**, 385-389.

— Nyhan. W. L. Further studies of the enzyme composition of mutant cells in X-linked uric aciduria. *Arch. Internat. Med.*, 1972; **130**, 214-220.

VanDerZee, S. P. M., Monnens, L. A. H., Schretlen, E. D. A. M. Hereditary disorder of purine metabolism with cerebral affection and megaloblastic anemia. *Nederlandse Tijdschritte voor Geneeskunde*, 1968; **112**, 1475-1481.

Wood, M. H., Fox, R. M., Vincent, L., Reye, C., O'Sullivan, W. J. The Lesch-Nyhan syndrome. Report of three cases. *Australian & New Zealand J. Med.*, 1972; **2**, 57-64.

Reprinted from *Develop. Med. & Child Neurol.*, 1982; **24**, 293-306 by kind permission of the authors and the publishers Spastics International Medical Publications, London NW3 5RN.

SELF-MUTILATIVE BEHAVIOR IN THE CORNELIA DE LANGE SYNDROME[1]

Yvonne Bryson, Nadia Sakati, William L. Nyhan, Charles H. Fish

Department of Pediatrics, University of California, San Diego, La Jolla, California and Fairview State Hospital, Costa Mesa, California

4 patients were observed with the Cornelia de Lange syndrome (Type II) in whom compulsive self-mutilation was a major feature. Each patient had a stereotyped pattern of abusive behavior in which there was repeated trauma to the same area. A total of 6 such patients have now been studied. Self-mutilation may represent a distinctive feature of this disorder and suggests a relationship between organic disease and the expression of human behavior.

The Cornelia de Lange syndrome (de Lange, 1933) is a readily recognizable clinical entity in which there are a number of characteristic features including low birth weight, retardation of growth and mental development, hirsutism, and a distinctive facies (de Lange, 1933; Jervis & Stimson, 1963; Ptacek, Opitz, Smith, Gerritsen, & Waisman, 1963). Synophrys is prominent as are long eyelashes, small nose, thin turned down lips, micrognathia, and general diminutiveness of the face and head. Micromelia of the hands and feet may be accompanied by absence or deformity of bones of the upper limbs. Clinodactyly, proximally placed thumbs, and abnormal dermatoglyphics occur regularly.

Two patients with the Cornelia de Lange syndrome have recently been studied in whom unusual self-mutilative behavior was a major manifestation (Shear, Nyhan, Kirman, & Stern, 1971). We therefore undertook a survey of all of the patients with the de Lange syndrome in the Fairview State Hospital. Four were found in whom some type of self-abusive behavior was prominent. These observations strengthen the association and indicate that self-mutilative behavior may be one of the characteristics of the de Lange syndrome.

Case 1

M. C. was an 18-year-old white female who was hospitalized at Fairview State Hospital because of problems of behavior associated with mental retardation.

She was the product of an 8-month gestation. Her birth weight of 1.2 kg was low for her gestational age. Her length was 35 cm. The child had always been small. She sat at 13 months and walked at 26 months. She was described as having an odd screeching cry and no speech. Her IQ was 20.

On physical examination, her height was 1.34 m (height age 9 years), and her weight was 38.3 kg. She was generally hirsute. She had high arched eyebrows, very faintly joined in the middle, and a low hairline. Her lips were thin and turned down. Micromelia was prominent with small hands and feet and small tapering fingers, proximally placed thumbs, and clinodactyly of the 5th fingers. Dermatoglyphic analysis revealed simian creases and marked hypoplasia of the dermal ridges. There was a distal axial triradius. The atd angle was 60° (This angle is formed by lines from the distal triradii, a.—under the index finger and, b.—under the fifth finger through the axial triradius. Normally it is 45°). The fingertip pattern was that of an ulnar loop in all but the index fingers, where there was an arch. There was a zygodactylous configeration in which the b and c triradii were absent.

She was institutionalized mainly because of her behavior problem which took the form of increasingly severe self-mutilative activity. This behavior began with a habit of picking at her eyes. This led to bleeding, excoriation, and repeated infections of the lids of both eyes. She then began to hit her face repeatedly with her knuckles, causing lacerations of her eyelids and an open wound under her chin which required sutures several times. This lesion also became secondarily infected and, with continued self-inflicted abuse, scarring and loss

[1]Aided by a grant from the National Foundation.

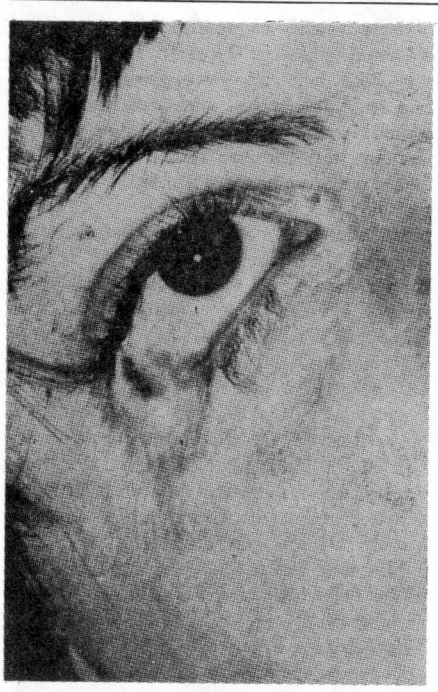

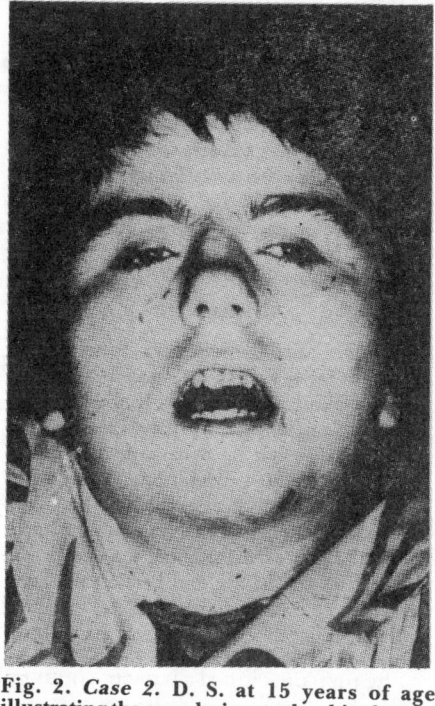

Fig. 1. *Case 1.* M. C. at 15 years illustrating the ectropion that resulted from picking at her lids.

Fig. 2. *Case 2.* D. S. at 15 years of age illustrating the open lesion on the chin that the patient produced by repeatedly hitting herself with her closed fist. Facial characteristics of the de Lange syndrome are also illustrated.

of tissue resulted. Many different approaches were tried to curb this self-mutilative behavior, including arm casts, a protective collar, and soft tie restraints. Numerous medications and electro-shock treatments were employed with no improvement. Her behavior progressed to biting her arms, resulting in infection and scarring. Severe biting of her tongue resulted in gross deformity and hypertrophy and scarring. She continued to pick at her eyes and developed an ectropian of each lower lid (Fig. 1) with exposure of conjunctiva. This was treated by skin grafting, but the graft was soon destroyed by her picking.

Case 2.

D. S. was a 15-year-old white female with the Cornelia de Lange syndrome who was referred to the Fairview State Hospital because of self-abusive behavior.

She was the 2.33 kg product of a 9-month pregnancy. She developed slowly, sitting alone at 1½ years and walking at 3 years. She had no speech development. Her IQ was estimated at 12.

Physical examination revealed a small girl, 1.27 m tall (height age 8½ years). Bushy eyebrows met in the midline. She had long eyelashes, a low hairline, microcephaly, thin turned down lips, and a high arched palate. She had very small hands, clinodactyly, and small feet, and her 2nd and 3rd toes were fused. She also had scoliosis of the spine and redundant skin over the nape of the neck. Dermatoglyphics revealed radial loops on the index and middle fingers and ulnar loops on the thumbs, ring, and fifth fingers. There was a distal axial triradius. The atd angle was 105°. There were simian lines.

She was noted from the age of 6 years to be severely self-destructive. She scratched her hands and bit her fingers and knees, causing the formation of ulcers. The back of her hands became excoriated and scarred from continual beating of her face and chin. Her parents became very concerned with her behavior, and this eventually led to her admission. Her behavior over the years had come to consist mainly of compulsive hitting of her face hard enough with her fists to cause a loud cracking sound and open bleeding wounds. Her hands have been restrained in an attempt to stop this behavior, but she has since managed to strike herself with her knees. She has been treated with numerous medications without success. Her open lesion has been present and intermittently secondarily infected for at least 3 years (Fig. 2).

Case 3.

B. M. was a 16½-year-old white female with mental retardation and self-abusive behavior.

She was the 2.30 kg product of a 42-week pregnancy and a normal delivery. She developed slowly, holding her head up at 8 months, sitting alone at one year and walking at two years. She had an estimated IQ of 20. She never developed speech but had a screeching cry. She had frequent episodes of pneumonitis and seizures starting at 3½ years of age which were controlled with dilantin and phenobarbital.

Physical examination revealed a small girl, 1.28 m tall, appearing much younger than her stated age. She had a high arched palate, an upturned nose, high arched eyebrows, and thin lips which were turned down at the edges. Her hair line was low, and she was hirsute. She had small hands with tapered fingers and clinodactyly. Her feet were very small, and the 3rd toe was aplastic bilaterally. Dermatoglyphics revealed hypoplasia of the dermal ridges. Hypoplasia of the ridges of the hypothenar eminence was striking. There was a simian line. The finger tip pattern was that of an ulnar loop on each finger. The atd angle was 58°.

This child was noted to have a tendency towards self-abusive behavior which was first evidenced by hitting her face and trunk with her fists. This caused numerous contusions and bruises on many different occasions.

She then developed a habit of continually rubbing her cheeks with the back of her hands.

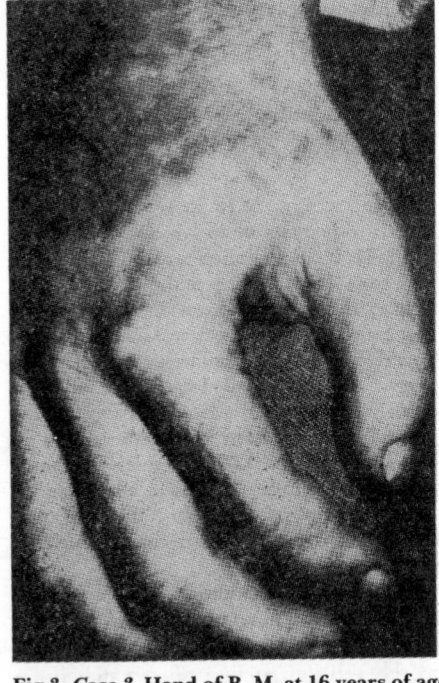

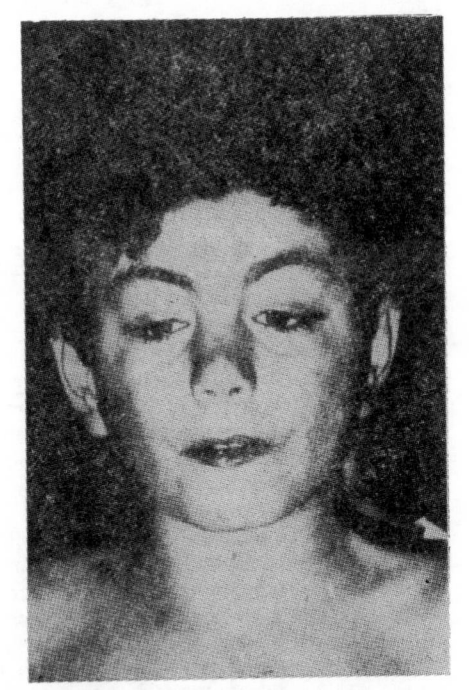

Fig 3. *Case 3.* Hand of B. M. at 16 years of age showing chronic dermatitis that resulted from rubbing.

Fig. 4. *Case 4.* K. S. at 16 years of age illustrating the facial characteristics of the de Lange syndrome. There were no open lesions at the time this photograph was taken.

She would lick her hands and then rub her cheeks for hours at a time. This caused reddening, excoriation, abrasion, bleeding, and secondary infection. She maintained this habit for years. The resultant chronic saliva dermatitis was treated with a variety of local medications, but all treatments failed to clear the dermatitis because her rubbing was persistent. This behavior also caused excoriation, reddening, thickening, and chronic skin changes on the backs of her hands (Fig. 3).

Case 4.

K. S. was a 16½-year-old male with mental retardation and self-abusive behavior.

He was the 2.36 kg product of a normal pregnancy and delivery. The child developed slowly, sitting at 8 months and walking at 21 months. He was found to have a heart murmur and was diagnosed as having a postductal coarctation of the aorta, which was corrected by surgery at 5 years of age. His IQ was 30.

On examination, he was a small boy (height 1.22 m, weight 26.10 kg). He had characteristic features of the de Lange syndrome (Fig. 4), including microcephaly, high arched eyebrows fused in the midline, high arched palate, thin turned down lips, and a very low hairline. He was very hirsute with hair covering his back, lumbosacral region, and legs. He had small feet and hands with tapering fingers and a small 5th finger. Dermatoglyphics revealed hypoplastic ridges and a low ridge count (84), a simian line, and a distal axial triradius. The atd angle was 75°. The fingertip patterns were those of ulnar loops except for the index finger which was an arch.

He was first intitutionalized in a home for the retarded at an early age and was found to be very aggressive. He was then transferred to Fairview State Hospital where his behavior was noted to take the form of tantrums in which he would arch his back and hit his hands and feet continually against the floor, causing bruises and scratches. He then began to pick and scratch his feet, causing ragged, gouged areas which became secondarily infected. He was treated on numerous occasions for self-inflicted injuries to his hands and for bites and scratches on his shoulders. Because of this behavior, he was treated with tranquilizers, which did not really alter his self-abusive activity. Soft restraints were also found to be unsatisfactory.

Discussion

Self-mutilative behavior in these patients occurred in a variety of forms. These included picking at the eyelids leading to ectropion, hitting the face with the knuckles of a closed fist causing an open wound, biting of the tongue producing deformity, biting of the arms, fingers, and knees, scratching the hands, picking and gouging the skin of the hands, feet, and other areas, rubbing the cheeks with the back of the hands, and beating the hands and feet against a hard surface. It seems probable that this list does not exhaust the forms of expression of self-directed aggressive activity in this syndrome. In the two patients we studied previously, a major manifestation was destructive biting of the lips (Shear, et al., 1971). This resulted in loss of tissue and an appearance about the mouth identical to that seen in the Lesch-Nyhan syndrome (Lesch & Nyhan, 1964). In each of the patients we have now observed, the self-mutilative behavior was stereotyped. Each repeated the same self-mutilative act over and over again, often reopening a single wound year in and year out. More than one pattern was seen in some of the patients, but each was a particular expression for that patient and was performed repeatedly. Neither the de Lange syndrome nor self-mutilation is common. These observations of self-mutilative activity in six patients with the syndrome indicate that the association between the two is too strong to be fortuitous.

Systematic quantitative data on the incidence of self-mutilation would be of interest in supporting the conclusion that there is an increased association between the de Lange syndrome and self-mutilation. There were seven patients with the de Lange syndrome at the Fairview State Hospital at the time this study was carried out. The observation of self-mutilation in four of them appears to us to constitute a high proportion. The total population of patients at this hospital approximates 2,000. Self-mutilation of some sort may be expected to occur in about 10 percent of these severely retarded patients.

No specific syndromes appear to be usually associated with self-mutilation other than those of de Lange and of Lesch-Nyhan. In the institutional population at large, most of the self-mutilation takes the form of head banging or of hitting some part of the body. These behaviors usually lead to hypertrophy of the injured tissue, with cauliflower ears and the like, rather than to loss of tissue. Loss of tissue rather than hypertrophy is the rule in the Lesch-Nyhan syndrome. It was therefore of considerable interest to encounter self-mutilation with loss of tissue in the de Lange syndrome. In the Lesch-Nyhan syndrome, self-mutilation may take a variety of forms, but it always includes severely destructive biting. Loss of tissue following biting of the lip is the rule. This may be seen in the de Lange syndrome, and the lips of our two previously described patients were identical to those seen in the Lesch-Nyhan syndrome. However, these four patients did not bite their lips. The actual process of mutilation also differs. In the de Lange syndrome it appears almost casual. In the Lesch-Nyhan syndrome it has a disturbing ferocity. These two apparent levels of severity may also be reflected in the relative ease of control, for in the de Lange syndrome a very aggressive program of operant conditioning may be effective.

A careful study of patients with the de Lange syndrome who mutilate has failed to reveal phenotypic differences from those with the syndrome who do not mutilate. The dermatoglyphic characteristics of these patients were typical of the de Lange syndrome. Of course the incidence of self-mutilation in our sample of patients is very high. We have recently observed that a younger patient, whom we have been following for 2 years, has begun to slap himself. He does not damage anything in this way, but this suggests that with careful observation aggressive behavior directed against self may be seen in other patients in whom mutilation has not been observed.

The time of onset of this unusual type of behavior is not assessable in most of these patients. In one it began at the age of 6 years; in the two previously studied it began at 3 and 4 years. It has not been observed in infancy. Self-mutilation is seen with some frequency in retarded children. It is generally considered that this represents an attention-getting mechanism in a large institution for the retarded in which rather natural human impulses lead the staff to reinforce the behavior. On the other hand, in these patients the history was regularly obtained that it was not the mental retardation or the other features of the syndrome that led to admission to the state institution but rather the behavior. Our previous patients had not been institutionalized. They lived at home in environments that appeared warm, understanding, and stimulative. It is, of course, always possible for an odd-looking retarded child to be treated in such a way that bizzare behavior results that is understandable on situational or psychologic grounds. This appears to us unlikely in this instance. Another hypothesis is that patients with a variety of structural abnormalities that are readily seen and with clear involvement of the central nervous system could well have anatomic or developmental abnormalities in areas of the nervous system that control this type of behavior. Elucidation of this type of abnormality could lead to a better understanding of behavior.

Self-mutilative behavior is only one manifestation of even stereotyped behavior. However, it may be a good point of departure, for it is seen in a number of conditions in which it might be considered a behavioural manifestation of organic disease. Among these conditions is the Lesch-Nyhan syndrome (Lesch & Nyhan, 1964), already discussed, in which aggressive, mutilative behavior is associated with mental retardation, athetoid cerebral palsy, hyperuricemia, and complete deficiency of the enxyme hypoxanthine guanine phosphoribosyl transferase (HGPRT). Two of these patients (B. M. and M. C.) have been studied from the point of view of purine metabolism. Their concentrations of uric acid in the plasma were 3.3 and 3.8 mg/100 ml respectively. The activities of HGPRT in their erythrocytes were 1211 and 1080 mμM/ml packed cells, respectively. These values are all within normal limits. Similarly, the two patients with the de Lange syndrome previously reported (Shear, *et al.*, 1971) were thoroughly investigated in this way and found to be normal. In addition, a detailed study of the excretion of purines and related compounds in the urine failed to reveal any abnormalities.

Self-mutilation is also found in familial dysautonomia. This has suggested the possibility of sensory abnormalities in these patients, although there is certainly no evidence of sensory abnormality in the Lesch-Nyhan or de Lange syndromes. Patients with established sensory neuropathies do sometimes mutilate (Landwirth, 1964). In general this appears to be accidental, not complusive, and not stereotyped. The patient may present with an unrecognized fracture of a major bone or burns of the finger and may look like a pugilist. Self-mutilation as a concomitant of rage has been observed in a boy with the XYY syndrome (Parker, *et al.*, 1970).

Control of these symptoms may be difficult. No medications have been useful. Restraints can be effective, but become less so as the patient gets older and stronger. An effective combination of restraint and attention requires a relatively small ratio of patients to staff. Operant approaches to behavioral modification using aversive stimulation in a highly structured environment has been successful in extinguishing this behavior in the de Lange syndrome (Shear, *et al.*, 1971). Recognition of the association of behavioral abnormalities in the de Lange syndrome and early vigorous intervention could be important in management. Self-mutilative behavior is a very difficult problem for parents and for the staff of an institution, as well as, of course, for the patient.

References

de Lange, C. Sur un type nouveau de degeneration (Typus Amstelodamensis). *Archives medicin des Enfanto*, 1933, **36**, 713.

Jervis, G. A., Stimson, D. W. de Lange syndrome. *Journal of Pediatrics*, 1963, **63**, 634.

Landwirth, J. Sensory radicular neuropathy and retinitis pigmentosa. *Pediatrics*, 1964, **34**, 519.

Lesch, M., Nyhan, W. L. A familial disorder of uric acid metabolism and central nervous system function. *American Journal of Medicine*, 1964, **36**, 561.

Parker, C. E., Mavalwala, J., Weise, P., Kock, R., Hatashita, A., & Cibilich, S. The 47 XYY syndrome in a boy with behavior problems and mental retardation. *American Journal of Mental Deficiency*, 1970, **74**, 660-665.

Ptacek, L. J., Opitz, J. M., Smith, D. W., Gerritsen, T., Waisman, H. A. The Cornelia de Lange syndrome. *Journal of Pediatrics*, 1963, **63**, 1000.

Shear, C. S., Nyhan, W. L., Kirman, B. H., Stern, J. Self-mutilative behavior as a feature of the de Lange syndrome. *Journal of Pediatrics*, 1971, **78**, 506.

Reprinted from *Am. J. Ment. Defic.*, 1971; **76**:3, 319-324 by kind permission of the authors and the publishers American Association on Mental Deficiency, Washington DC 20009.

CAUSES OF SEVERE SELF-INJURIOUS BEHAVIOR

J. A. Corbett, H. J. Campbell

The Bethlem Royal Hospital and the Maudsley Hospital and Institute of Psychiatry, Denmark Hill, London SE5 8AZ, England

Epidemiology

Stereotyped or repetitive, apparently purposeless motor activity is seen in about 40% of children under the age of 16 with severe mental retardation (Corbett, 1977) and in 18% of adults in contact with services for the mentally retarded (Corbett, 1979), suggesting that developmental factors play a part in its genesis. Stereotyped *self-injurious* behavior (SSIB) of relatively benign kind is less frequent but more persistent, occurring in 13% of children and adults. A recent regional survey (Corbett, in preparation) showed that *severe* SSIB (meriting specific medical or psychological intervention) is quite rare, of the order of 1 in 10,000 of the total mentally handicapped population.

Although severe SSIB, involving head to object and limb to head banging, eye punching and gouging, and/or biting of the extremities, may have its origins in the milder form of stereotyped behavior seen in normal infants (Shentoub and Soulairac, 1961; DeLissovoy, 1962) and may be perpetuated at some stage in its development by environmental deprivation, it is usually a cause rather than a result of long-term hospital care. However, it is one of the most problematic issues in the care of the mentally handicapped. As the late Professor Alistair Forrest pointed out (Corbett, 1975a), "Doctors, nurses, psychologists and other staff have certain role expectations, which are quite disrupted by a patient (allegedly under their care) who injures himself. This anxiety makes staff demand more intervention, whether by drugs, restraint or aversion therapy, and the increased (social) reinforcement (this entails) exacerbates the self-injury. This draws attention away from patients with less dramatic problems and leads to greater difficulty in staffing residential institutions." A similar situation occurs in schools and in families with a self-injuring member (Corbett, 1975a).

Clinical aspects

Most discussions terminate with the question, "But what is the cause?" indicating that our existing treatments are mainly empirical and inadequate. In order to obtain even a modicum of understanding, it is necessary to explain a number of clinical observations:

1. Severe SSIB can occur at high rates over long periods, resulting in irreversible mutilation, blindness, or brain injury. This suggests that the normal mechanisms for perceiving and responding to painful stimuli are disordered in people suffering from this condition.
2. This suggestion is reinforced by the observation that, although the subject seems generally oblivious to pain caused by the SSIB, he may seek out restraint or even the means of aversion. In the majority of cases, the sufferer seems to respond to other peripheral stimulation, e.g., pinprick, and these observations suggest that the disorder is a central rather than a peripheral one.
3. There is some element of "learning" in the behavior, because it may be increased by social reinforcement (Lovaas et al., 1965) and other operant techniques (Schaefer, 1970) and is reduced by procedures such as extinction, differential reinforcement of incompatible behaviors, and aversion (Corbett, 1975a). Moreover, the procedure of social learning is clearly more subtle than previously thought (Baumeister and Rollings, 1976; Romanczyk, 1979).
4. The effects of social reinforcement may be quite rapid, whereas aversion, using contingent, peripherally applied shock, may be considerably slower (Murphy and Wilson, this volume). Although this may reflect problems of technique or

This research was supported by donations from IBM (UK) and the Board of Governors of The Bethlem Royal Hospital and The Maudsley Hospital.

generalization or even spontaneous remission (Williams, 1979), it is also possible that it is due to differences in the neurophysiological or biochemical basis of the learning process that is involved.

5.   That biochemical factors are involved is supported by the finding that, although drug treatment is generally ineffective, certain pharmacological agents that are known to influence cerebral neurotransmitters may increase or decrease the behavior. Clinical example include:

   a.   The increase in some forms of stereotyped behavior with amphetamines, pemoline, and caffeine (Peters, 1967; Genovese et al., 1969), and their response to dopamine-blocking agents such as haloperidol or pimozide (Corbett, 1975b).

   b.   The finding that baclofen (Lioresal) (an analog of GABA) can alleviate severe SSIB (Primrose, this volume).

   c.   The alleviation of severe SSIB in the Lesch-Nyhan syndrome by means of 5-hydroxytryptophan combined with carbidopa (Nyhan, 1978).

The neurophysiological basis of self-injury

Until 1954 the best that could be said was that SSIB was in some way autoerotic or masochistic. Olds (1962), studying the alerting reaction in animals, placed stimulating electrodes in the limbic system and found that animals would press a switch at high rates

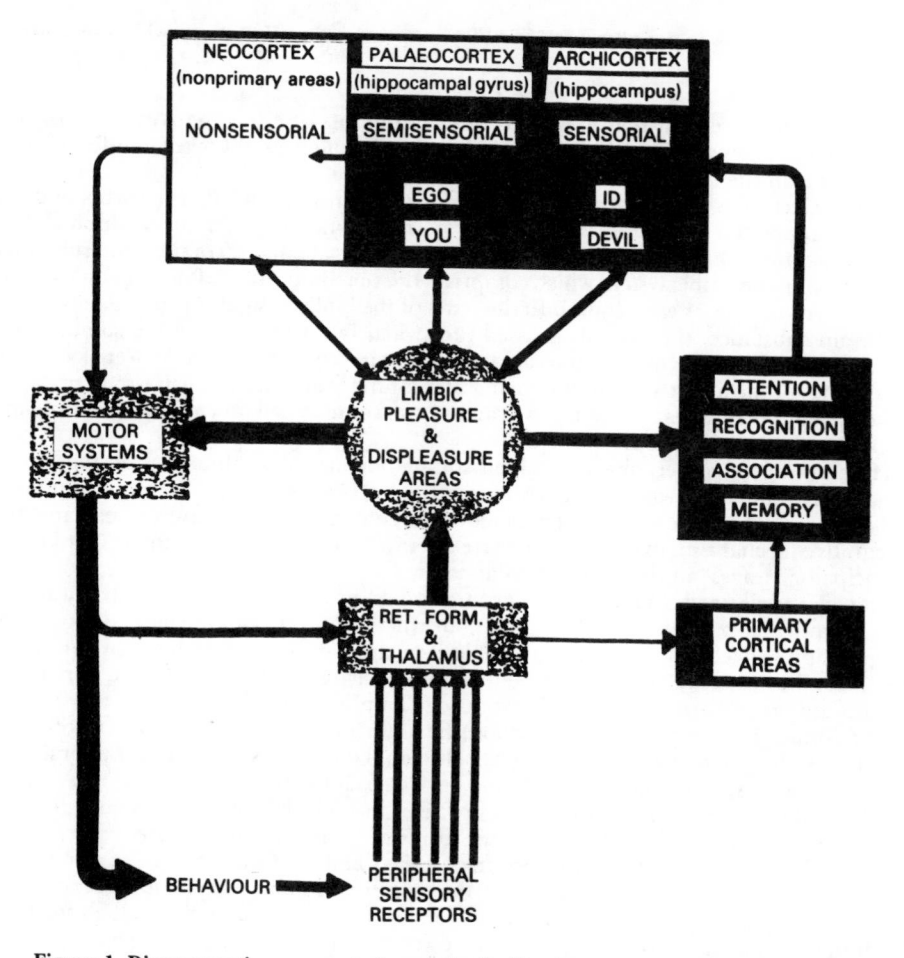

Figure 1. Diagrammatic representation of the limbic pleasure and displeasure areas.

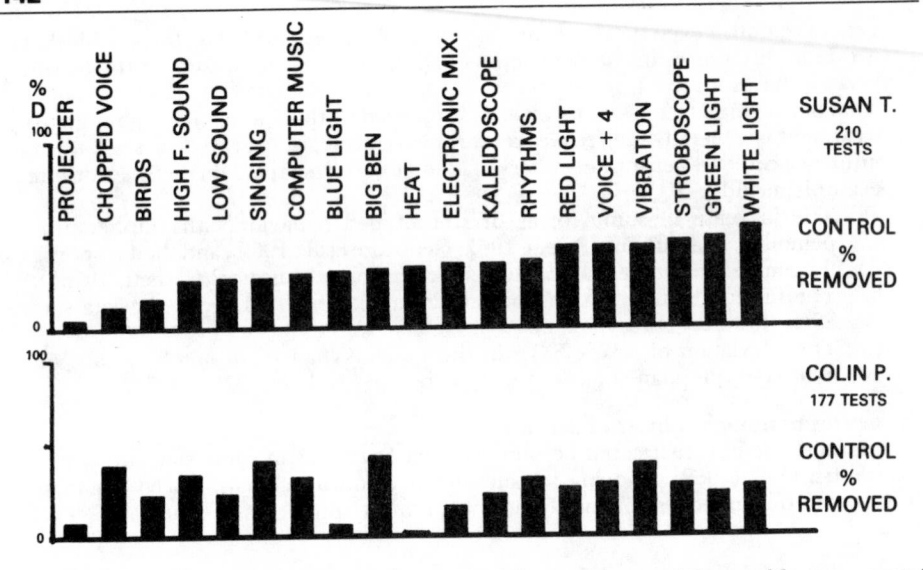

Figure 2. Differences in peripheral self-stimulation spectrum in two children with severe mental retardation.

until the point of exhaustion to obtain minute amounts of electric current. It was soon found that animals of many species and also humans would press the lever at different rates depending on the site of the electrodes.

When electrodes were placed in regions of the brain that include the cortex and the higher centers, the animal pressed the lever no more when the current was applied than when it was not. This neutral part of the brain comprises about 60% of the brain substance (Figure 1). In the limbic system which comprises the remaining 40% of the brain substance, two types of responses were found. In the parts of the limbic system occupying only 5% of the brain substance, the animals pressed the switch fewer times when the stimulus was provided and thereby avoided intracranial stimulation. When the electrodes were located in other parts of the limbic system (occupying 35% of the brain), the animals would press the switch at very high rates. These last two areas have come to be known as the pleasure and displeasure (pain) centers, respectively.

Human subjects undergoing central self-stimulation may to continue to press the switch, for a short time, even when the current is turned off. This may be due to some neural, self-feeding, cybernetic system of linkages between the limbic pleasure areas and the integrative mechanisms of the cerebral cortex, setting up something akin to the well-known "anticipatory waves" in the higher regions.

Moving the electrodes a few millimeters in animals can shift them from highly rewarding sites to undeniably unpleasurable regions, but when the electrodes are located roughly at the junction between the two types of limbic area, animals show an ambivalent attitude to the lever; they press it, run away, and return to press it again [the "stop it I like it" reaction or, the "go on you are hurting me" response (Campbell, 1973)].

The findings of Corbett (in preparation) fit in with the clinical experience of SSIB:

1.   The same phenomena as in central self-stimulation are seen with peripheral self-stimulation (PSS) in both animals and retarded children.
2.   Considerable individual differences are seen in both the rates of PSS and stimulus preferences in children with different forms of brain damage (Figure 2).
3.   PSS shows fluctuations over the course of days and weeks (Figure 3).

The studies of Heath (1976), suggesting that in humans subjective pleasure is correlated with activity in the septal region whereas adverse emotion is associated with the activity in the hippocampus, amygdala, mesencephalic tegmentum, and cingulate gyrus, provide further evidence for the areas of the limbic system involved in the appreciation of pleasure

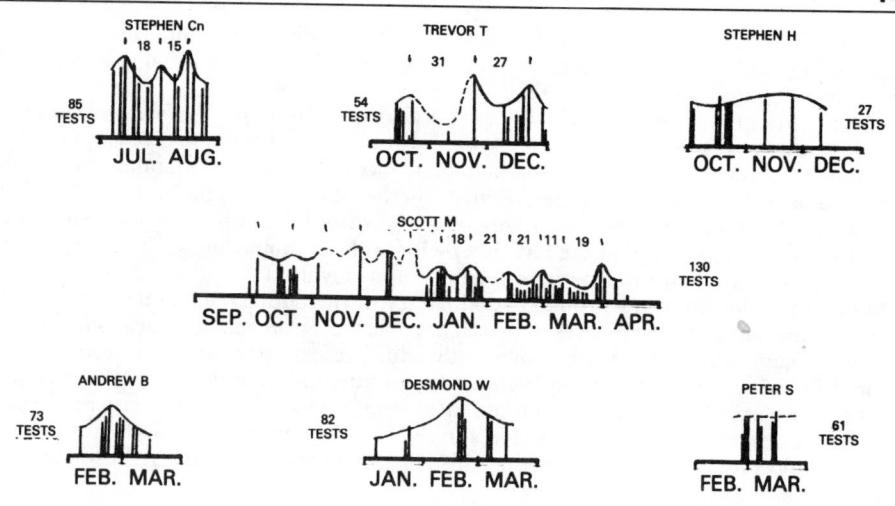

Figure 3. Cyclical variations in peripheral self-stimulation in seven children with severe mental handicap.

and pain. His demonstration of the alleviation of very severe emotional disorders using a cerebellar pacemaker suggests that abnormal responses involving the limbic system may be modulated without recourse to direct intracerebral stimulation (Heath, 1977).

Neuropharmacological aspects

Various hormones and psychotropic drugs have been shown to have marked influences on the rates of pleasure-seeking responses, although, until recently, attempts at pharmacological treatment of severe SSIB have been mainly empirical and unsuccessful. However, the recent explosion of interest in the neuropeptides and particularly the endorphins has shed light on the possible neurotransmitter agents involved in the limbic pleasure and displeasure areas, and recent reviews suggest a number of possible links between these substances and the clinical observations in SSIB and neurophysiological findings in both central and peripheral self-stimulation (Henry, 1978; Hughes, 1978; Miller et al., 1978).

Since Kosterlitz and Hughes (1975) originally suggested that the encephalins may be inhibitory neurotransmitters or neuromodulators and Hughes and coworkers described the structures of methionine and leucine-encephalin (Hughes et al., 1975), much has been discovered concerning the pharmacological and biochemical aspects of these substances and their distribution in the brain. It has been found that animals will press a lever to obtain intraventricular injections of encephalin and that electrical self-stimulation is suppressed by the opiate antagonist naloxone and by noradrenaline (Beluzzi and Stein, 1977). Further experiments with naloxone suggest that an endogenous morphine-like factor is released centrally during dental extraction (Levine et al., 1978) and this is consistent with the observation in man that analgesia produced by diencephalic stimulation (Hosobucki et al., 1977) or by acupuncture (Mayer et al., 1977) is reversed by naloxone.

Research into centrally acting peptides has been associated with renewed interest into the possible transmitter function of substance P, first identified in 1934 (Gaddum and Schild, 1934), and it has been suggested that opiates inhibit the release of substance P, at least at a spinal level (Jessell and Iverson, 1977). Great difficulty has been encountered in a search for specific antagonists for amino acids and peptides in particular, although Saito et al. (1975) suggested that baclofen exhibited a specific antagonism of substance P. It is interesting to speculate whether this could explain the effect described by Primrose (this volume) of suppression of SSIB by baclofen. Although it seems likely that the effect of baclofen is mainly on primary afferent transmission rather than on postsynaptic neurons (Pierau and

Zimmerman, 1973), it does have a nonselective postsynaptic depressant effect on central neuronal excitability, and it therefore seems unlikely that it is a specific substance P antagonist (Renaud and Padjen, 1978).

Linking the alleviation of SSIB in Lesch-Nyhan syndrome by 5-hydroxytryptophan (5-HT) is the finding by Way et al. (1968) that 5-HT is involved in the processes concerned with the development of tolerance to and dependence on morphine. A causal role has not been established, nor has it been determined whether the association is direct or indirect. However, the fact that the 5-HT precursor tryptophan enhances tolerance and dependence development and the fact that p-chlorophenylamine blocks the effect argues strongly that more than just a remote relationship is involved.

Although endorphins are probably modulatory in their function, rather than strictly analgesic, this line of research does suggest a possible link between the clinical phenomena seen in narcotic addiction and the apparently addictive behavior of self-injurers.

The field of mental retardation is littered with attempts to link specific biochemical lesions with particular behavioral consequences, and it is too early to evaluate the lasting significance of these findings from endorphin research, but the research findings reported in this symposium on SSIB suggest that this is a potentially rewarding field for further research.

References

Baumeister, A. A. Rollings, J. P. Self-injurious behavior. *In:* Ellis, N. R. (Ed.). *International Review of Research in Mental Retardation,* (Vol. 8.) New York: Academic Press, Inc., 1976.

Beluzzi, J. D., Stein, L. Encephalin may mediate euphoria and drive reduction reward. *Nature,* 1977; **266**, 556.

Campbell, H. J. *The Pleasure Areas.* London: Methuen Books, 1973.

Corbett, J. A. Aversion for the treatment of self-injurious behaviour. *J. Ment. Defic. Res.,* 1975a; **19**, 79.

Corbett, J. A. Tics and Tourette's syndrome. *In:* Rutter, M., Hersov, L. (Eds.) *Child Psychiatry, Modern Approaches.* London: Blackwell Scientific Publications, 1975b.

Corbett, J. A. Mental retardation psychiatric aspects. *In:* Rutter, M., Hersov, L. (Eds.). *Child Psychiatry, Modern Approaches.* London: Blackwell Scientific Publications, 1977.

Corbett, J. A. Psychiatric morbidity. *In:* James, F. F., Snaith, R. B. (Eds.). *Psychiatric Illness and Mental Handicap.* London: Gaskell, 1979.

Corbett, J. A. *The epidemiology of severe stereotyped self-injurious behaviours in the mentally retarded.* (In preparation.).

deLissovoy, V. Headbanging in early childhood. *Child Dev.,* 1962; **33**, 43.

Gaddum, J. H., Schild, H. Depressor substances in extracts of intestines. *J. Physiol.,* 1934; **83**, 1.

Genovese, E., Napoli, P. A., Bolego-Zonta, N. Self aggressiveness. *Life Sci.,* 1969; **8**, 513.

Heath, R.G. Correlation of brain function with emotional behaviour. *Biol Psychiat.,* 1976; **11**, 463.

Heath, R. G. Modulation of emotion with a brain pacemaker. *J. Nerv. Ment. Dis.,* 1977; **165**, 300.

Henry, A. *Developments in Opiate Research.* New York: Marcel Dekker, 1978.

Hosobucki, Y., Adams, J. E. Linchitz, R. Pain relief by electric stimulation of the central grey matter in humans and its reversal by naloxone. *Science,* 1977; **197**, 183.

Hughes, J. (Ed.). *Centrally Acting Peptides.* London: Macmillan, 1978.

Hughes, J., Smith, T. W., Kosterlitz, H. W., Fothergill, L. A., Morgan, B. A., Morris, H. R. Identification of two related pentapeptides from the brain with potent opiate agonist activity. *Nature.,* 1975; **258**, 277.

Jessell, T. M., Iverson, L. L. Opiate analgesics inhibit substance P release from rat trigeminal nucleus. *Nature,* 1977; **268**, 549.

Kosterlitz, H. W., Hughes, J. Some thoughts on the significance of encephalin. The endogenous ligand. *Life Sci.,* 1975; **17**, 91.

Levine, J. D., Gordon, N. C. Jones, R. T., Fields, H. L. The narcotic antagonist naloxone enhances clinical pain. *Nature,* 1978; **272**, 826.

Lovaas, O. T., Freitag, G., Gould, O. J., Kassorla, I. C. Experimental studies in childhood schizophrenia: analysis of self destructive behaviour. *J. Exp. Child Psychol.,* 1965; **2**, 67.

Mayer, D. J., Price, D. D., Rafii, A. Antagonism of acupuncture analgesia in man by the narcotic antagonist naloxone. *Brain Res.,* 1977; **121**, 368.

Miller, L. H., Sandman, C. A., Kastin, A. J. (Eds.). *Neuropeptide Influences on the Brain and Behaviour.* New York: Raven Press, 1978.

Nyhan, W. L. The Lesch-Nyhan syndrome. *Dev. Med. & Child Neurol.,* 1978; **20**, 376.

Olds, J. Hypothalamic substrates of reward. *Physiol. Rev.,* 1962; **42**, 554.

Peters, J. M. Caffeine induced hemorrhagic auto mutilaion. *Arch. Int. Pharm. Ther.,* 1967; **169**, 139.

Pierau, P. K., Zimmerman, P. Action of a GABA-derivative on postsynaptic potentials and membrane properties of cats' spinal motoneurons. *Brain Res.*, 1973; **54**, 376.

Renaud, L. P., Padjen, A. Electrophysiological analysis of peptide actions in neural tissues. *In*: Hughes, J. (Ed.). *Centrally Acting Peptides.* London: Macmillan, 1978.

Romanczyk, R. G. *Self-injurious behaviour: a critique of the response class hypothesis and implications for treatment.* Paper presented at the 5th Congress of the IASSMD, Jerusalem, 1979.

Saito, K., Koniski, S., Otsuka, M. Antagonism between Lioresal and substance P in rat spinal cord. *Brain Res.*, 1975; **97**, 177.

Schaefer, H. H. Self-injurious behaviour: Shaping head banging in monkeys. *J. Appl. Behav. Anal.*, 1970; **3**, 111.

Shentoub, S. A., Soulairac, A. L'enfant auto mutilateur. *Psychiat. Enf.*, 1961; **3**, 119.

Way, E. L., Loh, H. H., Shen, F.H. Morphine tolerance, physical dependence and synthesis of brain 5-hydroxytryptamine. *Science.*, 1968; **162**, 1290.

Williams, C. E. *The development of severe repetitive, self-injurious behaviour.* Paper presented at the 5th Congress of the IASSMD, Jerusalem, 1979.

Reprinted from Mittler, P., de Jong, J. M. (Eds.). *Frontiers of Knowledge in Mental Retardation Vol. II - Biomedical Aspects* (pp.285-292), 1980 by kind permission of the authors and the publishers University Park Press, Baltimore, ML 21202.

A STUDY OF HEAD-BANGING IN INFANTS AND CHILDREN

Harvey Kravitz, Vin Rosenthal, Zelda Teplitz, John B. Murphy, Raymond E. Lesser

Introduction

Head-banging is defined as a rhythmic motor habit characterized by repeated striking of the head against a solid object; it is probably the most spectacular motor rhythm seen in infants and children, yet, little detailed information is available in the pediatric, neurologic, and psychiatric literature on the phenomenon. One of the reasons for this is that it is difficult to study infants and children with this disorder. Although the parents and frequently the neighbors, are acutely aware of the child's head-banging very few physicians have actually witnessed the acts. The sight of a child rocking back and forth on all fours and pounding his skull against the headboard of a bed, 60 to 80 times a minute is certainly most alarming to the parents. Parents consult the physician because they fear the child will injure himself, or are concerned because the loud monotonous noise disturbs the household during sleeping hours. Also there is the fear that the behavior of the child indicates a serious neurological or psychiatric disorder. However, in many cases of head-banging the parents do not seek medical help.

We have studied 135 cases of head-banging which were encountered in our private practice of pediatrics, in terms of the natural history of the phenomenon. Because of the lack of detailed information on this subject, it was felt that such a study was a necessary first step before an understanding of the disorder could be obtained and a rational method of treatment developed. After presenting our findings, we will attempt to integrate them within the framework of current neurologic, psychologic and psychiatric theories of head-banging and of motor rhythms in general.

Review of the literature

Several theories have been advanced to explain the phenomenon of head-banging and associated motor rhythms. In an excellent discussion of the role of all rhythmic pattern in childhood, Lourie[1] in 1949, emphasized that these activities may be seen as a normal phenomenon satisfying instinctual need and facilitating motor and personality development. He states, "that rhythmic activities seem to serve the secondary function of the expression of pleasure, release of tension, or to give compensatory satisfaction." He reasons that the secondary values may cause the persistence of these patterns past the infantile period. Although his study was based on 120 children in a pediatric clinic, Lourie did not break down the number of head-bangers, body-rockers, or head-rollers in his series. He presented no detailed information on the head-bangers as a group except to note the importance of auditory stimuli in these cases.

Spitz[2] makes no reference to head-banging in describing a series of 87 body-rockers in an institution. He found the highest incidence of body-rockers to be between six and eight months. Only 12 cases occurred before six months. He felt that a disturbed relationship existed between the infant and the mother and that rocking was a symptom of the lack of emotional interchange between the mother and child. He felt that body-rocking is a pleasurable and narcissistic activity and a solace to the child. It is surprising to note that Spitz uncovered no head-bangers in his study.

In another study of motor rhythms Mittelman[3] felt that motor rhythms in general are the consequence of inherent rhythmic drives or motor urges. It is interesting to note that in a study of motor rhythms in animals, including monkeys and apes, Harlow[4] noted rhythmic rocking movements but specifically noted no head-banging activities in any of his animals.

Presented at the Chicago Neurologic Society, January 13, 1959.
From the Department of Pediatrics, University of Illinois, and the Department of Pediatrics, St. Francis Hospital, Evanston, Illinois.

Richmond[5] in a study of one head-banger noted the onset of body-rocking on hands and knees sometime after $4\frac{1}{2}$ months of age. Head-banging and body-rocking continued in the all fours position until ten months, when the patient began rocking in a sitting position and began head-banging occipitally. Richmond noticed an early interest in, and fondness for music and rhythms in this stage. He, also, observed that the child, after one year, head-banged as an attention getting device. He, also, noted a delay in the onset of speech. He concluded that there is no one specific etiological factor in head-banging but that a multiplicity of factors may be involved.

Anna Freud[6] mentioned head-banging occurring in six cases of children in an institution. She attributed head-banging to self-directed aggression towards the child's own body and felt it was affected by institutional life.

Teplitz and Bromberg[7] in a psychodynamic study of head-banging in 12 children and their parents, stressed the auditory and strong tactile stimulation in head-banging which they feel is a distinguishing characteristic of head-banging as opposed to body-rocking. They feel that head-banging is a purposeful reponse to internal or external sources of tension, in that it brings the tension under the control of the infant's own body and musculature. Interest in human response is given up during the period of head-banging, since the external inanimate object does not itself react, initiate emotional response, or otherwise participate in the activity. They mentioned teething as an internal source of tension which may be associated with head-banging.

Fitzherbert[8] in a study of one case, advanced the theory that head-banging represents the infant's attempt to re-experience the mother's heart beat when it is held in her arms. She presented no experimental data to support this theory, however.

Ilg and Ames[9] list a series of personality traits which they, on the basis of their clinical experience, feel are characteristic of head-bangers. These authors feel that head-bangers frequently show unusual interest in sounds and music and sing on pitch at an early age. (This is also our experience.) They may be ritualistic and compulsively neat. Although they have considerable energy, they are slow to approach a strange person or a new activity and slow to give it up. They may have temper tantrums and are considered to be poor sleepers.

Material and method

One hundred and thirty-five cases of head-banging were found by routinely questioning mothers, in private pediatric practice. In the cases studied by the authors and those contributed by other pediatricians, data on growth and development were obtained by examining the office records. A good number of additional cases were uncovered by asking the mother if she knew of head-banging infants or children among her friend's children. All cases reported to be head-bangers had the diagnosis confirmed by checking with the patient's physician. All of the cases studied came from white middle and low-income families. Infants with outstanding orthopedic, visual, and auditory abnormalities or those suspected of gross mental retardation or neurologic diseases were excluded from the study.

Psychometric studies were done in twelve of the cases studied by one of the authors, and are being reported in another paper.[7]

Head-banging is a relatively infrequently encountered problem. Without the co-operation of other pediatricians the number of cases compiled in this study could never have been accomplished.

Electroencephalographic studies were done on seven of our cases, by Gibbs and Gibbs. At our request they reviewed the electroencephalograms of 21 cases referred to their laboratory with a diagnosis of head-banging. The data on all these cases is included in the present study.

Results

No studies are available regarding the incidence of head-banging in infants and children. The incidence of head-banging in the senior author's private practice of pediatrics was calculated to be 3.6% with 1168 infants and children studied. De Lissovoy[13] calculated head-banging in a group of 825 children to be 6.5% In the total sample of 135 cases, males predominated over females 105 to 30, a ratio approximately 3.5 to 1, an obviously significant difference. This 3.5 to 1 ratio was also noted in the senior author's cases.

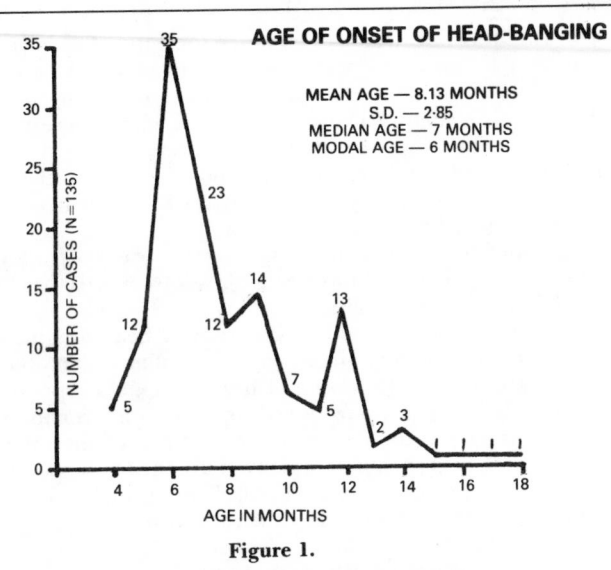

Figure 1.

Head-banging begins at a mean age of eight months, with a standard deviation of 2.5 months, indicating that the vast majority of cases begin head-banging between the ages of five and 11 months (see Figure 1). There were only nine cases that began head-banging after the age of twelve months.

Head-banging occurred most frequently, in 78% of the cases, at bed time, usually at night, but also during daytime naps. Approximately 50% of the children in our sample engaged in this activity for less than 15 minutes at a time. While there is considerable variability in this facet of the problem, 26% of the group are reported to head-bang for one hour or longer at a time. When one considers that these children have been observed by us to head-bang between 60 to 70 bangs per minute, the total number of head-bangs each night is extremely large. Although head-banging usually occurs in children who are awake, 35% of the children in the sample were also observed to head-bang while asleep. Of this group, over half also head-bang while awake.

In keeping with the findings that most head-banging occurs in connection with bed-time activities, 100 cases in our sample were found to bang against the head-board of the bed (see Figure 2). One-third of the children in our sample show multiple head-banging, that is, they

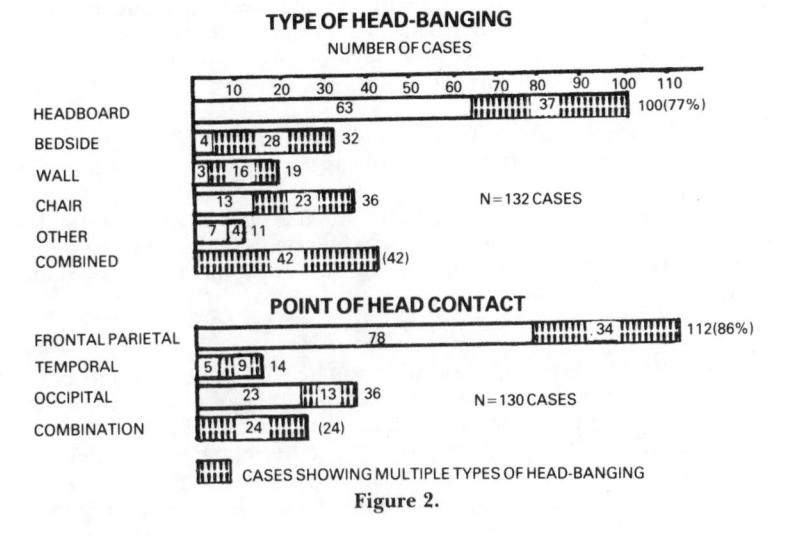

Figure 2.

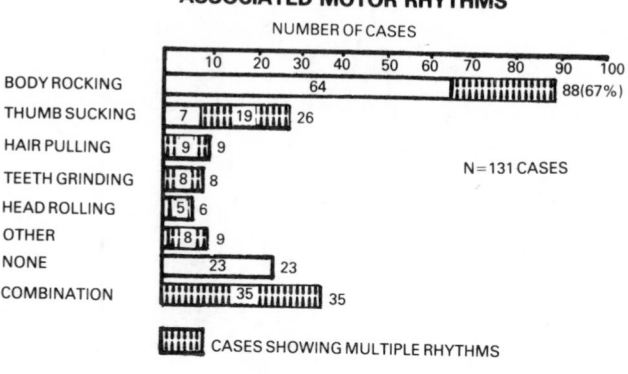

Figure 3.

bang against the head-board and the side of the bed, on the wall near the bed, and the back of chairs. It was found that 86% of the cases head-bang on all fours in the mid-frontal region. The next most common group were those who banged in the sitting position, 18% of the cases being occipital bangers exclusively.

Figure 3 illustrates the presence of associated motor rhythms in children who head-bang. It is clear that the large majority of the group, 67%, also indulge in body rocking. A clinical note at this point: body-rocking often precedes the onset of head-banging and may continue after the head-banging has ceased. Obviously, in these cases of frontal banging, in which the children are on all fours, the body-rocking movement is an integral part of the head-banging activity. Figure 3 shows that 27% of the children show combined associated motor rhythms, and that approximately 18% are reported to show no motor rhythms other than the head-banging. It is important to note that only 9% of our cases were thumb-suckers. According to Traisman[14] 45.6% of normal healthy infants seen in a pediatric practice were reported to be thumb-suckers

In evaluating the relationship of head-banging with other behavior, 91% of the cases show no crying associated with head-banging (see Figure 4), 68% showed no temper

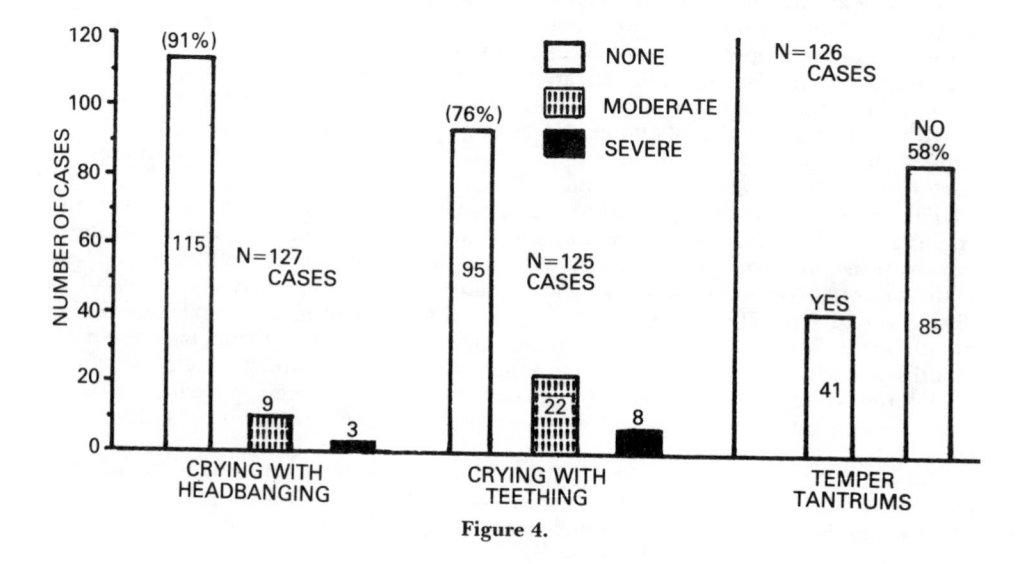

Figure 4.

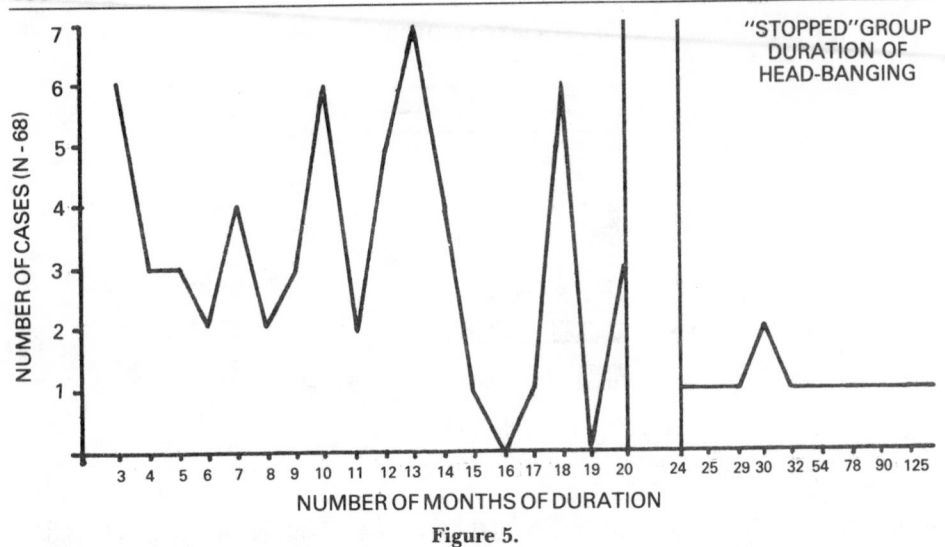

Figure 5.

tantrums; 66% of the children showed no night crying in combination with teething. It is important to note that the average age of eruption of the central and lateral incisors was 7.5 months and 9.85 months respectively, a range in which the onset of head-banging occurs. In several cases, head-banging would stop and again start with the eruption of a new group of teeth.

In evaluating family factors related to head-banging, the following facts were found: 1) Head-banging occurred in other children of the family in only 20% of the cases. 2) Head-banging occurs somewhat more frequently in families with two children, but may be said to be almost evenly distributed among families containing either one, two, or three children. 3) Head-banging occurs in the first child of the family in 53% of the cases, and in the second child in the family in 32% of the cases. 4) Separation of mother and child by virtue of hospitalization of either, or by divorce or separation, or mother working occurred in only 27% of the cases, indicating that by and large, the head-banging children are not significantly separated from their mothers.

Although the evaluation of the mother-child relationship by the pediatrician represents only a gross approximation of this relationship, 68% of the cases were felt to show a good mother-child relationship, 15% were felt to have fair mother-child relationship and 17% were felt to have a poor mother-child relationship.

In our series, head-banging disappeared in 54% of the cases, with a mean chronologic age of 47.4 months at the time of our contact with them. Among these children it was found that the duration of the phenomenon averaged 17 months, continuing to a mean chonologic age of 24.8 months (see Figure 5). Less than 20% of this group continued head-banging for longer than 18 months.

Of the other 46% of our cases, head-banging persisted up to the end of the present study. In this group the mean duration of the head-banging was 27.3 months, and the children were a mean chronologic age of 34.6 months at the time of our contact with them. Analysis of the data on this group showed that among children still banging, there were actually two distinct sub-groups. The first consisted of 32 children with a mean chronologic age of 17.6 months at the time of contact who had begun to head-bang at a mean chronologic age of 7.9 months, and who had continued for a mean duration of 10.1 months. Thus, this is a group of children who have not completed the course of the symptom, so to speak, and could probably be regarded as a "normal" group in comparison with the group in which head-banging had already stopped.

The second sub-group consisted of 25 children with a mean chronologic age of 56.4 months who began head-banging at a mean chronologic age of 8.16 months and who continued to head-bang for a mean duration of 48.3 months. This latter group, coupled with those 13 children who are no longer head-bangers, but who continued for more than 18 months, constitute the chronic or persistent cases. Thus, approximately 30% of the infants and children in our sample are or have been chronic head-bangers. Unlike the first group, in which head-banging lasts for a period of about 18 months, children in this latter group may continue head-banging for as long as 10½ years. However, inspection of our data on our chronic head-bangers shows no fundamental distinguishing characteristics which would set them apart from the other group.

In regard to the question of the EEG finding in cases of head-banging, Gibbs and Gibbs[12] have uncovered 21 cases of head-bangers referred specifically for EEG because of persistent head-banging. All cases have been reported as normal. In reviewing our own data, we have found an additional seven cases which also were described as having normal EEG. The absence of abnormal electroencephalograms in these cases suggests that head-banging is not an epileptic or epileptiform disorder and is not related to an acute or progressive cortical disorder. Also, it should be stated that we have not had one case of severe or permanent intracranial injury in 135 cases reported in this study. However, abrasions and contusions about the mid-frontal and occipital region have been noted. On the other hand, no evidence of acquired injury to the brain has been noted clinically or on EEG.

Discussion

Perhaps the outstanding feature which all the theories of head-banging advanced in the literature have in common, is the absence of clear cut experimental evidence to support them. The uniformity of onset of this phenomenon at age 8 months in all sub-groups in our population could be taken as support for the theory that head-banging reflects a maturational pattern emerging as an inherent function of the organism in the transitional phase from sitting to crawling. The fact that the age of onset also tends to correspond to the period of eruption of central and lateral incisors may indicate the role that tension reduction may play in the development of head-banging behavior. Because of the early age of onset, it is unlikely that attention seeking as a primary factor in head-banging can be argued, but in the chronic cases this secondary value may be significant. The absence of crying associated with head-banging and the apparent absence of pain raises a question about the acceptability of the idea that this act is a form of self-inflicted aggression against the body. However, it may be argued that the absence of overt response to pain during head-banging does not rule out the fact that pain may be present, but neutralized by kinesthetic, auditory, rhythmic pleasures.

These children tend to show various motor rhythms in combination with head-banging. Thus, they may be a group which is hypersensitive to tactile, kinesthetic and auditory stimulation, responding to these stimuli through the modality of body rhythms rather than, say verbal activities. Although no electroencephalographic abnormalities have been found in head-bangers it seems likely that hyperactivity of some type, possibly in deep centers, gives rise to this phenomenon. A normal electroencephalogram is found in children with choreoathetosis, with Sydenham's chorea and in patients with Parkinsonism. The electrical activity of at least two-thirds of the brain is not recorded in the electroencephalogram. Furthermore, there are types of neuronal function which are not electrogenic or which, at least, produce nothing that can be recorded in the electroencephalogram. The behavior pattern of these head-bangers indicates that they constitute a group in which some inherent central nervous rhythmicity is more strongly expressed than in the majority of infants of their age.

Treatment

Head-banging in infancy is a benign disorder which requires no medical treatment beyond reassurance of the mother that the child will outgrow the symptom and that no injury to the brain will result. In the severe chronic cases of head-banging persisting beyond the age of three years, it is our opinion that a neurologic and psychiatric evaluation is needed. We have employed various sedatives and tranquilizing drugs in a series of severe chronic head-bangers and have been impressed with the benefit obtained in some cases. It is our opinion that drug therapy is indicated in selected cases of persistent head-banging.

Conclusion

The average head-banger usually is a male child who begins head-banging at about 8 months of age, continuing for about 17 months until he is 25 months of age. He is usually awake and in bed at the time of head-banging, usually banging against the headboard while rocking on all fours and hitting his head in the mid-frontal area. The average head-banger does not cry in association with his head-banging, he generally shows no evidence of temper tantrums. Crying in connection with teething is rare. He is most often also a body-rocker which often preceded the head-banging. He does very little thumb-sucking. His central and lateral incisors tend to erupt at a period which marks the onset of the head-banging phenomenon. Head-banging is more frequent in the first child in the family. He has not been significantly separated from his mother. His relationship with the mother is generally regarded as adequate.

Acknowledgments: The authors wish to thank Dr. Frederic A. Gibbs and Dr. Erna Gibbs for making available the electroencephalograms in the cases of head-banging referred to their laboratory and for their help in reviewing this manuscript.

The authors also wish to thank Dr. Hayworth Sanford, Dr. Noel G. Shaw and Dr. Jack Metcoff for their aid in preparing this paper.

Bibliography
1. Lourie, R. S.. *Am. J. Psychiat.*, 1949; **105**, 653.
2. Spitz, R. A., Wolf, K. M. *The Psychoanalytic Study of the Child.* (3-4, p. 85.) 1949.
3. Mittelman, B. *The Psychoanalytic Study of the Child.* (9, p. 142.) 1954.
4. Harlow, H. Personal communication.
5. Richmond, J. B., Lipton, E. L. Emotional Problems of Childhood. *Lippincott.* (p. 17.) 1958.
6. Freud, A., Burlingham, D. *Infants Without Families.* New York: International University Press, 1944.
7. Teplitz, Z., Bromberg, R. L. *Am. J. Orthopsy.* (In press.).
8. FitzHerbert, J. *J. Ment. Sci.*, 1950; **96**, 793.
9. Ilg, F. L., and Ames, L. B. *Child Behavior.* (p. 141.) Harper and Brothers, 1955.
10. Kubie, L. S. *Psychoanal. Quart.*, 1941; **10**, 23.
11. Freeman, W., Watts, J. W. *Yale J. Biol. and Med.*, 1939; **11**, 527.
12. Gibbs, F., Gibbs, E. Personal communication.
13. Gibbs, F., Gibbs, E.: Personal communication.
13. de Lissovoy, V. Personal communication.
14. Traisman, A. S., Traisman, H. S. *J. Pediat.*, 1958; **52**, 566.

Reprinted from *Diseases of the Nervous System*, 1960; **21**, 203-208 by kind permission of the publishers Physicians Postgraduate Press, Memphis, TN 38124.

HEAD BANGING IN EARLY CHILDHOOD

Vladimir de Lissovoy*

Pennsylvania State University, University Park, Pennsylvania

Summary

This study describes head banging behavior of normal, not hospitalized young children. Thirty-three head bangers were observed under normal bedtime conditions. Four characteristic positions of head banging were defined: hands and knees, sitting, prone, and standing or kneeling. The age of onset ranged from 3 to 12 months, and all of the subjects had a history of other rhythmic activities, such as head or body rolling, prior to head banging. Most of the head banging took place at bedtime and in the morning when the subjects awakened. The regularity was described by 25 mothers as "every night" or "almost every night." Head banging sessions lasted between one half hour and four hours. The tempo of head banging ranged from 19 to 52 head object contacts per minute for girls and 26 to 121 for boys. Reaction of subjects exposed to metronome-stimulus varied from complete indifference to dramatic cessation of activity.

In a follow-up study of this sample of subjects it was found that 14 ceased head banging between 27 and 48 months of age. All of the former head bangers were described by mothers as active children, prone to rhythmic activity in response to musical stimuli. Coordination of the great majority of the children was described as "excellent."

Head banging is a curious behavior pattern sometimes seen in infants and young children. This activity is characterized by repetitive movements marked by a definite rhythm and monotonous continuity. The head is struck rhythmically against the head board, side railing of the crib, or other objects. This is not a tantrum type of behavior but is marked by an almost compulsive repetitiveness. Characteristically, it appears to commence sometime in the last half of the first year and is usually preceded by other less dramatic rhythmic motor behavior such as head or body rolling and crib rocking.

While this behavior has come to the attention of medical practitioners, very little in the way of descriptive material or controlled research has been done. Gesell states, "Rocking on hands and knees and bedshaking are common forms of deviation. Head banging and head rolling also have their origins in this period from 40 weeks to 21 months" (5, p.308). Spock (12) discusses this rhythmic behavior under the subheading of "Common Nervous Symptoms." Lourie (10) noted head banging in a study of 130 children who manifested a variety of rhythmic patterns. Other writers have noted this behavior, and references appear in medical, psychological and popular literature (1, 2, 4, 6, 7, 8, 9, 13).

The purpose of this paper is to describe systematically head banging behavior of normal, not hospitalized young children. Specifically, this report describes the positions in which head banging takes place, the age of onset, the frequency and persistency, the tempo, and related factors. In addition, reaction to metronome stimulus and a follow-up study of behavioral patterns of a portion of the sample are described.[1]

Thirty-three head bangers were observed under normal bedtime conditions; 23 were boys and 10 were girls. The age range for the total group was from 10 to 49 months; average age was 26.6 months. All of the observations described in this report took place in the homes of the subjects. Twenty-six of the 33 subjects in this sample were obtained from referrals of practicing physicians in cities of upstate New York. Seven cases were found through personal contacts.

*Department of Child Development and Family Relationships, Pennsylvania State University, University Park.

[1]This article is based on research conducted for a thesis which was submitted to Cornell University in partial fulfillment of the requirements for the degree of Doctor of Philosophy. The writer wishes to express his gratitude to Professors Robert M. Dalton, Mary N. Ford, Henry N. Ricciuti, and Gordon F. Streib for valuable criticism and help in this research.

Figure 1—Hands and knees position. Rocking motion usually involving the entire body. The forehead or the cranial cap strikes the headboard on forward motion.

Positions of head bangers

The most common forms of head banging noted by the investigator were as follows:

Hands and Knees Position (Fig. 1). Child stands on hands and knees and rocks forward and back; on the forward motion the forehead or the cranial cap is struck against the crib headboard. The propelling distance varies as does the tempo and the force of the motion. While some children actually stand "on all fours," others tend to sit more on their "haunches" and strike the headboard with a "salaaming" action. In four cases observed the child managed to support himself in such a manner that his weight rested on his knees, one hand, and an elbow; in this manner he banged his head while sucking his thumb. One subject lay in a knee-chest position sucking his thumb and holding the lapel of his pajamas with his other hand while rhythmically striking the cranial cap against the headboard of the crib.

Sitting Position (Fig. 2). Subject is in sitting position braced or sitting against side of crib or the headboard. The knees are drawn up or the legs may be straight out. The arms and hands serve to brace the body in motion. The motion is primarily a trunk movement or it is limited to throwing the head repeatedly to the rear, thus striking the object of support. As in the previous description, the distance, tempo, and force vary to some extent; however, the

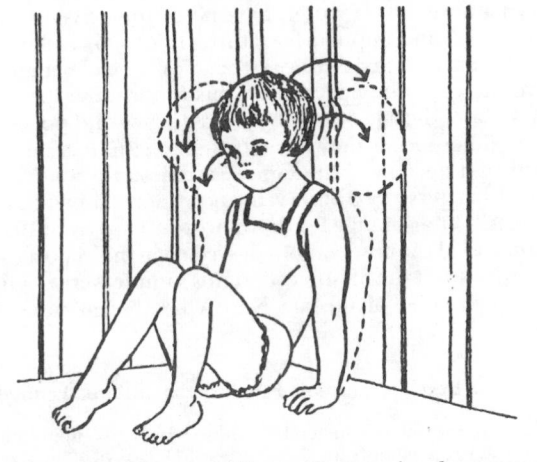

Figure 2—Occipital head banger. The motion may involve upper portion of body or may be primarily focused upon the head.

Figure 3—Prone position. The head is dropped or brought down with force.

impression of the observer is that subjects using this position were generally more violent in their actions. Eight of the 15 subjects observed in this position sucked their thumbs and held a stuffed toy, a blanket, or other piece of material. In all cases, it was possible to note that the eyes were closed while in motion, although it was not possible to determine if the subjects were asleep. Two cases were noted in which the subjects gradually slipped downward as they banged. In each case, the subjects stopped, moved back to the sitting position, and resumed head banging.

Prone Position (Fig. 3). Subject is lying in the prone position. The head is raised and "dropped" on the pillow or mattress. In some instances, the head appeared to be dropped, but at other times the head was brought down with considerable force. A variation of this method was noted in one subject who raised his torso as if doing "push ups" at the same time bringing his head down with force and letting his body fall. This was repeated with remarkable continuity and rhythm for over one half hour by a 10-month-old boy. The youngest head banger (3 months) reported to the investigator by parents followed this pattern.

Multiple Position (Fig. 4). Child kneels, stands, or sits as he holds on to the bars or the railing of the crib while striking his forehead. This appears to be the most dramatic type of

Figure 4—Multiple position. The forehead strikes side of crib (subject may kneel or sit).

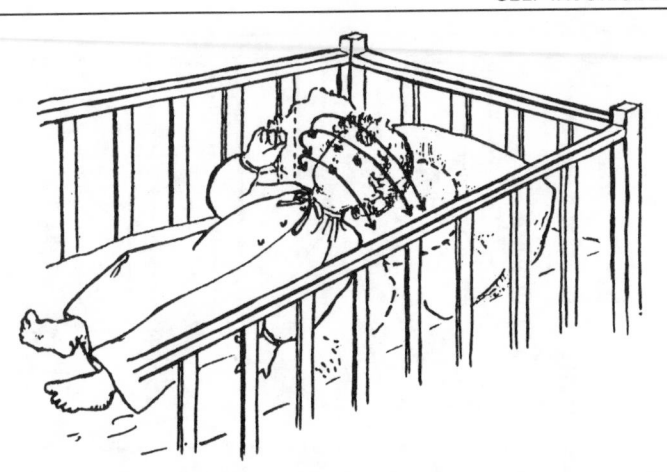

Figure 5—Supine position. Head rolling—child strikes sides of crib.

head banging because of the violence of the action and the evident tissue damage. One subject was observed striking his forehead repeatedly on the railing of the crib while holding a blanket and the support with one hand while sucking the thumb of the other hand. The five subjects observed using this position had their eyes closed. This type of action is not to be confused with the purposeful tantrum type of head knocking often seen in young children. The latter are usually conscious of the presence of an adult and often use this behavior as an attention-getting device. The head bangers observed appeared to be in a somnambulant state. This type of head banging is also to be noted at other times besides bedtime. The mother of four of the five subjects observed informed the investigator that the children follow this pattern of action upon awakening in the morning or, sometimes, upon awakening from naps. A curious aspect of this type of head banging appears in what could be interpreted as an attempt by the child to inflict pain upon himself. This was noted in one case where the child deliberately sought out parts of the crib that were not padded or tried to tear off the padding in an apparent effort to find a hard part against which to hit his forehead.

Supine Position (Fig. 5). Subject is in supine position. The head is rolled from side to side and, in some cases, the whole body is rolled from side to side with the head striking the sides of the crib or bed. The head contact is a templar one and, presumably, is painful. While head rolling has been observed by the investigator, templar head banging has never been witnessed. This position is included in the discussion because of reports to the writer by competent investigators and because of the notations of cranial jactitation in medical literature (11).

Discussion

Ten head bangers were observed in the hands and knees position (Fig. 1), 13 in the sitting position (Fig. 2), two in the prone position (Fig. 3), and four in the standing or kneeling (Fig. 4) position. Four of the children were seen in a variation of positions. According to the information supplied by mothers, head banging positions varied more than indicated by the investigator, but generally speaking the hand and knees and the sitting position tended to be favored by most head bangers.

Age of onset

Parental impression of the age at which head banging was first noted is indicated in Table 1. The age of onset of head banging follows the observations noted by other investigators. It was found, however, that parents were not always certain of the exact month when this activity commenced and their answers represent, at best, an honest estimate of the age of onset.

Table 1. Age of child when head banging commenced

Age in Months	Boys	Girls	Total Sample
3	1	—	1
4	—	—	—
5	1	—	1
6	2	1	3
7	4	—	4
8	3	3	6
9	2	2	4
10	2	1	3
11	—	1	1
12	—	1	1
	15	9	24
Did not know	8	1	9
Total	23	10	33

It was interesting to note that the answer to the query as to the age of onset brought out the fact that there was other rhythmic behavior present prior to head banging; the onset of the latter behavior was then estimated. For example, one mother stated as follows:

Well, she was a tense baby even right after we brought her home from the hospital. She thrashed around a lot and would stiffen if she was picked up suddenly. She used to move her head to and fro when she was very tiny. I'd say 2 or 3 months but she didn't rock until she was, oh, I'd say about 9 or 10 months. That's when she started to whack her head.

The presence of some type of rhythmic activity early in infancy prior to head banging was noted by all of the mothers although the age of such activity could not always be determined. Mothers' answers in this regard are noted in Table 2.

Table 2. Rhythmic activity noted by mothers prior to onset of head banging

Type of Rhythmic Activity Noted by Mothers	Number of Cases
Head rolling	10
Rocking	5
Swaying in high chair	5
Body rolling	2
More than one rhythmic pattern	11
Total	33

While seven mothers could not estimate the age of the child when rhythmic behavior, other than head banging, took place, 26 were able to do so. Eighteen mothers noted such behavior within the first 3 months. Six mothers noted some rhythmic action between 4 and 6 months. Two mothers mentioned noting rocking at 7 and 8 months, respectively. The most prevalent persistent rhythmic activity noted in the first 3 months was head rolling. The following represent some observations made by the mothers in this regard:

Case 5—When he was 3 months old, when I put him on his stomach he would raise his head and drop it. He would do this over and over.

Case 10—Well, she used to rock and hum, I'd say, when she first was able to get on her hands and knees, oh, sometime about 6 months.

Case 27—I first noticed it when he rolled his head while feeding (child was breast fed). He sucked and moved back and forth—he'd do it right after feeding too. He used to roll his body from side to side before he could turn over—that was before 3 months. He was a real heavy rocker before he could sit up.

Case 38—I know exactly when he started (head banging)—I write everything down. (Mother referred to a "Baby Book.") He started to knock his head at 6 months but he used to

Table 3. Mothers' answers to query regarding head banging at times other than at bedtime

Mothers' Answers	Number of Answers
Primarily at bedtime, very little at other times...	27
Bedtime and in the morning when child awakens..	10
During the night...	6
When child awakens from nap during the day..	4
Sometimes during the day when child sits on the sofa, chair; when in the play pen or riding in a car	12

Note.—Some of the subjects were head bangers at times other than bedtime, hence, the total answers number more than the *N* (33).

do all kinds of acrobatics before that. (This mother—a registered nurse—noted head rolling a 2 months and hand and knee rocking at 5 months.)

From the study of 33 cases in this investigation it seems clear that head banging does not start spontaneously but has a history of antecedent rhythmical behavior patterns that can be noted as early as the first month of life.

Frequency and persistency

In 27 of the 33 cases observed, head banging occurred primarily at bedtime. This is a common occurrence and has been noted by other observers. Gesell (5), in commenting on this behavior, refers to it as a "relaxational expedient" before falling asleep. In the observations it was not possible to determine whether the children were asleep. In two cases, mentioned in the discussion of reactions to the metronome stimulus, the children who ceased their activity remained, apparently, asleep. In two other cases, the mother picked up the child (both hands and knees cranial-cap head banger [Fig. 1]), and placed them on their side in the crib. Neither child resumed the activity.

As has been previously noted, all of the cases herein observed were seen in action during their "bedtime sessions." Mothers were queried about head banging at other times and their answers are noted in Table 3. From the answers given in Table 3 it is apparent that most of the head banging took place primarily at bedtime. It can readily be seen, however, that head banging does occur at other times. Two mothers noted that, if their children start head banging during the night, it is a signal that they need changing. After a diaper change, head banging ceased in both of these cases.

Mothers were asked regarding the regularity of head banging. The distribution of their answers is shown in Table 4. It will be seen from Table 4 that in 25 cases head banging took place nightly or "almost every night". This confirms the observations of Gesell (5) and Lourie (10).

In the majority of the cases the bedtime head banging sessions lasted between one half hour and an hour and a half (23 cases). Five cases averaged "about a half hour more or less," and in five cases the children continued this activity for as long as three and four hours.

Because the investigator deemed it desirable to know if head banging increased under unusual circumstances, the following question was asked of all mothers: "Does he tend to do this more at some of the times than others? For example, have you noted this during a cold or any other illnesses?" Mothers' answers are tabulated in Table 5.

Table 4. Regularity of head banging

Mothers' Answers	Number of Answers
Every night...	12
Almost every night	13
Several times a week	5
Twice a week or so	2
Several days in a row but he can go as long as a week without doing it	1
Total...	33

Table 5. Tendency to increase head banging during colds or illness

Mothers' Answers	Number of Answers
No increase in head banging	15
Definite increase	7
Not certain	4
Mother does not recall	2
Increased when child is tired	1
Increased when child is wet or dirty	1
Increased when child was excited or was anticipating something (before Christmas)	2
Increased when child returned from hospital	1
Total	33

Tempo

The tempo of head banging was measured by counting the number of times the child struck the side of the crib, headboard, or other object of contact in one minute of action. At least five such counts were taken during the observations. These measures were taken at approximately five-minute intervals, but they cannot be regarded as true time samples in as much as they were not distributed throughout the total time of head banging. The tendency throughout was to concentrate the tempo measures at the beginning of the observation time. This was done because the investigator had no way of knowing how long the head banging period would last; for the purpose of comparison the first five measures of all the children were used. In several cases, additional measures were recorded because of prolonged activity. No comparison of position is attempted. In other words, an occipital head banger and a hands and knees head banger are compared in tempos regardless the position. Table 6 presents the observed tempo of 33 head bangers.

The nonsignificant t value suggests that difference in tempo cannot be attributed to sex difference in this sample. Three cases of particularly exaggerated tempo were noted in boys only (64, 80, and 121 beats per minute).

Table 6. Tempo of head bangers based on the average of five one-minute counts*

	Boys	Girls
Range	26-121	19.3-52
Mean beats per minute	44.4	36.2
Standard deviation	20.1	10.5

* $t=1.16$.

Relation of tempo to heart rate and age

Lourie (10) states:

In the great majority of the children who rock, roll, bang, or sway the pacemaker is the heart beat. Possibly this also has an auditory component since . . . a great many individuals can distinctly hear their own pulses with the sound localized to their ears (p.657).

It was not possible to measure the heart rate while the children were head banging, but, since a minimal heart rate was recorded in terms of seconds for 0 to 20 systolic impulses for 15 of the 33 head bangers, the time in seconds was correlated with the tempo.[2] The correlation of minimal heart rate and head banging rate proved to be .25 (nonsignificant). It should be noted that, since the value of the correlation is positive, it follows that there is a tendency for the time interval to *increase* with the increase of rate per minute of head banging. Since the time interval increases while the measured heartbeat (0 to 20 systolic impulses) remains constant, it means that it takes longer to register the given number of

[2]Minimal heart rate is defined here as a time measure of intersystolic impulses obtained while the subject is asleep under normal but controlled conditions.

beats. Thus, even though the correlation is not statistically significant, its direction in terms of the heart as the pacemaker does not support the "pacemaking" hypothesis of the heart in this sample of head bangers.

In order to determine the relationship of age in months to tempo of head banging, these two variables were correlated. Because control over the body increases with age, it seemed plausible to expect that the tempo of head banging would be positively related to chronological age. This was not the case. The correlation for boys was .14; for the girls it was .20. The tempo of head banging, then, does not appear to be related to either the minimal heart rate nor chronological age.

Metronome reactions

In his study of rhythmic patterns in children, Lourie performed a series of experiments in which a metronome was set in action at the bedside of four children. ". . . two diurnal, purposeful head bangers and two children who banged their heads in their sleep" (10, p.657). It was found that when the tempo of the metronome was set at the speed the child was using in its action, head banging ceased. Lourie writes as follows:

The sleeping children remained asleep but quiet. When the metronome was stopped, only the daytime head bangers sooner or later (3 to 15 minutes) resumed the head banging. When the metronome beat was slowed, one of the awake and consciously aware children returned to its own preferred rhythmic tempo. . . . When the metronome was speeded up, they all stopped their movement but resumed it within 15 minutes after the superimposed rhythm was stopped (p.657).

Lourie's experiment was prompted by Titchener's (14) suggestions of the linkage of the kinesthetic sensation to auditory stimulation. The nexus of stimulation appears to be the

. . . contraction of the tensor tympani of the middle ear. This thesis seems to be borne out by the head banger in whom the auditory sensation produced by its activity is not only an integral part of the rhythmic movement but appears to be its most important component, although the vestibular apparatus is also concerned (p.657).

During the period of observation of head bangers, after initial observations, sketches, and time sampling of the tempo were recorded, a metronome, set at the speed of the child's rhythmic rate, was introduced. In each case, either the mother or the investigator placed the metronome under the crib or bed of the child in such a manner that the pendulum would not be visible to the child and the stimulus would remain an auditory one. This procedure was followed in 28 subjects.

Of the 28 subjects there was no noticeable reaction in 13 children. Seven manifested curiosity or fear; they cried or attempted to climb out of their cribs or beds to explore the source of the noise.

Eight cases expressed several types of reactions which ranged from some modification of rhythm to a dramatic cessation of all rhythmic activities. These reactions are noted in the following summary:

Boy 30 months: At first no apparent reaction followed by aggravation of head banging with increased force but same tempo.

Boy 42 months: Subject stopped activity, opened his eyes and asked, "What's that noise?" Examiner replied, "Listen." Child listened, did not resume head banging. Mother repeated procedure on the following night and reported that child went to sleep without head banging. A loud ticking alarm clock was placed on the dresser in the child's room and he was told to listen to the "tic." Mother stated that there was no further rocking or head banging. Three months later the investigator had the occasion to see the mother and she reported a complete absence of all rhythmic movement.

Boy 16 months: Activity ceased upon the introduction of metronome. Mother reported the same effect on the following night. Head banging commenced again on the third night after the initial introduction of the metronome (mother's report). The metronome had no subsequent effect upon head banging behavior.

Girl 26 months: Subject stopped head banging and appeared to listen. Sat up in crib, clutched a blanket. Commenced rocking and head banging but stopped every few seconds to listen. Rolled over on stomach and appeared to be listening, and fell asleep in this manner. Mother reported violent head banging in the morning and after nap; she stated to the investigator that while the metronome helped at night, ". . . she made up for it in the morning." Metronome was used by the mother on six nights with a marked decrease in rhythmic action, but subject returned to previous pattern after metronome was removed. There was no apparent reaction to a loudly ticking alarm clock.

Follow-up of head bangers

The data for this study were collected over a period of several years. It was thus possible to secure information about behavioral patterns of some of the subjects up to 5½ years after the initial contact. This was done by means of a short questionnaire which was sent to all of the mothers in the original study.

An attempt was made to obtain information in the following areas of growth and behavior: (a) the subjects' current status in school (if of school age]; (b) the activity level and lability of the subject; (c) an estimate of the subjects' coordination; (d) an estimate by mothers of the rhythmic response to music by the subjects; (e) the incidence and description of prevalent nervous habits; (f) age at which head banging ceased. Also, a question was included asking about the onset and the duration of head banging.

A total of 19 replies were received. The age of termination of head banging as reported by mothers is given in Table 7. The actual figure in months is used in this table with no attempt to group the answers.

Table 7. Age of termination of head banging given by mothers in the follow-up study ($N=18$)*

Age of Termination (months)	Number of Mothers
27	1
30	1
36	6
42	3
48	3
Total	14†

* One mother denied that her child was a head banger.
† Four children were still head banging at the time of the follow-up study (ages in months: 37, 42, 60, and 104).

It will be noted that 14 head bangers terminated this activity at or before the fourth year. It is very interesting to note that of the four children still head banging, one is much older than the average age of termination. The mother of this child (boy, age 96 months) enclosed a note with her reply. An excerpt from this follows:

X was seriously ill last June being hospitalized for two weeks . . . his head banging has become more consistent. It has stopped at bedtime but occasionally during the day when he is too tired to play, or there seems to have been a problem (either in school or just playing a game), he will come in and "pump" as he calls it. If he is left alone for a little while, he is soon over it.

The follow-up questionnaire was designed so that most of the answers could be checked by mothers on a five-point scale with three points descriptively designated. The answers were averaged with the following numerical values representing the mean scores for all of the mothers checking the question:

Activity ($N=19$). (1) Deliberate in anything he does (3) About average in terms of activity (5) Very active, energetic, and quick moving. Mean score 4.0.

Temperament ($N=19$). (1) Generally easy going and very patient (3) About average in patience (5) Tends to be impatient, can't seem to wait. Mean score 3.4.

Lability ($N=19$). (1) Quick to anger, becomes frustrated easily (3) Has occasional flareups but is generally even tempered (5) Usually even tempered, takes things in stride. Mean score 3.0.

It is evident that, although the mothers regarded their children to be above average in activity, temperament and lability were not so designated.

All of the 11 school aged children were found to be in the normal grade in terms of their age. Mothers' estimates of coordination suggested that 16 teachers felt that this was no problem and they judged their children as excellent in this factor. Three mothers stated that there was difficulty in coordination; all three subjects were under 5 years of age. Five children were nail biters; 14 did not do this.

Indication of rhythmic response to music was noted by 13 mothers; these said that the children could not sit still when music was playing but would sway, dance, jump, or hop. No response to music was noted in six cases. Nervous habits listed by mothers include five cases of nail biting, one "picks his nose," one "constant rocking on the sofa or in the car." The two traits of the subjects that were observed in the previous contact with the mothers that were indicated as being present in the follow-up study were activity and rhythmic response. There was no indication in this group of children that activity was associated with lability nor was there a suggestion of prevalence of nervous habits.

References
1 Bundesen, H. Babies' bedtime antics. (Syndicated column) *Binghamton (N.Y.) Press,* July 13, 1955.
2 Dean, C. A. For better health. (Syndicated column) *Oneonta (N.Y.) Star,* May 1, 1958.
3 deLissovoy, V. *Head banging in early childhood, an exploratory study of an atypical behavior pattern.* (Unpublished doctoral dissertation.) Cornell Univer., 1959.
4 Gee, S. Miscellanies. *St. Bartholomew's Hosp. Rep.,* 1886; **22**, 96-97.
5 Gesell, A., Ilg, F. L. *Infant and child in the culture of today.* Harper, 1943.
6 Holt, L. E., Jr. The children's center. Nervous habits. *Good Housekeeping,* May 1955.
7 Ilg, F. L., Ames, L. B. *Child behavior.* Dell, 1955.
8 Langford, W. S. Common psychopathological symptoms and syndromes—motor disorders. *In* E. L. Holt, Jr., R. McIntosh (Eds.). *Holt's Diseases of Infancy and Childhood.* (11th edn.). Appleton-Century, 1940.
9 Langford, W. S. Psychopathological problems. *In* E. L. Holt, Jr., R. McIntosh (Eds.), *Holt's Diseases of Infancy and Childhood.* (12th edn.). Appleton-Century, 1953.
10 Lourie, R. S. The role of rhythmic patterns in childhood. *Am. J. Psychiat.,* 1949; **105**, 653-660.
11 Schacter, M. Étude sur les rhythmies du jour ou du sommeil chez l'enfant. *Encephale,* 1954; **43**, 173-192.
12 Spock, B. *The pocket book of baby and child care.* Pocket Books, 1952.
13 Teicher, J. How to handle eight common behavior problems. *Parents Mag.,* 1953; **28**, 43-46.
14 Titchener, E. B. *Textbook of psychology.* Macmillan, 1919.

Reprinted from *Child Development,* 1962; **33**, 43-56 by kind permission of Vladimir de Lissovoy and the publishers The Society for Research in Child Development Inc., Chicago, Illinois 60637.

HEAD BANGING IN EARLY CHILDHOOD: A SUGGESTED CAUSE

Vladimir de Lissovoy

Pennsylvania State University, University Park, Pennsylvania

Summary

Fifteen head bangers were matched with a control group of subjects who did not manifest any dramatic rhythmic activities. Eleven boys and four girls ranging in age from 10 to 42 months were in each group. Age, sex, weight, type of birth and other relevant variables were matched. A statistically significantly higher incidence of otitis media was found in the head banging group.

Etiology of head banging is examined in terms of possible stress reaction or as a form of distraction and pain relief.

A. Introduction

Head banging is characterized by repetitive movements marked by a definite rhythm and monotonous continuity. The head is struck rhythmically against the headboard, side of crib or other objects. This is not a tantrum type of behavior but is marked by an almost compulsive repetitiveness. The incidence of this behavior among normal non-hospitalized children has been estimated to be five to 15 per cent (7). A description of this behavior based upon observation of 33 head bangers appears in another publication (6).

A wide variety of theories regarding the etiology of head banging appear in the literature. Most of these are not supported by empirical data or are based upon a very small sample of children.

According to Ribble (20), gentle motion or rocking is beneficial to infants because it ameliorates the shock of transition from a liquid to air environment. It is through such rhythmic activity that the neonate overcomes the "innate sensitivity of fear of falling" and such kinaesthetic experience is important in establishing the affective tie between mother and child. In a follow-up of some of the babies in her study Ribble noted, "Many of those who did not get this form of mothering frequently substituted it themselves with head rolling, body rolling, or other hyperkinetic manifestations during periods of stress."

Langford (15) notes that rockers and head bangers satisfy some basic need for rhythm and the common denominator of all rhythmic activities seems to rest in the pleasure of movement and the release of tension. A similar conclusion is drawn by Lourie (17) after an examination of available studies and observations of 130 children:

. . . It is suggested that rhythm and movement serve similar roles and complement each other in their association to further growth, express tension and pleasure, and achieve relaxation.

Theories regarding etiology of dramatic rhythmic movements can be classified under the following general headings: Autoerotism (3, 12, 24), aggression (8, 9, 10, 11), motor release (4, 13, 14, 16, 18, 19), parent-child relationships (1, 8, 20), intracranial irritations (2, 8, 9, 10, 21).

Of the above references none was oriented to the testing of hypotheses. The psychoanalytic generalizations of Clark and Uniker (3) were based on analyses of two children. Fitz-Herbert (9, 10) observed six cases. Lourie (17) based his comments upon observations of 130 children but it is not possible to determine whether such observations were made in the clinic, at the home of the child or whether they were in any way controlled.

The purpose of this paper is to present one aspect of a larger study of head banging and to suggest a possible etiology.

B. The study

Fifteen head bangers were matched with a control group of subjects who did not manifest any dramatic rhythmic activities. The following variables were controlled: age, sex, weight,

Table 1. Otitis media in the first year of life, diagnosed and treated

	Yes	No	Total
Head bangers	6*	9	15
Non-head bangers	1	14	15

*Two cases recurring attacks
$P < .05$ (Fisher Exact Probability Test -) (23).

Table 2. Age of treatment of otitis in relation to the age of onset of head banging

Case no.	Age of treatment for otitis	Age of onset of head banging (months)
8	9 and 11 months*	10
9	11	12
14	8	?**
11	8	12
1	2 weeks and 22 months*	7
29	11 and 12 months*	6

* Recurring attacks.
** Mother did not recall.

race, type of birth (spontaneous, instrumental, or section), birth order, socio-economic status and family structure. The age range was from 10 to 42 months; there were 11 boys and four girls in each group.

Each of the head bangers was observed in the process of head banging with a careful record made of the tempo and severity of the action. All of these children were observed in their homes. An interview with the mothers disclosed that in every case some form of rhythmic activity, such as head or body rolling, was present prior to the first birthday.

The revised form of the Stanford-Binet Scale was administered to 24 children in the matched groups. After the initial testing on Form L, a retest on Form M followed in one to three weeks. The scores obtained were adjusted for age differences in IQ variability and were averaged. The mean score for head bangers was 109.2; for non head bangers the mean score was 113.8. (This difference is not statistically significant). The Gesell Developmental Schedule was administered to the six younger children and no differences were noted between the head bangers and the matched group.

In checking the health histories of the children, it was found that, according to the reports of attending physicians, six head bangers were treated for otitis media within the first year of life (two of these cases had recurring attacks). Only one case of otitis was noted in the non head banging group.

The relationship between otitis media and head banging has been noted by Podosky (21). He states, "Of three children who had had otitis media, two developed head banging of the purely aggressive type, and a third that of a mixed or ambivalent kind."

Since the physicians in this study indicated the date of treatment of otitis it was possible to relate age at treatment to mothers' estimates of the onset of head banging. This is shown in Table 2.

It will be seen that in four cases otitis preceded the onset of head banging. The children who had recurring attacks of otitis were observed to be the most severe head bangers based on the tempo and the force of their blows. In the one case in which the mother could not recall the exact age of onset, she estimated that it was before the first birthday of the child. The subject in question was a head roller at three months and continued this action until head banging commenced.

C. Discussion

It has been shown that the head bangers in this study had a statistically significantly higher rate of diagnosed otitis media than the matched group children. It will be noted that these were diagnosed and treated cases and not maternal impressions. It should also be borne in mind that a mild middle ear infection, painful though it may be, is often undetected in very young children. In such cases the pain would cause fretfulness and crying and the relief or amelioration of the discomfort would largely depend upon maternal perception and sympathy.

The response repertory of the infant is a limited one. In the first three months of life physical activity is characterized by an undifferentiated pattern of behavior as noted in the mass movement of extremities, lack of control and generally undirected activity. Reaction to intruding stimuli, be it noise, hunger, pain or other discomforts, elicits random activity modified by the constitutional differences of children.

The earliest gross muscle rhythmic activity patterns noted in this investigation was head rolling. It is proposed that this activity was accidentally discovered and found to be rewarding. Its early discovery is clearly associated with the fact that control of the head is the first differentiation in the cephalo-caudal progression of development. Once the discovery was made, its repetition was insured because of its intrinsic rewarding experience or because it served to obtain mother's attention. Subsequent frustration encouraged the repetition of the satisfying act increasing its habit strength.

In terms of primary causal factors no reason can be suggested for otitis to be related to head banging insofar as physiological or neurological relationships is concerned. It is apparent that the pain generated by this infection could have served to increase the state of tension thus raising the level of excitability and reactivity. The differential constitutional structure of the children could have been a mediating factor in response to such a stimulus, thus, the higher activity level of the head bangers could have produced a correspondingly more acute reaction pattern.

Reactions to stress are often marked by compulsive repetitive behavior. Foot tapping and drumming of fingers are excellent examples of nervous discharges that are characterized by simplicity or primitiveness in comparison with the workings of the normal mature nervous system. Reinforcement of this tendency for repetition may come from regularly repeated stimulations or from the reward that is obtained when the repetitive movement decreases the intensity of the primary stimulus. In folk parlance one notes the expression, "to rock with pain," this illustrates the possible contention that the pain stimulus served to release from the inhibitive control of the cortex normally meaningless movements and the reward of the lowering of the threshold of pain served to foster repetitiveness. The stimulus of an earache could produce such a reaction.

There is another possible relation of head banging to otitis. An ancient practice in the primitive days of dentistry was said to include the "pepper in the eyes" cure for a toothache. Be this truth or legend, the principle behind it is sound; the intensity of the primary source of pain is decreased with the introduction of a distracting pain stimulus. This conjecture suggests the possibility that head banging may actually be a form of pain relief. A child in pain may have hit his head in a shaking random movement and, finding that this contact relieved the exacerbating irritation caused by otitis, the movement was repeated for its rewarding experience. In such a situation the primary stimulus of pain served to establish the habit of head banging. The reward of pain relief or decrease in pain, served to strengthen the habit pattern of head banging. Through the mechanism of generalization, other negative stimuli were relieved by a return to the "rewarding" behavior of head banging.

References
1 Bender, L., Yarnell, H. An observation nursery: a study of 250 children in the psychiatric division of Bellevue Hospital. *Am. J. Psychiat.*, 1941; **97**, 1170.
2 Cameron, C. H. *The Nervous Child*. New York: Oxford Univ. Press, 1924.
3 Clark, L. P., Uniker, T. E. An analytic study of stereotyped habit movements in children. *J. Nerv. Ment. Dis.*, 1927; **66**, 46-50.

4 Coleman, W. M. Psychological significance of the body rhythms. *J. Comp. Psychol.*, 1921; **1**, 213-225
5 de Lissovoy, V. Head banging in early childhood; an exploratory study of an atypical behavior pattern. *(Unpublished thesis).* Cornell, 1959.
6 ————. Head banging in early childhood. *Child Dev.*, 1962; **33**, 43-56
7 ————. Head banging in early childhood; a study of incidence. *J. Pediat.*, 1961; **58**, 803-805
8 English, O. S., Pearson, G. H. Common Neuroses of Children and Adults. New York: Norton, 1937.
9 Fitz-Herbert, J. The origin of head banging; a suggested explanation with an illustrated case history. *J. Ment. Sci.*, 1950; **96**, 793-795
10 ————. Head banging and allied behavior; further observation. *J. Ment. Sci.*, 1952; **98**, 330-333
11 Freud, A. Aggression in relation to emotional development: normal and pathological. *In The Psychoanalytic Study of the Child.* (Vols. III-IV.). New York: International Univ. Press, 1949.
12 ————. *Three contributions to the theory of sex. The Basic Writings of Sigmund Freud.* New York: Modern Library, 1938.
13 Gesell, A. Infant and Child in the Culture of Today. New York: Harper, 1943.
14 Greenacre, P. Infant reactions to restraint. *In* Kluckhohn, C., & Murray, H. A. *(Eds.). Personality in Nature, Society and Culture.* New York: Knopf, 1931.
15 Langford, W. S. Psychopathological problems. *In* Holt, L. E. & McIntosh, I. *(Eds.). Holt's Diseases of Infancy and Childhood* (12th Ed.). New York: Appleton-Century, 1953.
16 Levy, D. M., & Patrick, H. T. Relations of infantile convulsions, head banging and breath holding to fainting and headaches in the parents. *Arch. Neurol. Psychiat.*, 1928; **19**, 867-887
17 Lourie, R. S. The role of rhythmic patterns in childhood. *Amer. J. Psychiat.*, 1949; **105**, 653-660
18 Mahler, M. Ego psychology applied to behavior problems. *In* Lewis, N. D., Pacella, B. L. *(Eds.). Modern Trends in Child Psychiatry.* New York: International Univ. Press, 1945.
19 Mittleman, B. Psychodynamics of motility. *Int. J. Psycho-Anal.*, 1958; **38**, 197-201.
20 Morse, J. L. *Clinical Pediatrics.* New York: Saunders, 1926.
21 Podolsky, E. (Ed.). *Encylopedia of Abberations.* New York: Philosophical Library, 1953.
22 Ribble, M. A. Infantile experience in relation to personality development. *In* Hunt, J. Mc.V. (Ed.). *Personality and Behavior Disorders, V.* New York: Ronald Press, 1944.
23 Siegel, S. Non-Parametric Statistics for the Behavioral Sciences. New York: McGraw-Hill, 1956.
24 Spitz, R., & Wolf, K. M. Autoerotism: Some empirical findings and hypotheses on three of its manifestations in the first year of life. *The Psychoanalytic Study of the Child, Vols. III-IV.* New York: International Univ. Press, 1949.

Reprinted from *J. Genetic Psychology*, 1963; **102**, 109-114 by kind permission of Vladimir de Lissovoy and the publishers The Journal Press, Provincetown, MA 02657.

SOCIAL CONTROL OF SELF-INJURIOUS BEHAVIOR OF ORGANIC ETIOLOGY

Edward G. Carr
State University of New York at Stony Brook

Jack J. McDowell
Emory University

The self-injurious scratching behavior of a normal 10-year-old child was successfully treated using a combination of time out for scratching plus tangible reinforcement for reductions in the number of body sores. The efficacy of this treatment was demonstrated using a reversal design. A 9-month follow-up revealed that the number of body sores was negligible. Although the scratching was initially elicited by organic factors (contact dermatitis), a detailed analysis suggested that the behavior was currently influenced by social reinforcement. These data support the general principle that many problems which have an organic etiology may acquire operant characteristics and therefore become amenable to behavioral intervention.

The severity of some medical conditions is strongly influenced by social-environmental factors. Recently, behavior modification techniques have been successfully used to ameliorate, in selected cases, such physical problems as seizures (Zlutnick, Mayville, & Moffat, 1975), migraine headaches (Sargent, Walters, & Green, 1973), and asthma (Neisworth & Moore, 1972). Physical conditions other than those listed above may also potentially benefit from behavioral analysis and intervention. For example, some individuals engage in severe and chronic self-injurious scratching which produces numerous excoriations. The physical damage caused by such behavior has been reversed by applying techniques such as extinction (Allen & Harris, 1966; Walton, 1960) or punishment (Drabman, 1978) directly to the scratching behavior. These studies are suggestive and useful but they share one common limitation, namely that the analysis reported is descriptive rather than experimental. In the present study an attempt was made for the first time to provide a detailed experimental analysis of the treatment of severe self-injurious scratching in a young, normal child. Unlike previously reported cases of excoriation, in which the origin of the problem was unknown, this child's scratching had a clear organic etiology, namely poison oak dermatitis. The observation that the scratching, which was originally controlled by organic factors, now appeared to be strongly influenced by social and stimulus control factors, provided an additional dimension of interest.

Method

Subject. Jim was a 10-year-old boy who lived at home with his parents and an older sister and attended a remedial classroom because of his poor performance in the regular classroom. His IQ on the WISC-R was 84. Motor milestones were within normal limits.

Jim began scratching in September 1973 at which time the family physician diagnosed the condition as contact dermatitis caused by poison oak. Standard treatment with neomycin sulfate was successful and the dermatitis cleared after a few weeks. The scratching, however, continued with varying degrees of severity until the child was brought to our clinic. In October 1976, at the time of intake, Jim's skin was covered with scars and lesions. At one point, Jim's teacher wanted to exclude him from class because she mistook

Portions of this paper were presented at the Annual Convention of the Association for Advancement of Behavior Therapy, San Francisco, December 1979. The authors thank Jody Binkoff, Crighton Newsom, and Harry Kalish for their helpful criticism. The encouragement and support of Jim's parents during the course of this study are gratefully acknowledged. Requests for reprints should be sent to Edward Carr, Department of Psychology, SUNY at Stony Brook, Stony Brook NY 11794.

the condition of his skin as evidence of a contagious disease. Classmates ridiculed him, and he was developing a reputation as a "freak."

Procedure. The study consisted of three phases. In the assessment phase, data were collected to identify the situations in which scratching was most likely to occur. In the functional analysis phase, social attention for scratching was systematically manipulated to see what effect this variable would have on the frequency of scratching. Finally, in the treatment phase, a combination of time out for scratching plus positive reinforcement for reductions in the total count of body sores was applied to ameliorate the problem.

Assessment phase. Virtually all of the scratching occurred at home. Through parental interviews, three activities were identified during which scratching reliably occurred from day to day: *Play, TV,* and *Talk. Play* involved interacting with neighborhood friends in outdoor backyard activities or indoor games, depending on the weather. *TV* involved watching any of several television programs. *Talk* referred to a period of time in which the family got together to discuss what each individual did during that day. On a given day, the duration of each activity might vary from 10 to 45 min with a median of 24 min.

Jim was observed each weekday after dinner for a period of 7 days. During the observation period, the frequency of scratching was counted for each activity that occurred on a particular night. Scratching was defined as any repetitive rubbing (using the nails) or picking at the face, scalp, or exposed arms. The behavior had to have lasted at least 2 sec to be counted. A separate instance of scratching was recorded whenever the time between bursts of the above behavior exceeded 2 sec. In addition, the observer recorded the frequency of social attention delivered contingent on scratching. Social attention was defined as any verbal statement concerning the scratching (e.g., "Jim, stop scratching") made either during the behavior or within 2 sec of its termination. Social attention was also defined as any attempt to restrain Jim's hands during an episode of scratching. Multiple occurrences of social attention during or after a given episode of scratching were counted as only a single instance of social attention. Each time that either scratching or social attention occurred, the observer made a tally mark on a sheet that was divided into 5-min intervals. Only completed 5-min intervals were used in the final computations.

Functional analysis phase. We attempted to systematically manipulate the frequency of contingent social attention during Talk time to assess the effect of this variable on the frequency of scratching. Because there was a risk that the increase in scratching brought about through contingent social attention might conceivably reopen old sores, we decided to restrict the analysis to a single 65 min session to minimize any physical damage that might occur. This phase of the study was conducted in a reversal design as follows: 15 min of extinction, followed by 30 min of social attention, followed by 20 min of extinction. The experimenter cued each change of condition for the parents by means of an inconspicuous hand signal. Prior to the start of the session, the parents were given the following instructions: "During extinction, do not make any comment to Jim when he scratches and do not attempt to restrain him physically from scratching. During social attention, each time that you see Jim scratching himself, tell him to stop."

Treatment phase. Since the above functional analysis suggested that scratching was an operant maintained by social attention, we began treatment by describing our results to Jim's parents in an attempt to motivate them to implement the program described below. The treatment phase was carried out over a 1½-year period. Since the original presenting problem was the presence of sores on various parts of the body, treatment success was defined in terms of a reduction in the number of body sores.

A baseline sore count was taken on two occasions spaced 3 weeks apart. Next, treatment was instituted for a period of 2 months. There were two components to the treatment package. First, the parents were told to send Jim to the time out room (a utility room located in one corner of the house) for 20 min each time that they observed his scratching. Time out was used instead of extinction because Jim's scratching annoyed his parents to such a degree that they were unable to ignore it for long periods of time. The second component of treatment involved positive reinforcement contingency.. At the start of each week, Jim was asked to choose a reinforcer to work for (e.g., a trip to the science museum, roller skating, etc.). He was told that he would earn the reinforcer at the end of the week provided that there was a reduction of at least two sores on his body compared to the sore count at the start

Table 1. Rate of scratching per min (numbers without parentheses) and rate of social attention per min (numbers in parentheses) during three different activities

Session	Activity		
	Play	Talk	TV
1	0.10 (0.00)	0.36 (0.00)	1.67 (0.50)
2	*	*	1.36 **
3	0.00 (0.00)	*	*
4	*	0.00 (0.00)	*
5	0.00 (0.00)	0.07 (0.07)	0.58 (0.13)
6	*	0.52 (0.08)	2.25 (0.95)
7	*	0.36 (0.00)	*
Mean	0.04 (0.00)	0.32 (0.03)	1.36 (0.42)

* Activity did not occur.
** Data lost due to a recording error.

of the week. If he did not reach this goal, he could earn the reinforcer at the end of the next week provided the requisite reduction in sores occurred, and so on. Once a reinforcer was earned, the sore count had to decrease by two more in order for the next reinforcer to be earned.

The next 2½ months constituted a natural reversal. Both parents lost their jobs and no longer had the money or the time to continue the treatment contingencies since they were out looking for new jobs. When the father got a new job, treatment was reinstated for a period of 4½ months. Finally, a 9-month follow-up period was carried out during which both time out and tangible reinforcement were discontinued.

During the treatment periods, sores were counted by the mother once per week whenever possible. During the reversal, two sore counts were made, spaced 3 weeks apart. Finally, during follow-up, sore counts were made every 1 or 2 months whenever it was convenient for the family to do so.

Reliability. During the assessment phase, reliability was taken by a second observer, naive to the purposes of the study, during four sessions, at least once for each type of activity. Inter-observer reliability was computed by dividing the smaller total frequency for each 5-min interval by the larger and multiplying by 100 to get a percent. Thus, each session yielded as many reliability counts as there were completed 5-min intervals. The mean reliability for scratching was 85% (range: 75% to 100%) and for social attention, 94% (range: 88% to 100%). During the functional analysis phase, the same reliability procedures were used. The mean reliability (assessed for each 5-min interval) was 82% for scratching (range: 72% to 100%) and 89% for social attention (range: 75% to 100%). Finally, during the treatment phase, 28 sore counts were made by the mother. For 10 of these (at least one for each condition), one of the experimenters counted sores for reliability purposes. A sore was defined as any red or pink lesion, or a scab. The reliability index was computed by dividing the smaller sore count by the larger and multiplying by 100 to get a percent. The mean reliability was 92% (range: 75% to 100%).

Results

The assessment phase data are summarized in Table 1. The rate of scratching was negligible during Play, moderate during Talk, and high during TV. Also the rate of scratching was highly corrrelated with the rate of contingent social attention (Pearson r = 0.96). Next, Fig. 1 shows the data for the functional analysis. The rate of scratching was negligible during the first extinction, increased sharply during social attention (i.e., the reversal), and decreased again to near zero in the final extinction. There was a strong correlation between rate of scratching and rate of programmed social attention (Pearson r = 0.98). Finally, Fig. 2 shows the data for the treatment phase. Sore counts were elevated during the baseline and reversal conditions and decreased to low levels during the treatment conditions. These trends are evident from the horizontal dotted lines which show the median sore count for each condition. (In treatment, sore counts low enough to merit

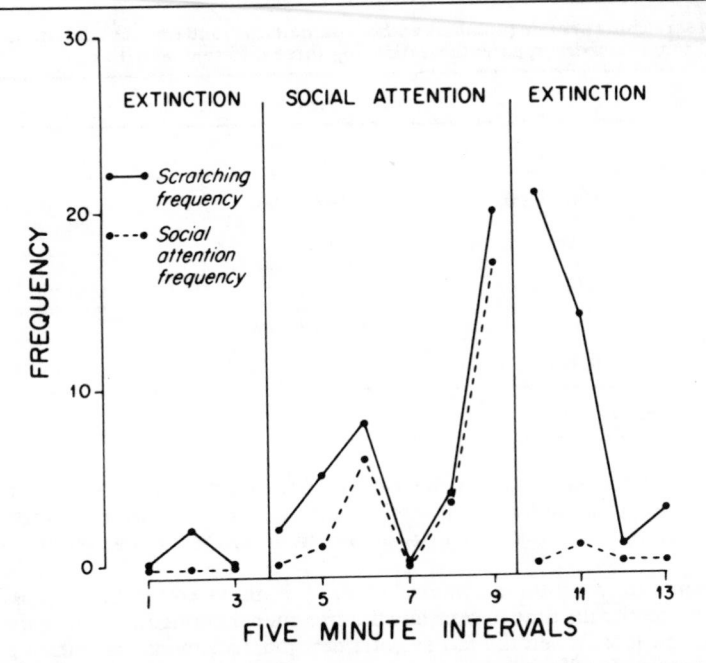

Fig. 1. Frequency of scratching during consecutive 5-min intervals. In the extinction condition, the parents were instructed to ignore the child's scratching. In the social attention condition, the parents were instructed to tell the child to stop scratching each time that he engaged in the behavior.

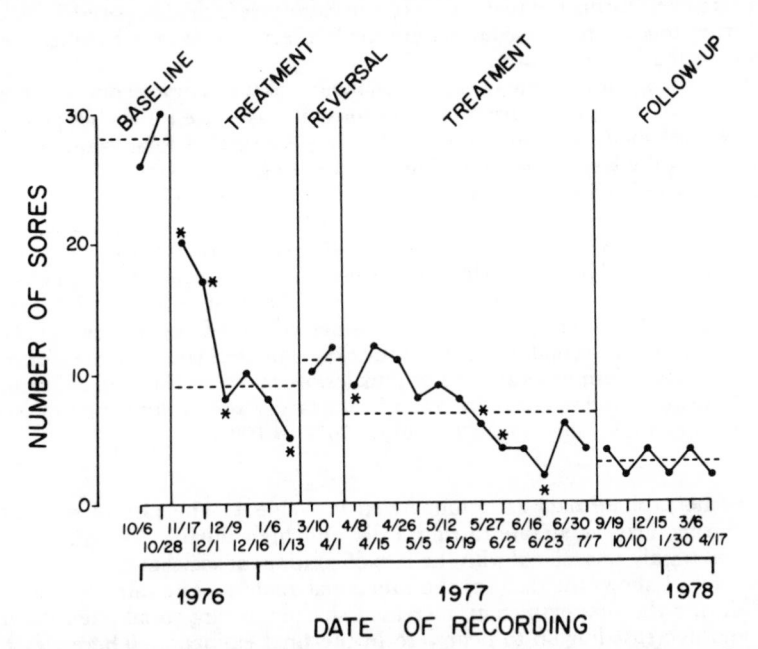

Fig. 2. Number of body sores recorded over a 1½-year period. During baseline and reversal, no treatment contingencies were in effect. During treatment, the child received time out for scratching plus positive reinforcement for reductions in the sore count. Sore counts low enough to merit reinforcement are indicated on the figure by an asterisk. The horizontal dotted lines represent the median sore count in each condition. Note that the recording dates shown on the abscissa are not equally spaced in time.

reinforcement are indicated on the figure by an asterisk.) During the 9-month follow-up, the sore count remained low. By the end of the study, Jim had only two sores, and these were almost completely healed.

Discussion

The present study is the first *experimental* demonstration, to the authors' knowledge, that self-injurious scratching in a normal individual can be eliminated using an operant, treatment package, which in this case consisted of a combination of time out for scratching plus positive reinforcement for sore count reduction. The reversal design· in Fig. 2 demonstrated that the elimination of the sores was the result of our treatment intervention and not simply a maturational effect. Just as importantly, treatment gains were maintained over a 9-month follow-up period. Anecdotal observations suggested that maintenance was the result of substantial social reinforcement from peers delivered as a consequence of Jim's improved physical appearance.

A second point of interest is that self-injurious scratching, initially elicited by organic factors, was found later to be influenced by social reinforcement. The rate of scratching was positively correlated with the rate of social attention (Table 1) and, more importantly, it could be systematically increased or decreased by the respective presentation or withdrawal of contingent social reinforcement (Fig. 1).

Other studies have demonstrated that self-injurious behavior can function as an operant, maintained by either positive reinforcement (Lovaas, Freitag, Gold, & Kassorla, 1965) or negative reinforcement (Carr, Newsom, & Binkoff, 1976). The present study makes an additional point, namely that even when self-injury has a distinct organic etiology (in this case, contact dermatitis), the behavior may nonetheless come to be influenced by social reinforcement factors. One can speculate that some children who injure themselves initially because of organic factors soon gain considerable social reinforcement by their unusual behavior. In this way, the behavior is perpetuated by social factors long after the original organic cause is gone (Carr, 1977). Interestingly, other investigators have also presented data which support the role of social reinforcement factors in maintaining problem behaviors of organic origin. Thus, asthmatic responding (Neisworth & Moore, 1972) and pain behavior (Fordyce, Fowler, Lehmann, & DeLateur, 1968) have been shown to be susceptible to reinforcement control. These data, as well as the data of the present study, suggest that many problems which have a clear organic etiology may acquire operant characteristics and therefore become amenable to behavioral intervention.

References

Allen, K. E., Harris, F. R. Eliminating a child's scratching by training the mother in reinforcement procedures. *Behav. Res. & Ther.*, 1966; **4**, 79-84.

Carr, E. G. The motivation of self-injurious behavior: A review of some hypotheses. *Psychol. Bull.*, 1977; **84**, 800-816.

Carr, E. G., Newsom, C. D., Binkoff, J. A. Stimulus control of self-destructive behavior in a psychotic child. *J. Abnorm. Child Psychol.*, 1976; **4**, 139-153.

Drabman, R. S. Decreasing the self-injurious behavior of a 3½-year-old from an economically underprivileged family through contingent soaking. *Behav. Ther.*, 1978; **1**, 19-20.

Fordyce, W. E., Fowler, R. S., Lehmann, J. F., deLateur, B. J. Some implications of learning in problems of chronic pain. *J. Chronic Diseas.*, 1968; **21**, 179-190.

Lovaas, O. I., Freitag, G., Gold, V. J., Kassorla, I. Experimental studies in childhood schizophrenia. I. Analysis of self-destructive behavior. *J. Experi. Child Psychol.*, 1965; **2**, 67-84.

Neisworth, J. T., Moore, F. Operant treatment of asthmatic responding with the parent as therapist. *Behav. Ther.*, 1972; **3**, 95-99.

Sargent, J. D., Walters, D. E., Green, E. E. Psychosomatic self-regulation of migraine headaches. *Seminars in Psychiat.*, 1973; **5**, 415-428.

Walton, D. The application of learning theory to the treatment of a case of neuro-dermatitis. *In* Eysenck, H. J. (Ed.), *Behavior therapy and the neuroses.* New York:Pergamon Press, 1960.

Zlutnick, S., Mayville, W. J., Moffat, S. Modification of seizure disorders: the interruption of behavioral chains. *J. Appl. Behav. Anal.*, 1975; **8**, 1-12.

Reprinted from *Behaviour Therapy*, 1980; **11**, 402-409 by kind permission of the authors and the publishers Association for Advancement of Behavior Therapy, New York, NY 10018.

EFFECT OF VIBRATORY STIMULATION ON A RETARDATE'S SELF-INJURIOUS BEHAVIOR[1]

Jon Bailey[2], Lee Meyerson

Arizona State University

Brief 1) response-contingent and 2) continuous, non-contingent vibration conditions were presented to a profoundly retarded, crib-bound child who exhibited several persistent self-injurious behaviors. Lever pressing, reinforced by six seconds of vibration, proved to be incompatible with these self-injurious behaviors and reduced them from baseline levels. Free continuous vibration, however, was even more effective. During the time it was in effect, self-injurious behavior in this subject was almost completely eliminated.

A continuing problem in institutions for the retarded are children who engage in self-injurious behavior (SIB). The generic term covers a long list of topographies including, among others, head-banging, face-slapping, hair pulling, biting or sucking skin from the extremities, scratching and tearing of flesh.

Prescription of sedatives or tranquilizers appears to be a common treatment for SIB but, unlike the mental hospital where the forced immobilization of patients has virtually disappeared, chemical restraints have not replaced the strait jacket, the strangulation cord, and other forms of physical restraint in institutions for the retarded. If drug therapy fails to reduce SIB, and alternative treatments are not readily available, the self-injurious retardate may be placed in restraints for long periods — possibly for a lifetime.

An obvious behavioral approach to the control of SIB is the positive reinforcement of an incompatible response. Lovaas, Freitag, Gold, and Kassorla (1965), Allen and Harris (1966), and Peterson and Peterson (1968) reported that social approval for behavior that was different from, or incompatible with, SIB was effective in reducing SIB in the cases they studied. Breland (1965) and others have observed that both aggressive and self-injurious behaviors decrease if reinforcement is available for constructive activities. In extending this approach, however, it is not clear what stimulus might serve as a convenient and effective reinforcer for deteriorated, crib-bound, self-injurious retardates who appear to be oblivious to social stimuli.

The present investigation was stimulated by a demonstration that contingent, vibratory reinforcement maintained consistent, long-term lever pressing in a seven-year-old, crib-bound, self-injurious retardate (Bailey and Meyerson, 1969). In this report, the effects on SIB of contingent and non-contingent vibratory stimulation are presented.

Method

Subject. The subject, whose descriptive characteristics were reported previously (Meyerson, Kerr and Michael, 1967; Bailey and Meyerson, 1969) engaged almost constantly during his waking hours in self-stimulatory and self-injurious behavior unless he was physically restrained. The SIBs, which resulted in visible tissue damage, were chewing on fingers and hands, and hitting head or feet against the bars of his crib.

The subject had been conditioned previously to press a lever which activated a vibrator attached to his bed. He was not restrained, receiving medication or involved in any other therapy during this study.

Apparatus. An industrial vibrator (Model DVE-10, Martin Engineering Co., Salt Lake City) was mounted on the underside of the springs of the subject's crib. It was activated, by

1. This paper is based on a thesis submitted by the senior author in partial fulfillment of the M.A. degree at Arizona State University. This investigation was supported in part by Office of Education Grant No. 5-0415. Preparation of the manuscript was partially supported by NICHHD grant HD-00183-03 to the Bureau of Child Research, University of Kansas. The authors are indebted to Brian Jacobson whose technical assistance was invaluable for this study.

2. Now at Florida State University.

wiring to appropriate electro-mechanical programming equipment, for six seconds by one press of a leather-padded oval lever (8.5″ x 5.5″) which was attached to the subject's crib within easy reach of his hand; or, alternatively, for 10 minutes by an experimenter-controlled switch.

Lever presses were counted and recorded on a Gerbrands cumulative recorder. SIBs, as they occurred, were recorded by an observer by means of a hand-held microswitch connected to a second Gerbrands recorder. A six-pen event recorder was used to assess the reliability of recording SIB events.

Procedure. During seven sessions of 30 to 60 minutes each, vibratory stimulation was provided under two conditions:

1) Response-contingent: six seconds of vibration each time the subject activated his lever if the vibrator was not already operating. Additional presses while the vibrator was running did not extend the vibration time resulting from the first press.

2) Non-contingent: 10 minutes of free, continuous vibration.

Under each condition, an observer stood near the child's crib and recorded SIBs via a hand-held switch connected to a cumulative recorder. A hand-chewing response was recorded when the subject inserted a finger or hand into his mouth, at least up to the knuckle, and lateral jaw movements were observed. A hit of head or foot to the bars of the crib was counted when the sound of these extremities being struck against the bars could be heard five feet away.

Operant levels of SIBs and of unreinforced lever pressing were obtained in the first 10 minutes of each session. In subsequent 10 minute periods, one of three conditions was in effect: response contingent vibration, non-contingent vibration, or extinction.

The reliability of recording SIBs was assessed by two observers independently, but simultaneously, observing the subject and recording SIB events on separate, parallel channels of a multi-pen event recorder. An agreement was counted if both observers activated their pens within a one-second interval. Reliability was calculated by dividing the number of such agreements by the sum of agreements and disagreements.

Results

Three reliability checks with two observers were made on two separate days. Agreement ranged from 75% to 91% and averaged 86%.

Figure 1 shows the typical relationship between total SIBs and lever pressing during operant level, response contingent vibration and extinction. It can be seen that SIB varied inversely with lever pressing. When vibratory stimulation was contingent on lever pressing, the rate of lever pressing was high and SIB was low. In comparison with operant levels and extinction conditions, the functional incompatability of lever pressing and SIB is evident.

Figure 2 displays the results of a typical session when response contingent vibration followed a 10-minute period of free vibration. It is apparent from this comparison that free vibration was much more effective in reducing the frequency of SIB than was response contingent vibration.

Figure 3, a record of one of the longer experimental sessions, shows that regardless whether response-contingent vibration preceded or followed a period of free vibration, non-contingent vibration resulted in fewer SIBs. Response contingent vibration reduced SIB below the initial operant level, but free vibration had the effect of almost completely eliminating SIB.

Discussion

The results supported the expectation that the frequency of SIB would be reduced if the presentation of a reinforcing stimulus was made contingent upon a response temporally and functionally incompatible with a self-injurious response. What was surprising, however, was the strikingly greater control over SIB that was obtained by the presentation of free, non-contingent vibratory stimuli.

The data lend support to some speculations in the literature that self-injurious responses in some retardates represent attempts to obtain sensory input under extremely restrictive environmental conditions such as exist in some institutions (McKinney, 1962; Provence and Ritvo, 1961); attempts to overcome some physiological barrier to perceiving stimulus input

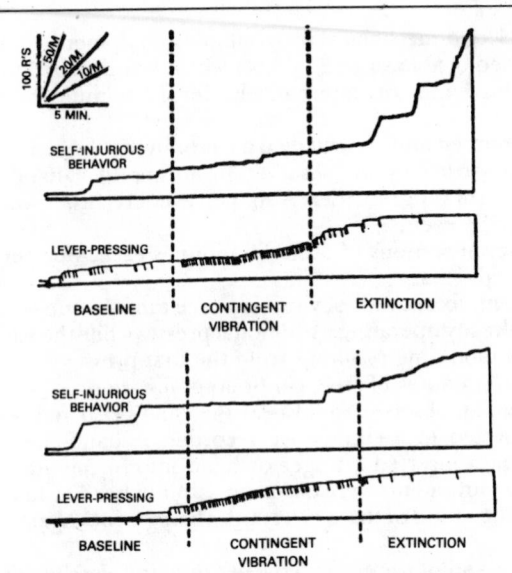

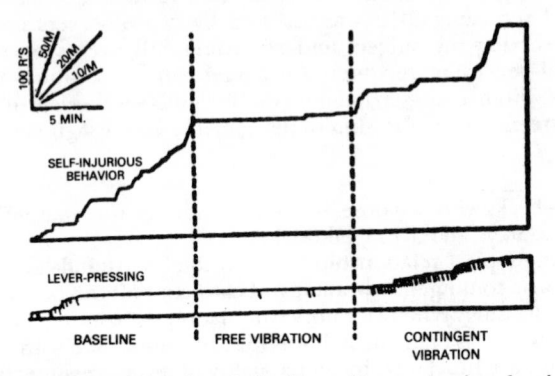

Fig. 1. Cumulative records of self-injurious behavior and lever pressing for two sessions showing the effect of vibratory reinforcement of lever pressing on concomitant self-injurious behavior.

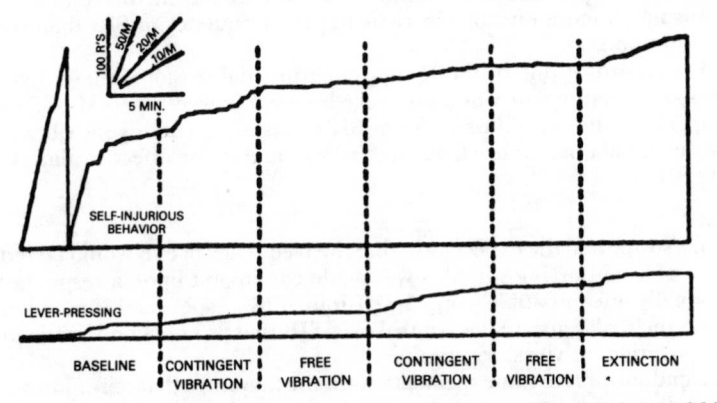

Fig. 2. Cumulative records of self-injurious behavior and lever pressing showing the effects of free continuous vibration and vibratory reinforcement of lever pressing on self-injurious behavior.

Fig. 3. Cumulative records of self-injurious behavior and lever pressing showing a within session comparison of response-contingent vibration and free, continuous vibration on self-injurious behavior.

such as may exist in some organically defective organisms (DeLissovoy, 1963; Kravitz, Rosenthal, Teplitz, Murphy and Lesser, 1960); or some combination of the two. These speculations are compatible with the experimental literature on sensory deprivation in man (Bexton, Heron and Scott, 1954) and animals (Butler, 1953; Butler and Alexander, 1955) which suggests that sensory input may function as a primary reinforcer. (See also Kish, 1966 for a review of this literature).

From a practical standpoint, and because of its potentially wider theoretical import also, further research to determine the long-term durability and the relevant parameters of non-contingent, sensory stimulation in reducing the SIBs of retardates would be desirable.

References

Bailey, J., Meyerson, L. Vibration as a reinforcer with a profoundly retarded child. *J. Appl. Behav. Anal.*, 1969; **2**, 135-137.

Bexton, W. H., Heron, W., Scott, T. H. Effects of decreased variation in the sensory environment. *Canadian J. Psychol.*, 1954; **8**, 70-76.

Breland, M. *In* Bensberg, G. (Ed.). *Teaching the Mentally Retarded.* Atlanta: Southern Regional Education Board, 1965.

Butler, R. A. Discrimination learning by rhesus monkeys to visual-exploration motivation. *J. Comparat. & Physiol. Psychol.*, 1953; **46**, 95-98.

Butler, R. A., Alexander, H. M. Daily patterns of visual exploratory behavior in the monkey. *J. Comparat. & Physiol. Psychol.*, 1955; **48**, 247-249.

deLissovoy, V. Head-banging in early childhood, a suggested cause. *J. Genet. Psychol.*, 1963; **102**, 109-114.

Kish, G. Studies of sensory reinforcement. *In* Honig, W. K. (Ed.). *Operant Behavior: areas of research and application.* (pp.109-159). New York: Appleton-Century-Crofts, 1966.

Kravitz, M., Rosenthal, V., Teplitz, Z., Murphy, J., Lesser, R. A study of head-banging in infants and children. *Diseas. Nerv. Syst.*, 1960; **21**, 203-208.

Lovaas, O. I., Freitag, G., Gold, V. J., Kassorla, I. C. Experimental studies in childhood schizophrenia: analysis of self destructive behavior. *J. Exper. Child Psychol.*, 1965; **2**, 67-84.

McKinney, J. A multidimensional study of the behavior of severely retarded boys. *Child Dev.*, 1962; **33**, 923-938.

Meyerson, L., Kerr, N., Michael, J. L. Behavior modification in rehabilitation. *In* Bijou, S., Baer, D. (Eds.). *Child Development: readings in experimental analysis.* (pp214-239). New York: Appleton-Century-Crofts, 1967.

Peterson, R. F., Peterson, L. R. Use of positive reinforcement in the control of self destructive behavior in a retarded boy. *J. Experi. Child Psychol.*, 1968; **6**, 351-360.

Provence, S., Ritvo, S. Effects of deprivation on institutionalized infants. *In The Psychoanalytic Study of the Child.* (Vol. XVI). ,New York: International University Press, Inc., 1961.

Reprinted from *Psychol. Aspects of Disabil.*, 1970; **17**:3, 133-137 by kind permission of the authors and the American Psychological Association, Arizona State University, Tempe, Arizona 85281.

SENSORY EXTINCTION: A PROCEDURE FOR ELIMINATING SELF-STIMULATORY BEHAVIOR IN DEVELOPMENTALLY DISABLED CHILDREN[1]

Arnold Rincover[2]

University of North Carolina at Greensboro

This study was designed to investigate the role of sensory reinforcement in the motivation of self-stimulation. If self-stimulatory behavior is maintained by its sensory consequences, such as the proprioceptive, auditory, or visual stimulation it produces, then such behavior should extinguish when those sensory consequences are not permitted. The present study introduces a new procedure, Sensory Extinction, in which certain sensory consequences are masked or removed, to examine whether self-stimulation is operant behavior maintained by sensory reinforcement. The effectiveness of Sensory Extinction was assessed by a reversal design for each of three autistic children, and the results showed the following. First, self-stimulation reliably extinguished when a certain sensory consequence was removed, then increased when that consequence was permitted. This was replicable within and across children. Second, different Sensory Extinction procedures were required for different self-stimulatory behaviors, since the sensory reinforcers supporting them were idiosyncratic across children. Finally, regarding clinical gains, the data suggest that Sensory Extinction may be a relatively convenient and rapid alternative for the treatment of self-stimulation. The present findings extend the efficacy of extinction as a behavior-modification technique to instances in which the reinforcer is purely sensory. The implications of these results for the treatment of other forms of deviant behavior are discussed.

One of the most salient and bizarre characteristics of psychotic children is self-stimulatory behavior. Such activity, typically described as persistent, stereotyped, repetitive mannerisms, is considered one of the defining characteristics of autism (Rimland, 1964) and has been observed in approximately two-thirds of the institutionalized retarded population (Berkson & Davenport, 1962; Kaufman & Levitt, 1965). These children may spend virtually all of their waking hours spinning objects, flapping their fingers or arms, rhythmically rocking back and forth, echoing, and the like.

Self-stimulation represents one of the most formidable obstacles to the treatment of psychotic children. Such behavior appears to provide no external consequences and has been notoriously resistant to extinction (Newsom, Carr, & Lovaas, 1977). Despite some success with various punishment procedures (Baumeister & Forehand, 1972; Foxx & Azrin, 1973; Lovaas, Schaeffer, & Simmons, 1965) and differential reinforcement of alternative behavior (Repp, Deitz, & Speir, 1974), the generalized, durable elimination of self-stimulatory behavior remains difficult to obtain (cf. Forehand & Baumeister, 1976). This resistance to treatment is particularly unfortunate in that a number of positive "side effects" have been observed when self-stimulation is even temporarily reduced. Risley (1968) and Lovaas and Newsom (1976) discuss various prosocial and attentional behaviors that seem to arise as a product of suppressing self-stimulation, while others have reported that discrimination learning (Koegel & Covert, 1972) and appropriate play (Koegel, Firestone, Kramme, & Dunlap, 1974) may increase when self-stimulation is restrained. Lovaas, Litrownik, and Mann (1971) observed that previously established stimulus control

[1] This investigation was supported in part by an Excellence Fund Faculty Research Fellowship from the University of North Carolina and grant no. G007802084 from the Office of Education. The author would like to acknowledge the helpful comments of Drs. Edward Carr and Crighton Newsom on an earlier version of this manuscript, and the valuable discussions of Drs. Steven Hayes and Rosemary Nelson.
[2] Address all correspondence to Arnold Rincover, Department of Psychology, University of North Carolina, Greensboro, North Carolina 27412.

was disrupted during episodes of self-stimulation, yet recovered when self-stimulation was absent. Solnick, Rincover, and Peterson, and Peterson (1977, Experiment 1) found that a *reinforcing* effect of time-out, on tantrum behavior, was due to the opportunity to engage in self-stimulation during the time-out interval, and tantrums were then eliminated when self-stimulation was restrained contingent upon tantrums. Equally important, excessive self-stimulation is socially stigmatizing; it looks bizarre and undoubtedly repels many potentially beneficial social contacts.

Since self-stimulation is common among psychotic children, and clearly interferes with many classes of adaptive behavior, it would appear worthwhile to investigate the variables that may maintain and support this behavior. Various motivational theories have been proposed to account for self-stimulatory behavior, including dysfunctioning connections between the vestibular system and the cerebellum or brainstem (Ornitz, 1974), frustration (Forehand & Baumeister, 1971), social deprivation (Harlow & Harlow, 1971), superstitious conditioning (Spradlin & Girardeau, 1966), overarousal (Ritvo, Ornitz, & LaFranchi, 1968), underarousal (Ellis, 1973), and alternating states of arousal (Sroufe, Steucher, & Stutzer, 1973). At this time, none of these hypotheses can yet be discarded or held up as a valid explanation of the etiology or maintenance of self-stimulation (cf. Newsom et al., 1977).

Recently, however, a relatively new proposal has surfaced, which at first glance appears to provide a parsimonious explanation of much of the literature: The notion is that self-stimulation is operant behavior maintained by its *sensory* consequences (Azrin, Kaplan, & Foxx, 1973; Rincover, Newsom, Lovaas, & Koegel, 1977). To illustrate, repetitive finger flapping might be conceptualized as being maintained by the specific proprioceptive stimulation it produces, while persistent delayed echolalia, on the other hand, may be motivated by its preferred auditory feedback. A substantial amount of data has accumulated which demonstrates such a functional relationship between operant behavior and its sensory consequences (Hunt & Quay, 1961), an operation described as "sensory reinforcement" (Kish, 1966). Furthermore, a sensory reinforcement explanation has been offered to account for several phenomena observed in psychotic children, including an inverse relationship between self-stimulation and appropriate play (Koegel et al., 1974), the durability of operant responding for sensory stimulation (Rincover et al., 1977), and the immediate and dramatic increase in other self-stimulatory behaviors when a predominant self-stimulatory behavior is suppressed (Newsom, 1974).

An investigation of the role of sensory reinforcement in self-stimulation may increase both our understanding and our ability to treat self-stimulatory behavior in developmentally disabled children. Specifically, if sensory consequences reinforce self-stimulation, then their removal should lead to a reduction in this behavior. The present study introduces a new procedure, Sensory Extinction, in which certain sensory consequences are masked or removed in an attempt to assess whether self-stimulation is operant behavior maintained by sensory reinforcement.

Method

Subjects

Three developmentally delayed children, two boys (Reggie and Robert) and one girl (Brenda), participated in this experiment. Each child was living at home and attending our experimental classroom program at UNC-G during the day (described in Koegel & Rincover, 1974; Rincover & Koegel, 1977a, b). All were severely psychotic, displaying minimal, if any, intelligible verbal behavior, large amounts of self-stimulatory behavior, and minimal responsiveness to instruction. Brenda was mute, evidencing only a limited set of vowel sounds and no words. Robert displayed immediate echolalia, as he meaninglessly repeated words or phrases said to him. Reggie, who was severely visually impaired, was primarily echolalic, although the meaningful use of words has been observed on occasion. Two children, Brenda and Robert, were found to be untestable when administered the Leiter International Performance Scale by an independent agency, while Reggie achieved an MA of 3.9. Brenda, age 7, and Robert, age 10, had been diagnosed autistic by an independent agency, while Reggie, age 14, was classified profoundly retarded.

Thèse three children were selected for this study on the basis of their high rates of self-stimulatory behavior. In each case, parents, previous teachers, and/or psychologists reported that self-stimulation was dominant in the child's repertoire for a minimum of the past 5 years.

Selection of sensory consequences to be tested

We observed each child throughout the day and consulted with the teachers in an attempt to identify possible sensory consequences of their self-stimulatory behavior. We found that Reggie would incessantly spin objects, particularly a plate, in a stereotyped, repetitive manner. However, when he twirled the plate, he would also cock his head to the side and lean toward it, seeming to listen to the plate as it was spinning. This suggested that the auditory feedback may have been an important consequence of Reggie's self-stimulation. Robert engaged in excessive finger flapping, in which he had one or both hands in front of his face and vigorously moved the fingers (but not the arms) back and forth. In this case, two sensory consequences were identified for testing: the visual feedback from watching the finger movements, and the proprioceptive stimulation from the finger movement itself. Brenda's self-stimulatory behavior consisted of twirling objects, such as a feather or a string of beads, in front of her eyes. For Brenda, as with Robert, both the visual and the proprioceptive components were targeted for testing.

On this basis we constructed three types of Sensory Extinction procedures for children in this study: one to eliminate the auditory feedback from plate spinning (Reggie); a second to mask the proprioceptive stimulation, from both finger flapping (Robert) and object manipulation (Brenda); and a third procedure to remove the visual feedback for all three children.

Setting and apparatus

Each session, lasting 20 min, was conducted in a 2.5×2.5m experimental classroom. A child was seated at a circular table, .9m in diameter, situated in the center of the classroom. On the table was the preferred object a child used to engage in self-stimulatory behavior: a plate for Reggie and a string of beads for Brenda. Standing in the corner of the room, facing the child, was an experimentally naive undergraduate psychology major who recorded self-stimulatory behavior.

During Sensory Extinction sessions we attempted to eliminate a particular sensory consequence of a given self-stimulatory behavior. Three types of Sensory Extinction procedures were used, corresponding to the three types of sensory feedback identified for testing (auditory, visual, and proprioceptive). First, in order to eliminate the auditory feedback from Reggie's plate spinning, carpeting was installed atop the table in the classroom. The carpeting was .6cm thick and completely covered the surface of the table. The surface of the carpet was hard and flat so as not to restrict the plate from spinning: however, four naive observers each reported that no sound was audible from spinning the plate on the carpeted table. A second Sensory Extinction procedure was designed to mask the proprioceptive stimulation from finger flapping (Robert) and object manipulation (Brenda). A small vibratory mechanism was taped to the back of a child's hand, generating a repetitive low-intensity, high-frequency pulsation. The vibrator (Pollenex, Model No. 123927ND) was cylindrical in shape, approximately 2.5cm in diameter and 7.6cm long, and was driven by two small ("D") batteries. Significantly, the vibrator did not physically restrict self-stimulatory behavior. The final Sensory Extinction procedure involved removing the visual consequences for each of the three children. For this purpose a blindfold was introduced, consisting of a handkerchief, once folded, snugly placed over the child's eyes and tied behind his head.

Design and procedures

Baseline sessions were alternated with Sensory Extinction sessions, in a reversal design, to assess whether self-stimulation would decrease when one of its sensory consequences was removed. In addition, a multiple-baseline design was used across subjects in which Sensory Extinction was introduced at different times for different children.

During Baseline no attempt was made to interfere with self-stimulatory behavior. At the beginning of each session, an undergraduate psychology student brought the child into the room, sat him at the table, and then moved to a corner of the room to record self-stimulation. There were no further interactions for the remainder of the 20-min session. On the table and within arm's reach was the child's preferred object of self-stimulation, a plate for Reggie and a string of beads for Brenda.

Sensory Extinction sessions were identical to baseline, with one exception: the addition of a stimulus designed to eliminate a particular sensory consequence of the child's self-stimulatory behavior. The "Sensory Extinction:Auditory" condition, used only with Reggie, denotes that the table was carpeted to eliminate the auditory feedback from plate spinning. The "Sensory Extinction:Proprioceptive" condition, used with Brenda and Robert, refers to the use of a vibrator to mask the proprioceptive stimulation from bead twirling and finger flapping. In the "Sensory Extinction:Visual" condition, a blindfold was used to mask the visual feedback from plate spinning, bead twirling, and finger flapping.

When a Sensory Extinction procedure was found to be effective for a given child, follow-up sessions were planned. These sessions were designed simply to assess whether the Sensory Extinction procedure would remain useful over an extended period of time. During the follow-up phase the Sensory Extinction procedure was in effect for the duration of each session (20 min), and sessions were conducted daily (5 days per week). Data were recorded at approximately 2-week intervals for each child.

Recording and reliability

Self-stimulatory behavior was defined individually for each child: plate-spinning was recorded for Reggie, finger flapping for Robert, and twirling for Brenda. (In addition, an "Other" category was included for each child in order to monitor the occurrence of new forms of self-stimulation; however, other forms of self-stimulation were rarely observed and consequently these data are not presented in the results). A time-sampling recording procedure was used, in which an observer alternately watched the child for 5 sec then recorded for 15 sec, resulting in a total of 60 observations per (20 min) session. If self-stimulation was noted at any time during a 5-sec recording interval, the observer placed a $\sqrt{}$ mark in the appropriate box on a precoded data sheet. After each session occurrences were totaled and then divided by 60, in order to calculate the percent of self-stimulation for that session.

The reliability of recording was assessed in the following manner. Two experimentally naive observers independently recorded self-stimulation, with one observer in the classroom and the other seated in the adjoining observation room. Using a "bug in the ear" device one observer said "Start" and "Stop" to signal the beginning and end of each 5-sec observation interval in the time-sampling procedure. Each observer recorded the presence ($\sqrt{}$) or absence (0) of self-stimulation during each of the 60 observations. A total of 18 reliability sessions were conducted, with at least one reliability measure for each condition of each child. Reliability was calculated for each session by dividing the total number of observer agreements by 60, and then multiplying by 100. The average reliability for recording self-stimulation was .83 (range: .73 to 1.00).

Results

The results of the Sensory Extinction procedure are shown for each child in Figure 1. The percent of self-stimulation is presented on the ordinate of each graph and sessions are presented on the abscissa. The Sensory Extinction:Auditory condition signifies that the table was carpeted to remove the auditory feedback, the Sensory Extinction:Visual condition represents sessions in which the child was blindfolded, and the Sensory Extinction:Proprioceptive condition denotes sessions with the vibrator.

Looking first at Reggie's (upper graph), it is apparent that removing the auditory feedback from plate spinning produced a substantial decrease in self-stimulation. During two initial Baseline sessions self-stimulation occurred at a relatively high rate, 42 and 72%, respectively. The Sensory Extinction procedure was then introduced, specifically removing the auditory feedback, and Reggie's self-stimulatory behavior decreased to 0 and remained

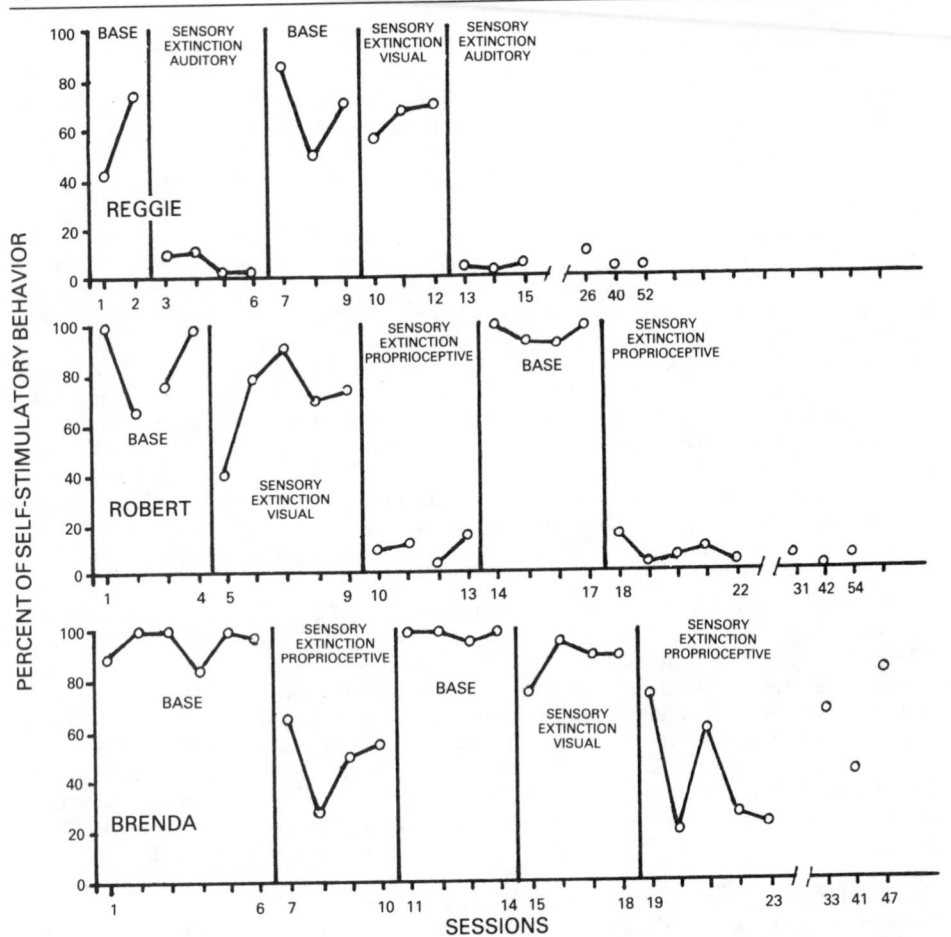

Fig. 1. Percent occurrence of self-stimulation, during Baseline and Sensory Extinction conditions, is plotted on the ordinate for Reggie, Robert, and Brenda. The Sensory Extinction:Auditory condition signifies that the auditory sensory consequences of self-stimulation were removed, while the Sensory Extinction:Proprioceptive and Sensory Extinction:Visual conditions signify that the proprioceptive and visual consequences were removed, respectively.

very low for four consecutive sessions (range 0-7%). When the Baseline condition was subsequently reinstituted in session 7, self-stimulation increased to 83% and remained at a high rate for three consecutive sessions (range: 52-83%). At that point, the visual feedback from plate spinning was removed for the first time, in order to assess whether the visual consequences were instrumental in maintaining Reggie's self-stimulation. The Sensory Extinction:Visual condition shows that self-stimulation remained at a relatively high rate over the next three sessions, averaging 58%, which suggests that visual stimulation did not reinforce Reggie's self-stimulatory behavior. Beginning with session 13 the Sensory Extinction:Auditory condition was reintroduced, and the extinction of plate spinning was replicated, as self-stimulation immediately decreased and stabilized at 0 over the next three sessions. Subsequent follow-up data (sessions 26, 40 and 52) show that self-stimulatory behavior was maintained at or near 0 over a period of 2 months, suggesting that the sensory extinction procedure remained effective over an extended period of time. Overall, the data suggest that Reggie's self-stimulation was maintained by its auditory consequences and could be extinguished by removing those auditory consequences.

The data for Robert show a similar effect of Sensory Extinction. During four Baseline sessions, finger flapping averaged 83% (range: 65-98%). When the visual consequences were then removed, in sessions 5-9, self-stimulation initially dropped a bit but then increased to 78% and remained at a high rate over four consecutive sessions. At this point the Sensory Extinction:Proprioceptive condition was introduced for the first time, and self-stimulation immediately decreased to 5% and remained low for four consecutive sessions (range: 0-12%). Additional sessions are presented in which first Baseline and then Sensory Extinction:Proprioceptive sessions were reintroduced, and the effect of the Sensory Extinction procedure was replicated. Data obtained during follow-up observations in sessions 31, 42, and 54 show that this procedure retained its effectiveness over several weeks. In short, the data suggest that Robert's self-stimulation, like Reggie's, was maintained by sensory reinforcement and could be extinguished by removing those sensory consequences. In Robert's case, however, the sensory reinforcers appeared to be proprioceptive.

The data obtained for Brenda (lower graph) also show that Sensory Extinction produced a decrease in self-stimulation, although the change was not as dramatic as that found for the other two children. Object twirling averaged 95% during Baseline and subsequently decreased to an average of 49% when the proprioceptive feedback was masked. After the base rate was recovered, the visual consequences were then removed, and little if any change in self-stimulation was noted. When the Sensory Extinction:Proprioceptive condition was then introduced for the second time, a decrease in self-stimulation was replicated as object twirling decreased to an average of 40%. Follow-up measures obtained over the next 2 months revealed that object twirling was observed during 70, 42, and 83% of sessions 33, 41, and 47, respectively.

Discussion

The main purpose of this study was to assess the role of sensory reinforcement in self-stimulation. The results may be summarized as follows. First, the data show that self-stimulation was reliably decreased when a certain sensory consequence was removed, then increased when that consequence was permitted. Importantly, this was found to be replicable within and across children. Second, it is notable that different Sensory extinction procedures were required for different self-stimulatory behaviors, since the sensory reinforcers supporting them were idiosyncratic across children. Finally, regarding clinical gains, the data show that the Sensory Extinction procedure was a relatively rapid and durable technique for suppressing self-stimulatory behavior.

The present results support the notion that self-stimulation is operant behavior maintained by sensory reinforcement, since such behavior decreased or was eliminated when one of its sensory consequences was removed. Current theories suggesting that self-stimulation emerges when the child is "underaroused" or "overaroused" do not easily account for these data, primarily because the suppressive effect of removing sensory consequences was specific to a particular sensory modality. For example, Robert's hand flapping decreased when its proprioceptive consequences were removed but not when the visual consequences were removed, suggesting that the general level of arousal, per se, was not instrumental in the decrement observed. Rather, the data suggest that such stereotypic behavior is more a function of the *type* of sensory stimulation (i.e., its reinforcing properties) than the *amount* of stimulation, although a more substantial change in stimulation level might produce results more in keeping with arousal hypotheses (e.g., Zubeck, 1969).

Clinically speaking, these data may suggest that Sensory Extinction procedures could be useful in the treatment of self-stimulation. The Sensory Extinction procedures used in this study virtually eliminated self-stimulatory behavior in two children and reduced it by approximately 50% in the third. In addition, the Sensory Extinction procedures appeared to be relatively efficient, requiring minimal staff training and child surveillance, producing rapid results, and retaining its effectiveness over time. Given the many detrimental effects of self-stimulation on learning (e.g., Koegel & Covert, 1972), and the oft-cited difficulty in eliminating self-stimulation in a durable manner (Forehand & Baumeister, 1976; Newsom, 1974), we viewed the present data as encouraging. At the same time, however, several questions remain to be explored. First, although a decrease in Brenda's self-stimulation was observed during Sensory Extinction, it was not as substantial as that found for the other two children. One explanation might be that Brenda's object twirling was maintained by multiple sensory reinforcers (e.g., proprioceptive plus tactile), while only one was removed in this study. If multiply determined, then removing additional sensory consequences might produce a greater decrease in self-stimulation. Second, in the present study naive observers were exposed to a Sensory Extinction procedure in an attempt to determine whether the intervention did in fact mask or remove the sensory consequences targeted; it would of course be more instructive to have an independent measure that directly assesses the degree of masking for each child. Third, further research is obviously needed, with additional children and self-stimulatory topographies, before any statement can be made regarding the generality of Sensory Extinction procedures. The conditions under which Sensory Extinction may be the treatment of choice for self-stimulatory behavior can only be clarified by future research addressed to issues such as these.

The second and perhaps more important implication for treatment is that the Sensory Extinction procedure may serve to *identify potent reinforcers* for teaching autistic children. For example, the data showing that Reggie's plate spinning was maintained by its auditory consequences suggest that such auditory stimuli are extremely powerful reinforcers for him, since they were capable of supporting so much self-stimulatory behavior. The implication is that auditory consequences might profitably be used for educational purposes, to teach and support a large amount of adaptive behavior. If these sensory reinforcers can be used in treatment to sustain a high level of motivation, then it should follow that the treatment gains obtained with these children may be substantially increased. Preliminary results have in fact shown that external sensory reinforcers can be programmed to shape appropriate behavior (Fineman, 1968; Rincover et al., 1977), and that they are more resitant to satiation than the more commonly used edible reinforcers (Rincover & Berry, 1977).

Prior to this study, the use of extinction has been restricted almost exclusively to behaviors maintained by social reinforcement (e.g., Baer and Wolf, 1970; Bandura, 1969, pp. 355-423). The present findings extend the efficacy of extinction as a behavior-modification technique to instances in which the reinforcer is purely sensory. Furthermore, since previous authors have suggested that sensory consequences may play an important motivational role in several forms of psychopathology, including certain sexual disorders, hallucinations, and compulsions (e.g., Lovaas & Newsom, 1976), investigations of the generality of Sensory Extinction procedures may be a profitable area of future research.

Reference Note
1 Rincover, A., & Berry, K. *Comparing the motivational properties of sensory and edible reinforcers in the treatment of autistic children.* Paper presented at the annual meeting of the Association for the Advancement of Behavior Therapy, Atlanta, 1977.

References
Azrin, N. H., Kaplan, S. J., Foxx, R. M. Autism reversal: Eliminating stereotyped self-stimulation of retarded individuals. *Am. J. Ment. Defic.*, 1973; **78**, 241-248.
Baer, D. B., Wolf, M. M. Recent examples of behavior modification in preschool settings. *In* Neuringer, C., Michael, J. L. (Eds.). *Behavior Modification in Clinical Psychology.* New York: Appleton-Century-Crofts, 1970.
Bandura, A. *Principles of Behavior Modification.* New York: Holt, Rinehart & Winston, 1969.
Baumeister, A. A., Forehand, R. Effects of contingent shock and verbal command on body rocking of retardates. *J. Clin. Psychol.*, 1972; **28**, 586-590.
Berkson, G., Davenport, R. K. Stereotyped movements in mental defectives: I. Initial survey. *Am. J. Ment. Defic.*, 1962; **66**, 849-852.
Davison, G. C., Neale, J. M. *Abnormal psychology: an experimental clinical approach.* New York: Wiley, 1974.
Ellis, M. J. *Why people play.* Englewood Cliffs, N. J.: Prentice-Hall, 1973.
Fineman, F. R. Shaping and increasing verbalizations in an autistic child in response to visual-color stimulation. *Percept. & Motor Skills*, 1968: **27**, 1071-1074.
Forehand, R., Baumeister, A. A. Rate of stereotyped body rocking of severe retardates as a function of frustration of a goal-directed behavior. *J. Abnorm. Psychol.*, 1971; **78**, 35-42.
Forehand, R., Baumeister, A. A. Deceleration of aberrant behavior among retarded individuals. *In* Hersen, M., Eisler, R., Miller, P. (Eds.). *Progress in Behavior Modification.* New York: Academic Press, 1976.

Foxx, R. M., Azrin, N. H. The elimination of autistic self-stimulatory behavior by overcorrecuon. *J. Appl. Behav. Anal.*, 1973; **6**, 1-14.

Harlow, H. F., Harlow, M. K. Psychopathology in monkeys. *In* Kimmel, H. D. (Ed.). *Experimental Psychopathology: recent research and theory.* New York: Academic Press, 1971.

Hunt, J. McV., Quay, H. C. Early vibratory experience and the question of innate reinforcement value of vibration and other stimuli: a limitation on the discrepancy (burnt soup) principles in motivation. *Psychol. Rev.*, 1961; **68**, 149-156.

Kaufman, M. E., Levitt, H. A study of three stereotyped behaviors in institutionalized mental defectives. *Am. J. Ment. Defic.*, 1965; **69**, 467-473.

Kish, G. B. Studies of sensory reinforcement. *In* Honig, W. K. (Ed.). *Operant Behavior: areas of research and application.* New York: Appleton-Century-Crofts, 1966.

Koegel, R. L., Covert, A. The relationship of self-stimulation to learning in autistic children. *J. Appl. Behav. Anal.*, 1972; **5**, 381-387.

Koegel, R. L., Firestone, P. B., Kramme, K. W., Dunlap, G. Increasing spontaneous play by suppressing self-stimulation in autistic children. *J. Appl. Behav. Anal.*, 1974; **7**, 521-528.

Koegel, R. L., Rincover, A. Classroom treatment of psychotic children: I. Learning in a large group. *J. Appl. Behav. Anal.*, 1974; **7**, 45-59.

Lovaas, O. I. *Language Acquisition Programs for Nonlinguistic Children.* New York: Irvington Publishers, 1976.

Lovaas, O. I., Lintrownik, A., Mann, R. Response latencies to auditory stimuli in autistic children engaged in self-stimulatory behavior. *Behav. Res. & Ther.*, 1971; **9**, 39-49.

Lovaas, O. I., Newsom, C. D. Behavior modification with psychotic children. *In* Leitenberg, H. (Ed.). *Handbook of Behavior Modification and Therapy.* Englewood Cliffs, New Jersey: Prentice-Hall, 1976.

Lovaas, O. I., Schaeffer, B., Simmons, J. Q. Building social behavior in autistic children by the use of electric shock. *J. Experi. Res. Personal.*, 1965; **1**, 99-109.

Newsom, C. D. *The role of sensory reinforcement in self-stimulatory behavior.* (Unpublished doctoral dissertation). UCLA, 1974.

Newsom, C. D., Carr, E. G., Lovaas, O. I. Experimental analyses and modification of autistic behavior. *In* Davidson, R. S., (Ed.). *Experimental Analysis of Clinical Phenomena.* New York: Gardner Press, 1977.

Ornitz, E. M. The modulation of sensory input and motor output in autistic children. *J. Autism & Child. Schiz.*, 1974; **4**, 197-215.

Repp, A. C., Deitz, S. M., Speir, N. C. Reducing stereotypic responding of retarded persons by the differential reinforcement of other behaviors. *Am. J. Ment. Defic.*, 1974; **79**, 279-284.

Rimland, B. *Infantile Autism.* New York: Appleton-Century-Crofts, 1964.

Rimland, B. The differentiation of childhood psychoses: an analysis of checklists for 2,218 psychotic children. *J. Autism & Child. Schiz.*, 1971; **1**, 161-174.

Rincover, A., Koegel, R. L. Research on the education of autistic children: recent advances and future directions. *In* Lahey, B. B., Kazdin, A. E. (Eds.). *Advances in Clinical Child Psychology.* New York: Plenum Press, 1977a.

Rincover, A., Koegel, R. L. Classroom treatment of autistic children: II. Individualized instruction in a group. *J. Abnorm. Child Psychol.*, 1977(b); **5**, 113-126.

Rincover, A., Newsom, C. D., Lovaas, O. I. Koegel, R. L. Some motivational properties of sensory reinforcement with psychotic children. *J. Experi. Child Psychol.*, 1977; **24**, 312-323.

Rincover, A., Peoples, A., Packard, D. Using sensory extinction and sensory reinforcement principles for programming response generalization. *J. Appl. Behav. Anal.* 1978 (in press).

Risley, T. R. The effects and side effects of punishing the autistic behaviors of a deviant child. *J. Appl. Behav. Anal.*, 1968; **1**, 21-34.

Ritvo, E. R., Ornitz, E. M., LaFranchi, S. Frequency of repetitive behaviors in early autism and its variants. *Arch. Gen. Psychiat.*, 1968; **19**, 341-347.

Solnick, J. V., Rincover, A., Peterson, C. R. Some determinants of the reinforcing and punishing effects of time-out. *J. Appl. Behav. Anal.*, 1977; **10**, 415-424.

Spradlin, J. E., Girardeau, F. L. The behavior of moderately and severely retarded persons. *In* Ellis, N. R. (ed.). *International Review of Research in Mental Retardation.* (Vol. 1). New York: Academic Press, 1966.

Sroufe, L. A., Steucher, H. V., Stutzer, W. The functional significance of autistic behaviors for the psychotic child. *J. Abnorm. Child Psychol.*, 1973; **1**, 225-240.

Zubeck, J. P. *Sensory deprivation: Fifteen years of research.* New York: Appleton-Century-Crofts, 1969.

Reprinted from *J. Abnormal Child Psychol.*, 1978; **6**:3, 299-310 by kind permission of the publishers Plenum Publishing Corp., New York, NY 10013.

SELF-INJURIOUS BEHAVIOR AS LEARNED BEHAVIOR

Alfred A. Baumeister
George Peabody College, Vanderbilt University, Nashville, Tennessee
John Paul Rollings
Partlow State School and Hospital, Tuscaloosa, Alabama

Of the various efforts to explain SIB the most recent and, perhaps, currently most popular center on principles of instrumental conditioning. Within this view the initiating and maintaining conditions for SIB are determined by contingent relationships between the environment, the behavior, and the consequences of the behavior. Learning theory, by far, offers the most explicit (and testable) hypotheses concerning the origin and maintenance of SIB. Furthermore, it is the application of learning principles that has proven to be the only consistently useful procedure for the modification of these behaviors. Actually, there are two fairly distinct approaches to the explanation of SIB on the basis of learning variables: (1) the *avoidance* hypothesis and (2) the *discriminative stimulus* hypothesis (Bachman, 1972). Both were originally suggested by Skinner (1953).

1. Avoidance learning

Skinner proposed that self-injury may function as a response mechanism by which the organism might avoid more aversive events including conditioned fear responses. According to this view, stimuli that are associated with the presentation of an aversive stimulus develop conditioned aversive properties. Extended exposure to these conditioned events may be more aversive to the individual than the nominal aversive stimulus. The anxiety or fear responses associated with continued exposure to the conditioned aversive stimulus is thus reduced by self-punishment if such behavior results in avoidance or escape. Along similar lines, Bucher and Lovaas (1968) suggested that cues associated with punishing stimuli develop conditioned aversive properties capable of eliciting "emotional" responses, as well as escape and avoidance reactions.

Tangential support of a correlational nature for the avoidance interpretation of SIB was reported by Green (1968), who found a significant relationship between physical abuse in the first 2 years of life and later head-banging behavior in schizophrenic children. One may hypothesize that some of these children may have avoided parental abuse by hitting themselves. Fear and avoidance of fear-producing situations may be a powerful variable controlling SIB. Self-injuring individuals often exhibit high rates of SIB upon release from restraints or when exposed to social contact (Bucher & Lovaas, 1968; Corte, Wolf, & Locke, 1971; Peterson & Peterson, 1968; Tate, 1972; Tate & Baroff, 1966). Tate (1972) reported that upon release from restraints a young female subject would appear "frightened" and perform "emotional" behaviors including SIB until the restraints were replaced. This is not at all an uncommon phenomenon. In fact, the authors have observed cases in which the patient will attempt to retie restraints from which he has been released.

It is possible to imagine situations in which a retarded or autistic individual could avoid or escape from unpleasant situations by performing SIB. On initial reflection it may seem strange that an individual would resort to such extreme measures to escape or avoid other unpleasant conditions. Yet, the extreme character of this behavior may make it particularly adaptive as an avoidance behavior, because adults find it difficult to ignore. In addition, the behavioral repertoire of many of these individuals is very limited. Moreover, cues associated with the unpleasant situation would become conditioned aversive stimuli capable of eliciting escape or avoidance behavior, including SIB. SIB would thus be reinforced by the escape from or avoidance of "aversive" situations. An explanation of this nature could account for a phenomenon reported by Rollings, Baumeister, and Baumeister (in press). They observed that the application of mild punishment procedures (overcorrection) to suppress stereotypic body rocking exhibited by a male retardate was associated with markedly increased self-hitting early in training. However, the rate of SIB decreased with extended training suggesting extinction of self-hitting in the training environment. Self-hitting may have occurred during treatment because SIB had been successful in avoiding or escaping from unpleasant situations in the past. The self-hitting then extinguished in the training environment because it was ineffective in preventing escape from the aversive situation. These interpretations, of course, are merely suggestive. There is more direct experimental evidence that punishment can facilitate and maintain behavior.

One of the most compelling studies for an avoidance interpretation was reported by Bandura (1969) who described unpublished research by Sandler and Quagliano which directly demonstrated such avoidance behavior with monkeys. In effect, they were able to stimulate "masochistic" behavior through an avoidance conditioning paradigm. Subsequent to avoidance training, in which shock was averted by lever pressing, a shock of lesser magnitude was made contingent upon the avoidance response. The animal was caught between two "evils." He could only avoid the more painful shock by administering a less painful shock to himself. The magnitude of the contingent shocks was gradually increased to the level of the avoided shock but with no concomitant deceleration of avoidance responding. Furthermore, punished responding continued *after* the avoidance contingency was terminated and no shock was delivered for failure to avoid. The nature of the avoidance conditioning paradigm is that it does not usually lead to rapid extinction of the avoidance behavior, because the subject is not apt to "take the chance." This study clearly shows that the conditions under which a stimulus is presented are important in predicting its subsequent effects on behavior.

Several other investigators have systematically demonstrated that punishment of avoidance and escape responding is capable of maintaining such behavior in animals (Bender, 1969; Brown, Martin, & Morrow, 1964; Rollings & Melvin, 1970; Sandler & Davidson, 1971). This seemingly maladaptive behavior is sometimes referred to as the "vicious circle effect." Sandler & Davidson (1971) observed that subjects with long avoidance-training histories would continue the avoidance response learned initially, even though that response was later punished with strong shock and even though an alternate nonpunished response was available. Similar effects have been experimentally produced with retarded subjects. Corte *et al.* (1971) reported that the use of mild shock contingent upon the SIB exhibited by a retarded female subject was associated with "markedly" increased rates of SIB, again suggesting that children may engage in the SIB to avert other stimuli.

The facilitation of SIB under conditions of mild punishment poses some theoretical questions. Is the facilitation of SIB with mild shock related to the same processes which maintain avoidance responding under conditions of punishment (e.g. Sandler & Davidson, 1971)? Can SIB be shaped and maintained by escape under controlled experimental conditions? Can SIB be brought under the control of highly discriminated stimuli?

2. Discriminative function

One of the most perplexing aspects of SIB is the failure of the apparently painful self-injurious responses (e.g., pulling the fingernails out by their roots, head-banging) to suppress further self-injury. Skinner (1953) suggested that an aversive stimulus could function as a conditioned positive reinforcer if contingencies were such that the aversive stimulus was selectively associated with or predicted positive reinforcement. Thus, the aversive stimulus (possibly the pain) may be *discriminative* for subsequent positive reinforcement. This "cue" theory essentially describes a situation in which the retarded individual can learn to identify stimuli that reliably signal either reward or punishment. In the process the aversive event itself may become positively reinforcing. In fact, we offer the generalization that given the appropriate conditions, *any* stimulus can become a positive conditioned reinforcer. Moreover, if the "training" were accomplished through intermittent schedules of reinforcement, then we should expect the behavior to be maintained over long periods of time without additional reinforcement. Expressly dealing with the problem of SIB in children, Lovaas and Simmons (1969) speculated that the pain associated with self-injurious responding could become discriminative for the social reinforcers that presumably follow SIB. Lovaas *et al.* (1965) had previously demonstrated that contingent social reinforcers in the form of adult attention effectively increased the rate of SIB in a psychotic girl. Furthermore, Lovaas and Simmons (1969) reported that adult attention contingent upon SIB was associated with increased self-injurious responding compared to a previous condition in which no attention was given. Ample experimental evidence exists for the view that nominally punishing stimuli can also function as discriminative cues.

The discriminative properties of punishment have been reliably demonstrated in pigeons (Holz & Azrin, 1961), monkeys (Sandler, 1962), and in humans (Ayllon & Azrin, 1966). Ayllon and Azrin established discriminative and conditioned properties of an aversive noise with chronic schizophrenic females. The aversive properties of the noise were first demonstrated in a conventional two-response operant situation. Subsequently, when the noise was associated with positive reinforcement (tokens), the subjects responded to produce the noise. Finally, a new response (button pushing) was shaped utilizing noise alone as the reinforcer.

Obviously, it is necesssary to examine the reinforcement history of the subject, including his experience with both positive and negative stimuli, in the analysis of the etiology of SIB (Sandler & Davidson, 1971). The discriminative stimulus hypothesis of SIB takes into account the stimulus properties of the behavior (SIB) and its relation to the system of rewards and punishers that function in the environment of the individual.

Many instances of SIB occur within the context of specific environmental events (Bachman, 1972). For example, release from restraints has been shown to be discriminative for the occurrence of SIB (Bucher & Lovaas, 1968; Corte et al., 1971; Lovaas & Simmons, 1969; Tate, 1972; Tate & Baroff, 1966; Thomas and Howard, 1971; Yeakel, Salisbury, Greer, & Marcus, 1970). Thomas & Howard (1971) reported that upon release from restraints a retarded male subject would immediately engage in SIB (head-banging and face hitting). Similarly, Yeakel et al. (1970) observed that a female autistic child would immediately begin hitting her head subsequent to the removal of shock electrodes from her arm.

Peterson and Peterson (1968) reported that the withdrawal of the favorite blanket of a young retarded male subject was associated with increased SIB (head banging, self-hitting)relative to periods when the blanket was in the child's possession. Possibly the blanket functioned as a powerful reinforcer for the subject and that removal of the blanket became discriminative for SIB. Likewise, Lovaas et al. (1965) demonstrated that the withdrawal of social reinforcers (praise) from a previously reinforced response (appropriate music behaviors) was discriminative for SIB (e.g., head banging, self-hitting) in a young schizophrenic girl. Additionally , the extinction of another socially reinforced response (bar pressing) was associated with increased SIB relative to the acquisition of the bar-pressing response. Lovaas and his associates suggested that the SIB as well as the appropriate music and bar-pressing behaviors were maintained by social reward. Extinction of the previously reinforced behavior (bar pressing, music behaviors) became the discriminative stimulus for other behaviors (SIB) which were also under the control of social reinforcers. The subject exhausted her repertoire of socially reinforced behaviors according to a hierarchy. The most recently learned behaviors (e.g., bar pressing) extinguished first followed by behaviors which were well established in the response hierarchy. Thus, when bar pressing and appropriate music behaviors were extinguished, the subject performed behaviors (SIB) successful in obtaining social reward in the past.

Procedures designed to suppress stereotyped behaviors have been observed, on occasion, to cause an increase in occurrence of SIB. For example, J. C. White and Taylor (1967) noted the occurrence of SIB (arm biting) when shock procedures were utilized to suppress rumination and vomiting behaviors exhibited by young retarded females. Rollings et al. (in press) found that the application of overcorrection procedures to suppress stereotypic head weaving exhibited by a severely retarded male subject was associated with the occurrence of SIB (self-pinching, self-scratching, head banging). Furthermore, the use of overcorrection procedures to eliminate high-rate rocking behavior of another subject was associated with increased self-hitting behavior. The suppression of certain high-rate stereotyped behaviors may become discriminative for other forms of stereotypic responding including SIB.

Moreover, these can be very fine discriminations. In a more tightly conducted study Rollings (1975) demonstrated that self-hitting could be brought under control of visual stimuli. Following baseline procedures, a multiple schedule of punishment was utilized to train retarded subjects to discriminate lights arranged linearly on a stimulus panel directly in front of the subject. Two of the lights, located on either end of the stimulus panel, served as training stimuli and the remainder functioned as test stimuli. During presentation of the "punishment stimulus" (one or the other end lights) target stereotypies were punished by overcorrection procedures. No contingencies were in effect during presentation of the "safe" stimuli (the remaining lights). Subsequent to discrimination training all of the test and training stimuli were presented in extinction. The essential question concerned the extent to which the subject could form discriminations between the end lights (signaling punishment for the stereotypy) and the middle lights (signaling that it was "safe" to engage in the stereotypy). Steep gradients of inhibition were obtained for the target stereotypies with minimum stereotyped responding at test values in close spatial proximity to the "punishment" stimulus. The further the test stimulus from the punishment stimulus, the greater the rate of stereotyped responding. Furthermore, nontarget stereotypies, including SIB, also appeared to be under stimulus control. Orderly gradients were obtained for these behaviors under test conditions. The gradients for the collateral behaviors were the inverse of gradients observed for the target stereotypies, with greater SIB exhibited during presentations of "punishment" stimuli relative to "safe" correlated stimuli. In addition, the same trend was recorded during the discrimination training phase of the experiment.

The situational nature of SIB has also been demonstrated in primates. Levinson (1970) noted that head banging of a young rhesus monkey appeared with "aversive" events such as termination of handling by the trainer.

The finding that self-injurious responding often occurs under tight environmental control offers strong support for the avoidance and discriminative stimulus accounts of SIB. Whether SIB is an avoidance behavior or a socially reinforced behavior or still another class of behavior is an issue that requires further study utilizing rigid experimental procedures. It is conceivable that SIB may actually serve both avoidance and discriminative functions. For example, self-injurious responding may function as an attention-getting device under certain conditions of social deprivation. Additionally, SIB may serve to avoid certain events (e.g., participation in training situations) which may be aversive to the individual.

In attempting to differentiate among the various theoretical perspectives regarding SIB, we have not made a fine or precise distinction between conditions from which the behaviors originate and those conditions that maintain the behavior. Indeed, the genesis of the behavior may be quite a different matter from the maintenance of the behavior. We believe this to be the case, particularly with respect to the role of learning. To put it simply, we are not at all sure what caused the behavior in the first place, but we are willing to state that in most cases the behavior is maintained by instrumental conditioning. Furthermore, the very fact that one can decelerate these behaviors by arranging contingencies certainly does not prove that either the avoidance conditioning or the discriminative stimulus theories is correct.

References

Ayllon, T., Azrin, N. H. Punishment as a discriminative conditioned reinforcer with humans. *J. Experi. Anal. Behav.*, 1966; **9**, 411-419.

Bachman, J. A. Self-injurious behavior: A behavioral analysis. *J. Abnorm. Psychol.*, 1972; **80**, 211-224.

Bandura, A. *Principles of behavior modification.* New York: Holt, 1969.

Bender, L. Secondary punishment and self-punitive avoidance behavior in the rat. *J. Compara. & Physiol. Psychol.*, 1969; **69**, 261-266.

Brown, J. S., Martin, R. C., Morrow, M. W. Self-punitive behavior in the rat: facilitative effects of punishment on resistance to extinction. *J. Compara. & Physiol. Psychol.*, 1964; **57**, 127-133.

Bucher, B., Lovaas, O. I. Use of aversive stimulation in behavior modification. *In* Jones, M. R. (Ed.): *Miami symposium on the prediction of behavior, 1967: Aversive stimulation.* (pp 77-145). Coral Gables, Fla.; Univ. Miami Press, 1968.

Corte, H. E., Wolf, M. M., Locke, B. J. A comparison of procedures for eliminating self-injurious behavior of retarded adolescents. *J. Appl. Behav. Anal.*, 1971; **4**, 201-213.

Green, A. Self-destructive behavior in physically abused schizophrenic children. *Arch. Gen. Psychiat.*, 1968; **19**, 171-179.

Holz, W. C., Azrin, N. H. Discriminative properties of punishment. *J. Experi. Anal. Behav.*, 1961; **4**, 225-232.

Levinson, C. The development of head banging in a young rhesus monkey. *Amer. J. Ment. Defic.*, 1970; **75**, 323-328.

Lovaas, O. I., Frietag, G., Gold, V. J., Kassorla, I. C. Experimental studies in childhood schizophrenia: Analysis of self-destructive behavior. *J. Experi. Child Psychol.*, 1965; **2**, 67-84.

Lovaas, O. I., Simmons, J. Q. Manipulation of self-destruction in three retarded children. *J. Appl. Behav. Anal.*, 1969; **2**, 143-157.

Peterson, R. F., Peterson, L. R. The use of positive reinforcement in the control of self-destructive behavior in a·retarded body. *J. Experi. Child Psychol.*, 1968; **6**, 351-360.

Rollings, J. P. The establishment of extroceptive stimulus control of stereotypic responding exhibited by two profoundly retarded males. Unpubl. doctoral dissert. Univ. Alabama, 1975.

Rollings, J. P., Baumeister, A. A., Baumeister, A. A. The use of overcorrection procedures to eliminate the stereotyped behaviors of retarded individuals: An analysis of collateral behaviors and generalization of suppression effects. *Behav. Mod.*, in press.

Rollings, J. P., Melvin, K. B. Effects of a punitive noise on self-punitive running established with shock. *Psychon. Sci.*, 1970; **21**, 313-314.

Sandler, J. Reinforcement combinations and masochistic behavior: A preliminary report. *Psychol. Reports*, 1962; **11**, 110.

Sandler, J., Davidson, R. S. Psychopathology: An analysis of response consequences. *In* Kimmel, H. D. (Ed.). *Experimental psychopathology: recent research and theory.* (pp 71-93). New York: Academic Press, 1971.

Skinner, B. F. *Science and human behavior.* New York: Macmillan, 1953.

Tate, B. G. Case Study: Control of chronic self-injurious behavior by conditioning procedures. *Behav. Ther.*, 1972; **3**, 72-83.

Tate, B. G., Baroff, G. S. Aversive control of self-injurious behavior in a psychotic boy. *Behav. Res. & Ther.*, 1966; **4**, 281-287.

Thomas, R. L., Howard, G. A. A treatment program for a self-destructive child. *Ment. Retard.*, 1971; **9**, 16-18.

White, J. C., Jr., Taylor, D. J. Noxious conditioning as a treatment for rumination. *Ment. Retard.*, 1967; **5**, 30-33.

Yeakel, M. H., Salisbury, L. L., Greer, S. L., Marcus, L. F. An appliance for autoinduced adverse control of self-injurious behavior. *J. Experi. Child Psychol.*, 1970; **10**, 159-169.

Reprinted from Ellis, N. R. (Ed.). *International Review of Research in Mental Retardation, Vol. III* (pp10-16), 1976 by kind permission of Alfred Baumeister, George Peabody College, Nashville, TN 37203, J. Paul Rollings, State of Florida, Dept. of Health and Rehabilitative Services, Fort Myers, Florida 33905, and the publishers Academic Press Inc., Fifth Avenue, New York, NY 10003.

SELF-INJURIOUS BEHAVIOR: SHAPING "HEAD-BANGING" IN MONKEYS[1]

H. H. Schaefer

Patton State Hospital

Head-banging, a common phenomenon among the mentally retarded, was shaped, brought under stimulus control, extinguished, and re-established in two monkeys through reinforcement and discrimination procedures of operant conditioning. The behavior was stable and led to lacerations, a condition that qualifies head-banging as self-injurious. The principles of the analysis of behavior used here may well be of value in the etiology and treatment of some human head-banging.

Head-banging, the slapping or hitting of the head or face by oneself, or the hittting (banging) of the head against objects in the environment, is a phenomenon as yet little understood among mentally retarded and occasionally also of the mentally ill patients. An excellent summary of traditional views has been given by Lovaas, Freitag, Gold, and Kassorla (1965).

It is quite conceivable that at least some forms of head-banging are simply linked to reinforcing features of the environment. In this view, the behavior is an operant maintained most typically by the attention it evokes from other persons. In support of this view, Wolf, Risley, and Mees (1964) reported that extinction and timeout procedures successfully reduced head-banging. Similarly Lovaas et al. (1965), in a series of studies with self-injurious behavior in a schizophrenic child, presented evidence that suggested that the self-injurious behaviour was learned. Tate and Baroff (1966) provided further evidence to support this view. They used the presentation and withdrawal of physical human contact, as well as punishment procedures, to modify the severe self-injurious behavior of a 9-yr-old psychotic boy. Lest it be thought that only part of the armatory of the analysis of behavior be applicable to this problem it is interesting to note the ingenious use of a positive reinforcer in the control of self-destructive behavior reported by Peterson and Peterson (1968). They used brief walks across a room and access to a blanket as effective reinforcers for establishing behaviors that were incompatible with head-banging.

Thus, as Wolf et al. (1964) pointed out, procedures established originally with lower organisms can be successful with, and are increasingly applied to human problems. Yet, head-banging as such has never been explored *experimentally* with lower animals. At the same time, it is well to point out that the behavioral laws that were developed in animal laboratories are indeed so general that they can be applied to novel situations. But even so, to shed further light on this particular problem would require experiments with lower animals where a degree of control, which cannot be exercised with humans, is possible. In particular, it would be interesting to see under what conditions this behavior can be acquired. To explore this question was one objective of the present study.

Extensive self-injurious behavior has been observed in lower primates. Yerkes and Yerkes (1929) reported chest-beating, severe self-scratching, and hair-tearing of apes as expressions of anger. Finch (1942) described hair-tearing and severe scratching of primates as apparent frustration responses. Hebb (1947) related "anus picking to the point of gross self-injury" in a female monkey to the deprivation of the preferred cell mate. Tinklepaugh (1928) similarly observed paw biting and scrotum ripping with resulting severe lacerations

[1] I gratefully acknowledge the generous, able, and patient assistance of Miss Katherine Johnson in assisting with the present work. This research was in part supported by Grant #67-11-13 awarded by the Department of Mental Hygiene of the State of California. This manuscript has not been reviewed for publication by the Department of Mental Hygiene and the author is solely responsible for content. I feel deeply indebted to Nathan Azrin whose critical comments not only improved this paper (especially the graphs), but also provided insights beyond the pale of the experimentation reported. In addition, I would like to express my deepest gratitude to one of the reviewers of JABA—unknown to me— who took extraordinary pains in offering helpful suggestions without which this paper would not exist. Both he and Dr. Azrin are not, to be sure, responsible for any shortcomings this presentation might have. Reprints may be obtained from the author, Patton State Hospital, Patton, California 92369.

to be a result of sexual starvation and laboratory imposed interferences with the happy sex life of a male monkey. He reported too, that this behavior later generalized to other situations. Cain (1961) quoted a statement by G. Cuvier dating back to 1811 to the effect that "impatience is the cause of the animal's throwing himself on the floor and striking his head on the floor."

Whether self-injury in primates is "merely" reflexive, physiologically occasioned, accidental, or whether it is an operant that can be controlled by discriminative stimuli is an empirical question. To explore whether head-banging could be brought under stimulus control was the second objective of the present study.

Subjects and general procedure

Two male rhesus monkeys, I and II, 7- and 2-yr-old respectively, had been raised from age one by the author and were tame to him, e.g., he could enter the small cage of each animal and handle them ungloved. The animals were kept in separate rooms and could hear, but not see each other. For the procedures of shaping and maintaining the experimentally desired behavior, standard banana pellets (Ciba), half sections of monkey chow (Purina), slices of bananas and apples, grapes and peanuts were used as the scheduled consequences for hitting the head with a forepaw (for Exp. I) and hitting the wall of the cage with the head (for Exp. II). The words: "Poor boy! Don't do that! You'll hurt yourself!" spoken by the experimenter in various combinations were used as a stimulus in the presence of which the behavior would be reinforced (S^D); the absence of these word's constituted S^Δ.

Experiment I

For the first shaping session, the experimenter seated himself in front of the 4 by 4 by 4ft (1.2 by 1.2 by 1.2m) cage which was enclosed on top, bottom, and on the right side with wire mesh, with galvanized steel on the rear and left side, and on the front with a door consisting of ⅜in. stainless steel bars spaced vertically 1.5in. (3.8cm) apart mounted in a square frame. The animals were deprived of food for 24hr before the session.

At first, the raising of the animal's paw was followed by presentation of a single pellet of food. By successive approximations, the positioning of the paw above the head and finally the bringing down of the paw upon the head was followed by the food. The complete motion of touching the head was shaped in the adult monkey within 12 min; in the younger monkey, it took about 20 min. The first session was terminated after each animal had touched its head 30 times.

The second session constituted the first discrimination session. Now a stimulus ("Poor boy! . . . etc.") was presented continuously. After food pellets were presented for the 10 initial responses, the food pellets were scheduled to follow every other response for the next 10 responses, then every fifth response. Each response and food pellet was recorded via a noiseless handswitch connected to a standard cumulative recorder located in another room. The performance of both animals was very similar. The only difference was that the younger monkey emitted a total of 105 responses as compared to 140 responses for the older monkey during the 25-min session.

For this first discrimnation session, the S^D and S^Δ periods were signalled to the experimenter by the appearance of a dim signal light out of sight of the animal, controlled by a tape program to be off or on in irregular multiples of 30 sec, such that the total S^D time was equal to the S^Δ time. Again, the record for both animals is similar, except that from this session on, the younger animal always responded at a greater rate than the older monkey.

At that time it became evident that considerably greater sophistication in instrumentation would be required to achieve a clear distinction between the stimulus complex, which the presence of the experimenter and his actions afforded on the one hand, and the spoken words "poor boy . . . etc.", which were intended as the control stimulus. In particular, the operation of the handswitch necessary during S^Δ intervals and the continued holding of the right hand in the lab coat pocket bulging with food seemed to sustain responding. Rather than interrupt the study for the building of such apparatus, the following procedure was adopted: for both animals the sole supply of food for the next 10 days was made contingent upon head-hitting during repeated brief sessions in the course of a day, rather than during a single 25-min session.

No records were kept during this 10-day period. S$^\triangle$ sessions consisted of the experimenter sitting or standing in front of the animals' cages, hand in coat pocket containing food, or else walking by the cages in the course of regular lab routine work without speaking the control words; the S^D sessions were in every respect the same except that the control stimulus words were spoken during this condition and the food consequences were given for every tenth response (FR 10).

At the end of this 10-day training period, another 25-min session was held for each animal. The data for both animals are shown in Fig. 1. During this session an assistant, observing both experimenter and animal from another room through a window, operated the recording equipment. Scheduling of S^D and S$^\triangle$ was the same for both animals. Figure 1

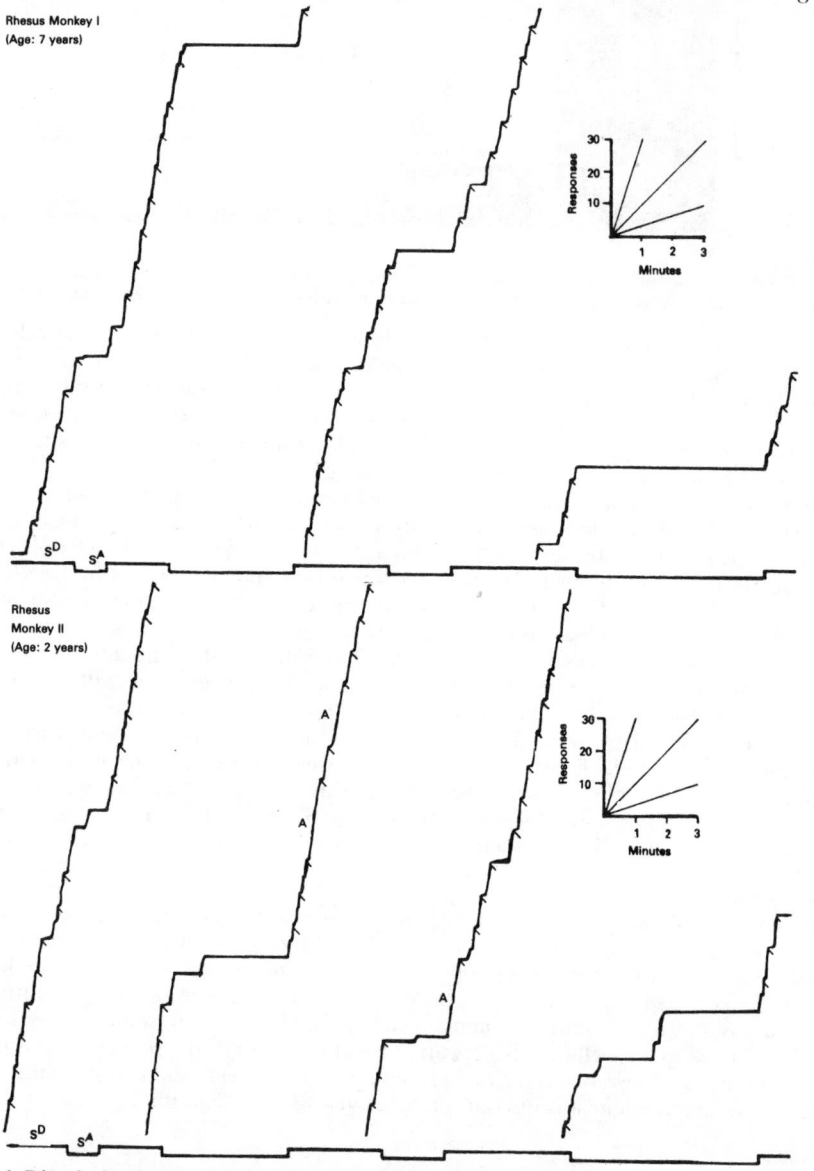

Fig. 1. Discrimination formation after 10 days (see text) for two rhesus monkeys 7 (I) and 2 (II) yr of age; self-head-hitting was reinforced (on FR 10) in the presence of the spoken words ("Don't do that! . . . etc.").

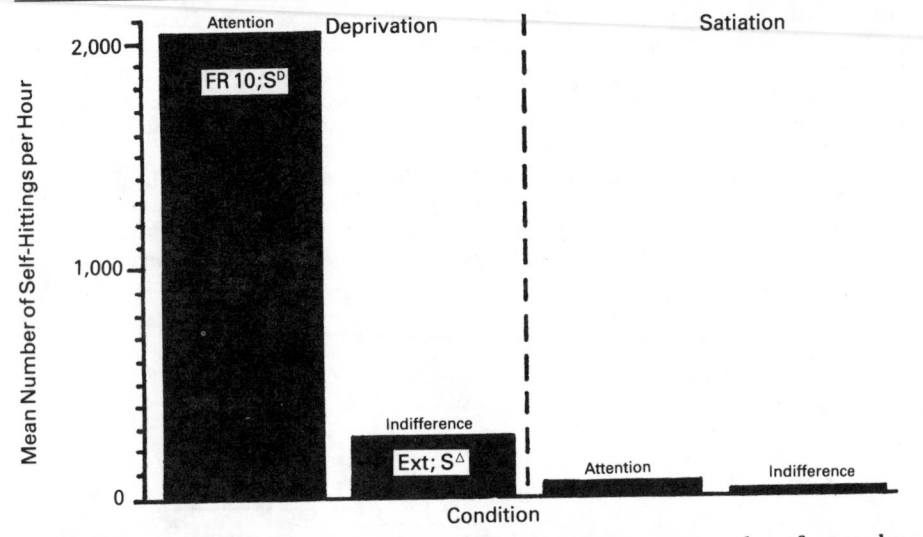

Fig. 2. Number of self-hittings averaged as arithmetic mean responses per hour for two rhesus monkeys over several experimental sessions and four different conditions. See text for details.

shows that Monkey I, the adult, discriminated more neatly (*i.e.*, hit itself promptly upon presentation of S^D) than did Monkey II. Monkey II responded at a higher rate, and as shown at points A in the record in Fig. 1, continued to hit itself even when the experimenter proferred the reinforcer after the tenth response had been emitted. At such instances the animal was not looking at the experimenter. Instead, it appeared to be looking at the ceiling or at the assistant, whose face could be seen through the window.

After this session, both animals were returned to a free-feeding schedule for a period of four days. On the third and fourth days of this period, *i.e.*, when the animals were satiated with food, the experimenter seated himself for a 10-min period in front of each cage exactly as during the training sessions and emitted the control stimulus as called for by the S^D and $S^\triangle$ program. To a naive onlooker it might well have appeared that the experimenter showed extreme "compassion" or "attention" during the S^D periods, while he was "indifferent" during the $S^\triangle$ period. The older animal did not hit itself once during these sessions. The younger animal did emit the behavior 60 times during the S^D sessions and 40 times during all $S^\triangle$ sessions. Typically, it hit itself in bursts of several responses at a time. No records of these session were taken; instead a count of the frequency of the behavior during each 10-min session was made. Figure 2 allows a comparison of the rate of responding for both animals averaged for the recorded sessions of Day 3 (the first day of discrimination training), Day 14 (the recorded session after 10 days of discrimination training), and Days 17 and 18 (before and during which the animals were on free feeding).

Experiment II

Immediately following this experiment, a session was begun with the older monkey to hit a wall of its cage with its paws to obtain a pellet of food. The intent was to replace the hitting paw(s) eventually by the head so as to make the food contingent not on touching the wall with the paws but with the forehead. The animal learned the new behavior of hitting the wall with paws within 20 reinforcements. During the same session, reinforcement for its head being close to the wall was also begun. Table 1 summarizes the procedures employed in the course of the next 40 days. None of these procedures were successful. At the end of this time, the experiment was discontinued because of lack of funding.

Discussion

An important aspect of this study is the reliability of the behavior: at one time the younger animal was presented to professional audiences in medical schools and universities in California and finally at a convention of the Western Psychological Association. The

Table 1. Sequence of procedures used in successively approximating head-banging against cage wall in adult rhesus monkey

Day	Contingency	Success	Remarks
1	One pellet for every touch of wall with hands	Excellent	
2-7	One pellet for every 10 hits with hands, close to wall	Excellent	Responses increase in intensity
8-10	One pellet for every movement of head away from and back to wall	Poor	Much screaming
11	Hold cage door bars with both hands and move head toward hitting wall	Excellent	
12-20	One pellet for every 10 moves like Day 11	Excellent	
21-30	One pellet for every contact sound made in touching head to wall while holding bars	Nil	Much screaming
31	One pellet for moving head close to wall opposite hitting wall *and* then toward hitting wall	Excellent	
32-35	Increase speed of head movement and reinforce for contact noise	Nil	Speed did increase but no contact
36-40	Like previous, but reinforce close proximity to hitting wall (within 0.25in.) of head at end of movement	Poor	Screaming again

behavior proved extremely stable: not merely the experimenter, but any member of the audience could evoke the behavior, although the sight of a banana even without the control stimulus at these occasions was sometimes sufficient to produce the behavior.

There are additional observations in connection with Exp. I that are difficult to quantify *post facto,* but which easily could be subjected to the methods of the analysis of behavior. For example, as mentioned the younger monkey could not be brought under the same degree of stimulus control as the older animal; but also during the period of free feeding it began hitting itself when it heard the research assistant before cage-cleaning time during which it would be taken on a leash outside. Also, the monkey was seen hitting itself when the food truck (with bananas) arrived. At no time during these instances was the control stimulus spoken. The older monkey never emitted the behavior after it had been placed on free feeding. When the bananas arrived, it screamed and rattled the cage walls as it had usually done before the experiment began. That poor experimental control is likely to be involved here is substantiated by two observations: discrimination in the older animal had been formed better than in the younger; and for the younger animal the experimenter himself, even the noises he made in moving about the lab (as before cage-cleaning time) had come to function as control stimuli. Longer discrimination training and/or more sophisticated instrumentation aimed at isolating the experimental control stimulus from the experimenter himself might have solved this problem.

In the failure to establish wall-hitting with the head in the older animal, it is likely that a poor program of successive approximation was used in attempting to shape this behavior and that the experiment was abandoned before every possible alternative was exhausted.

The work with these animals confirms the findings of investigators who have worked on the same problem with humans in that it demonstrates that self-destructive behavior can be brought under the control of environmental variables. Furthermore. in exploring the ways in which these variables initially acquire their influence over self-destructive behavior, it can now be said that the well-established procedures of the analysis of behavior are entirely justified for this problem: the behavior can be shaped by successive approximation, the reinforcer used must be effective to sustain the behavior, discriminations can be formed, *i.e.,* the behavior can be maintained while granting the reinforcer in the presence of one stimulus, and extinguished by withholding that same reinforcer in the presence of another stimulus.

On the strength of the present experimental evidence, it seems permissible and advisable to analyze each case of head-banging among humans for the presence of control-stimuli that set the stage for, and the presence of reinforcers that sustain this behavior. If these reinforcers are manipulable, then both extinction and satiation will lead to a cessation of the behavior. For example, if attention reinforces the behavior, then both continuous giving of these to an extreme degree, as well as their withholding when the behavior occurs, will diminish the behavior. It must be remembered, however, that there is no gradual weaning the organism of continuous attention. As soon as it is no longer given continuously, deprivation will increase and the behavior will reappear. Thus, from a clinical point of view it is much more advisable to use attention judiciously so as to avoid the inadvertant strengthening of undesirable or harmful behaviors.

References

Cain, A. C. The presuperego "turning-inward' of aggression. *Psychoanal. Quart.*, 1961; **30**, 171-208.

Finch, G. Chimpanzee frustration responses. *Psychosom. Med.*, 1942; **4**, 233-251.

Hebb, D. O. Spontaneous neurosis in chimpanzees: theoretical relations with clinical and experimental phenomena. *Psychosom. Med.*, 1947; **9**, 3-16.

Lovaas, O. I., Freitag, G., Gold, V. J., Kassorla, I. C. Experimental studies in childhood schizophrenia: analysis of self-destructive behavior. *J. Experi. Child Psychol.*, 1965; **2**, 67-84.

Peterson, R. F., Peterson, L. R. The use of positive reinforcement in the control of self-destructive behavior in a retarded boy. *J. Experi. Child Psychol.*, 1965; **6**, 351-360.

Tate, B. G., Baroff, G. S. Aversive control of self-injurious behavior in a psychotic boy. *Behav. Res. & Ther.*, 1966; **4**, 281-287.

Tinklepaugh, O. L. The self-mutilation of a male macacus rhesus monkey. *J. Mammalogy,* 1928; **9**, 293-300.

Wolf, M., Risley, T., Mees, H. Application of operant conditioning procedures to the behaviour problems of an autistic child. *Behav. Res. & Ther.*, 1964; **1**, 305-312.

Yerkes, R. M. and Yerkes, A. W. *The Great Apes.* New Haven: Yale University Press, 1929.

MANIPULATION OF SELF-DESTRUCTION IN THREE RETARDED CHILDREN[1]

O. Ivar Lovaas, James Q. Simmons

University of California, Los Angeles

The study attempted to isolate some of the environmental conditions that controlled the self-destructive behavior of three severely retarded and psychotic children. In the extinction study subjects were placed in a room where they were allowed to hurt themselves, isolated from interpersonal contact. They eventually ceased to hurt themselves in that situation, the rate of self-destruction falling gradually over successive days. In the punishment study, subjects were administered painful electric shock contingent on the self-destructive behavior. (1) The self-destructive behavior was immediately suppressed. (2) The behavior recurred when shock was removed. (3) The suppression was selective, both across physical locales and interpersonal situations, as a function of the presence of shock. (4) Generalized effects on other, non-shock behaviors, appeared in a clinically desirable direction. Finally, a study was reported where self-destructive behavior increased when certain social attentions were given contingent upon that behavior.

A significant number of children, who are diagnosed as psychotic or severely retarded, manifest, at one time or another in their lives, self-destructive behavior. This behavior consists primarily of "head-banging" (against walls and furniture), "arm-banging" (against sharp corners), beating themselves on their heads or in their faces with their fists or knees, and biting themselves on wrists, arms, and shoulders. In some children, the self-destructive behavior can be severe enough to pose a major problem for the child's safety. Thus, one can frequently see that such children have removed large quantities of flesh from their bodies, torn out their nails, opened wounds in their heads, broken their noses, *etc.* Such severe forms of self-destruction often require restraints, either in the form of camisoles ("straitjackets") or by tying the child's feet and arms to his bed. Sometimes the self-destructive behavior may be sporadic, at other times it is long-lasting, necessitating such prolonged use of restraints that one can observe structural changes, such as demineralization, and shortening of tendons, and arrested motor development, secondary to disuse of limbs.

Such children pose major problems for both their parents and the personnel who care for them. First of all, there is the immediate threat to the child, either directly through tissue damage or indirectly through infections. There are secondary problems associated with self-destructive behavior which center on the curtailment of growth, psychological and otherwise, in the child who has to be restrained. Finally, the self-destructive child poses major psychological problems for those who take care of him, in the form of anxiety, demoralization, and hopelessness. The authors know of no treatment that effectively alleviates self-destructive behavior. The most common form of treatment consists of some combination of drugs and supportive, interpersonal therapy, and occasional electro-convulsive therapy. There is no evidence to demonstrate that any of these forms of treatment are effective. Conceivably, some treatments could make the child worse. There are no systematic studies that would support either outcome.

[1]These studies were supported by PHS Research Grant No. MH-11440 from the National Institute of Mental Health. Aspects of this manuscript were presented with the purpose of illustrating the use of aversive stimuli in behavior therapy work, at the Miami Symposium on the Prediction of Behavior: Aversive Stimulation, Marshall R. Jones (Editor), University of Miami Press, 1968. We express our appreciation for the help of the nursing staff at the Neuro-psychiatric Institute at UCLA, and to the large number of students from the Department of Psychology who assisted in the project. We are particularly indebted to Mrs. Kathy Burnett, M.A., R.N., and Michael Clowers, of Southern Illinois University, for their valuable assistance in these studies. Reprints may be obtained from O. Ivar Lovaas, Department of Psychology, University of California, Los Angeles, California.

Finally, clinically speaking, such violent self-destruction forms an expression of a most severe psychotic state. If self-destruction is an expression of a psychosis, then an understanding of the events that effect self-destruction should throw some light on the psychosis itself.

An earlier paper (Lovaas, Freitag, Gold, and Kassorla, 1965a) reported an attempt to study self-destructive behavior in a systematic manner. Data were presented which indicated that the self-destructive behavior showed a great deal of lawfulness which could be accounted for by considering the self-destructive behavior as learned social behavior.

The present paper seeks to clarify further the variables that control self-destructive behavior. On the suggestion from the first study that such behavior is learned social behavior and is maintained by social reinforcement (e.g., attention), the following relationships could be expected to exist: (a) one should observe a decrease and eventual disappearance of self-destructive behavior if the social consequences were withheld (that is, self-destructive behavior should extinguish); (b) one should observe an increase in self-destructive behavior if that behavior resulted in social reinforcement; and (c) the delivery of aversive stimuli, contingent upon such behavior, should serve to suppress it.

Punishment by the use of aversive stimuli or extinction through withdrawal of effective reinforcers ("ignoring") involves purposefully exposing the child to pain and raises ethical problems of what to do. In addition to punishment and extinction procedures, we could have attempted to check the pathological behavior by establishing incompatible behavior. A previous study (Lovaas et al., 1965a) found that self-destructive behavior could be suppressed by building incompatible behaviors. Perhaps this would be the most humane procedure, since it involves exposing the child to minimal pain. However, the children to be treated here came from, and were to be returned to, state hospitals where maintaining incompatible behaviors was judged unfeasible. The wards were understaffed (a particular nurse having to deal with as many as 20 children) and were staffed by personnel unfamiliar with reinforcement procedures. In fact, the failure of the ward environment to provide reinforcement for alternative behaviors (coupled with the attention paid to the self-destruction) may have originally created, maintained, and increased the self-destruction. The viable alternatives, then center on extinction by "ignoring" *versus* suppression with severe aversive stimulation. The potential therapeutic value of this intervention, once the children were returned from our clinic to the state hospitals, will be discussed after the data on aversive stimulation has been presented.

Method

The three children reported here were obtained by requesting that two of the state hospitals in Southern California point out their worst cases of self-destructive children. We then requested transfer of the first three children referred to the Neuropsychiatric Institute at UCLA. These children were all known, in their respective hospitals, from among thousands of children for the severity of their self-destructive behavior. The children were hospitalized at UCLA for the explicit and limited purpose of investigating their self-destructive behavior.

The three children, John, Linda, and Gregg, can be described as follows. John was an 8-yr-old boy with a diagnosis of severe mental retardation (IQ = 24). There was no known organic basis for his retardation. He had no speech and showed only a very limited understanding of language, such as simple commands. He would visually attend to adults, but in general had minimal social behavior. He did not imitate, was not toilet trained, and did not dress himself. At various times in his life he had evidenced severe psychotic behaviors, such as smearing and eating of feces, drinking from the toilet bowl, mouthing of objects, rocking, etc. He had no play behavior. His self-destructive behavior started when he was 2-yr old. A medical examination at the time he was three noted that "his fists and knuckles were used to bang the temple and forehead area to a degree in which bruising and contusions are resulted". Apparently his parents were initially partly successful in suppressing self-destructive behavior by teaching incompatible behaviors. For example, during one of his psychological examinations, at age five, his mother had him hold a cup in each hand to prevent him from hitting himself. The self-destructive behavior worsened over time and caused the parents to hospitalize him at the age of seven. For six months before this study he had been in continuous restraints on both legs and arms. He would become extremely disturbed and refuse food if the restraints were removed. At this point in his development he needed complete care in feeding, hygiene, and all other aspects of his functioning. He had been on a combination of tranquilizers during his prior hospitalization with no visible effect on his self-abusive behavior. When admitted to UCLA, he had multiple scars all over his head and face. He was extremely agitated, kicked and screamed, and in general appeared extremely frightened and out of control, with a heart rate exceeding 200. Two days after hospitalization, he had settled down to the hospital routine, and the agitation and fear were seemingly gone but would reappear as soon as he was taken out of restraints.

Linda was 8 yr old at the time of hospitalization at UCLA. She had an IQ of 33 and was diagnosed as mentally retarded, etiology unknown. She evidenced some psychotic features, primarily in the form of self-stimulatory behavior. She had no speech and her understanding of speech was limited to correct responses to primitive commands. She had a viral infection at the age of two, at which point she stopped walking for three months and subsequently evidenced a bizarre gait. She was not toilet trained, could not feed herself, and in general needed complete nursing care. Unlike John, she resisted affectionate contact. She had bilateral cataracts, thought to be congenital, and was effectively blind. Her self-destructive behavior went back to her seventeenth month, and had become so severe that she had been kept in continuous restraints for 1.5 yr before her admission to UCLA. When she came to UCLA her left ear was bleeding, she had multiple scabs on both ears, and multiple bruises on both legs. Unlike John, she did not seem apprehensive upon admission, and her heart rate was within normal range, although she laughed excessively and inappropriately. She wore wrist restraints, tied around her thighs in such a fashion as to prevent her from hitting her ears. To prevent her knees from reaching her head, and thereby damaging herself, she had been placed on her abdomen while in bed, where she would lie quietly for most of the day, flopping her foot up and down rhythmically.

The third child, Gregg, was 11 yr old. He was diagnosed as having craniostenosis with motoric impairment and severe retardation (IQ = 13). He had been hospitalized since the age of 3.5 yr. As a child he was described as hyperactive and irritable. He was not toilet trained and could not dress himself. His self-destructive behavior started when he was 2 yr old. He had spent most of the two preceding years in restraints, tied on legs and arms to the four corners of his bed. He appeared unable to walk and was confined to a wheelchair. He had shortened Achilles tendons and some demineralization secondary to disuse. When placed on the floor he would stand still on his toes, hunched over, with his back bent, but it was judged physically possible for him to walk. He did not talk, but evidenced considerably delayed echolalia, particularly when upset. His social development was as limited as his intellectual, although he enjoyed physical contact, such as tickling and stroking. Upon admission to UCLA, he had about the same amount of scar tissue on his face and scalp as had Linda and John. Our informal probes revealed that none of the children responded appropriately to the word "no". It is important to note that these children came from, and would return to, settings where available treatments had failed and probably would continue to do so. Unless an effective technique was discovered, in all likelihood these children would remain self-destructive.

All experiments were conducted in sparsely furnished wardrooms that contained a bed, chest of drawers, a chair, and an occasional table. Some of these rooms had adjoining observation rooms connected by one-way mirrors and sound equipment, permitting observation and recording of the child's behavior. Recordings were made on a button panel, where each button corresponded to a particular behavior, the panel being wired into an Esterline Angus multiple pen recorder. A more detailed account of this observation technique has been given in a previous paper (Lovaas et al., 1965b). The observers were instructed to depress the button corresponding to a particular behavior and keep it depressed for the duration of that behavior. Three observers were randomly assigned to record at various times throughout the study, so as to rule out changes in the recordings being associated with peculiarities in any one observer.

The observers met with experimenters, who defined the behaviors in the presence of the child. If the observers did not exceed 90% agreement on any one behavior before the actual recordings, they were trained to do so. In no instance did the training exceed 1 hr. If agreement was not achieved in that time, the response was redefined.

The following behaviors were recorded (although all behaviors were not recorded in any one study): *Self-destructive behavior* was particularly unambiguous in its occurrence. The child would strike his head with his fists or hit his head against the side of the bed, the blows generating considerable noise; the observers agreed that this would have caused considerable pain to them they had done likewise. Their agreement in recording this behavior exceeded 95% without training. Two additional behaviors were recorded, in an attempt to measure more generalized changes which might help determine whether a particular form of intervention, such as aversive stimulation, should be employed. In particular, changes were recorded in withdrawal from attending adults. The adult would attempt to maintain close physical proximity to the child (less than 1 ft) and re-establish that contact as soon as the child moved away. *Withdrawal* was scored when the child was in the process of moving away from the adult [certain instances of this behavior were quite unambiguous, such as the child struggling to get off the adult's lap (*cf.* John on lap), or to withdraw a hand (*cf.* Linda during walk)]. An instance of emotional behavior, *whining*, was also recorded. The child would emit an annoying, screeching sound, without tears, and without communicating sadness or apprehension, but rather anger.

The three studies performed on these children, extinction through removal of interpersonal consequences, suppression by the use of painful shock, and increasing self-destruction through attention, are presented separately.

Extinction study

If the self-destructive behavior had been originally shaped by its effect on the social environment and if the maintenance of the behavior was dependent upon its producing social effects or consequences, then the removal of such consequences should weaken, and eventually stop, the self-destruction. That is, the behavior should extinguish. We had previously attempted extinction, in an informal manner, on another self-destructive boy, Rick (attending personnel were instructed not to give him attention when he hit himself, and to leave his room if he started self-destruction while they were present). Rick eventually did stop hitting himself under this arrangement, but the reduction in self-destruction was not immediate, and even took a turn for the worse when the extinction was first initiated, causing considerable bleeding and apparent physical discomfort. We feared, therefore, for the children's safety, and decided not to expose Linda to this treatment (her ears were already badly damaged), limiting the extinction to John and Gregg.

Extinction was carried out in a small, 12 by 12-ft experimental room with a bed and occasional furniture. The experimental room was connected to an adjoining observation room by one-way screens and sound equipment. The extinction sessions were conducted in the morning, on consecutive days. Each session lasted for 1.5 hr. The child was placed on the bed and his restraints removed; then the attending adults left the child alone. An observer in the observation room recorded each act of self-destructive behavior.

Figure 1 shows the extinction data on John and Gregg in terms of total frequency over days of extinction. The abscissa gives successive days of extinction and the ordinate gives the total number of self-destructive acts on any one day. John started with a high rate of 2750 self-destructive acts in the first 1.5 hr of extinction, declining to zero by the tenth session. John hit himself almost 9000 times before he quit. The data on Gregg are consistent with those of John: from a high of more than 900 self-destructive acts during the early part of extinction, his rate fell gradually to a low of 30 acts during the last part of extinction. It was different from John's in two respects: Gregg took more sessions for extinction and showed more irregularity. Actually, only the first 17 days of extinction represented "true" extinction, since certain experimental manipulations were superimposed upon the extinction from Session 18 on. These are discussed more fully in the subsequent section.

We have replicated the extinction operations on other institutionalized children, with similar, but not as intense, self-destructive behaviors as those of John and Gregg. In each instance, the self-destructive behavior showed a very gradual drop over time, being particularly vicious in the early stages of extinction. Our data are consistent with those reported by others. For example, Wolf, Risley, and Mees (1964) observed a similar cessation

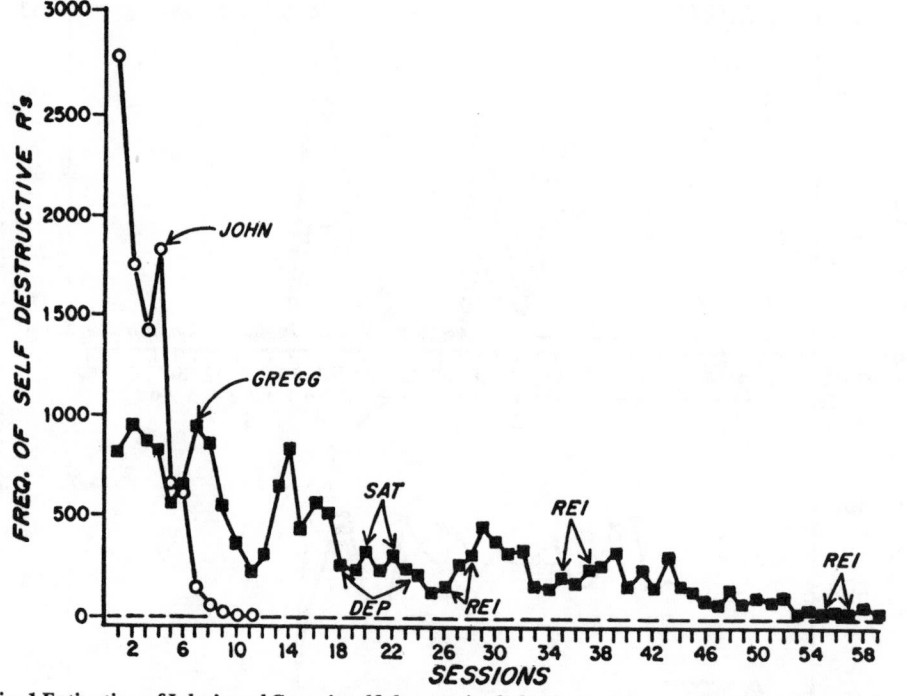

Fig. 1 Extinction of John's and Gregg's self-destructive behavior, over successive days of extinction, during 90-min sessions with total number of self-destructive acts on any one day given on the ordinate. SAT stands for satiation, DEP for deprivation, and REI for reinforcement.

of tantrumous and self-destructive behavior in an autistic child when the child was isolated from interpersonal contact contingent upon such behavior.

In summary, we can conclude that although extinction seemingly works, it is not an ideal form of treatment because the large amount of self-destructive behavior during the early stages of extinction subjects the child to much apparent discomfort. For some children extinction is ill-advised because the self-destructive behavior is severe enough to pose a high risk of severe or fatal damage, for example in children who bite themselves, tearing tissue.

Another disturbing feature of the extinction data pertains to the highly situational nature of effectiveness: while the self-destructive behavior fell to zero in the room used for extinction, it remained unaffected in other situations (these data are presented below). It is likely, therefore, that the child has to undergo extinction in a variety of situations. In view of these considerations, it was judged appropriate to investigate punishment (painful electric shock) as a way to suppress this behavior.

Punishment study

While John received extinction for self-destructive behavior in the first situation, the bedroom, we recorded his self-destruction in two other situations, referred to as "John during lap", and "John during room". In the first situation, "John during lap", John's restraints were removed, and the attending nurse sat him sideways on her lap, placing one arm behind his back for support and the other on his knees. Although he was allowed as much freedom of movement as possible, he was not allowed to get off her lap. These observations took place in the same ward, but in a different room from that used during his extinction. They were made on a daily basis, each observation lasting 5 min. In addition to recording the frequency of his self-destructive behavior, a record was also kept of the amount of time that he attempted to avoid the nurse (defined as struggle to get off her lap) and the amount of time whining.

The data on John during the lap sessions are presented in the upper half of Fig. 2. The abscissa gives the days, the kind of experimenter (one of four adults) present during that

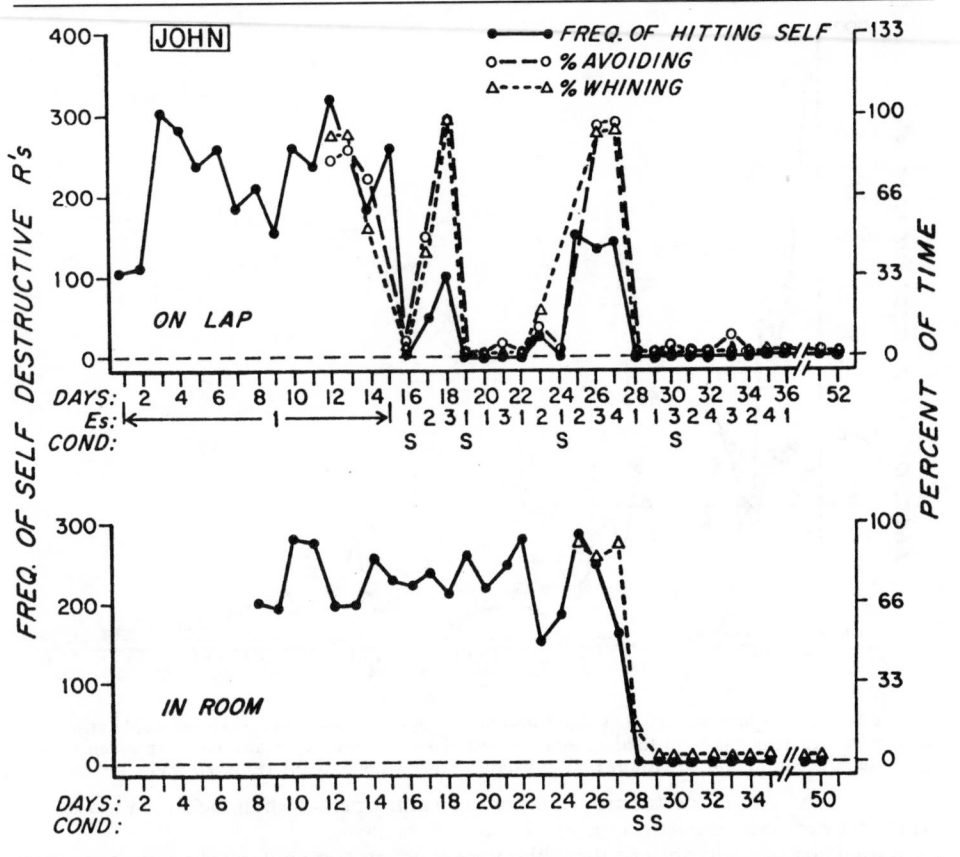

Fig. 2. Frequency of John's self-destructive behavior and the percentage of avoiding adults and whining, as a function of shock. Data are presented for two situations: daily 5-min sessions "on the lap" (upper half), and daily 10-min sessions "in the room" (lower half). The ordinate gives the particular experimenter (attending adult) present, condition (cond.) which shows when shock (S) was administered, and days, which are the same for the two situations, enabling comparison between the two situations. Shock was given by Experimenter 1 on Days 16, 19, and 24, and by Experimenter 3 on Day 30, in the lap situation. It was given on Days 28 and 29 in the room.

particular session, and condition: [S (shock)]. The ordinate gives either frequency of self-destructive behavior or per cent of time that John was avoiding and whining during the session. (Because of mechanical failures in the apparatus, some data are missing for some sessions.) The first 15 days were used to obtain his base rates. As can be observed, his rates stayed about the same over these 15 days, neither improving nor getting worse. It is important to note that the extinction of John's self-destructive behavior in the experimental room, as presented in Fig. 1, was going on during this time, and while he had reached Session 10 in the lap situation, he was effectively extinguished in the experimental room. The extinction, then, did not generalize to this situation. Punishment, in the form of a 1-sec electric shock, was delivered by a hand-held inductorium ("Hot-shot", by Hot-shot Products Company, Inc., Savage, Minnesota). The inductorium was a 1-ft long rod, with two electrodes, 0.75 in. apart, protruding from its end. The shock, delivered from five 1.5-v flashlight batteries, had spikes as high as 1400 v at 50,000 ohms resistance. It was definitely painful to the experimenter, like a dentist drilling on a unanesthetized tooth, but the pain terminated when shock ended. As soon as (within 1 sec) the child hit himself, the experimenter, holding the inductorium, reached over and applied it to the child's leg. The punishment (S in the figure) was introduced in Session 16 with dramatic results. John received a total of 12 shocks distributed over Sessions 16, 19, 24, and 30. There was a two-week span between Sessions 36 and 51, and it can be observed that his rate was low, even without shock, after that time period.

Two additional observations are of interest. The first pertains to the generalization of the suppression effect across experimenters. Up to Session 29, he was punished only by Experimenter 1. The suppression effected by Experimenter 1 generalized only partly to the other experimenters. By Sessions 25, 26, and 27 it can be observed that his rate of self-destructive behavior with the non-punishing adults was climbing alarmingly. In other words, he started to form a discrimination between the adult who punished him for self-destruction, and those who did not. In Session 30, Experimenter 3 also punished John for self-destruction, with the effect of producing generalization across other experimenters.

The second observation of interest pertained to the generalization of the shock effects to behaviors that were not punished. As self-destructive behavior was brought down by shock, John avoided the attending adult less and also whined less. Apparently, avoiding, whining, and self-destructive behavior fell within the same response class. These data indicated that the side effects of punishment were desirable. Informal clinical observations further confirmed the finding (John was observed by some 20 staff members), the nurse's notes reporting less distance and less fussing.

Perhaps the most significant changes that took place in John after he was freed from restraints were the ones we were unable to quantify. He was removed from restraints and shocked at 9 a.m. He appeared extremely frightened and agitated (apparently not by the shock but from the absence of restraints). He sat slumped on the floor, close to the wall and underneath the washbasin in a corner of his room. At 9:25 he moved out from the wall, peeked into a cupboard in the room, and then darted back to his original place of departure. He repeated this behavior at 9:40 and 9:50. At 10:00 and 10:30 he moved, in very gradual steps, from his room into the corridor and adjoining room. He became very rambunctious, running up and down the hallway, seemingly insatiable. Freedom from restraint also permitted him many other apparently reinforcing discoveries: that first afternoon he allowed himself a full hour of scratching himself, a luxury he had not been allowed while his hands were tied behind his back. He had been so self-destructive that it had been almost impossible to give him a bath in a tub. Freed of self-destructive behavior, he behaved much like a seal when he was placed in a tub, screaming in happiness and scooting underneath the water with his face up and eyes open.

The hallway and the bath were immediately adjacent to the location in which he was shocked, and maintained the suppression. The effect of shock did not generalize to rooms some distance away (e.g., in another part of the ward) from the punishment situation. For example, it did not generalize to the other situation where we kept a record of his self-destruction, called "John during room". In this situation, he was left free to wander around a small dormitory room in the company of two or three adults. The sessions lasted for 10 min each, and were conducted once each day; during this time the rates of his self-destructive behavior and his whining were recorded.

Data from this study are presented in the lower half of Fig. 2. The days along the abscissa in the lower half correspond to those in the upper half, so that his behaviors in the two situations can be readily compared. Twenty days (Days 8 through 27) of pre-experimental measurements were obtained. They show that his self-destruction was essentially unaffected by what occurred in the lap situation, where his self-destruction had been esssentially eliminated by Day 16. (It should be pointed out that the pre-experimental sessions in Fig. 2, as in Fig. 3 and 4, approximate extinction sessions, since self-destruction was left unattended. Apparently 10 min sessions were too short for extinction, probably reflecting the thinness of the schedule of reinforcement, less than VI 10-min, which had supported the self-destruction in the past.)

He was given two 1-sec shocks on Days 28 and 29. This brought his self-destructive behavior down to zero and retained it at that level until the end of the experiment, some 18 days later. At the same time as his self-destructive behavior was decreasing, whining also disappeared. In general, these data are identical to those observed during the first shock session, except that fewer shocks were necessasry to suppress the behavior.

At the end of this last experiment, shock was introduced in all other situations. It is

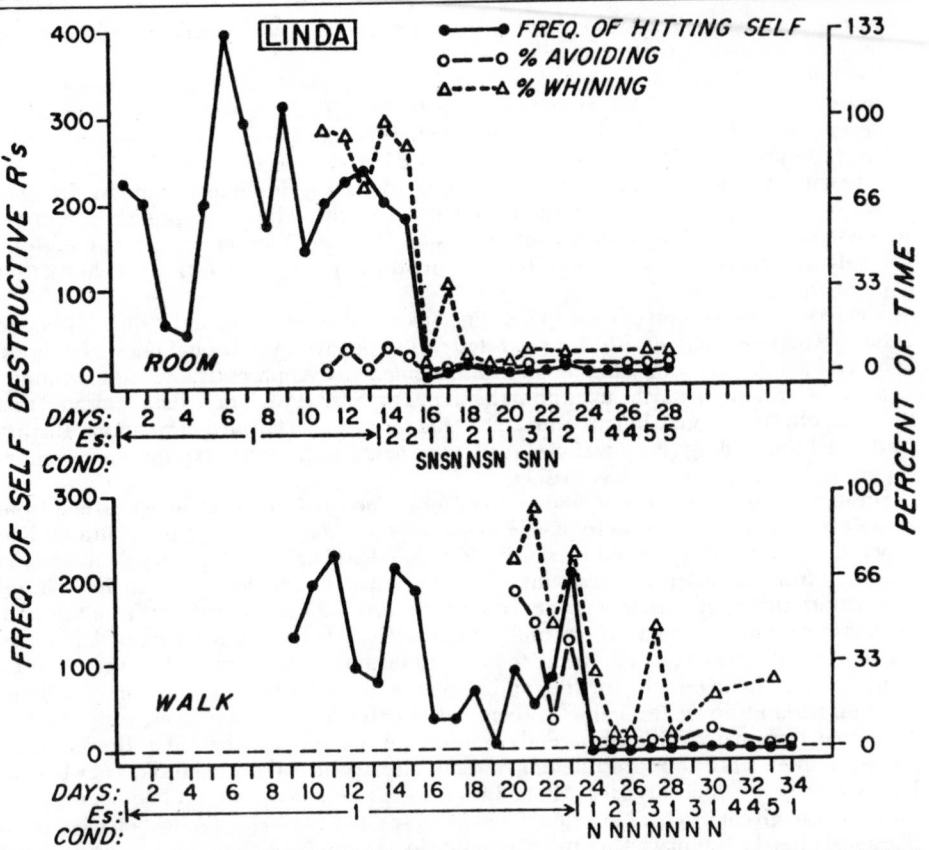

Fig. 3. Frequency of Linda's self-destructive behavior and the percentage of avoiding adults and whining as a function of shock (S) and of "No" (N). Data are from the two situations: daily 5-min sessions "in the room" (upper half), and daily 5-min sessions "on the walk" (lower half). The days in the two situations are the same, enabling comparison between situations.

notable that John was effectively freed from self-destructive behavior after five shocks in other (on the ward and on the street) situations. In other words, it was possible to achieve suppression of his self-destructive behavior in a large variety of situations using only a few shocks.

We attempted to study the effect of shock on Linda's self-destructive behavior in the same manner as John had been studied. The effect of shock on Linda was observed in two situations. The first situation, "Linda during room", consisted of 5-min sessions, one session per day. The data from this experiment are presented in the upper half of Fig. 3. The abscissa gives number of days, kind of experimenter (one of five) present during that session, and conditions. The first 15 days served as base-rate measures. There was considerable variability in these sessions, but they showed neither a worsening nor an improvement in her self-destruction. Experimenter 1 administered a 1-sec shock (S) to her while at the same time she gave the patient a loud "no" (denoted by the letter N on the abscissa). She received one shock on each of Days 16, 17, 19, and 21, and it is apparent that her rate fell to zero or near-zero immediately, with the shock effects generalizing across experimenters. During Days 18 and 22, she received merely the word "no". "No" had been tested for suppressing properties for Linda before its pairing with shock (on Days 14 and 15) and was demonstrated to be neutral (*i.e.*, ineffective).

One can observe the same change in non-punished behaviors with Linda as was the case with John: there was a substantial decrease in both avoiding of the attending adults and whining after shock was administered.

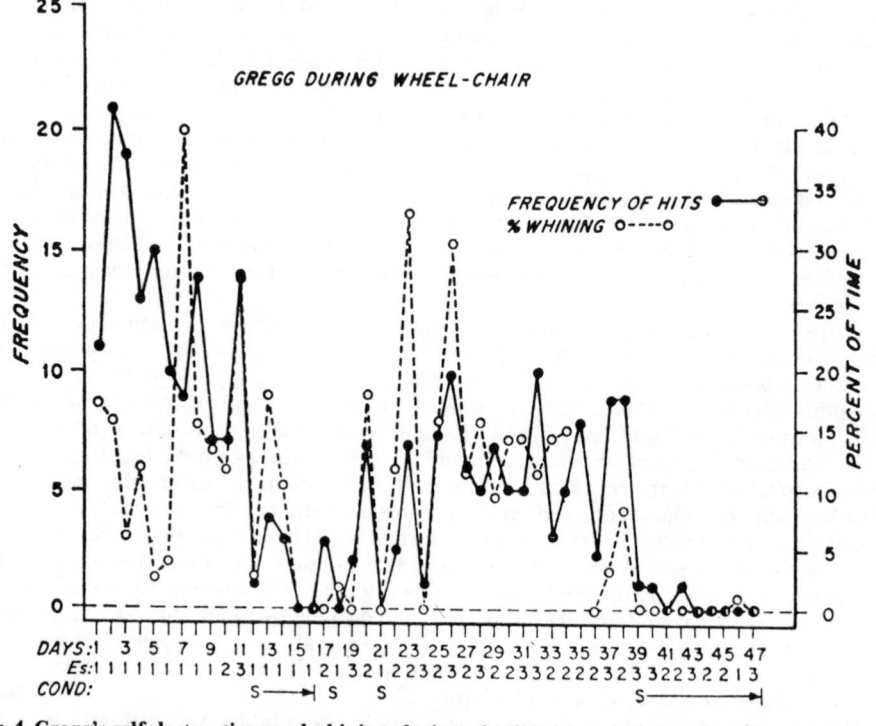

Fig. 4. Gregg's self-destructions and whining, during wheelchair sessions, as a function of shock (S) and the attending adult (E) who delivered shock. Each session ran 2.5 min.

The other situation in which Linda was studied is referred to as "Linda during walk". In these sessions the experimenter and Linda walked together up and down a corridor for a 5-min period. The experimenter held Linda's hand; if Linda pulled away, which was scored as avoiding, the experimenter would let her go and then restablish hand-to-hand contact. We were particularly interested in whether the word "no", which had been paired with shock during the room sessions, had acquired suppressing properties.

The data are presented in the lower half of Fig. 3. The abscissa shows which experimenter was attending to her. The days correspond to those in the upper half of the figure (Room sessions) so that her behaviors in the two situations can be readily compared. In addition to keeping track of her self -destructive behavior and her whining, avoiding behavior defined as pulling away from the experimenter's hand, was recorded. The first 15 days (9 through 23) served as baseline. As we had already observed with John, there was no effective generalization from shock in the room (Day 16 on) to the walk situation. On days 16 through 21, a loud "no" was given contingent upon self-destructive behavior, and it served to bring that behavior to zero level. The effects generalized across experimenters (4 and 5). The correlated behavior changes were the same as in the other studies reported: a concurrent suppression of whining and avoiding behavior.

Gregg was the last child with whom we observed the effect of shock under these controlled conditions. He was studied during one situation referred to as "Gregg during wheelchair". These sessions took place one week after extinction and the accompanying seven sessions of reinforcement for self-destruction (to be discussed later) had been completed. The sessions lasted for 2.5 min. He was placed in a standard wheelchair on one side of the experimental room (he was placed in a wheelchair because he did not walk). His self-destruction was so violent that the arms of the chair had to be padded. An attending adult sat directly in front of and facing him.

The data on Gregg in the wheelchair are presented in Fig. 4. The first 11 sessions served to establish the base rate, and produced no apparent change in his behavior. He was given shock by Experimenter 1 in each of Sessions 12, 13, and 14. His self-destruction was almost immediately suppressed during these sessions. Experimenter 2 and Experimenter 3 did not punish him at this time and it can be observed that his self-destructive behavior increased in their presence over the next several sessions (Sessions 22 through 38). In other words, he formed a discrimination between Experimenter 1 and other experimenters as had John (Fig. 2). He was punished with shock by the other experimenters starting at Session 39 and the result shows an unambiguous drop in self-destruction. It was consistent with the data obtained on Linda and John, *i.e.,* as self-destructive behavior was brought down by the use of shock, there was a concomitant drop in whining. In the case of Gregg, we also recorded his physical contact with the attending adults and his vocalizations, but these were not systematically related to the experimental operations or correlated with the other behaviors.

In the case of both Gregg and John (Fig. 4 and 2 respectively) we replicated the effect of the noxious stimulus in a single subject design. Considering also the replication across subjects and situations, we no doubt are dealing with a reliable phenomenon.

Additional data on self-destruction, from more casual recording procedures, support the data on John, Linda, and Gregg. One of the most severe cases seen was Marilyn.[2] She was a 16-yr-old child diagnosed as retarded (moderate range) with psychotic features. She had been hospitalized for the previous 2 yr, and had been self-injurious since she was 2 yr old. The referring complaint centered on the parents' inability to control her self-destructive behavior. During her 2 yr of hospitalization she had been kept in a camisole in an attempt to prevent this behavior. When removed from the camisole, or when she removed the camisole herself by using her teeth, she would bite her hands so severely that at one time the little finger on her right hand had to be amputated to the first joint. She would similarly, with her teeth, remove her nails by their roots. She was also a head-banger; her scalp was covered with scar tissue. She would fall to the ground without apparent reason, scream, and occasionally aggress toward others by biting them.

Her base rate of "spontaneous" injury was very low, and in that way different from the other children's. That is, self-destructive acts were highly discriminated: she would mutilate herself only whenever the experimenter gave her affection, such as comforting her or praising her (33 self-injurious behaviors out of the 36 such interactions with her before shock). The first session lasted for about 2 hr; half way into the session she was given shock for self-destructive behavior. A total of five shocks (on the first, fourth, fifth, and fifteenth presentation of the affectionate interaction) brought her biting and head-banging to zero, and it remained at zero-level for the rest of the session. The suppression data on Marilyn were virtually identical to the others.

Because of the extreme severity of her self-injurious behavior, Marilyn demonstrated why it is impossible to place such a child on extinction. Marilyn could have inflicted serious self-injury or even killed herself during the extinction run.

While the immediate generalized behavior change due to shock was very favorable, there is some reason to believe that her aggression toward other children on the ward increased at a later time. Apparently, the reinforcers that maintained the self-destructive behavior were still operative, and since she did not develop a more acceptable behavior form, which seems to be the case in most children, and was not explicitly trained to behave otherwise, she returned to a form of behavior which also yielded large quantities of attention.

The data on shock can be summarized as follows. First, the use of shock, given contingent upon self-destructive behavior, brings about an immediate cessation of that behavior. Second, the effect of shock appears specific to the situations in which it is administered. If a child is shocked in one room and not in another, or by one person and not another, he sometimes will form a discrimination between these situations. Finally, both in the changes that we were able to record objectively and in the clinical observations, there was every evidence that the side effects of punishment, instead of being undesirable, were judged to be therapeutically desirable.

[2]Thomas Ball, Ph.D., Chief Psychologist at Pacific State Hospital in Pomona, California, and Lawrence Dameron, Ph.D., formerly on the staff at Pacific State, had the major responsibility for the research with Marilyn.

Worsening the self-destructive behavior

It is apparent from the data presented above that considerable changes can be effected in destructive behavior, either by extinction or punishment. That there must be other variables that control self-destructive behavior is apparent on inspection of the great amount of variability present in all our baselines. Consider, as an example, the variability in the extinction data on Gregg, which was presented in Fig. 1. Within a matter of three or four days, his rate of self-destruction fell from more than 900 (Session 7) to less than 300 (Session 11) and then increased to more than 800 hits per session. Such large shifts in amount of self-destructive behavior surely must be related to powerful variables and it is, therefore, appropriate to search for them.

We had some reason to suspect that these fluctuations in self-destructive behavior were caused by changes in the kinds of nursing care received on any one day. In particular, the early peaks in self-destruction occurred on Mondays, and we knew that the nursing personnel who cared for him over the weekend approached him differently from those who cared for him during the week. The nature of this difference was unknown, however, and could be a function of deprivation of interpersonal relationships, satiation of such relationships, or an undue amount of attention being paid to his self-destruction. Of course, a large number of other dimensions in interpersonal relationships could be responsible for the rise and fall in his self-destructive behavior.

In an attempt to identify some of the sources responsible for the magnitude of his self-destructive behavior, certain probes were initiated. First, we considered that deprivation of attention was responsible for a rise in self-destruction. Therefore, he was placed on a 24-hr period of social deprivation before Sessions 18 and 24 (DEP in Fig. 1). Essentially, Gregg was left alone in his room except for being changed and fed. He would lie the entire day on his bed in restraints, much as a typical day in a state hospital. The rate of self-destructive behavior after these deprivation operations was not different, however, from other days. To check further on the effectiveness of such operations of availability of social stimulation, we instigated two days of social satiation. During the 24-hr periods before Sessions 20 and 22 (SAT also in Fig. 1), Gregg was given continual attention during his waking hours, such as being talked to, touched, tickled, hugged and kissed, walked, and generally stimulated an excessive amount. However, there was no significant change in his self-destructive behavior accompanying such periods of social stimulation. We concluded, therefore, that the availability of interpersonal stimulation (*per se*) had no appreciable effect upon his self-destruction.

One form of nursing intervention of particular interest to us centered on the nurse's reaction to the child when he was self-destructive. We observed that the great majority of nursing personnel would be particularly likely to interact with him contingent upon his self-destruction. Anyone who has been around self-destructive children has experienced an urge to attend to such children when they hurt themnselves, in an attempt to nurse their suffering. In fact, nursing personnel, as well as parents, are typically given explicit directions by the doctors and nurses in charge of the case to respond to self-destructive behavior with warmth and "understanding", attempting to reassure the child that they are in attendance, that he need not be afraid, and other words and gestures to that effect.

We tested the effects of this kind of intervention during Sessions 26 and 28 (REI in Fig. 1) Half an hour into the session, an adult would enter the room contingent upon Gregg's self-destructive behavior, hold Gregg's hands and say in a pleading voice, "don't do that, Gregg, everything is OK" and other comments to that effect. This contact lasted for approximately 30 sec, at the end of which the attending person would again leave. The adult would appear on the average of every third time Gregg hit himself. If one considers Sessions 25 through 34, it looked as if his self-destructive behavior temporarily worsened (acquisition followed by extinction). We replicated these operations (REI) in Sessions 35 and 37. Again, there seemed to be some worsening of his self-destructive behavior following these operations. However, when these operations were reintroduced a third time during Sessions 55 and 57, we did not replicate the observations.

On the basis of these data, we entertained the possibility that his self-destructive behavior was under the control of the attention paid to that behavior, but that the attention he did receive was a rather weak consequence which lost its reinforcing properties over time: that

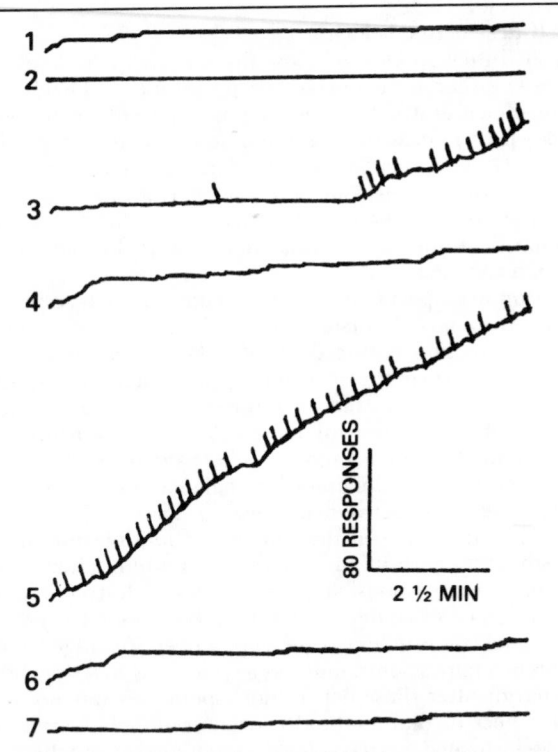

Fig. 5. Gregg's self-destruction, as cumulative response curves, over successive sessions (1 through 7). The upward moving hatchmarks in Sessions 3 and 5 mark delivery of sympathetic comments, play, *etc.*, contingent on self-destruction.

is, it lost its reinforcing properties as its S^D properties extinguished. This led us to investigate whether there were other consequences that would lead to greater control over his self-destruction.

The day after the last extinction day (Session 59 in Fig. 1), we obtained a new base rate of Gregg's self-destructive behavior in the same situation where he had undergone extinction. The new base rate data are presented in Fig. 5 as cumulative curves. Numbers 1 and 2 refer to the first and second 10-min sessions that formed the base rate of self-destruction: he was left to hit himself and no one did anything about it. The number 3 refers to the third 10-min session where approach was changed as follows. On an average of every fifth time that Gregg hit himself, we would take him out of the crib for about 30 to 60 sec and, in addition to comforting him, would allow him to play with some drawers, closet doors, and wooden blocks, which we knew that he liked to play with. On the average of every fifth reinforcement, we would take him for a 5-min walk (with the experimenter's physical assistance) from his bedroom to the day room. Again, Gregg very much enjoyed to be taken for a walk. This 10-min reinforcement period (referred to as number 3 in Fig. 5) was followed by a 10-min extinction session (number 4 in Fig. 5). This extinction session was similar to the pre-experimental operation denoted with number 1 and 2. The next day, we again gave attention and play contingent upon self-destructive behavior (number 5 in Fig. 5). Finally, we ended with 2 hr of extinction with the first 10 min and the last 10 min presented as 6 and 7, respectively.

It is apparent that this approach, trying, in a sense, to "understand" what Gregg wanted and to give it to him when he was self-destructive, is a very dangerous form of treatment. His rate went up the first time we did this (number 3) and climbed alarmingly the second time (number 5). In fact, the attending adults agreed that if we had continued to attend to his self-destruction, we could have hurt him badly. This could have been true particularly if we had given attention contingent upon larger and larger amounts of self-destruction, as might happen when a parent or attendant becomes "used to", or adapted to, a particular level of self-destructive behavior.

This finding was consistent with one reported earlier (Lovaas *et al.*, 1965a) where a child's self-destructive behavior worsened when we attempted to communicate sympathy and reassurance contingent upon such behavior. Such therapy is typically prescribed for such children when tne therapist attempts to address himself to the alleviation of some internal pathology, such as anxiety, for which the self-destruction is seen as an expression. Reinforcing attention is also likely to be given spontaneously by adults, since it is extremely difficult to withhold expressions of concern when a child appears to hurt himself. If our data are reliable, then it is such expressions which keep the child in restraints. Said differently, in this instance the expression of "love" contingent upon self-destructive behavior benefits only the giver.

The great majority of studies on treatment attempt to isolate the conditions under which a particular problem can be alleviated. There is also some value in attempting to assess whether aspects of current treatments do in fact worsen the patient's condition. Ideally, such studies help change old treatments.

Discussion

Our data can be summarized as follows. Two procedures effectively terminated the self-destructive behavior. The first procedure, carried out with two of the children, involved an extinction paradigm, whereby the child was allowed to hurt himself, isolated from personal contact. In both these instances, the self-destructive behavior was terminated. Our data are consistent with those obtained by Risley *et al.* (1964), who used extinction procedures to reduce the self-destructive behavior of a 3.5-yr-old boy. Additional data which support this kind of intervention have been reviewed by Gardner (1967).

This procedure of withdrawing or making potential reinforcers unavailable has an undesirable attribute, in that it is not immediately effective and temporarily exposes the child to the danger of severe damage from his own self-destruction, which is particularly intense during the early stages of the extinction run. In some cases of severe self-destruction, it is ill-advised to place the child on extinction. Marilyn (reviewed above), for example, could have inflicted serious self-injury or possibly even killed herself during an extinction run.

We reported five studies, carried out on three children, in which we observed an immediate suppression of self-destructive behavior when aversive stimuli were given contingent upon that behavior. This finding is consistent with data from previous work with aversive stimuli (Lovaas, Schaeffer, and Simmons, 1965) which reported the suppression of tantrums and self-destruction in two 5-yr-old autistic boys. Risley (1968), Tate and Baroff (1967), and others (as reviewed by Bucher and Lovaas, 1967) have reported similar findings.

The effects of shock appear to be specific to the situation in which shock is used, with respect to both physical locales and attending adults. This implies that if punishment to suppress self-destruction is to be maximally therapeutic (*i.e.*, durable and general) it has to be administered by more than one person, in more than one setting. Our data amply suggest that each child would revert to self-destruction as soon as he returned to the treatment settings from which he came, unless his treatment under those conditions was made consistent with our procedures. The children, in other words, formed discriminations. Figure 2 illustrates how quickly such discriminations can come about. Again, our previous work and the work of others (*e.g.*, Risley, 1968; Hamilton and Standahl, 1967) is consistent on the highly discriminated stimulus control of shock. We observed also that the children did not become generally fearful of the adults who administer the punishment, but showed fear of the adult only when the adult gave signs of disapproval (looking angry and verbalizing anger, as he does when he administers punishment) or when they are in the act of self-destruction. That observation also supports the specificity of the shock-effects. Most likely, such discriminations come about because of the adults' differential treatment. Should the adult administer only punishment, then it seems likely that the child would become generally fearful of him. However, the adult who administered punishment for self-destruction was associated with the child in a number of situations, as a caretaking and parental person, administering love when the child acted appropriately. Watson (1967) made this point explicitly in discussing punishment effects.

One of the surprising findings on the use of shock pertains to the immediate increase in socially directed behavior, such as eye-to-eye contact and physical contact, as well as the simultaneous decrease in a large variety of inappropriate behaviors, such as whining, fussing, and facial grimacing. Such response generalization has also been reported by others: Risley (1968) made specific efforts to record some of these. Hamilton, Stevens, and Allen (1967) described their children, after punishment, ". . . to be more socially outgoing, happier, and better adjusted in the ward setting . . ." (p. 856). White and Taylor (1967) reported, as a consequence of shock, that their patients ". . . appeared to be more aware of and interact more with the examiner . . ." (p. 32). We reported similar findings in an earlier study (Lovaas et al., 1965c). We have a filmed record that quite dramatically portrays the changes in John.

Some of these behavioral changes might occur for rather "mechanical" reasons: that is, it is difficult for a child who whines to smile simultaneously. It is easier for a child, removed from the restraints of his bed, to come into contact with more rewarding aspects of his environment, etc. Some of the beneficial changes will be specific to certain children. For example, the suppression of self-destruction (largely head-banging) in Linda permitted surgery for her cataracts, with resultant alleviation of her restricted vision. Some of the behavioral changes accompanying shock probably occur because reinforcements have been given to the child for behaving appropriately when faced with aversive stimuli in the past. Finally, certain behaviors may be elicited by shock as an unconditioned stimulus: that is, certain kinds of stress, fears, or pains may call forth socially oriented behavior at a purely biological level. A number of interesting questions await research in that area.

Although the immediate "side-effects" of punishment point in a desirable direction, one should be less optimistic about long-term behavioral change under certain conditions. We can supply few data which exceed a couple of months follow-up, and in the case of only two children have we had the opportunity to conduct follow-ups for as much as 1 yr, while the suppression of self-destruction was being maintained. It seems reasonable that if social reinforcement controlled the self-destructive behavior in the first place, then that reinforcement being unaltered in strength through punishment operations, should retain the power to build other, equally undesirable, behaviors. If the child had to go to such extremes as self-destruction to gain some attention from his attending adults, then it seems but reasonable that these adults, unless they were taught to respond to more appropriate behavior, would repeat themselves and begin shaping some similarly alarming behavior, such as feces smearing or eating, aggression toward other children, etc. Within reinforcement theory terms, the suppression of one behavior may be discriminative for a large number of other behaviors, some more and some less desirable than the suppressed one.

These children have demonstrated through their self-destruction, that they will apparently withstand considerable pain to get attention, and that they may have considerable experience with pain adaptation. To avoid selecting a neutral shock, or a weak one to which the children could adapt quickly, we have used a strong shock which guaranteed quick suppression. By a strong shock is meant a shock which the experimenters experienced as definitely painful (smarted like a whip, or a dentist drilling on an unanesthetized tooth), and to which the subjects gave every sign of fear and apprehension. The question is sometimes raised as to how, in view of the much more severe pain associated with self-destruction (e.g., pulling own nails out with teeth), the shock works in the first place. We can offer two guesses in this regard: the child has not had an opportunity to adapt to shock, nor has the shock been associated with positive reinforcement, both of which may have occurred with the painful stimuli generated by the self-destruction.

References

Bucher, B., Lovaas, O. I. Use of aversive stimulation in behavior modification. In Jones, M. R. (Ed.). Miami symposium on the prediction of behavior 1967: aversive stimulation. (pp.77-145.) Coral Gables, Florida: University of Miami Press, 1968.

Gardner, J. E. Behavior therapy treatment approach to a psychogenic seizure case. *J. Consult. Psychol.*, 1967;; **31**, 209-212.

Hamilton, H., Stephens, L., Allen, P. Controlling aggressive and destructive behavior in severely retarded institutionalized residents. *Am. J. Ment. Defic.*, 1967; **71**, 852-856.

Hamilton, J., Standahl, J. *Suppression of stereotyped screaming behavior in a profoundly retarded institutionalized female.* (Unpublished paper.) Georgia: Gracewood State School, 1967.

Lovaas, O. I., Freitag, G., Gold, Vivian J., Kassorla, Irene C. Experimental studies in childhood schizophrenia: analysis of self-destructive behavior. *J. Experi. Child Psychol.*, 1965(a); **2**, 67-84.

Lovaas, O. I., Freitag, G., Gold, Vivian J., Kassorla, Irene C. A recording method and observations of behaviors of normal and autistic children in free play settings. *J. Experi. Child Psychol.*, 1965(b); **2**, 108-120.

Lovaas, O. I. Schaeffer, B., Simmons, J. Q. Experimental studies in childhood schizophrenia: building social behavior in autistic children by the use of electric shock. *J. Experi. Research Personnel.*, 1965; **1**, 99-109.

Risley, T. The effects and side effects of punishing the autistic behaviors of a deviant child. *J. Appl. Behav. Anal.*, 1968; **1**, 21-35.

Tate, B. G., Baroff, G. S. Aversive control of self-injurious behavior in a psychotic boy. *Behav. Res. & Ther.*, 1966; **4**, 281-287.

Watson, L. S. Application of operant conditioning techniques to institutionalized severely and profoundly retarded children. *Ment. Retard. Abstr.*, 1967; **4**, 1-18.

White, J. C., Jnr., Taylor, D. Noxious conditioning as a treatment for rumination. *Ment. Retard.*, 1967; **6**, 30-33.

Wolf, M., Risley, T., Mees, H. Application of operant conditioning procedures to the behavior problems of an autistic child. *Behav. Res. & Ther.*, 1964; **1**, 305-312.

Reprinted from *J. Appl. Behav. Anal.*, 1969; **2**:3, 143-157 by kind permission of JABA, University of Kansas, Lawrence, Kansas 66045. Copyright 1969 by the Society for the Experimental Analysis of Behavior Inc.

STIMULUS CONTROL OF SELF-DESTRUCTIVE BEHAVIOR IN A PSYCHOTIC CHILD[1]

Edward G. Carr[2]
University of California, Los Angeles

Crighton D. Newsom
Camarillo State Hospital

Jody A. Binkoff
University of California, Santa Barbara

This study attempted to isolate some of the stimulus variables that controlled the self-destructive behavior of a psychotic child. In Experiment 1, the child was exposed to several demand and nondemand situations. In Experiment 2, the situation containing demands was modified so that demands now occurred in the context of a positive, ongoing interaction between the child and the adult therapist. The rates of self-destructive behavior underwent several orderly changes: (1) rates were high in demand situations and low in nondemend and modified-demand situations; (2) rates decreased sharply when a stimulus correlated with the termination of demands was introduced; and (3) rates of self-destruction typically showed gradual increases within each of those sessions which contained only demands. These results were interpreted as suggesting that (1) self-destruction, under certain circumstances, may be conceptualized as an escape response which is negatively reinforced by the termination of a demand situation and (2) certain modifications of the social environment may provide discriminative stimuli for behaviors other than self-destruction, thereby decreasing this behavior.

A number of children diagnosed as psychotic, retarded, or brain-damaged exhibit self-destructive behavior, that is, behavior which results in physical injury to the child's own body. The most prevalent forms of self-destruction are head-banging, face-slapping, and biting of the hands, arms, or shoulders. Because such behavior poses a physical threat to the child's well-being, as well as preventing him from participating in normal social and academic activities, the problem has been the focus of a great deal of research. The majority of such research has been concerned with altering the *consequences* of self-destructive behavior. Thus, investigators have reduced the frequency of self-destructive behaviors by utilizing extinction (Lovaas & Simmons, 1969); timeout (Wolf, Risley, & Mees, 1964; Hamilton, Stephens, & Allen, 1967); positive reinforcement of behaviors incompatible with self-destruction (Lovaas, Freitag, Gold, & Kassorla, 1965; Peterson & Peterson, 1968); and punishment (Tate & Baroff, 1966; Lovaas & Simmons, 1969; Corte, Wolf, & Locke, 1971).

The literature cited above makes it clear that by manipulating the consequences of self-destruction, it is possible to achieve considerable control over this behavior. Nevertheless, one occasionally encounters children who, for various reasons, respond poorly to some or all of the above interventions (Bachman, 1972). The present study dealt with just such a child. The treatment failures cited underline our imperfect understanding of self-destructive behavior and provide an incentive to seek new interventions. In the present case, the casual observation that the child's self-destructive behavior appeared to worsen considerably whenever he was placed in a demand situation led us to consider the

[1]This investigation was supported in part by USPHS Research Grant 11440 from the National Institute of Mental Health. The research was conducted while the first author held a postdoctoral fellowship from the Medical Research Council of Canada. The authors thank John and Lynn Killion and Dennis Russo for their help in data collection and Ivar Lovaas, Laura Schreibman, and Robert Koegel for their many helpful criticisms. The encouragement and support of Tim's parents during the course of this study are sincerely appreciated.

[2]Requests for reprints should be sent to Edward Carr, Lovaas Laboratory, Department of Psychology, UCLA, Los Angeles, California 90024.

possibility of an intervention based on appropriate manipulations of antecedent stimuli (such as demands) rather than consequences. By concentrating the experimental analysis on antecedent stimulus variables, it might be possible not only to develop effective procedures for decreasing self-destruction but also to discover new functional relationships relating to the motivation of self-destructive behavior. Accordingly, we designed two experiments to study the effects of stimulus variables on self-destructive behavior. In Experiment 1 we attempted to isolate those stimulus situations which seemed to be particularly conducive to high rates of self-destructive behavior. In Experiment 2 we sought to modify the stimulus properties of those situations so as to reduce the frequency of this behavior.

EXPERIMENT 1

Method

Subject

Tim was 8 years old and had a diagnosis of schizophrenia, childhood type, with associated mental retardation. His Stanford-Binet IQ was 66 (mildly retarded range). He had limited expressive and receptive speech and understood only simple commands and requests. He had some social behavior; for example, he would occasionally talk to adults or show signs of affection such as kissing. He could imitate rather extensively and had adequate self-care skills. Visual hallucinations may have been present, since he was occasionally observed to stare into space while talking and gesticulating vigorously. He often engaged in self-stimulatory behavior (primarily body rocking). His self-destruction began when he was 2 years old. Typically, he would hit his head and face with his closed fist or the palm of his hand at various times throughout the day. The intensity of his self-destructive behavior was seldom great but he would often bruise or cut his face through the cumulative effect of many hours of hitting. Before we saw Tim, he had received several unsuccessful forms of treatment for his hitting, including drugs (Mellaril, Ritalin, and Thorazine), restraints (hands tied behind the back), contingent electric shock, extinction, timeout, and reinforcement of incompatible behaviors. We were alerted to Tim's problem by his teachers, who complained that his self-destructive behavior worsened considerably whenever he was put in a classroom situation.

Apparatus and recording technique

All sessions were conducted in one of two 2.4- by 3.7-m experimental rooms, one with a red carpet and one with a brown carpet. Henceforth, these rooms will be referred to as the red room and the brown room, respectively. At one end of each room was a one-way mirror. On the ceiling behind the child and out of his sight was a small, 6-w, green light bulb which was used to signal the start and finish of each session to the adult (experimenter). During sessions, the door to the room was locked. In all sessions, the adult and the child sat facing each other near the one-way mirror, except during the Free Time condition (see below), in which Tim was not required to sit in his chair.

In the observation rooms adjacent to each experimental room, recordings were made on button panels wired to an Esterline Angus multiple pen recorder in a soundproof box. Six observers (four of whom were naive to the purposes of the study) were randomly assigned to record at various times throughout the study.

Two behaviors were recorded: self-hitting and compliance. Self-hitting was defined as any blow delivered to the face or head with the closed fist or the palm of the hand. Compliance was defined as a correct response to a command within 5 sec; the list of commands is given below. Hitting and compliance were not mutually exclusive behaviors: It was possible for Tim to hit himself while in the act of complying and, in fact, he sometimes did.

A minimum of one reliability check was taken during each condition of an experiment. In Experiment 1 there was a total of 15 reliability checks, and in Experiment 2, there were 10. Each reliability observer was naive to the purpose of the experiment in progress. The response definitions were communicated verbally to each of the observers a few minutes before the start of a session. The reliability index was the percentage of agreement between the two observers calculated by dividing the smaller total frequency by the larger total frequency. In Experiment 1, the mean interobserver reliability for hitting frequency was 91% (range: 75% to 100%) and for compliance to mands, 100%. In Experiment 2, reliability on hitting was 99% (range: 95% to 100%) and for mand compliance, 100%.

Procedure

In Experiment 1, we assessed the effects of three different stimulus conditions on the rate of Tim's hitting. These conditions were the following.

Free Time. This condition was intended to approximate those periods of the day on the ward when Tim was not engaged in any structured activity. He was free to roam about the room, to sit, or to lie down. If he talked to the adult, the adult would answer him politely and briefly, avoiding a conversation. (This restriction also held for the Tacts and Mands conditions described below). Such interactions were rare. At all other times, the adult would avoid eye contact or talking. No demands were placed on Tim.

Tacts. This condition served as a control for the effects of verbalizations per se on self-destructive behavior. The adult presented a series of simple declarative sentences, none of which required a response from Tim (e.g., "The grass is green"). A list of these tacts (Skinner, 1957) appears in Table 1. Each session consisted of 20 tact presentations whose order changed daily. The adult presented the tacts at the rate of once every 30 sec on the average, irrespective of Tim's ongoing behavior. The adult would call the child's name, look him in the eye, smile, and deliver the tact. The adult would then look away and avoid eye contact or talking.

Mands. This condition was intended to approximate a structured classroom or therapy situation. Tim was presented with a series of 20 commands (e.g., "Point to the door"), which appear in Table 1. These mands (Skinner, 1957) were very similar to mands we had observed Tim to carry out correctly and easily on the ward. The method and order of presenting the mands was the same as that described for the tacts with the following modifications. If Tim responded correctly to a mand, the adult would pat him on the leg and praise him. (In other, nonexperimental situations, we found this combination of social reinforcers to be effective for Tim). If he responded incorrectly or failed to respond within 5 sec, the adult would look away from him. When the adult was not presenting mands to Tim, he would avoid eye contact or talking with Tim.

The sessions in each of the above three conditions were conducted in the following manner. Tim was brought to either the red or the brown room first (the order varying from day to day) and a 10-min component would be run. At the end of the first component, the adult would announce, "Okay, let's go," and unlock the door to the room. The adult and child would then walk down a hall to the other room and the next component would begin 3-5 min later. Each set of two components constituted a session. Sessions were carried out 5 days per week, one or two sessions per day, the minimum time between sessions being 4 hours.

The experimental design used to assess the effects of mands on self-destructive behavior was a multiple schedule design (Leitenberg, 1973) with reversals in each component. The red and brown rooms constituted the two stimulus components of the multiple schedule. In each component, the Free Time condition served as the baseline. The mands condition was introduced into and removed from one of the components at a time while the baseline condition was in effect in the other. The Mands condition was replicated across components (i.e., in both the red and the brown room). The Tacts condition, as noted above, served as a control for the effects of verbalizations per se on self-hitting, and was conducted in the brown room. (This point is discussed further below). Finally, during sessions 6 and 20-27, an adult who was naive to the purpose of the study carried out the various conditions. (For all other sessions, the adult in the room with Tim was knowledgeable about the purpose of the experiment).

Marker Stimulus Sessions. During the course of Experiment 1, it became clear that the verbal stimulus used by the adult to end the sessions had a profound effect on rate of self-hitting. Therefore, after the three conditions described above had been completed, a fourth condition was conducted (in the red room) to assess the effect of this stimulus on

Table 1. Stimuli used in experiments 1 and 2

List of tact stimuli

The walls are white.	The birds are singing.
My pants are soft.	The lights are on.
There are flowers in the garden.	The grass is green.
It's sunny today.	I have two eyes.

List of mand stimuli

Do this (hold arms out).	Do this (touch knees).
Point to the window.	Point to the door.
Touch your leg.	Touch your shoe.
Do this (clap hands).	Do this (arms up in the air).

self-hitting. The first 10 min of each session were identical to the Mands condition described above. However, at the 10-min point in each session, the adult presented a marker stimulus (so named because it was used to "mark" the 10-min point). For two of the sessions the marker stimulus was "Okay, let's go," the stimulus which normally ended all sessions. For the remaining two sessions the marker stimulus was "The sky is blue," a stimulus which had never been used before to end a session. Once the marker stimulus was presented, no more mands were given but hits were recorded for an additional minute, during which the adult would remain seated. Thus, these sessions lasted for 11 min, at the end of which the adult would unlock the door to the room and leave with Tim. The order of the marker stimulus sessions was: "Okay, let's go" (first and fourth sessions), and "The sky is blue" (second and third sessions).

Results and discussion

Figure 1 shows the number of hits per min, over sessions, in the brown and red rooms (top and bottom panels, respectively) for the various experimental conditions. Hitting

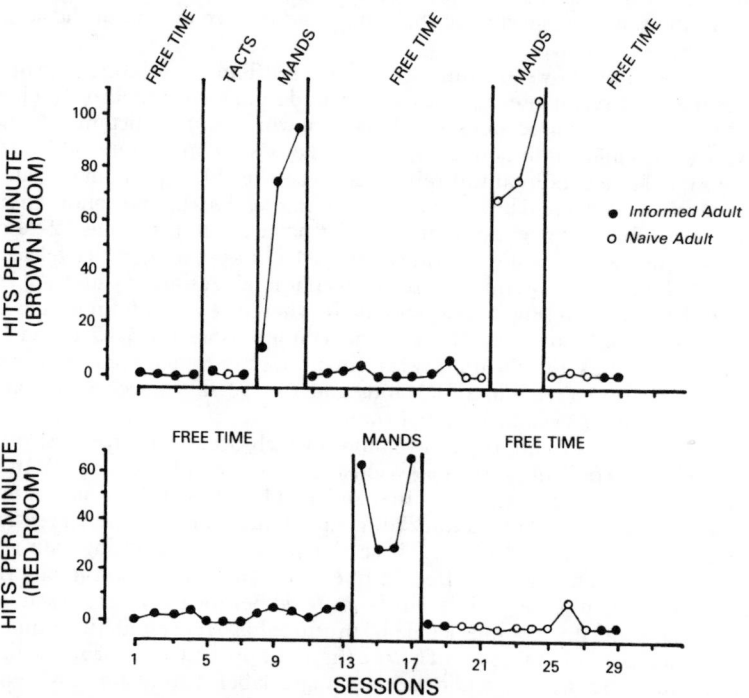

Fig 1. Number of hits per min, over sessions, in the brown and red rooms (top and bottom panels, respectively) for the various experimental conditions. The filled circles are the data for the informed adult and the open circles are the data for the naive adult.

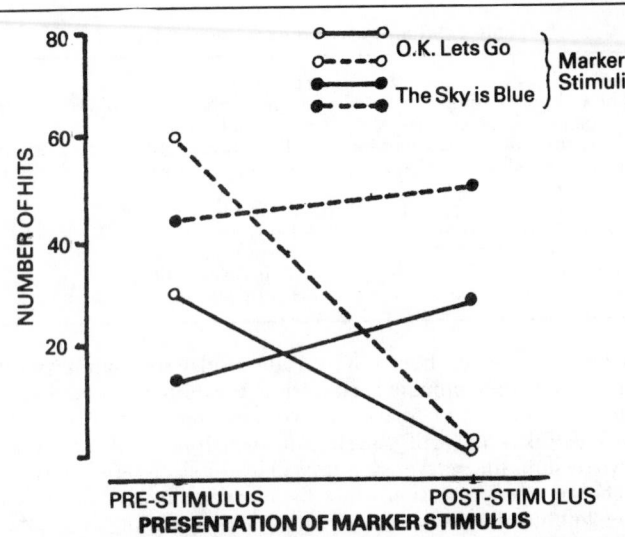

Fig. 2. Number of hits occurring before and after presentation of the marker stimuli. Data points labeled "prestimulus" represent the number of hits during the 1-min period *before* the adult presented the marker stimulus; data points labeled "poststimulus" represent the number of hits during the 1-min period *after* the adult presented the marker stimulus. The open circles are the data for the stimulus "O.K., let's go" and the filled circles are for the stimulus "The sky is blue." The solid lines are for the first session (presentation) of a given stimulus and the dotted lines are for the second session (presentation) of the same stimulus.

occurred at a high rate during the Mands conditions and at a near-zero rate during the Free Time and Tacts conditions. The effects of the Mands and Free Time conditions on rate of hitting were the same irrespective of the room used (brown or red) or the adult who was present (informed or naive).

Figure 1 (top panel) shows that during the first Free Time condition in the brown room, hitting occurred at a mean rate of .5 hits per min and remained at that level (.4 hits per min) during the Tacts condition (sessions 5-7). However, with the introduction of Mands, hitting abruptly increased and continued to rise over sessions 8-10 (mean rate, 60.5 hits per min). When the Free Time condition was reinstated in session 11, hitting immediately fell to a near-zero level and remained low over the remaining sessions in that condition (mean rate, .9 hits per min). Reinstatement of Mands by the naive adult in sessions 22-24 resulted in another sharp increase in hitting rate (mean rate, 84.1 hits per min), which fell again during the final Free Time condition (mean rate, .5 hits per min). A similar pattern of responding was seen in the red room (Fig. 1, bottom panel), where the mean hitting rates during the first Free Time, Mands, and second Free Time conditions were 1.3, 47.1, and 1.2 hits per min, respectively. Thus, the abrupt reversals in hitting rate which occurred across sessions with the change from Free Time to Mands and vice versa were characteristic of Tim's behavior in both the brown and the red room.

Perhaps even more striking than the changes which occurred *across* sessions were the changes which occurred *within* sessions. Consider, for example, session 22. In the brown room, a Mands conditions was in effect first and Tim hit himself 711 times. A few minutes later, the second component of session 22 was run in the red room where Free Time was in effect, and Tim hit himself 3 times. These sharp reversals in hitting rate were *always* obtained when Free Time was in effect in one room and Mands, in the other.

Figure 2 shows the number of hits which occurred before and after presentation of the marker stimuli. The data points labeled "prestimulus" represent the number of hits occurring during the 1-minute period *before* the adult presented the marker stimulus (i.e., the 10th minute of the session) while the data points labeled "poststimulus" represent the number of hits during the 1-minute period *after* the adult presented the marker stimulus (i.e., the 11th minute of the session). The open circles are for the stimulus "Okay, let's go", and the filled circles are for the stimulus "The sky is blue." Finally, the solid lines on the graph are for the first session with a given stimulus and the dotted lines are for the second session with the same stimulus.

The figure shows that when the marker stimulus which normally ended the session ("Okay, let's go") was presented, the number of hits abruptly decreased to a near-zero level. The hitting decreased from 29 to 59 hits in the prestimulus period to 1 and 2 hits, respectively, in the poststimulus period. However, when a marker stimulus which had not previously been used to end a session ("The sky is blue") was presented, the number of hits increased somewhat. The hitting increased from 14 and 43 hits in the prestimulus period to 29 and 49 hits, respectively, in the poststimulus period.

Experiment 1 demonstrated that a situation in which demands occur can be discriminative for high rates of self-destructive behavior. It was possible, of course, that any differences in the rate of self-destructive behavior in the Mands versus Free Time conditions might have been due simply to the fact that the adult presented verbal stimuli to Tim during the Mands condition but not during Free Time. Thus it might be that *any* verbal stimuli (whether they were mands or not) would have increased hitting. To control for this possibility, we had an adult present tacts to Tim. The fact that Tim's hitting was negligible in the Tact condition is evidence that not *all* verbal stimuli are discriminative for self-destruction.

Another important point is that the naive adult was able to replicate the results of the informed adult. This fact demonstrates that the data which were generated were not a function of some idiosyncracy in the informed adult's manner of conducting the sessions.

EXPERIMENT 2

In Experiment 1, we isolated a stimulus situation, namely the presentation of demands, which was discriminative for high rates of self-destructive behavior. In Experiment 2, we sought to modify the demand situation so as to bring the hitting under control.

Method

The subject, apparatus, and reliability measurement were the same as in Experiment 1.

Procedure

In Experiment 2, we assessed the effect of two different methods of mand presentation on the rate of Tim's hitting. These methods were as follows.

Mands. This condition was identical to the Mands condition of Experiment 1 (see above).

Mands Plus Positive Context. This condition was the same as the mands condition with one important exception. When the adult was not presenting a mand to Tim, the adult, instead of remaining silent, would relate a simple story to him which concerned some familiar object or event (such as going swimming). The adult was instructed to deliver the story in an animated, cheerful manner, and to be as entertaining as possible. Each story was elaborated upon long enough to fill the entire intermand interval. There were 10 such stories. The order of story presentation and the specific wording of each story varied from session to session but the themes of the stories did not. Each story was presented twice in a session. When a mand was due to be presented, the adult simply stopping telling the story and delivered the mand. In a sense, the mands were "slipped into" a positive context.

All sessions were conducted in the red room. Each session was of 10-min duration, at the end of which the adult would announce, "Okay let's go." Sessions were run 5 days per week, no more than twice a day, with the minimum time between sessions being 4 hours.

We employed a reversal design to study the effects of Mands versus Mands Plus Positive Context (with an informed adult conducting the sessions). The Mands condition served as the baseline for six sessions, and was followed by the Mands Plus Positive Context condition for four sessions, and finally, the Mands condition was reinstated for two sessions. The pattern of alternating between Mands and Mands Plus Positive Context was repeated with a naive adult conducting the sessions.

Results and Discussion

Figure 3 shows the number of hits per min, over sessions, for the experimental

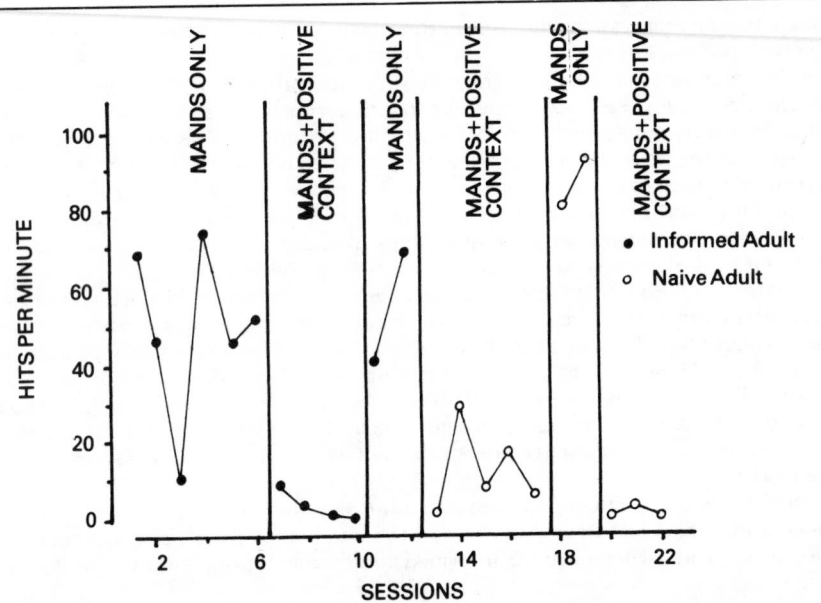

Fig. 3. Number of hits per min, over sessions, for the Mands versus Mands Plus Positive Context conditions. The filled circles are the data for the informed adult and the open circles, the data for the naive adult.

conditions. Hitting occurred at a high rate during Mands and generally at a low rate during Mands Plus Positive Context. The mean hitting rates for the first, second, and third Mands conditions were 50.3, 55.0, and 84.1 hits per min, respectively, while the mean rates for the corresponding Mands Plus Positive Context conditions were 4.0, 11.7, and 2.0 hits per min, respectively. The change from Mands to Mands Plus Positive Context was *always marked by an abrupt decrease in hitting rate while the change from Mands Plus Positive Context to Mands was always* marked by an abrupt increase. These relationships were the same whether the adult who was present was informed or naive.

The Pearson product — moment correlation coefficient computed for the relationship between frequency of hitting and frequency of compliance was — .82. There was thus a

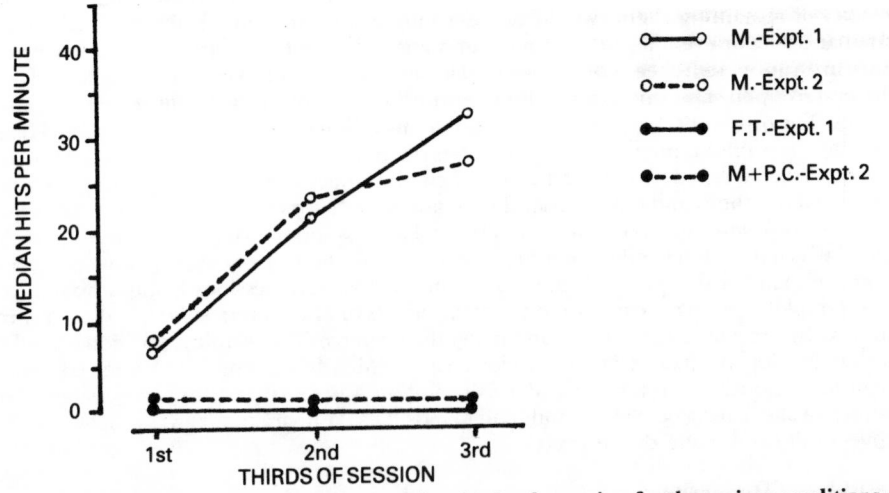

Fig. 4. Median hits per min during successive thirds of a session for the various conditions of Experiments 1 and 2. M=Mands; F.T.=Free Time; M.+P.C.=Mands Plus Positive Context.

strong tendency for high hitting rates to be associated with low compliance rates and vice versa. Mean compliance was 96% during Mands Plus Positive Context and 45% during Mands. It should be noted that whenever Tim did comply, he made the correct response and was reinforced.

Figure 4 shows the median hits per min during successive thirds of a session for the various experimental conditions. The median rates reported for the Mands and Free Time conditions of Experiment 1 were a combination of all the data collected for each of these conditions and were not separated according to which room the session was conducted in. This averaging was justifiable since Tim's performance under a given condition was essentially the same in the two rooms.

During the Mands conditions, the median rate of hitting increased steadily from a low level during the first third of a session to a high level by the final third of a session. In Experiment 1, the median rates in the first, second, and final thirds of a session were 6.6, 21.3, and 32.1 hits per min, respectively, and in Experiment 2, the rates were 7.5, 22.6, and 26.5 hits per min, respectively. This pattern of gradually increasing hitting through the course of a session occurred for 70% of the Mands sessions in both Experiments 1 and 2. In contrast, the rate of hitting in the Free Time and Mands Plus Positive Context conditions remained essentially the same across thirds of a session. The median rates in the first, second, and final thirds of a session in the Free Time condition were .1, .2, and .2 hits per min, respectively, and the corresponding rates in the Mands Plus Positive Context condition were 1.3, 1.1, and 1.4 hits per min, respectively. Only 28% of the sessions in the Free Time condition and 17% of the sessions in the Mands Plus Positive Context condition showed the pattern of gradually increasing hitting which characterized the majority of the sessions in the Mands conditions.

In Experiment 2, we showed that by altering the stimulus properties of a demand situation (i.e., presenting the demands in the context of a cheerful, positive, ongoing interaction), it was possible to bring the problem behavior under control without sacrificing the opportunity of presenting demands to the child, as is essential in teaching situations. Additionally, our naive adult control demonstrated that the changes in Tim's behavior were not an artifact of the informed adult's manner of conducting the sessions.

We can speculate on how stimulus changes such as those occurring during the Mands Plus Positive Context condition of Experiment 2 might work to control self-destructive behavior in a demand situation. It will be recalled that commands were a salient feature of the Mands conditions and that these stimuli were discriminative for high rates of hitting. Once Tim started such hitting, he generally continued throughout the session. It is plausible that high rates of self-destructive responding are discriminative stimuli for additional self-destructive responses and that such responses become chained to one another in a manner analogous to that reported for lower organisms in the reinforcement schedule literature (Ferster & Skinner, 1957; Reynolds, 1968). If this hypothesis is true, it may be that the major role of the stories in the Mands Plus Positive Context condition was that of providing stimuli for behaviors *other* than self-destruction (thus breaking up the response chain). The laughing, smiling, and talking which Tim exhibited during the Mands Plus Positive Context sessions may be examples of just such behaviors. Our results may also be related to those typically obtained in counterconditioning studies (Jones, 1924; Wolpe, 1958), in which certain stimuli, known to control behaviors incompatible with an undesirable target behavior, are deliberately introduced into the therapeutic setting.

General discussion

It should be noted that Tim differed from many self-destructive children described in the literature in that he was only mildly retarded and had language as well as some social skills. His pattern of self-destruction might therefore be more characteristic of higher functioning children. Given this possible limitation, the data presented above on the stimulus control of self-destructive behavior may nevertheless have implications for theories of the motivation of self-destructive behavior. Specifically, several aspects of the data suggest that Tim's self-destructive behavior in the Mands conditions may best be conceptualized as *escape responding*. The strongest evidence for this interpretation are the data of Figures 2 and 4.

First, Tim's rate of hitting dropped dramatically following presentation of the stimulus "Okay, let's go" (Figure 2). This stimulus was always used to terminate sessions and was thus highly discriminative for the termination of demands. A stimulus which is consistently paired with the absence of an aversive event is technically referred to as a "safety signal." Typically, operant escape responding is reduced in the presence of a safety signal (Azrin, Hake, Holz, & Hutchinson, 1965; Hineline & Rachlin, 1969). The fact that Tim abruptly stopped hitting himself whenever the adult said, "Okay, let's go," suggests that the stimulus functioned as a safety signal for him, indicating that the demands had ended and no further escape responses (self-hits) were necessary. Further, it is important to note that the stimulus "The sky is blue" (which was never before used to terminate sessions and therefore could not have become a safety signal) did not reduce the rate of hitting.

Secondly, if one regards as a negative reinforcer the termination of a session which contained demands, then it is possible to think of each session (in the Mands conditions) as a fixed-inteval 10-min schedule of escape. That is, after a fixed interval of 10 min the session ended, and any hitting which occurred at that time was negatively reinforced by the termination of the demands. In the animal literature, fixed-interval schedules of escape have been shown to generate a rate of responding which gradually increases throughout the fixed interval (Azrin et al., 1965; Hineline & Rachlin, 1969). Examination of Figure 4 shows that during the Mands conditions of Experiments 1 and 2, Tim's rate of hitting gradually increased throughout the session, a fact which is again consistent with an escape hypothesis. It is noteworthy that in the Free Time condition (which did not contain demands and therefore would not be expected to generate escape responding) Tim's rate of hitting remained unchanged throughout the session. Finally, we may consider the self-destructive behavior in the Mands Plus Positive Context condition. If we make the plausible assumption that the cheerful, amusing stories which the adult told to Tim in this condition prevented that condition from becoming aversive as the Mands conditions were assumed to be, then again we would expect no motivation for escape responding. The unchanging rate of hitting for this condition, shown in Figure 4, may reflect the lack of aversiveness of the Mands Plus Positive Context condition.

Third, if the demand situations are aversive, as an escape interpretation requires, one might expect considerable negative emotional behavior in these situations. In fact, we noticed that Tim appeared very "anxious" and whined a great deal during the Mands conditions. On the other hand, in the Free Time Tacts, and Mands Plus Positive Context conditions, which we have suggested were not aversive, he smiled and laughed and, in general, seemed quite happy. These observations are hampered, of course, by the fact that they are only anecdotal and must therefore be interpreted with caution. However, these observations do suggest one direction for further research. It is possible that through continued association with a positive context, the mands might eventually lose their aversive properties and the positive context could be faded out. If this effect could be produced, it might no longer be necessary to establish routinely a positive context each time the child was placed in a demand situation.

The most prevalent conceptualization of self-destructive behavior states that this behavior is maintained by positive social reinforcement such as adult attention (Lovaas et al., 1965; Lovaas & Simmons, 1969). We suggest that in some cases it may be that self-destruction serves an escape function and is maintained by the negative reinforcement which is produced by the termination of a demand situation. The possibility of multiple determination of self-destructive behavior has an important treatment implication. If self-destruction which is in fact being maintained by negative reinforcement is incorrectly assumed to be maintained by positive reinforcement, the therapist may treat the problem with extinction or timeout, techniques which involve removing all attention from the child: Unfortunately these procedures also involve the termination of all demands, and thus the therapist would inadvertently be negatively reinforcing self-destructive behavior, making it worse. Thus, the teacher who dismisses a child from the classroom because the child is hitting himself may, in a sense, be giving the child just what he wants. This analysis should make clear the importance of always performing a functional analysis of such behaviors and not merely assuming that all behaviors which share a similar topography also share a similar set of controlling variables.

References

Azrin, N. H., Hake, D. F., Holz, W. C., Hutchinson, R.R. Motivational aspects of escape from punishment. *J. Experi. Anal. Behav.*, 1965; **8**, 31-44.

Bachman, J. A. Self-injurious behavior: a behavioral analysis. *J. Abnorm. Psychol.*, 1972; **80**, 211-224.

Corte, H. E., Wolf, M. M., Locke, B. J. A comparison of procedures for eliminating self-injurious behavior of retarded adolescents. *J. Appl. Behav. Anal.*, 1971; **4**, 201-213.

Ferster, C. B., Skinner, B. F. *Schedules of Reinforcement.* New York: Appleton-Century-Crofts, 1957.

Hamilton, J., Stephens, L., Allen, P. Controlling aggressive and destructive behavior in severely retarded institutionalized residents. *Am. J. Ment. Defic.*, 1967; **71**, 852-856.

Hineline, P. N., Rachlin, H. Notes on fixed-ratio and fixed-interval escape responding in the pigeon. *J. Experi. Anal. of Behav.*, 1969; **12**, 397-401.

Jones, M. C. The elimination of children's fears. *J. Experi. Psychol.*, 1924; **7**, 382-390.

Leitenberg, H. The use of single-case methodology in psychotherapy research. *J. Abnorm. Psychol.*, 1973; **82**, 87-101.

Lovaas, O. I., Freitag, G., Gold, V. J., Kassorla, I. C. Experimental studies in childhood schizophrenia. I. Analysis of self-destructive behavior. *J. Experi. Child Psychol.*, 1965; **2**, 67-84.

Lovaas, O. I., Simmons, J. Q. Manipulation of self-destruction in three retarded children. *J. Appl. Behav. Anal.*, 1969; **2**, 143-157.

Peterson, R. F., Peterson, L. R. The use of positive reinforcement in the control of self-destructive behavior in a retarded boy. *J. Experi. Child Psychol.*, 1968; **6**, 351-360.

Reynolds, G. S. *A Primer of Operant Conditioning.* Glenview, Illinois: Scott, Foresman, 1968.

Skinner, B. F. *Verbal Behavior.* New York: Appleton-Century-Crofts, 1957.

Tate, B. G., Baroff, G. S. Aversive control of self-injurious behavior in a psychotic boy. *Behav. Res. & Ther.*, 1966; **4**, 281-287.

Wolf, M. M., Risley, T. R., Mees, H. Application of operant conditioning procedures to the behavior problems of an autistic child. *Behav. Res. & Ther.*, 1964; **1**, 305-312.

Wolpe, J. *Psychotherapy by Reciprocal Inhibition.* Stanford, California: Stanford University Press, 1958.

Reprinted from *J. Abnorm. Child Psychol.*, 1976; **4**:2, 139-153 by kind permission of the authors and the publishers Plenum Publishing Corp., New York, NY 10013. Edward Carr is now at the State University of New York, Stony Brook, NY 11794.

TOWARD A FUNCTIONAL ANALYSIS OF SELF-INJURY

Brian A. Iwata, Michael F. Dorsey, Keith J. Slifer, Kenneth E. Bauman, Gina S. Richman

The John F. Kennedy Institute and The Johns Hopkins University School of Medicine

This study describes the use of an operant methodology to assess functional relationships between self-injury and specific environmental events. The self-injurious behaviors of nine developmentally disabled subjects were observed during periods of brief, repeated exposure to a series of analogue conditions. Each condition differed along one or more of the following dimensions: (1) play materials (present vs absent), (2) experimenter demands (high vs low), and (3) social attention (absent vs noncontingent vs contingent). Results showed a great deal of both between and within-subject variability. However, in six of the nine subjects, higher levels of self-injury were consistently associated with a specific stimulus condition, suggesting that within-subject variability was a function of distinct features of the social and/or physical environment. These data are discussed in light of previously suggested hypotheses for the motivation of self-injury, with particular emphasis on their implications for the selection of suitable treatments.

The description, incidence and damaging effects of self-injury, as well as numerous attempts to control it, have been repeatedly documented in the literature. Self-injury is a bizarre and often chronic form of aberrant behavior, the etiology of which is at best poorly understood. It poses serious risks to those who engage in the behavior, and it represents a formidable challenge to those who are responsible for treating it.

Most of the research on self-injury over the past 15 years has focused on discovering means for its effective elimination. The greatest success has been found using methods based on operant conditioning principles (Bachman, 1972; Baumeister & Rollings, 1976; Frankel & Simmons, 1976; Johnson & Baumeister, 1978; Romanczyk & Goren, 1975; Schroeder, Schroeder, Rojahn & Mulick, 1981; Smolev, 1871). However, some mixed findings have been noted with almost all of the behavioral interventions. For example, although a number of studies have shown that the reinforcement of incompatible or other behavior (DRI/DRO) reduced self-injury (Allen & Harris, 1966; Frankel, Moss, Schofield, & Simmons, 1976; Lovaas, Freitag, Gold, and Kassorla, 1965; Tarpley & Schroeder, 1979), others have reported poor results with DRO/DRI (Corte, Wolf, & Locke, 1971; Measel, & Alfieri, 1976; Young & Wincze, 1974). Extinction has been effective in some instances (Jones, Simmons, & Frankel, 1974; Lovaas & Simmons, 1969) but not in others (Corte et al, 1971; Myers, 1975), and conflicting findings also have been reported with both timeout (Adams, Klinge, & Keiser, 1973; Corte et al, 1971; Duker, 1975; Solnick, Rincover, & Peterson, 1977), and overcorrection (Azrin, Gottlieb, Hughart, Wesolowski, & Rahn, 1975; Foxx & Martin, 1975; Harris & Romanczyk, 1976; Measel & Alfieri, 1976).

The only treatments that have been consistently effective in treating self-injury are those based on punishment in the form of aversive stimulation (Birnbrauer, 1968; Corte et al., 1971; Dorsey, Iwata, Ong, & McSween, 1980; Sajwaj, Libet, & Agras, 1974; Tanner & Zeiler, 1975). However, due to concerns regarding the appropriate and safe use of "restrictive" or "intrusive" treatments (e.g., ACFMR, 1971), it has been recommended that punishment be limited to those situations in which other interventions have failed (May, Risley, Twardosz, Friedman, Bijou, Wexler et al., 1975). It is therefore important to conduct research that may eventually identify the limiting conditions of the various treatments for self-injury. It would be especially useful if these conditions were known *prior* to initiating what otherwise might be an arbitrarily determined and seemingly endless series

Reprint requests may be addressed to Brian A. Iwata, Division of Behavioral Psychology, The John F. Kennedy Institute, 707 North Broadway, Baltimore, MD 21205.

of interventions.

Recent reviews (Carr, 1977; Johnson & Baumeister, 1978) have suggested that some of the treatment failures and inconsistencies reported throughout the literature may reflect a lack of understanding regarding the variables that either produce or maintain self-injury. In discussing a number of hypotheses for the motivation of self-injury, Carr (1977) indicated that the behavior may be reinforced through extrinsic sources (e.g., through positive reinforcement such as attention, or negative reinforcement such as the termination of demands), or that the behavior itself may produce some form of intrinsic reinforcement (e.g., sensory stimulation, pain reduction). This conceptualization of self-injury as a multiply controlled operant would indicate that no single form of treatment can be expected to produce consistent positive results, and it suggests that one means of selecting a potentially effective treatment would consist of first determining what events are currently maintaining the behavior.[1]

For several reasons, very little behavioral research has focused on the environmental determinants of self-injury. First, in light of data from numerous sources suggesting that self-injury is a learned phenomenon, behavioral researchers and clinicians generally have dismissed the importance of etiology, since the conditions that are necessary to develop or maintain a response may be totally unrelated to the conditions that are sufficient to alter or eliminate it. Second, with respect to the initial development of self-injury, functional analyses have been limited to animal studies (Holz & Azrin, 1961; Schaeffer, 1970), since experimental attempts to induce self-injury in humans when it does not already exist would be regarded as unacceptable from the standpoint of subject risk/benefit. Third, the apparent severity of the behavior often suggests the need for immediate attention, thereby discouraging attempts to identify features of the social and physical environment that may serve to maintain self-injury (see Carr, Newsom, & Binkoff, 1976, for a notable exception).

Over the past two years, we have been working toward the development and refinement of an operant methodology whose application might prove useful in identifying the functional properties of self-injury on a pretreatment basis. This article describes and presents the results obtained with our initial assessment protocol, in which subjects' behavior was repeatedly observed across several well-defined analogue environments. Similar approaches have been used to examine the effects of physical aspects of the environment on behaviors such as stereotypy (Adams, Tallon, & Stangl, 1980) and pica (Madden, Russo, & Cataldo, 1980). In the present study, environmental events consisted of both physical and social manipulations that might differentially affect the occurrence of self-injury.

Method

Subjects and setting

Nine subjects participated in the study. All showed some degree of developmental delay, and were admitted for inpatient evaluation and/or treatment to The John F. Kennedy Institute, a pediatric hospital affiliated with the Johns Hopkins University School of Medicine. Interviews and direct observations conducted prior to admission indicated that each subject exhibited moderate to high rates of self-injurious behavior. Demographic information for each subject is provided in Table 1. Sessions were conducted in 3.0m by 3.0m therapy rooms, equipped with tables and chairs, a variety of games and toys, and either floor carpeting or a mat. Each therapy room was adjoined to a 3.0m by 1.5m observation room via a one-way mirror.

Human subjects protection

In order to assess the differential effects of environment on self-injury, the present study required that subjects be allowed to engage in self-injurious behavior while free from

---

[1]Punishment would be an exceptional case, since its effectiveness does not depend on its ability to alter a reinforcement contingency. Rather, punishment is effective due to the fact that its "aversive" properties are sufficient to overcome *whatever* source of reinforcement is maintaining the behavior (Azrin & Holz, 1966). Given the types of stimuli that typically have been used as punishing events (e.g., electric shock, aromatic ammonia), it is not surprising to find that punishment has been found to be the most effective treatment for self-injury.

Table 1. Demographic characteristics of subjects

Subject	Sex	Age in Years	Developmental Level	Motor Involvement	Diagnosis	Self-Injury
1	F	4-9/12	2-3-½ yr	Normal	Mild to moderate mental retardation	Self-biting, head banging
2	M	5-10/12	8-12 mo	Spastic cerebral palsy, delayed	Congenital rubella syndrome, profound mental retardation, blind, hearing deficit	Eye gouging, head banging
3	M	13	8-10 mo	Normal (restricted by arm restraints)	Profound mental retardation, Down's syndrome	Ear pulling, head banging
4	M	6-8/12	10-15 mo	Normal	Profound mental retardation, autistic-like behavior	Head banging, head hitting
5	M	13-1/12	2-3 yr	Poor ambulation, abnormal gait, delayed	Severe to profound mental retardation, Rubenstein-Taybi syndrome	Face slapping, head banging, hand biting
6	M	1-7/12	6-9 mo	Delayed	Developmental delay, cranio-synostosis	Hand mouthing
7	M	17-2/12	15-24 mo	Mild cerebral palsy, delayed	Congenital rubella syndrome, profound mental retardation	Head hitting, head banging, arm biting, self-choking, hair pulling
8	M	4-9/12	2-14 mo	Delayed	Profound mental retardation, Down's syndrome	Head hitting, head banging
9	M	3-7/12	6-12 mo	Cerebral palsy, left hemiplegia, delayed	Profound mental retardation	Head hitting, head banging

mechanical, physical or chemical restraint. All procedures were reviewed and approved by a human subjects committee, and the following safeguards were employed to reduce the risk of physical damage as a function of self-injury exhibited during the observation sessions. First, each subject received a complete medical examination by a physician, as well as other diagnostic consultations (e.g., neurological, audiological, visual). The purpose of

Table 2. Observer definitions of subjects' self-injury

Response	Definition	Subjects
Ear pulling & gouging	Closure of fingers, fingernails or hand on ear with a pulling or digging motion	3
Eye gouging	Any contact of any part of hand within the ocular area	2
Face slapping	Forceful contact of the open hand with the face	6
Hair pulling	Closure of the fingers and thumb on hair with a pulling motion away from the head	7
Handmouthing	Insertion of one or more fingers into the mouth	6
Head banging	Forceful contact of the head with a stationary environmental object	1–9
Head hitting	Forceful contact of the hand with any part of the head	4,5,7,9
Neck choking	Forceful closure of both hands around the neck	7
Self-biting	Closure of the upper and lower teeth on the flesh of any portion of the body	1,5,7

the examination was to assess current physical status and to rule out organic factors that might be associated with or exacerbated by self-injury. Potential subjects who presented an immediate risk of severe physical damage due to self-injury were not included in the study. Second, each subject's physician recommended a criterion (expressed in terms of either degree of injury or level of responding or both) for terminating observation sessions due to physical risk. Physicians and nurses observed sessions intermittently in order to assess subjects' self-injury as it occurred and, if necessary, to modify the criterion. Third, if a subject's physical condition or level of responding met the criterion for terminating a session, (s)he was removed from the therapy room, self-injury was interrupted via brief physical or mechanical restraint, and a physician or nurse examined the subject and either approved continuation or recommended postponement of the sessions. Fourth, following each set of four observation sessions, subjects were routinely examined by a nurse who noted any changes in physical status as a result of self-injury. Finally, each subject's case was reviewed at least weekly in both departmental case conferences and interdisciplinary rounds.

In light of the above procedures, it was felt that the degree of risk to which subjects were exposed was no greater (and perhaps considerably less) than that found in their natural environment. During the course of the study, subjects often engaged in self-injury to the extent that minor bleeding or swelling occurred; however, at no time did subjects require any medical care due to their self-injury other than routine cleaning and/or topical dressing by a nurse. On three occasions, a session was terminated prematurely for subject 7, due to an extremely high rate of forceful head banging against the floor of the observation room. However, self-injury was never severe enough to require the termination of a session for other subjects, and no subject was ever excluded from participation in sessions due to residual effects of accumulated self-injury.

Response definitions and measurement

Observations conducted prior to and upon admission indicated that all subjects engaged in two or more self-injurious topographies, with head banging the most prevalent. Table 2 contains a listing of the specific self-injurious responses observed for each subject, along with operational definitions used in collecting data.

During each session, an observer recorded the occurrence or nonoccurrence of self-injurious behavior from the observation room during continuous, 10-sec intervals (Powell,

Table 3. Interobserver agreement data

Subject	Percent of Observations for which Observer Agreement was Measured	Overall		Occurrence		Nonoccurrence	
		X%	Range	X%	Range	X%	Range
1	26.6	99.8	98–100	84.3	50–100	99.7	97–100
2	67.0	88.0	63–100	80.4	41–100	63.2	27–100
3	32.0	98.8	88–100	95.0	75–100	97.8	83–100
4	17.0	96.3	94–99	86.8	78–95	80.0	39–99
5	25.0	99.7	97–100	93.5	75–100	99.3	98–100
6	17.0	100	100	100	100	100	100
7	61.3	92.4	73–100	72.9	21–100	88.8	61–100
8	45.0	97.0	91–100	85.5	43–100	97.5	90–100
9	30.3	99.2	96–100	46.9	0–100	99.0	95–100

Martindale, & Kulp, 1975). Interval changeovers were signalled by a cassette tape containing pre-recorded prompts. The dependent variable of interest consisted of the percentage of intervals during which one or more self-injurious responses were scored, and was calculated by dividing the number of positively scored intervals by the total number of intervals, and multiplying by 100.

Interobserver agreement

Two observers independently scored responses during 35% of the sessions (the range for individuals was 17% to 67%). Overall, occurrence, and nonoccurrence reliability percentages were calculated on an interval-by-interval basis by dividing the number of agreements by the number of agreements plus disagreements, and multiplying by 100 (Bailey & Bostow, 1979; Hawkins & Dotson, 1975). Overall, occurrence, and nonoccurrence agreement averaged 96.8%, 82.8%, and 91.7%, respectively. Individual means and ranges for each subject are presented in Table 3. Lower agreement percentages were obtained during sessions in which subjects exhibited either extremely high or extremely low levels of responding.

Staff training

All observers and experimenters who participated in the study had previous coursework and experience in the use of behavioral interventions with developmentally disabled children. In addition, specific training activities were employed to ensure that staff could reliably observe behavior and respond appropriately during sessions in which they served as an experimenter. Each staff member received written instructions describing the observation procedure and experimental protocol. After reading and reviewing these materials with an experienced staff member, a new staff member was assigned to conduct informal observations, reliability observations, and primary data observations for approximately five sessions each. Persons serving as experimenters (i.e., those conducting sessions) did so only after demonstrating competence as an observer. At least one of the authors was present during each session and provided feedback regarding compliance with the procedures as needed.

Experimental conditions

Eight of the nine subjects were exposed to each of four different conditions in an experimental design that used a multielement manipulation (Barlow & Hayes, 1979; Sidman, 1960; Ulman & Sulzer-Azaroff, 1975). Subject 1, who served as a pilot, was exposed to three of the four conditions. Eight sessions (two per condition) were conducted each day, with four sessions occurring in the morning and four in the afternoon. The order of presentation for each series of four sessions was determined by random drawing. Each session lasted for 15 min, with the exception of the three occasions noted earlier. For those conditions requiring the presence of an experimenter in the room with a subject, at least three different persons were trained to conduct sessions for each subject, and were rotated to control the experimenter-specific effects. Within each series of conditions, experimenters were changed between sessions, and subjects were briefly removed from the room.

Social disapproval. The experimenter and subject entered the therapy room together, where a variety of toys were available on a table and the floor, within easy reach of the subject. The experimenter directed the subject to "play with the toys" while the experimenter "does some work." If the subject had questionable receptive language or poor hearing, the experimenter initially placed the subject in physical contact with the toys. The experimenter then sat in a chair across the room and assumed the appearance of reading a book or magazine. Attention was given to the subject contingent upon each episode of self-injury (either a single response or a rapid burst of responses), and took the form of statements of concern and disapproval (e.g., "Don't do that, you're going to hurt yourself"; "Look at your hand, don't hit yourself"; etc), paired with brief physical contact of a non-punitive nature (e.g., hand on shoulder). All other responses exhibited by the subject were ignored. This condition was designed to approximate one type of reinforcement contingency that might maintain self-injury. In the natural environment, especially in institutional settings having low staff-to-client ratios, self-injury often produces much emotional behavior and attention from caregivers, while other behavior receives relatively little attention (Frankel & Simmons, 1976; Lovaas et al., 1965; Lovaas & Simmons, 1969; Risley, 1968). Thus, statements of concern and social disapproval paired with physical contact contingent upon self-injury may maintain the behavior via inadvertent delivery of positive reinforcement.

Academic demand. Educational activities appropriate for each subject were selected on the basis of a special education evaluation conducted upon admission, or from an individual education program plan obtained from the subject's current school or institutional placement. Examples of the educational tasks included: placing plastic rings on a peg, stacking wooden blocks or placing them in a bucket, putting pieces in a wooden puzzle, threading large plastic beads on a string, grasping and holding small objects, and touching various body parts upon request. The tasks were judged to have a low probability of occurrence, in that subjects never completed them spontaneously. In addition, the tasks were apparently difficult for subjects to perform even when physically guided.

During the academic session, the experimenter and subject were seated at a table, and the experimenter presented learning trials using a graduated, three-prompt procedure (Horner & Keilitz, 1975; Tucker & Berry, 1980). The experimenter initially gave a verbal instruction and allowed the subject 5 sec to initiate a response. If, after the 5 sec, the subject failed to initiate an appropriate response, the experimenter repeated the instruction, modeled the correct response, and waited an additional 5 sec. If no response occurred at that point, the experimenter repeated the instruction and physically guided the subject through the response, using the least amount of contact necessary to complete it. Appropriate modification and/or elimination in the first two steps occurred for subjects with auditory or visual deficits. Social praise was delivered upon completion of the response, regardless of whether or not modeling or physical guidance were required, and the next trial was begun. Contingent upon the occurrence of self-injury at any time during the session, the experimenter immediately terminated the trial and turned away from the subject for 30 sec, with an additional 30-sec change-over delay for repeated self-injury. While such a consequence for self-injury might resemble an extinction procedure, it was actually designed to assess whether or not self-injury was maintained through negative reinforcement as a result of escaping or avoiding demand situations (Carr, 1977; Carr et al., 1976; Jones, Simmons, & Frankel, 1974; Measel & Alfieri, 1976; Wolf, Risley, Johnston, Harris, & Allen, 1967).

Unstructured play. As in the two previous conditions, an experimenter and subject were present in the room. No educational tasks were presented, and a variety of toys were available within the subject's reach. Throughout the session the experimenter maintained close proximity to the subject (i.e., within 1m when both were seated), allowed the subject to engage in spontaneous isolate or cooperative toy play or to move freely about the room, and periodically presented toys to the subject without making any demands. The experimenter delivered social praise and brief physical contact contingent upon appropriate behavior — the absence of self-injury — at least once every 30 sec. Self-injurious behavior was ignored, unless its severity reached the point where the session was terminated. This condition served as a còntrol procedure for the presence of an experimenter, the availability of potentially stimulating materials, the absence of demands, the delivery of social approval for appropriate behavior, and the lack of approval for self-injury. Additionally, it was designed to serve the function of an "enriched environment" (Horner, 1980), in which relatively little self-injury might be expected to occur.

Alone. The child was placed in the therapy room alone, without access to toys or any other materials that might serve as external sources of stimulation. The purpose of this condition was to approximate a situation that would be considered "impoverished" or "austere" from a social and physical standpoint (Horner, 1980). There is growing evidence to suggest that self-stimulatory behavior is motivated through self-produced reinforcement of a sensory nature (Rincover, 1978; Rincover, Cook, Peoples, & Packard, 1979), and it is possible that self-injury may be similarly maintained (Carr, 1977; Dorsey, Iwata, Reid, & Davis, in press; Favell, McGimsey, & Schell, 1982; Parrish, Aguerrevere, Dorsey, Iwata, 1980; Rincover & Devany, 1982). If so, one might expect to observe higher levels of self-injury in situations where minimal amounts of stimulation are provided by the environment.

The above procedures continued until: (1) apparent stability in the level of self-injury was observed, (2) unstable levels of responding persisted in all conditions for 5 days, or (3) 12 days of sessions were completed. The length of subject participation in this study averaged 8 days (range = 4–11), while the total number of sessions run per subject averaged 30 (range = 24–53).

Results

Figure 1 summarizes the results for the nine subjects. For each subject, the numerical data in Figure 1 indicate the overall mean percent of intervals of self-injury and its standard deviation, and means for the separate experimental conditions. These data allow for an examination of overall responding between subjects, as well as condition-by-condition comparisons within subjects. However, in light of the rather large differences observed in subjects' overall level of self-injury, it is difficult to make condition-by-condition comparisons between subjects on the basis of absolute data alone (e.g., 81.3% vs 44.4% vs 8.9% self-injury for subjects 4, 7, and 9, respectively, during the Alone condition). For this reason, the condition means for individual subjects are also portrayed graphically in standard deviation units above or below a subject's overall mean. Thus, Figure 1 provides a summary of both absolute level and relative variability of subjects' self-injurious behavior.

Several differences can be seen in the present data. First, the level of responding varied widely *across* subjects, with the overall mean percent of intervals of self-injury ranging from a low of 4.5% (subjects 1 and 9) to a high of 91.2% (subject 6). Second, considerable variability was observed *within* subjects across the different experimental conditions. The within-subject variability was evident regardless of a subject's overall level of responding. For example, subjects 1 and 6, who displayed markedly different overall levels of self-injury, both showed variable responding across conditions. Third, within-subject *patterns* of responding did not appear related to the overall level of self-injury. For example, subjects 3 and 9, both of whom displayed relatively little self-injury, differed with respect to the condition in which self-injury was found to be the greatest.

In spite of the above differences, the data provide information regarding specific conditions that may affect self-injury, and the results shown in Figure 1 suggest five general patterns of responding for the present subjects. The first pattern was characterized by a relatively low level of self-injury during the Unstructured play condition. For all of the eight subjects exposed to this condition (subject 1 was excluded), self-injury during Unstructured play was at or below their overall mean level, and four of the subjects (subjects 2,4,5,9) showed less self-injury during Unstructured play when compared to any of the other conditions. A second pattern was reflected in the data for subjects 4,6,7, and 9. For these individuals, self-injury was greatest during the Alone condition, in which access to external sources of stimulation was minimized. This pattern is most clearly evident in subject 4's data. However, subjects 6 and 9, whose overall level of self-injury differed considerably, also displayed more self-injury during the Alone condition. A third pattern of results was

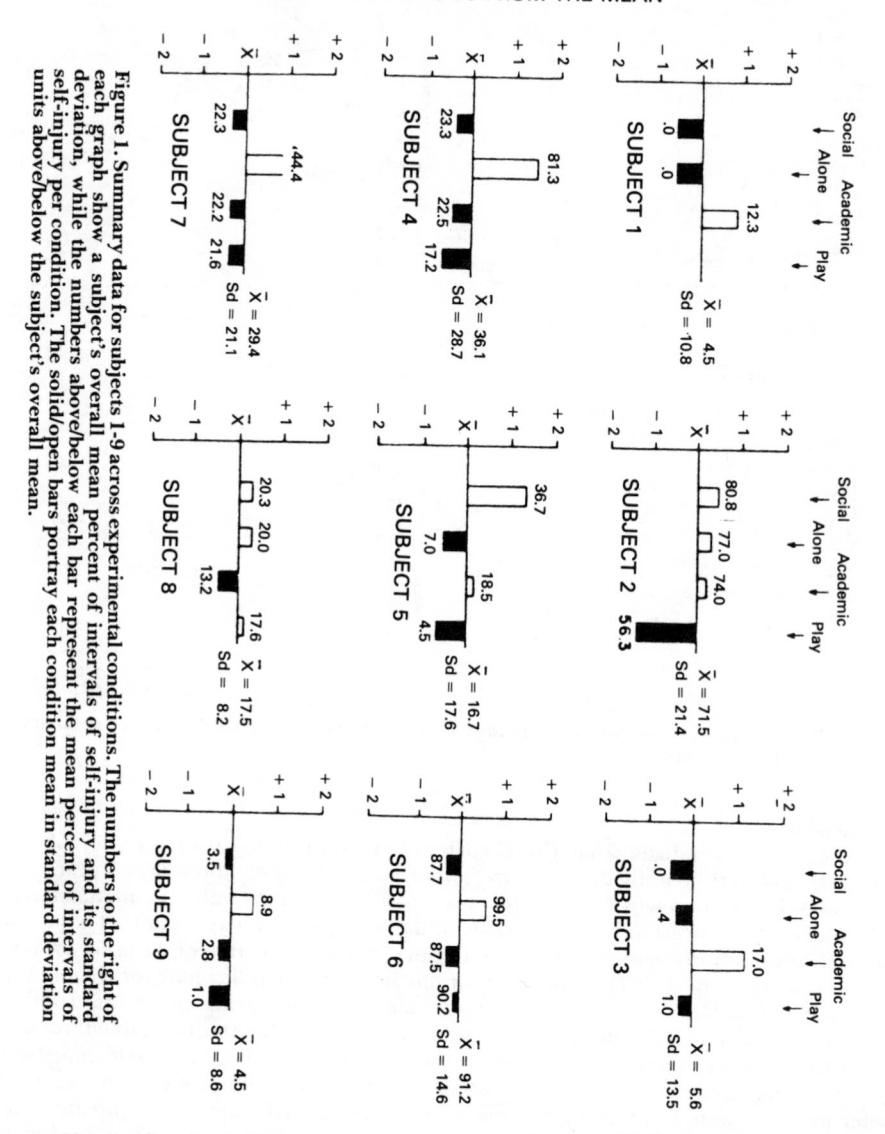

Figure 1. Summary data for subjects 1-9 across experimental conditions. The numbers to the right of each graph show a subject's overall mean percent of intervals of self-injury and its standard deviation, while the numbers above/below each bar represent the mean percent of intervals of self-injury per condition. The solid/open bars portray each condition mean in standard deviation units above/below the subject's overall mean.

suggested by the data for subjects 1 and 3. Both of these of individuals exhibited little or no self-injury during all but one of the conditions — the High demand situation. Subject 5 exemplified a fourth pattern in which self-injury occurred most often during the Social disapproval condition. Finally, the data for subjects 2 and 8 showed an undifferentiated pattern, in that they exhibited either very high (subject 2) or similar (subject 8) amounts of self-injury across two or more conditions. Subject 6's data might also be considered an example of undifferentiated responding merely because he exhibited very high levels of self-injury across all conditions, even though the greatest amount was seen during the Alone condition.

Figure 2 presents session-by-session data for four subjects whose results are characteristic of different response patterns. Subjects 1,4, and 5 exhibited higher levels of self-injury during the Academic demand, Alone, and Social disapproval conditions, respectively, while subject 2 engaged in relatively high levels of self-injury across all experimental conditions.

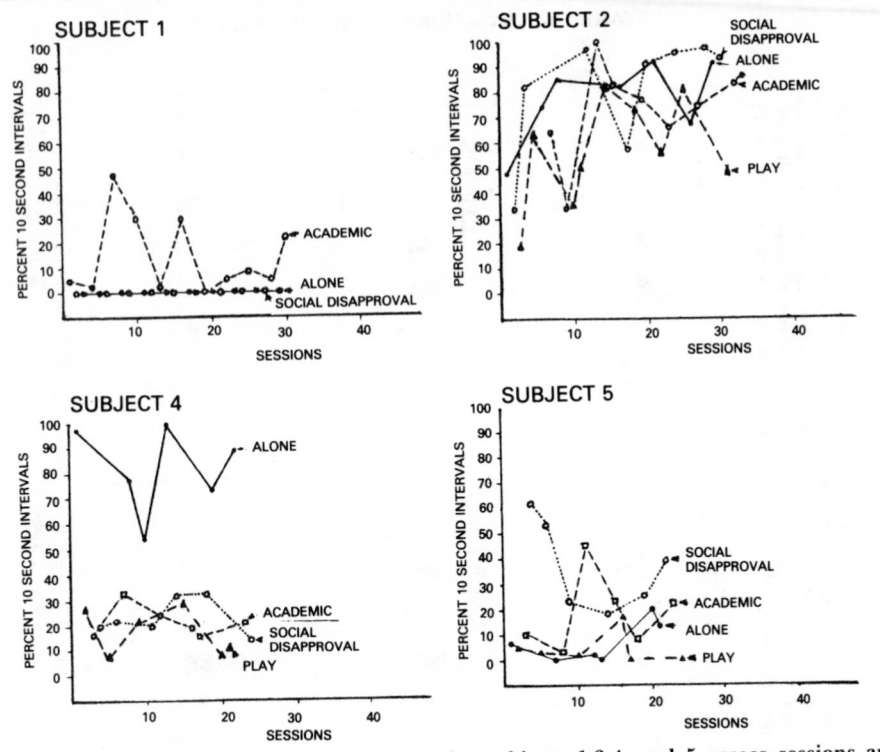

Figure 2. Percent of intervals of self-injury for subjects 1,2,4, and 5 across sessions and experimental conditions.

Discussion

Present results indicate that the occurrence of self-injury varies considerably, both between and within individuals. More importantly, the data show that within-subject variability is not merely a random process. In six of the nine subjects, higher levels of self-injury were consistently associated with a specific stimulus condition. These results provide direct empirical evidence that self-injury may be a function of different sources of reinforcement (Carr, 1977), a finding that has significant implications for treatment.

In four of our subjects, self-injury was relatively high during the Alone condition, suggesting a form of self-stimulation as a motivational variable. Assuming that this analysis is a correct one, knowledge of the specific reinforcing event provided by self-injury would greatly enhance the effectiveness of reinforcement procedures designed to reduce the behavior. For example, on several occasions, we have noticed that visually impaired clients engage in eye-poking that probably intensifies visual stimulation. Intervention for such individuals might include the use of bright flashing lights, massage to the ocular area, etc., that is delivered contingent upon the absence of self-injury, or produced by a response that is incompatible with self-injury (Favell et al., 1982). Alternatively, effective extinction procedures may not require the withholding of social consequences but, instead, the elimination or attenuation of sensory stimulation derived from the response (e.g., Dorsey et al., in press; Rincover, 1978; Rincover et al., 1979; Rincover & Devany, 1982).

Two subjects exhibited more self-injury during the Academic sessions, where the behavior functioned to briefly terminate demands made by an experimenter. The pattern of behavior shown by these subjects resembles that described by Carr et al. (1976) who were able to reduce self-injury by including non-demand periods (reading entertaining stories to the subject) during a demand condition. The use of "guided compliance" trials, in which a client's self-injury is followed by physical assistance in completing the desired academic response and continuation of the session until a performance criterion is reached, might also be effective in "extinguishing" the negative reinforcement provided through escape responding. On the other hand, a typical extinction technique — the contingent withdrawal of attention — would be expected to strengthen the behavior.

Only one subject in the present study showed higher levels of self-injury during the Social disapproval condition. This finding was rather surprising in light of the fact that social attention often has been suggested as a likely source of reinforcement for self-injury. However, in situations where it can be determined that clients engage in self-injury for the attention that it produces, extinction (ignoring), timeout, and DRO would seem to be the most effective treatments.

Three of the subjects showed either undifferentiated patterns or high levels of self-injury across all stimulus conditions. Although it is impossible to determine what may have accounted for these results, several possibilities appear likely. Each of these subjects was either quite young or profoundly retarded, and it is possible that the different conditions were not clearly discriminable to them. Alternatively, the behavior may have been a function of variables that were not controlled in the present study. Finally, self-injury in these individuals may represent a response that serves multiple functions — providing stimulation when little is available, producing attention from others, and terminating undesirable situations. The latter possibility is most significant in that it suggests the need for different treatments applied to the same individual, depending upon the situation in which self-injury is observed.

Although clear differences were observed in a majority of our subjects, the present data must be regarded as limited in two respects. First, our methodology did not control for very subtle aspects of contingencies that may affect behavior. For example, assuming that the attention provided during the Social disapproval condition serves a reinforcing function, the reinforcement is provided on a very frequent basis.[2] The Alone condition differed from the Social attention condition in at least two respects: it not only represented a condition of stimulus deprivation, but also eliminated access to all social attention. In light of the fact that an operant response may occur at higher rates during the initial stages of extinction than during a CRF condition, a high level of self-injury during the Alone condition *might not* be maintained by reinforcement of a self-stimulatory nature, but by the withdrawal of social reinforcement. Thus, our methodology does not isolate conclusively the exact nature of the contingency responsible for maintaining self-injury, and we foresee the need for constructing an extended series of conditions that progressively analyzes variables such as reinforcement schedules. A second limitation can be found in the incompleteness of our analysis. For example, if subjects exhibit self-injury primarily in demand situations, a reduction of self-injury following a reversal of the apparent contingency operating in that environment (i.e., the elimination of escape as a consequence for self-injury) would provide stronger evidence that the behavior was, in fact, maintained through negative reinforcement. Furthermore, a comparison of that technique to one whose use is unrelated to the concept of negative reinforcement for self-injury (e.g., timeout, DRO) would provide the ultimate test of the clinical utility of the assessment procedure in selecting effective treatments. Although no treatment data are included in this study, all of the present subjects were provided a therapy program following the completion of their assessment. During the course of that treatment, we have conducted several types of intervention analyses, the results of which have been very encouraging in cases where self-injury was clearly differentiated during the assessment period.

In addition to the above limitations, several distinctive features of the present study are worth noting. The use of environments that may not closely resemble naturalistic situations was based on our experience that it is often difficult to either precisely identify or control naturally occurring events related to self-injury. Also, by using well-defined analogue environments, it was possible to limit subjects' inclusion in the study to an amount of time no

[2]The use of these schedules raises the question of whether or not procedures in this study could have contributed to the development of self-injury in our subjects. Data indicating an increasing function across time would have suggested that learning or acquisition was taking place. However, only the data for subject 2 showed any increase across sessions, and it can be seen (Figure 2) that this subject's self-injury was occurring at high levels during initial sessions.

greater than that of a typical baseline period, yet provide data on a number of variables that may affect self-injury. Both of these features (operational definition of the environment and limited duration) should increase the likelihood that the present methodology, or one similar to it, could be incorporated into the design of most intervention research. Procedures for minimizing risks to the subjects were also carefully considered, and provide a model for screening and monitoring that might be considered essential in research of this type. In, particular, the independent monitoring system was seen as a safeguard to experimenters as well as subjects, and should be employed whenever possible.

The major focus of the present study was on the identification of variables that are associated with (and may serve to maintain) the occurrence of self-injury. However, it is important to note that lower levels of self-injury were consistently associated with the control condition, which included the availability of toys, the relative absence of demands, and reinforcement for behavior that was generally incompatible with self-injury. This finding is consistent with previous data (Horner, 1980) suggesting that physical and social characteristics associated with an "enriched environment" may produce a number of beneficial outcomes, including reductions in self-injury. In addition to enrichment, in cases where individuals exhibit few adaptive behaviors, successful treatment of self-injury may include the active shaping and/or reinforcement of specific appropriate responses, such as toy play (Favell et al., 1982).

In summary, the present study offers a methodology for examining the multiple effects of environment on the occurrence of self-injury. Whether or not it will contribute to a more thorough understanding of the etiology of self-injury remains to be seen.[3] However, it is clear that improvements are needed in our approach to the treatment of self-injury. The present results suggest that it may be possible to empirically identify variables that affect self-injury prior to implementing lengthy treatment conditions. If so, we can no longer afford to conduct clinical research in which the baseline data provide information regarding behavior in a single invariant situation, or to make treatment decisions based on a "best guess" as to what might constitute the most effective means of intervention.

Acknowledgement—This research was supported in part by Grant# 000917-15-0 from the Maternal and Child Health Service. We thank Michael Cataldo for his support; Pamela Fabry, H. Richard Waranch and Eric Ward for their valuable input during the early stages of protocol development; Luis Aguerrevere, Patricia Davis, Rebecca Deal, Harvey Jacobs, John Parrish, Belinda Traughber, and Tim Wysocki for their assistance in conducting the study; and Tom Thompson for his helpful comments on a previous draft of the manuscript.

References

Accreditation Council for Facilities for the Mentally Retarded. *Standards for residential facilities for the mentally retarded.* Chicago: Joint Commission on Accreditation of Hospitals, 1971.

Adams, G. L. Tallon, R. J. Stangl, J. M. Environmental influences on self-stimulatory behavior. *Am. J. Ment. Defic.*, 1980; **85**, 171-175.

Adams, K. M., Klinge, V., Keiser, T. W. The extinction of a self-injurious behavior in an epileptic child. *Behav. Res. & Ther.*, 1973; **11**, 351-356.

Allen, K. E., Harris, F. R. Elimination of a child's excessive scratching by training the mother in reinforcement procedures. *Behav. Res. & Ther.*, 1966; **4**, 79-84.

Azrin, N. H., Gottlieb, L., Hughart, K., Wesolowski, M. D., Rahn, T. Eliminating self-injurious behavior by educative procedures. *Behav. Res. & Therapy*, 1975; **13**, 101-111.

Azrin, N. H., Holz, W. C. Punishment. *In* Honig, W. K. (Ed.). *Operant behavior: Areas of research and application.* New York: Appleton-Century-Crofts, 1966.

Bachman, J. A. Self-injurious behavior: A behavioral analysis. *J. Abnorm. Psychol.*, 1972; **80**, 211-224.

Bailey, J. S., Bostow, D. E. *Research methods in applied behavior analysis.* Tallahassee, FL.: Copy Grafix, 1979.

Barlow, D. H., Hayes, S. C. Alternating treatments design: One strategy for comparing the effects of two treatments in a single subject. *J. Appl. Behav. Anal.*, 1979; **12**, 199-210.

---

[3]The present study does not address the issue of environmental versus physiological determinants of self-injury. However, assuming that there may be a physiological basis for the development or maintenance of self-injury, research of the present type should suggest ways to reduce the effects of environmental variance when conducting biobehavioral investigations.

Baumeister, A. A., Rollings, J. P. Self-injurious behavior. *In* Ellis, N. R. (Ed.). *International review of research in mental retardation*. New York: Academic Press, 1976.

Birnbrauer, J. Generalization of punishment effects — A case study. *J. Appl. Behav. Anal.*, 1968; **1**, 201-211.

Carr, E. G. The motivation of self-injurious behavior: A review of some hypotheses. *Psychol. Bull.*, 1977; **84**, 800-816.

Carr, E. G., Newsom, C. D., Binkoff, J. A. Stimulus control of self-destructive behavior in a psychotic child. *J. Abnorm. Child Psychol.*, 1976; **4**, 139-152.

Corte, H. E., Wolf, M. M., Locke, B. J. A comparison of procedures for eliminating self-injurious behavior of retarded adolescents. *J. Appl. Behav. Anal.*, 1971; **4**, 201-213.

Dorsey, M. F., Iwata, B. A., Ong, P., McSween, T. E. Treatment of self-injurious behavior using a water mist: Initial response suppression and generalization. *J. Appl. Behav. Anal.*, 1980; **13**, 343-353.

Dorsey, M. F., Iwata, B. A., Reid, D. H., Davis, P. A. Protective equipment: Continuous and contingent application in the treatment of self-injurious behavior. *J. Appl. Behav. Anal.*, in press.

Duker, P. Intra-subject controlled time-out (social isolation) in the modification of self-injurious behavior. *J. Ment. Defic. Res.*, 1975; **19**, 107-112.

Favell, J. E., McGimsey, J. F., Schell, R. M. Treatment of self-injury by providing alternative sensory activities. *Anal. & Intervent. in Develop. Disabil.*, 1982; **2**, 83-104.

Foxx, R. M., Martin, E. D. Treatment of scavenging behavior (coprophagy and pica) by over-correction. *Behav. Res. & Ther.*, 1975; **13**, 153-162.

Frankel, F., Moss, D., Schofield, S., Simmons, J. Q. Case study: use of differential reinforcement to suppress self-injurious and aggressive behavior. *Psychol. Reports*, 1976; **39**, 843-849.

Frankel, F., Simmons, J. Q. Self-injurious behavior in schizophrenic and retarded children. *Am. J. Ment. Defic.*, 1976; **80**, 512-522.

Harris, S. L., Romanczyk, R. G. Treating self-injurious behavior of a retarded child by over-correction. *Behav. Ther.*, 1976; **7**, 235-239.

Hawkins, R. P., Dotson, V. A. Reliability scores that delude: An "Alice in Wonderland" trip through the misleading characteristics of interobserver agreement scores in interval recording. *In* Ramp, E., Semb, G. (Eds.). *Behavior analysis: Areas of research and application*. Englewood Cliffs, New Jersey: Prentice-Hall, 1975.

Holz, W. C., Azrin, N. H. Discriminative properties of punishment. *J. Experi. Anal. Behav.*, 1961; **4**, 225-232.

Horner, R. D. The effects of an environmental "enrichment" program on the behavior of institutionalized profoundly retarded children. *J. Appl. Behav. Anal.*, 1980; **13**, 473-491.

Horner, R. D., Keilitz, I. Training mentally retarded adolescents to brush their teeth. *J. Appl. Behav. Anal.*, 1975; **8**, 301-309.

Johnson, W. L., Baumeister, A. Self-injurious behavior: A review and analysis of methodological details of published research. *Behav. Modific.*, 1978; **2**, 465-484.

Jones, F. H., Simmons, J. Q., Frankel, F. An extinction procedure for eliminating self-destructive behavior in a 9-year-old autistic girl. *J. Aut. & Child. Schiz.*, 1974; **4**, 214-250.

Lovaas, O. I., Freitag, G., Gold, V. J., Kassorla, I. C. Experimental studies in childhood schizophrenia: Analysis of self-destructive behavior. *J. Experi. Child Psychol.*, 1965; **2**, 67-84.

Lovaas, O. I., Simmons, J. Q. Manipulation of self-destruction in three retarded children. *J. Appl. Behav. Anal.*, 1969; **2**, 143-157.

Madden, N. A., Russo, D. C., Cataldo, M. F. Environmental influences on mouthing in children with lead intoxification. *J. Pediatr. Psychol.*, 1980; **5**, 207-216.

May, J. G., Risley, T. R., Twardosz, S., Friedman, P., Bijou, S., Wexler, D., et al. Guidelines for the use of behavioral procedures in state programs for the retarded. NARC Monograph, *M. R. Research*, 1975, **1**.

Measel, C. J., Alfieri, P. A. Treatment of self-injurious behavior by a combination of reinforcement for incompatible behavior and overcorrection. *Am. J. Ment. Defic.*, 1976; **81**, 147-153.

Myers, D. V. Extinction, DRO, and response cost procedures for eliminating self-injurious behavior: A case study. *Behav. Res. & Ther.*, 1975; **13**, 189-191.

Parrish, J. M., Aguerrevere, L., Dorsey, M. F., Iwata, B. A. The effects of protective equipment on self-injurious behavior. *Behav. Ther.*, 1980; **3**, 28-29.

Powell, J., Martindale, A., Kulp, S. An evaluation of time-sampling measures of behavior. *J. Appl. Behav. Anal.*, 1975; **8**, 463-469.

Rincover, A. Sensory extinction: A procedure for eliminating self-stimulatory behavior in psychotic children. *J. Abnorm. Child Psychol.*, 1978; **6**, 299-310.

Rincover, A., Cook, R., Peoples, A., Packard, D. Sensory extinction and sensory reinforcement principles for programming multiple adaptive behavior change. *J. Appl. Behav. Anal.*, 1979; **12**, 221-233.

Rincover, A., Devany, J. Using sensory reinforcement and sensory extinction principles in the treatment of self-injury. *Anal. & Intervent. Develop. Disabil.*, 1982; **2**, 67-81.

Risley, T. R. The effects and side effects of punishing the autistic behaviors of a deviant child. *J. Appl. Behav. Anal.*, 1968; **1**, 21-34.

Romanczyk, R. G., Goren, E. R. Severe self-injurious behavior: The problem of clinical control. *J. Consult. & Clin. Psychol.*, 1975; **43**, 730-739.

Sajwaj, T., Libet, J., Agras, S. Lemon-juice therapy: The control of life-threatening rumination in a six-month-old infant. *J. Appl. Behav. Anal.*, 1974; **7**, 557-563.

Schaeffer, H. H. Self-injurious behavior: Shaping "head banging" in monkeys. *J. Appl. Behav. Anal.*,

1970; **3**, 111-116.

Schroeder, S. R., Schroeder, C. S., Rojahn, J., Mulick, J. A. Self-injurious behavior: An analysis of behavior management techniques. *In* Matson, J. L., McCartney, J. R. (Eds.). *Handbook of behavior modification with the mentally retarded.* New York: Plenum Press, 1981.

Sidman, M. *Tactics of scientific research.* New York: Basic Books, 1960.

Smolev, S. R. Use of operant techniques for the modification of self-injurious behavior. *Am. J. Ment. Defic.,* 1971; **76**, 295-305.

Solnick, J. V., Rincover, A., Peterson, C. R. Some determinants of the reinforcing and punishing effects of timeout. *J. Appl. Behav. Anal.,* 1977; **10**, 415-424.

Tanner, B. A., Zeiler, M. Punishment of self-injurious behavior using aromatic ammonia as the aversive stimulus. *J. Appl. Behav. Anal.,* 1975; **8**, 53-57.

Tarpley, H. D., Schroeder, S. R. Comparison of DRO and DRI on rate of self-injurious behavior. *Am. J. Ment. Defic.,* 1979; **84**, 188-194.

Tucker, D. J., Berry, G. W. Teaching severely multihandicapped students to put on their own hearing aids. *J. Appl. Behav. Anal.,* 1980; **13**, 65-75.

Ulman, J. D., Sulzer-Azaroff, B. Multielement baseline design in educational research. *In* Ramp, E., Semb, G. (Eds.). *Behav. anal.: Areas of research and application.* Englewood Cliffs, New Jersey: Prentice-Hall, 1975.

Wolf, M. M., Risley, T., Johnston, M., Harris, F., Allen, E. Application of operant conditioning procedures to the behavior problems of an autistic child: A follow-up and extension. *Behav. Res. & Ther.,* 1967; **5**, 103-111.

Young, J. A., Wincze, J. P. The effects of the reinforcement of compatible and incompatible alternative behaviors on the self-injurious and related behaviors of a profoundly retarded female adult. *Behav. Ther.,* 1974; **5**, 614-623.

Reprinted from *Analysis & Intervention in Dev. Disabil.,* 1982; **2**, 3-20 by kind permission of Brian A. Iwata and the publishers Pergamon Press Ltd., Oxford OX3 0BN.

SECTION III

Treatment of self-injurious behaviour in individuals who are mentally handicapped or autistic

Introduction

In this final section we shall describe a range of treatments used to reduce or eliminate self-injurious behaviour in people who are mentally handicapped or autistic.

We begin with what is probably the most widely used method of controlling SIB, namely, the use of restraints or protective clothing of some kind. Restraints may range from simply putting mittens on a person's hands to prevent hand biting, through to using bandages or straps to tie an individual to a bed for most of the day and night. In the latter case bone deformities and muscle weakness will inevitably occur. In between these two extremes people can be found wearing helmets, collars, arm splints, and so forth. Restraints of this kind are not used as a treatment to eliminate self-injurious behaviour but rather to prevent the behaviour occurring at all, or to terminate an episode of self-injury once it has occurred, or to prevent tissue damage if the behaviour persists. The use of restraint and protective devices is widespread and, because of this and the fact that such measures are usually the first to be employed in instances of self-injurious behaviour, this section begins with two papers describing such devices.

These are followed by a group of papers on pharmacological or drug treatments, for such treatment is often the second method considered by those responsible for the well-being of the child or adult who severely self-injures. Schroeder, Schroeder, Smith, and Dalldorf (1978), included in the previous section, found that drugs appeared to benefit some 32 per cent of the mixed group of individuals who self-injured that they studied. A controversy exists about the effectiveness of drugs on the self-injurious behaviour of individuals with Lesch-Nyhan syndrome, and papers for and against drug treatment are included.

The subsequent collection of papers covers the behavioural treatments which are often tried in desperation after restraints and drugs have failed to control self-injury. Behavioural treatments involve a wide range of techniques and, perhaps, offer the best hope of improvement for the majority of individuals who self-injure. Schroeder, Schroeder, Smith, and Dalldorf (1978), for example, reported that 94 per cent of their sample responded to behaviour modification programmes.

We had hoped to include one or two papers on psychoanalytical or psychotherapeutic treatments for, although we are not convinced that these are of benefit in the treatment of self-injurious behaviour, we wanted to be as comprehensive as possible. However, whilst it was possible to unearth papers favouring a psychodynamic *explanation* of SIB we were unable to find any papers on treatment or intervention using this approach — at least as far as the mentally handicapped population is concerned. There are accounts of a psychodynamic approach in the treatment of self-injury in people who are not mentally handicapped (see, for example, Slawson and Davidson, 1964). Also excluded from this section are papers on surgical treatment for self-injurious behaviour, although we know that this irreversible procedure is sometimes carried out (Kiloh, Gye, Rushworth, Bell, and White, 1974). As Singh (1981) points out, evidence for the effectiveness of surgical intervention is weak.

Some guidelines on selecting the most appropriate treatment for a particular type of self-injurious behaviour or a particular individual may be found in the following papers, but it is impossible to state categorically that a given treatment should be used in a given circumstance. As stated in Section II, if the causes leading to the development of SIB can be determined, these may provide guidelines as to the most suitable treatment in any one case. Thus, for example, if social attention has led to self-injurious behaviour, then removal of attention for that particular behaviour may result in a reduction of its occurrence. If attention is reinforcing for the individual then it should still be given for more acceptable or adaptive behaviour, but *not* for self-injurious behaviour.

Unfortunately, as we pointed out in Section II, it is rarely easy to determine the factors that led to the emergence of self-injurious behaviour in the first place. Neither is it always the factors that originally caused SIB to develop which maintain it once it *has* developed. In such circumstances an attempt should be made to remove the factors which are maintaining SIB rather than the causal factors.

Whilst it is true that reading published reports of successful and unsuccessful self-injurious behaviour treatments may be of help in the selection of appropriate intervention strategies, readers should be warned that a treatment which has worked with one person may not work with another in a seemingly identical situation; the reason for this being that the range of contributing circumstances can be so varied and subtly different. A proper functional analysis with a linked treatment design will probably provide the best solution, as discussed in Section II (Iwata, Dorsey, Slifer, Bauman, and Richman, 1982; Murphy, 1985).

More group studies are needed to find out the percentage of people who respond to each kind of treatment and, to some extent, surveys such as those carried out by Schroeder, Schroeder, Smith, and Dalldorf (1978) and Maisto, Baumeister, and Maisto (1978) are useful. However, these were retrospective studies which did not include controlled treatment trials. It is, of course, difficult to undertake experimentally sound treatment studies because, fortunately, severe self-injurious behaviour is rare. Group studies also have their failings. They usually provide information about group means and averages, and not about individual responses. Single case experimental designs (see, for example, Lutzker, 1978) provide more useful information about an individual's response to treatment, but they cannot inform us about the selection of treatment in the first place.

It is possible that some progress in this area can be made by focusing on common features present in the individuals who self-injure, their problems, and the treatments they receive. In each case a functional analysis of the self-injurious behaviour should be carried out, that is, an investigation into the antecedents and consequences of the behaviour, and a *precise* description of the form of the self-injury should be given. For example, if an episode of SIB is usually preceded by the mother wanting to bath the child (the antecedent) and followed by the child being allowed to remain unbathed (the consequence), then treatment based on a learning theory or behavioural approach would probably be the method of choice. On the other hand, if the self-injurious behaviour is preceded by an earache then antibiotics or painkillers would probably required. At the same time care should be taken not to inadvertently reinforce the self-injurious behaviour with attention. Such reinforcement should be administered when the individual is *not* self-injuring. Or, to take another example, if the person is injuring for self-stimulation, then the method of choice might be to search for a more acceptable form of stimulation, perhaps involving vibration, touch, sound, or smell. Alternatively, with a very anxious person, systematic desensitisation might be considered (see Carr (1980 (b)) for a description of desensitisation).

As we have seen earlier in this book, the belief that people who injure themselves need more tender loving care can be dangerous. We would be the last to deny such individuals tender loving care, but it should not be contingent on the self-injurious behaviour because, as Lovaas and Simmons (1969) demonstrated, this can increase the very behaviour we are trying to reduce.

Ethical considerations also enter into the decision about which treatment to select. Restraint may prevent or restrict opportunities for learning; drugs may result in unpleasant side effects, such as reduced levels of consciousness; and many of the behavioural approaches could possibly be employed to adapt people who are mentally handicapped or autistic to unacceptable environments and living conditions. All approaches are open to abuse and, as people who are mentally handicapped are unable to argue their own case, it is up to parents and therapists to make sure that treatment is not a euphemism for physical, pharmacological, or behavioural imprisonment. On the other hand, every individual has the right to the most effective treatment available, and to deny treatment because of misguided beliefs, or lack of interest, or shortage of staff, is also unethical. Contingent electric shock, for example, often causes great controversy, yet this may be life saving treatment the first time it is used. It can be argued that to withhold shock under certain conditions (for example, if a person is suffering brain damage from severe head banging, or deformities through permanent restraint) is more unethical than to use contingent shock. The majority of people working with individuals who self-injure, however, would use shock only as a last resort after other methods have been tried and failed. We shall return to the problem of selecting the best treatment in the Summary.

Restraints and protective clothing

Protection is a vitally important aspect in the management of self-injurious behaviour. Even though it is not, strictly speaking, a treatment procedure, people who injure themselves severely have to be protected and most staff working with such people will need to use protective restraint at some time. We begin this section with an extract from Nyhan (1976), who discusses some simple protective devices for children with Lesch-Nyhan syndrome. These devices are also suitable for use with other individuals who self-injure. The second paper, by Spain, Hart, and Corbett (1984), is a more detailed description of some helmets, collars, and arm splints which have been used in the management of self-injurious behaviour. The guiding principle here is to choose the least restrictive appliance compatible with prevention of self-injury. Thus, if arm splints are used to prevent hand to head banging, the person should be able to move his arms freely to within a few centimetres of the head.

Sometimes it is necessary to have a range of protective devices available to avoid irritation to the skin of a particular area. Helmets and plastic neck collars, for example, may be alternated each day or every few days to avoid skin rashes. However, even with these practical precautions, other dangers may arise when restraint is used purely for protection and not as part of a treatment programme. In some people restraint may actually increase self-injurious behaviour by acting as positive reinforcement (see Section II for a discussion of the role of restraint in the development and maintenance of SIB). In other situations and with other people restraint may serve as a punisher and lead to a decrease in self-injurious behaviour. It is also possible to provide devices or clothing which will enable individuals who self-injure to practise self-restraint, whilst leaving their hands free in between times to carry on their normal lives. Restraints as reinforcement, punishment, and self-control are discussed later under the heading Behavioural treatments.

Pharmacological treatments

Four papers are included under this heading. The first, by Mizuno and Yugari (1974), reports the use of L-5 hydroxytryptophan with four children with Lesch-Nyhan syndrome aged between one year eight months and twelve years three months. The authors report that self-injurious behaviour ceased in all cases but reappeared within 12-15 hours of the medication being stopped. Unfortunately, as we learn in the following paper by Frith, Johnstone, Joseph, Powell, and Watts (1976), in a more carefully designed double blind trial, Mizuno and Yugari's findings were not replicated. Frith, Johnstone, Joseph, Powell, and Watts's study was a single case investigation, but there is other evidence from Nyhan (1978) (not included in this book) to suggest that L-5 HTP does not result in significant reduction of self-injury in children with Lesch-Nyhan syndrome. Nyhan feels that combining L-5 HTP with a decarboxylase inhibitor is more likely to result in injury free periods*, but considers that tolerance rapidly develops so that the effect is short-lived. Nevertheless, Nyhan feels optimistic about the future of pharmacological therapy for the treatment of self-injurious behaviour in children with Lesch-Nyhan syndrome.

The third drug treatment paper, by Primrose (1979), describes the use of baclofen in the treatment of a large, mixed group of patients exhibiting self-injurious behaviour. This study is interesting because it is one of the few large scale studies in the field of treatment of SIB. In a double blind trial 28 patients were treated, and 22 of these were said to have improved. Improvement was judged by nurses' ratings. Unfortunately, the paper provides too little information both on the original rates of SIB and on the amount of change following baclofen, for us to know the true extent of the drug's effectiveness.

The final paper in this section is a case study by Richardson and Zaleski (1983). Their 15-year-old boy had a long history of self-mutilation and was treated by an infusion of naloxone, an opiate antagonist. The authors argue that the resulting reduction in self-injury was evidence in favour of the hypothesis that individuals who self-injure release high levels of endorphins during their self-injurious behaviour, since the blocking of endorphin receptors (by naloxone) led to a drop in SIB in their patient. Unfortunately, this is the only case report of its type in the literature to date. Clearly the findings need to be replicated.

Given that many researchers believe there may be a causal link between the organic or biochemical status of certain mentally handicapped people and their self-injurious behaviour (see Section II), then drugs may have a large part to play in the future treatment of SIB. At present, however, their role is unclear although combining drugs with the use of behavioural techniques could prove to be a useful treatment approach. Such an approach has been used by Durand (1982) whose paper is included later, under Combined treatments.

Behavioural treatments

This term covers a wide range of approaches, many of which are illustrated in the following papers. We subdivide behavioural treatments into:

(a) Positive reinforcement and differential reinforcement of other (non-self-injurious) behaviour

(b) Relaxation and systematic desensitisation

(c) Extinction

*Nyhan, Johnson, Kaufman, and Jones (1980) tried this with some success.

(d)   Time out from positive reinforcement

(e)   Overcorrection

(f)   Aversive tastes and smells

(g)   Contingent electric shock.

For readers wanting further explanations of these terms Carr (1980 (b)) and Yule and Carr (1980) are both recommended. The former is written especially for parents of children who are mentally handicapped, and the latter for professionals and others interested in behaviour modification. In the same way as the guiding principle in using protective restraint is to select the least restrictive appliance, so in behavioural treatments most therapists seek the least punitive forms of treatment first.

(a)   POSITIVE REINFORCEMENT AND DIFFERENTIAL REINFORCEMENT OF OTHER BEHAVIOUR (DRO)

The simplest treatment, and perhaps the most powerful tool in behaviour modification, is positive reinforcement, that is, in the context of treatment of self-injurious behaviour, reinforcing or strengthening any behaviour that is not self-injurious. The first paper in this section, by Young and Wincze (1974) illustrates this approach. The patient showed two kinds of self injury: she banged her head on the bed rail and hit her head with her hand. At first the therapists reinforced her for making eye contact with them. This had the effect of increasing the amount of eye contact she made, but did not affect the SIB. Following this, she was reinforced for holding her hands at her sides, that is, for behaviour incompatible with hand to head banging which, in consequence, decreased. Unfortunately, the head to bed rail banging (not incompatible with hands at sides) increased. This paper illustrates some of the difficulties encountered in treating people who self-injure: the effects are often specific to one situation or therapist, and one type of behaviour may improve whilst others deteriorate. Positive reinforcement alone rarely seems effective for severe self-injury and usually has to be combined with other procedures.

In a DRO approach positive reinforcement may be given for all types of non-self-injurious behaviour, or specifically for behaviour that is incompatible with self-injury. In the second behavioural paper, Fleming and Nolley (1981) compare several different procedures, including DRO, used with a mildly mentally handicapped woman who scratched her skin. The most successful method was a combination of differential reinforcement of incompatible behaviour (for example, letter writing and doing puzzles) together with restraint (the wearing of boxing gloves). Neither of these approaches alone, nor several others, had effectively stopped the self-injury. The authors argue that the period spent wearing boxing gloves signalled to the patient that reinforcement for SIB was not available, and that when the gloves were removed it was necessary to reinforce incompatible behaviour such as letter writing and puzzle making. This woman was not typical of the majority of patients who severely self-injure in that she was only mildly mentally handicapped, highly verbal, sociable, and had a fairly rich repertoire of behaviours available to her.

(b) RELAXATION AND SYSTEMATIC DESENSITISATION

In the third paper Steen and Zuriff (1977) were also trying to establish a new behaviour incompatible with self-injurious behaviour. They chose relaxation as the incompatible response. Their patient, another young woman, was taught to relax first one hand and then the other. Self-injurious behaviour of 13 years' standing almost disappeared after 17 hours of treatment. The treatment was interesting, imaginative, and very acceptable. It is possible that many patients would benefit from such an approach and, as with many of the studies referred to in this book, further and larger scale investigations are necessary.

Bull and La Vecchio (1978) also used relaxation, but as a prelude to systematic desensitisation for treatment of a 10-year-old boy with Lesch-Nyhan syndrome. He was said to have a "phobic reaction" to removal of restraints. This attachment to restraints is a frequently reported phenomenon in self-injurious behaviour and will be commented on again in this section. Bull and La Vecchio first removed the restraints which led to the least distress and then progressed to those which had resulted in the boy's most severe "phobic reactions". This is another example of imaginative treatment and, again, it is possible that systematic desensitisation will work with other individuals who self-injure including those with Lesch-Nyhan syndrome.

(c) EXTINCTION

Extinction means the non-presentation of positive reinforcement. If a self-injurious behaviour is maintained by some kind of positive reinforcement, such as attention or escape from an activity, then non-reinforcement of that self-injurious behaviour should, eventually, lead to its disappearance.

Extinction can certainly be an effective treatment (see, for example, Lovaas and Simmons (1969) in Section II). However, it is often not possible to use this method because, firstly, the individual might seriously damage himself before the self-injurious behaviour disappears. This might be days, weeks, or even months later. Secondly, if self-stimulation or sensory stimulation is maintaining the self-injurious behaviour, the reinforcement cannot be removed. For example, if eye poking resulting in stimulation to the optic nerve is reinforcing, it is impossible to remove the source of reinforcement.

Thirdly, because there is often an increase in any behaviour before it is extinguished, self-injurious behaviour might become so much more severe during the extinction phase that it would be necessary to intervene for the person's safety. In this case the end result would be to extinguish less severe self-injurious behaviour and reinforce extremely severe self-injurious behaviour. If protective restraints were very reliable, and protection of the individual could be guaranteed, then it might be possible to engage in an extinction programme. Nevertheless, it would almost certainly be necessary to combine extinction with DRO in order to ensure no overall drop in the amount of reinforcement received by the individual.

Punishment procedures

The following four techniques are all punishment procedures and here we use the term "punishment" to mean an intervention which decreases the likelihood of a particular behaviour occurring again. This may be something obviously unpleasant, like a shock, but sometimes an event most people would consider pleasant can be punishing for some individuals. For example, giving a cuddle to some autistic children may be very unpleasant for them because they find physical contact aversive, and may stop them them from doing what we want them to do. Although most people trying to help individuals who self-injure prefer the non-punishment techniques of positive reinforcement, extinction, relaxation, and desensitisation, these are not always successful. In many cases they are less effective than punishment, which may be quicker and might lead to greater reduction in the behaviour. It goes without saying that punishment procedures should always be combined with reinforcement of desirable and non-injurious behaviours.

Still following the principle of the least restrictive alternative, some punishment procedures are less painful than others, as well as being more acceptable to staff and relatives. This does not necessarily mean they are less aversive or unpleasant for the recipients. Over-correction, for example, is probably more acceptable to most people than shock because of its presumed re-educative value, but Murphy (1978), in a review of over-correction, considers that to view it as an educative procedure is unwarranted and that it is effective because it is a powerful punishment technique. A good review of punishment and its alternatives may be found in Harris and Ersner-Hershfield (1978).

(d) TIME-OUT FROM POSITIVE REINFORCEMENT

Time-out and extinction are very similar procedures, because they both involve non-presentation of the reinforcer. The difference is that, in time-out, reinforcement becomes completely unavailable for a set period of time, whereas in an extinction programme the target behaviour (in this case self-injurious behaviour) is simply not reinforced, though positive reinforcement may still be available for other behaviours (see Carr, 1980(b); Murphy, 1980).

Time-out can be classified as a punishment technique (Leitenberg, 1965) and some of the punishment techniques used in the treatment of self-injurious behaviour can be seen as essentially time-out, for example, facial screening. This procedure usually means covering the individual's face with a terry towelling cloth for a brief period of time. Lutzker (1978) voices the opinion of many people working in the field of self-injury: that we need treatment procedures that do not cause pain and are aesthetically and ethically acceptable. In a multiple baseline across settings design,

Lutzker covered the face of a 20-year-old mentally handicapped young man with a cloth bib for three seconds every time self-injurious behaviour occurred. It is not clear whether the procedure worked because it resulted in time-out from positive reinforcement, or because it was a response contingent aversive stimulus, or because both of these conditions were in operation.

We include here a paper by Singh, Beale, and Dawson (1981) who investigated the duration of facial screening using three time intervals (three seconds, one minute, and three minutes) in order to determine which was the most effective in reducing self-injurious behaviour, and in generalisation to other situations. The one-minute interval was the most effective. This paper is interesting because of the use of an alternating treatments design. This has the major advantage of allowing simultaneous investigation of several treatment procedures or variations of procedure.

(e) OVER-CORRECTION

Over-correction, as mentioned above, is also a punishment procedure. It often involves two separate steps: restitution and positive practice (Murphy, 1978). Restitution means putting the situation to rights; positive practice means practising more appropriate behaviour. Thus, for a child who has tipped his full potty over the floor, restitution might involve mopping and scrubbing the floor and positive practice might consist of tipping the potty down the lavatory.

Sometimes restitution is not possible. Take, for example, the case of a child who moves his hands around inappropriately. For such stereotyped behaviour restitution is inappropriate. Nevertheless, positive practice of appropriate hand movements is possible. A series of hand exercises has proved effective in reducing stereotyped hand and foot movements in two children (Epstein, Doke, Sajwaj, Sorrell, and Rimmer, 1974).

The biggest disadvantage of the over-correction procedure is that it is time consuming and demanding on therapists, particularly if they work in a busy, understaffed ward or school. However, it has been shown to be effective for many different problems (Murphy, 1978) as well as for self-injurious behaviour. The paper by Azrin, Gottlieb, Hughart, Wesolowski, and Rahn (1975) is one of the few papers using a relatively large number of subjects. They treated an unselected sample of 11 institutionalised patients who self-injured, using required relaxation and/or hand awareness training. There was a 90 per cent reduction in SIB after one day's treatment. After three months self-injurious behaviour was virtually eliminated in four of the patients, and the other seven showed a reduced rate of SIB.

Borreson (1980) used a forced running exercise to reduce wrist and forearm biting in a 22-year-old man. (Although, strictly speaking, this is different from over-correction it would appear to work in a similar way to the hand exercises described above by Epstein, Doke, Sajwaj, Sorrell, and Rimmer, 1974.) Several other treatments had been tried before the forced running procedure. Using an ABAB design and several follow ups

Borreson showed that the procedure was very successful. Unfortunately, we are not told why this particular response was chosen.

Several other published reports of over-correction exist which are not included in this book. For example, De Catanzaro and Baldwin (1978) used a forced arm exercise to treat two boys. They used a reversal design whereby, following baselines, one boy was required to do arm exercises whenever he self-injured. This was followed by a return to baseline, after which positive reinforcement alone was tried. In the next stage arm exercises and reinforcement were combined. Treatment for the other boy was similar, although reinforcement on its own was not tried. Dramatic improvements were noted in both boys particularly when reinforcement was combined with the arm exercises but only two months' follow up was reported. Duker and Seys (1977) were able to eliminate vomiting by a mentally handicapped woman by use of restitutional over-correction, in which the patient was made to wash her face, the walls, and the floor for 20 minutes following self-induced vomiting. Measel and Alfieri (1976) and Matson, Stephens, and Smith (1978) give further accounts of over-correction procedures in the reduction of self-injurious behaviour.

Not all over-correction treatments are successful. For example, Azrin, Gottlieb, Hughart, Wesolowski, and Rahn (1975) reported that one or two subjects were made worse by over-correction, probably because the procedure used — that is, required relaxation — was reinforcing for those individuals. Measel and Alfieri (1976) also found that self-injurious behaviour was made worse in a study which combined positive reinforcement of other behaviour with over-correction of the SIB.

f) AVERSIVE TASTES AND SMELLS

Aversive tastes and smells have been successfully used as treatments for self-injurious behaviour. In 1974 Sajwaj, Libet, and Agras described lemon juice therapy to control life threatening rumination in a six-month-old infant. Lemon juice was squirted into the infant's mouth whenever tongue and lip movements (precursors of rumination) occurred. The treatment was successful and easy to use. The author discusses the advantages and disadvantages of this therapy and says evaluation with other individuals who ruminate is needed. Marholin, Luiselli, Robinson, and Lott (1980), in a paper not included here, successfully used lemon juice for reducing rumination in a 16-year old boy, but with another boy — an 11-year-old — they found that although the juice worked initially it ceased being so effective over a period of time. The introduction of Tabasco sauce, however, resulted in a further reduction of the ruminative vomiting.

Rapoff, Altman, and Christophersen (1980) used both lemon juice and ammonia with a five-year-old boy who was deaf-blind and who poked his face with his thumb. Lemon juice reduced, but did not eliminate, the self-injurious behaviour. Ammonia was then introduced, and this did eliminate the behaviour. This paper uses an elegant multiple baseline across settings combined with reversal design. The authors report that staff found the procedure more acceptable with lemon juice than ammonia, and that there was little potential for abuse or misuse with lemon juice. Ammonia is more likely to produce side effects and, as we said before, the general rule is to choose the least aversive alternative. In any case, ammonia should only be used after careful consideration and under close supervision.

The next paper in this section is that by Tanner and Zeiler (1975) who describe the use of ammonia with a 20-year-old woman with autism, who had received contingent electric shock for self-injurious behaviour in the past. Shock had initially been successful, but then the self-injurious behaviour had returned. The woman was successfully treated with aromatic ammonia, but the follow up was only for a period of 20 days. Further self-injurious behaviour may well have occurred at a later stage. Tanner and Zeiler claim that ammonia has one big advantage over shock, and that is the capsules can be more easily hidden than the shock apparatus so the subject is less able to discriminate between the punishers and the others. In other words, the procedure will be less person or situation specific and more likely to work with a variety of therapists and in different settings.

(g) CONTINGENT ELECTRIC SHOCK

In spite of the reluctance to use shock there is a widely held belief that it is the most effective and rapid treatment for severe self-injurious behaviour (see, for example, Azrin, Gottlieb, Hughart, Wesolowski, and Rahn, 1974; and Baumeister and Rollings, 1976). It is certainly more rapid than extinction and there can be little doubt that, as a first time treatment, shock can be very effective in reducing or eliminating self-injurious behaviour for a 6 - 12 month period. It can, therefore, be a valuable life saver in some cases.

Lovaas and Simmons (1969) (see the paper included in Section II) demonstrate the rapidity and effectiveness of shock for their patients and point out the positive side effects of this treatment. The paper by Tate and Baroff (1966) describes a successful use of shock paired with DRO for the treatment of self-injurious behaviour in a nine-year-old boy suffering from blindness and psychosis. Lang and Melamed (1969) were similarly successful when they used shock with a nine-month-old infant whose life was seriously endangered by persistent vomiting and chronic rumination.

There are problems with shock, however. Jones, Simmons, and Frankel (1974) describe its unsuccessful use with a nine-year-old girl with autism. The shock treatment in that instance resulted in an increase of self-injurious behaviour, the suppression of self-feeding, and the necessity for constant physical restraint. Shock also seems to be unsuccessful in some individuals with Lesch-Nyhan syndrome (see, for example, Anderson, Dancis, Alpert, and Herrmann, 1977).

Often, shock seems to be partially successful in one setting but not in another; or, as Romanczyk and Goren (1975) demonstrate, shock can make it possible to gain experimental but not clinical control (that is, self-injurious behaviour can sometimes be eliminated or reduced in the laboratory or in certain specific situations, but not always in natural, everyday environments). The paper by Romanczyk and Goren describes the treatment of severe self-injury in one patient over a period of 10 months. It is a good illustration of many of the problems which arise with individuals who severely self-injure and, in particular, it shows how difficult it is to generalise from one treatment setting to another. The next paper in this section, by Williams and Surtees (1975), reiterates the difficulty with clinical control and demonstrates that, although short term solutions may be found, the self-injurious behaviour may reappear in the long term. In Williams and Surtees' study escape avoidance conditioning was used. A buzzer preceded the shock which was avoidable if the patient engaged in behaviour incompatible with self-injury (holding a toy in both hands). This method was superior to straightforward contingent shock for self-injurious behaviour. Incidentally, the shock used was punishment and *not* negative reinforcement as the authors claim.

We also include in this section a discussion of the side effects of shock by Lichstein and Schriebman (1976) who confirm the views of others (for example, Lovaas and Simmons, 1969) that the majority of side effects are favourable — such as increased smiling and decreased whining. However, the long term effects of contingent shock treatment are uncertain. The final paper in this section is a survey of the long term outcomes of such treatment (Murphy and Wilson, 1981). This survey indicated that shock is not a widely used procedure, particularly in Great Britain where only a handful of cases could be traced, and that its effects are short-lived.

Designing and organising a successful shock treatment programme is extremely difficult, as we hope the papers we have included show. Since it may be helpful to summarise some of the major problems, we will now discuss them briefly.

At the outset lengthy discussions are necessary, both with the handicapped individual's parents or guardians and with staff who will be involved in the programme, to ensure that there is a general agreement about the need for a contingent shock technique. In many units it is also necessary to clear the procedure with an ethical committee, whose job it is to ascertain that all other forms of treatment have failed and that, therefore, in view of the present condition of the patient, contingent shock is an acceptable form of treatment. It is unlikely that any ethical committee would agree to a shock programme if the individual were not producing severe tissue damage through self-injury (though not all committees would take the view that self-injury had to be life-endangering before agreeing to shock treatment). It is important that such discussions take place *before* instituting a shock programme: contingent shock is an extreme form of punishment and, even when combined with DRO schedules, it should not be undertaken lightly.

If the patient's parents or guardians, the ethical committee, and the team of staff responsible are all agreed that a contingent shock programme is necessary, the next stage is to design the programme in outline. First and foremost, consideration must be given to the positive reinforcement programme that is to be combined with the contingent shock treatment. Secondly, the shock delivery apparatus must be devised. Early shock programmes employed simple, hand held devices, but these pieces of equipment have several disadvantages. It is common for individuals who self-injure to discriminate strongly between situations in which they will be shocked and those in which they will not be shocked (hence the need for careful programming of generalisation in any shock programme). While the hand held equipment is visible, therefore, the individual may well learn to cease, or to reduce his self-injurious behaviour (because he has discovered that shocks will follow such behaviour). However, if the equipment is absent from a room the individual's self-injury often rapidly increases. Even though it is sometimes possible to reduce this kind of discrimination by hiding the equipment within the room, a further problem remains. The application of shock by means of a hand held device may well entail an unpleasant struggle between the staff member and the individual who is to receive the shock. Moreover, the clear association of the adult and the delivery of the shock might give the adult aversive properties as far as the patient is concerned, something which should be avoided if possible.

The alternatives to hand held devices include remote (radio) controlled and automatic equipment. In the former case, an adult still triggers the shock delivery, but from a position remote from the patient (who wears the necessary equipment on his back). This obviates the need for a struggle to apply the shock and reduces the likelihood of the shock being associated with one person. With automatic equipment, the self-injurious response (such as a head bang) itself triggers the shock delivery, without members of staff being involved. This may sound an attractive proposition, but such equipment needs to be very carefully designed and maintained to prevent accidental shock delivery for non-injurious responses. For example, if the patient trips and bangs his head on the floor it is difficult to avoid the automatic presentation of a shock.

There are a number of other technical difficulties which apply to any piece of contingent shock equipment, not the least of which is the problem of voltage levels. Although the voltage partly determines the current, because of the complexities of human physiology it is difficult to be precise about the level of current applied (as discussed in Butterfield, 1975). Most therapists decide to try the shock on themselves and to employ a level which they find bearable but painful. This, of course, assumes that the self-injuring individual has a similar pain threshold, which may not be the case.

Finally, the details of the shock programme need to be determined. It is usual to begin with brief treatment sessions in a specified room and then slowly to generalise the programme in a planned way. Decisions need to be made regarding the training of staff (and parents) in the use of the equipment, and arrangements for the maintenance and repair of the devices are essential. It is not unknown for programmes to fail following equipment breakdowns (Romanczyk and Goren, 1975) and it may be best to have two sets of equipment available in order to avoid this problem. Perhaps most crucial of all, it will be necessary to arrange for data collection on the rate and intensity of the individual's self-injury, to ensure that the programme is effective or, if it is not, to modify the procedures used or stop the programme completely.

In a follow-up of the long-term outcome of contingent shock programmes, we discovered that about two-thirds of individuals who self-injured relapse within a year from the end of the shock programme (Murphy and Wilson, 1981). Sometimes a further programme is successful; but these figures should alert those considering such treatment régimes to the fact that relapse is the most likely eventual outcome. Contingent shock may only provide a breathing space for individuals who injure themselves severely.

Combined treatments

Some of the treatments already described (for example, Fleming and Nolley, 1981) combined two or more behavioural approaches with greater success than one approach used alone. In addition, there are several treatment reports combining methods from different areas, and this may prove to be a particularly useful approach in the future.

One such approach is to use protective restraints, such as those described earlier in this section, as part of a behavioural programme. The restraints could gradually be faded out, that is they could be reduced in size or frequency of use, in much the same way as shaping or chaining procedures are used to teach new behaviours (see, for example Yule and Carr, 1980). The boy described by Corbett (1975) often wore a large, strong helmet to prevent him from head banging. During one of the many attempts to treat this boy (Corbett, personal communication) parts of his helmet were removed one piece at a time (for example, the visor, the chin strap, and so forth). Eventually, the boy was wearing a symbolic skull cap on his head in place of the helmet. A similar procedure was used by Williams (personal communication) who used a copy of *The Times* as an arm splint to prevent hand to head banging in another boy. Treatment consisted of removing sheets of the newspaper one at a time over a period of several weeks without the self-injurious behaviour recurring. The air splints described by Paul and Romanczyk (1973) also readily lend themselves to gradual fading.

For some children the gradual removal of restraints may work in a similar way to desensitisation, described earlier. The child has a chance to adapt gradually to less and less control, and the full blown anxiety and panic which can appear with complete or sudden removal of restraints is thus avoided. At the same time, some part of the restraint is retained to act as a reminder or safety signal which is sufficient to prevent self-injury. Some children may never be able to manage without a symbolic safety signal of this nature.

Self-control is another way in which restraints and a behavioural approach to treatment may be combined. It can be argued that the aim of every behavioural programme is to enable the individual being treated to eventually gain control of his own behaviour. Self-control techniques are widely used in behavioural treatments for such disorders as phobias, over-eating, and ruminative thoughts. Kazdin (1975, p. 192) defines self-control as "those behaviours an individual deliberately undertakes to achieve self-selected outcomes". If we can provide the means to enable individuals who show severe self-injurious behaviour to control their own SIB then we may have a simple, effective tool to help a considerable number of such people.

This approach may prove particularly valuable in view of the frequent reports of people who self-injure who do attempt to restrain themselves, by such means as wrapping themselves in blankets or sitting on their hands. We can, for example, provide special clothing which allows hands to be removed easily for certain activities but restrains them during dangerous or inactive periods. One six-year-old boy known to us was provided with a muff to allow him to practise self-restraint. Initially, one muff dramatically reduced his hand to head banging. After a few weeks he restrained one hand in the muff but used the other to bang his head. A second muff solved the problem for another few weeks until this, too, became ineffective. Novelty may, in some cases, be an essential part of treatment, and therapists should, therefore, be prepared to use a variety of treatments. We have included the paper by Rojahn, Mulick, McCoy, and Schroeder (1978) to illustrate how the provision of special clothing may allow self-control of self-injurious behaviour.

The next two papers, by Favell, McGimsey, Jones, and Cannon (1981) and Dorsey, Iwata, Reid, and Davis (1982) discuss the influence of restraint and protective equipment in self-injurious behaviour from a different standpoint. Favell, McGimsey, Jones, and Cannon demonstrate that individuals who self-injure can be reinforced by restraint, that is, they injure themselves in order to gain access to the restraint which they enjoy. This may be an important factor in the maintenance of self-injurious behaviour. Dorsey, Iwata, Reid, and Davis, on the other hand, in a multiple baseline across settings design, suggest that protective equipment may lead to rapid and substantial decreases in self-injurious behaviour together with increases in desirable behaviour. In other words, restraint may work as a punisher too. It is possible that people who attempt to restrain themselves find externally imposed restraints reinforcing, and those who do not attempt self-restraint find such restraints punishing. This is probably too simplistic; but certainly some people find any restriction of movement very aversive, and others seem thankful for anything which prevents their compulsive self-injury. The last two papers mentioned both provide good discussions on the advantages and pitfalls of the use of physical restraints in the management of self-injurious behaviour.

Pharmacological treatments may also be combined with behavioural methods to enhance the effectiveness of intervention strategies. We conclude this section with a paper by Durand (1982(a)). This is an important paper, because it compares a drug treatment alone with a behavioural treatment alone, and with a combined drug and behavioural treatment. This single case study, using a reversal design, concludes that neither the drug (haloperidol) alone nor the behavioural treatment alone (in this case, punishment) was successful; but when used together self-injurious behaviour was dramatically reduced.

Summary

It seems that no single approach to treatment will be effective with all people engaging in self-injurious behaviour; nor is it likely to be possible to discover one approach which will suit each particular type of self-injurious behaviour (for example, head banging, eye gouging, or face picking). For certain problems the treatment selected will depend on how the self-injurious behaviour originally developed and what factors maintain it. In the majority of cases it will not be easy to determine the causes and maintaining factors. Nevertheless, we would agree with Durand (1982) that a careful analysis of each individual's self-injurious behaviour is always required.

For the majority of people who self-injure it is likely that behavioural approaches to treatment will be most appropriate and we remind the reader of Schroeder, Shroeder, Smith, and Dalldorf's (1978) survey which suggested that 94 per cent of individuals on a behaviour modification programme appeared to improve. This is not altogether surprising in view of the fact that the learned behaviour hypothesis is one of the most convincing hypotheses for explaining the development of self-injurious behaviour (see Section II). A learning theory approach might, therefore be expected to be one of the most effective ways of changing such behaviour.

It is likely that in the future we shall see new developments in chemical treatments for self-injury and, in view of the strong relationship between some organic disorders and self-injurious behaviour, this may be particularly valuable for certain groups of self-injuring individuals, such as those with the Lesch-Nyhan or De Lange syndrome.

With regard to the use of restraints, we have pointed out that to use these purely as protection is, at best, of limited value — although restraints may stop serious tissue damage from occurring they make no attempt to enable the person to live without them. At worst, restraints can lead to an increase in self-injurious behaviour, where the individual self-injures in order to be placed in the restraints. On the other hand, when combined with a behavioural approach, restraints or special clothing which enable self-control of self-injurious behaviour are likely to prove a simple, straightforward, and successful management technique for a substantial group of self-injuring individuals — at least for a period of time. Other combinations of treatment methods, such as drugs used with a behavioural approach, also seem promising. Finally, as self-injurious behaviour often reappears after an apparently successful treatment programme, it may be necessary for parents and therapists to accept the need to switch from one approach to another every few weeks or months, as novelty may be an important aspect of treatment for many behaviour disorders.

The relative rarity of severe self-injury means that any one psychologist, psychiatrist, teacher, or nurse will probably have limited experience of the problem. It would seem, therefore, that referral to special treatment centres might be advisable for individuals showing severe self-injurious behaviour. However, experience in this country (at Hilda Lewis House) and in America (Schroeder, Schroeder, Smith, and Dalldorf, 1982) suggests that admission of people who self-injure to specialised units is a mistake. Even when successful programmes are set up in the treatment centre there is no guarantee that they will be effective in the referring hospital, hostel, or home environment, once the person being treated returns to that setting. It is often very difficult to transfer a programme from the one situation to the other, even despite frequent and lengthy visits, because of the inherent situational differences (for example, in staffing ratios, staff attitudes and training, and so on). Certainly, regional advice centres are needed but it is preferable for them to operate entirely in the original environment of the individual referred instead of admitting that person for treatment of self-injury to an unfamiliar and distant unit.

BEHAVIOR IN THE LESCH-NYHAN SYNDROME[1]

William L. Nyhan[2]

Department of Pediatrics, University of California, San Diego

The Lesch-Nyhan syndrome is a heritable disorder of the metabolism of uric acid in which behavioral manifestations are prominent and among the most provocative. The mutated or variant gene that determines this disorder is carried on the X chromosome. The disease is expressed exclusively in males. The molecular expression of the abnormal gene is in the completely defective activity of the enzyme hypoxanthine guanine phosphoribosyl transferase. As a result these patients overproduce uric acid and may develop early in life many of the clinical findings we associate with gout. They have in addition a variety of neurological abnormalities including mental retardation, spastic cerebral palsy, and involuntary, choreoathetoid movements. Involved patients have unusual, compulsive, aggressive behavior. Its most prominent but by no means exclusive feature is self-mutilation. The central feature in the management of this behavior is physical restraint. A number of practical procedures have been learned which facilitate the care and feeding of these patients. Promising new findings suggest that behavioral modification using extinction techniques and pharmacologic methods utilizing agents designed to increase the effective cerebral content of serotonin may each have a place in the management of behavior in this syndrome.

Introduction

The Lesch-Nyhan syndrome (Lesch & Nyhan, 1964) is an inborn error of purine metabolism in which abnormal behavior is a major manifestation. The disorder is determined by a gene on the X chromosome and affects only males. The primary product of the abnormal gene is a variant enzyme, hypoxanthine guanine phosphoribosyl transferase (Seegmiller, Rosenbloom, & Kelley, 1967; Sweetman & Nyhan, 1972). This enzyme, which is present in every cell in the body, normally converts hypoxanthine and guanine to their respective nucleotides, inosinic acid and guanylic acid. In patients with the Lesch-Nyhan syndrome the activity of this enzyme is completely lacking. The metabolic consequences of this defect are an enormous overproduction of uric acid and accumulation of large amounts of uric acid in body fluids. Hypoxanthine also accumulates, particularly in the cerebrospinal fluid (Sweetman, 1968) where concentrations of uric acid are never high. Uric acid is not formed in the central nervous system and it is effectively excluded by the blood-brain barrier.

As a result of their uric acid excess, these patients may develop any of the manifestations of gout. They may have arthritis tophi, renal stone disease, and nephropathy (Nyhan, 1968, 1973, 1974; Howard & Walzak, 1967). Urate nephropathy may lead to renal failure. This was the rule, usually with death in childhood, until the advent of treatment with allopurinol (Sweetman & Nyhan, 1967; Balis, Krakoff, Berman, & Dancis, 1967). These patients also have a variety of abnormalities that are clearly unrelated to the presence of large amounts of uric acid in body fluids. A severe degree of mental retardation is one of the cardinal features of the disease. IQs are usually below 50 and none learn to walk. On the other hand, we have regularly felt that most of these patients were more intelligent than test scores indicated. Tests of IQ were certainly not developed with children like these in mind. The neurological defect makes it difficult for these children to perform adequately. Writing is out of the question. Furthermore, the behavior disorder imposes a virtually unique problem for

[1]Supported by research grants from the Public Health Service (DHEW), General Clinical Research Center #RR00827; from the National Institute of General Medical Sciences, National Institutes of Health, #GM 17702; and from the National Foundation-March of Dimes, #NF1377.
[2]Requests for reprints should be sent to Dr. William L. Nyhan, Department of Pediatrics, University of California, San Diego, La Jolla, California 92093.

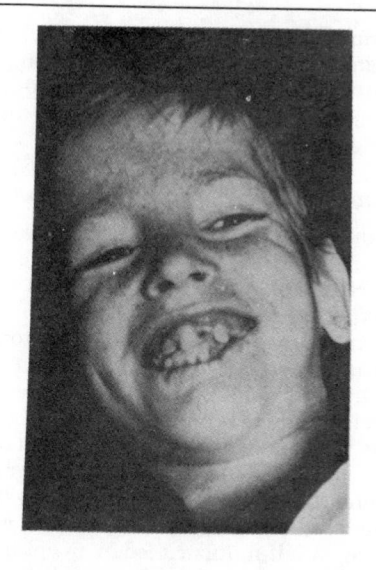

Fig 1. A patient with Lesch-Nyhan syndrome, illustrating the characteristic loss of tissue about the lips.

adequate testing. All of these children have bright, understanding eyes. They relate unusually well to people and they are usually felt by those closest to them to understand everything that is said to them. They all learn speech, and some communicate quite well. A few of our patients have been thought by parents, teachers, or psychologists to be functioning at a normal level of intelligence. One patient has been reported in whom performance of selected psychological tests was within normal limits (Scherzer & Ilson, 1969).

All of the patients have cerebral palsy and display a very marked choreoathetosis. Increase in muscle tone may be the earliest neurological manifestation. Abnormal movements usually begin by 8 to 12 months of age. They are increased by tension or excitement. Opisthotonic or extensor spasms of the trunk are characteristic. Speech is notably dysarthric. Athetoid dysphagia is another problem. These patients are difficult to feed. They vomit frequently. In a crowded State hospital, or elsewhere, these features can lead to aspiration or to inanition, either of which may be fatal. Convulsive seizures are seen occasionally, but not uniformly in this syndrome.

Among the inborn errors of metabolism, this disease is relatively common. In collections of patients with mental retardation it is our experience to find this disease second in frequency to phenylketonuria and more common than other heritable metabolic diseases.

The abnormal behavior (Lesch & Nyhan, 1964; Nyhan, 1968) of patients with the Lesch-Nyhan syndrome is generally first manifest with the eruption of teeth. Patients begin biting themselves, and self-mutilation through biting continues as the single most unsettling feature of the disease to parents and others responsible for the care of these children (Lesch & Nyhan, 1964; Nyhan, 1972a; Reed & Fish, 1966; Hoefnagel, 1965). The biting is ferocious. Partial amputations of fingers are common. There have also been some who have produced a partial amputation of the tongue. Most patients have lost a considerable amount of tissue about the lips. The hallmark of this syndrome is a distinct absence of tissue about the upper or lower lip (Figure 1). In some patients there is destruction of both. It is rare to see a patient with this disease in whom there is not permanent damage to the lips, unless the primary teeth have been removed early. As they grow and develop, this behavior becomes more varied. These children find other ways of self-mutilating, such as picking with their fingers, scalding in hot water, and catching themselves in braces employed for cerebral palsy or in the spokes of a wheelchair. They will bite others but this is limited by the motor defect.

In working with handicapped children it is clear that many of them have highly specific patterns of behavior. We have proposed the idea that there are behavioral phenotypes (Nyhan, 1972b) or syndromes just as there are patterns of somatic expression. It is furthermore clear that it is the child's behavior rather than his IQ or motor capacities that determines whether he must be institutionalized. Among deviant behaviors, self-mutilative behavior is one of the most difficult to live with. Most patients with the Lesch-Nyhan syndrome are ultimately admitted to institution, although they are otherwise quite engaging children.

Self-mutilative behavior in pediatric patients

The differential diagnosis of self-mutilation in childhood is not large. We have reported self-mutilation in the DeLange syndrome (Shear, Nyhan, Kirman, & Stern, 1971; Bryson, Sakati, Nyhan, & Fish, 1971). Children with the DeLange syndrome have a behavioral phenotype (Johnson, Nyhan, Shear, Ekman, & Friesen, 1976) in which quite a number of behaviors are seen regularly in the syndrome. Aversive, self-stimulatory behavior appears to be an integral component of this phenotype. Some of the children acquire malformations of the lip, indistinguishable from those of patients with the Lesch-Nyhan syndrome. However, the mutilation is much less severe than in the Lesch-Nyhan syndrome; loss of tissue is rare and seems almost accidental. The behavior is readily extinguished, using aversive operant methods which are never effective in the Lesch-Nyhan syndrome. At the same time the behavior of the patient with the DeLange syndrome may lead to serious consequences. We followed one patient with the DeLange syndrome who shortly after beginning to self-mutilate died in an episode that was interpreted as suicide. Another was murdered by another retarded child shortly after being admitted to a state institution (Johnson et al., 1976). Self-mutilative activity is also seen in children with sensory neuropathies. The pattern in these children is quite different. The trauma is clearly accidental. These patients began to look like pugilists. They have many unrecognized fractures. They have trophic changes or burns which result in the loss of the ends of fingers or toes. The nasal septum is particularly subject to traumatic loss. Patients with dysautonomia may also have self-mutilation. In these patients the problem appears also to result from abnormalities in innervation, although they may have abnormalities in other aspects of behavior. Autistic children and children with nonspecific mental retardation may have self-mutilative behavior, especially after long institutionalization. The pattern of mutilation in these patients is usually quite different from that of the Lesch-Nyhan syndrome. Head banging is its most common form. Hitting is next, and picking and biting are much less common. The activity tends to be chronic and low grade. It therefore leads not to losses of tissue but to hypertrophies in the area of trauma. The cauliflower ear is a common example. Such a patient may develop partial or complete blindness due to trauma to an eye, but serious consequence of the behavior is the exception rather than the rule. In sum, self-mutilation is seen in a variety of children with mental retardation but it is rare. When examined closely this behavior almost never resembles that of the patient with the Lesch-Nyhan syndrome.

Behavior of the patient with the Lesch-Nyhan syndrome

The self-mutilative behavior of the patient with the Lesch-Nyhan syndrome is remarkable for its effectiveness in producing loss of tissue. In no other type of patient is self-aversive behavior so dramatic or so effectively mutilative. Amputations of digits often include the entire bone of a phalanx. One of our patients now has an acquired cleft of the palate. It is also remarkable for its lightninglike rapidity. When one of these patients gets out of restraints, the hand goes instantly to the mouth. The hand may be quicker than the eye if the eye is not trained through experience with these patients, and one quick trip to the mouth can produce a considerable amount of damage. It is a source of continued surprise that patients so athetoid, who have so much difficulty controlling the simplest hand movements, can so quickly and so accurately get the hand to the mouth and bite or lacerate it on a tooth.

Sensory modalities are all intact in these patients. They definitely perceive pain. They do not want to bite themselves and scream in pain when they do. These are usually engaging children. When they are restrained securely, they are relaxed and good-humored, and they smile easily. They tend to look quite a bit alike. Athetoid children in general resemble each other, but these children are reminiscent of the principal character of the ballet "Petroushka" with their admixture of good humor and tragedy, unusual posturing, and the usual mittenlike coverings on their hands.

When protective coverings or restraints are removed, the patient's personality undergoes a dramatic change. He appears terrified. He screams, I think, for help, to protect him against himself. Older patients are sometimes able to get help, to get them back in restraints before they damage themselves. A corollary of this involves sleeping behavior. We have frequently obtained the history that a child with this syndrome has never slept properly since the time his teeth came in. Neither had the family, because he screamed all night. We interpreted this as a call for help and protection against himself. Patients restrained securely, with all four extremities tied for sleep, sleep very well. Parents have sometimes had to be convinced of this by an overnight admission to hospital. However it is done, teaching parents or guardians to restrain the patient securely in bed obliterates this problem of sleeping behavior.

It is paradoxical that the self-mutilative behavior is uncontrollable, but nevertheless very much within the patient's consciousness. Furthermore, it changes with time; as a patient gets older he gets better at finding ways, especially enlisting the help of others in protecting him against himself. We have thought that the basic urge that drives him to mutilate is a chemical consequence of the disease, while the various methods that individual patients learn to attempt control are like the modulations any of us employ in civilizing primitive behavioral impulses.

Mutilation in these patients does not come only from biting. They may pick at a wound or work on it with their tongues. A tooth may be combined with a hard surface or even a bed sheet to injure an interposed lip. Patients may find hot water faucets and burn themselves. One patient burned himself in a dry ice acetone bath left unattended by an investigator in a clinical research center. The extensor spasms of the trunk in which the head is thrown back forcibly may lead to injury if the head meets a hard surface.

More often this extension behavior injures someone else. Nurses and others caring for these children learn to be careful when they are behind them. The back of the head is hard and it is thrown back with considerable force. Patients are less effective with other outer-directed aggressive behavior, but it is clear that the behavior of these children is not simply self-mutilative. It is a generally compulsive aggressiveness that the patient cannot control. He is as remorseful if he succeeds in hurting another as when he hurts himself, but he cannot help continuing to pursue it. They do bite, but the unwary must be very close for this to be effective, and those that get very close to these patients quickly become wary. They hit with their hands and kick with their feet. Attendants are better off with plastic glasses so that they do not break when they are knocked off. One of our patients was visited at Christmas by his mother, whom he had not seen for some months as she lived in another state. When he saw her come in the room he was overjoyed. Nevertheless, he promptly threw a truck he had received as a present across the room at her and lacerated her ankle. Some of these patients spit at people. They all vomit, and certainly this is not all self-induced; possibly not even much of it is, but some of it appears at least semivoluntary. They do seem to vomit situationally. Some have vomited on others, especially those feeding them. Some of our older patients have developed aggressive patterns of behavior with sexual overtones, pinching or grabbing the bottoms or the genitalia of those that come near them. Verbal forms of aggression develop in most of them. Four-letter Anglo-Saxon expressions are commonly used, especially in the presence of those that seem upset by them. One of our patients developed more subtle forms of aggression, telling for instance his mother, as she left to drive somewhere, that he hoped she'd get in an accident and die. This boy lived at home and loved his mother more than anyone else in the world. It was she who received the worst of his behavior. Another patient we observed was expert at turning one of the nurses in the unit against another. He manufactured things to tell one, saying that another had said this about her. Nurses experienced with this patient learned never to believe the things he attributed to another staff member.

The behavior of these patients is a striking and provocative element in the syndrome. It is the first instance in which a stereotyped pattern of human behavior has been associated with a distinct biochemical abnormality. Understanding of mechanism could contribute to an understanding of behavior and its biochemical basis.

Day-to-day management and nursing care

Over the years we have learned a number of things about the care and feeding of these children that may be useful to parents or others responsible for their care. Feeding is a problem. Many have mouths made inefficient by mutilation or the removal of teeth. Swallowing is inefficient and they vomit frequently. Consequently, some degree of inanition is the usual situation. We have admitted to hospital some patients in whom this was the chief complaint. Most patients with the syndrome have a retardation of linear growth and the bone age, but the defect in weight gain is always greater. The reasons for this are not clear, and endocrinologic evaluation is negative (Skyler, Neelon, Arnold, Kelley, & Lebovitz, 1974). We have felt that the etiology is nutritional. One argument for this hypothesis is the fact that those children who have grown and developed best have been those who have lived at home and who had the best nutrition.

We have been very successful in improving the nutrition of even some very advanced cases who were skin and bones at the start. For such a patient we have emphasized small, frequent, high-caloric liquid feedings. Milk, to which egg or ice cream is added, makes an excellent between-meals and bed-time supplement. We refeed within one hour for vomiting. Few of these patients can do much chewing, so that solids should be mashed up very soft and contain no chunks on which to choke. It is not necessary to use purees. We have used spoons exclusively, avoiding knives and forks, which may be dangerous. The food is placed well back on the tongue. Paper or plastic cups are preferable to glass, which patients can break even with their teeth. Syringe feeding of liquids or medications may be useful. It is ideal to have one person, or a very few, feed the patient so that each becomes accustomed to the routine. Eating is one of the few real pleasures these children can enjoy. It is worth devoting some effort to making mealtime pleasant, arranging the food attractively, and serving things that he likes.

It is preferable to have these patients up in a chair most of the day. This permits them to use many of their muscles, and to participate in the environment. They like to be where the action is, whether it is the kitchen or playroom at home or the nurses' station. They enjoy television, radio, and recordings. Most will ultimately profit by an individually built chair. It is well to start with an ordinary wheelchair, the smaller and narrower the better, and learn what works with an individual patient before embarking on something elaborate. The organization of restraints in the chair is important. These patients cannot sit up unless tied in securely. Once in place they can do a lot, including playing with toys and getting

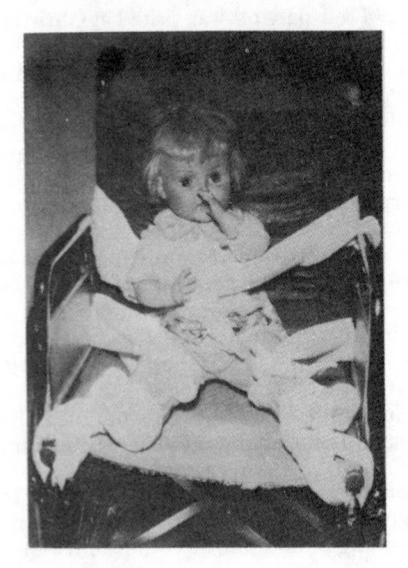

Fig. 2. Pattern of restraint using ordinary cloth diapers and an ordinary wheelchair, permitting a patient with the Lesch-Nyhan syndrome to be up and about.

Fig. 3. Patient with the syndrome in a specially designed wheelchair, small and narrow enough to fit him. The integral central bar on the seat and the seat belt above were enough to keep him upright in the chair. He was illustrating with his right hand his ability to move the chair.

themselves around.

Cloth diapers provide the mainstay for restraints and it is possible to function quite well, especially in hospital, with nothing more complex than cloth diapers. They are ideally tied rather than pinned. Pins come apart more easily, and they can be dangerous. The chair is gradually built up with diapers, one around each thigh and fastened to the poles on the back of the chair. The forearms are tied to the back of the chair, leaving the hands free. There is a tie around the chest. The ties around the arms are brought under this and tied to the back of the chair. Any hard surface is padded. The principle is illustrated in Figure 2 with an ordinary wheelchair. Figure 3 illustrates a patient in a specially constructed wheelchair with a built-in seat belt and a central bar in the seat, which were enough to keep this boy upright in the chair. Figure 4 illustrates a more elaborate individually constructed stationary chair. A much more elaborate chair was designed by Letts and Hobson (1975) which is removable from the wheeled frame, permitting service as a car seat. A clear plastic arm and hand enclosure reminiscent of the side of an isolette has portholes from which the child cannot withdraw his arms because the back of the chair prevents extension of the humeri. Objects

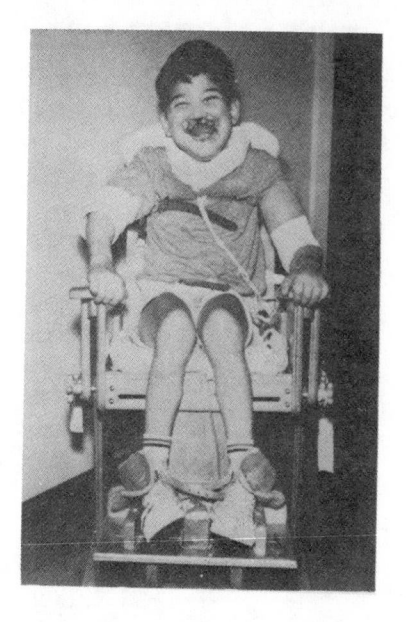

Fig. 4. Patient in a more elaborate specially built stationary chair. This patient could get himself to a standing position using this chair. A desk-top-type work table could be added in front. One of our patients who wore leg braces had a specially constructed wooden stand table at which he could stand and work or play.

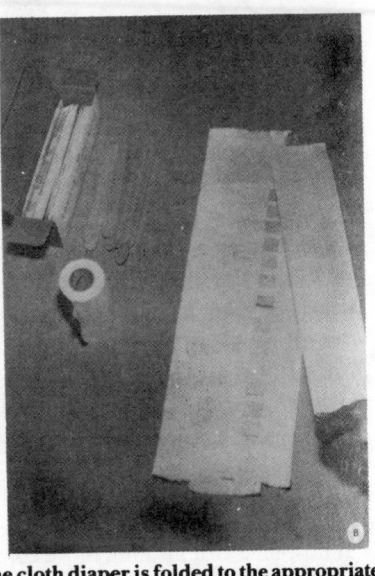

Fig. 5. The fashioning of elbow restraints. In 5A the cloth diaper is folded to the appropriate size and taped, and the tongue depressors are placed in a row. In 5B the diaper is folded over and taped with wide adhesive tape. The restraint is then placed around the elbow and taped circumferentially to itself.

can be placed in the enclosure permitting the patient to use his hands and arms to manipulate them without fear of getting a hand to the mouth.

In Figures 3 and 4 the patient's hands are shown free, permitting their use in locomotion, play, or learning. This illustrates the utility of elbow restraints which prevent flexion of the elbow, making it impossible for a hand to get to the mouth. These restraints are the most valuable in permitting a child maximum use of his hands. Two forms are shown. The simplest, in Figure 4, can be made using cloth diapers, wooden tongue depressors, and adhesive tape. The manufacture of one of these restraints is shown in Figure 5. Patients of ours have had similar devices fashioned of leather with intrinsic staves and a zipper closure.

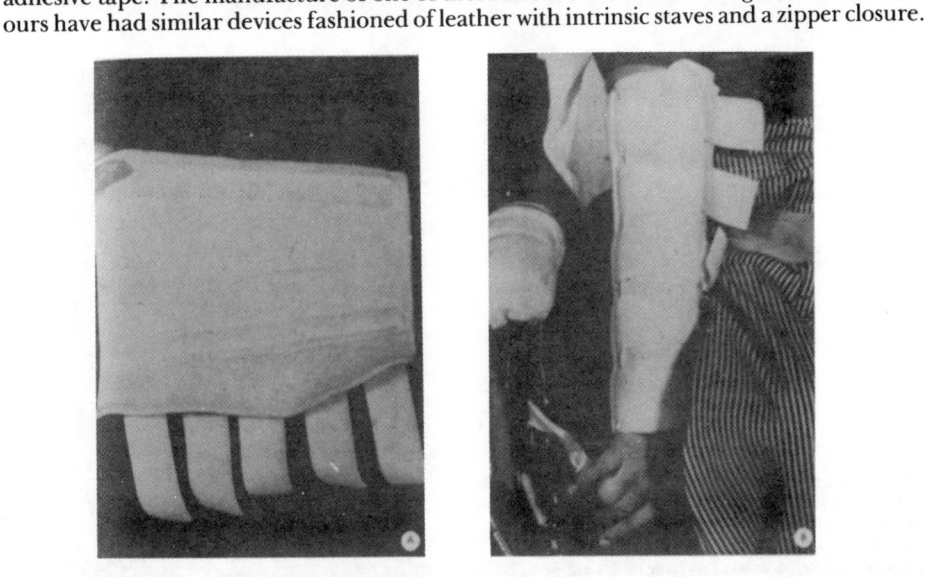

Fig. 6. Cloth and plastic elbow restraint. A—open. B—partially attached to illustrate the method of closure.

We have employed plastic elbow splints (Figure 3) made on order for individual patients.[3] A close-up is shown in Figure 6.

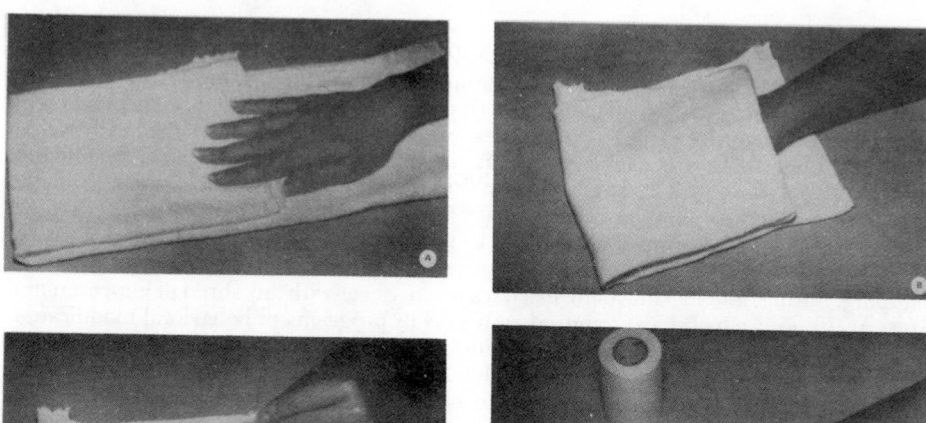

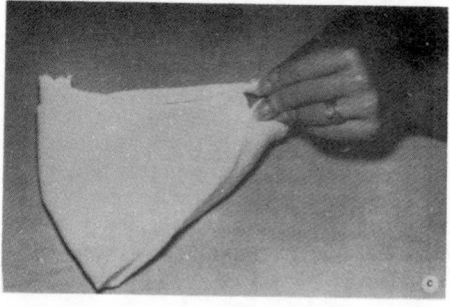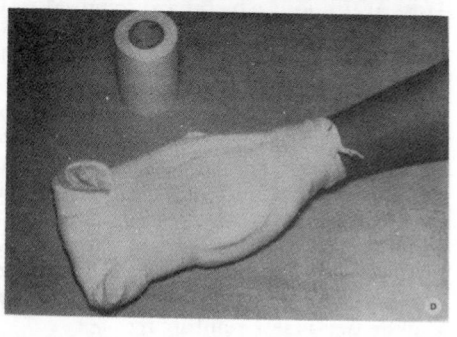

Fig. 7. Cloth mittens fashioned from diapers and adhesive tape. A—Folded diaper with hand in place. B—Cloth is folded over to enclose the hand. C—Sides are drawn in to make mitten. D—Adhesive tape completes the closure.

Most patients cannot be maintained continuously in elbow restraints or they begin to develop abrasions at the edges. This can become a form of self-mutilation. Therefore, it is useful to alternate them with some form of mitten. Quite a variety is effective in individual children. Again, the simplest and most effective can be fashioned from cloth diapers (Figure 7). These are tough and withstand the most vigorous efforts of the child. We have used actual boxing gloves and they are highly effective, but they are airless and lead to maceration. Any heavy cloth mitten will usually do nicely. Some children need only rather thin cotton mittens, or even socks, more as a reminder than true protection, but effective in some. Most are highly specific about a finger or two, which are repeatedly damaged and sometimes covering only the dangerous finger suffices. Plastic hair rollers have been used with success. These individual variations among children are reminiscent of variations in behaviour among normal children. Among our patients with this syndrome some are basically very gentle people, on whom, as it were, an irresistible impulse has been grafted. These are the ones for whom thin mittens suffice. There is a spectrum of behavior in the syndrome, as there is among normal individuals.

At night most patients are best tied with all four extremities to the bed using heavy diapers. A jacket restraint or tieback vest[4] is often very useful for restraint in bed. This can also be used in the chair.

We have tried and discarded helmets. Most of our patients have not enjoyed being on the floor. Bathing usually requires two people. A large sink may be easier on their backs than the usual bathtub. In any case, the spigots should be covered to protect against direct injury or turning on the water at an inopportune time. For the attendant who can maintain a sense

[3]In San Diego these may be obtained from Abbey Rents, 2110 El Cajon Boulevard, San Diego, California, Attention: Mr. Ron Morton.

[4]Posey Company, 39 South Santa Anita Avenue, Pasadena, California.

of humor, these are interesting children to care for. They provide considerably more feedback than virtually any child with a similar degree of physical and mental handicap.

Behavior Modification

Self-mutilative behavior in mentally retarded patients has been considered a learned response and as such subject to unlearning with suitable techniques of behavioral modification. In many retarded patients this type of behavior has been thought to reflect an attention-getting device. This has seemed less reasonable in patients with the Lesch-Nyhan syndrome, but there are elements of this in the behavior. Mild aversive techniques, including mild shock with a prod, have been very effective in, for instance, patients with the DeLange syndrome. They have been totally ineffective in the Lesch-Nyhan syndrome. Most observers have found the behavior to worsen with aversive techniques. We have encountered patients who have been subjected to extreme aversive techniques, such as slapping, hitting, and locking alone in a dark room, never with any shred of improvement. Most institutions which have removed restraints in programs of behavioral modification have ended up with extreme examples of mutilation that were very upsetting for the family and the staff, and, of course, the patient. This approach to behavior modification is known as extinction. It is generally considered to be undesirable in the management of self-mutilation. Increase in the rate of deviant behavior in the early stages of such a program is characteristic. Severe losses of tissue and blindness have been observed under these circumstances in mentally retarded, self-mutilative patients (Duker, 1975). Nevertheless, it has generally been observed in patients with the Lesch-Nyhan syndrome that mutilative behavior increases under some circumstances. Some conditions appear to reinforce it. These include the responses of parents, attendants, nurses, and others to the behavior and its attendant pain, blood, and horror. The crying of the child in response to his pain elicits reponses which are reinforcing. The sight of the patient's injured part, or of his own blood, may be perversely reinforcing.

Extinction therapy in which the patient was ignored when he bit without restraints was reported to be successful in a patient with the Lesch-Nyhan syndrome reported by Duker (1975). Extinction was combined with removal to a new environment, and the rate of biting behavior was documented to decrease. This patient also was a head banger and the therapy failed to decrease that behavior; instead it increased. The report is not a convincing success. However, a similar extinction in biting behavior was documented in a number of patients by Anderson, Herrmann, Alpert, and Dancis (1975), whose technique was to turn away when the patient went to bite himself. These investigators reported an increase in biting behavior with aversive stimulation, so that there was a distinct difference in response to extinction therapy. We have recently studied a patient who was the product of an independent program of extinction therapy conceived for him by the staff at the Arizona Training Program in Tucson, Arizona. There is no question that biting of the hands was not a problem for this boy, and it was of considerable advantage to him not to have his hands restrained. His primary teeth had been removed prior to the start of this program. He developed a single lower tooth and proceeded to lacerate his lower lip. This tooth was removed to prevent disfigurement, for he continually worked at the area. Furthermore, he slept only fitfully at night until he was restrained for sleep.

The results obtained to date are mildly encouraging. They indicate that the behavior is subject to some modification. On the other hand, it is clearly not a complete therapy, and there may even be displacement from an area of abnormal behavior improved to one that develops or worsens. The approach merits intensive further investigation.

Chemical Approaches to the Modification of Behavior

Understanding of the molecular feature of the Lesch-Nyhan syndrome and its metabolic consequences led to highly effective therapy for those aspects of the disease that are directly related to uric acid. Treatment with allopurinol which inhibits xanthine oxidase regularly lowers the concentrations of uric acid in the blood and urine. It is in this way possible to prevent arthritis tophi, renal stones, and fatal nephropathy. This treatment has not influenced the neurologic, cerebral, or behavioral manifestations of the disease. These observations, along with the fact that a number of patients have now been treated with allopurinol from birth and never had significant elevations of uric acid (Marks, Baum, Keele, Kay, & MacFarlen, 1968), indicate clearly that the cerebral and behavioral aspects of this disease are not a consequence of elevated concentrations of uric acid.

In a recent communication from Japan (Mizuno & Yugari, 1974) the oral administration of L-5-hydroxytryptophan was associated with a marked reduction in the rate of self-mutilative behavior in patients with the Lesch-Nyhan syndrome. Four patients were treated with 1-8 mg of hydroxytryptophan per kg of body weight per day for 36 weeks. It was said that mutilation ceased within 1-3 days of the initiation of treatment. There were no adverse effects. Mutilation reappeared within 12-15 hours of the discontinuation of treatment.

There is information from a variety of other sources which provides a rationale for serotonergic influences in self-mutilative behavior. Self-mutilation has been induced in rats and rabbits by the administration of caffeine or theophylline (Boyd, Dolman, Knight, & Sheppard, 1965; Morgan, Schneiderman, & Nyhan, 1970). Aggressive behavior has been observed in experimental animals following the administration of psychotomimetic drugs (Valzelli, 1967). In rats aggression has been studied in an assay, the end point of which is the killing of a mouse introduced into the cage. Some rats are spontaneously muricidal. Aggressiveness may also be induced by the production of lesions that transsect the olfactory pathways. In studies in which serotonin turnover was blocked by monoamine oxidase inhibitors such as pargyline, analysis of the content of serotonin in the brain was significantly lower in aggressive animals than in normal animals (Valzelli, 1967). Increased aggressive behavior was reported in rats given p-chlorophenylalanine which inhibits the synthesis of serotonin (Dichiara, Camba, & Spano, 1971). The administration of 5-hydroxytryptophan, which is the immediate precursor of serotonin, to rats made highly muricidal by olfactory bulbotomy significantly reduced this aggressive behavior (Dichiara et al., 1971). A dose of 30 mg/kg was employed. Rats selected for their muricidal behavior were found to lose this in response to treatment with 200 mg/kg of 5-hydroxytryptophan (Kulkarni & Bocknik, 1973). The data provide a background for the use of measures calculated to increase the cerebral content of serotonin in an approach to the management of patients with self-mutilation

Recent experience with the use of 5-hydroxytryptophan in man indicates that large amounts may be administered with safety. Its combination with a peripheral aromatic amino acid decarboxylase inhibitor is pharmacologically rational. Like dopamine, 5-hydroxytryptamine cannot enter the brain directly. Rather the free acid, 5-hydroxytryptophan, crosses into the brain where it is converted to serotonin. Yet, in the presence of an active decarboxylase, most hydroxytryptophan administered is converted peripherally to serotonin and thus lost to the central nervous system. Carbidopa (MK-486) is a highly effective inhibitor of the decarboxylase and it does not cross the blood-brain barrier. Thus it is a peripheral decarboxylase inhibitor. It has been used predominantly, along with dopa, in the treatment of Parkinson's disease. Wyatt and colleagues (Wyatt, Vaughan, Galanter, Kaplan, & Green, 1972; Wyatt, Kaplan, & Vaughan, 1973; Wyatt & Gillin, 1974) have employed 5-hydroxtryptophan in the management of patients with schizophrenia. These investigators gave 5-hydroxytryptophan along with carbidopa in doses up to 6 g and 150 mg per day, respectively. If the dose of hydroxytryptophan was increased slowly, side effects were minimal or absent. Rapid increase in dosage or abrupt discontinuation of 5-hydroxytryptophan produced side effects, including nausea, vomiting, diarrhea, diaphoresis, and mild diastolic hypotension. Two patients had grand mal seizures on abrupt withdrawal of the drug. Coleman (1971) has treated a large series of infants with Down's syndrome with 5-hydroxytryptophan. She has reported doses of 1-10 mg/kg even from the first days of life. As many as 15% of these infants developed seizures resembling infantile spasms. The electroencephalogram was that of hypsarrhythmia.

A positive effect of pharmacologic therapy on self-mutilative behavior in patients with the Lesch-Nyhan syndrome would be readily apparent. The patient usually cannot be released from restraint even for seconds without biting himself. The rapidity and ferocity with which biting takes place are difficult to overemphasize. This inhibits quantitation, for one tends to hold the patient after restraints are removed, and the data may reflect the frequency of release by the attendant rather than patient-generated rates. We have therefore undertaken to obtain quantitative behavioral data using timed videotape recordings of facial expression and body movement under standardized conditions. This provides hard copy records for scoring behavior. It permits independent scorers or coders, and reexamination from time to time in analyses using the VIDR system of Ekman and Friesen (1969).

It is clear from results to date that the administration of 5-hydroxytryptophan can lead to a modification in behavior. A successfully treated patient is able in the presence of the drug to tolerate being without restraint for short periods of time. Two hours is about maximal, and someone must be with the patient at all times when the restraints are off. The patient usually prefers to hold something to immobilize himself while restraints are off. Thus we have seen an effect from treatment. However, the results are considerably less encouraging than the Japenese workers implied (Mizuno & Yugari, 1974). Furthermore, we have observed any therapeutic effect at all in only one patient treated with 5-hydroxytryptophan alone. Much of the hydroxytryptophan administered is decarbocylated. A major portion appears in the urine as 5-hydroxyindoleacetic acid, and increasing the dose does not reliably increase the effect.

For these reasons we have turned our attention to the decarboxylase inhibitor. We have now had experience with a small number of patients treated with carbidopa and hydroxytryptophan. The results are considerably more interesting. A therapeutic effect is regularly achievable. Periods up to 8 hours have been readily tolerated without restraint. The patient has been observed under conditions in which he thought he was alone without any biting behavior. It is not inconsistent that most patients do not respond to 5-hydroxytryptophan alone while most seem to respond to 5-hydroxytryptophan when it is combined with a peripheral decarboxylase inhibitor. Only the dicarboxylic acid 5-hydroxytryptophan can cross the blood-brain barrier. Our data on urinary 5-hydroxyindoleacetic acid indicate that in the absence of the decarboxylase inhibitor very little 5-hydroxytryptophan must get into the central nervous system. Our results are preliminary. It is already apparent that tolerance develops rapidly to these regimens of treatment. Nevertheless, the results are encouraging. They indicate that the problem is researchable and that the behavior is subject to chemical modification. It is possible that combinations of pharmacologic and psychologic approaches to treatment might be combined to create a therapeutic environment for these patients.

References

Anderson, L. T., Herrmann, L., Alpert, M., Dancis, J. Elimination of self-mutilation in Lesch-Nyhan disease (Abstr.). *Pediat. Res.*, 1975; **9**, 257.

Balis, M. E., Krakoff, I. H., Berman, P. H., Dancis, J. Urinary metabolites in congenital hyperuricosuria. *Science*, 1967; **156**, 1122-1123.

Boyd, E. M., Dolman, M., Knight, L. M., Sheppard, E. P. The chronic oral toxity of caffeine. *Canadian J. Physiol. Pharmacol.*, 1965; **43**, 995.

Bryson, Y., Sakati, N., Nyhan, W. L., Fish, C. H. Self-mutilative behavior in the Cornelia DeLange syndrome. *Am. J. Ment. Defic.*, 1971; **76**, 319-324.

Coleman, M. Infantile spasms association with 5-hydroxtryptophan administration in patients with Down's syndrome. *Neurology*, 1971; **21**, 911-919.

Dichiara, G., Camba, R., Spano, P. F. Evidence for inhibition by brain serotonin of mouse killing behaviour in rats. *Nature*, 1971; **233**, 272.

Duker, P. Behaviour control of self-biting in a Lesch-Nyhan patient. *J. Ment. Defic. Res.*, 1975; **19**, 11-19.

Ekman, P., Friesen, W. A tool for the analysis of motion picture film or videotape. *Am. Psychol.*, 1969; **24**, 240-243.

Hoefnagel, D. The syndrome of athetoid cerebral palsy, mental deficiency, self-mutilation and hyperuricemia. *J. Ment. Defic. Res.*, 1965; **9**, 69-74.

Howard, R. S., Walzak, M. P. A new cause for uric acid stones in childhood. *J. Urology*, 1967; **98**, 639-642.

Johnson, H. G., Nyhan, W. L., Shear, C., Ekman, P., Friesen., W. A behavioral phenotype in the DeLange syndrome. *Pediat. Res.* 1976; **10**.

Kulkarni, R. G. R., Bocknik, S. E. Muricidal block induced by 5-hydroxytryptophan in the rat. *Arch. Internat. de Pharmacodynamie et de Therapie*, 1973; **201**, 308-313.

Lesch, M., Nyhan, W. L. A familial disorder of uric acid metabolism and central nervous system function. *Am. J. Med.*, 1964; **36**, 561-570.

Letts, R. M., Hobson, D. A. Special devices as aids in the management of child self-mutilation in the Lesch-Nyhan syndrome. *Pediatrics*, 1975; **55**, 853-855.

Marks, J. F., Baum, J., Keele, D. K., Kay, J. L., MacFarlen, A. Lesch-Nyhan syndrome treated from the early neonatal period. *Pediatrics,* 1968; **42**, 357-359.

Mizuno, T.-I., Yugari, Y. Self-mutilation in the Lesch-Nyhan syndrome. *Lancet,* 1974; **1**, 761.

Morgan, L. L., Schneiderman, N., Nyhan, W. L. Theophyline: induction of self-biting in rabbits. *Psychonom. Sci.,* 1970; **19**, 37-38.

Nyhan, W. L. Introduction, clinical and genetic features. *In* Bland, J. H. (Ed.). *Seminars on the Lesch-Nyhan syndrome. (Federal Proceedings),* 1968; **27**, 1027-1033.

Nyhan, W. L. Clinical features of the Lesch-Nyhan syndrome. *Archiv. Internal Med.,* 1972a; **130,** 186-192.

Nyhan, W. L. Behavioral phenotypes in organic genetic disease. Presidential address to the Society for Pediatric Research, May 1, 1971. *Pediat. Res.,* 1972b; **6,** 1-9.

Nyhan, W. L. The Lesch-Nyhan syndrome. *In* Creger, W. P. (Ed.). *Annual Reviews, Annual Review of Medicine,* 1973; **24,** 41-60.

Nyhan, W. L. The Lesch-Nyhan syndrome. *In* Hamburger, J., Crosnier, J., Maxwell, M. H. (Eds.). *Advances in Nephrology* (Vol. 3), (pp.59-70). Chicago: Yearbook Medical Publishers, 1974.

Reed, W. B., Fish, C. H. Hyperuricemia with self-mutilation and choreoathetosis. *Arch. of Dermatol.,* 1966; **94,** 194-195.

Scherzer, A. L., Ilson, J. B. Normal intelligence in the Lesch-Nyhan syndrome. *Pediatrics,* 1969; **44,** 116-120.

Seegmiller, J. E., Rosenbloom, F. M., Kelley, W. N. Enzyme defect associated with a sex-linked human neurological disorder and excessive purine synthesis. *Science,* 1967; **155,** 1682.

Shear, C. S., Nyhan, W. L., Kirman, B. H., Stern, J. Self-mutilative behavior as a feature of the DeLange syndrome. *J. Pediat.,* 1971; **78,** 506-509.

Skyler, J. S., Neelon, F. A., Arnold, W. J., Kelley, W. N., & Lebovitz, H. E. Growth retardation in the Lesch-Nyhan syndrome. *Acta. Endocrinologica.,* 1974; **75,** 3-10.

Sweetman, L. Urinary and CSF oxypurine levels and Allopurinol metabolism in the Lesch-Nyhan syndrome. *Federal Proceedings,* 1968; **27,** 1055-1059.

Sweetman, L., Nyhan, W. L. Excretion of hypoxanthine and xanthine in a genetic disease of purine metabolism. *Nature,* 1967; **215,** 859-860.

Sweetman, L., Nyhan, W. L. Further studies of the enzyme composition of mutant cells in X-linked uric aciduria. *Archiv. Internal Med.,* 1972; **130,** 214-220.

Valzeilli, L. Drugs and aggressiveness. *Adv. Pharmacol.,* 1967; **5,** 79-108.

Wyatt, R. J., Gillin, J. C. The development of tolerance to and dependence on endogenous neurotransmitters. *In* Mandell, A. J. (Ed.). *Neurobiological mechanisms of adaptation and Behavior.* New York: Raven Press, 1974.

Wyatt, R. J., Kaplan, J., Vaughan, T. Tolerance and dependence to serotonin, a speculation. *Arch. Gen. Psychiat.,* 1973; **29,** 597-599.

Wyatt, R., Vaughan, T., Galanter, M., Kaplan, J., Green, R. Behavioral changes of chronic schizophrenic patients given L-5-hydroxytryptophan. *Science,* 1972; **177,** 1124-1126.

Reprinted from *J. Autism & Child. Schiz.,* 1976; **6**:3, 235-252 by kind permission of William L. Nyhan and the publishers Plenum Publishing Corp., New York, NY 10013.

THE USE OF APPLIANCES IN THE TREATMENT OF SEVERE SELF-INJURIOUS BEHAVIOUR

Bernie Spain, Sally Ann Hart, John Corbett

Hilda Lewis House, Bethlem Royal Hospital, London

Summary

While protective appliances may be of considerable value in the management and treatment of self-injurious behaviour, they should be used with caution and only as part of a general behavioural programme. This article describes a variety of equipment which has been found to be useful with individuals who self-injure, in preventing tissue damage during treatment programmes designed to reduce their self-injurious behaviour.

Introduction

Protective appliances of various kinds may be useful in the management of severe self-injurious behaviour (SSIB) in order to prevent tissue damage, but it is important to be quite clear what function they are to serve. It is essential that protective appliances are only used as part of a general strategy aimed to decrease the SSIB and replace it with alternative behaviours, so as to allow the person to lead a more satisfactory life and to promote skill development.

It is often possible to manage self-injurious behaviour in some other way, wihout recourse to appliances, especially in young children. Usually it is only necessary to provide protective appliances when the self-injury is particularly severe.

Forrest (1975) discussed the anxiety felt by staff in the presence of self-injury and how such anxiety may lead to demands for drugs or restraints. It is necessary to be particularly cautious about providing an appliance simply to allay staff anxiety. However, it may be justifiable to do so on the understanding that the appliance is for emergency use only. Staff may be more willing to undertake a behavioural programme if they know that there is an appliance available which can be used if the self-injury becomes too severe. In such circumstances it is especially important to give clear instruction about its use and to insist that records are kept of the frequency, circumstances and duration of use.

The question that needs to be asked is whether there is any alternative way of preventing damage: which would be non-reinforcing (of the SSIB); which would allow the person to engage in other activities; and which would be feasible in practice, given realistic staffing levels. If the answer is that there is not, then protection would appear to be the only means of preventing tissue damage. However, even if staffing levels do make physically holding the person a realistic option, it may be preferable to use material rather than human restraints since human physical contact may itself be a powerful reinforcer to maintaining the self-injurious behaviour. An analysis of the particular contingencies for each individual who self-injures is essential before deciding on an intervention strategy. Quite different stimuli appear to be responsible for maintaining self-injurious behaviour in different clients (Carr, 1977; Schroeder et al., 1980), even though the behaviour usually appears to be a learned strategy to coerce adult attention (Frankel and Simmons, 1976).

Sometimes staff are reluctant to consider a protective device because they fear that the person may become dependent upon it. As Corbett (1975) has pointed out, this is a real possibility which needs to be considered from the outset, balancing this danger against the possible effects of the unprotected SSIB. Undesirable collateral behaviour may also develop in some individuals (Baumeister et al., 1976).

This account describes protective appliances which have been found useful at Hilda Lewis House, a unit for children with mental and physical handicaps, and gives some examples of how they were used. They are divided into three categories in order of degree of restriction: (A) protective environments; (B) protective appliances which restrict the movements involved in the self-injuring behaviour; (C) protective helmets.

(A) Protective environments

It may be possible to protect a person merely by adapting or altering his environment in some way so that the self-injurious behaviour can be ignored. This option should always be considered first. The following examples provide some ideas, which could be adapted to suit the circumstances in which the behaviour occurs.

COT PADDING

Cot padding can be used to protect a head banging child from self-injuring when in his cot.

Materials. ½-inch coloured plastazote, four pieces to fit cot sides. Nylon-webbing attached to plastazote with plastic rivets, and velcro fixed to the webbing straps to hold the plastazote in place.

Case study. S was a 2½-year-old child who persisted in head to object banging prior to sleep and during temper tantrums. In the padded cot the behaviour could be ignored. It became a safe place in which to leave *S* during a temper tantrum.

PADDED CHAIRS

A child who head bangs, or bangs his trunk or limbs when seated, may be offered additional protection by specifically padding appropriate areas on the chair.

Materials. ½-inch plastazote. One layer is generally thick enough, but this can be easily reinforced by heat welding extra pieces on to the first layer. The plastazote can be fixed either by spot welding using an old iron (plastazote to plastazote), or by fixing webbing straps riveted at each end. Padding may be faded by gradually reducing the thickness of layers.

PLASTAZOTE CUSHION

Materials. ¾-inch plastazote 12″ × 9″, with a hole punched in the corner to hang it up for ease of access. Thicker plastazote can be used if the banging is particularly severe.

Case study. G was a young child who sought out floor areas on which to bang her forehead. Immediately she began to bang an adult approached her from behind and placed the cushion between her forehead and the floor, with a verbal instruction of "No *G*".

(B) Minimal physical restraint(s) to prevent movement

These appliances can be used with children with hand to body SSIB. The aim is to prevent the children's hands from reaching parts of the body which they tend to injure.

MUFFS

These are particularly appropriate for people who already use their clothing as a form of self-restraint (when they may be best used in conjunction with a catsuit) but they may be useful to consider for others as well. They may be made of any soft material, for example towelling, and they should allow the person to free the hands for play.

Materials. Towelling, brightly coloured. Design details are shown in Figure 1.

Case study. C was 13-year-old boy who was mentally handicapped and autistic who used his own clothing, especially a T-shirt or jersey, to wrap around his hands to prevent self-injury. Initially a long towelling muff was made, with holes through which his hands could emerge for play. A catsuit prevented use of other clothing. A second stage muff consisted of two small towelling muffs joined by a third short piece of material. This reduced the amount of material that could be used for hand wrapping. (A muff with an elasticated middle was unsuccessful because the child wrapped this so tightly that it inhibited the blood supply to his wrists.) In the third stage the appliance consisted of wrist cuffs only. the process took three months to achieve. Several pairs of muffs and cuffs were needed to allow for frequent washing.

MITTENS

These can be useful for a child who bites his hands, fingers, or wrists, or who probes fingers into the nose, mouth, or anus. Mittens with a thumb piece are generally

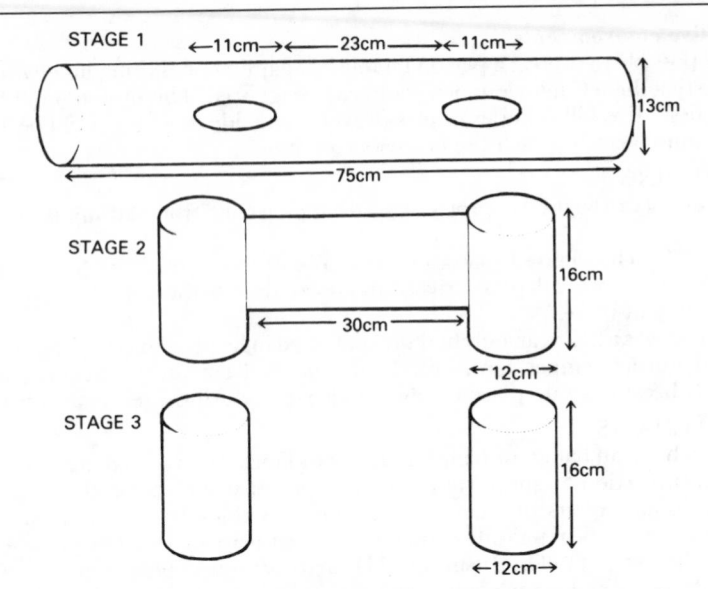

Figure 1. The three stages of the towelling muffs

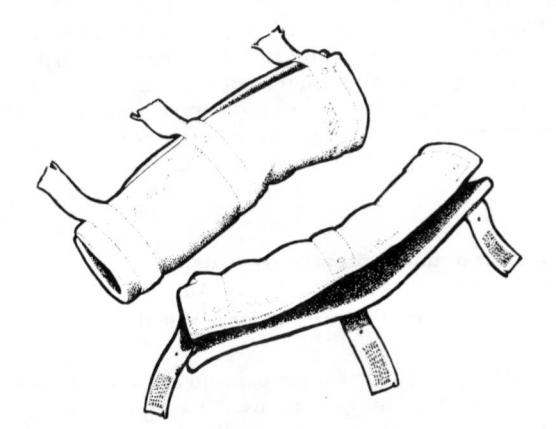

Figure 2. Plastazote elbow splints

Figure 3. Variable hinged arm splints

preferable to gloves. The main problems are keeping them on an active child, and the fact that they restrict the child's ability to use his hands. Several pairs are needed to allow for frequent washing.

Materials. Terry towelling, moleskin, cotton. To keep them in place either: (a) elasticate the wrists; (b) join the mittens together with elastic which goes under the client's shirt or top; or (c) extend the mittens to the elbow and fasten them above the elbow joint.

ELBOW SPLINTS

These can be useful for children who damage the head, face, or eyes with fist or fingers, or who pick open slow healing scars. They are preferable to mittens because they allow full use of the hands. We have used four types made from the following materials:

(a) *Plastazote* with webbing straps and velcro fasteners at the wrist, and below and above the elbow, fixed by plastic rivets. These splints may be reinforced with vitrathene if necessary (see Figure 2).

(b) *Canvas* with stiffeners, webbing, and velcro fasteners.

(c) *Lightweight foam elbow cuffs* cut to size with velcro straps attached by plastic rivets.

(d) *Variable hinged arm splints* which reduce access of hand to head but allow elbow flexion for feeding or other purposes (see Figure 3). Each of these splints can be faded by gradually reducing its size.

Materials. Polypropylene lined with plastazote, with either a polypropylene hinge with leather straps and velcro fastening, or a metal hinge with Fastex fastenings.

Design. Upper and lower cuffs joined by hinged joints. The joints have fixed straps to limit the degree of flexion at the elbow, depending on the need. When worn with the fastenings on the *anterior* surface of the arm free movement is obtained between full extension and approximately 110° of flexion. This means that the child can just manage to feed himself with a spoon but is unable to self-injure. When worn with fasteners on the *posterior* surface of the arm, a lesser range of movement can be obtained (approx. 0° to 45° flexion). These splints are light to wear, especially if polypropylene hinges are used. The metal hinged variety is stronger and less easy to open, but is slightly heavier.

Arm measurements needed for any type of arm splint:
(1) elbow circumference;
(2) mid-forearm circumference;
(3) mid-upper arm circumference;
(4) length between 1 and 2, and 2 and 3.

Case study. P was a young man with DeLange's syndrome who persistently self-injured by fist to head banging. With these splints P was unable to reach his face with his hands although the hands were free to play or eat. The splints enabled the problem to be contained during bouts of severe self-injury.

"WATCH" OR PALM SPLINTS

These may be useful for a client who bites wrists and hands, or who engages in other finger activity requiring free hand movements, such as plucking hair or picking at the palm. They are illustrated in Figure 4.

Materials. Plastazote, velcro, plastic rivets.

Case study. C was a young child who bit her wrist. This was prevented by wearing the splint on the wrist. She also bit her hand and pulled out her hair. This was prevented by placing the pad over the palm rather than the wrist. She learned to pull on the splints herself to prevent the self-injury.

CAPES

These can be useful for a person who engages in fist to head banging, head to shoulder jerking, or other damage to the face or head. They have the advantage that the person has full movement of the hands, and can raise his arms high enough to feed himself using a spoon or other long handled implement, but is prevented from

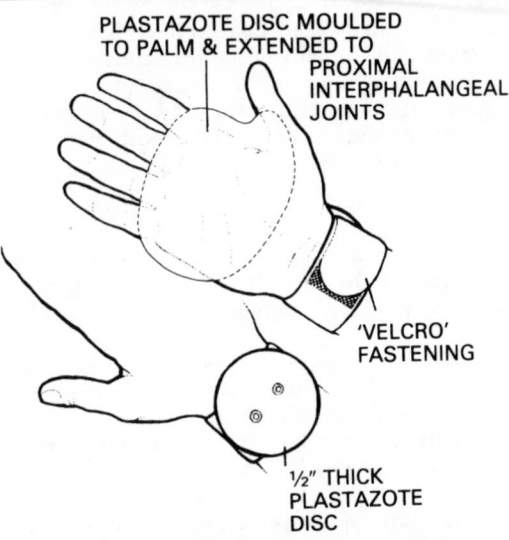

PLASTAZOTE DISC MOULDED
TO PALM & EXTENDED TO
PROXIMAL
INTERPHALANGEAL
JOINTS

'VELCRO'
FASTENING

½" THICK
PLASTAZOTE
DISC

Figure 4. Plastazote "watch" or palm splint

reaching any closer to his face (see Figure 5).

Materials. Plastazote with velcro fastenings (spot welded), moulded to fit over the shoulder and end just below the elbow, with a curved lip at the base. The fastenings are usually at the front. (For one child with additional head to shoulder jerking a moulded collar was also necessary, and back fastenings were more convenient. The moulded neck piece was also secured with velcro at the back.)

Case study. N was an eight-year-old child with severe fist to head banging. He appeared to find the cape comforting and did not attempt to get his fist to his head while wearing it. He was able to engage in more activities than previously while wearing the cape.

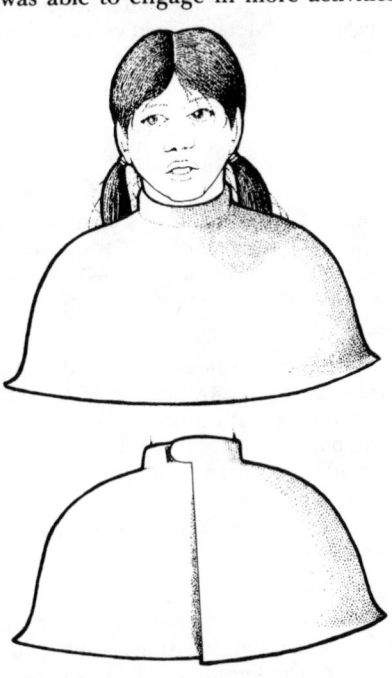

Figure 5. Plastazote cape

Figure 6. Lip splint

LIP SPLINT (MOUTH GUARD)

This device can be useful for children who bite the lips or tongue very severely. Following a number of earlier developments with gum shields to prevent lip biting, a lip splint was designed for a child with Lesch Nyhan syndrome to prevent him from biting his lower lip (see Figure 6).

Design. Full details of the design and materials are given elsewhere (Smith, 1984). *Case study. D* was a 12-year-old child with Lesch Nyhan syndrome. He had severely bitten his lower lip necessitating removal of his first dentition. The biting recurred with his second dentition, necessitating considerable restraint and total nursing care by his parents. The splint was faded successfully after a period of six months.

(C) Protective helmets

These can be useful with children who engage in severe head to object banging which cannot be controlled in any way other than attention and human physical restraint which may itself reinforce the SSIB. The lightest type of helmet should be considered first. Only if this fails should a more restrictive type be adopted. Two custom made helmets are discussed below, and then commercially made helmets are considered.

PLASTAZOTE HELMET

Plastazote has the advantage over other materials in that it can be cut to size and then quickly heated and moulded to the head with minimal fuss, making the experience less traumatic for someone who is already very anxious. It is available in different thicknesses and colours. As with all appliances the therapist's attitude and approach to the child are all important in gaining cooperation.

A full description of the plastazote helmet is given elsewhere (Patterson, 1982), together with examples of its use in conjunction with a behavioural programme.

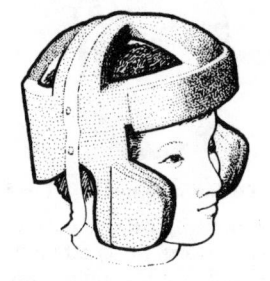

Figure 7. Plastazote helmet with "dew drop pieces"

Briefly it comprises a piece of plastazote which encircles the head, with a crosspiece over the top to form a hat. This is held in place by a webbing strap which goes over the head and fastens under the chin or, preferably, over the cheek to reduce discomfort. This helmet is light and can provide good protection but, since it is difficult to fit with really secure fastenings, it may not be suitable for all children who self-injure. A really determined child is likely to be able to remove this type of helmet by himself.

This basic design can be altered in the following ways, depending on the type of self-injury or the shape of the head.

1. For hand to face slapping, maxillary protection can be provided by the addition of "dew drop pieces" (see Figure 7).
2. Sometimes a band alone is sufficient if the problem is confined to head to object banging.
3. Additional protection can be provided to particularly vulnerable spots by adding an extra thickness of plastazote.
4. For a child with chin banging, a moulded ¼- to ½- inch thick plastazote chin piece can be added.

Our experience with plastazote suggests that: welding is stronger than glueing — glued joints come unstuck when heated; a glued joint needs a wedge in it; a welded joint remains strong when reheated; heated and moulded plastazote can be welded together; and a piece stuck on when heated remains stuck. Plastazote helmets can be made more cosmetically attractive using various coverings, for example, a sun hat in summer, a woolly hat in winter.

ORTHOTIC HELMETS

Plastazote helmets have mainly been constructed for short term use and in specific behavioural programmes during the stages of fading (for example, gradual removal of restraint) and generalisation (for example, extending newly earned alternative behaviours into new situations). More substantial helmets for longer term use have been made by specialist appliance makers (orthotists), and may be necessary when the self-injury is very severe. Examples are shown in Figures 8 and 9.

Figure 8. Orthotic helmet with side fastening

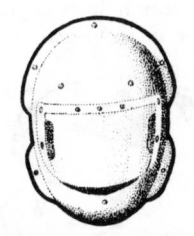

Figure 9. Orthotic helmet fixed by bolts

There are several advantages in using experienced orthotists to make up a helmet to occupational therapists' specifications, the chief being that they have the necessary materials and equipment. The main disadvantages are the time spent in travelling and fittings, and the costs (which may limit their use in some clinical situations).

COMMERCIAL HELMETS

These often need modification but they are usually cheaper and more quickly available than helmets custom made by orthotists. They are also aesthetically more pleasing. However, they are basically designed to protect people suffering from epilepsy or participating in hazardous sporting activities and so may not be strong enough to protect against severe repetitive head to object banging. They are not as secure as the orthotists' models previously described if the person has good manipulation and determination. One example is shown in Figure 10 but there are many on the market.

Figure 10. Commercial helmet

Fastenings and cosmetic implications

The fastenings on all helmets require careful consideration. They must be comfortable and secure, yet allow for easy removal by staff. Fastex release buckles are very suitable but to avoid chafing the skin they may need to be lined with moleskin or placed against the cheek rather than under the chin. If a child is determined to remove the helmet the fastening should be at the side (see Figure 8) or the helmet should be fixed by bolts (see Figure 9). Additionally several straps can be attached so that even if one is undone the others keep the helmet in place. It is important that two helmets or bands are made if they are in continual use in order that one can be worn whilst the other is washed.

All helmets should be made to look as attractive as possible both for the child's sake and for the sake of people who come into contact with him. The child must not be shunned on account of being unattractive to work with because he his wearing a helmet. It is important that his non-injurious behaviour is reinforced with appropriate staff attention.

Plastazote helmets can be decorated with felt tip pens and other trimmings for children. Alternatively helmets for children or adults can be almost completely covered by a suitable hat, according to the time of year (see Figure 11).

Figure 11. Hat worn over Plastazote helmet
for cosmetic reasons

Orthotic and commercial helmets are not as easy to render cosmetically pleasing, but in life saving instances this is not the major consideration. However, the Muckamore helmet is one example of an orthotic helmet which is more cosmetically appropriate. This was described by Barker (1981).

Discussion

In considering the use of a protective appliance, the following points must be borne in mind.

1. Protective appliances should be chosen only after a careful functional analysis of a person's behaviour and environment. There are no standard appliances as such, and any of the devices described here may need to be adapted for use with individual children or adults who self-injure.

2. Once an appliance has been agreed upon for an individual, it is important to consider how it is to be used as part of a general strategy of teaching alternative skills, and clear instructions must be given to care staff about its use. Baselines should be established before introducing the appliance and recording of behaviour should be continued after its introduction, partly to ensure that it is used only in the agreed way, and partly to monitor whether the use of the appliance affects the frequency or intensity of the person's SSIB.

3. SSIB is distressing to witness and it raises anxiety among care staff and parents. As a result the tendency is often to protect or restrict excessively, but this will not promote the long-term aims of helping the child or adult to become independent and cease the self-injurious behaviour. Equipment that is too restrictive may also produce contractures or arrested motor development (Lovaas and Simmons, 1969).

Any strategy for intervention must aim to restrict movement minimally, while at the same time preventing tissue damage. This applies equally whether the SSIB is prevented by physically holding the person or by a protective appliance. The first choice must always supply the minimum protection required; only if this fails should more restrictive appliances be considered. All too frequently protective equipment prevents the wearer from participating in activities (Rojahn, Schroeder, and Mulick, 1980).

It must be possible for the person wearing the appliance to engage in other activities, for a large part of the day, which can be strongly rewarded. Attempts merely to eliminate the SSIB without at the same time encouraging alternative behaviours are unlikely to be successful; particularly as it is often found that SSIB is contingent upon staff requiring some activity from the self-injuring individual (Edelson, Taubman, and Lovaas, 1983).

4. Any intervention programme must aim to ensure that SSIB does not produce effects that are enjoyed by the self-injurer. Protective appliances used in the programme must, therefore, be easy to put on and must not involve prolonged physical contact which the child might find reinforcing.

5. Although the main aim of an appliance is simply to protect, it is important to know whether the equipment itself is perceived by the individual as aversive or rewarding, and to take this into account in designing any programme. Restraints are perceived as reinforcing by a few individuals (Flavell, McGimsey, Jones, and Cannon, 1981) and contingent restraint will result in increased SSIB in such cases.

6. Consideration should be given from the outset as to how the use of the appliance can be gradually reduced or faded over time. If possible the appliance should be designed in such a way as to facilitate fading its use.

7. The length of time for which the appliance is used contingent upon the SSIB is important. Short periods have been found to be more effective than longer periods (Singh, Dawson, and Manning, 1981). No-one should ever be left unattended for long periods wearing restrictive equipment.

8. The effect of any appliance must be assessed and reviewed at frequent intervals, with the aim of reducing its use. Appliances should never be provided without review and follow-up.

9. Any appliance should look ordinary and pleasing. The possibility of adapting some everyday article of clothing should always be considered.

Acknowledgements

Grateful thanks are due: to all occupational therapists who have worked at Hilda Lewis House, including particularly Mrs. Sheena Wickings, Miss Pat Raley, and Miss Patricia Patterson; to Ms. Pat Cook for typing the manuscript; to Ms. Peta Smith, Senior Lecturer, King's College Hospital Dental School; and the following orthotists: Mr. Kim Barton, Chailey Heritage, Chailey, Sussex; S. H. Camp & Co. Ltd., 116, Tower Bridge Road, London, SE1 3AE; U. Williams & Co. Ltd., 23-25, Wyche Grove Street, Croydon.

Finally our thanks to the children of Hilda Lewis House and their parents for patience and understanding during the development of these appliances.

References

Barker, R. J. Construction of the Muckamore Abbey Cosmetic Helmet for the protection of special care patients. *Physiotherapy.*, 1981; **67**, 47-49.

Baumeister, A. A., Rollings, J. P. Self-injurious behavior. *In* Ellis, N. R. (Ed.). *International Review of Research in Mental Retardation.* (Vol. 8.) New York: Academic Press, 1976.

Carr, E. G. The motivation of self injurious behaviour: a review of some hypotheses. *Psychol. Bull.*, 1977; **84**, 800-816.

Corbett, J. Aversion for the treatment of self injurious behaviour. *J. Ment. Defic. Res.*, 1975; **19**, 79-95.

Edelson, S. M., Taubman, M. T., Lovaas, O. I., Some social contexts of self destructive behavior. *J. Abnor. Child Psychol.*, 1983; **11**, 2, 299-312.

Flavell, J., McGimsey, J. F., Jones, K. L., Cannon, P. R. Physical restraint as positive reinforcement. *Am. J. Ment. Defic.*, 1981; **85**, 425-432.

Forrest, Personal communication. 1975.

Frankel, F., Simmons, J. Q. Self injurious behavior in schizophrenic and retarded children. *Am. J. Ment. Defic.*, 1976; **80**, 5, 512-522.

Lovaas, L. O., Simmons, J. Manipulation of self destruction in three children. *J. Appl. Behav. Anal.*, 1969; **2**, 143-157.

Patterson, P. M. Making a plastazote helmet — its use and mini-case history. *Occupat. Ther.*, 1982; **45**, 131-133.

Rojahn, J., Schroeder, S. R., Mulick, J. A. Ecological assessment of self-protective devices in three profoundly retarded adults. *J. Autism & Dev. Dis.*, 1980; **10**, 59-66.

Schroeder, C., Rojahn, J., Mulick, J. A. Self injurious behavior: an analysis of behavior management techniques. *In* Matson, J. L., McCartney, J. R. (Eds.). *Handbook of Behaviour Modification with the Mentally Retarded.* New York: Plenum Press, 1980.

Singh, N. N., Dawson, M. J., Manning, P. J. The effects of physical restraint on self injurious behaviour. *J. Ment. Defic. Res.*, 1981; **25**, 207-216.

Smith, P. Dental protection and severe self injurious behaviour. (In preparation). 1984.

BIMH Publications was pleased to give permission for this original paper to first appear in *Occupational Therapy*, 1984; Nov., 353-357.

SELF-MUTILATION IN LESCH-NYHAN SYNDROME

Tei-ichi Mizuno
Health Service Centre, Ockanomizu University, Tokyo

Yasumi Yugari
Research Institute for Life Sciences, Ajinomoto Co. Inc., Yokohama, Japan

SIR,—Lesch-Nyhan syndrome is an inborn error of purine metabolism—specifically, a defect in hypoxanthineguanine phosphoribosyltransferase. Its manifestations include hyperuricaemia, choreoathetoid movement, self-mutilation, and mental retardation. Self-mutilation is the most miserable symptom of this disease, and no suitable treatment has yet been reported.

We assumed that self-mutilation was an aggressive behaviour directed by patients towards themselves. Reports[1] that aggressive behaviour, induced in rats or mice by isolation or transection of the olfactory bulbs, was alleviated by administration of L-5-hydroxytryptophan (L-5-H.T.P.) supported our idea of treating self-mutilation with L-5-H.T.P.

Four patients with the Lesch-Nyhan syndrome found in the Tokyo area (aged 1 year 7 months, 8 years 4 months, 8 years 10 months, and 12 years 3 months) were given orally 1-8mg. of L-5-H.T.P. per kg. body-weight per day for 36 weeks. 50mg. of L-tryptophan per kg. or 15-30 mg. of levodopa per kg. was administered as a control, and lactose as a placebo. Severity of self-mutilation was graded from 0 to 5 (see accompanying table). Urinary 5-hydroxyindoleacetic acid (5-H.I.A.A.) was estimated by Ho's method.[2]

Table 1. Treatment of self-mutilation and urinary excretion of 5-H.I.A.A. in Case 3

—			Dose (mg./kg. B.W./DAY)	SCORE OF SELF-MUTILATION*	Urinary 5-H.I.A.A.† (mg./kg. B.W./24 hr.)
Before treatment	..		..	5	0.09-0.14
Placebo (lactose)	..		..	5	0.09-0.10
L-tryptophan	..	..	50	3	0.27-0.36
Levodopa	..	..	26	2	0.03
L-5-H.T.P.	..	..	1	0	0.23
			4	0-1	0.17-11.4
			6	0-1	1.3-2.0

* 0, none; 1, scarcely any; 2, 1-4 times a day; 3, 5-9 times while awake; 4, 10-20 times a day while awake; 5, almost continuously.
† Control children; 0.09-0.15 mg./kg. B.W./24 hr.

On the first medication, self-mutilation completely disappeared at a daily dose of 1.2 mg. of L-5-H.T.P. per kg. body-weight in case 3 (see table). However, after a control period on levodopa and L-tryptophan the effective dose increased, and 5-7 mg. per kg. body-weight per day was required to obtain a rapid and definite effect. After a lag period of 1 to 3 days, self-mutilation stopped in every case. Maintaining the L-5-H.T.P. dose at this level, self-mutilation was controlled in all four cases without any adverse effects. When treatment was discontinued, self-mutilation reappeared within 12 to 15 hours without exception. Administration of placebo (lactose) or L-tryptophan 50 mg. per kg. daily was ineffective. Levodopa (15-30 mg. per kg. per day) had some effect in alleviating self-mutilation in some cases but its effect was temporary and incomplete.

In case 3 urinary excretion of 5-H.I.A.A. before treatment was found to be 0.09—0.14 mg. per kg. per day, which is not significantly different from that in control children. Oral administration of L-5-H.T.P. or L-tryptophan caused increase in urinary excretion of 5-H.I.A.A., and this did not improve symptoms. These results suggest that the metabolism of L-tryptophan and L-5-H.T.P. in these patients is not generally impaired, and the error of purine metabolism in this syndrome causes decreased serotonin levels in some areas of the brain and induces self-mutilation.

In summary, self-mutilation in the Lesch-Nyhan syndrome can be controlled by oral administration of L-5-H.T.P. without any adverse effects.

References

1 Valzelli, L. *Adv. Pharmac.*, 1967; **5** 79; DiChiara, G., *et al. Nature*, 1971; 233, 272; Kulkarni, A. S., *et al. Arch. Int. Pharmacodyn.*, 1973; **201,** 308.
2 Ho, B. T., *et al. Biochem. Med.* 1971; **5,** 521.
3 Nakamura, T. *Acta Schol. Med. Gifu,* 1971; **18,** 875.

Reprinted from *The Lancet*, 1974; April 20, 761 by kind permission of the publishers The Lancet Ltd., London WC2N 6AD.

DOUBLE-BLIND CLINICAL TRIAL OF 5-HYDROXYTRYP-TOPHAN IN A CASE OF LESCH-NYHAN SYNDROME

C. D. Frith, Eve C. Johnstone, M. H. Joseph, R. J. Powell, R. W. E. Watts

From the Divisions of Psychiatry and Inherited Metabolic Diseases, MRC Clinical Research Centre, Watford Road, Harrow, Middlesex

SYNOPSIS 5-Hydroxytryptophan (5-HTP) treatment of a single case of Lesch-Nyhan syndrome showing compulsive self-mutilation, athetoid movements, and characteristic clinical biochemical picture was studied on a double-blind basis. 5-HTP or placebo was administered for seven fortnightly treatment blocks. 5-HTP produced a significant reduction of athetoid movement and a sedative effect but did not improve the patient's mood or reduce self-mutilation.

The Lesch-Nyhan syndrome (Lesch and Nyhan, 1964), as originally described, comprised mental retardation, choreoathetosis, spasticity, compulsive self-mutilation, aggressiveness, hyperuricaemia, hyperuricaciduria, urinary calculi, and juvenile gout. Some patients also have megaloblastic anaemia. The syndrome is associated with a gross deficiency, and often undetectable levels, of hypoxanthine phosphoribosyltransferase (HGPRT, EC 2.4.2.8) activity in the patient's erythrocytes and other tissues, although the catalytically incompetent enzyme can be demonstrated immunologically (Arnold et al., 1972; Müller and Steinberger, 1974). However, the degree of any residual enzyme activity demonstrable in erythrocytes does not closely relate to the severity of the clinical manifestations.

The compulsive self-mutilation is a most striking and particularly distressing feature of the syndrome. Mizuno and Yugari (1974) reported an open trial of 5-hydroxytryptophan (5-HTP) in which self-mutilation was completely relieved in four cases of Lesch-Nyhan syndrome. A decision to treat with 5-hydroxytryptophan would probably involve committing the child to a lifelong course of medication with a new psychotropic drug, and we therefore considered that every effort should be made to establish firmly the efficacy of the drug in such a way that subjective factors were as far as possible excluded from the judgements of the observers. This would seem to be particularly important since it is well known that the severity of the manifestations of this disorder fluctuate in intensity and that apparent improvement sometimes occurs if the child's environment is changed, especially when he is admitted to a paediatric ward for a period of investigation or for treatment of an intercurrent condition.

This paper reports the design and results of a double-blind trial of 5-hydroxytryptophan treatment in conjunction with a peripheral decarboxylase inhibitor in a case of the Lesch-Nyhan syndrome using an objective rating procedure.

Methods

Analytical Uric acid, creatinine, and protein were determined as previously reported (Watts *et al.*, 1974); erythrocyte hypoxanthine phosphoribosyltransferase and adenine phosphoribosyltransferase (APRT, EC 2.4.2.7) as described by Craft *et al.* (1970) but using pH 8.0 rather than pH 7.5 tris-Cl buffer (0.1 M); erythrocyte ribosephosphate pyrophosphokinase (PRPP synthetase, EC 2.7.6.1) as described by Fox and Kelley (1971); erythrocyte phosphoribosylpyrophosphate (PRPP) as described by Gordon *et al.* (1974). The immunoassay of the catalytically incompetent HGPRT protein cross-reacting material or CRIM (Arnold *et al.*, 1972) was kindly performed by Professor W. N. Kelley, Department of Medicine, Duke University, Durham, North Carolina, U.S.A. Plasma 5-HTP levels were determined by the method of Joseph and Baker (in preparation). 5-HTP was extracted into acid butanol, back extracted into dilute acid, and separated from 5-HT using a liquid cation exchange reagent. Quantitation was via fluorimetric assay after condensation with o-phthalaldehyde (Maickel and Miller, 1966) with the addition of cysteine.

Patient

The patient (D.H.) is the 6½ year old boy previously described by Watts *et al.* (1974) when he was 4½ years old. He remains choreoathetoid and markedly hypotonic. Compulsive self-mutilation continues and the patient now shows evidence of insight into this aspect of his condition. Megaloblastic anaemia, renal complications, and gout have not developed. Psychometric examination (Miss S. Gilbert) using a slightly modified Peabody Picture Vocabulary Test gave a raw score of 44 and a mental age of 4 years 3 months when his chronological age was 6 years 5 months. This result may be an underestimate because of the patient's difficulty with expressive language and his inevitably limited experience. It seems likely that this child's prognosis will be governed more by his physical than by his mental handicap. The present studies were undertaken when he was taking allopurinol (100 mg daily). The biochemical findings, which are characteristic of the Lesch-Nyhan syndrome, are presented in Table 1.

Table 1. Diagnostic biochemistry

	Patient	Normal range in our laboratory
HGPRT (nmol·mg·protein^{-1}·hour^{-1})	0	103 (SD=18; n=13)
APRT (nmol·mg·protein^{-1}·hour^{-1})	54	19 (SD=3.0; n=31)
PRPP synthetase (nmol·mg·protein^{-1}·hour^{-1})	23	25 (SD=6.3; n=10)
PRPP (pmol·mg·protein^{-1})	97	16 (SD=2.6; n=31)
Serum uric acid (mg·dl^{-1}) (μM)	9.0 536	1.2-6.8* 72-405
Urine uric acid/creatinine	3.2	1.8†
CRIM‡	+	+

* Data reported by Harkness and Nicol (1969) for boys age 0-13 years, these workers used the method of Liddle *et al.* (1959). The values obtained for younger children are in the lower part of this range with a fairly abrupt rise as puberty approaches.

† The limit of the upper range for boys of this patient's age (Kaufman *et al.*, 1968).

‡ CRIM +=patient's red cells contain protein which cross-reacts with antiserum prepared against purified hypoxanthine phosphoribosyl-transferase (HGPRT EC 2.4.2.8) (Arnold *et al.*, 1972).

DESIGN OF TRIAL The trial was divided into a series of fortnightly blocks during each of which the patient received either drug or placebo. These treatments were assigned on a random basis which was unknown to the patient, his parents, the ward staff, or those responsible for assessing changes in behaviour. For the first half of each fortnight the patient was at home and for the second half in hospital. The major assessments of behaviour change were made in hospital during the second week of each treatment block at which time it was considered that drug effects would have stabilized and transient changes in behaviour would have ceased.

DRUG ADMINISTRATION Drugs were administered in gelatine capsules; placebos for each drug contained lactose. 5-HTP (Cambrian Chemicals, Croydon) was administered at a dose of 100 mg/day in four equal doses, Carbidopa (Merck, Sharp and Dohme; Hoddesdon) at a dose of 50 mg/day in two equal doses. This amount of 5-HTP is equivalent to the maximum dose (8 mg/kg) used in the study by Mizuno and Yugari (1974) and pilot studies had shown that this was well tolerated by our patient. A peripheral decarboxylase inhibitor was not used in their study; it should potentiate the central effects of 5-HTP and therefore enhance

Table 2. Scale of speech quality

Speech impairment scale
(Evoked speech occurs in response to question)

0. Both spontaneous and evoked speech comprehensible and minimally
   disturbed
1. Spontaneous speech difficult to understand
2. Only evoked speech understandable to any extent
3. Only a few expected words understandable ('yes', 'no', names of
   requested toys, etc.)
4. All speech incomprehensible *or* no speech in spite of attempts to elicit
   it

any effects on behaviour. Placebo tablets for both drugs were administered during non-treatment weeks.

After 14 weeks (seven treatment blocks, four on drug and three on placebo) it was clear that there was no obvious difference in behaviour between treatment and no treatment periods, particularly with regard to self-mutilation. In addition the weekly shuttle between home and hospital was becoming distressing both for the patient and his parents. It was therefore decided to terminate the trial.

ASSESSMENT OF BEHAVIOUR CHANGE Six behavioural rating scales were designed specifically for the patient on the basis of observations made before the start of the trial. Two scales related to abnormal behaviour, self-mutilation, and choreoathetoid movement, and the others concerned normal behaviour, mood, attention, voluntary movement, and speech quality. The scales were modelled on the Goldberg Psychiatric rating scales (Goldberg *et al.*, 1970) and consisted of five points each defined by concrete examples of behaviour. The scales ranged from the worst example of the particular behaviour (score 4) observed during the pre-trial observation period to the best improvement in behaviour that might be expected if the treatment were successful (score 0). Table 2 lists the five levels of behaviour for the scale of the speech quality. During his weeks in hospital the patient was rated independently by six observers each day. The ratings were based on a 15-minute observation period during which time the patient was generally playing with ward staff or the observers. To obtain a measure of the reliability of the rating scales, uncontaminated by genuine fluctuations of the patient's behaviour, four of the observers worked in pairs observing the same behaviour, but arriving at independent ratings of it.

In addition to the rating scales, an objective index of movement was provided by an activity meter consisting of a modified self-winding wrist-watch which was attached to the patient's left ankle for 10 minutes each day. Since the patient is confined to a wheel-chair with his legs hanging freely, readings from this meter were an index of amount of athetoid movement. It was also noted each day which of the various measures adopted to prevent self-mutilation was being used. These varied from splints and bandages on both arms and hands to no restraint on either arm and hand. These measures were a further indication of the tendency to self-mutilation.

Results

DRUG LEVELS As expected, 5-hydroxytryptophan was not detectable in plasma before treatment, or in any of the placebo periods (Table 3). It was detectable, however, as long as 10 hours after administration of 5-HTP. A higher level was observed 0.5 hr after administration; the results reported are consistent with potentiation of the 5-HTP by inhibition of peripheral decarboxylation, but ethical considerations precluded more detailed pharmacokinetic analysis.

OVERALL MOOD It was found that a number of the rating scales were related closely to one another. An unhappy mood was associated with lapses of attention, poor voluntary movement, and unclear speech. Therefore these four scales were combined to give one index of overall mood. The reliability of this scale was 0.57 (based on 20 observations) when the ratings being compared were of the same behaviour. However, the correlations between ratings made at different times of the same day fell to 0.21, suggesting that there were

Table 3. Plasma Levels of 5-Hydroxytryptophan

Date	Treatment period	Carbidopa (mg/day)	5-HTP (mg/day)	Plasma 5-HTP (μg/ml, 10 h post-drug)
6 Jan. 75		0	0	ND
13 Feb. 75		0	30	0.07
14 Mar. 75		50	100	0.68
19 May 75	1	0	0	ND
5 June 75	2	50	100	0.31
17 June 75	3	50	100	0.42
1 July 75	4	0	0	ND
15 July 75	5	50	100	(1.79, ½ h post-drug)
29 July 75	6	0	0	ND
12 Aug. 75	7	50	100	0.36

ND=not detectable.

considerable fluctuations in mood during the course of a day. Overall mood was somewhat worse during drug periods than during placebo periods, but not significantly so (Fig. 1), indicating that 5-HTP did not improve this patient's overall mood.

It was apparent from the parent's ratings when the patient was at home that there was a worsening of mood at the beginning of each placebo period (and hence immediately after the patient had stopped taking 5-HTP). There was not enough data for this effect to be significant, but it suggests that some mild withdrawal effect was occurring.

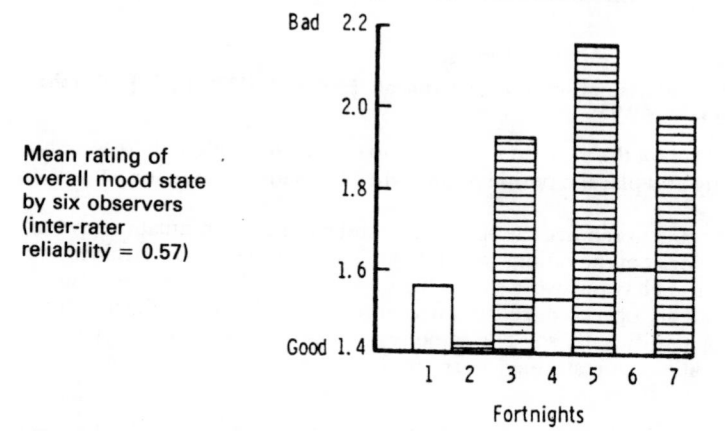

Fig. 1. Effects of 5-HTP on overall mood. Treatment: ▦ =5-HTP. ☐ =Placebo. No significant effect of 5-HTP on mood.

ATHETOID MOVEMENT Ratings of athetoid movement were fairly reliable ($r=0.68$) and the daily fluctuations were relatively small ($r=0.54$). Furthermore, there was close agreement between the ratings and the readings of the wrist watch activity meter ($r=0.61$). The activity meter indicated that there was significantly less athetoid movement during periods on drug (Mann-Whitney U test, $P <0.05$). Thus 5-HTP reduced athetoid movement in this patient (Fig. 2).

Certain spontaneous observations made by the raters were related to this finding. At least three observers commented that the patient appeared sleepy, quiescent, or flaccid during each drug period; no such comments were made during placebo periods (Fig. 3). Thus 5-HTP was having a significant sedative effect on this patient (Mann-Whitney U test, $P <0.05$).

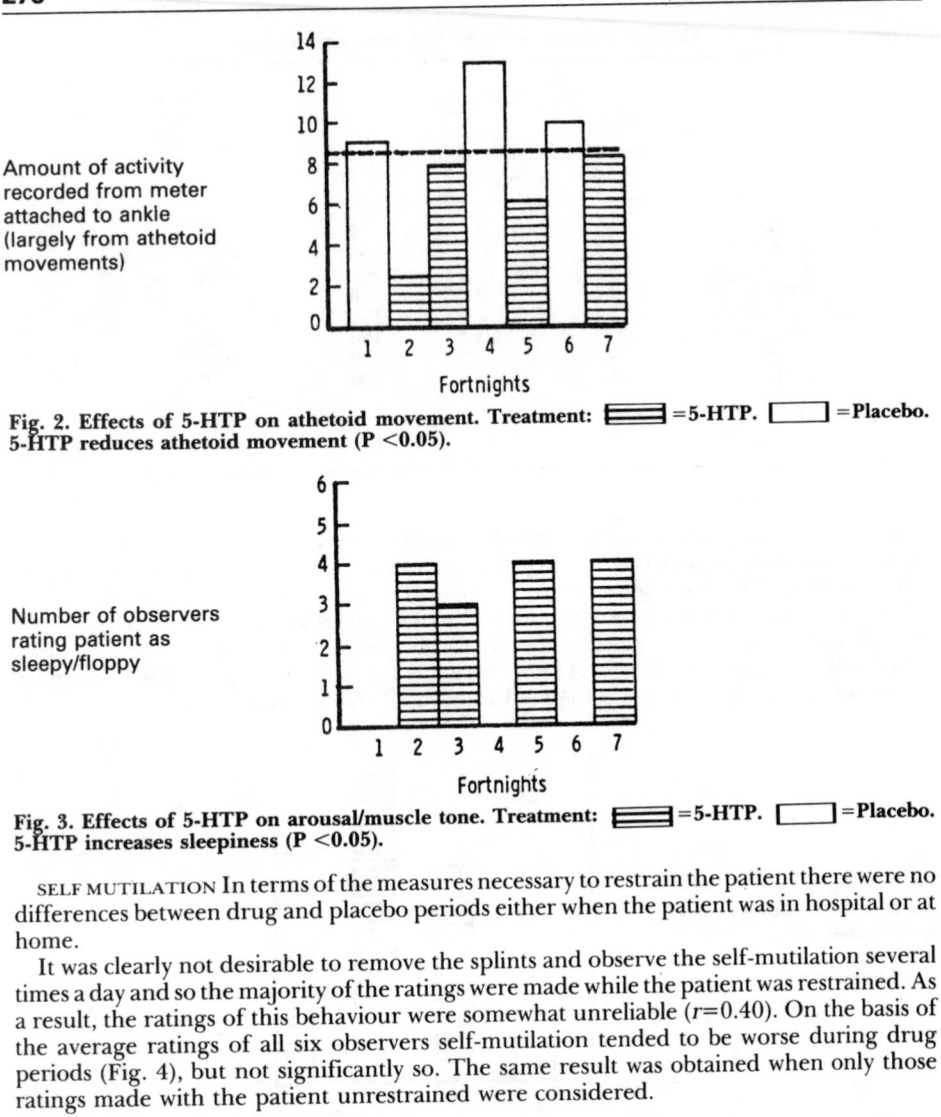

Fig. 2. Effects of 5-HTP on athetoid movement. Treatment: ▤▤=5-HTP. ☐=Placebo. 5-HTP reduces athetoid movement (P <0.05).

Fig. 3. Effects of 5-HTP on arousal/muscle tone. Treatment: ▤▤=5-HTP. ☐=Placebo. 5-HTP increases sleepiness (P <0.05).

SELF MUTILATION In terms of the measures necessary to restrain the patient there were no differences between drug and placebo periods either when the patient was in hospital or at home.

It was clearly not desirable to remove the splints and observe the self-mutilation several times a day and so the majority of the ratings were made while the patient was restrained. As a result, the ratings of this behaviour were somewhat unreliable ($r=0.40$). On the basis of the average ratings of all six observers self-mutilation tended to be worse during drug periods (Fig. 4), but not significantly so. The same result was obtained when only those ratings made with the patient unrestrained were considered.

Discussion

Mizuno and Yugari (1974) used 5-HTP to treat self-mutilation on the basis that this was an autoaggressive phenomenon, and that 5-HTP prevented the development of isolation-induced aggressive behaviour in rats and mice. Although we feel that self-mutilation in Lesch-Nyhan syndrome should not be regarded simply as autoaggressive behaviour, since physical restraint appears to prevent it without frustration or displacement to other autoaggressive behaviours, we did feel that there was additional experimental work supporting a possible beneficial action of 5-HTP. The presence of HGPRT in well-washed synaptosomes (Gutensohn and Guroff, 1972) points to a possible role of purine salvage in synaptic transmission. The lack of HGPRT in the Lesch-Nyhan syndrome will lead to a deficiency of GMP, and hence of GTP in vulnerable tissues such as the brain and bone marrow. This would in turn lead to a deficiency of cyclic GMP. This nucleotide is thought to be a modulator of certain metabolic processes including cell division (Hadden et al., 1972; Shields, 1974), cholinergic receptor action (Weight et al., 1974; Kebabian et al., 1975), and, at least extracerebrally (Sandler et al., 1975), of serotonergic receptor action. Thus, a

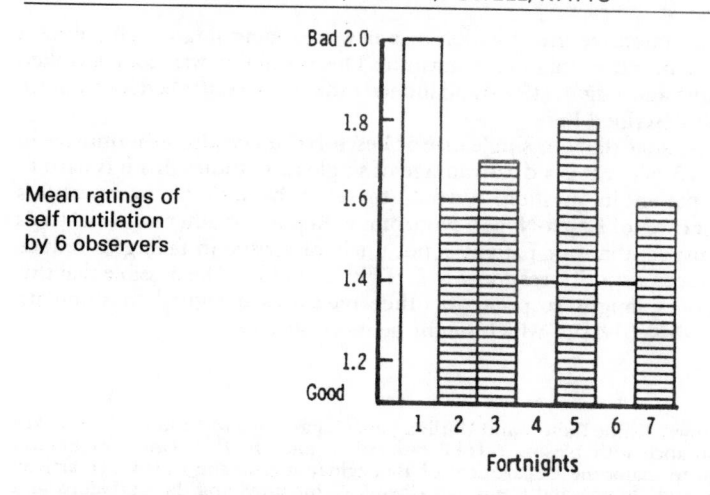

Fig. 4. Effects of 5-HTP on self-mutilation. Treatment: ▦ = 5-HTP. ☐ = Placebo. 5-HTP
does not reduce self-mutilation.

disturbance in the balance between cyclic nucleotides or between serotonergic and
catecholaminergic systems in Lesch-Nyhan syndrome might be restored by increased 5-HT
synthesis and receptor stimulation. The reports of increased dopamine - ß hydroxylase
(dopamine - ß -mono-oxygenase, EC 1.13.17.1) activity in the Lesch-Nyhan syndrome
(Rockson *et al.*, 1974), of the production of compulsive gnawing, and stereotyped
behaviours in rats and cats by amphetamine (Randrup and Munkvad, 1966; Wallach and
Gershon, 1971), and of the production of autoaggression in experimental animals by
feeding caffeine and theophylline (Nyhan, 1968; Morgan *et al.*, 1970), which block the
degradation of cAMP and cGMP by inhibition of 3' : 5'-cyclic AMP phosphodiesterase (EC
3.1.4.17) would be broadly consistent with this formulation.

However, in the present study, although it was clear that 5-HTP affected the behaviour of
this patient, it did not reduce self-mutilation behaviour, nor did it improve the patient's
overall mood. It seems unlikely that this failure to affect self-mutilation was due to an
insufficient dose of 5-HTP. The dose the patient received was equal to the maximum dose
used by Mizuno and Yugari (1974). The plasma levels of 5-HTP that were measured
confirmed that the patient in fact received the active drugs and placebo in accordance with
the design of the trial, that the 5-HTP was absorbed, and that raised plasma levels persisted
until the next dose was administered. It is possible that the addition of Carbidopa, by
inhibiting peripheral effects, also prevented an effect on self-mutilation behaviour.
However, a previous uncontrolled study suggested that 5-HTP alone administered for six
weeks had equally little effect on this patient's self-mutilation.

5-HTP did reduce our patient's involuntary movements and produce a general
appearance of sleepiness. It is possible that a sufficiently large dose of 5-HTP would reduce
self-mutilation as a secondary consequence of this sedating effect. Such an effect might
account for the results of Mizuno and Yugari (1974).

Self-mutilation varied markedly in our patient. It increased when he was frightened or
frustrated and reduced when he was concentrating on some interesting occupation. The
patient is very much aware of the undesirability of the self-mutilation. He becomes very
agitated if the restraining splints or bandages are removed from his hands and can only be
calmed by their replacement. He will try and impose his own restraints by such measures as
sitting on his hands. Some of this behaviour is in line with Duker's (1975) suggestion that
self-mutilation behaviour is learned by Lesch-Nyhan patients as a method of gaining
attention. Duker has demonstrated that the behaviour is under the control of
environmental influences and has achieved some success in reducing self-mutilation using
behaviour modification techniques. If self-mutilation is indeed influenced by the patient's
environment, then the marked change in environment brought about when the patient is

moved to hospital for an intensive investigation of a new treatment might well induce a similarly marked change in self-mutilation behaviour. This possibility was not controlled for in the study by Mizuno and Yugari (1974) and indeed can only be controlled for by using a double-blind study as described here.

Lastly, it is of course possible that our single case of Lesch-Nyhan syndrome is unusual in his failure to respond to 5-HTP. It is a disadvantage of single case studies that it is hard to generalize beyond the patient in question. It would therefore be desirable to repeat this kind of study with other cases of Lesch-Nyhan syndromne. Reports of other informal trials of 5-HTP lead us to suspect that our patient is not uncharacteristic in failing to reduce self-mutilation behaviour as a specific response to 5-HTP. It would still be possible that this patient, or indeed others, might respond to other measures designed to stimulate serotonergic neurones, the effects of which might be more specific.

Acknowledgements
We wish to thank Edna Brown, Lynne Dalton, and Marilyn James for assisting with ratings, H. F. Baker for skilful technical assistance with plasma 5-HTP estimation, and Dr T. J. Crow for helpful discussions. We also wish to thank the Department of Bioengineering for the wrist-watch activity meter, and Merck Sharp and Dohme and Cambrian Chemicals for providing the Carbidopa and 5-HTP respectively. Particular thanks are due to our patient, his parents, and the nursing staff of Carol Ward.

References
Arnold, W. J., Meade, T. J., Kelley, W. N. Hypoxanthine-guanine phosphoribosyl transferase: characteristics of the mutant enzyme in erythrocytes from patients with the Lesch-Nyhan syndrome. *J. Clin. Invest.*, 1972; **51**, 1805-1812.
Craft, J. A., Dean, B. M., Watts, R. W. E., Westwick, W. J. Studies on human erythrocyte IMP: pyrophosphate phosphoribosyl-transferase. *European J. Biochem.*, 1970; **15**, 367-373.
Duker, P. Behaviour control of self-biting in a Lesch-Nyhan patient. *J. Ment. Defic. Res.*, 1975; **19**, 11-19.
Fox, I. H., Kelley, W. N. Human phosphoribosyl pyrophosphate synthetase: distribution, purification and properties. *J. Biolog. Chem.*, 1971; **246**, 5739-5748.
Goldberg, D. P., Cooper, B., Eastwood, M. R., Kedward, H. B., Shepherd, M. A standardised psychiatric interview for use in community surveys. *Br. J. Prevent. & Soc. Med.*, 1970; **24**, 18-23.
Gordon, R. B., Thompson, L., Emerson, B. T. Erythrocyte phosphoribosylpyrophosphate concentrations in heterozygotes for hypoxanthine-guanine phosphoribosyltransferase deficiency. metabolism. 1974; **23**, 921-927.
Gutensohn, W., Guroff, G. Hypoxanthine-guanine-phosphoribosyl transferase from rat brain (purification, kinetic properties, development and distribution). *J. Neurochem.*, 1972; **19**, 2139-2150.
Hadden, J. W., Hadden, E. M., Haddox, M. K., Goldberg, N. D. Guanosine 3':5'-cyclic monophosphate: a possible intracellular mediator of mitogenic influences in lymphocytes. *Proceed. Nat. Acad. Sc., USA.*, 1972; **69**, 3024-3027.
Harkness, R. A., Nicol, A. D. Plasma uric acid levels in children. *Arch. Dis. in Child.*, 1969; **44**, 773-778.
Kaufman, J. M., Greene, M. L., Seegmiller, J. E. Urine uric acid to creatinine ratio—a screening test for inherited disorders of purine metabolism. *J. Paediatrics.*, 1968; **73**, 583-588.
Kebabian, J. W., Bloom, F. E., Steiner, A., Greengard, P. Neurotransmitters increase cyclic nucleotides in postganglionic neurons: immunocytochemical demonstration. *Science*, 1975; **190**, 151-159.
Lesch, M., Nyhan, W. L. A familial disorder of uric acid metabolism and central nervous system function. *Am. J. Med.*, 1964; **36**, 561-570.
Liddle, L., Seegmiller, J. E., Laster, L. Enzymatic spectrophotometric method for determination of uric acid. *J. Laborat. Clin. Med.*, 1959; **54**, 903-908.
Maickel, R. P., Miller, F. P. Fluorescent products formed by reaction of indole derivatives and o-phthalaldehyde. *Analyt. Chem.*, 1966; **38**, 1937-1938.
Mizuno, T., Yugari, Y. Self mutilation in the Lesch-Nyhan syndrome. *Lancet.*, 1974; **1**, 761.
Morgan, L. L., Schneidermann, N., Nyhan, W. L. Theophylline; induction of self biting in rabbits. *Psychonom. Sc.*, 1970; **19**, 37-38.
Müller, M. M., Steinberger, H. Biochemische und immunologische Untersuchungen der Hypoxanthin-Guanin-Phosphoribosyltransferase in den Erythrozyten von Lesch-Nyhan Patienten. *Wiener klinische Wochenschrift.*, 1974; **86**, 127-131.
Nyhan, W. L. Seminars in the Lesch-Nyhan syndrome: pathology and pathologic physiology, discussion. *Federation Proceed.*, 1968; **27**, 1044-1046.
Randrup, A., Munkvad, I. Role of catecholamines in the amphetamine excitatory response. *Nature.*, 1966; **211**, 540.
Rockson, S., Stone, R., van der Weyden, M., Kelly, W. N. Lesch-Nyhan syndrome: evidence for abnormal adrenergic function. *Science*, 1974; **186**, 934-935.

Sandler, J. A., Clyman, R. I., Manganiello, V. C., and Vaughan, M. The effect of serotonin (5-hydroxytryptamine) and derivatives on guanosine 3′,5′-monophosphate in human monocytes. *J. Clin. Invest.*, 1975; **55**, 431-435.

Shields, R. Control of cell growth by the cyclic nucleotide seesaw. *Nature*, 1974; **252**, 11-12.

Wallach, M. B., Gershon, S. Induction and antagonism of stereotyped behaviour in cats. *Pharmacologist*, 1971; **13**, 230.

Watts, R. W. E., McKeran, R. O., Brown, E., Andrews, T. M., Griffiths, M. I. Clinical and biochemical studies on treatment of Lesch-Nyhan syndrome. *Arch. Dis. in Child.*, 1974; **49**, 693-702.

Weight, F. F., Petzold, G., and Greengard, P. Guanosine 3′,5′-monophosphate in sympathetic ganglia:increase associated with synaptic transmission. *Science*, 1974; **186**, 942-944.

Reprinted from *J. Neurol. Neurosurg. & Psychiat.*, 1976; **39**, 656-662 by kind permission of the authors, the Editor of *J. Neurol. Neurosurg. & Psychiat.*, and the publishers British Medical Association, London WC1H 9JR.

TREATMENT OF SELF-INJURIOUS BEHAVIOUR WITH A GABA (GAMMA-AMINOBUTYRIC ACID) ANALOGUE

D. A. Primrose

The Royal Scottish National Hospital, Larbert, Stirlingshire, Scotland

Summary
    Self-injurious and other undesirable behaviour is described in twenty-eight mental defectives in hospital. The effect of treatment with a GABA analogue, baclofen, is given. Twenty-two of the patients who are severely subnormal, and whose behaviour had improved after commencing baclofen, were then followed up for twenty weeks in a double-blind cross-over trial. The results, including side effects, are discussed. There is significant improvement in the behaviour of many of the patients. In some the improvement seems to be dependent on continuing the baclofen, whilst in others it has been maintained after stopping the drug, thus indicating that behaviour modification has taken place. It has been possible to discontinue, or reduce, other medication in some of the patients.

Self-injurious behaviour (SIB) is not uncommon in the severely subnormal. Corbett (1975) found the incidence in several reported series to vary between 3.5 per cent and almost 40 per cent, and Van Velzen (1973), in a survey of ten institutions in the Netherlands, found it present in 584 patients out of almost 2,000 (30.3 per cent). Treatment is notoriously difficult and many kinds have been tried including physical restraint, drug regimes, and electric shock aversion therapy. An account is given here of a drug trial using baclofen, a gamma-aminobutyric acid (GABA) analogue that crosses the blood brain barrier. GABA, in addition to being a muscle relaxant, is also a major inhibitor in many areas of the brain, including the cortex and basal ganglia (Callingham, 1972) and it was presumed by the author that some severely subnormal defectives have damage in these areas and hence might be deficient in this inhibitor.
    The trial commenced with a preliminary period during which the reactions of patients to the drug at different dose levels were observed. This was followed by a double-blind cross-over trial in patients who had already shown improvement.

Preliminary trial
    The trial was commenced with four patients (Nos. 2, 9, 14 and 17 in Table 1), two of whom (Nos. 9 and 14) have phenylketonuria (PKU). Of these, one had made himself blind by hitting his head and causing bilateral retinal detachments and cataracts. To prevent further injury it had been necessary for his arms to be restrained for a considerable period of time. Many drugs, a low phenylalanine diet, and behaviour modification by the psychologist had already been tried with no sustained improvement. The second patient with PKU frequently banged her head on the ground and bit her hands. The other two patients have no specific diagnosis, but one (No. 2) required padded cot sides because of head banging, and patient No. 17 frequently scratched and caused his face to bleed.
    After a month, two of these patients (Nos. 2 and 17) showed some improvement and so, over a period of a few months, a further eighteen patients with long-standing SIB or other difficult behaviour, who had not responded satisfactorily to other treatments, were brought into the trial. These patients, with one exception (No. 22), had been in hospital for more than two years and their pattern of behaviour was well known. They were in eleven different wards and no particular change was made in their environment. Details of the patients are shown in Table 1, from which it can be seen that twenty-one exhibit SIB, four are aggressive to other patients and staff, such as by biting, scratching or hitting them, and ten are hyperkinetic. Sixteen have a history of epilepsy, nineteen have no significant speech (sixteen mute), five are blind and two of these are also deaf. All the patients except one (No. 3) are severely subnormal (IQ < 50).

Table 1. Details of patients showing disabilities and behaviour prior to treatment

Patient No.	Sex	Age (years)	Duration in hospital (years)	Epilepsy	Speech	Blind-ness	Deaf-ness	Hyper-kinetic	Self-injury			Other
									Bites	Scratches	Bangs, slaps, etc.	
1	M	16	9	+	Occ. words	−	−	−	Hands			
2	M	31	25	+	No	−	−	−			Head	
3	M	31	15	+	Yes	+	−	+			Head	Aggression
4	M	16	9	+	Occ. words	+	−	+				Aggression
5	M	13	8	−	No	+	−	+	Hands	Face	Head	
6	F	17	10	−	No	−	−	+	Hands		Face, head	
7	M	12	2	+	No	−	−	+	Hands		Head	Aggression
8	M	14	8	+	No	+	+	−		Face, body, arms	Head, eyes, ears	
9	M	28	12	−	No	+	−	−			Head	
10	M	34	20	+	Yes	−	+	−		Body/limbs		
11	F	37	22	+	No	+	−	−			Head, ears	
12	M	17	9	+	No	−	−	−			Head, face	
13	F	34	29	−	Echolalia	−	−	+	Hands		Face	Aggression
14	F	20	13	+	No	−	−	+			Head	
15	M	31	20	+	No	−	−	−			Face	
16	M	9	4	+	No	−	−	−		Face	Face, eyes	
17	M	23	25	+	No	−	−	+	Hands, arms		Face, eyes	
18	M	23	11	+	NO	−	−	−		Face		Coprophilia
19	F	22	9	+	No	−	−	+			Head	Aggression
20	M	24	14	−	Yes	−	−	+			Head	
21	M	24	17	+	No	−	+	−			Head	Coprophilia
22	F	16	5/12	−	No	−	−	+	Hands	Face	Face	Coprophilia

Table 2. First changes in mood observed by nursing staff

Patient No.	Period	A/B/C*	Comment by nursing staff
1	Within 5 days	A	Happier, quieter, more settled.
2	11	A	Much happier.
3	3	B	Quieter and happier.
4	2	B	Happier and dancing.
5	12	A	Quieter.
6	6 }	A	Quieter, smiling.
	3 }	B	Smiling.
7	13	B	Quieter and happier.
8	9	A	Quieter.
9	13	B	Quieter, smiling, happier.
10	9	B	More settled, communicative, co-operative.
11			No change.
12	10	A	Happier, laughing.
13	9	A	Happier, laughing.
14	10	B	Happier.
15			No change in mood.
16	3 }	A	Quieter.
		C	Happier (treatment reduced because of nausea).
	21 }	B	Quieter, happier.
		B	Ceases to make himself vomit after dinner.
17	9	A	Co-operative, affectionate, happier, no longer makes herself vomit.
18	9		
19	9	B	Much quieter, fewer outbursts.
		A	Much quieter.
20	15	A	Quieter.
21	4		
22	2		

A = Time after treatment commenced.
B = Time after dose was increased.
C = Time after dose was decreased.

Treatment was usually commenced with 10 mgm (one tablet) three times daily and, if there were no apparent effects after two weeks, this was increased. Patients and ward staff were seen weekly by the author, who recorded any changes in the behaviour of the patients. The first changes noticed after the commencement of treatment are shown in Table 2, along with an indication of the time taken to produce them. There was some evidence of drug tolerance in that the beneficial effects were not maintained in many patients, and therefore further increases were made in the dosage until, at doses varying from 20 mgm to 200 mgm daily, in divided doses, there appeared to be improvement in behaviour maintained for more than a month in most of the patients.

Side effects (discussed later) led to the withdrawal of baclofen in patient No. 22 after five days, and in patient No. 5 after twenty-nine days. After patient No. 15 had been in the trial for eighty-five days, and shown considerable improvement in his behaviour, he died suddenly from asphyxia due to the aspiration of vomitus after the evening meal.

Double-blind trial

It was decided to carry out a double-blind trial in severely subnormal patients whose behaviour had apparently improved on the drug. Patients Nos. 11 and 20 were excluded as they had not shown any sustained improvement, and patient No. 3 was also rejected because he was not severely defective. This left sixteen patients; to these were added a further six who had started treatment with baclofen subsequent to the preliminary trial, and had shown some improvement. These six patients are all severely subnormal and five of them had exhibited SIB, whilst in the sixth the main problem was coprophilia. They have been numbered 3A, 5A, 11A (female), and 15A, 20A, 22A (male); the original sixteen patients retained their former numbers. Patient No. 15A is aged thirteen years, the others are adult. At the commencement of this part of the trial, eighteen of the twenty-two patients had been on baclofen for more than six months and the other four for more than three months.

Baclofen is produced commercially as Lioresal and the makers randomly allocated the patients to one of two groups (A and B) and supplied tablets of either placebo, or active drug, in separate containers for each patient. The dose schedule and grouping of the patients is shown in Table 3.

No person in the hospital knew which was being given to any particular patient and each patient was given an eight-weeks period of either placebo or drug, followed by a further eight-weeks period of drug or placebo, and then all patients were given the active drug for a further four weeks. The author interviewed ward staff weekly (except for a holiday absence of two weeks in the middle of one of the periods), and at the end of the twenty-week period the code was broken and the behaviour pattern which had been recorded for each period was compared according to whether drug or placebo had been taken.

Results

The results from the twenty-two patients in the cross-over trial are summarised in Table 4, from which it can be seen that all the patients show some improvement from the pre-trial state. Nine deteriorated during the placebo period, improved during the baclofen period, and maintained this improvement during the final four-week period. One of these, who had shown marked deterioration, fell in the fourth week of her placebo period and fractured her left femur and treatment for this required transfer from her original ward. A tenth patient (No. 3A) did not appear to deteriorate during the placebo period, but after the subsequent changeover to baclofen an improvement was noted. A further eight whose SIB had improved on baclofen prior to starting the control trial, maintained the improvement throughout the trial with no deterioration during the placebo period. Three of the patients seemed to be slightly worse during the eight-week period with baclofen, but there was still a considerable improvement when compared with their behaviour prior to the exhibition of baclofen. The remaining patient (No. 22A) had coprophilia and used to urinate on the ward radiators. After starting the drug there was less coprophilia, and he urinated appropriately in the toilet. He showed a further slight improvement during the placebo period.

Routine blood count at the end of the trial was normal for all these patients.

Other medication

In addition to anti-epileptic drugs where necessary, the patients had previously been tried with many different tranquillisers, anti-depressants and sedatives, e.g. phenothiazines, benzodiazepines, tricyclic anti-depressants, and other preparations, such as lithium. At the commencement of the trial, fifteen of the original twenty-two patients were on routine phenothiazines, five on benzodiazepines, two on tricyclic anti-depressants, two on chlormethiazole, one on haloperidol and one on lithium.

When baclofen was commenced whatever medication was already being given was continued. In some patients, once there appeared to be an improvement, the concurrent medication was reduced or stopped. For example, five of those on phenothiazines (Nos. 2, 3, 4, 5 and 22) had these discontinued, but in patient No. 5 there was such a deterioration that the phenothiazine was reintroduced, the baclofen stopped, and the patient removed from the trial. In another five (Nos. 6, 10, 18, 19 and 21) the dose of phenothiazine was reduced, but patient No. 19 deteriorated and so her original dose was restored. Other drugs were also able to be reduced, or stopped altogether in some of the patients. During the placebo period patients No. 9 and 13 became very disturbed and additional sedation was required, but this has since been discontinued in patient No. 13.

Side effects

It is recognised that baclofen may increase the frequency of epileptic seizures (Meldrum, 1978). Sixteen of the patients in the original series were known to have had epilepsy but this was well controlled. In patient No. 4, after commencing the trial, there was an increase in the frequency of his seizures but in view of the substantial reduction in his biting and scratching, it was decided to continue the baclofen, and after some weeks his seizure pattern returned to the pre-trial state. In one other patient (No. 22), not previously known to have seizures, these occurred at a dose level of 10 mgm t.i.d., and the baclofen was stopped. Since

Table 3. Daily dose of Baclofen or placebo at commencement of double-blind trial

Group A (Placebo followed by Baclofen)	Daily dose (mgm)
Patient No. 1	30
2	30
3A	90
4	260
8	90
9	300
13	60
16	20 (increased to 40)
18	90
20A	90
21	90

Group B (Baclofen followed by placebo)	
Patient No. 5A	30
6	90
7	60
10	60
11A	30 (increased to 90)
12	30
14	40 (increased to 80)
15A	90
17	120
19	90
22A	60

Table 4. Results of double-blind trial in patients already showing improvement since introduction of Baclofen

Patient No.	8 Weeks Placebo	8 Weeks Baclofen	4 Weeks Baclofen	Comparison with original behaviour
1	No change	No change	No change	Less SIB. Still hyperkinetic.
2	No change	No change	No change	SIB completely stopped. Protective padding no longer required.
3A	No change	Better	Maintained	Much less SIB. Less aggression.
4	No change	Worse	Improved	Much less aggression.
5A	Better	Worse	Improved	Less SIB. Much better behaved and co-operative.
6	No change	No change	No change	Much less SIB. Now interested and co-operative. Hand wounds healed.
7	No change	No change	No change	Less SIB, less aggression. Hyperkinesis unchanged.
8	No change	No change	No change	Less SIB. Better behaved.
9	Worse	Better	Maintained	Much less SIB. Now no restraint. Face wounds healed.
10	No change	No change	No change	Less SIB.
11A	Worse	Better	Maintained	Less SIB. Hand wounds healed.
12	Worse	Better	Maintained	SIB completely stopped. Some aggression.
13	Worse	Better	Maintained	Much calmer, less aggression.
14	Worse	Better	Maintained	Much less SIB. Hand wounds healed.
15A	No change	No change	No change	Less SIB. Happier and co-operative.
16	Worse	Better	Maintained	Less SIB.
17	Worse	Better	Maintained	Much less SIB. Face wounds healed.
18	No change	No change	No change	Much less SIB. Less coprophilia.
19	Better	Worse	No change	Much less SIB. Less aggression and seclusion required much less.
20A	Worse	Better	Maintained	Less SIB.
21	Worse	Better	Maintained	Less aggression, less coprophilia and will now use toilet.
22A	Better	No change	No change	Quieter. Less coprophilia, and uses toilet for micturition.

her behaviour had improved on the drug it was started again at 5 mgm t.i.d., but again she had seizures and it was discontinued and the patient removed from the trial. In none of the other patients has there been any increase in epileptic seizures.

Transient anorexia was noted in four patients and, following an increase in dosage, vomiting after meals lasting for two days occurred in another. Sphincter control was upset in three patients. In one of these there was urgency of micturition which lasted for one day and in another it was a week before he regained bladder control. The third patient was incontinent and usually constipated and she developed increased frequency of bladder and bowel movements which lasted for about two weeks.

Drowsiness was noted in several patients but this wore off, usually after a few days. During the controlled trial, the sudden change in Group A from placebo to a full dose of the drug made patients 3A and 9 so drowsy that it had to be stopped for a few days and then reintroduced gradually.

Patient 3A, a forty-seven-year-old female who punches and bangs her head, and kicks and scratches other people, had a large pigmented lesion, present for many years, on the left buttock, and in addition there are other smaller pigmented skin lesions. She commenced baclofen on 2nd February, 1978, and had been on 90 mgm daily from 19th May. On 9th October, whilst being bathed, the lesion on the buttock was found to be hard and more discoloured. It was removed surgically and histologically "shows malignant change in an extensive dermal naevo-cellular naevus". It is not known whether there could be any relationship between the malignant change and the use of baclofen, but no similar cases have been reported in relation to this drug, which has been in clinical use since 1972.

Discussion

During the initial trial with baclofen there was an obvious improvement in the mood and behaviour of many of the patients (Primrose, 1977). These patients continued in the usual ward routine and the addition of an extra drug to their existing medication did not alter this routine or single them out for special attention. Patients who were upset by the baclofen, or who had not shown any sustained improvement, were not continued in the trial, so that the subsequent double-blind trial started with patients who had already shown improvement. As can be seen from Table 4, the behaviour of all the patients at the end of the double-blind trial is still better than before baclofen was introduced. In patients Nos. 2, 4, 5A, 6, 9, 12, 13, 14, 17 and 19 the improvement is remarkable. Three of these patients have biochemical disorders (PKU in nos. 9 and 14, and porphyria in No. 13); three may have had viral encephalitis (Nos. 4, 5A and 13); No. 12 has many autistic features, and No. 17 has arrested hydrocephalus. No cause for the mental deficiency is known in the other three.

Of the remaining twelve patients, the only one with a known probably aetiology is No. 8, where it is likely to have been maternal rubella. In these twelve patients the improvement is less dramatic, but in four of them (Nos. 11A, 16, 20A and 21) there was an obvious deterioration during the placebo period, with subsequent sustained improvement on recommencing baclofen.

From the first observed changes in these patients (Table 1), it would seem that the drug improved their sense of well-being and in many it has increased their voluntary involvement with nursing staff and other patients, usually in a co-operative way, but patient No. 12 became aggressive to other patients although his SIB ceased. Two patients (Nos. 18 and 20A) who routinely vomited after meals have ceased to do so and two (Nos. 21 and 22A) have changed to more appropriate toilet behaviour. In three patients (Nos. 6, 11A and 14) chronic self-inflicted wounds of their hands have healed, and in two (Nos. 9 and 17) facial wounds have been allowed to heal, and in others frequent bruising is no longer evident.

At the end of the trial baclofen was stopped in those patients who did not deteriorate during the placebo period. The behaviour of all the patients in the control trial has been recorded for a further eight weeks, and because of deterioration in her behaviour, baclofen has been recommenced in patient No. 5A. Twenty of these patients have now been monitored for more than a year and the other two for more than nine months.

It is hoped that some of those patients who deteriorated during the placebo period will, after a further time on the drug, establish a more acceptable pattern of behaviour which will likewise continue after withdrawal of the drug.

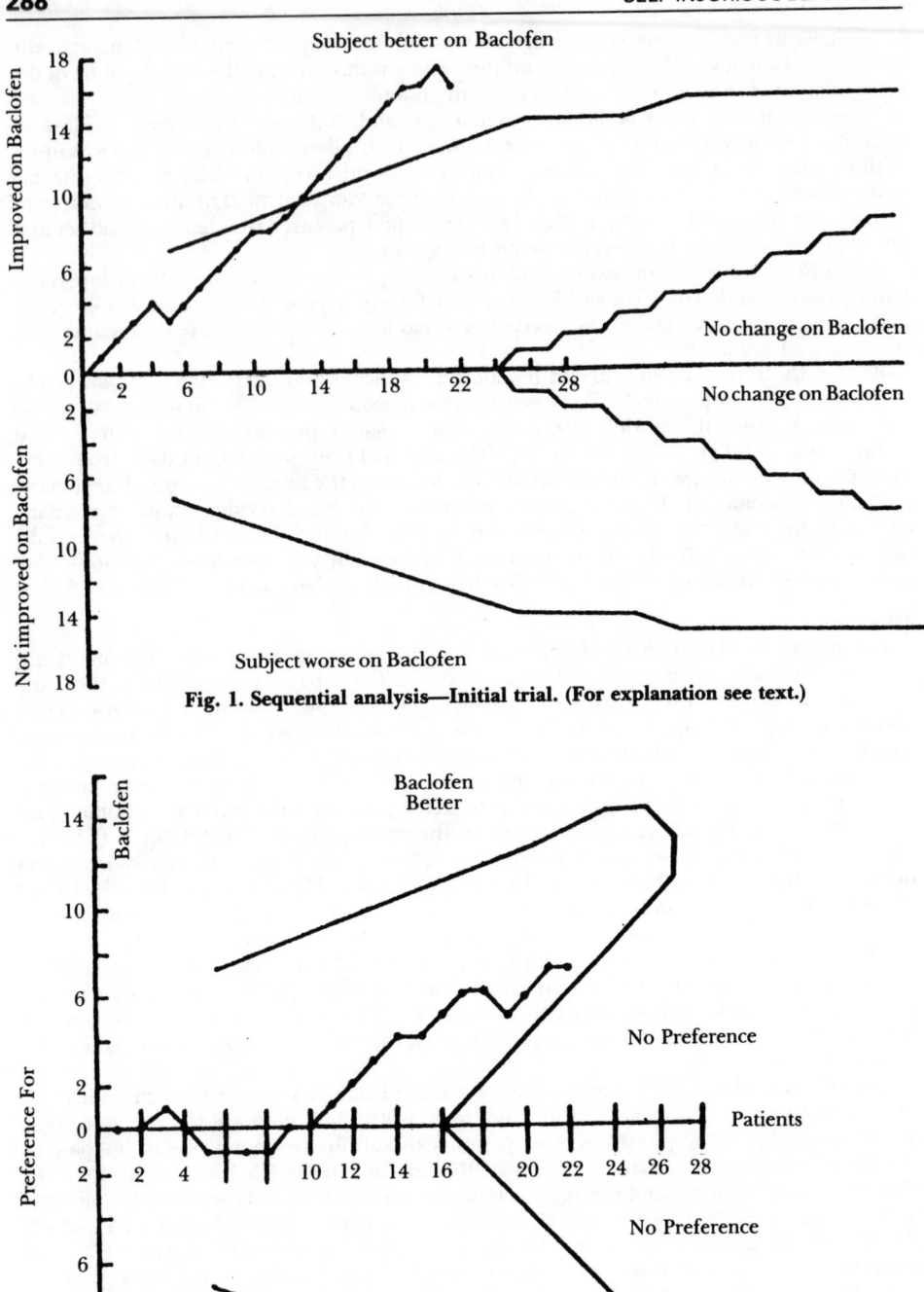

Fig. 1. Sequential analysis—Initial trial. (For explanation see text.)

Fig. 2. Sequential analysis—Cross-over trial. (For explanation see text.)

Statistical analysis of preliminary and double-blind trials

A study of this kind is difficult to analyse by the more common parametric statistical methods, partly because of the wide range of behavioural problems encountered among the severely mentally retarded, and also because of their innate inability to express valid observations. Under these circumstances it was only possible, after introducing the drug, to give a general rating as to whether the behaviour was better, the same, or worse. In the context of "worse" it was felt necessary to include those patients who showed adverse side effects. Sequential analysis is designed to compare data of this type and full details of the method are admirably summarised by Armitage (1960), and its use in blind cross-over trials has been adopted elsewhere (Sainsbury and Lucas, 1959).

In both the initial trial and the subsequent cross-over trial restricted sequential designs were adopted. For the initial trial the design of Snell and Armitage (1957) was used with $2a$ = 0.05, and this is shown in Figure 1. From this figure the conclusion can be drawn that at p = 0.05 baclofen improved behaviour, with the boundary in favour of the drug being reached at N = 14.

For the double-blind trial the design adopted was the "plan B" closed design of Bross (1952) with $2a$ = 0.098. This is shown in Figure 2 with a direct comparison between the eight weeks placebo and the eight weeks on baclofen. In Figure 2 it will be seen that the middle boundary is crossed at N = 22 which means there is now no significant difference in behaviour of the group whether on baclofen or on placebo. This confirms the clinical observations that in nine patients the improvement of behaviour continued even after removal of the drug, indicating that a form of behaviour modification had taken place.

Acknowledgements

I would like to thank the nursing staff of the Royal Scottish National Hospital for their co-operation in this trial, and also Messrs Ciba for supplying the drug and placebo tablets. Thanks are also due to Dr A. T. Rundle of St Lawrence's Hospital, Caterham, Surrey, for contributing the statistical analysis.

Permission for the above trial was obtained from the Department of Health and Social Security.

References

Armitage, P. *Sequential Medical Trials*. Oxford: Blackwell, 1960.

Bross, I. Sequential medical plans. *Biometrics*, 1952; **8**, 188.

Callingham, B. A. Current aspects of pharmacology — GABA. *Pharm. J.*, 1972; **209**, 423.

Corbett, J. Aversion for the treatment of self-injurious behaviour. *J. Ment. Defic. Res.*, 1975; **19**, 79.

Meldrum, B. S. Gamma-amino-butyric acid and the search for new anti-convulsant drugs. *Lancet*, 1978; **2**, 304.

Primrose, D. A. Self-injury in the severely defective. *Br. J. Psychiat.*, 1977; **132**, 413.

Sainsbury, P., Lucas, C. J. Sequential methods applied to the study of prochlorperazine. *Br. Med. J.*, 1959; **2**, 737.

Snell, E. S., Armitage, P. Clinical comparison of diamorphine and pholcodine as cough suppressants, by a new method of sequential analysis. *Lancet*, 1957; **1**, 860.

Van Velzen, W. J. Autoplexy or self-destructive behaviour in mental retardation: In Primrose, D. A. (Ed.) *Proc. 3rd Congr. Int. Ass. Sci. Study Ment. Defic.*, 1973; **1**, 734. Polish Medical Publishers. Also obtainable from Swets and Zeitlinger, Amsterdam.

NALOXONE AND SELF-MUTILATION

J. S. Richardson[1,3], W. A. Zaleski[2]

A 15-year-old male with a long history of self-mutilation resembling the Lesch-Nyhan syndrome, but with normal uric acid levels, was treated with naloxone. Pain-inducing behavior decreased in the evenings following infusion of the drug, and was markedly reduced for 2 days following the treatment period. Though not recommended as therapy, the observations suggest that naloxone may play a role in the regulation of endorphin/enkephalin neural systems.

Various endorphins are released in increased amounts following vigorous exercise (Bortz et al., 1981), painful stimulation (Willer et al., 1981), and other stressful situations (Dubois et al., 1981). A general neurochemical observation is that the chronic activation of neurotransmitter receptors leads to a down-regulation of the reactivity of those receptors and they become subsensitive and non-responsive to usual levels of the agonist neurotransmitter. Such alterations in endorphin receptor sensitivity may underlie the development of tolerance and addiction to opiate analgesics and may explain the persistence of such paradoxical behavioral syndromes as self-mutilation and chronic long-distance running. If pain-inducing behaviour is being reinforced by the release of endorphins onto opiate receptors, then blocking those receptors should prevent the reinforcing consequences of the behavior and allow extinction to occur. The results of a trial of the opiate antagonist naloxone in a patient with a history of self-mutilation are consistent with the involvement of endorphin receptors in the maintenance of pain-inducing behavior.

Methods

The patient was a 15-year-old male with a long-standing history of continuous and vigorous self-mutilation. Behaviorally, this patient is very similar to people with the Lesch-Nyhan syndrome but has normal blood and urine uric acid levels rather than the hyperuricemia that is characteristic of the Lesch-Nyhan syndrome. At various times over the last 10 to 12 years this patient has received numerous medications including most antipsychotics, antianxiety agents, antidepressents, sedatives, hypnotics, anticonvulsants, and other drugs such as methylphenidate. In addition, long periods of behavior modification have been tried on several occasions. None of these interventions had a beneficial effect. Constant nursing attention was required.

During the period of the naloxone trial, the patient was observed continuously and his behaviour was recorded in 15-min blocks. Naloxone, dissolved in normal saline, was given by intravenous infusion over a 6-hr period during midday on 2 successive days.

Results and discussion

The Pain-inducing Behavior Index in Table I represents the ratio of the number of blocks during which self-mutilation was attempted (serious self-harm was prevented by the nursing staff at all times) to the total number of blocks of the observation period. Compared to pre-naloxone periods, pain-inducing behavior went up during the naloxone infusion but fell dramatically during the evening after naloxone infusion. The increase in pain-inducing behavior during the naloxone administration is consistent with a naloxone-induced reduction in the reinforcement maintaining the self-mutilation and suggests that the naloxone was producing a period of nonreward. The increased frequency or magnitude of a behavior during initial periods of nonreward was described as the extinction burst by

[1]Departments of Pharmacology and Psychiatry, University of Saskatchewan College of Medicine, Saskatoon, Saskachewan, Canada.
[2]Department of Pediatrics, University of Saskatchewan College of Medicine, Sasakatoon, Saskatchewan, Canada.
[3]All correspondence should be sent to Dr. J. S. Richardson, Departments of Pharmacology and Psychiatry, University of Saskatchewan College of Medicine, Saskatoon, Saskatchewan, S7N 0W0, Canada.

Table 1

Naloxone	Pain-inducing Behavior Index		
	During naloxone	Post naloxone	
Day (mg/hr)	Midday	Evening	Night
1 0	—	0.57	0.77
2 1 mg/30 ml	0.95	0.37	0.37
3 2 mg/30 ml	1.0	0.33	0.25

Skinner (1938) and as the Frustration Effect by Amsel and Roussel (1952).

However, in the evenings after the naloxone infusion was stopped, and for several days thereafter, the frequency and severity of the self-mutilation attempts dropped to a level much below the pre-drug base line. This reduction continued for about 2 days after the second naloxone administration with nurses' comments such as "behavior much more settled today" and "no physical restraining by staff today," entered on the patient's chart. But by the 3rd day, pain-inducing behavior increased again as reflected by nurses' comments such as "kicking at leg frequently," "arm restraints applied," and "restless this shift." This pattern of behavior is consistent with a rapid (Eisenberg, 1982) antagonist-induced development of supersensitive receptors (Creese and Sibley, 1981) such that after naloxone treatment, the endorphine receptors would be responsive to lesser amounts of endorphins.

Lloyd et al. (1981) recently reported alterations in various neurotransmitter parameters in the brains of Lesch-Nyhan patients, but these authors did not investigate the endorphin/enkephalin neural systems. Our preliminary findings indicate that the functional activity of enkephalin neurons may be altered as well. Although current evidence is not sufficient to allow definite conclusions, the speculation that the paradoxical pain-inducing behavior of these patients and of long-distance runners maintains elevated endorphin/enkephalin levels thereby preventing a morphinelike withdrawal syndrome is consistent with the behavioral observations. While naloxone may not be a useful therapeutic agent, our results suggest that additional research into the role of enkephalinergic neurons in self-mutilating syndromes may prove rewarding.

References

Amsel, A., Roussel, J. Motivational properties of frustration: 1 Effect on a running response of the addition of frustration to the motivational complex. *J. Exptl. Psychol.*, 1952; **43**, 363-368.

Bortz, W. M., Angivin, P., Mefford, I. N., Boarder, M. R., Noyce, N., Barchas, J. D. Catecholamines, dopamine, and endorphin levels during extreme exercise. *New Engl. J. Med.*, 1981; **305**, 466-467.

Creese, I., Sibley, D. R. Receptor adaptations to centrally acting drugs. *Ann Rev. Pharmacol. Toxicol*, 1981; **21**, 357-391.

Dubois, M., Pickar, D., Cohen, M. R., Roth, Y. F., Macnamara, T., Bunney, W. E. Surgical stress in humans is accompanied by an increase in plasma beta-endorphin immunoreactivity. *Life Sci.*, 1981; **29**, 1249-1254.

Eisenberg, R. M. Short-term tolerance to morphine: Effects of indomethacin. *Life Sci.*, 1982, **30**, 399-405.

Lloyd, K. G., Hornykiewicz, O., Davidson, L., Shannak, K., Farley, I., Goldstein, M., Shibuya, M., Kelley, W. N., Fox, I. H. Biochemical evidence of dysfunction of brain neurotransmitters in the Lesch-Nyhan syndrome. *New Engl. J. Med.*, 1981; **305**, 1106-1111.

Skinner, B. F. *The Behavior of Organisms*. New York: Appleton-Century-Crofts, 1938.

Willer, J. C., Dehen, H., Cambier, J. Stress-induced analgesia in humans: Endogenous opiods and naloxone-reversible depression of pain reflexes. *Science*, 1981; **212**, 680-691.

Reprinted From *Biological Psychiatry*, 1983;**18**:1, 99-101 by kind permission of the publishers Plenum Publishing Corp., New York, NY 10013.

THE EFFECTS OF THE REINFORCEMENT OF COMPAT-IBLE AND INCOMPATIBLE ALTERNATIVE BEHAVIORS ON THE SELF-INJURIOUS AND RELATED BEHAVIORS OF A PROFOUNDLY RETARDED FEMALE ADULT[1]

James A. Young, John P. Wincze[2]

Dalhousie University

An attempt was made to compare the effects of the reinforcement of compatible and incompatible alternative behaviors on the self-injurious and related behaviors of a profoundly retarded female adult. This subject banged her head on the metal rails of a hospital bed and hit her head with her fists. Methodologically, the experimental procedure followed a multiple-baseline, within-subject design. The reinforcement of a physically compatible target behavior (eye contact with the experimenter) resulted in a systematic increase in this behavior but no decrease in self-injurious behaviors. The reinforcement of a physically incompatible target behavior (sitting erect with hands lowered) also resulted in its increase over baseline level. Under this condition, one class of self-injurious behavior increased in frequency while another class decreased.

The experimental data indicate that the mere presence of any particular alternative behavior (whether compatible or incompatible) that is effective in obtaining reinforcement is not sufficient in itself to reduce self-injurious behavior.

During a final phase of this study, response contingent shock was introduced. This procedure was effective in suppressing the class of self-injurious behavior to which it was applied. Self-injurious behavior which was not punished continued at baseline level.

Tate and Baroff (1966), Bucher and Lovaas (1968), Lovaas and Simons (1969) and Corte, Wolf, and Locke (1971) have suppressed self-injurious behavior in children by using response-contingent aversive stimulation. Other investigators have used a method of treatment involving the withdrawal of positive reinforcers contingent upon a self-injurious response (Hamilton, Stephens, and Allen, 1967; Tate and Baroff, 1966) while others have used the positive reinforcement of alternative behaviors (Allen & Harris, 1966; Corte et al., 1971; Lovaas, Frietag, Gold & Kassorla, 1965; Peterson & Peterson, 1968). (See Bachman's 1972 review).

In this latter procedure, alternative behaviors can be of two types: compatible and incompatible with the self-injurious response. In the strictest definition, compatible behavior may be defined as any behavior that can be physically performed simultaneously with the self-injurious behavior. Conversely, incompatible behavior is any behavior that is physically impossible to carry out while making a self-injurious response. Incompatible behavior should not be confused with behavior that, by chance, never occurs with self-injurious behavior. For example, laughing behavior may occur at a high rate in a patient's behavioral repertoire but never while making self-injurious behaviors. Laughing, however would still be considered as physically compatible. Some researchers have used DRO schedules in attempting to decrease the frequency of self-injurious behavior (Allen & Harris, 1966; Corte et al., 1971; Peterson & Peterson, 1968). In a DRO schedule, reinforcement is given for any behavior which is occurring when the self-injurious behavior

[1] This research was supported in part by Dalhousie University Grant RDF 1200-450-025 and in part by Dalhousie University Grant RDF 1200-450-029 both awarded to John P. Wincze.
[2] The authors gratefully acknowledge the invaluable help of Paul Curren who assisted in the recording of the data. The cooperation of the staff and medical director, John Tainsh, of the Abbey Lane Memorial Hospital is gratefully acknowledged. Reprint requests should be sent to John P. Wincze, Department of Psychology, Dalhousie University, Halifax, Nova Scotia, Canada.

is not occurring. Reinforcement under a DRO schedule may or may not be physically incompatible with the self-injurious behavior. Most studies which have used reinforcement to reduce the frequency of self-injurious behavior have used DRO schedules and have measured success in terms of a reduction of self-injurious behavior and have not measured increases in desirable behaviors. Only three studies in the literature have looked at the effects of reinforcement of specific desired behavior on the occurence of self-injurious behavior (Lovaas et al., 1965; Peterson & Peterson, 1968; Risley, 1968).

Lovaas et al. (1965) and Peterson and Peterson (1968) indicated that providing a subject with an alternative response that is efficient in producing positive reinforcement will produce a subsequent decrease in self-injurious behavior. In none of the research reported in the literature, however, is any indication given as to what kind of reinforced alternative behavior, if any, would be most effective in reducing self-injurious behavior. Risley (1968), using the reinforcement of incompatible alternative behavior, found no decrease in the undesirable behavior of his subject. His suggestion that the elimination of deviant behaviors may be a necessary prerequisite to the establishment of new behaviors is contradictory to the findings of Lovaas et al. (1965) and of Peterson and Peterson (1968), in that these experimenters did establish new behaviors without first eliminating self-injurious behaviors.

In attempting to reduce self-injurious behavior by reinforcing compatible alternative behaviors, it is possible that self-injurious behaviors can occur simultaneously with the alternative behavior and thus be coincidently reinforced and strengthened. Because of this possibility, it would seem to be more efficient to reinforce incompatible behaviors in attempting to reduce the occurence of self-injurious behavior. Research to date, however, has not looked at this issue. The purpose of the present experiment was to assess the effects of the positive reinforcement of compatible and incompatible behavior on the self-injurious and associative behaviors of a mentally retarded hospitalized adult.

Method
Subject

Brenda, a 21-yr-old girl, had been hospitalized continuously for 18 years and diagnosed as profoundly retarded. She was restrained in bed to prevent self-injury. After participation in a previous experiment (Wincze and Bachman, 1972), she was allowed to play without restraints for short periods on the ward. Wincze and Bachman's (1972) experiment was completed 3 wk prior to the commencement of the present study. She was neither toilet trained nor able to feed herself, and possessed no verbal language skill.

Setting and Apparatus

Brenda was observed in an experimental room located two floors below the ward. The room contained a standard hospital bed similar to the subject's own bed, a Sony black and white video camera on a tripod, a Sony microphone suspended from the ceiling, a number of wires entering the room from a wall conduit, a two-way mirror and a wire leading under the door to a footswitch in front of the experimenter's chair. Brenda was brought to and from the room in a standard hospital wheelchair. This wheelchair was stabilized in a position facing the camera and the experimenter seated 3ft directly in front of the subject. The wheelchair was placed 1 ft from the bed, allowing Brenda easily to bang her head. A waist restraint prevented her from leaving the wheelchair.

An observation-control room, located beside the experimental room, contained all the electromechanical relay equipment used to record data plus a Sony video recorder and monitor (model AV 3600) which permitted an assistant to view the subject and record behavior. The data recording apparatus included an Esterline-Angus 10-pen event recorder, a Lafayette data recorder, two Lafayette 100-sec timers, and a Lafayette predetermining counter.

A remote-controlled shock-delivery system (Lehigh Valley Electronics, no 551-13) was used to deliver electric shocks to the subject. This system consisted of two units; a battery-powered transmitter and a lightweight, battery-powered receiver/shocker. This was activated by an external source through input jacks in a manner such that when a head-to-rail response was recorded a shock could be delivered automatically if so desired. The transmitter at this time emitted a specific, high-frequency radio signal that was detectable by the receiver/shocker unit up to 1000 yd away. The shocker generated a fixed-intensity stream of shock pulses at a rate of 15-20 pulses/sec for the 0.5 sec duration that the transmitter was activated. The 700-V output of the shocker produced pain but no physical injury.

Procedure

A multiple baseline experimental design was used to evaluate the effects of the reinforcement of compatible and incompatible target behaviors on the self-injurious and associated responses of the subject. Because of the undesirable effects of the reinforcement of incompatible behavior in phase 4 (i.e., high rates of head-to-rail; see Fig. 1), two additional phases employing contingent shock were added to suppress unwanted high rates of head banging and to satisfy ethical therapeutic commitments.

All sessions in the first four phases of the study were 15 min in length, but in contingent shock phases (5 and 6) sessions were reduced to 10 min to decrease any unnecessary stress caused by shock. All sessions of the experiment were conducted at 1600 hr, 3½ hr after Brenda's lunch to insure approximately the same moderate state of hunger (deprivation) throughout the experiment.

The design included the following phases:

Phase 1: Baseline. Baseline observation sessions were conducted to determine the rate of occurrence of the subject's self-injurious and associated behaviors. This phase was carried out for 6 days, at which time the experimenters were confident that eye contact, the first behavior to which contingencies were applied, was stable. Since this was a multiple baseline experimental design, all other behaviors were observed for longer periods of time before contingencies were applied.

During the baseline phase the experimenter, present in the experimental room, sat motionless and said nothing.

Phase 2: Reinforcement of compatible behavior (eye contact). In the second phase the subject was reinforced with a small amount of ice cream on a spoon, and praise, contingent upon 1.0 sec of eye contact after the experimenter's verbal command "look at me." This verbal command was given every 5 sec or, when reinforced, 5 sec after the subject received her ice cream. After a correct response the experimenter immediately fed the subject and said "Good, Brenda." The experimenter, after reinforcing the subject, put more ice cream on the spoon and, while giving the verbal command, at first held the ice cream up to his eyes in order to prompt the subject's eye contact. Gradually, with more correct trials, the experimenter progressively lowered the spoon away from the direct line of eye contact and eventually kept the ice cream hidden behind his hand. Reinforcement was contingent only upon eye contact and thus, being compatible, Brenda could be reinforced while performing any other simultaneous behavior such as head-to-rail or fist-to-head responses.

Phase 3: Baseline. The third phase consisted of baseline recovery sessions. During this phase, ice cream was no longer available to the subject for eye contact behavior. It was felt that a return to the original baseline conditions was necessary at this time to demonstrate clearly the effectiveness of reinforcement. Since sitting erect with hands-on-chair might facilitate eye contact, a further increase in eye contact might have been observed when reinforcement was applied to hands-on-chair. If this increase in eye contact occurred, it would have obscured the reinforcement effect in phase two.

Phase 4: Reinforcement of incompatible behavior (hands-on-chair). Phase 4 employed ice cream and praise reinforcement contingent on the previously defined hands-on-chair behavior. This phase began with three sessions of prompting the subject. Brenda's hands were held on the wheels of the chair for 3 sec by the experimenter and then, while still holding one hand down (preventing head-to-rail responses), the experimenter reinforced her.

After three prompting sessions, hands-on-chair was required in a free-operant situation. No verbal command was given and the subject was never reinforced while making a self-injurious response. A 5-sec time-out was inserted after each head-to-rail, or fist-to-head response in an attempt to hinder any superstitious chaining of self-injurious behavior. No ice cream was visible to Brenda during this time-out period, or any other time, unless the target behavior occurred.

Phase 5: Contingent punishment. In the fifth phase, the subject received a half-second electric shock, delivered through the receiver/shocker strapped to her right calf, contingent upon any head-to-rail responses made during the experimental sessions. The risk of extremely high rates of head-to-rail banging, and hence possible serious physical injury, precluded the introduction of a baseline phase after phase 4. (The number of head-to-rail bangs in phase 4 systematically increased from 23 in Session 25 to a peak of 126 bangs in Session 33). Therapeutic commitments also made it necessary to introduce response-contingent shock. The experimenter did not interact with Brenda in any way during this phase and no ice cream was given for hands-on-chair behavior.

Phase 6: Contingent punishment and reinforcement of incompatible behavior (hands-on-chair). The sixth phase consisted of ice cream and praise reinforcement contingent on the target behavior of hands-on-chair, and contingent shock for each head-to-rail response. The procedure in this phase was exactly the same as that used in the last six sessions of Phase 4 (reinforcement of incompatible behavior in a free-operant situation).

Recording procedures

An observer, in the control room, equipped with push buttons that activated an event recorder recorded all responses except eye contact. The television system was used in the control room by this observer to monitor all of the sessions and to record about 25% of them. Since the eye-contact response required eye contact with the experimenter in the experimental room, only he could accurately monitor this response. The experimenter was equipped with a foot push button which also activated the event recorder.

Prior to phase 4, the measurement of hands-on-chair behavior was recorded from available video tape records to yield seven baseline points.

Definition of the responses

A head-to-rail bang was defined as any forceful contact of less than 1-sec duration made between Brenda's head and the rail of the bed or back handle of the wheelchair.

A fist-to-head bang was defined as any contact made between either of the subject's closed fists and her head for a duration of less than 1-sec. The frequency of this response was measured.

Eye contact was defined as fixation of the subject's eyes on the experimenter's eyes for a duration of more than 1.0 sec. That is, a glance or a mere scanning of the room in the experimenter's direction was not considered as an instance of eye contact. Eye contact was selected as a compatible target behavior because it could be maintained while the subject performed other behaviors.

Crying was defined as any outburst of the subject's high pitched scream or crying that lasted for more than 1.0 sec. The duration of this response was recorded.

Hands-in-pants was defined as either of the subject's hands being inside her leotards, under her diaper, for more than one second. The duration of this response was important because little or no self-injurious behavior occurred concomitantly.

Hands-on-chair was a target behavior that was defined as the subject sitting erect with her hands either on the arms of the wheelchair, the side of the chair, or on her lap for a duration of at least 1.0 sec. (This did not include any "fidgeting behavior" such as tugging at her waist restraint or ripping buttons from her blouse). Hands-on-chair behavior was, therefore, incompatible with self-injurious behavior.

Reliability measurements

About 25% of the experimental sessions were recorded on video tape. An independent naive observer was asked at the conclusion of the experiment to monitor the taped sessions and to record by the same procedure the responses that had been recorded previously by the control room observer. The independent observer's records were compared with the records obtained during the experiment proper. For behaviors measured by frequency count, reliability was calculated by totalling the number of agreements between the two sets of recorded occurrences of the behavior, multiplying this by two, and dividing the sum by the total number of recorded occurrences of the behavior for both observers. Thus, the denominator contained all recorded occurrences of the behavior whether there was agreement or disagreement between the two judges. For behaviors measured by duration, reliability was calculated by totalling the number of seconds of agreement between the two sets of data, multiplying this by two, and dividing the sum by the total number of seconds of recorded occurrences of the behavior for both observers.

Results

The mean number of self-injurious responses per minute for each session of each phase is presented in Fig. 1. The mean duration of desirable target behaviors (eye contact and

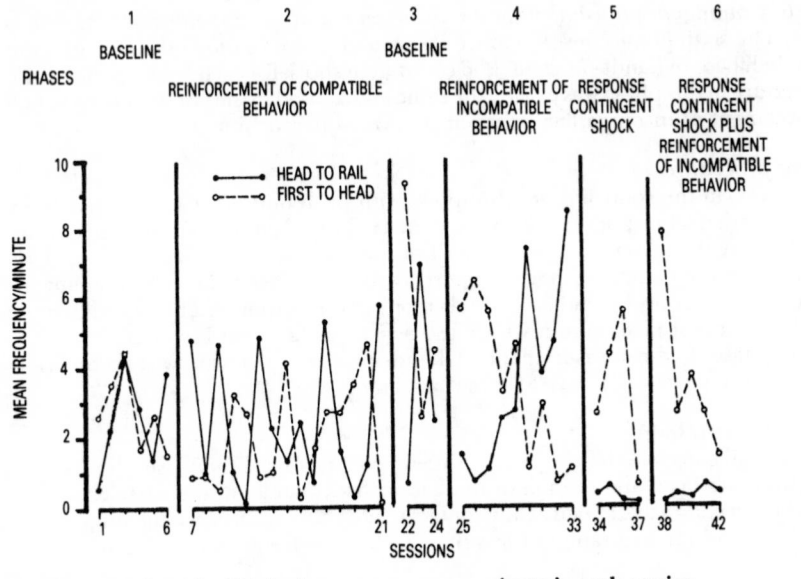

Fig. 1. **Mean number of self-injurious responses per minute in each session.**

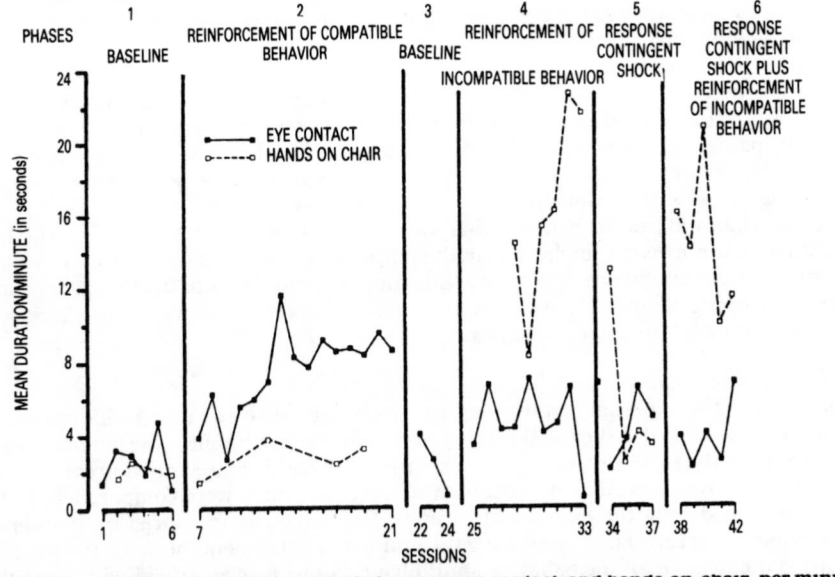

Fig. 2. **Mean duration of desirable target behaviors, eye contact, and hands-on-chair, per minute (in seconds) for each session. Data points for hands-on-chair behavior are not reported for sessions 25, 26, and 27 because this response was being shaped during these sessions.**

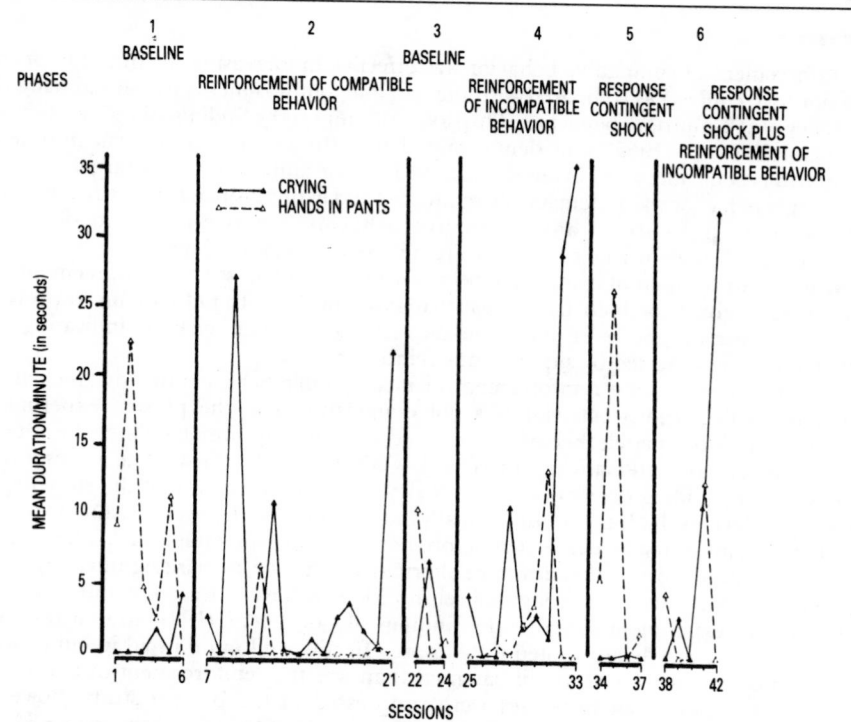

Fig. 3. Mean duration of non-self-injurious undesirable behaviors, crying and hands-in-pants, per minute (in seconds) for each session.

hands-on-chair) per minute for each session of each phase is shown in Fig. 2, and Fig. 3 presents the mean duration of crying and hands-in-pants for each session of each phase.

When eye contact was reinforced, it increased about 200% over baseline, but then returned to its baseline rate when reinforcement was withdrawn in phase 3. Neither class of self-injurious behavior nor any associated behaviours showed any systematic changes in frequency as eye contact increased. Hands-in-pants continued to decrease during phase 2 following a decreasing trend observed in phase 1.

In phase 4 hands-on-chair was reinforced and increased more than 600% over its previous baseline rate. As hands-on-chair behaviour increased, one class of self-injurious behavior, fist-to-head, decreased in frequency while another class, head-to-rail, increased. Crying, which correlated positively with head-to-rail banging also increased in phase 4 while eye contact remained at baseline level.

With the introduction of contingent shock for head-to-rail responses in phase 5, head-to-rail responses decreased steadily. Crying also decreased steadily during this phase while fist-to-head responding showed no specific trend and fluctuated at its previous baseline level. Hands-on-chair was no longer reinforced in this phase and decreased to its former rate of occurrence.

In phase 6 contingent shock for head-to-rail responses and the reintroduction of reinforcement for the hands-on-chair behavior, resulted in a continued low level of head-to-rail responses and an increase in the duration of hands-on-chair behavior. Fist-to-head responding decreased steadily throughout this phase and eye contact remained stable at baseline level. Crying increased throughout this final phase.

Reliability measurements. The percentage agreement between the experimenter's original observations of the subject's behavior and the independent observer's observations was calculated. There was 98% agreement for fist-to-head banging, 95% agreement for hands-on-chair behavior, 90% agreement for crying, and 99% agreement for hands-in-pants behavior.

Discussion

Reinforcement of compatible behavior was effective in increasing the duration of that behavior (eye contact) as compared with the baseline, but was ineffective in reducing the frequency of self-injurious behaviors. This does not support the findings of Lovaas, Freitag, Gold, and Kassorla (1965) who demonstrated that the occurrence and magnitude of self-injurious behavior varied inversely with the increase and decrease of a target behavior as the target behavior was systematically reinforced and extinguished. Present data indicate that the mere presence of any alternative behavior that is effective in obtaining reinforcement is not sufficient in itself to reduce self-injurious behavior.

During reinforcement of compatible behavior in the present study, reinforcement was coincidentally given for both fist-to-head banging and head-to-rail banging on several occasions. There was, however, no systematic increase in either behavior, indicating that neither was being affected by superstitious reinforcement.

The effectiveness of the reinforcement of incompatible behavior (hands-on-chair) in eliminating self-injurious behavior was not demonstrated in the present experiment. Although this incompatible behavior increased significantly over baseline, the rate of head-to-rail bangs systematically increased while the rate of fist-to-head responses decreased. This finding does not support Risley's (1968) statement that the stereotyped behaviors of deviant children are "functionally incompatible" with the establishment of new behaviors and must first be eliminated before new behaviors are established. The present results are contradictory in that desirable alternative behavior increase significantly when contingently reinforced even though all self-injurious behaviors were not eliminated.

The present experiment supports the findings of Corte et al. (1971) in that response contingent shock was demonstrated to be more effective and more rapid in eliminating self-injurious behavior (head-to-rail banging) than was the reinforcement of alternative behaviors. As head-to-rail responses were suppressed in the present study, however, fist-to-head responses increased in frequency (cf sessions 20, 31, 32, 33, with sessions 34, 35, 36). This finding may be one example of symptom substitution as predicted by a behavioral model. Dunham (1971) predicted that the punishment of a more probable response in an organism's behavioral repertoire, and thus its suppression, would produce an increase in the rates of less probable responses. The present results, and those of Wincze and Bachman (1972) support this prediction.

Future research should focus on discovering what kind of alternative behaviors are optimum in interfering with self-injurious behavior. This experiment attempted to explore the compatible-incompatible distinction but other factors may be important. For example, Green (1967) postulated that self-mutilation and self-injury may serve to increase sensory input in unstimulating environments. Thus, it might be more worthwhile to reinforce a target behavior that requires a self-injurious subject to "perform" some action and increase sensory input and relieve boredom.

References
Allen, K. E., Harris, F. R. Elimination of a child's excessive scratching by training the mother in reinforcement procedures. *Behav. Res. & Ther.*, 1966; **4**, 79-84.
Bachman, J. A. Self-injurious behavior: a behavioral analysis. *J. Abnorm. Psychol.*, 1972; **80**, 211-224.
Bucher, B., Lovaas, O. I. Use of aversive stimulation in behavior modification. In Jones, M. (Ed.). *Miami symposium on the prediction of behavior, 1967: Aversive stimulation*. (pp77-145). Coral Gables, Florida: Univerisy of Miami Press, 1968.
Corte, H. E., Wolf, M. M., Locke, B. J. A comparison of procedures for eliminating self-injurious behavior of retarded adolescents. *J. Appl. Behav. Anal.*, 1971; **4**, 201-213.
Dunham, P. J. Punishment: method and theory. *Psychol. Rev.*, 1971; **78**, 58-70.
Green, A. H. Self-mutilation in schizophrenic children. *Arch. Gen. Psychiat.*, 1967; **17**, 234-244.
Hamilton, J., Stephens, L., Allen, P. Controlling aggressive and destructive behavior in severely retarded institutionalised residents. *Am. J. Ment. Defic.*, 1967; **71**, 852-856.
Lovaas, O. I., Freitag, G., Gold, V. J., Kassorla, T. Experimental studies in childhood schizophrenia: analysis of self-destructive behavior. *J. Experi. Child Psychol.*, 1965; **2**, 67-84.
Lovaas, O. I., Simmons, J. Q. Manipulation of self-destruction in three retarded children. *J. Appl. Behav. Anal.*, 1969; **2**, 143-157.

Peterson, R., Peterson, L. The use of positive reinforcement in the control of self-destructive behavior in a retarded boy. *J. Experi. Child Psychol.*, 1968; **6**, 351-360.

Risley, T. R. The effects and side effects of punishing the autistic behaviors of a deviant child. *J. Appl. Behav. Anal.*, 1968; **1**, 21-34.

Tate, B. G., Baroff, G. S. Aversive control of self-injurious behavior in a psychotic boy. *Behav. Res. & Ther.*, 1966; **4**, 281-287.

Wincze, J. P., Bachman, J. *The effects of contingent and noncontingent electric shock punishment on self-injurious and associated behaviors.* (Unpublished manuscript). Dalhousie University, 1972.

Reprinted from *Behavior Therapy*, 1974; **5**, 614-623 by kind permission of the publishers Association for Advancement of Behavior Therapy, New York, NY 10170.

A COMPARISON OF TECHNIQUES FOR THE ELIMINATION OF SELF-INJURIOUS BEHAVIOR IN A MILDLY RETARDED WOMAN*

Arthur Fleming, David Nolley

Oakdale Regional Center for Developmental Disabilities, Lapeer, Michigan

Summary
The self-injurious behavior of an institutionalized, highly social, highly verbal, mildly retarded woman was successfully treated through the use of boxing glove restraints over a 30-week period after unsuccessful, less-intrusive means were attempted. Application of the restraint was conditioned to be an (S-delta), contrasted with an expanding Differential Reinforcement of Incompatible behavior (DRI) during periods of restraint removal. Absence of self-injury was maintained at 18 month follow-up by which time she had been discharged to a community placement.

Most reports of the incidence and treatment of self-injurious behavior (SIB) have described the behavior in severely autistic or quite disturbed schizophrenic or severely or profoundly retarded children (Green, 1967; Shodell & Reiter, 1968; Bartak and Rutter, 1976; Baumeister and Rollings, 1976; Schroeder et al., 1978). In contrast, clinical case studies of self-injury in more intellectually capable clientele generally take the form of psychiatric treatment of attempted suicide (e.g. Menninger, 1938), although there have been exceptions (Roback et al., 1972; Stabler and Warren, 1974). This clinical case study is unique in reporting successful results of treating severe SIB in a highly social, highly verbal, mildly retarded woman, using clinical behavior therapeutic treatments implemented by direct-care staff in a state institution.

Subject
Lorne, a 47 yr old mildly mentally retarded woman (Wechsler Full-Scale Adult IQ = 51), was returned to the institution due to SIB after 3 years in an otherwise successful community placement. The SIB was described as "continual scratching and picking at her skin" which, according to the dermatologist, had resulted in "multiple excoriations of the face, arms and legs". He also reported that she had ". . . multiple punched out excoriated ulcers scattered all over her body". The dependent variable chosen for study and treatment was any occasion when Lorne's fingertips were touching any part of her body. Reliable data on the severity of the behavior was elusive because Lorne continued to pick her skin even when she was alone using the bathroom and when she was supposedly sleeping. Therefore her bed was moved out to a lighted area under the direct observation of staff during the night. No formal measures of reliability were taken. Keeping a count of new lesions was found not to represent reliably the severity of the behavior as Lorne often chose to enlarge lesions she had already made. Physical examinations and laboratory tests had ruled out parasites, skin disease, renal disease, diabetes, carcinomatosis and hormonal inbalance. Psychiatric evaluation had ruled out psychotic depression. She also received unsuccessful treatment with Tofranil on the hypothesis that she suffered from neurotic depression. After 17 months of unsuccessful treatment by various means (see below) she was proposed by the psychiatrist for treatment of the SIB by means of contingent electric shock, because of severe anemia which had resulted from the SIB. A less intrusive treatment, viewed to be the last step before proposing contingent shock, was then implemented.

*A preliminary version of this paper was presented at the meeting of the Association of Advancement of Behavior Therapy, San Francisco, California, December, 1979.
Requests for reprints should be addressed to Arthur Fleming, M.S.W., Oakdale Regional Center for Developmental Disabilities, Lapeer, Michigan 48446. David Nolley is now at Metropolitan Regional Recipient Rights Office, State of Michigan Plaza, Detroit, Michigan.

Procedures and results

Treatment Five was to be the last attempt at treatment before approval could be sought for use of contingent electric shock. Prior to the implementation of Treatment Five, four different treatment techniques were attempted and shown not completely to suppress the behavior. Each treatment was approved by an interdisciplinary team and her guardian, and the facility's aversive techniques committee (similar to a Human Rights Committee) which had been constituted in time to review and approve the last four treatments.

Treatment One consisted of a typical institutional control technique, contingent mechanical restraint, but used concurrently with a program of omission training utilizing Differential Reinforcement of Other Behavior (DRO) on a 30-min schedule of social reinforcement. Although a 60% reduction in frequency (from 8.5/day during the first month to 3.3/day during the last month of treatment) was realized, as shown in Fig. 1, the severity of the behavior continued and gross excoriations were still present.

Therefore, after 34 weeks without complete suppression, a shift was made to Treatment Two, a program of Differential Reinforcement of Incompatible behavior (DRI). This program used virtually continuous social reinforcement in the form of praise, and polite one-to-one conversation was provided for fine motor activities geared to hand tasks such as embroidery, needle-point, writing, puzzles, etc. and this was combined with contingent restraint. Treatment over 19 weeks resulted in a frequency of 2.6/day over the last 3 weeks, which was still regarded to be insufficient suppression because excoriations continued to occur.

Treatment Three consisted of a verbal request to stop at the first observed occurrence of the SIB. If the SIB did not immediately cease, then a camisole jacket was applied for 15 min. Concurrently, a form of overcorrection was tried in which Lorne was required to prepare and apply her own dressings and to cover and treat her wounds twice daily. After nine weeks, the frequency of SIB had escalated to 12.3/day and the treatment was therefore terminated.

Treatment Four was DRO on a 60-min schedule using social reinforcement concurrent with contingent restraint for the first exhibition of SIB, daily fingernail trimming, and the application of vaseline to her fingernails and fingertips in the hope of reducing friction caused by rubbing and/or digging. After 12 weeks the resulting frequency was 7.0/day including 1 week of complete suppression. Between the seventh and eighth week of this treatment in her living unit Lorne spent almost two months in the institution's hospital in 24 hr restraints in the hope that all her wounds would be allowed to heal, thus allowing fewer discriminative stimuli for SIB. Upon discharge from the institution's hospital, rates decreased to 0.0/day in the ninth week. From the ninth to the twelfth week, however, rates soared again to 7.0/day.

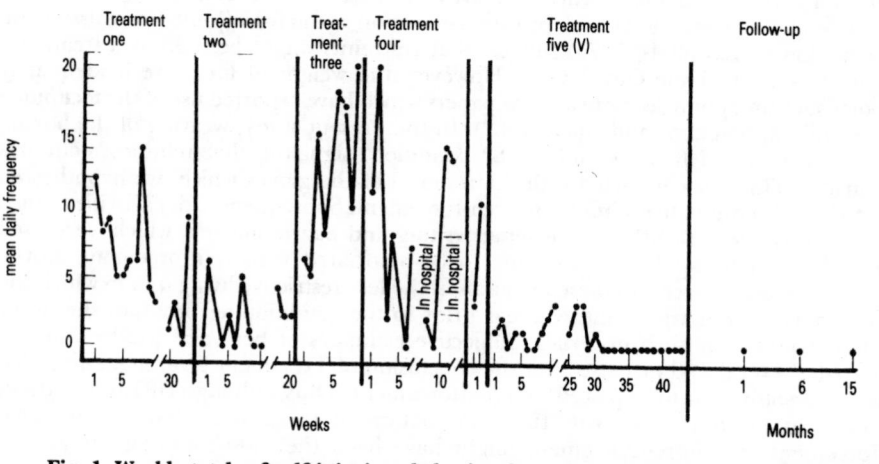

Fig. 1. **Weekly totals of self-injurious behavior throughout the five phases of treatment.**

An additional hospitalization followed for a period of 33 days for the same reasons cited above. Then, a reversal to Treatment One: the use of contingent restraint for the first incident of SIB concurrent with omission training on a thirty minute schedule was reinstated on her living unit while approval was sought for the use of Treatment Five. At no time could a no-treatment baseline or reversal be conducted, since Michigan state law specifically provides that self or other injurious behavior *must* receive intervention.

Treatment Five consisted of the application of 24-hr boxing glove restraints in order to control SIB. For 15 min every 2 hr (8 times per day) a resident care aid (institution worker) engaged Lorne in fine motor activities on a continuous schedule of social reinforcement for appropriate use of hands (DRI). After the 15 min had elapsed, the boxing gloves were reapplied. For the 105 min between sessions, all of Lorne's behavior was placed on extinction whether the behavior was appropriate or not. If she tried to engage in appropriate vocal behavior while wearing the boxing gloves, for example, she was ignored. All other behaviors emitted while wearing boxing gloves were ignored with the intent that wearing the boxing gloves should become a stimulus signaling non-exclusionary time-out (Foxx and Shapiro, 1978). If SIB occurred during the 15 min DRI session, manual restraint was applied for the duration of the session and subsequently the boxing gloves were applied. Criteria were established for the expansion of the DRI sessions based upon a maximum of SIB incidents per day, averaged over the week. When Lorne met the first criterion (no more than an average of three SIB incidents daily over one week, while out of restraints), the DRI sessions were expanded to 20 min out of restraints. When she met the second criterion (no more than an average of two SIB incidents daily over 1 week), the sessions were expanded to 30 min of DRI. When the third criterion was met (no more than an average of one SIB incident daily over one week), the sessions were expanded to 45 min, divided into a 30 min DRI and 15 min of supervised free time in order to reacquaint her with the more typical density of DRO existing in her program unit. When the fourth criterion was met (no more than three SIB incidents in an entire week), the sessions were expanded to 60 min, divided into a 30 min DRI and 30 min of supervised free time. As shown in Fig. 1, complete suppression of SIB was attained by the thirtieth week of treatment and was subsequently maintained in the least restrictive living unit at the facility, without the benefit of a specified intervention program for SIB. One, six and fifteen month follow-ups in the less-restrictive environment found Lorne without incidents of SIB. An 18 month follow-up (in a community placement) found Lorne without SIB.

Discussion

Mechanical restraints such as leather cuffs, camisole jackets, and wrist ties are ordinarily conceived to be means only of controlling behavior, infrequently with treatment implications. Use of such means are ordinarily associated with treatment failure. Federal law (Federal Register, 1974) and private association standards (Joint Commission on Accreditation of Hospitals, 1975) suggest that restraints might be used as a treatment technique — as a "Time Out device". However, the weight of literature inadequately supports such an option, as there are few papers which have reported use of the technique (e.g. Hamilton, Stephens and Allen, 1967). In the present study, wearing of the boxing gloves was intended to constitute an S^Δ condition, signaling that reinforcement was unavailable. This was contrasted with the removal of the gloves which, we hypothesize, came to be a discriminative stimulus for reinforcement. Subsequently, the activities which were incompatible with SIB such as letter writing and puzzle making, which were used during the expanding DRI, also came to be associated with reinforcement. Lorne frequently asked for access to these materials in the less-restrictive living unit to which she was transferred after treatment, whereas prior to the conditioning program she never initiated requests for such materials. Subjective estimates of her vocal production also suggested a several-fold increase after the conclusion of Treatment Five, suggesting that conversation also came to be paired with reinforcement. Thus, although DRI and restraint had been attempted previously, the combination of the two procedures to signal reinforcement or non-reinforcement might have been the most important treatment variable. At the least, prior experience with restraint and DRI might have contributed to the success seen during Treatment Five, as a result of "Carry-over" or sequence effects. In this case, successful treatment results were sought at the expense of research results which a reversal after Treatment Five might have yielded.

Alternatively, the literature suggests that mechanical restraints have been used to control SIB between therapy sessions and that they, over time, as therapy progressed toward success, could be faded out (Bucher and Lovaas, 1968; Corte, Wolfe and Locke, 1971; Lovaas and Simmons, 1969; Tate, 1972; Tate and Baroff, 1966; Thomas and Howard, 1971; Yeakel *et al.*, 1970). This study possibly evaluated an extension of that literature to a client unique in terms of intellectual capability. This study was also unique since the essentially behavioral technique used was implemented entirely by relatively untrained workers in a state institution.

As the various regulations and standards suggest, and this study confirmed, mechanical restraints can have a role in remediating severe behavior disorders *if* they are employed within an overall treatment program. Even in poorly staffed state institutions where professional staffing levels are also thin, treatment through the use of restraints can occur if it is simple, measurable, and as easy to follow as this program was.

References

Bartak, L., Rutter, M. Differences between mentally retarded and normally intelligent autistic children. *J. Aut. & Child. Schiz.*, 1976; **6**, 109-120.

Baumeister, A. A., Rollings, J. P. Self-injurious behavior. *In* Ellis, N. R. (Ed.). *International Review of Research in Mental Retardation*. New York: Academic Press, 1976.

Bucher, B., Lovaas, O. I. Use of aversive stimulation in behavior modification. *In* Jones, M. R. (Ed.). *Miami Symposium on the Prediction of Behavior*. Coral Gabels, Fla: University of Miami, 1967.

Corte, H. D., Wolf, M. M., Locke, B. J. A comparison of procedures for eliminating self-injurious behavior of retarded adolescents. *J. Appl. Behav. Anal.*, 1971; **4**, 201-213.

Federal register Department of Health, Education & Welfare, Thursday, 17 January 1974; **39**: 12, Part II. Medical Assistance Program, Intermediate Care Facility Service.

Foxx, R. M., Shapiro, S. T. The timeout ribbon: a non-exclusionary timeout procedure. *J. Appl. Behav. Anal.*, 1978; **11**, 125-136.

Green, A. Self-mutilation in schizophrenic children. *Arch. Gen. Psychiat.*, 1967; **17**, 234-244.

Hamilton, J., Stephens, L., Allen, P. Controlling aggressive and destructive behavior in severely retarded institutionalized residents. *Am. J. Ment. Defic.*, 1967; **71**, 852-856.

Joint Commission on Accreditation of Hospitals. *Standards for Residential Facilities for the Mentally Retarded*. 5th printing, 1975.

Lovaas, O. I., Simmons, J. Q. Manipulation of self-destruction in three retarded children. *J. Appl. Behav. Anal.*, 1969; **2**, 143-157.

Menninger, K. *Man Against Himself*. New York: Harcourt, 1938.

Roback, H., Frayn, D., Gunby, L., Tuters, K. A multifactorial approach to the treatment and ward management of a self-mutilating patient. *J. Behav. Ther. & Exp. Psychiat.*, 1972; **3**, 189-193.

Schroeder, S. R., Schroeder, C. S., Smith, B., Dalldorf, J. Prevalence of self-injurious behaviors in a large state facility for the retarded: a three-year follow-up study. *J. Aut. & Child. Schiz.*, 1978; **8**, 261-269.

Shodell, M., Reiter, H. Self-mutilative behavior in verbal and non-verbal schizophrenic children. *Arch. Gen. Psychiat.*, 1968; **19**, 453-455.

Stabler, B., Warren, A. B. Behavioral contracting in treating Trichotillomania: case note. *Psychol. Rep.*, 1974; **34**, 401-402.

Tate, B. G. Case study: Control of chronic self-injurious behavior by conditioning procedures. *Behav. Ther.*, 1972; **3**, 72-83.

Tate, B. G., Baroff, G. S. Aversive control of self-injurious behavior in a psychotic boy. *Behav. Res. & Ther.*, 1966; **4**, 281-287.

Thomas, R. L., Howard, G. A. A treatment program for a self-destructive child. *Ment. Retard.*, 1971; **9**, 16-18.

Yeakel, M. H., Salisbury, L. L., Greer, S. L., Marcus, L. F. An appliance for autoinduced adverse control of self-injurious behavior. *J. Exp. Child Psychol.*, 1970; **10**, 159-169.

Reprinted from *J. Behav. Ther. & Exp. Psychiat.*, 1981; **12**, 81-85 by kind permission of the authors and the publishers Pergamon Press Ltd., Oxford OX3 0BN.

THE USE OF RELAXATION IN THE TREATMENT OF SELF-INJURIOUS BEHAVIOR

P. L. Steen, G. E. Zuriff

Wheaton College

Summary
A severely self-injurious, profoundly retarded woman was taught to relax her hands and arms while still in full restraints. As relaxation was gradually learned, the restraints were gradually removed. By the end of training the subject had learned to relax when released from restraints with virtually no self-injurious behavior occurring throughout the training.

Methods developed to eliminate self-injurious behavior include the reinforcement of alternate behaviors (Lovaas *et al.*, 1965), time-out (Meyers and Deibert, 1971), extinction (Lovaas and Simmons, 1969), punishment (Tate and Baroff, 1966), and the "educative procedures" of Azrin *et al.*, (1975). A major problem with these methods is that self-injurious behavior occurs during treatment, especially during the time immediately following release from restraints. This study tested a technique to minimize self-injurious behavior during a brief period when restraints are removed so that appropriate behavior can be learned. Because relaxation (Jacobson, 1938; Bruno, 1975) is an incompatible response that can be conditioned while the patient is still in restraints, treatment can occur without self-injurious behavior.

Case history
A twenty-one-year-old non-verbal, profoundly retarded, female resident of the Wrentham State School emitted self-injurious behavior including finger biting and scratching of the legs, face and scalp. For three years prior to treatment she was kept in full restraints, with ankles and wrists tied to the bed.

Method
Reinforcement consisted of candies, verbal praise, and physical contact. Dependent variables were the rates of scratches and bites. For an initial baseline, the subject was released from all restraints for five minutes while on her bed, and response frequencies were recorded. Because of the severity of the self-injurious behavior, only one baseline session was possible.

Following preliminary shaping of eye contact, relaxation training was begun on the subject's right hand while she was in full restraints. The experimenter placed her index finger in the subject's palm and directed "Tighten up!" while simultaneously reaching her other hand around the subject's fingers and wrapping them around the index finger. The subject's fingers were held in place by the experimenter's thumb. The experimenter then gave the direction "Relax!", unwrapped the subject's fingers, and massaged the subject's hand until it was limp enough for the experimenter's finger to be rolled off the subject's fingers without applying any pressure. The subject was reinforced for each correct trial in a ten-trial session. Manual guidance was gradually faded out until only slight touches to the backs or tips of the fingers were needed.

In the eleventh session, the right arm was released from restraints. The experimenter placed her finger in the subject's right hand and directed "Tighten up!". As the subject tightened, the experimenter raised her own arm to above the subject's shoulder, moved it back and forth, and applied a slight pressure downward. If the subject had grasped the

---

*This report is based on a B.A. thesis by the first author submitted to the faculty of Wheaton College in partial fulfillment of the requirements for Honors in Psychology. Requests for reprints should be addressed to G. E. Zuriff, Wheaton College, Norton, Mass. 02766, U.S.A.

finger tightly enough to hold it as it was brought up and offered resistance to the experimenter's pressure, she was reinforced.

Then the subject was directed "Relax!". The experimenter relaxed her own arm, giving a slight push so that the subject's arm would flop to its original position with her hand slightly below her shoulder level. If she successfully dropped her arm and the experimenter was able to roll her finger off the subject's fingers, the subject was reinforced.

By the twenty-first session the subject had learned to relax the right arm, and the procedure was repeated on the left arm with the right arm unrestrained. Beginning with session 79, the subject learned to relax both arms simultaneously from a sitting position. The technique was similar to that in the lying position except that when tightening, the subject brought her arms over her head.

The inhibitory strength of the relaxation response was assessed at various stages by occasional probes which began with two reinforced trials of relaxation. Then the subject was released from restraints whether or not she had reached the point of being released from restraints during relaxation training sessions. Self-injurious behavior was then recorded for five minutes. Because of the danger of self-injurious behavior, probes were carried out infrequently at first, but nearly daily later.

After 115 relaxation training sessions, self-injurious behavior during probes was virtually eliminated, and it was possible to release the subject safely. However, all new teaching of appropriate behavior was delayed several weeks for a follow-up assessment of the effects of the relaxation training alone. During five follow-up probes, the subject was left unrestrained and given directions and prompts to relax, but no reinforcements, while self-injurious behavior was recorded for 5 min.

Results and discussion

By termination, the subject had learned to relax both arms and hands while in a sitting position. During the trials of the 115 relaxation training sessions, no scratches and only seven bites occurred. The results of the probes are presented in Fig. 1 showing the number of scratches and bites during 5-min recording periods. Starting with an initial baseline of 9, the frequency of scratching gradually declined until the sixth probe when scratching was eliminated. From a baseline of 117 bites, the frequency of biting declined by the 19th probe to a stable zero rate. Compared to scratching, biting began at a far higher rate of response,

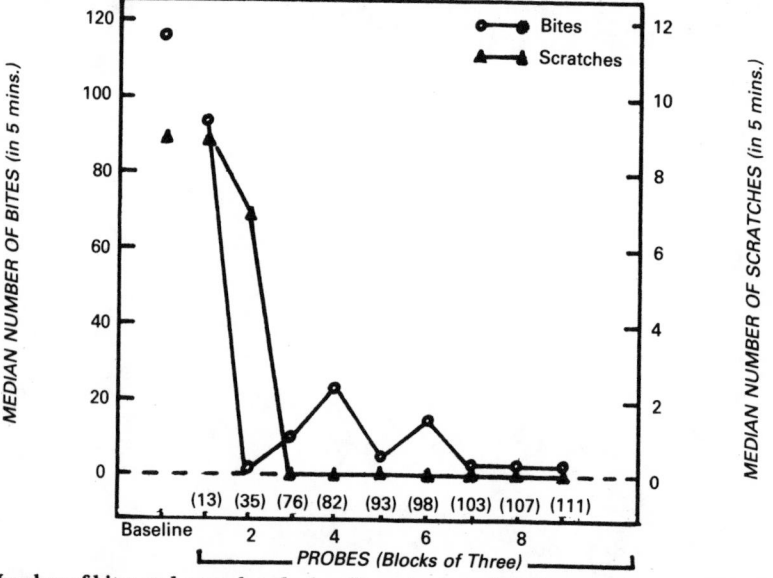

Fig. 1. Number of bites and scratches during five-minute probes. Data are the medians of blocks of three probes. The number of relaxation training sessions prior to the median probe is in parenthesis. Note that the ordinate scales for bites and scratches are different.

showed greater variability, and took longer to eliminate. During the five follow-up probes no scratches and only three bites occurred. Once the subject could be briefly released from restraints without self-injurious behavior several programs were instituted to train her in self-help skills. One year after the present study of relaxation was completed staff reports indicated that self-injurious behavior remained at low levels, and the subject was no longer kept in restraints.

The present method is advantageous because self-injurious behavior does not occur during treatment, and because it can be carried out without special apparatus. In purely therapeutic situations, the probes are unnecessary, and no self-injurious behavior need occur at all. Only about 17 hr of relaxation training were required to eliminate behaviors that had been occurring for 13 years.

Acknowledgements
We thank Dr. Paul Jansen and Ms. Karen Gitlin for their guidance and Ms. Betty Maloney and Ms. Carol Beaumont for their cooperation.

References
Azrin, N. H., Gottlieb, L., Hughart, L., Weslowski, M. D., Rahn, T. Eliminating self-injurious behavior by educative procedures. *Behav. Res. & Ther.*, 1975; **13**, 101-111.
Bruno, B. Progressive relaxation training for children: a guide for parents and teachers, Part II. *Spec. Child.*, 1975; **2**, 38-46.
Jacobson, E. *Progressive Relaxation.* Chicago: University of Chicago Press, 1938.
Lovaas, O. I., Frietag, G., Gold, V. J., Kassorla, I. C. Experimental studies in childhood schizophrenia: analysis of self-destructive behavior. *J. Exp. Child Psych.*, 1965; **2**, 67-84.
Lovaas, O. I., Simmons, J. Q. Manipulation of self-destruction in three retarded children. *J. Appl. Beh. Anal.*, 1969; **2**, 143-157.
Meyers, J. J., Deibert, A. N. Reduction of self-abusive behavior in a blind child by using a feeding response. *J. Behav. Ther. & Exp. Psychiat.*, 1971; **2**, 141-144.
Tate, B. G., Baroff, G. S. Aversive control of self-injurious behavior in a psychotic boy. *Behav. Res. & Ther.*, 1966; **4**, 281-287.

BEHAVIOR THERAPY FOR A CHILD WITH LESCH-NYHAN SYNDROME

Marilyn Bull, Francesca LaVecchio

Summary

The behavioral symptoms in a 10-year-old boy with Lesch-Nyhan syndrome were effectively ameliorated by the behavior therapy techniques of systematic desensitization and extinction. Therapy was undertaken in a highly controlled environment. The hypothesis that the self-destructive behaviors in this syndrome were voluntary and maintained through continuous reinforcement was confirmed. Characteristic biting and other maladaptive behaviors were extinguished. Over a period of time it was possible to remove all the physical restraints previously used to prevent the boy injuring himself. During treatment his anxiety, associated with phobic reaction to being unrestrained, was reduced by nitrous oxide. At 1½ years follow-up the boy continues to be symptom-free. He attends a special class at school and is learning to walk with crutches.

It is emphasised that a trained and experienced therapist and a controlled environment are essential for the success of this form of behavior therapy, and the dangers inherent in this method of treatment are discussed.

Introduction

It has recently been demonstrated that methods of operant conditioning are effective in children with Lesch-Nyhan syndrome (Anderson *et al.,* 1975). The purpose of this paper is to present the results of behavioral treatment in the management of a 10-year-old boy affected with this condition.

Lesch-Nyhan syndrome is a rare, X-linked, recessive disorder characterized by neurological abnormalities, psychomotor retardation, self-mutilating behavior, hyperuricemia (Lesch and Nyhan 1964, Nyhan 1973), and absent activity of the enzyme hypoxanthine-guanine phosphoribosyltransferase (HGPRT) in erythrocytes, lymphocytes and skin fibroblasts of affected individuals (Seegmiller *et al.,* 1967, Geerdink *et al.,* 1973).

Affected individuals appear to be normal at birth and may develop normally for as long as six to eight months (Nyhan and Sakati 1976). Subsequently neurological manifestations develop, including spasticity, choreoathetosis, athetoid dysarthria, opisthontonic posturing and in some instances, seizures (Dreifuss *et al.,* 1967). The majority of patients attain IQs of less than 50.

Self-mutilation is a characteristic behavior. Biting, which occurs frequently, usually begins between two and three years of age. The lips, buccal mucosa, and subsequently fingers, arms, and toes are most frequently involved. There is no evidence of insensitivity to pain, and the child usually screams or cries and occasionally verbalizes about his pain (Nyhan 1973).

Management of patients with this condition has previously consisted of prevention of renal failure by pharmacological reduction of hyperuricemia and attempts to minimize self-mutilation. Hyperuricemia is characteristically present in all patients. The concentration of uric acid in plasma is between 9 and 12mg/100ml. Those patients with greater amounts of uric acid in body fluids may develop gout. Untreated, the majority of patients develop urate nephropathy and die from renal failure before the end of the first

Authors' Appointments

Marilyn Bull, M.D., Indiana University School of Medicine, James Witcomb Riley Hospital for Children, 1100 West Michigan Street, Room P120, Indianapolis, Indiana 46202. (Formerly at New England Medical Center — Birth Defects Center.)
Francesca LaVecchio, Ph.D. (Candidate), Tufts-New England Medical Center, Department of Neuropsychology, 260 Tremont Street, Boston, Massachusetts 02111.

Correspondence to Francesca LaVecchio.

decade of life. Those who survive usually develop tophi (Nyhan and Sakati 1976). The use of restraints and other special devices has been recommended to restrict mobility (Letts and Hobson 1975). Extraction of teeth has also been used to prevent self-injury (Watts *et al.*, 1974). Traditional medication to reduce anxiety and spasticity has not been beneficial, even at high dosages (Watts *et al.*, 1974). Furthermore, treatment of hyperuricemia prior to the onset of biting has not prevented the development of self-mutilation (Marks *et al.*, 1968).

Case report

The patient was adopted by his family at eight weeks of age, and little is known of his prenatal, neonatal or family history. He was reported to be the product of a normal delivery with a birthweight of 13·7kg, and appeared to develop normally until 3½ months of age, when developmental delay was first suspected. He was not sitting at eight months of age, and at nine months the diagnosis of cerebral palsy was made. From age 10 months to three years he was involved in a patterning program, which was discontinued because of the onset of biting. By that time he had developed a sight vocabulary of 300 words and was able to perform age-appropriate fine motor functions.

Maladaptive behavior subsequently increased significantly and interfered with developmental progress. Eventually, extensive restraints were required to prevent self-injury. He was confined to a wheel-chair with his arms restrained in extension by splints, wore a helmet and shoulder pads, and at night was restrained in bed by a jacket and safety straps. In addition to biting, other maladaptive behaviors developed, including breath-holding, removing finger and toe nails, throwing himself from chairs and bed, screaming, spitting, neck snapping, projectile vomiting, banging his head and limbs, and vulgar language (coprolalia). These behaviors were forceful and potentially life-threatening, as well as occurring very frequently and for extended periods of time. Hypermobility of joints made it possible for him to inflict wounds to his shoulders, knees and toes, as well as lips and fingers. Exposure of bone as a result of biting predisposed him to infection.

A characteristic verbal pattern also developed, and during self-infliction of wounds he would cry "I hate myself". When injuring others, he would apologize frequently. Sentences indicating ambivalence were commonly repeated in rapid succession, such as "I hate you, I love you, I hate you, I love you", and "Yes, no, yes, no". During these times he appeared to be experiencing a classic approach-avoidance conflict in desiring a particular goal object, yet being overcome by fear. When his anxiety reached what he perceived to be an uncontrollable level, he would scream, cry and mutilate himself.

At age six years the diagnosis of Lesch-Nyhan syndrome was suspected. Serum uric acid determinations ranged from 6 to 7mg/100ml. The diagnosis was confirmed by erythrocyte HGPRT specific gravity activity which was 0(μmol/mg prot/hr).

On neurological assessment his speech was noted to be dysarthric; he had spastic diplegia with choreoathetoid movements, occasional myoclonic jerks and movements interpreted as being hemiballismus.

Self-help skills were minimal, and although enrolled in a special class in public school his academic progress was negligible. He became increasingly dependent and employed his self-injurious behavior in a manipulative fashion to gain assistance and attention from family members and school personnel. A maintenance dose of allopurinol (50mg twice daily) reduced his uric acid from 8·3 to 2·3mg/100ml. Treatment with diazepam (2·5 to 5mg twice daily) had no apparent effect. An electroencephalogram was normal. His Binet IQ scores (Form L-M, 1960 revision) ranged from 61 to 69, but these measures were believed to be influenced by his emotional lability, and therefore reflected a minimal estimate of his intellectual ability.

Method

The design of the experimental treatment plan was based on the hypothesis that the maladaptive behaviors exhibited were voluntary and had been maintained by a continuous reinforcement of fixed ratio schedule of reinforcement. Both positive and negative reinforcement served to magnify his maladaptive behavior, including its frequency, duration and intensity. Although the circumstances of the initial incident of biting is unknown, it is recognized that it was immediately reinforced by the attention received.

Further, the anxiety level was observed to be directly related to a phobic reaction to being unrestrained. Indications of anxiety, in addition to verbally expressed ambivalence, were noted when the patient realised that his safety was threatened; these included increased respiratory rate, pulse, perspiration, facial rubor, grimacing, screaming and crying. His response to any anxiety-provoking stimulus was self-mutilation. Maladaptive behaviors were also employed in a manipulative fashion when he wished to be left alone or when he did not want to participate in any activity.

The behavioral technique of systematic desensitization was chosen as the method of treatment for our 10-year-old patient's phobic reaction to lack of restraint. Before treatment began, objects which the patient regarded as restrictive were rated according to their anxiety-provoking value and were arranged in a hierarchical fashion by observing the patient's relative anxiety level in response to removal or attempted removal of each item. Initial training sessions involved exercises in relaxation, which was induced by inhalation of a mixture of 60 per cent CO_2 and 40 per cent O_2. It was actually during these initial sessions and prior to formal treatment that the patient allowed the removal of low anxiety-provoking restraints (*e.g.* socks). however, the CO_2O_2 mixture induced the perception of heat, an unpleasant taste and hyperventilation, which appeared to disturb the patient and thereby interfered with the relaxation process. Therefore nitrous oxide was administered intermittently to induce relaxation during subsequent treatment sessions. Restraints were removed during these sessions, proceeding from lesser anxiety-provoking objects (*e.g.* shirt) to high anxiety-value objects (*e.g.* arm splints).

During and between treatment sessions, 'extinction' was employed to eliminate biting and other maladaptive behaviors. Initially, extinction was accomplished by the therapist leaving the room and re-entering it only when the maladaptive behavior had ceased. The patient was observed through a one-way mirror, and he consistently ceased his self-destructive activity after the therapist left the room. By the third day of treatment the therapist had only to turn away from the patient for the behavior to cease; a participant-observer stationed outside the room would sound a tone to signal the therapist to turn back to face the patient when self-mutilation had ceased. In addition to recording the frequencies of maladaptive behaviors, the participant-observer also recorded the duration and intensity of all responses charted. For example, biting was rated as 1 (mild) to indicate bumping of the skin with teeth or lips; 2 (moderate) to indicate biting without breaking the skin, but possibly bruising it; or 3 (severe) to indicate biting which broke the skin or drew blood. Because of the severity of the behaviors being treated and to prevent unnecessary injury, accurate frequency baselines were not secured prior to beginning formal treatment; instead, frequencies of each behavior were assumed to occur at dangerously high levels. However, prior to admission for treatment, baseline frequency for biting was 3·1 per minute; this frequency was elicited merely by informing the patient that his shirt was to be removed. This baseline was secured under conditions of attention, *i.e.*, facing the patient and at times physically restraining him to prevent injury, and therefore under conditions of reinforcement. Unlike other schedules of reinforcement in which responses can occur without reinforcement (intermittent schedules) and where extinction is actually taking place during acquisition, in the continuous reinforcement schedule all behaviors are reinforced constantly. It was therefore expected that extinction would occur rapidly, with incidents of spontaneous recovery, when the patient was returned to the acquisition-extinction environment in the presence of previously reinforcing individuals.

It was observed that biting and all other maladaptive behaviors did not occur when the patient was alone, which indicates that the behaviors were not in themselves gratifying. It was also observed that attention given to the inflicted wounds was especially reinforcing; therefore all injuries inflicted during the therapy were treated under anesthesia. Osteomyelitis developed in one of these wounds following discharge from the hospital, and amputation of the distal phalanx of the right index finger was necessary.

Traditional play therapy was used after behavioral treatments were completed in order to encourage the patient to verbalize his fears, perceptions and feelings, and to achieve an understanding and acceptance of himself. These sessions became particularly appropriate when maladaptive behaviors had ceased and depression occurred, apparently because the patient experienced the loss of his primary mode of interaction with his environment.

All hospital personnel involved in the treatment were trained in operant conditioning, and all medical procedures were performed under these conditions. Parents and family were excluded during the initial stages of treatment and were then gradually reintroduced as co-therapists.

Results
One-hour treatment sessions were conducted by the therapist, with the assistance of the participant-observer. The following behavioral responses were charted during each session: (1) biting; (2) biting attempts; (3) head banging; (4) spitting; (5) neck snapping; (6) vomiting; (7) injury to others; and (8) damage to body, exclusive of biting (*e.g.* pulling fingernails). Figs. 1 and 2 illustrate the frequencies of specific behaviors during the 15 treatment sessions. All restraints were removed by the seventh day, and by the tenth day biting had ceased. Treatment sessions were terminated after five consecutive days of no biting.

In Fig. 1A the increase in biting responses during treatment session 9 was specifically related to attention paid by the nursing staff to an infected wound which had been inflicted during treatment session 1. The patient had become extremely anxious and exhibited a transient regression.

In addition to a gradual decline in frequency of maladaptive behavior, analysis of descriptive accounts of each behavior therapy session revealed a decrease in the patient's observable anxiety level, in the duration of each response, and in the intensity of each response — from severe to moderate to mild, and ultimately to cessation. However, since anxiety remained relatively high, the less severe maladaptive behaviors, such as spitting, transiently increased in frequency and then gradually declined both during and outside treatment sessions.

The described treatment appears to have ameliorated the classical maladaptive behavior manifested in this child with Lesch-Nyhan syndrome. During the first seven months after treatment occasional regressive acts were observed in high-anxiety situations. In addition to the cessation of self-destructive behavior an increase in verbal fluency also occurred, so that the patient became increasingly capable of expressing his needs, fears and emotions. Apparent relaxation of musculature and subsequent increased control of movement has also become apparent. Follow-up neurological examination revealed no choreoathetosis or ballistic movements, and his gross movements were noted to be clearly purposeful.

On standardized IQ testing (WISC-R), the patient scored in the moderately retarded range (IQ 54). In addition to the expected lowered score attributable to the difference between the WISC-R and 1960 Revised Binet, his measured intelligence level appears to reflect a lack of exposure to social situations, practical problem-solving situations, and formal academic training. In an attempt to gain some valid measure of his cognitive level, a Peabody Picture Vocabulary Test was administered, which gave a score in the normal range IQ 91).

Without restraints, the patient is able to feed himself and to manipulate his own wheelchair. The achievement of these skills alone represents much greater independence, and the family feels that the improvement justified the risks assumed and the difficulties encountered.

At 1½-year follow-up the patient exhibited no regressive behavior. In addition to cessation of biting, he no longer engages in verbal ambivalence or coprolalia. He has come to express his needs and concerns verbally, in contrast to his previous self-mutilation. He is at present enrolled in a behavior-oriented classroom in a public school, where he is attaining academic and self-help skills. He no longer requires a body brace for support and is learning to walk with crutches.

Conclusions and implications
Several important variables should be considered in selecting a patient for this method of treatment. A trained and experienced therapist and a highly controlled treatment environment are essential for successful therapy. Equally important are involved parents, capable of being trained to execute the procedures after formal treatment has ended. They must be thoroughly acquainted with each segment of the treatment regimen and supported

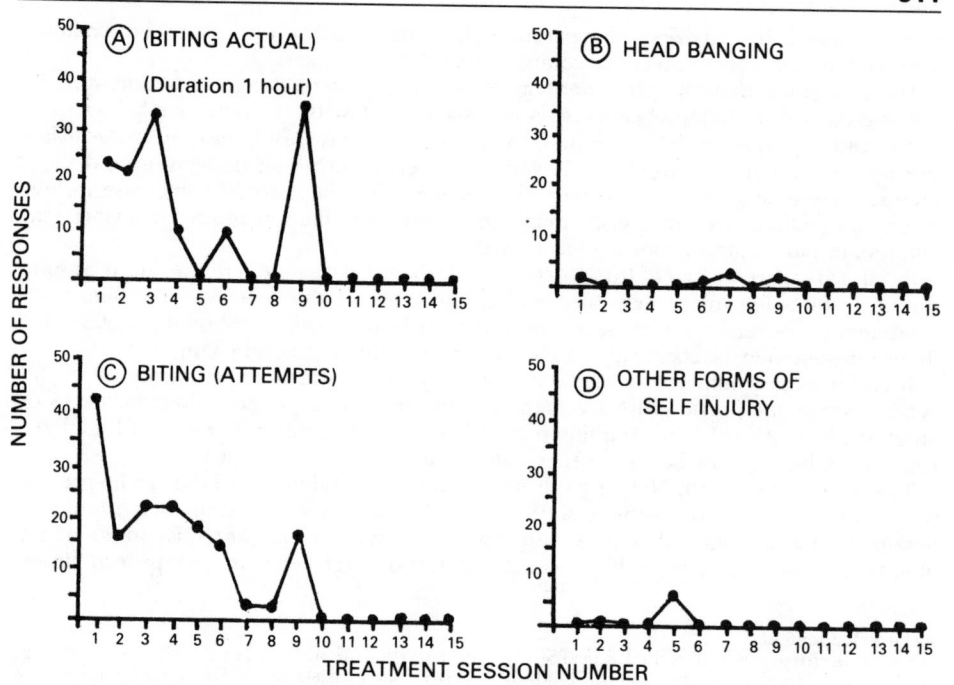

Fig. 1. Responses during 15 treatment sessions in relation to actual biting, head banging, attempts at biting and other forms of self-injury.

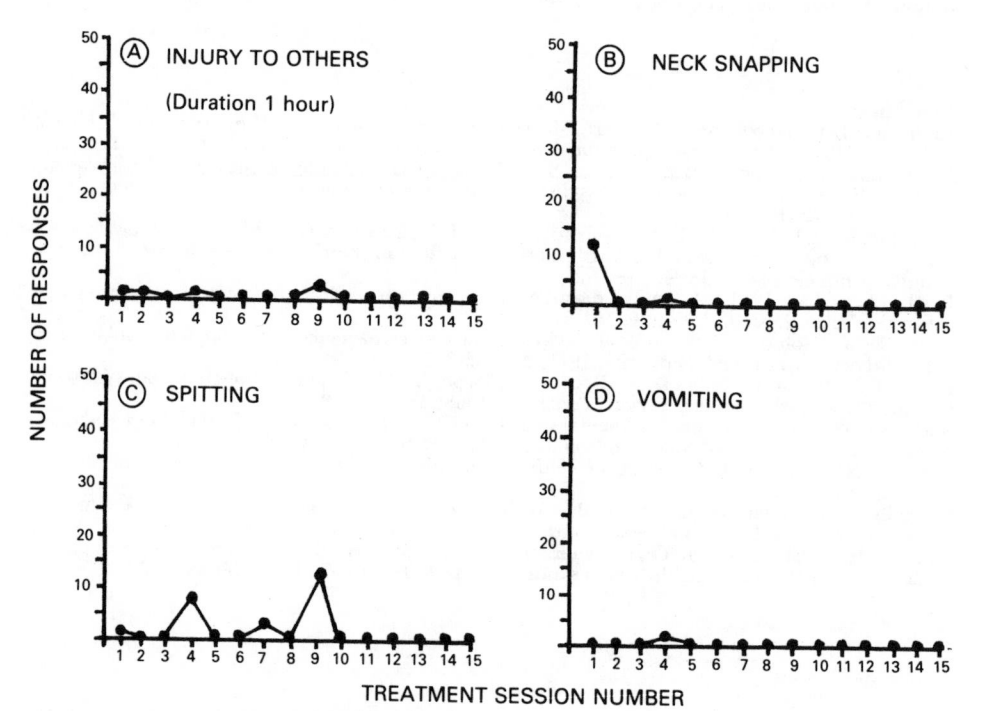

Fig. 2. Responses during 15 treatment sessions in relation to injury to others, neck snapping, spitting and vomiting.

through the difficult period of separation. A medical facility with a multi-disciplinary approach is desirable to meet the complex needs of the patient.

We recognize that the treatment method has inherent dangers, which must be considered before therapy begins. It is necessary to allow the maladaptive behaviors to occur during treatment, and injury to the patient may result despite appropriate precautions. Emotional problems of variable severity, including depression and night terrors, may emerge soon after extinction of the target behavior. An increase in low-frequency maladaptive responses may occur, and new inappropriate behaviors may emerge, in particular after biting has ceased.

Several areas are worthy of further research. Behavioral treatment of the family prior to the onset of biting might help to elucidate the cause of this behavior. Pre- and post-treatment measurements of uric acid, serotonin, BUN and creatinine should be obtained to determine whether biochemical changes occur with the behavioral changes.

It is our clinical impression that some of the neurological findings attributed to this syndrome may be purposeful movements which are misinterpreted as hemiballismus or athetosis. Patients with this condition may also manifest a significant degree of functional retardation but actually be less intellectually retarded than they appear.

The diagnosis of Lesch-Nyhan syndrome should be considered for infants who present with spasticity and choreoathetosis. If indicated, a uric acid determination should be obtained to facilitate early diagnosis. Behavior problems in patients with this condition may in some cases be treated, or perhaps even prevented, through behavior therapy techniques.

Acknowledgements:
We are grateful to the staff of the Clinical Study Unit: to Catherine Bove, R.N., Dr. Michael Goldberg, Dr. Seymour Zimbler and Dr. Eugene Solod for their invaluable assistance; to Dr. K. Itiaba of Victoria Hospital (Montreal) for performing the HGPRT determination; to Dr. Murray Feingold for advice in preparation of the manuscript; and especially to our patient for have the courage to change. This study was performed at the Clinical Study Unit, Tufts-New England Medical Center, and was funded by National Institutes of Health Grant no. RR00054.

References
Anderson, L.T., Herrmann, L., Alpert, M., Dancis, J. 'An anlaysis of self-injury in Lesch-Nyhan disease', (1975). *Paper presented at the American Psychiatric Society Annual Meeting, May 1975.*
Dreifuss, F. E., Newcombe, D. S., Shapiro, S. L., Shepperd, G. C. 'X-Linked primary hyperuricaemia (hypoxanthine-guanine phosphoribosyl transferase deficiency) encephalopathy'. *J. Ment. Defic. Res.*, 1967; **12**, 100-107.
Geerdink, R. A., DeVries, W. H. M., Willemse, J., Oei, T. L., DeBruyn, C. H. M. M. 'An atypical case of hypoxanthine guanine phosphoribosyl transferase deficiency (Lesch-Nyhan syndrome). 1. Clinical study'. *Clin. Genets.*, 1973; **4**, 348-352.
Lesch, M., Nyhan, W. L. 'A familial disorder of uric acid metabolism and central nervous system function'. *Am. J. Med.*, 1964; **36**, 561-570.
Letts, R. M., Hobson, D. A. 'Special devices as aids to management of child self-mutilation in Lesch-Nyhan syndrome'. *Pediatrics*, 1975; **55**, 853-855.
Marks, J. F., Baum, J., Keele, D. K., Doman, K., Jacob, K., MacFarlen, A. 'Lesch-Nyhan syndrome treated from early neonatal period'. *Pediatrics,* 1968; **42**, 357-359.
Michener, W. 'Hyperuricemia and mental retardation'. *Am. J. Diseases Child.*, 1967; **113**, 195-206.
Nyhan, W. L. 'The Lesch-Nyhan syndrome'. *An. Rev. Med.*, 1973; **24**, 41-60.
— Sakati, N. *Genetic and Malformation Syndromes in Clinical Medicine.* Chicago: Yearbook Medical Publishers, 1976.
Seegmiller, J. E., Rosenbloom, F. M., Kelley, W. N. 'Enzyme defect associated with a sex-linked human neurological disorders and excessive purine synthesis'. *Science,* 1967; **155**, 1682-1684.
Watts, R. W. E., McKernan, R. O., Brown, E., Andrews, T. M., Griffiths, M. 'Clinical and biochemical studies on treatment of Lesch-Nyhan syndrome'. *Arch. Disease Child.*, 1974; **49**, 693-702.

DURATION OF FACIAL SCREENING AND SUPPRESSION OF SELF-INJURIOUS BEHAVIOR: ANALYSIS USING AN ALTERNATING TREATMENTS DESIGN

Nirbhay N. Singh
University of Canterbury

Ivan L. Beale
University of Auckland
and
Maryan J. Dawson
Mangere Hospital and Training School

Facial screening has been shown to be effective in reducing certain classes of maladaptive behavior in children. In the present study, an alternating treatments design was used to measure the differential impact of three durations of facial screening on the self-injurious behavior of a severely retarded child. Each occurrence of self-injurious behavior was followed by facial screening of 3-sec, 1-min, or 3-min duration. Results showed 1-min duration to be most effective in terms of both immediate response reduction and short-term generalization. The study demonstrates the advantages of an alternating treatments design for comparative evaluation of the clinical utility of two or more treatments, using a single client.

Self-injurious behavior (SIB) is an intransingent problem in institutionalized severely and profoundly mentally retarded persons (Baumeister & Rollings, 1976). It can be defined as any self-inflicted repetitive action which leads to lacerations, bruising, or abrasions of the patient's own body. Prevalence estimates of self-injury in institutionalized retarded persons range from 5 to 23% (Singh, in press), with greatest prevalence in severely and profoundly retarded persons (Maisto, Baumeister, & Maisto, 1978).

Various treatments have been developed to reduce SIB, the most effective of which ususally involve some form of punishment. In response to a growing concern in the area of treatment ethics and in line with the least restrictive treatment model (May, Risley, Twardosz, Friedman, Bijou, Wexler et al., 1975), however, several relatively innocuous procedures have recently been investigated. Facial screening (Lutzker & Spencer, Note 1) is a mildly aversive procedure in which the subject's face is covered with a terry-cloth bib for a few seconds following a maladaptive response. It has been shown to be effective in the suppression of a number of topographically different maladaptive behaviors, such as out-of-seat behavior (Jenkins & Becker, Note 2), persistent disruptive hand clapping (Zegiob, Jenkins, Becker, and Bristow, 1976), and self-injurious behavior (Lutzker, 1978; Singh, 1980; Zegiob, Alford, & House, 1978).

Despite its demonstrated efficacy, however, few studies have focused on specific parameters of the facial screening procedure. In partial component analysis, Zegiob et al. (1978) found that presenting the bib without actually covering the subject's face was not effective in the suppression of self-injurious behavior and that holding the subject's head in the same position as used for facial screening was not effective. They speculated that the critical component of facial screening may be the actual blocking of vision. This has been confirmed in a more recent study (Singh, Dawson, & Manning, Note 3) which showed that self-injury was suppressed only when the subject's vision was blocked.

The suppressive effects of various durations of facial screening is another variable which has not been investigated. Previous studies using facial screening have arbitrarily used durations of 3 to 10 sec, but none has specifically investigated the time parameter of this

Requests for reprints should be addressed to Nirbhay Singh, Department of Psychology, University of Canterbury, Private Bag, Christchurch 1, New Zealand.

procedure within a single subject. Clinically, duration is a variable of interest since the efficacy and the ease with which the procedure can be implemented may depend on it. To test for the differential effects of various durations, three time periods (including one very short and one fairly long) were chosen for this study. The present study was designed to test the efficacy of facial screening for controlling self-injurious behavior under three time durations, using an alternating treatments design.

The alternating treatments design

In the present experiment, the effects of three durations of facial screening on self-injurious behavior were evaluated. A rather complex research strategy is required when one wishes to measure simultaneously the effects of three values of an independent variable. There are important limitations to the commonly used reversal and multiple-baseline designs for investigations of this sort, mainly in terms of sequence and treatment interaction effects, the difficulty in reversing certain treatment conditions, and the prolonged length of the overall intervention.

A design which circumvents most of these problems has been variously termed a simultaneous treatment design (Browning, 1967; Kazdin & Hartmann, 1978; McCullough, Cornell, McDaniel, & Mueller, 1974), alternating treatments design (Barlow & Hayes, 1979), multiple schedule design (Leitenberg, 1973), multi-element baseline design (Sidman, 1960), and a randomization design (Edgington, 1967). In line with Barlow & Hayes' (1979) recommendations, in this paper, we will use the term alternating treatments design.

In the alternating treatments design, two or more interventions are concurrently implemented in the experimental phase following the baseline phase to alter a single target response. The design is characterized by "the fast alternation of two different treatments or conditions, each associated with a distinct and discriminative stimulus" (Barlow & Hayes, 1979, p. 200). Typically the two treatments are alternated, usually within each session or between sessions in the same experimental phase, independently of changes in behavior. The frequent alternation of the treatments minimizes time-correlated artifacts that might occur when each of the two or more treatments is tested serially as in reversal or multiple-baseline designs. Stimulus conditions, other than the programmed treatments, which might affect the data (e.g., time and location of treatment, therapists or experimenters) are counterbalanced so that their effects can be separated from the effects of the programmed treatments. The experimental phase is terminated when the target behavior stabilizes under the separate treatment conditions. Usually, the more (or most) effective treatment is then implemented for clinical purposes in the final phase.

Method

Subject

The subject was an 18-year-old severely retarded girl who had been institutionalized for the preceding 13 years. The etiology of her retardation was unknown. Her social age on the Vineland Social Maturity Scale was equivalent to 2.2 years and her behavioral age on the Fairview Self-help Scale was 16.9 months. She had no receptive language and showed only minimal responsiveness to simple verbal commands. Her nursing notes showed that she could feed herself and was toilet trained by habit. Physically she was in good condition apart from her walking which tended to be splay-footed. Medical case notes showed that she had at least a 11-year history of self-injurious behavior, which consisted mainly of hitting herself about the face and lower jaw. Over the last several years she had been tried on several psychotropic drugs with no apparent improvement.

Response measurement and reliability

Data were collected by one of a pool of four observers, randomly assigned on a daily basis. There were three 1-hour experimental sessions daily. An interval-recording technique was utilized in which each session was divided into 360 10-sec observational intervals. The observer, who was equipped with a timer that signalled through earphones the end of successive 10-sec periods, recorded the number of self-injurious responses since the preceding signal. An instance of self-injurious behavior was defined as a punch to the jaw or face with either hand, with each fist-to-jaw (or face) movement being counted as a separate response.

All observers were trained in the use of the behavioral observation system for approximately four weeks preceding this study, until their interobserver agreement with a randomly assigned partner was above 85%. To minimize observer drift, the third author met regularly with the observers during the study for practice and discussion. An agreement was reached when both observers recorded the same number of target responses during the same interval. The number of agreements between observers divided by the number of agreements plus disagreements and multiplied by 100 served as a percentage measure of reliability. Reliability checks were made on 15% of the observation periods distributed across each phase. Interobserver agreement ranged from 86.4 to 93.7% (median = 91%). Only the data from a randomly assigned primary observer for each day were included in the study.

Experimental procedure

The study consisted of three experimental phases conducted over 45 consecutive days. The phases were: (a) baseline (15 days), (b) first treatment phase with three separate time durations (15 days), and (c) second treatment phase with the most effective time duration. An alternating treatments design was used in the first treatment phase to test the efficacy of three durations of facial screening on self-injurious behavior.

Baseline. Behavioral recordings of self-injurious behavior were made during the first 15 days of the study three times a day (8:30–9:30 am, 11:00 am–12:00 pm, 1:30–2:30 pm). Baseline observations were arbitrarily divided into two consecutive 30 minute observation sessions. The first corresponded to the treatment periods and the second to the generalization periods during the intervention phases. The conditions during baseline represented the usual ward procedures.

Facial screening: Phase 1. At the beginning of each treatment session, a terry-cloth bib (30cm × 25cm wide) was tied around the subject's neck by a behaviorally trained nurse who served as the therapist. Each instance of self-injury resulted in the bib being quickly placed over the subject's face and head and held loosely at the back of the head. Three durations of facial screening were used: 3 sec, 1 min, and 3 min. Except for treatment durations, the three treatments were procedurally identical. The durations were randomly alternated between sessions on a daily basis. All interventions were programmed only for the first 30 min of each session, followed by a 30-min observation period. The observation periods were identical in procedure to the baseline phase and served as a measure of short-term generalization of response suppression.

Facial screening: Phase 2. The most effective of the three treatment durations was used during the three daily sessions in this phase to demonstrate clinical control. As in the previous phase, the treatment was limited to the first 30 min of each session followed by a 30-min observation period.

Results

Figure 1 shows the rate of self-injurious responses per minute across baseline and the two treatment phases. Each data point was derived by dividing the total number of self-injurious responses by the observation time per session, which yielded self-injurious responses per minute (rate). In all cases, the time the subject's face was screened was subtracted from the total observation time (30 min) before rate was calculated. For example, if the subject exhibited 5 SIB's during the session when 1-min facial screening was in effect, the rate was obtained by dividing the frequency by 25 rather than 30.

Overall effects

The data in Figure 1 can be combined across all stimulus conditions to give an indication of the overall effects during treatment and generalization sessions. The mean rate of self-injurious responses during the baseline (corresponding to the treatment session in the intervention phases) was 6.18 responses per minute ($R = 4.8$–7.4). Self-injury decreased to a mean of 0.33 responses per minute ($R = 0.0$–0.9) when the three interventions were implemented in the first experimental phase. Finally, the rate of SIB decreased in the second intervention phase to 0.11 responses per minute ($R = 0.0$–0.2) when the most

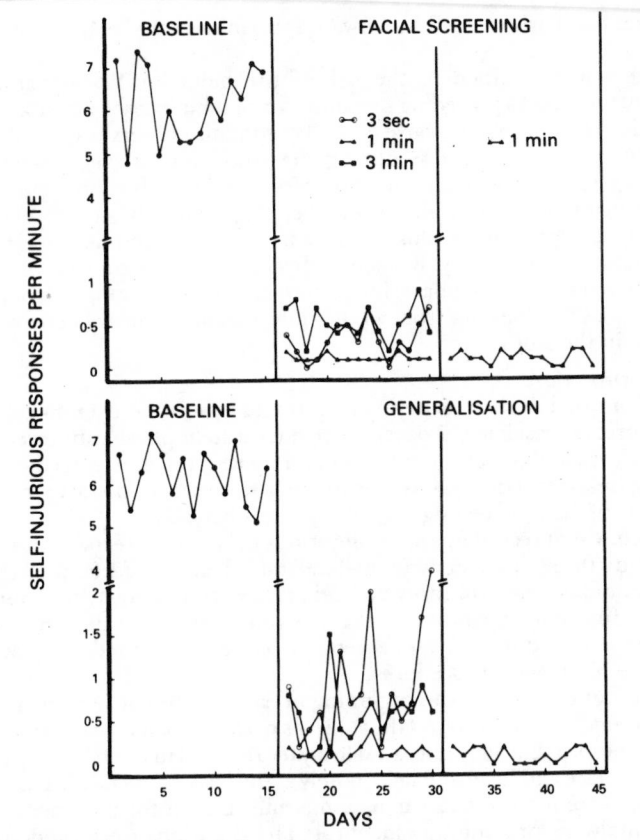

Fig. 1. Number of self-injurious responses per minute during treatment (top panel) and generalization (bottom panel).

effective intervention (facial screening for 1 min) was implemented across all time periods.

The rate of self-injurious behavior during baseline sessions (corresponding to the generalization sessions in the intervention phases) was 6.2 responses per minute ($R = 5.1$–7.2). Overall, self-injury decreased to a mean of 0.58 responses per minute ($R = 0.0$–4.0) during the generalization sessions in the first intervention phase. The rate of SIB decreased even further in the second intervention phase to 0.11 responses per minute ($R = 0.0$–0.2).

Alternating treatments analysis

A visual analysis of Figure 1 shows that a 1 min duration of facial screening produced the most consistent response suppression ($M = 0.12$), followed by a 3-sec duration ($M = 0.33$) and finally by a 3 min duration ($M = 0.53$). Rates of self-injurious responses under the three treatments were compared using the Friedman Test (Siegel, 1956), which showed that rates during the three conditions were significantly different ($X_r^2 = 20.1$, $df = 2$, $p < .001$).

In terms of short-term generalization of treatment effects, a visual analysis reveals that 1-min facial screening was most effective ($M = 0.14$), followed by a 3-min ($M = 0.59$) and finally by 3-sec ($M = 0.99$). Rates of self-injurious responses under the three treatments were compared using the Friedman Test (Siegel, 1956), which showed that rates during the three conditions were significantly different ($X_r^2 = 19.25$, $df = 2$, $p < .001$).

Overall, the data from the treatment and generalization sessions show that a 1-min duration of facial screening was the most effective time parameter for the present subject. Rates under the 1-min treatment condition were not significantly different from those under the related generalization (Friedman Test, $X_r^2 = .07$, $df = 1$, $p > .8$).

Discussion

The present results showed that self-injurious behavior of a severely retarded girl was rapidly suppressed by the contingent application of a mild aversive stimulus, facial screening. In addition, the short-term generalization data showed that self-injurious behavior was suppressed over time even when generalization was not explicitly programmed. Although data were not formally collected, ward staff reported a general decrease in the rate of SIB during the time observational recording was not taking place. Following the termination of the second treatment phase, a maintenance program was introduced during which all the staff on the ward were instructed in the use of the 1-min facial screening and therapy was scheduled for the subject's entire day. Unfortunately, maintenance data are available for only six months since the subject was then included in a drug study (Singh & Aman, in press). The mean rate of SIB was 0.17 responses per minute over the six-month period.

As found in other studies (Singh, 1980; Zegiob et al., 1976), the present subject showed some initial resistance to facial screening. However, this disappeared within the first two days of treatment. Furthermore, no differential avoidance behaviors due to the different durations of facial screening were observed.

The generality of the present results is obviously limited, given the single-subject nature of the study and the focus of treatment being on only one type of maladaptive behavior. Replications with other subjects and with other maladaptive behaviors should strengthen the generality of the present findings.

Several issues were considered before selecting the design for this study. The first requirement was that the design be robust enough in terms of internal validity to allow for the measurement of the impact of three separate values of an independent variable on a given dependent variable. Secondly, the design should be able to ovecome the possibility of time-correlated artifacts which usually occur when two or more values of an independent variable are tested serially for several sessions, as in reversal and multiple baseline designs. In addition, the design should facilitate the implementation of the treatment within an institutional setting where the child's behavior occurs under various stimulus conditions (e.g., across time, therapists, and location of treatment).

The alternating treatments design was chosen because it met the above requirements, allowing for the comparison of two or more "treatments" in the intervention phase and overcoming the problem of sequence effects by programming frequent alternation of treatments within or between sessions. Furthermore, all stimulus conditions, other than the programmed "treatments," are counterbalanced so that the relative effects of separate interventions can be unambiguously measured. In effect, the alternating treatments design ensures that all uncontrolled temporal variables would have a constant effect across all intervention conditions.

As argued elsewhere (cf. Barlow & Hayes, 1979), the alternating treatments design is an internally valid design. However, data from an experiment such as the present one may be questionable in terms of external validity because of multiple-treatment interference (Campbell & Stanley, 1963) or condition change interactions (Ulman & Sulzer-Azaroff, 1975). Is the potency of one intervention influenced by the presence of the other intervention and how can such effects be measured?

In terms of the present study, to what extent is the response suppression attributed to one duration of facial screening a function of the presence of the other two durations? For example, would the 1-min duration achieve a response suppression of the same magnitude if it had been presented alone? Previous research on the effects of various durations of timeout are pertinent here. White, Nielson, & Johnson (1972) examined the effectiveness of 1, 15, and 30-min durations of timeout and found that the efficacy of 1-min timeout decreased in its suppressive effect only when it followed longer durations of timeout. That is, the efficacy of the 1-min timeout decreased only when it was contrasted with 15-min and 30-min durations. Similar contrast effects have been noted in other studies (Burchard & Barrera, 1972; Johnson, Bolstad, & Lobitz, 1976; Kendall, Nay, & Jeffers, 1975). Future research might address itself to the role of contrast effects in the efficacy of different treatments within an alternating treatments design. For example, it would be instructive clinically to know how long this effect persists when other treatments have been withdrawn.

The present study did not attempt to measure the magnitude of multiple treatment interference, although interference may have been present. Several experimental techniques have been suggested which make it possible for this to be done (see Barlow & Hayes, 1979, for a review), but we know of no studies which have systematically examined the magnitude of treatment interaction in an alternating treatments design. Future research might well address itself to this issue.

In summary, the present results add to the growing literature which attests to the potency of facial screening as a generally effective means of reducing certain maladaptive behaviors in children. Furthermore, the present study suggests that an alternating treatments design is not only a viable research methodology, but is also of immediate relevance in clinical settings, since it allows an effective comparison of two of more treatment options before the more (most) effective alternative is implemented.

Acknowledgements
We would like to thank Dr. D. J. Woods and Mr. Alan Chapman for their support and encouragement, the ward staff for carrying out this program of research, and Mrs. Judy Singh for preparing the figure.

Reference notes
1. Lutzker, J. R., Spencer, T. *Punishment of self-injurious behavior in retardates by brief application of a harmless face cover.* Paper presented at the meeting of the American Psychological Association, New Orleans, 1974.
2. Jenkins, J., Becker, J. *Positive reinforcementt, overcorrection, and punishment in the management of out-of-seat behavior.* Paper presented at the meeting of the Southeastern Psychological Association, Atlanta, Georgia, 1975.
3. Singh, N.N., Dawson, M.J., Manning, P. *Treatment of self-injurious behavior by facial screening: Is visual blocking a necessary component?* Manuscript in preparation, 1980.

References
Barlow, D. H., Hayes, S. C. Alternating treatments design: one strategy for comparing the effects of two treatments in a single subject. *J. Appl. Behav. Anal.,* 1979; **12**, 199-210.
Baumeister, A. A., Rollings, J. P. Self-injurious behavior. In Ellis, N. R. (Ed.). *International Review of Research in Mental Retardation* (Vol. 8). New York: Academic Press, 1976.
Browning, R. M. A same subject design for simultaneous comparison of three reinforcement contingencies. *Behav. Res. & Ther.,* 1967; **5**, 237-243.
Burchard, J. D., Barrera, F. A. An analysis of timeout and response cost in a programmed environment. *J. Appl. Behav. Anal.,* 1972; **5**, 271-282.
Campbell, D. T., Stanley, J. C. Experimental and quasi-experimental designs for research. In Gage, N. L. (Ed.). *Handbook of Research on Teaching.* Chicago: Rand McNally, 1963.
Edgington, E. S. Statistical inference from N = 1 experiments. *J. Psychol.,* 1967; **65**, 195-199.
Johnson, S. M., Bolstad, O. D., Lobitz, G. K. Generalization and contrast phenomena in behavior modification with children. In Mash, E. J., Hamerlynck, L. A., Handy, L. C. (Eds.). *Behavior Modification and Families.* New York: Brunner/Mazel, 1976.
Kazdin, A. E., Hartmann, D. P. The simultaneous-treatment design. *Behav. Ther.,* 1978; **9**, 912-922.
Kendall, P. C., Nay, W. R., Jeffers, J. Time-out duration and contrast effects: a systematic evaluation of a successive treatment design. *Behav. Ther.,* 1975; **6**, 609-615.
Leitenberg, H. The use of single-case methodology in psychotherapy research. *J. Abnorm. Psychol.,* 1973; **82**, 87-101.
Lutzker, J. R. Reducing self-injurious behavior by facial screening. *Am. J. Ment. Defic.,* 1978; **82**, 510-513.
Maisto, C. R., Baumeister, A. A., Maisto, A. A. Analysis of variables related to self-injurious behavior among institutionalized retarded persons. *J. Ment. Defic. Res.,* 1978; **22**, 27-36.
May, J. G., Risley, T. R., Twardosz, S., Friedman, P., Bijou, S. W., Wexler, D., *et al.* Guidelines for the use of behavioral procedures in state programs for retarded persons. *MR Research,* 1975, **1**.
McCullough, J. P., Cornell, J. E., McDaniel, M. H., Mueller, R. K. Utilization of the simultaneous treatment design to improve student behavior in a first-grade classroom. *J. Consult. & Clin. Psychol.,* 1974; **42**, 288-292.
Sidman, M. *Tactics of Scientific Research.* New York: Basic Books, 1960.
Siegel, S. *Nonparametric Statistics for the Behavioral Sciences.* New York: McGraw-Hill, 1956.
Singh, N. N. The effects of facial screening on infant self-injury. *J. Behav. Ther. & Experi. Psychiat.,* 1980; **11**, 131-134.
Singh, N. N. Current trends in the treatment of self-injurious behavior: an evaluative review. In Barnes, L. A. (Ed.). *Advances in Pediatrics* (Vol. 28). Chicago: Year Book Medical Publishers. (In press).

Singh, N. N., Aman, M. G. Effects of thioridazine dosage on the behavior of severely retarded persons. *Am. J. Ment. Defic.* (In press).

Ulman, J. D., & Sulzer-Azaroft, B. Multi-element baseline design in educational research. *In* Ramp, E., Semb, G. (Eds.). *Behavior analysis: areas of research and application.* Englewood Cliffs, N. J.: Prentice-Hall, 1975.

White, G. D., Nielson, G., Johnson, S. M. Timeout duration and suppression of deviant behavior in children. *J. Appl. Behav. Anal.,* 1972; **5**, 111-120.

Zegiob, L. E., Alford, G. S., House, A. Response suppressive and generalization effects of facial screening on multiple self-injurious behavior in a retarded boy. *Behav. Ther.,* 1978; **9**, 688.

Zegiob, L. E., Jenkins, J., Becker, J., Bristow, A. Facial screening: Effects of appropriate and inappropriate behaviors. *J. Behav. Ther. & Experi. Psychiat.,* 1976; **7**, 355-357.

Reprinted from *Behavioral Assessment,* 1981; **3**, 411 by kind permission of the authors and the publishers Pergamon Press Ltd., Oxford OX3 0BN.

ELIMINATING SELF-INJURIOUS BEHAVIOR BY EDUCATIVE PROCEDURES

N. H. Azrin*, L. Gottlieb, L. Hughart, M. D. Wesolowski, T. Rahn†

Anna State Hospital

Summary
Self-injury is a common problem among autistic and severely retarded persons. The most effective treatment has been pain-shock punishment. To provide a possible alternative treatment, modifications were made in previously developed treatments for autistic behavior. The revised method included positive reinforcement for non-self-injurious behavior, a period of required relaxation or incompatible postures upon each occurrence of a self-injurious episode, and a hand-awareness training procedure. The treatment procedure was used with 11 clients, ten of whom were very severely retarded. No clients were excluded. The mean number of self-injurious episodes was reduced by 90 per cent on the first day, by 96 per cent at the end of one week and by 99 per cent by the end of three months. For four of the clients self-injury was eliminated almost entirely. The new procedure appears to be an effective method of treating self-injurious behavior and avoids the general reluctance to use pain-shock.

Self-injurious behavior by the profoundly retarded or mentally ill is one of the most severe psychological disorders since physical injury always results and sometimes, even death, if ignored. Yet, this problem persists in spite of a large number of recent reports of effective treatment by learning therapy procedures. One frequently used method is pain-shock punishment which has been effectively used by Risley (1968), Tate and Baroff (1966), Yeakel et al. (1970), Corte, Wolf and Locke (1971), and see review by Bucher and Lovaas (1968). A second method of treating self-injury is timeout from positive reinforcement which has been used effectively by Wolf, Risley and Mees (1964), Hamilton, Stephens and Allen (1967), Myers and Deibert (1971), Wolf et al. (1967), but has been fairly ineffective in studies by Corte, Wolf and Locke (1971), Risley (1968) and Tate and Baroff (1966). In a few instances, effective treatment has resulted from a third method, that of reinforcement for non-injurious behavior (Lovaas et al., 1965; Lane and Domrath, 1970; Peterson and Peterson, 1968).

Unfortunately, the general applicability of the above treatments is an open question since all of the above reported applications have been case studies in which only one selected client was used, except for two reports where the same method was used with three clients (Bucher and Lovaas, 1968) and four clients (Corte et al., 1971). Also, most of the studies have eliminated the self-injurious behavior during restricted time periods of an hour or less per day. Exceptions are the all-day elimination obtained by Tate and Baroff (1966), Hamilton et al. (1967), Wolf et al. (1964).

Of the three methods, shock seems to have the advantage of extreme rapidity in eliminating self-injury, often within 1 hr. Perhaps the greatest restraint on the use of shock has been the reluctance of therapists to resort to this physical punishment (see discussion by Bucher and Lovaas, 1968, and Risley, 1968). As Lovaas and Bucher have stated, regarding the use of shock-punishment by the ward staff members, "all have approached the task with extreme reluctance and anxiety" (p. 140). In addition, the spectre of a ward attendant carrying an electric prod discourages the widespread use of this demonstrably effective and rapid treatment.

The alternatives to shock have been less satisfactory. Physical restraint by tying the client to a chair (Lane and Domrath, 1970) is not as rapid a treatment as shock and also suffers

* Author from whom reprints may be obtained, at Behavior Research Laboratory, Anna State Hospital, Anna, Illinois 62906, U.S.A.
† Currently at St. Lawrence State Hospital, Ogdensburg, New York 13669, U.S.A.

from the characteristic of being excessively aversive. Timeout from positive reinforcement has not been as rapid or as effective as shock and seems to suffer from the disadvantage that the client can continue to injure himself during the timeout, thereby precluding its use with severe self-injury (Corte *et al.*, 1971). Reinforcement of incompatible behavior has the advantage of being totally non-aversive but has not been used effectively alone, only in combination with other methods (Lane *et al.*, 1970, and Lovaas *et al.*, 1965).

The present study devised a new treatment program based largely on three recently developed procedures that appear to hold promise as a relatively non-aversive treatment for self-injury. The first method is that of Autism Reversal (Azrin, Kaplan and Foxx, 1973; Foxx and Azrin, 1972) which has been found to be effective as a general treatment for autistic behavior, of which self-injury may be considered a sub-class and is based on the Overcorrection principle (Foxx and Azrin, 1972; Foxx and Azrin, 1973). In the Autism Reversal procedure, the client is required by instruction and manual guidance to engage in several different fixed postures which are non-self-stimulatory. This required practice is given upon each self-stimulatory episode on a response contingent basis. When the client is not self-stimulating, he is given positive reinforcement for alternative, incompatible activities. The second promising method, the Required Relaxation procedure, is also derived from the Overcorrection principle, and has been effectively used to eliminate a variety of agitative-disruptive behavior, including one client who injured himself (Webster and Azrin, 1973). This Required Relaxation procedure was found to be especially favored by hospital ward staff as a humane and meaningful type of treatment. The third promising procedure was Hand-Awareness Training. In a recent treatment developed for eliminating nervous habits of normal clients (Azrin and Nunn, 1973), the lack of awareness by the client of the location of his hands seemed to be contributing toward nervous habits involving the hands. Consequently the normal clients were given training in being continually aware of the position of their hands as part of the treatment. Since self-injury almost always includes striking oneself with the hands, the Hand-Awareness Training might be expected to help the self-injurious client to control this problem.

The present study modified these three promising procedures of Required Relaxation, Autism Reversal, and Hand-Awareness Training for use with a larger number of self-injurious clients in an attempt to eliminate self-injury on an all-day basis.

Method

Clients

Eleven clients were obtained in response to an offer to several institutions to provide assistance in treating clients who repeatedly inflicted injury on themselves that resulted in evident tissue damage. No clients were excluded. Five were from the same institution, the remaining six from four other institutions. Treatment was given in the client's institution. Table 1 shows the age, sex, diagnosis, IQ, years of institutionalization, years of exhibiting self-injury, the type of self-injury and the frequency of the behavior. Ten clients were diagnosed as severe or profoundly retarded, having an average IQ of 13, the highest IQ being 26 and the lowest was 6. The 11th client was diagnosed as schizophrenia, childhood type with an IQ of 89; he exhibited many of the diagnostic signs of autism. The retarded clients had an average age of 30 yr with an average duration of institutionalization of 18 yr, all having been institutionalized before the age of 15. Self-injury was reported to have been a problem for an average of 12 yr except for the schizophrenic boy who developed the problem only a year earlier. One noteworthy instance was the 18-year-old female who was reported in her records to have started hitting her head against the sides of her crib at 2 yr of age and had evidently self-inflicted scratches on her cheeks and ears during her first year of life. All clients had visible swelling and most also had scratches, scabs, bruises, or open wounds. All clients struck themselves on the face or head or on one part of their head such as the ears, side of the face, or eyes, usually with their fist or open hand. In addition, 2 clients banged their head on a floor or wall (listed as head-banging in Table 1), one of them as his predominant method of self-injury. Five of the clients had been given protective clothing such as a helmet or gloves or put in physical restraints such as special jacket or wrist restraints. Ten of the 11 clients were receiving tranquilizing or sedative medication. For 4 of the clients, treatment has also been given previously in the form of Electro Convulsive

Table 1. Description and frequency of occurrence of the self-injurious behaviors for each of the 11 clients

Client age and sex	Diagnosis	IQ	Years inst'd	Years exhibiting self-injury	Nature of injury	Pre-treatment frequency of behavior
28-yr-old male	Mentally retarded profound	11	22	14	face hitting, self-choking, biting, kicking	32/day
44-yr-old female	Mentally retarded profound	8	31	6	face slapping	6/day
26-yr-old female	Mentally retarded severe	26	19	6	scratching, face slapping	9/day
25-yr-old male	Mentally retarded profound	14	20	20	face and head slapping, punching	748/day
32-yr-old female	Mentally retarded profound	6	19	8	eye gouging	86% of the day
46-yr-old female	Mentally retarded profound	11	31	31	face, arm, leg slapping, finger biting	200/day
24-yr-old male	Mentally retarded profound	12	14	20	hand biting, head hitting and banging	25/day
10-yr-old male	Mentally retarded profound	9	9	7	ear punching	3528/day
18-yr-old female	Mentally retarded profound	6	18	18	face, ear, and head slapping	3500/day
15-yr-old male	Schizophrenia, childhood type	89	3	0.65	face punching	48/day
17-yr-old male	Mentally retarded profound	8	8	7	head banging	41/day

Shock therapy or timeout seclusion, or manually holding the client's hands behind the back. For 2 of the clients, the ward staff was only mildy interested in treating the problem. For one of these clients they felt that the protective helmet was adequately preventing self-injury; for the other client, the problem of eye-gouging usually was subordinated to other pressing ward problems.

Recording

The extent of self-injurious behavior prior to treatment was directly recorded by observing the client for as long as was feasible. For 2 clients who were in restraints or protective clothing, the restraint or clothing was removed and the client observed until the self-injury responses appeared to be causing damage. For one of these clients, only 10 min of observation was feasible; for the other, 38 min. For the other 9 clients, the duration of observation was adjusted to the frequency of the behavior. One client who hit himself continuously was observed for 30 min, whereas another client who had a few episodes per day was observed for 8 hr per day for 12 days, by a time-sample procedure. A response was considered self-injurious if the client struck, bit or scratched himself. The nature of the behavior was so unusual that the observers felt little difficulty in differentiating these self-injurious actions from normal on-going activities. In every instance, the ward staff reported that the recorded frequency was representative of the client's usual frequency. For one client, the self-injurious response was static, namely pressing her hand hard against her eyeball; this response was recorded in terms of duration. When the self-injury consisted of spaced blows, the measure was number of blows. If the self-injury consisted of a rapid flurry of blows, the measure was the number of such episodes (see last column of Table 1).

Response detection

After treatment was initiated, two instructors continually observed the client for about 12hr/day for the first 2 or 3 days, always keeping the client in full view, and within arms' length since the instructors were required to give continuing positive reinforcement for appropriate non-injurious behavior. Members of the ward staff assisted the instructors in recording and carrying out the treatment during these first few days and were encouraged to assume this responsibility when the instructors were absent. For 5 of the clients, the special instructors were present for at least 2 weeks. For the other 6 clients who were at remote institutions, the instructors returned periodically for direct confirmatory observation of reported benefits.

Duration of treatment

On each ward, the special instructor taught those employees who were interested how to conduct the procedure and supervised their performance. The instructors role-played the procedure with the staff members prior to application of the procedure to a client. The staff was advised of the importance of using the procedure immediately upon detection of a self-injurious response and upon every self-injurious response. One ward employee was typically designated as the coordinator but all were instructed to record the self-injurious behavior and to initiate the treatment procedure. The ward staff was advised to continue the treatment for several weeks after the special instructor departed but his role was advisory only. Telephone contact was made daily with the employees to encourage their continuation of the treatment. For all clients, the treatment lasted for at least 12 days. For 4 clients, the ward employees were not motivated to continue the procedure after the special instructors were absent. The ward employees discontinued treatment for 1 client after 12 days, another after 1 month, and the third and fourth clients after 2 months.

Positive reinforcement for outward-directed activities

The client was given positive reinforcers for engaging in a variety of outward-directed and incompatible responses. For the clients whose behavior was most 'inner-directed' these activities included eye contact with the instructor, looking at specific objects when instructed, sitting down or arising from a chair when instructed, walking, banging drumsticks together, grasping the armrests of their chair, catching and throwing a ball, or even simply sitting still without injuring themselves. For the clients who were more 'outward-directed', the responses included playing with a jig-saw puzzle, educational games, toileting, dressing, grooming, washing oneself, word recognition, ward cleaning chores, making beds, trips to the ward commissary, playing with simple music-making instruments, group recreational activities, swimming at a local pool, and bus rides. The guiding principle was to select those responses that involved active interaction with the physical and social environment, especially responses that were functional and could be expected to be maintained later because of their potential enjoyment or utility in their own right. If the ward program included regular supervised activities or classes, every attempt was made to enroll the client in these activities or classes. The reinforcers selected for use included verbal praise, back-stroking, and desired snack items such as candy, pudding, coffee, and juice. The ward staff usually knew what was reinforcing for a given client. In general, the snack items proved to be the best reinforcers for the more inward-directed clients. Reinforcers were delivered very frequently at first, the verbal praise was almost continuous. Once the client began spending extended periods without self-injury, the reinforcers were made more intermittent by reinforcing for longer response sequences.

Required relaxation

The Required Relaxation was essentially the same as described elsewhere as a treatment for agitative-disruptive conduct (Webster and Azrin, 1973). When the client injured himself, he was told that he was over-excited and agitated and was required to go relax in his bed. He was assisted in putting on a hospital gown and directed to his own bed where he remained for 2 hr. The instructor stood behind the head of the bed and assured that the client did not leave the bed.

A modification in the previously described procedure was made because of the severe nature of the self-injurious conduct. The client was required not only to remain in bed but to maintain his arms in an extended downward position with the hands alongside his legs away from his head, a position that was incompatible with striking one's head. The instructor used verbal instruction and gentle manual guidance, according to the Graduated Guidance Method which provides no more manual contact than is minimally necessary to obtain the required posture. This gentleness of contact as prescribed by the Graduated Guidance procedure was essential; otherwise great resistance resulted. His fixed posture was required for an uninterrupted 10 min in this arms-extended position. If he moved his hands toward his head or hit himself, 10 more min were required. All clients required considerable manual guidance initially, but after 1 or 2 days they usually performed the Required Relaxation Procedure upon verbal direction and with minimal manual contact. After the client began spending several hours on the ward without injuring himself, the Required Relaxation was given for any emotional or agitated conduct that was found to be a usual precursor to self-injury, such as excitedly pacing or rocking, muttering, screaming, or cursing in which case the Required Relaxation was given only for 10 min, again explaining to the client that he was overexcited and had to calm himself. The instructor's presence at bedside was usually required only during the first 1 or 2 days until the client learned to lay fairly still with the arms extended. Thereafter, the instructor usually remained with the client for only about 5 min until he was assured that the client was resting in the correct posture. The instructor, or any other staff member passing by the open door, could determine whether the client was resting as required. The pressure-sensitive device attached to the leg of the bed, and described previously (Webster and Azrin, 1973), sounded a signal to the staff if the client left the bed.

Hand control

The Hand Control Procedure was very similar to the arm exercises described in the previous report (Azrin et al., 1973) for eliminating hand autisms. In the previous report, when the client exhibited an autism he was immediately reprimanded and told that he must now practice holding his hands away from his body. The instructor stood behind him and guided him. The client was required to hold his arms extended at his sides, then outstretched horizontally to the front, then to the side, then extended over his head. Thirty seconds was required in each position preceded by a verbal instruction prior to each change in position. This cycle was repeated for 20 min in the standing posture. No conversation occurred between the instructor and the client, except the instruction every 30 sec as to the change in hand posture. The client received no praise or cajoling from the instructor during the exercises.

Several modifications were made in the above procedure to make it suitable for use with self-injurious clients. The arms-forward position was eliminated since a head-striking movement could be made easily from that position leaving only the arms down, side, and up position. Secondly, the arm-down position was modified to include clasping of the hands together behind one's back in order to make the response more incompatible with striking oneself than was the hands-by side position. This clasping of the hands also seemed easier to teach and seemed to be used spontaneously after training by the clients as a method of self control. Another modification was to require a position change every 10 sec rather than every 30 sec in order to have the client more active and to give more opportunity to react to the instructions. A fourth modification was to conduct the exercises in the sitting posture rather than standing for those clients who were physically unable to stand easily or who became too fatigued or emotionally upset by having to stand. A fifth modification was omission of the head-orientation exercises at the start of the practice period since the self-injurious clients could easily hit themselves while the instructor was manually guiding their head. A sixth modification was to terminate the arm exercise period while the client was in the arms-down position since this posture merged more naturally with his usual posture. This last posture was maintained for a longer period, 30 sec to 1 min, until the client was standing calmly with his arms down with no need for the instructor to hold his arm there. As in the previous report, the clients usually learned after 1 or 2 days to move their arms to the new position upon hearing the verbal instruction with a need for only minimal manual guidance.

In the event that the client became very upset during the Hand Control exercises, the instructor attempted to continue but paying special note to the need for gentleness of contact during the Graduated Guidance. If the agitation still persisted, the client was seated in a chair and the practice continued. In the event the agitation still persisted, the client was given the Required Relaxation procedure in his bed for a few minutes, until he was calm, at which time he completed the remainder of the 20-min practice period. The general rule was that the client should learn that the full 20 min of practice would be required whenever he injured himself.

Hand-awareness training

The Hand-Awareness Training procedure of Azrin and Nunn (1973) was modified for use with the present type of clients. At the start of treatment the instructor continually made comments to the client regarding the need to position his hands away from his head. The instructor used gestures, pointing, and touching as well as verbal statements. When the hands were away from the client's head, the instructor praised him for keeping them there. Conversely, when his hand moved upward for any reason, the instructor directed him to lower them. To maintain awareness of their hands, the clients were instructed to walk with their hands clasped behind their back and to clasp the armrests of their chairs while seated. As in the other procedures, the reinforcers were snack treats, praise, and stroking. As the client learned to maintain his hands away from his head, the instructor commented on the client's hand position progressively less often, but after having commented almost continuously for the first 2 days. This awareness was also being taught indirectly as an integral part of the Hand Control procedure when the client changed his hand position every 10 sec in response to the direct instruction regarding his hands. Similarly, in the Positive Reinforcement procedure, the client was being reinforced for using his hands in a functional manner.

Sequence

At the start of treatment, the protective helmet or mittens were removed and the client was given the Hand-Awareness training, and the Positive Reinforcement for outward-directed activities. When the client injured himself, the instructor immediately reprimanded him in a stern tone of voice that conveyed his displeasure and gave the Hand Control Procedure for 20 min or the Required Relaxation procedure for 2 hr. (See Results section as to which clients received which procedure.) The Positive Reinforcement for outgoing behaviors and the hand-awareness training were then reinstated after indicating to the client that he should not injure himself and that the Hand Control or Required Relaxation would be needed if he did injure himself. Initially, all instruction was conducted in special locations on the ward to obtain a more distraction-free atmosphere. After a few trials the locations were varied so that the client would learn that the procedure would eventually be applied in any locations in which he might self-injure.

Fading out of treatment

In both the Required Relaxation and Hand Control procedures, the instructor 'faded out' the need for his guidance or even his presence. In the Required Relaxation procedure, once the client attained the fixed-posture, and his behavior was agitation-free while in bed, the instructor moved himself gradually to the rear of the client, and eventually completely out of the client's view. In the Hand Control procedure, once the client was responding to the postural instructions and maintaining the positions unassisted, the instructor reduced his guidance of the client's arms to merely a touch and then to just 'shadowing' the client's movements.

When the client had spent one day without self-injury, the duration of the scheduled Required Relaxation or Hand Control was reduced to about 5 min on the next day, then to 2 min, and then to a simple warning on successive days, providing no self-injurious responses had occurred on the preceding day. Even in the final stage, a warning or reminder was given to the client for any attempt at self-injury.

Results

Figure 1 shows the change in self-injurious conduct averaged for the 11 clients. Each data point is expressed as a percentage of the baseline level. On the first day of training the

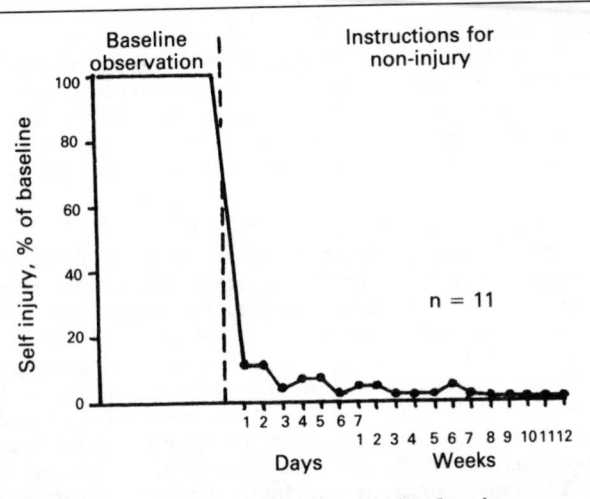

Fig. 1. Self-injurious behavior of 10 retarded and 1 schizophrenic persons. The frequency of self-injury is expressed as a percentage of the frequency recorded prior to treatment. The self-injury prior to treatment (Baseline Observation) was recorded for varying durations dictated by the safety of the client and the frequency of the behavior. The data points are for the average number per day for the first 7 days and weekly thereafter. Each data point is for 11 clients for the first 2 weeks, 9 clients for the 3rd week, 8 for the 4th to 7th weeks and 7 clients thereafter. During the 'Baseline Observation', the self-injury was simply recorded; during the 'Interruptions for Non-Injury', the instructors used positive reinforcement for non-injurious behavior, a Required Relaxation procedure for agitated states, a Hand Control procedure for self-injury and a Hand-Awareness procedure. The vertical dashed line designates the time that the treatment procedure started.

self-injurious responses decreased by 90 per cent from the pre-treatment level and decreased further by about 96 per cent by the end of the first week. By the fourth week of training, the self-injurious responses had decreased by 98 per cent and by 99 per cent by the third month. A t-test of differences showed that all of the data points were significantly less than the baseline level ($p < 0.001$). (Four clients received no treatment by the ward staff after the special instructors were absent. The data for these 4 clients are therefore included only up to the date that treatment was terminated.)

The Relaxation Procedure was used as the treatment for the first 6 clients. For 3 of these clients, the Relaxation Procedure was very effective, but none of the other 3 clients was benefitted substantially and 2 of them began injuring themselves in a seemingly deliberate fashion in order to obtain the bed-rest indicating that the bed-rest involved in the procedure was serving as a reinforcer for self-injury. In addition, these 3 clients continued to attempt to injure themselves while in bed unless very closely supervised. Consequently, the Relaxation Procedure was discontinued for these 3 clients and the Hand Control procedure substituted for it. The last 5 clients were given only the Hand Control procedure and no Relaxation Training. The data treatment points in Fig. 1 are for the Hand Control procedure for all but the first 3 clients whose data points are for the Relaxation Procedure.

Analysis of the individual benefits showed that 4 of the 11 clients were almost totally free of the self-injurious responses, either having no further self-injurious responses or less than one per week. One of these was discharged to a shelter-care facility where the operators reported he has not exhibited any self-injury. Each of the other 7 clients averaged less than 4 self-injurious responses per day by the second week of treatment. The client who had exhibited self-injurious behavior for the longest period, 31 yr, had the highest level of self-injury after 2 weeks, an average of four self-injurious responses per day. The client who had exhibited self-injurious responses shortly after birth, and a high pre-treatment rate of 3500 responses per day, exhibited an average of only one self-injurious response per week after 2 months of treatment.

Three of the clients often physically aggressed against other residents or staff members at the same time that they exhibited self-injury. The physical aggression by all 3 clients decreased substantially once treatment was initiated for the self-injury.

General improvements in the clients' overall manner were evident when the self-injurious behavior was decreased. Ten of the 11 clients seemed to greatly increase their social interactions and social responsiveness. The notable exception was one client located on a ward with virtually no programmed activities and whose pre-treatment routine was to sit limply in a chair or to lie in a corner asleep wearing his protective helmet. He exhibited little muscle tone when the instructor manually guided him during attempts at reinforcement during the treatment phase.

Discussion

The new procedure was effective in eliminating, or greatly reducing, the self-injurious behavior of the mentally ill and retarded clients. The treatment was fairly rapid as seen by the average reduction of about 90 per cent on the first day and about 96 per cent by the seventh day. The treatment appears applicable to the general population of self-injurious clients as seen by its effectiveness with all 11 clients in the present unselected sample. The extent of the benefit was substantial in that after three months of treatment, the self-injurious behavior was reduced by an average of 99 per cent. Self-injury was virtually eliminated for all 4 clients. The general acceptability of the treatment was evidenced by the positive reaction of the clinical personnel in all five institutions in which the clients were treated.

Speculatively, the degree of benefit for a given client seemed to be greater if he had a pre-existing high level of outward-directed behavior, or if the ward environment strongly encouraged outward-directed activity. All 4 of the clients who were virtually 'cured' had considerable social and attention-getting behavior, including aggression toward others by three of them, whereas the clients who benefitted less, were seemingly oblivious to the presence or actions of others. The 'custodial' type of wards in which little attention was paid to residents often abandoned the treatment effort, whereas the clients in the treatment-oriented ward situations continued to receive the instruction and continued to benefit. The Required Relaxation procedure seemed most appropriate for the outward-directed client whereas the Hand Control procedure seemed more appropriate with the inward-directed client. The 3 clients with whom the Required Relaxation was successful were all of the outward-directed type, whereas the 3 clients with whom it was unsuccessful were inward-directed.

Comparison of the present procedure with alternative procedures must be somewhat tentative since the clients treated in the previous reports are of unknown comparability. Nevertheless, the present method appears to be more acceptable as a treatment than either shock or timeout seclusion, in that no physical punishment is used and the emphasis is on instruction and adding reinforcers. In all of the institutions included in this study, shock was viewed as a last resort and the staff were apprehensive about its abuse. They were eager to use this procedure before considering shock punishment. With respect to the speed of treatment, the present method appears at least as rapid as has been reported for the alternative methods but far less rapid than the almost instantaneous benefit obtained in most reports of shock (Bucher and Lovaas, 1968; Corte *et al.*, 1971; Tate and Baroff, 1966; Risley, 1968). With respect to general applicability to a variety of clients, the present method would be considered superior at this time if only because the previous reports have been case studies that have not as yet reported results for a large number of unselected clients. In general, the present method seems to provide many advantages over the alternative methods.

Acknowledgements

This research was supported by the Illinois Department of Mental Health. Grateful acknowledgement is given to the many staff members of the several institutions in the State of Illinois who participated in this project.

References

Azrin, N. H., Kaplan, S. J., Foxx, R. M. Autism reversal: eliminating stereotyped self-stimulation of retarded individuals. *Am. J. Ment. Defic.*, 1973; **78**, 241-248.

Azrin, N. H., Nunn, R. G. Habit-reversal: a method of eliminating nervous habits and tics. *Behav. Res. & Ther.*, 1973; **11**, 619-628.

Bucher, B., Lovaas, O. I. Use of aversive stimulation in behavior modification. *In* Jones, M. R. (Ed.). *Miami Symposium on the Prediction of Behavior, 1967: Aversive Stimulation.* (pp. 77-145.) Florida: University of Miami Press, 1968.

Corte, H. E., Wolf, M. M., Locke, B. J. A comparison of procedures for eliminating self-injurious behavior of retarded adolescents. *J. Appl. Behav. Anal.*, 1971; **4**, 201-213.

Foxx, R. M., Azrin, N. H. Restitution: a method of eliminating aggressive-disruptive behavior of retarded and brain damaged patients. *Behav. Res. & Ther.*, 1972; **10**, 15-27.

Foxx, R. M., Azrin, N. H. The elimination of autistic self-stimulatory behavior by overcorrection. *J. Appl. Behav. Anal.*, 1973; **6**, 1-14.

Hamilton, J., Stephens, L., Allen, P. Controlling aggressive and destructive behavior in severely retarded institutionalized residents. *Am. J. Ment. Defic.*, 1967; **71**, 852-856.

Lane, R. G., Domrath, R. P. Behavior Therapy: a case history. *Hosp. & Commun. Psychiat.*, 1970; **21**, 150-153.

Lovaas, O. I., Freitag, G., Gold, V. J., Kassorla, I. C. Experimental studies in childhood schizophrenia: analysis of self-destructive behavior. *Behav. Res. & Ther.*, 1965; **2**, 67-84.

Myers, J. J., Deibert, A. N. Reduction of self-abusive behavior in a blind child by using a feeding response. *J. Behav. Ther. & Exp. Psychiat.*, 1971; **2**, 141-144.

Peterson, R. F., Peterson, L. R. The use of positive reinforcement in the control of self-destructive behavior in a retarded boy. *J. Exp. Child Psychol.*, 1968; **6**, 351-360.

Risley, T. The effects of punishing the autistic behaviors of a deviant child. *J. Appl. Behav. Anal.*, 1968; **1**, 21-34.

Tate, B. G., Baroff, G. S. Aversive control of self-injurious behavior in a psychotic boy. *Behav. Res. & Ther.*, 1966; **4**, 281-287.

Webster, D. R., Azrin, N. H. Required relaxation: a method of inhibiting agitative-disruptive behavior of retardates. *Behav. Res. & Ther.*, 1972; **11**, 67-78.

Wolf, M., Risley, T., Johnston, M., Harris, F., Allen, E. Application of operant conditioning procedures to the behavior problems of an autistic child: a follow-up and extension. *Behav. Res. & Ther.*, 1967; **5**, 103-111.

Wolf, M., Risley, T., Mees, H. Application of operant conditioning procedures to the behavior problems of an autistic child. *Behav. Res. & Ther.*, 1964; **1**, 305-312.

Yeakel, M. H., Salisbury, L. L., Greer, S. L., Marcus, L. F. An appliance for autoinduced adverse control of self-injurious behavior. *J. Exp. Child Psychol.*, 1970; **10**, 159-169.

Reprinted from *Behav. Res. & Ther.*, 1975; **13**, 101-111 by kind permission of N. H. Azrin and the publishers Pergamon Press Ltd., Oxford OX3 0BN.

THE ELIMINATION OF A SELF-INJURIOUS AVOIDANCE RESPONSE THROUGH A FORCED RUNNING CONSEQUENCE*

Paul M. Borreson

Intermediate School District # 347, Willmar Public Schools, Willmar, MN

Abstract

The self-injurious avoidance responses of a 22 year old profoundly mentally retarded male were eliminated through a forced running consequence. The effects were reversible as demonstrated in an A-B-A-B design. Several positive side effects were noted. Generalization was quickly achieved when the punishment procedure was implemented in the residential setting. The results were maintained over a period of two years.

Self-injurious behavior (SIB) is a common phenomena in severely and profoundly mentally retarded (MR) institutionalized individuals. The most common forms include scratching, head banging, and gouging. A variety of procedures have been employed to effectively reduce the severity of the problem or entirely eliminate it in some individuals (see Frankel and Simmons, 1976 for a review). However, there is a paucity of research on procedures successful in treating the subject who responds with SIB in high demand situations. The purpose of the present study was to evaluate the efficacy of forced running as a punishing consequence for the self-injurious avoidance responses of an MR adult.

Method

Setting

The investigation was conducted in a day school program for severely and profoundly MR children and adults operated by the Willmar Public Schools, Willmar, Minnesota. S was one of six students in a classroom with one-to-two staff to student ratio. Classes were in session five days a week, six hours per day. The study was conducted for the entire school day over a period of four months.

Subject

S was a 22 year old profoundly retarded male admitted to an institution for MR persons in west central Minnesota at age 19. Psychological testing within the last year yielded a Slossen Intelligence Quotient of 10 and a Mental Age of 18 months. He received a Social Quotient of 10 and a Social Age of 2 years 4 months on the Vineland Social Maturity Scale. Physically, S was in good health. He alternated feet up and down stairways, displayed normal range of motion and would run independently displaying a shuffling gait with no heel strike. Because of the latter characteristic the school nurse and residential medical staff observed and examined his feet and ankles before and after engaging in the forced running consequence. Neither pain nor physical problems were observed. Subsequently, the treatment procedure was approved by both school and residential based Human Rights Committees.

S possessed only rudimentary self-care skills and no expressive language, but did have receptive language for basic commands. His instructional program consisted of self-care, fine and gross motor skill acquisition, and receptive language training. He engaged in a high rate of self-injurious avoidance behavior involving the biting of hands, wrists and forearms, accompanied by a loud growling noise. S would engage in SIB to avoid instructional demands. Several different systematic programs consistent with the principle

* The author expresses appreciation to Carmen Bailey, Karen Hendricksen, Jane Hjelle, and Adeline Nelson for their consistent efforts in implementing the procedures and to Jean Anderson, Program Coordinator, for her administrative support throughout the entirety of the study.

of the least restrictive alternative had been attempted. A five minute Differential Reinforcement of Other behavior (D.R.O.) program was the first to be implemented using food and social praise as reinforcers. No significant change was observed from this treatment. Subsequently, a plan involving reinforcement for incompatible behavior was implemented using attention and food as reinforcers. The behavior remained at its high baseline level. Extinction was attempted but resulted in no change. A ten minute mechanical restraint program paired with reinforcement for incompatible behavior had reduced the frequency initially but became less effective over several months. On rare occasions S's hands and wrists would require medical attention after intense biting sessions. The most probable antecedent for S emitting the target behavior was in response to instructional commands (e.g. "put your shoes on.") Two other lower probability situations that stimulated the SIB response included his approaching staff members to obtain attention and also when discouraged from the simultaneous hugging and hair pulling of a staff member. S manipulated adult attention in the precise way hypothesized by Frankel and Simmons (1976) in their operant model for self-injurious behavior. Specifically, he elicited adult attention through SIB and reduced adult attention in high demand situations through SIB. S also frequently engaged in other hand-to-mouth behaviors that gave the appearance of "threading a needle." This movement involved moving his hands in a brief circular motion followed by touching his protruding tongue.

Procedure

Whenever S displayed the biting behavior the instructional task was immediately terminated, as the command "no biting" was issued. S was immediately guided up and down a four-step training stairway. The physical guidance was provided to increase the rate of stair climbing to a faster than normal rate. A minimum of two staff members implemented the consequence with one providing the inertia through pushing S while the other followed closely behind or at the side of the stairway insuring proper positioning of the feet on the risers to guard against injuries. It required less than one minute to be removed from the instructional activity, physically guided up and down the stairway twice, return to the classroom and resume the instructional activity that was interrupted. The same instructional request that precipitated the avoidance response was immediately delivered again. On the less frequent occasions when he would bite himself while approaching a staff member or when discouraged from hugging and hair pulling he would be physically guided through the training staircase and returned to the specific area of the classroom where the self-injurious response occurred as there was no specific instructional request. If SIB occurred when not in close proximity to the training stair, the staircase in closest proximity was used. S was reinforced with edibles for incompatible behaviors of responding to instructional requests, toy play, appropriate social contact and manipulation of instructional materials throughout all conditions of the study.

A self-injurious biting response was operationally defined as any finger, palm, wrist, or forearm either entering the mouth to the extent that it was placed between the upper and lower teeth, or positioned on the lips or teeth for greater than two seconds and then removed from contact with the mouth. Consequently, the hand-to-mouth behavior having the appearance of "threading a needle" was not consequated due to the short contact of the fingers with the mouth.

Recording

Frequency counts of the self-injurious biting response was made throughout the course of the six hour school day. Data collected during the A_1 baseline condition are based on frequency counts during six fifteen minute intervals. These intervals were spaced at one per hour throughout the day. This information was extrapolated to make it comparable to the continuous full day data collected in the remaining conditions. Reliability was calculated for one fifteen minute period in each phase of the study by the author. Frequency counts of the SIB were compared for each minute. Agreement was defined as having an identical SIB count at the end of each minute interval resulting in fifteen one minute interval comparisons. Reliabiity was calculated using a percent agreement formula. Percent agreement ranged from a low of 86 to a high of 100, yielding a mean of 97.

Experimental design

The experimental design consisted of an A-B-A-B phase sequence, with A denoting baseline conditions and B treatment conditions.The independent variable was the application of forced running contingent upon the occurrence of the dependent variable, the biting response. During baseline conditions when S engaged in self-injurious behavior it was ignored if it did not interfere with training. If his biting interrupted an instructional task his hands were guided back toward the instructional activity. No verbal directions were provided.

Results

The effect of forced running on SIB responding is shown in Figure 1. In the A_1 baseline condition S displayed a mean SIB frequency of 1,236 per day. During the first five days of

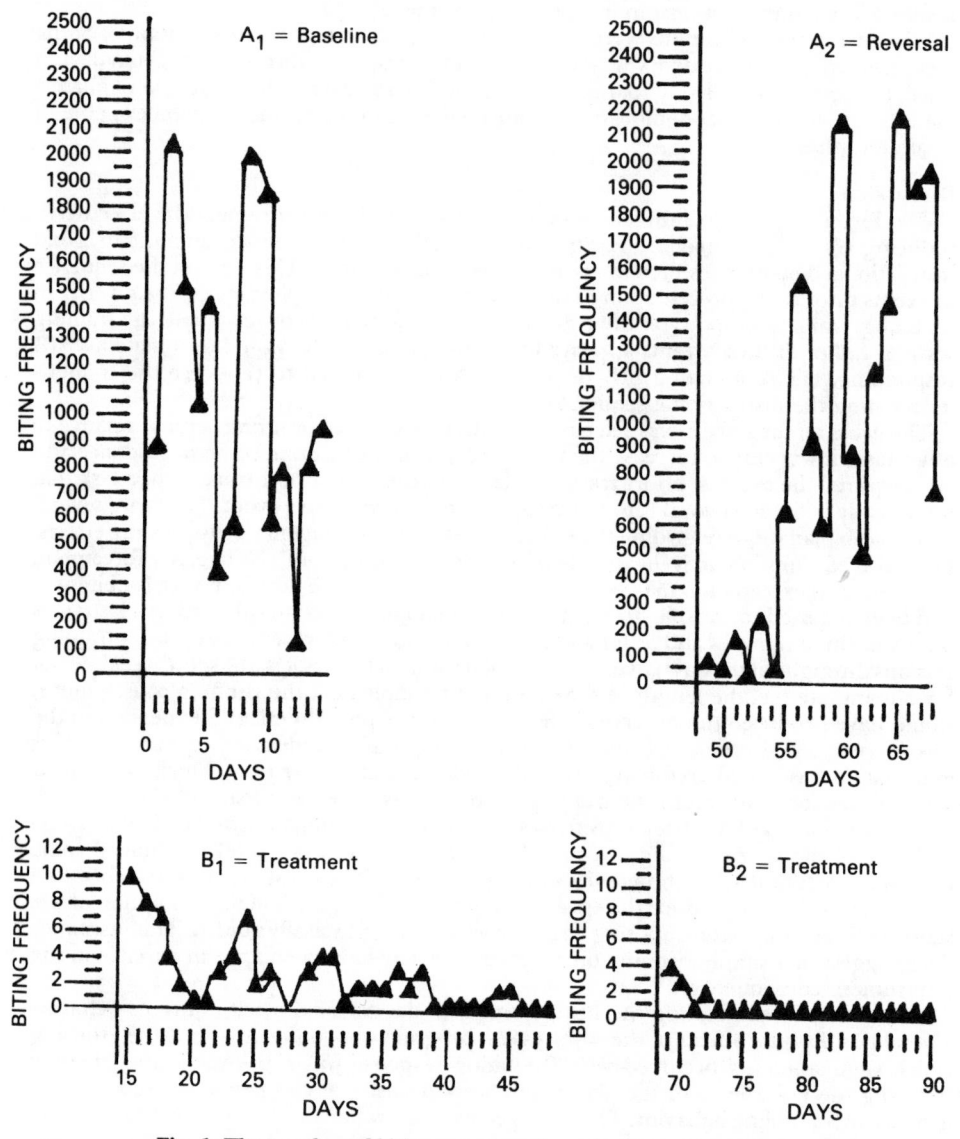

Fig. 1. The number of biting responses in a six-hour school day.

the B₁ treatment phase there was a steady decline in S's rate of biting behavior, reaching a frequency of zero by the sixth treatment day. Days 22, 23 and 24 revealed slight rate increases to a maximum of six biting occurrences on the 24th day, returning to zero by the 27th day. From days 39 to 48 S only bit himself twice. During the first treatment phase lasting a total of 34 days S only bit himself 58 times yielding a mean of less than twice/day.

The reversal phase commenced on day 49 and lasted through day 68. With the exception of the first day of the reversal condition when S made no biting responses, response rate climbed dramatically reaching a peak in excess of 2100 responses on days 59 and 65. During the 19 day A_2 condition S exhibited a total of 17,692 self-injurious biting responses yielding a mean of 842 per day. Instructional programming became exceedingly difficult during this phase, as it had been during the A_1 baseline condition. Although the rate of SIB in the A_2 condition did not return to the same level as the initial baseline, control of the behavior was demonstrated when the B_2 phase was implemented. A longer A_2 phase may have resulted in a closer relationship in the A_1 and A_2 means.

When treatment conditions were reinstated on day 69 an immediate cessation of biting was observed. Biting frequency was reduced to seven responses during the first ten days of the B_2 treatment phase. In comparison, during the first ten days of the B_1 treatment phase S made 37 biting responses demonstrating much faster learning of the contingency in the B_2 treatment phase.

Discussion

The forced running contingency for avoidance behavior was dramatically effective in reducing S's biting behavior. He quickly learned that biting in an attempt to avoid instructional demands resulted in greater behavioral demands. This was not the sequence of events prior to the presentation of the treatment strategy. Depending on the severity of S's biting, trainers would typically provide fewer training trials or terminate the training session. Either of these events appeared to reinforce S since he would terminate his SIB responding. His terminating SIB responding also functioned to reinforce the trainer's terminating the instructional sequence.

The gross motor activity was selected from his instructional program because relative to other tasks it was easy to increase the rate of performance through physical guidance and also required the greatest effort from S. Increasing the rate of performance of a task that was already in S's behavioral repertoire functioned as an aversive event. There are several plausible explanations regarding the effectiveness of the contingency's suppressing effects. First, forced running may have functioned as time out from positive reinforcement. However, this explanation may be faulted by examining S's treatment history for biting. S had been exposed to various time outs using human and mechanical restraints lasting as briefly as three minutes and as long as twenty-four hours interspersed with brief training sessions throughout the day. Given this type of treatment history it is unlikely that a time out for one minute (i.e. the length of time required to implement the running consequence) would have produced the observed effect. Second, the physical effort S expended in the forced running consequence may have been physically unpleasant or aversive. This explanation has added credibility given the sedentary character of S. Third, the rate at which S was forced through the training staircase may have been fear inducing. Finally, forced running may have been effective as a result of the combination of the physical stress and fear of the stair climbing activity when performed at a fast rate. S exhibited some resistance each time the contingency was implemented. The resistance was usually in the form of attempting to reduce the speed of movement down the hall to the location of the staircase by leaning in the opposing direction while being physically guided. This resistance does suggest that simple running on a flat surface may have been a major variable in the punishment consequence.

In addition to eliminating the obvious medical danger of the self-injurious behavior several positive side effects of the suppression program were observed. First, the growling which simultaneously occurred with the biting response was suppressed, also, thereby reducing the noise level in the classroom. Second, instructional personnel reported an increase in S's smiling behavior. Third, subjective observations suggested an increased rate in ascending and descending the training staircase independently. Finally, S began to make progress on his instructional objectives at a much faster pace than previously, since training sessions were no longer terminated to stop S from biting.

Generalizations of the suppressive effect across individual trainers and settings was not spontaneously obtained. On days 22, 23 and 24 of the B_1 treatment phase a substitute instructional aide was involved in S's programming. This led to slight temporary increases in response rate. During the entirety of the B_1 and B_2 treatment phases self-injurious response rate did not decrease during non-school hours in the residential setting. Once the treatment variable was instituted in the residential setting rapid suppression of the SIB response was achieved. Birnbrauer (1968) observed similar generalization effects utilizing response contingent electric shock as the aversive stimulus.

Follow-up One

During the three monts following the completion of the B_2 treatment phase S manifested only one SIB response in the school setting. S's response rate in the residential setting had also been maintained at an equally low level. As a consequence S's hands, wrists, and forearms had healed completely, and the heavy calouses had disappeared and been replaced by forearm hair.

Follow-up Two

Six months following completion of the B_2 treatment phase S had manifested only four SIB responses in the school setting. At this time a second component of the therapy program was initiated. Previously, S had not been consequated for the hand-to-mouth behavior that gave the appearance of "threading a needle", since the behavior was not physically injurious. However, this behavior represented an approximation to the original SIB response and was therefore consequated in a similar manner. At this time when S engaged in any hand-to-mouth movements he was immediately physically guided in a running response on a flat surface and was not physically guided through a staircase. A response reduction pattern nearly identical to the experimental phases of the original experiment was observed. This data lends some support to the differential effects of the stair-climbing exercise and rate components of the original program. That is, rapid movement may have been the aversive component responsible for the response reduction rather than stair climbing. However, in the absence of a thorough component analysis the issue remains clouded.

Follow-up Three

Two years following the final treatment phase S remained in good health and had not engaged in self-injurious behavior or any approximations thereof in the school setting. He has acquired several self-care skills, is compliant in training situations and appears to be well adjusted.

References

Birnbrauer, J. S. Generalization of punishment effects: a case study. *J. Appl. Behav. Anal.*, 1968; **1**, 63-71.

Frankel, F., Simmons, J. Q. Self-injurious behavior in schizophrenic and retarded children. *Am. J. Ment. Defic.*, 1976; **80**, 512-522.

Reprinted from *Mental Retardation*, 1980; **18**; 73-77 by kind permission of Paul M. Borreson and the publishers American Association on Mental Deficiency, Washington DC 20009.

LEMON-JUICE THERAPY: THE CONTROL OF LIFE-THREATENING RUMINATION IN A SIX-MONTH-OLD INFANT[1]

Thomas Sajwaj, Julian Libet[2], Stewart Agras[3]
University of Mississippi Medical Center

Summary
Chronic, life-threatening rumination was eliminated in a six-month-old infant by squirting a small amount of lemon juice into her mouth whenever rumination or its precursors were detected. A brief suspension of this therapy demonstrated its crucial role. Lemon-juice therapy offers a practical and acceptable alternative to other therapies for rumination, namely electric shock and massive noncontingent attention. However, since this study is limited to a single case, claims as to the effectiveness of this therapy across children are premature.

Chronic rumination is a behavior of considerable clinical significance in infants. Kanner (1957,p.484) defined it as . . . "bringing up food without nausea, retching, or disgust. The food is then ejected from the mouth (if liquid, allowed to run out) or reswallowed". This behavior appears to be "voluntary", that is, children actively engage in behaviors that induce the rumination, e.g., infants are observed to strain vigorously to bring food back to their mouth. The incidence of rumination in the general population is unknown, since it is typically confused with food allergies, especially to milk. Serious clinical problems, such as malnutrition, dehydration, and lowered resistance to disease, may prompt a life-threatening condition if significant amounts of food are lost. Kanner (1957) noted that 11 of 52 ruminating babies in one group died; Gaddini and Gaddini (1959) reported death in one of six cases. Within the first author's experience, one of eight referred ruminating children died.

Treatment procedures for infantile rumination are diverse. Kanner (1957) noted the use of surgery, drugs, mechanical devices (e.g., chin straps, esophagus blocks), thickened feedings with farina, and very high levels of attention, with the last treatment producing the most positive effects. Typically, an adult is assigned to provide the ruminating child with his undivided attention for at least 8 hr a day. Fullerton (1963), Gaddini and Gaddini (1959), Hollowell and Gardner (1965), Menking, Wagnitz, Burton, Coddington, and Sotos (1969), Richmond, Eddy, and Green (1958), and Stein, Rausen, and Blau (1959) all reported reductions in rumination and increases in weight coincident with the onset of high levels of attention. One difficulty with this treatment is that cessation of rumination is usually slow. Hollowell and Gardner (1965), Menking et al. (1958), and Stein et al. (1969), reported that rumination gradually disappeared over four to eight weeks. In contrast, Fullerton (1963) reported cessation in four days for one infant.

Since rumination is often life-threatening, a more rapid treatment has been sought. White and Taylor (1967) apparently were the first to use contingent electric shock for rumination. Although they did not report adequate quantitative data, they concluded that shock did significantly interfere with rumination. Galbraith, Byrick, and Rutledge (1970), Lang and Melamed (1969), and Luckey, Watson, and Musick (1968) reported cessation of vomiting and rumination within two to four days when shock was used. Kohlenberg (1970)

[1]This clinical case study was supported in part by the Avery Fund for Research in the Behavioral Sciences. The authors wish to express their most grateful appreciation to Dr. Blair Bateson and his staff of the Department of Pediatrics for their most gracious cooperation. Reprints may be obtained from Thomas Sajwaj, North Mississipi Retardation Center, Oxford, Mississipi 38655.
[2]Now at the Department of Psychiatry and Behavior Sciences, Medical University of South Carolina, Charleston, South Carolina.
[3]Now at the Department of Psychiatry, Stanford University School of Medicine, Stanford, California.

shocked stomach tension that preceded vomiting. Elimination of stomach tension and vomiting occurred within one day. Bright and Whaley (1969) first attempted to eliminate regurgitation and vomiting in a retarded boy with Tabasco brand peppersauce before resorting to shock. The peppersauce was sprinkled on the vomitus. Very substantial reductions in regurgitation and rumination resulted, but neither was eliminated. Shock then eliminated both behaviors within three days.

The present paper reports the successful treatment of life-threatening rumination in an infant through the use of lemon juice as a punisher. Even though the infant's physical condition was serious, the authors were reluctant to resort to shock, since they felt that it might jeopardize co-operation with the pediatrics ward staff. Further, successful treatment might require the use of shock after hospital discharge by the parents, but there was evidence of family instability and neglect of the child.

Method

Child

Sandra was born on September 6, 1971, to an economically marginal, rural family after an unplanned, uncomplicated pregnancy. She was delivered at home by a nurse-midwife and weighed eight pounds. The next day she was admitted to the University Hospital for feeding difficulties associated with a cleft palate and lip. These difficulties were rectified with gastric tube feedings, and Sandra was discharged to her aunt nine days after admission. During the next four months, weight gain was below average, although neither mother nor aunt reported any further feeding difficulties. There were, however, indications of neglect and Sandra was cared for during this period by a number of different individuals, including neighborhood children.

Sandra was admitted to the University Hospital for the second time on February 29, 1972, at the age of about six months by the aunt because of a failure to gain weight associated with rumination. On examination, she was emaciated and unresponsive to her environment. There was very little grasping of objects, no smiling, no babbling, no gross movements, and some crying. She was primarily lethargic and lay passively in her crib. Exhaustive medical examinations and laboratory analyses revealed no organic cause for her difficulties. Her weight, however, was falling rapidly and was below her birth weight and below the third percentile for infant girls. Malnutrition and dehydration were pressing problems, and death, resulting from possible complications, was a distinct possibility.

Measurement of rumination

Feeding consisted of a commercially prepared formula every 4 hr. Immediately after each feeding, ruminative behavior would begin. Sandra would open her mouth, elevate and fold her tongue, and then vigorously thrust her tongue forward and backward. Within a few seconds milk would appear at the back of her mouth and then slowly flow out. This behavior would continue for about 20 to 40 min until she apparently lost all of the milk she had previously consumed. No crying or evidence of pain and discomfort was observed during this behavior. Rumination could be interrupted by touches, pokes, or mild slaps, but would resume immediately.

This rumination behavior was recorded through the use of the 10-sec-block method (Allen, Hart, Buell, Harris, and Wolf, 1964). A check was made in each 10-sec interval for any occurrence of tongue thrusting with her mouth open. The tongue did not have to be elevated or folded, nor did milk need to be visible. A check of observer agreement was made with the help of an independent observer on one occasion in each of the four experimental conditions. Observers were about 3ft (0.9m) apart in full view of each other. Data sheets could not be readily seen and observers would mark each interval even if no coded behaviors occurred. An agreement was scored if both observers checked the occurrence of rumination in corresponding time intervals. A disagreement was scored if only one observer had scored rumination in an interval. Agreements on the nonoccurrence of rumination were not included in these computations. The four checks on the recording of rumination yielded indices (agreements divided by the sum of agreements plus disagreements) of: 91% (42/46), 100% (11/11), 95% (75/79), and 75% (12/16).

Sandra was observed for 20 min immediately following a feeding. The observational period started when the bottle was removed from her mouth for the last time. The period ended 20 min later whether or not rumination was continuing. During the first three experimental conditions, Sandra was observed after four to six feedings daily. During the final condition, observation was reduced to one to three times daily.

Sandra was weighed daily at roughly the same time in the morning while clothed only in diaper. The same scale was used throughout this study.

Procedure

Baseline conditions involved the usual circumstances and conditions of care given on the pediatrics ward. No one individual was assigned to care for Sandra. Rumination was not treated systematically, save for some intermittent mild slapping by ward staff when rumination was observed. However, no slapping was allowed during the five observation periods during the baseline condition or at any other time subsequently.

Lemon-juice therapy was initiated on March 15. This consisted of squirting about five to 10-cc of lemon juice (unsweetened Realemon brand) into her mouth with a 30-cc medical syringe as soon as vigorous tongue movements were detected. At the occurrence of each instance of tongue movements, her mouth was filled with lemon-juice. For the next 30-60 secs no more lemon juice was administered, although tongue movements might persist. Lemon juice was so omitted because it tended to produce some lip and tongue smacking. Then, lemon juice was reapplied, if ruminative tongue movements persisted or if a new episode started. During these 30- 60-sec periods, lip and tongue movements continued to be scored as ruminative behavior. Ward staff were carefully instructed in the use of lemon juice by observing the authors and by using the lemon juice while the authors were present to give feedback. Lemon juice was to be used at any time ruminative tongue movements were observed, whether or not the authors or observers were present. This responsibility was assigned to one of two specific ward staff for each shift, in addition to their normal duties. Reports from other ward staff and observation by the authors and observers indicated that the responsible staff correctly used the lemon juice.

After 16 feedings with lemon-juice therapy, the use of lemon juice was suspended for 8 hr, during which two feedings occurred. Lemon-juice therapy was then resumed immediately following the next feeding.

During the initial lemon-juice condition, informal observation by several individuals suggested that the amount of attention given Sandra by the ward staff began to increase spontaneously. To help control for this concurrent change the ward staff were instructed to continue this relatively higher level of attention throughout the reversal condition and into the resumption of lemon juice. The authors verified that the staff continued high levels of attention by casual observations during the 20-min postfeeding period and at other times of the day.

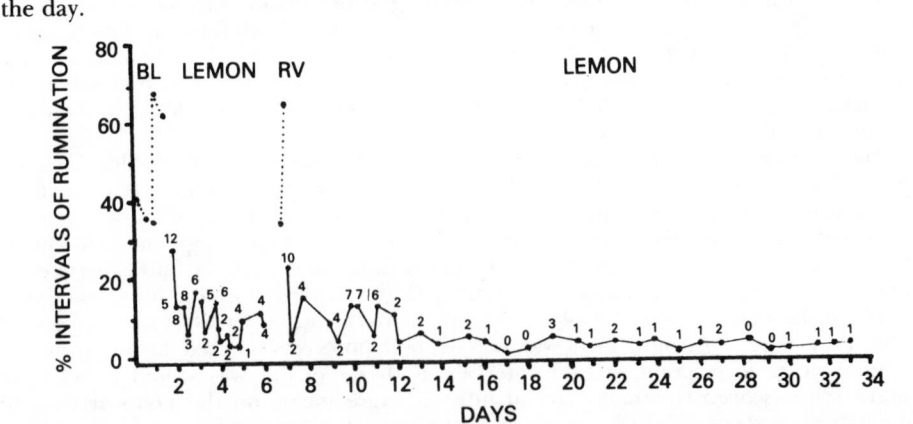

Fig. 1. Per cent intervals of Sandra's rumination during the 20-min postfeeding periods during baseline (BL), lemon-juice therapy periods (LEMON), and brief cessation of therapy (RV). The numbers over the data points refer to the number of applications of lemon juice after each feeding session.

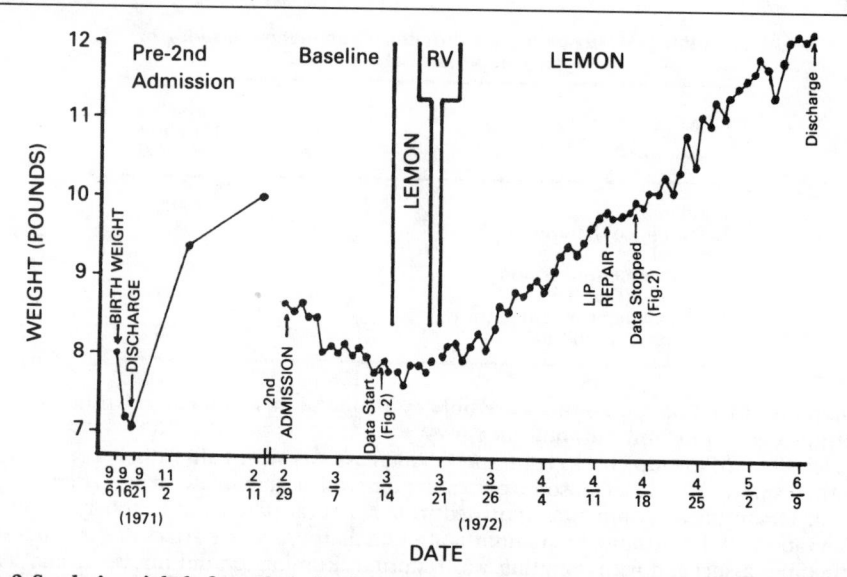

Fig. 2. Sandra's weight before admission for rumination (before second admission), during baseline before lemon-juice therapy, during lemon-juice therapy (LEMON), and during brief cessation of therapy (RV). Data shown were obtained between March 13 and April 16, 1972.

After eight weeks of lemon-juice therapy in the hospital, Sandra was discharged to the care of foster parents, who were carefully instructed in the use of lemon juice. Five months later custody was returned to her biological parents. Sandra was seen at seven follow-up visits over a 12- month period. At 10 months posthospitalization, the Denver Developmental Screening Test and the Vineland Social Maturity Scales were administered.

Results

The baseline of Figure 1 shows that the percent of 10-sec intervals of rumination was between 40% and 70% for the first 20 min following a feeding. Her weight was falling rapidly (baseline, Figure 2).

The initial use of lemon juice decreased rumination and vigorous tongue movements to below 10% of the 20-min period. The number of applications of lemon juice during these periods is shown on Figure 1. Weight ceased to fall and stabilized at just under eight pounds. The brief omission of therapy prompted a return to high levels of rumination (Figure 1). The resumption of the use of lemon juice again reduced rumination. After the twelfth day (Figure 1), no regurgitated milk was ever observed in her mouth. The slight rates after this time were due to what appeared to the observers as normal lip and tongue movements. However, since these met the definition of rumination, they were scored as such. These normal mouth and tongue movements were difficult for the ward staff to detect and, consequently, lemon juice was applied intermittently for them. After Day 33, the use of lemon juice was dropped altogether for them.

Weight began to increase and continued to do so until discharge (Figure 2). There was a temporary reduction of weight gain, when the cleft lip was surgically repaired. Sandra was discharged with a weight of 12 pounds and five ounces, a 54% increase from pretreatment weight.

Table 1 gives the number and duration of rumination episodes observed during the 20-min postfeeding periods of each experimental condition. An episode was defined as rumination occurring on one or more consecutive 10-sec intervals followed by one or more intervals in which rumination was not scored. Duration was the number of consecutive scored intervals of rumination in an episode multiplied by 10-sec. The table shows that the reduction in rumination level seen in Figure 1 was due to both a reduction in the number and in the duration of rumination episodes. It should be noted that these numbers and

Table 1. Mean number and duration of rumination episodes for each experimental condition

Condition	Mean Number	Mean Duration (seconds)
Baseline	9.6	60.6
Lemon-juice therapy	4.5	33.4
Reversal	6.0	106.0
Re-instatement of lemon-juice therapy (first half)	2.8	26.4
Re-instatement of lemon-juice therapy (second half)	0.9	9.8

durations of rumination episodes are only estimates because interval recording does not permit precise rate and duration measures.

Weight on follow-up checks continued to increase. Six weeks after discharge, the foster mother reported two brief episodes of rumination, which were followed immediately by the use of lemon juice. Sandra was returned to her natural parents in October, despite the reservations of the authors. Eight months after discharge, a severe attack of gastrointestinal difficulties associated with vomiting was reported. Rumination did not recur and lemon juice was not used. Weight on one-year follow up was just over 24 pounds, which placed her at about the twenty-fifth percentile for infant girls.

Concurrent with the reduction of rumination and with the increase of weight, changes in other behaviors were observed in the hospital. Sandra became more attentive of adults about her, smiling appeared, and she began grabbing at objects near her. Babbling also appeared for the first time. These behaviors continued to increase. During the follow-up visits, it was evident that motor, social, and speech development had continued. The Denver Developmental Screening Test and the Vineland Social Maturity Scale given 10 months after discharge when Sandra was about 19 months old, indicated only a slight developmental delay.

Discussion

Although the case studies cited in the introduction of this paper suggest two different treatment modes for infantile rumination, namely massive attention and electric shock, there are questions as to the effectiveness of these treatment procedures. A treatment procedure can be demonstrated unequivocally by either: (1) omitting the treatment after its initial use and then re-applying it, or (2) using a multiple baseline design where the treatment procedure is applied sequentially to different patients or to different behaviors within a single patient. Unfortunately, none of the above cited studies utilized either of these designs. Rather, the treatment procedures were applied after an initial period of observation. No further manipulations of the treatment procedures were attempted, and possible contaminations by other time-related factors are not eliminated. Luckey, et al. (1968) is a partial exception because rumination and vomiting in their patient recurred after contingent shock had apparently eliminated it. Shock was again used, and vomiting again rapidly disappeared.

Although the brief ommission of lemon-juice therapy demonstrated its critical role, the question arises as to the critical role of the lemon juice itself, since the therapy has several components. Other contributing factors may be the interruption of the ruminative behavior, the forceful injection of a fluid into the mouth, the temperature difference between the room-temperature lemon juice and the mouth fluids, and the attention accompanying the administration of the lemon juice. This case study does not attempt an analysis of the differential role of these components. However, subsequent preliminary work with other ruminating children suggests a central role for lemon juice *per se*.

One major strength of behavioral techniques has been the ability of paraprofessionals to use them effectively. Shock, however, as a prime treatment tactic for rumination and vomiting does not lend itself to use because of the pain and suffering it entails. Even when used, some individuals may not use the shock as consistently and often as is initially necessary for it to be effective. Related to this minimal social acceptance is the problem of potential abuse. Paraprofessionals should not be trained in the use of shock when there is any suspicion of possible abuse or neglect. Consequently, shock is limited to use by professional staff in restricted settings, and it will be avoided altogether by some institutions and agencies.

The use of lemon juice as a punisher avoids these problems. Lemon juice caused only mild discomfort, if any, to the infant, and the pediatrics staff were not adverse to its use. Further, abuse would be difficult, if not impossible, and its use could be taught to most parents without fear. However, the evaluation of the effectiveness of lemon-juice therapy is limited to this one case. Whether the therapy will prove effective with other ruminating children in other settings in differing circumstances remains to be demonstrated.

Two medical complications may arise from the use of lemon juice therapy. First, since lemon juice is acid, it will irritate the interior and immediate exterior of the mouth. This irritation is minimal and disappears rapidly as the use of lemon juice decreases. Second, aspiration of lemon juice into the lungs is a possibility with serious medical complications resulting. The risk of aspiration can be minimized by keeping the child's head upright or down, not back, when the lemon juice is injected, by reducing the amount of lemon juice injected, and by minimizing the force with which the lemon juice strikes the inside of the mouth. Neither aspiration or gagging were ever observed with Sandra.

References

Allen, K. E., Hart, B. M., Buell, J. S., Harris, F. R., Wolf, M. M. Effects of social reinforcement on isolate behavior of a nursery school child. *Child Development*, 1964, **35**, 511-518.

Bright, G. O., Whaley, D. L. Suppression of regurgitation and rumination with aversive events. *Michigan Mental Health Research Bulletin*, 1968; **11**, 17-20.

Fullerton, D. T. Infantile rumination: a case report. *Archives of General Psychiatry*, 1963, **9**, 593-600.

Gaddini, R., Gaddini, E. Rumination in infancy. In Jessner, C., Pavenstadt, E. (Eds.). *Dynamic psychopathology in childhood.* New York: Grune & Stratton, 1959. Pp.166-185.

Galbraith, D., Byrick, R., Rutledge, J. T. An aversive conditioning approach to the inhibition of chronic vomiting. *Canadian Psychiatric Association Journal*, 1970; **15**, 311-313.

Hollowell, J. R., Gardner, L. I. Rumination and growth failure in male fraternal twins: association with disturbed family environment. *Pediatrics*, 1965; **36**, 565-571.

Kanner, L. *Child psychiatry.* 3rd ed.; Springfield, Ill.; Charles C. Thomas, 1957.

Kohlenberg, R. J. The punishment of persistent vomiting: a case study. *J. Appl. Behav. Anal.*, 1970; **3**, 241-245.

Lang, P. J., Melamed, B. G. Avoidance conditioning therapy of an infant with chronic ruminative vomiting. *J. Abnorm. Behav.*, 1969; **74**, 139-142.

Luckey, R. E., Watson, C. M., Musick, J. K. Aversive conditioning as a means of inhibiting vomiting and rumination. *Am. J. Ment. Defic.*, 1968; **73**, 139-142.

Menking, M., Wagnitz, J., Burton, J., Coddington, R. D., Sotos, J. Rumination — A new fatal psychiatric disease of infancy. *New Engl. J. Med.*, 1969; **281**, 802-804.

Richmond, J. B., Eddy, E., Green, M. Rumination: A psychosomatic syndrome of infancy. *Pediatrics*, 1958; **22**, 49-54.

Stein, M. L., Rausen, A. R., Blau, A. Psychotherapy of an infant with rumination. *Am. Med. Assoc.*, 1959; **171**, 2309-2312.

White, J. C., Taylor, D. J. Noxious conditioning as a treatment for rumination. *Ment. Retard.*, 1967; **5**, 30-33.

Reprinted from *J. Appl. Behav. Anal.*, 1974; **7**, 557-563 by kind permission of the authors and JABA, University of Kansas, Lawrence, Kansas 66045. Copyright 1974 by the Society for the Experimental Analysis of Behavior Inc. Thomas Sajwaj is now at Tennessee Valley Authority, 112 Patten Towers, Chattanooga, Tennessee 37401.

SUPPRESSION OF SELF-INJURIOUS BEHAVIOUR: DETERMINING THE LEAST RESTRICTIVE ALTERNATIVE

M. A. Rapoff*, K. Altman, E. R. Christophersen

University of Kansas Medical Center, Kansas City, Kansas, U.S.A.

Summary
In keeping with recent ethical and legal guidelines regarding the use of aversive treatment procedures, a number of alternatives for the treatment of self-injury have been suggested. The present study provides an example of the determination of the least restrictive but most effective treatment with a case of self-injury. Employing a combination of multiple baseline and reversal designs, the effects of DRO, overcorrection, lemon juice, and aromatic ammonia on the rate of self-poking in a profoundly retarded child were examined. DRO and overcorrection were both ineffective. Although lemon juice suppressed and stabilised the rate of poking, aromatic ammonia produced greater suppression. Implications for the testing of treatments for SIB are discussed.

Introduction

A variety of procedures, both aversive and non-aversive, have been suggested in the treatment of self-injurious behaviour (SIB) (see Baumeister and Rollings, 1976, for a thorough review). It is agreed that non-aversive procedures should be tried first (Corbett, 1975). If these prove ineffective a combination of positive and aversive procedures should be considered. It has been suggested that shock is the most effective aversive procedure (Baumeister and Rollings, 1976). However, because of legal and ethical concerns, the utilisation of lesser aversive treatment alternatives seems to be in order (Martin, 1975; Repp and Deitz, 1978). Several alternatives to more aversive procedures (such as shock) have been reported in the literature. These alternatives include response-contingent overcorrection (Azrin, Gottlieb, Hughart, Wesolowski and Rahn, 1975), lemon juice (Flavell, McGimsey and Jones, 1978), and aromatic ammonia (Tanner and Zeiler, 1975).

Overcorrection procedures have been used to modify self-injurious and self-stimulatory behaviour. Overcorrection procedures are advantageous, because physical punishment is unnecessary, staff seem to accept the procedures, and they are as rapidly effective as other treatment alternatives with the exception of shock (Azrin et al., 1975). The procedures can be implemented by parents, and suppressive effects appear to be durable (Barnard, Christophersen and Wolf, 1976). Although often successful, overcorrection procedures may be too demanding for treatment staff to implement (Kelly and Drabman, 1977). In addition in some cases the procedures have not been found to be effective (Ollendick and Matson, 1978).

In the only published report where lemon juice was applied to SIB, Flavell et al. (1978) found that SIB was suppressed reliably but not to acceptable levels. Additional treatment was necessary. The contingent use of lemon juice has been effective in suppressing rumination (Sajwaj, Libet and Agras, 1974; Becker, Turner and Sajwaj, 1978) and public masturbation (Cook, Altman, Shaw and Blaylock, 1978). In these studies, from 5 to 10 ccs of lemon juice were squirted into the subjects' mouths contingent on emission of the target responses. The use of lemon juice in cases of self-injury appears promising; however further replications are needed.

A number of studies have suggested that aromatic ammonia (smelling salts) can function as an aversive stimulus in suppressing SIB. In the first published report of the use of

*Reprint requests to: M. A. Rapoff, Pediatric Research Institute, 4106 Francis Street, Kansas City, Kansas 66103, U.S.A.

aromatic ammonia to suppress SIB, Tanner and Zeiler (1975) demonstrated the effectiveness of this procedure in eliminating self-slapping in an adult autistic subject. Ammonia capsules were crushed and placed under the subject's nose each time she slapped herself and were removed when she stopped slapping. Baumeister and Baumeister (1978) completely suppressed SIB in two institutionalised retarded children using aromatic ammonia. This treatment of SIB was incorporated into the children's daily educational programme, with all staff having contact with the participating children. As a precautionary measure, a nurse examined the children daily to check for potential negative side effects. Altman, Haavik and Cook (1978) found that ammonia effectively suppressed hair-pulling and self-biting in two young retarded children.

The present study was designed to examine the effectiveness of several alternative treatment procedures, including differential reinforcement of other behaviour (DRO), overcorrection, lemon juice, and aromatic ammonia on SIB in a profoundly retarded child. Several procedures were introduced in order to find the most effective but least aversive treatment.

Method

Subject

Jason, a five-year-old deaf-blind non-ambulatory retarded child was referred by a physician to the Children's Rehabilitation Unit, University of Kansas Medical Center, for treatment of self-injurious behaviour. At the beginning of this study Jason had at least a nine-month history of poking himself with his right thumb around the facial area, particularly on the chin and left ear. This poking behaviour frequently came in bursts and resulted in lacerations, lesions, and multiple contusions. During bursts of self-injury, Jason would typically begin poking with minimal intensity and increase until he made contact with one part of his face numerous times. He would then stop and cry. Medical records indicated Jason had multiple congenital anomalies including megalocornea, congenital glaucoma, and retarded mental and motor development. Several physicians indicated Jason had a large percentage of the findings present in Hurler's disease. He was also considered to have very limited vision and hearing. A report by a psychologist indicated he was functioning in the profound range of retardation. He was able to reach and grasp, roll over, and in a prone position raise his head with arms extended. Jason could not sit unsupported and showed no evidence of functional productive or receptive language.

In previous attempts to suppress Jason's SIB his parents tried elbow restraints, physical punishment, and brief response-contingent interruption of feeding during mealtime. These procedures only temporarily reduced the behaviour. To minimise the intensity of the pokes, a sock was often tied to Jason's right hand.

Setting

The study was conducted in a preschool-like therapy room at the medical centre and in the subject's home. The therapy room was carpeted and equipped with toys, tables, chairs, a one-way observation window, and videotaping equipment. Portable videotaping equipment was used in the home setting. Treatment and baseline sessions were scheduled once or twice a week in both the medical centre and home settings. Data collection in the home was always done during the evening meal. In the therapy room, Jason was placed in two situations: on the floor and in a specially constructed chair with a tray, slanting support seat, and securing belts.

Recording and reliability

Poking was defined as striking the head, chin, ear, and/or facial area with the thumb and/or hand. For poking to be scored, the hand or thumb, in a position away from the face, had to make contact with the face, head, chin, and/or ear and return to a position away from the face. If the child made contact with the face, head, chin, and/or ear and the thumb or hand did not return to a position away from the face then a poke was not scored. The primary observers served alternately as trainers in this study. Observers were equipped with clipboards and data sheets divided into ten-second intervals. A cassette tape recorder signalled ten-second intervals throughout the study (Quilitch, 1972). The observers recorded the frequency of pokes *in vivo* or from videotapes per ten-second interval. For each session, these frequencies were converted to a rate per minute measure by dividing the frequencies by the total observation time (ten minutes per session).

Reliability assessments were made by a calibrating observer on a minimum of 20 per cent of the sessions for each setting. This included at least one reliability assessment in each condition across all settings. The calibrating observer recorded independently but in identical fashion as the primary observers. Most reliability assessments were made from videotapes. The records of the two observers were compared over one-minute intervals. For each one-minute interval, reliability estimates were calculated by dividing the smaller frequency by the larger frequency and multiplying by 100 (Bijou, Peterson, and Ault, 1968). Reliability assessments did not include data from one-minute intervals in which neither observer recorded the behaviour. The mean agreement for the chair setting was eighty-eight per cent, for the floor setting ninety-two per cent, and for the home setting eighty per cent.

Design

A combination of multiple baseline and reversal designs was used (Baer, Wolf and Risley, 1968). As can be seen in Table 1, a series of baseline and treatment conditions were introduced in the therapy room-chair setting, including a DRO, overcorrection, lemon juice, and ammonia procedure. In the therapy room-floor setting two baseline conditions and the lemon juice and ammonia procedures were introduced. Only baseline and ammonia conditions were introduced in the home setting. This sequence of baseline and treatment conditions was introduced in this order to determine the most effective but least aversive procedure. The level of aversiveness of procedures were determined in advance by a Committee on Legal and Ethical Protection.

Table 1. Sequence of conditions for each setting, with number of ten-minute sessions and of calendar days per condition.

Settings	Conditions	No. of ten-minute sessions	Calendar days
Therapy room chair	Baseline	5	2
	DRO	9	3
	Overcorrection	1*	1
	Lemon juice	27	7
	Reversal	6	2
	Ammonia	18	4
Therapy room floor	Baseline	10	6
	Lemon juice	16	5
	Reversal	4	2
	Ammonia	10	2
Home	Baseline	51	17
	Ammonia	6	2

*This was a forty-minute session.

Procedure

To minimise the amount of damage the subject could self-inflict, each baseline or treatment session in the therapy room setting was preceded and followed by a period when the subject had a sock tied over his right hand. During all conditions a preferred toy, a cloth lamb, was available to the child. He frequently would manipulate and mouth this object. This seemed to be a reasonable alternative response to poking and one which could be encouraged (Whaley and Tough, 1970). Every attempt was made to ensure that the lamb was within Jason's reach during all sessions except in the home setting during mealtimes.

Baseline. In both therapy room settings the lamb was placed within reach and data were collected by one or two nearby observers. As in other conditions, Jason's mother was always present.

Baseline sessions in the home were taken during meals. If the child began poking himself, his mother would often hold his arm briefly and distract him by offering a bite of food. No specific instructions were given to the mother.

DRO. Initially, every time ten seconds elapsed without any occurrence of poking, Jason was provided with any one of several potential reinforcers including tickling, flashing light, pudding, or a drink of water. Following ten consecutive ten-sec intervals without any poking, the schedule was increased to DRO-20 sec. Another ten consecutive ten-sec intervals without poking increased the schedule to DRO-30 sec, then forty sec, then sixty sec and finally 120 sec. The occurrence of poking in any two consecutive ten sec intervals reset the DRO to the previous schedule, eg, 20-sec to 10-sec. The ten-sec audio tape allowed trainers to switch schedules at appropriate times.

Overcorrection. During this condition any occurrence of poking resulted in five minutes of "functional movement" training (Foxx and Azrin, 1973). Training involved manually guiding the child's arms through two positions, arms above his head and arms straight out in front of him. The trainer would alternate these two positions every fifteen seconds until five minutes had elapsed. It was not possible to fade manual guidance.

Lemon juice. Lemon juice therapy involved squirting about 5 ccs of lemon juice (unsweetened Realemon brand) into the child's mouth contingent on any occurrence of poking. To minimise the possibility of aspiration, the trainer would hold the child's head forward and squirt the lemon juice on the inside cheek part of the mouth (Sajwaj *et al.,* 1974). Jason's face was often wiped during administrations to prevent him from rubbing the lemon juice in his eyes. Typically, in response to the lemon juice, Jason would pull on his teeth, grimace, and cry; however, these responses gradually diminished.

Aromatic ammonia. Contingent on any occurrence of poking, an unused capsule of aromatic ammonia was broken and immediately placed under the child's nose. With the exception of six sessions in the chair setting, all ammonia sessions involved a three-second administration for each occurrence of poking. During the first six sessions in the chair setting, ammonia was administrated for the duration of poking responses.

During most administrations, it was necessary to hold Jason's head in position as he typically turned away from the capsules and struggled. Care was taken to avoid direct contact with the skin to prevent possible irritation (Tanner and Zeiler, 1975). Prior to the introduction of treatment in the home the mother was trained to administer the ammonia capsules. The procedure was modelled for her and she implemented the procedure receiving feedback from the trainers.

The capsules used are available without prescription for 16 cents each. They are manufactured by the Burroughs Wellcome Co. with each capsule containing 0.33 cc ammonia and 36 per cent alcohol according to the package. The only cautionary note on the box stated: "Do not use if face is flushed." In conjunction with an earlier study (Altman *et al.,* 1978) a paediatrician and a paediatric neurologist were consulted regarding possible negative side effects. They both indicated that the procedure should be safe medically. Temporary nasal congestion, flushing, and tearing may follow ammonia administration. The paediatrician noted that prolonged use in a non-ventilated area could produce vomiting and diarrhoea. With the exception of some tears and coughing, Jason displayed no evidence of side effects. No adverse effects persisted. As a precautionary measure two different paediatricians agreed to be on call in case any adverse effects were observed. An average of 2.2 capsules were used for each session (range nought to six).

Prior to the introduction of lemon juice and ammonia conditions informed consent was obtained from the parents and the procedures were reviewed by a Committee on Legal and Ethical Protection (Cook, Altman and Haavik, 1978).

Results

The effects of positive and aversive treatment procedures on the rate of self-poking are shown in Figure 1. In the chair setting (upper position of the figure) the average rate of 6.8 self-pokes per minute was reduced slightly to 5.4 during DRO but increased to 12.0 during the subsequent overcorrection procedure. During overcorrection, thirty-eight minutes of this forty-minute procedure were spent manually guiding Jason. Thus, the response rate

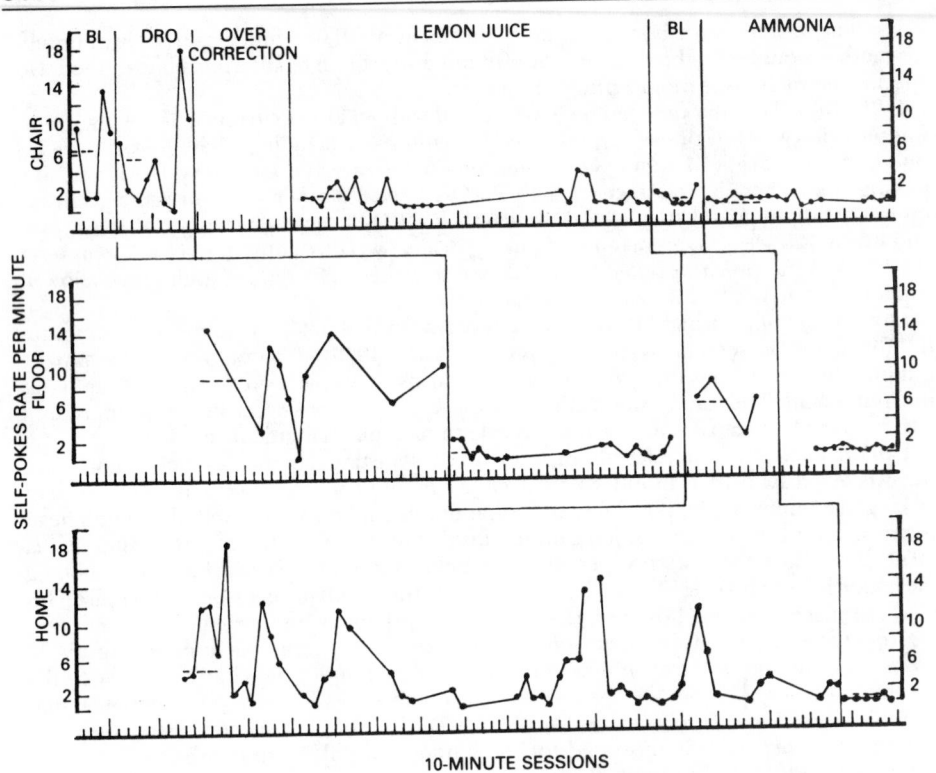

Fig. 1. The effects of positive and aversive treatment on rate of self-poking.

during overcorrection was based on the two minutes when self-poking was not precluded by manual guidance.

While lemon juice treatment in the chair setting substantially reduced and stabilised the rate of self-poking to an average of 1.3 responses per minute, simultaneous baselines in floor and home settings continued to show higher and more variable rates. Introduction of lemon juice to the floor setting (centre portion of Figure 1) also reduced and stabilised the rate of self-poking, this time to an average of 0.9 responses per minute compared with an average of 9.0 seen in the previous floor baseline condition and the somewhat reduced but still variable rates concurrently observed in the home setting.

In the chair setting (upper portion of Figure 1) an attempted return to baseline following lemon juice failed to demonstrate recovery of the initial baseline rates. Subsequently, it did not appear that the response-contingent aromatic ammonia condition substantially reduced the target behavior in the chair setting, i.e., from an average of 0.9 responses per minute in baseline 2 to an average of 0.4 responses per minute during aromatic ammonia. However, in the floor setting, self-poking was reduced from an average of 6.0 responses per minute in the previous baseline to an average of 0.5 responses per minute during aromatic ammonia treatment. Also, in the home setting, aromatic ammonia treatment reduced and stabilised the self-poking rate at an average of 0.2 responses per minute as compared to the average of 4.4 responses per minute seen in the previous baseline. It is especially noteworthy that four of the six ammonia treatment sessions in the home showed complete elimination of self-poking while in no previous home session had zero rates been observed.

Discussion

This study demonstrated the trial and elimination of several treatment alternatives for decreasing self-injury. Response-contingent lemon juice and ammonia were found effective in decreasing the SIB of a profoundly handicapped child. Though some reduction was obtained during the DRO condition, the procedure offered little promise in stabilising self-poking at zero or near-zero levels. The overcorrection procedure resulted in an increase in SIB as compared to baseline rates. Although this effect of overcorrection was unexpected, in some cases overcorrection has been found to increase SIB (Measel and Alfieri, 1976, Study 2). In this study overcorrection was only implemented during one calendar day; however, it was clear to the trainers that even if the overcorrection procedure proved to be effective over time it was quite time consuming and impractical. This is consistent with the finding of Kelly and Drabman (1977) who reported successful results using overcorrection procedures in reducing SIB though the procedures were abandoned as the response cost to treatment staff was too high.

The introduction of lemon juice reduced and stabilised the rate of poking in both the chair and floor settings. Although the behaviour remained below a rate of 2.0 responses per minute the lemon juice treatment was abandoned in favour of what was considered to be a more intensive procedure, aromatic ammonia. It was assumed that a more intensive aversive event might completely suppress the SIB. A multiple baseline design demonstrated that the introduction of aromatic ammonia decreased the rate of self-poking to less than 1.0 per minute across all settings.

It might be argued that the results obtained during the lemon juice and ammonia conditions are less convincing experimentally due to the problem of sequential treatment (order) effects and the failure to recover baseline rates during the reversal condition in the chair setting. In regard to lemon juice, it should be noted that though this procedure followed DRO and overcorrection conditions in the chair setting this was not the case in the floor setting. Thus, treatment order effects would seem to be controlled for as the rate of poking was similarly reduced and stabilised in both settings.

Although ammonia administration followed lemon juice in the floor and chair settings, similar reductions occurred in the home setting in which no previous treatment was introduced. Again, the necessity of preceding treatment conditions (i.e., lemon juice) appears contraindicated. Though base rates were not recovered in the chair setting reversal condition, a partial recovery was obtained in the floor setting reversal condition. The failure to obtain a similar recovery in the chair setting may have been due to the lengthy lemon juice treatment condition which preceded the reversal condition.

Shortly after the introduction of ammonia in the home setting the study was prematurely terminated as the subject was placed in a residential treatment facility. Anecdotal reports from staff and family indicated that during the child's three-month placement in residential treatment the rate of poking had increased, though not to pretreatment levels. In addition, the intensity of the behaviour had diminished.

The partial suppression of SIB obtained with lemon juice treatment is consistent with the findings of Flavell et al. (1978). There is some justification then for the use of lemon juice therapy in cases of self-injury. Personnel at the residential treatment facility indicated that lemon juice was a more socially acceptable procedure than ammonia. The procedure is safe, easily implemented, readily available, and has little potential for abuse or misuse.

The effectiveness of aromatic ammonia as demonstrated in this study systematically replicates the finding of others who have applied ammonia successfully to cases of self-injury (Tanner and Zeiler, 1975; Baumeister and Baumeister, 1978; Altman et al., 1978). The data in this study would suggest that greater suppression was obtained with ammonia when the procedure was introduced across all settings. There is some evidence for this suggestion in that the rate of self-poking was at zero for four of the six ammonia treatment sessions in the home setting. This is consistent with the findings of Baumeister and Baumeister (1978) who noted that generalisation of suppression was obtained in two cases of SIB when ammonia was introduced throughout the subject's entire environment. No serious side effects were observed with either the lemon juice or ammonia procedures, though, as recommended by Baumeister and Baumeister (1978), medical consultation was available in case side effects developed.

Thus, this study systematically compared the effectiveness of one positive procedure, DRO, and three mildly aversive procedures, overcorrection, lemon juice and aromatic ammonia, for treating SIB. Lemon juice and aromatic ammonia substantially reduced SIB,

DRO slightly decreased SIB, and overcorrection slightly increased SIB. This study proves one example of a means of selecting the least restrictive but most effective procedure for treating the SIB of a profoundly retarded individual. The use of brief (ten-minute) sessions in this study allowed for the testing of different treatments before one treatment was fully adopted. Other investigators and clinicians may find the use of brief sessions useful particularly with SIB cases. Effective procedures can be isolated within a short period of time thereby preventing further self-inflicted harm to the subject which can occur during longer treatment trial periods.

Acknowledgements
Preparation of this manuscript was partially supported by a grant from NICHD (HD 03144) to the Bureau of Child Research, University of Kansas. Salary support to the second author was provided by DHEW Grant MCT 000944. Space in which to conduct the project was made possible by NIH Grant No. HD 0258/10. The authors wish to thank Susan LeClaire and Suzanne Gleeson for their assistance in preparation of this manuscript.

References
Altman, K., Haavik, S., Cook, J. W. Punishment of self-injurious behavior in natural settings using contingent aromatic ammonia. *Behav. Res. & Ther.*, 1978; **16**, 85.
Azrin, N. H., Gottlieb, L., Hughart, L., Wesolowski, M. D., Rhan, T. Eliminating self-injurious behavior by educative procedures. *Behav. Res. & Ther.*, 1975; **13**, 101.
Baer, D. M., Wolf, M. M., Risley, T. R. Some current dimensions of applied behavior analysis. *J. Appl. Behav. Anal.*, 1968; **1**, 91.
Barnard, J. D., Christophersen, E. R., Wolf, M. M. Parent-mediated treatment of children's self-injurious behavior using overcorrection. *J. Ped. Psy.*, 1976; **1**, 56.
Baumeister, A. A., Baumeister, A. A. Suppression of repetitive self-injurious behavior by contingent inhalation of aromatic ammonia. *J. Aut. & Child. Schiz.*, 1978; **8**, 71.
Baumeister, A. A., Rollings, J. P. Self-injurious behavior. *In* Ellis, R. (Ed.). *International Review of Research in Mental Retardation*. (Vol. 8.). New York: Academic Press, 1976.
Becker, J. V., Turner, S. M., Sajwaj, T. E. Multiple behavioral effects of the use of lemon juice with a ruminating toddler-age child. *Behav. Mod.*, 1978; **2**, 267.
Bijou, S. W., Peterson, R. F., Ault, M. A method to integrate descriptive and experimental field studies at the level of data and empirical concepts. *J. Appl. Behav. Anal.*, 1968; **1**, 175.
Cook, J. W., Altman, K., Haavik, S. Consent for aversive treatment: a model form. *Ment. Retard.*, 1978; **16**, 47.
Cook, J. W., Altman, K., Shaw, J., Blaylock, M. Use of contingent lemon juice to eliminate public masturbation by a severely retarded boy. *Behav. Res. & Ther.*, 1978; **16**, 313.
Corbett, J. Aversion for the treatment of self-injurious behaviour. *J. Ment. Defic. Res.*, 1975; **19**, 79.
Flavell, J. E., McGimsey, J. F., Jones, M. L. The use of physical restraint in the treatment of self-injury and as positive reinforcement. *J. Appl. Behav. Anal.*, 1978; **11**, 225.
Foxx, R. M., Azrin, N. H. The elimination of autistic self-stimulatory behavior by overcorrection. *J. Appl. Behav. Anal.*, 1973; **6**, 1.
Kelly, J. A., Drabman, R. S. Overcorrection: an effective procedure that failed. *J. Clin. Child Psy.*, 1977; **6**, 38.
Martin, R. *Legal Challenges to Behavior Modification: trends in schools, corrections, and mental health*. Champaign, Ill.: Research Press, 1975.
Measel, C. J., Alfieri, P. A. Treatment of self-injurious behavior by a combination of reinforcement for incompatible behavior and overcorrection. *Am. J. Ment. Defic.*, 1976; **81**, 147.
Ollendick, T. H., Matson, J. R. Overcorrection: an overview. *Behav. Ther.*, 1978; **9**, 830.
Quilitch, H. R. A portable programmed audible timer. *J. Appl. Behav. Anal.*, 1972; **5**, 18.
Repp, A. C., Deitz, D. E. On the selective use of punishment — suggested guidelines for administrators. *Ment. Retard.*, 1978; **16**, 250.
Sajwaj, T., Libet, J., Agras, S. Lemon-juice therapy: the control of life-threatening rumination in a six-month-old infant. *J. Appl. Behav. Anal.*, 1974; **7**, 557.
Tanner, B. A., Zeiler, M. Punishment of self-injurious behavior using aromatic ammonia as the aversive stimulus. *J. Appl. Behav. Anal.*, 1975; **8**, 53.
Whaley, D. L., Tough, J. Treatment of a self-injuring mongoloid with shock-induced suppression and avoidance. *In* Ulrich, R., Stachnik, T., Mabry, J. (Eds.). *Control of Human Behavior.* (Vol. 2), Glenview, Ill.: Scott, Foresman and Co., 1970.

Reprinted from *J. Ment. Defic. Res.*, 1980; **24**, 37-46 by kind permission of Michael A. Rapoff, Edward R. Christophersen, and Karl Altman, University of Kansas Dept. of Pediatrics, Kansas City, Kansas 66103 USA and the publishers Blackwell Scientific Publications Ltd., Oxford OX2 0EL.

PUNISHMENT OF SELF-INJURIOUS BEHAVIOR USING AROMATIC AMMONIA AS THE AVERSIVE STIMULUS

Barry A. Tanner[1], Marlene Zeiler

Georgia Regional Hospital at Atlanta

Punishment with aromatic ammonia was used to eliminate self-injurious behavior of an autistic woman during experimental sessions. The effects were reversible but were limited to experimental sessions until staff used the ammonia on the ward at all times.

DESCRIPTORS: aversive control, aromatic ammonia, self-injurious behavior.

Punishment rapidly and effectively reduces self-injurious behavior (Lovaas, Schaeffer, and Simmons , 1965; Lovaas and Simmons, 1969; Risley, 1968; Tate, 1972; Tate and Baroff, 1966). In a comparison of three procedures, Corte, Wolf, and Locke (1971) reported that extinction was ineffective in reducing such behavior, differential reinforcement of a competing response was effective only under conditions of food deprivation, but punishment consistently reduced the frequency of self-injurious behavior. In addition, Smolev (1971) pointed out that while nonaversive procedures may be preferable to aversive control, because they involve less discomfort for the subject, such procedures may allow subjects to injure themselves, a behavior that might be quickly suppressed with punishment. Therefore, when danger to the subject, or staff limitations, preclude the use of extinction or differential reinforcement, punishment is indicated.

To be effective, punishment requires the use of an intense stimulus delivered immediately after the response (Azrin and Holz, 1966). Otherwise, responding will either not be affected, or will be only temporarily reduced. Electric shock is effective when applied appropriately, although it is not without problems. For example, ethical considerations preclude supplying shock stimulators to all staff whom a patient encounters. Thus, patients may discriminate when shock will or will not be forthcoming. Furthermore, not only may shock be administered indiscriminately, but the stimulator is usually visible enough to establish a discrimination. Justifiable concern over inflicting pain (American Psychological Association, 1971) may sometimes lead to an administrative decision to restrict or even ban the use of shock (Lucero, Voil, and Scherber, 1968).

Other forms of aversive stimuli have been used, for example, loud noise (Azrin, 1958; Flanagan, Goldiamond, and Azrin, 1958), but this is aversive to other patients and staff on the ward, and was only partially effective in reducing responding (Azrin and Holz, 1966). Other stimuli, such as a blast of air (Masserman, 1946) have been used with nonhumans. Aromatic ammonia was therefore tried in the present study because its fumes are very unpleasant, yet produce no lasting effect when used moderately, and in diluted form (Goodman and Gilman, 1965); unlike the fumes of household ammonia, aromatic ammonia does not annoy people more than about 2 ft (0.6 m) from the capsule. Immoderate use or an undiluted form would, however, be destructive to the nasal mucosa. The relative safety of ammonia capsules, their cost (2.5 cents per capsule), and their small size makes this stimulus a good candidate for distribution to all staff. It was expected that by having all staff conceal capsules on their person, a patient would have difficulty establishing a discrimination, and the punishment could be continued by staff beyond the end of the study. The present paper reports the use of aromatic ammonia to punish self-injurious behavior of an institutionalized adult.

---

[1]Reprints may be obtained from Barry A. Tanner, Northeast Guidance Center, 17000 East Warren, Detroit, Michigan 48224.

Method

Subject

The subject was a 20-yr-old autistic woman who slapped herself. Such slapping was sometimes accompanied by vocalizations and screams, but her verbalization was limited to imitating a few words when candy reinforcers were available. A former staff member had reported limited success in shaping verbalizations, but shaping was discontinued when this person resigned. The patient spent most of the day sleeping in a chair in front of the television, occasionally getting up to collect lint from the floor. Unless she was under constant observation, she would eat her own feces and urine. Shock had been successfully used previously to suppress her slapping, but responding had gradually recovered since the shock stimulator had been removed more than a year earlier. When this study began, the subject wore a padded helmet all day and occasionally had her arms restrained to a chair. She would sometimes remove her helmet and slap her face with both hands until staff restrained her again. There was no record of her slapping any other part of her body regularly. Her medication during the first six observation periods was 100 mg of chlorpromazine three times a day, and thereafter was 75 mg of chlorpromazine and 10 mg of trifluoperazine hydrochloride twice a day. Heavier doses of these and other drugs had previously had no effect on her self-injurious behavior, but had increased the amount of time she spent sleeping.

Apparatus

A capsule of aromatic ammonia was concealed in the experimenter's hand. The capsules are odorlesss until crushed, after which they retain their power for about 10 min (twice the length of the experimental session used). The fumes are mildly annoying up to about 2 ft (0.6 m) from the source, but are aversive only when the ampule is brought close to the nose. The capsule does not, however, have to come into contact with the nose in order to be highly aversive, and physical contact or prolonged exposure may result in damage to the skin or nasal mucosa. The crushable capsules are manufactured by Burrough's Wellcome Company, with each capsule containing a minimum of "5.41 (0.33 cc) alcohol 36%" according to the package.

Recording

Observation periods lasted from 3 to 5 min, with a maximum of one observation period per working day, since the experimenters felt it unwise initially to leave the subject unhelmeted longer than that. Most observation periods lasted the full 5 min, but one period during the baseline and one during return to baseline were terminated earlier because the subject began to bite herself. No record was kept of the biting because it was observed to be a problem only when the subject was allowed to hit herself at a high rate for more than two consecutive minutes; even under these conditions, biting seldom occurred. Observations were initially made in the day area where the unhelmeted subject occupied her usual chair in front of the television. However, at the request of the head nurse, we moved to an empty meeting room during baseline so that the subject's screamings and slapping would not disturb other patients.

Two independent observers, stationed so that they could neither hear nor see one another's counts, recorded the behavior during every observation session. The junior author generally observed the subject, with the senior author or the nursing supervisor providing a reliability check for the simple event recording. Per cent agreement among the observers was determined by dividing the larger grouped value recorded into the smaller grouped value recorded. Agreement ranged from 93% to 100%, with a mean of 98%. The rate plotted in Figure 1 was computed from the mean of the two frequencies recorded by the independent observers. A slap was defined as rapidly bringing one or both hands to the subject's face, with the palm in apparent contact with the face. The response was generally easily discriminable because slaps could be both heard and seen; disagreement sometimes occurred between observers when the slaps were emitted more quickly than they could be recorded.

Beginning with the second experimental phase, unit staff also recorded slapping outside of experimental sessions. They recorded the occurrence of each burst or incidence of

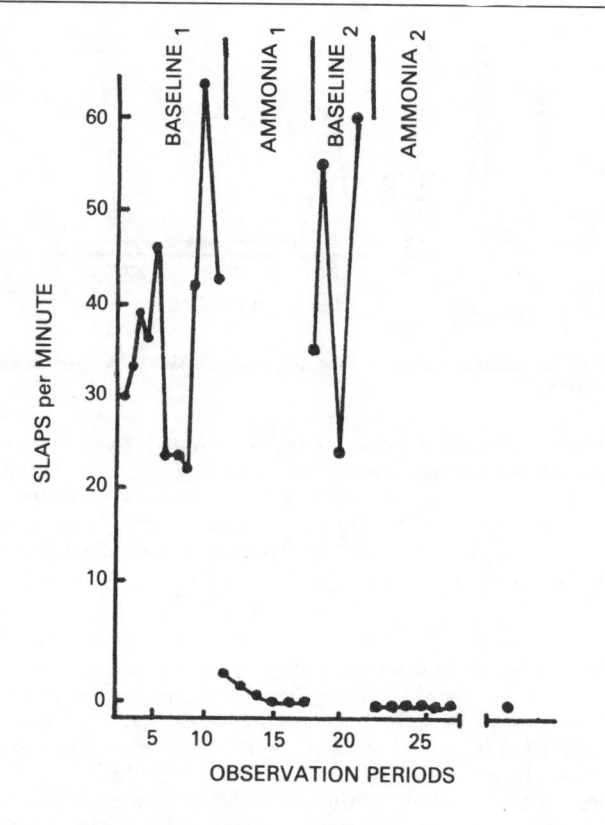

Fig. 1. A record of an autistic woman's face slapping during experimental sessions under baseline and punishment conditions.

slapping, rather than noting the number of slaps in each burst. This was done on a 24-hr-per-day basis.

Procedure

During the first baseline phase, the observers recorded the subject's behavior but otherwise did not respond to her during the 11 observation periods distributed over 21 calendar days. The subject's medication was changed after the sixth observation period in an attempt to suppress her face slapping. The first experimental phase began 10 calendar days (six observation days) after the medication change to allow the drugs time to take effect. During observation periods 12 to 14, a capsule of ammonia was crushed and thrust under the subject's nose when she slapped herself, and was withdrawn when she stopped. During observation periods 15 to 17, the ammonia was used whenever the subject brushed her hair back from her forehead, since it was observed that slapping was always preceded by this movement, although the movement was not always followed by slapping. A single capsule was used for each experimental session, as it maintained strength for more than enough time. The six observation periods of the first experimental phase were distributed over 16 calendar days. During observation periods 18 to 21, there was a return to the baseline conditions in which the experimenters again only recorded the subject's behavior. These four observation periods were distributed over 11 calendar days. Beginning with the twenty-second observation period, the experimental procedure was re-instituted, with one change. During the second experimental phase, all unit staff were instructed in the use of the ammonia and carried capsules with them. While only the senior author administered the ammonia during the experimental sessions, all staff administered it out on the ward,

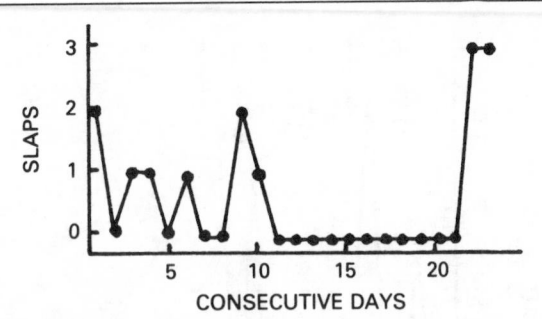

Fig. 2. A record of an autistic woman's face slapping outside of experimental sessions under punishment conditions.

and continued to do so after the experiment was terminated. This was done in the hope that the experimental results would no longer be person or situation specific. The subject's helmet and restraints were not worn during this phase nor were they used during the remainder of the subject's stay at the hospital. The six observation periods were distributed over seven calendar days. A follow-up observation period occurred 21 calendar days after the last experimental session.

Results

A record of the subject's face slapping during experimental sessions is presented in Figure 1. During the first six observation periods of baseline, the rate of this behavior ranged from 23 to 45 slaps ($\overline{X}$ = 34.3 per minute). Following the medication change, the rate ranged from 22 to 61 slaps per minute, ($\overline{X}$ = 38.4 per minute). The overall mean for the 11 observation periods of baseline was 36.2 slaps per minute.

During the first experimental phase, the rate of slapping ranged from 0.4 to 3 per minute ($\overline{X}$ = 1.3 per minute) when the experimenter contingently applied ammonia. For the last three observation periods of this phase, the experimenter applied the ammonia following the precursor of the face slapping, and no occurrences of the target behavior were observed. The overall mean for the six observation days of the first experimental phase was 0.7 slaps per minute.

During the return to baseline, the rate of responding recovered to a mean of 42.5 slaps per minute, with a range from 23 to 59 slaps per minute.

Face slapping was immediately eliminated during the second experimental phase. A follow-up observation 21 calendar days after the last experimental session once again found no occurrences of the target behavior.

A record of the subject's face slapping outside of experimental sessions during and after the second experimental phase is shown in Figure 2. During the 23 days of recording, the bursts of slapping ranged from zero to three per day, with a mean of 0.58 per 24 hr. While nursing staff did not record the number of slaps in each burst, they reported anecdotally that the number of slaps was substantially reduced compared to the pre-intervention rate.

Discussion

This study reports the first published use of ammonia to suppress self-injurious behavior. The procedure was quickly effective, and offers an alternative to the more commonly used stimulus, electric shock. Ammonia capsules could be easily carried by all staff in their pockets or pinned to their clothing, thereby involving more people in more places than is often the case. Possibly because capsules were generally concealed, the behavior was reported to have been substantially reduced outside of experimental sessions as well as during them. Unfortunately, no baseline was recorded outside of experimental sessions, as this recording was not introduced on the ward until the second experimental phase. Staff reported no other changes, desirable or undesirable, in the subject's behavior during the study. Because ward staff were able to continue the use of the ammonia, the reduction in slapping appears to have been maintained for the duration of the relatively brief follow-up. No long-term follow-up was possible because the subject was transferred to another institution shortly after the initial follow-up.

Slapping outside of experimental sessions could probably have been reduced further if staff had been more consistent in their use of the ammonia. Several staff were observed to approach the subject when she slapped herself, and then retreat without applying the ammonia if she stopped slapping upon observing their approach. Slapping decreased after the senior author discussed this with staff on the tenth day of staff use, instructing them always to apply the ammonia following a slapping incident. In addition, some staff stopped carrying the ammonia when no slapping had occurred for several days, and had to scurry for the capsules when the slapping began, e.g., Days 22 and 23. Obviously, discrimination was more of a problem than had been anticipated, and it appeared that punishment would have to be continued indefinitely in order to control the slapping.

The subject reacted violently to the ammonia, turning her head and struggling with the experimenter, although the capsule could be brought to within a few inches of her nose immediately following a slap or antecedent behavior, largely because the subject did not leave her chair. It would undoubtedly be more difficult to use ammonia with a stronger or more agile person. The experimenter and any patient sitting close to the subject were sometimes mildly irritated by the fumes, and the odor lingered on the experimenter's hands after each use. In addition, scabs appeared at the tip of the subject's nose during the second experimental phase, while she had a cold. It is not clear whether the scabs resulted from the cold or because a staff member placed the ammonia capsule in direct contact with the woman's nose. Still, this procedure offers promise, especially in situations where electric shock cannot easily be used.

References

American Psychological Association. Research ethics being revised. *APA Monitor*, 1971; **2**, 1.

Azrin, N. H. Some effects of noise on human behavior. *J. Experi. Anal. Behav.*, 1958; **1**, 183-200.

Azrin, N. H., Holz, W. C. Punishment. *In* Honig, W. K. (Ed.). *Operant Behavior: areas of research and application.* (pp 380-447.) New York: Appleton-Century-Crofts, 1966.

Corte, H. E., Wolf, M. M., Locke, B. J. A comparison of procedures for eliminating self-injurious behavior of retarded adolescents. *J. Appl. Behav. Anal.*, 1971; **4**, 201-213.

Flanagan, B., Goldiamond, I., Azrin, N. H. Operant stuttering: the control of stuttering through response-contingent consequences. *J. Experi. Anal. Behav.*, 1958; **1**, 173-177.

Goodman, L. S., Gilman, A. *The Pharmacological Basis of Therapeutics.* (3rd edn.) New York: MacMillan, 1965.

Lovaas, O. I., Schaeffer, B., Simmons, J. Q. Building social behavior in autistic children by use of electric shock. *J. Experi. Res. in Personality*, 1965; **1**, 99-109.

Lovaas, O. I., Simmons, J. Q. Manipulation of self-destruction in three retarded children. *J. Appl. Behav. Anal.*, 1969; **2**, 143-157.

Lucero, R. J., Vail, D. J., Scherber, J. Regulating operant-conditioning programs. *Hosp. & Commun. Psychiat.*, 1968; **19**, 53-54.

Masserman, J. H. *Principles of Dynamic Psychiatry.* Philadelphia: Saunders, 1946.

Risley, T. R. The effects and side-effects of punishing the autistic behaviors of a deviant child. *J. Appl. Behav. Anal.*, 1968; **1**, 21-34.

Smolev, S. R. Use of operant techniques for the modification of self-injurious behavior. *Am. J. Ment. Defic.*, 1971; **76**, 295-305.

Tate, B. G. Case study: control of chronic self-injurious behavior by conditioning procedures. *Behav. Ther.*, 1972; **3**, 72-82.

Tate, B. G., Baroff, G. S. Aversive control of self-injurious behavior in a psychotic boy. *Behav. Res. & Ther.*, 1966; **4**, 281-287.

AVERSIVE CONTROL OF SELF-INJURIOUS BEHAVIOR IN A PSYCHOTIC BOY

B. G. Tate, George S. Baroff

University of North Carolina at Chapel Hill, and Murdoch Center, Butner, North Carolina, U.S.A.

Summary
Two studies are reported which indicate how quickly and effectively chronic self-injurious behavior was controlled in a 9-yr-old blind psychotic boy. In the first study, the self-injurious responses were punished by contingent withdrawal of human physical contact. In the second study, response-contingent electric shock was employed.

Introduction

There have been many attempts to explain self-injurious behavior (Cain, 1961; Dollard et al., 1939; Freud, 1954; Goldfarb, 1945; Greenacre, 1954; Hartmann et al., 1949; Sandler, 1964). It has been labeled masochism, auto-aggression, self-aggression and self-destructive behavior. The present authors prefer the term self-injurious behavior because it is more descriptive and less interpretive. Self-injurious behavior (SIB) does not imply an attempt to destroy, nor does it suggest aggression; it simply means behavior which produces physical injury to the individual's own body. Typically SIB is composed of a series of self-injurious responses (SIRs) that are repetitive and sometimes rhythmical, often with no obvious reinforcers, and therefore similar to stereotyped behavior. Common types of SIB are forceful head-banging, face slapping, punching the face and head, and scratching and biting one's body.

A patient who emits SIRs at high frequency and/or magnitude is particularly difficult to work with because the behavior interferes with the production of more desirable responses and there is always the risk of severe and permanent physical injury, e.g. head and eye damage. Usually such patients must be physically restrained or maintained on heavy dosages of drugs. Lovaas et al. (1964), however, successfully employed punishment in the form of painful electric shock to dramatically reduce the frequency of SIRs in several schizophrenic children. Ball (1965) used the same technique with a severely retarded girl and achieved similar results.

The present paper describes two punishment procedures used to control SIB in a psychotic boy. In Study I, punishment was withdrawal of human physical contact contingent on a SIR. In Study II, punishment was response-contingent painful electric shock. Following a description of the subject, the procedures and results of Studies I and II are presented, followed by a report on related behavioral changes and a general discussion.

Subject

Sam was a 9-year-old, blind male who was transferred for evaluation and treatment on a research basis from an out-of-state psychiatric hospital to Murdoch Center, a state institution for the mentally retarded. At the age of 5 he was diagnosed as autistic and was hospitalized. For the next 4 years he received group and individual psychotherapy, and drug therapy with no long-term benefit. Drugs were used in an effort to control self-injurious behavior, screaming, and hyperactivity.

The SIB began at about the age of 4 and consisted of face slapping. By age 9, his SIB repertoire included banging his head forcefully against floors, walls, and other hard objects, slapping his face with his hands, punching his face and head with his fists, hitting his shoulder with his chin, and kicking himself. Infrequently he would also pinch, bite, and scratch others.

At age 8, bilateral cataracts, a complete detachment of the left retina, and partial detachment of the right retina were discovered. An ophthalmologist has suggested that the cataracts were probably congenital but were not noticed until they matured and that the retinal detachments were likely caused by head-banging. The cataract in the right eye was removed soon after its discovery, leaving Sam with some light-dark vision and possibly some movement perception.

Upon arrival at Murdoch Center, Sam was assigned a room in the infirmary and drugs were immediately discontinued. Casual observations were made for the first 2 weeks while he was adapting to his new environment. Following the adaptation period, eighteen 30-minute daily observation periods were conducted during which a female research assistant held Sam, tried to interest him in games, and ignored all SIRs. These observations yielded a median daily average SIR rate of 2.3/min (range: 0.9-7.9/min). A second type of observation consisted of 5-min periods four times a day at random intervals. Over a 26-day period the median daily average SIR rate was 1.7/min (range: 0.3-4.1/min). SIB, therefore, was a frequent form of behavior observed under a wide variety of situations.

Observations also revealed the following: Sam had a firm hematoma approximately 7 cm in diameter on his forehead — a result of previous head banging. His speech was limited to jargon and to approximately twenty words usually spoken in a high-pitched, whining manner and often inappropriately used. He was not considered autistic at this time because he obviously enjoyed and sought bodily contact with others. He would cling to people and try to wrap their arms around him, climb into their laps and mold himself to their contours. When left alone and free, he would cry, scream, flail his arms about, and hit himself or bang his head. When fully restrained in bed he was usually calm, but often engaged in head-rolling and hitting his chin against his shoulder.

Study I: Control by withdrawal and reinstatement of human physical contact

Early observations of Sam indicated that physical contact with people was reinforcing to him and that being alone, particularly when he was standing or walking, was aversive. Study I was undertaken in an effort to learn if a procedure of withdrawing physical contact when a SIR occurred and reinstating the contact after a brief interval during which no SIRs occurred could be used to control Sam's SIB.

Procedure

Study I began on the fourth day following the end of the 26-day observation period mentioned. During the 3 weeks preceding the commencement of the study Sam was restrained in his bed except for morning baths given by attendants and for daily walks around the campus and through the infirmary corridors with two female research assistants (Es). During the walks Es held Sam's hands and chatted to him and to each other and ignored SIRs.

Study I consisted of twenty daily 20-min sessions run at the same time each day by the same Es. There were five control sessions (SIRs were ignored), followed by five experimental sessions (SIRs were punished), five control sessions, and five experimental sessions.

Control sessions consisted of a walk around the campus with the two Es who chatted with Sam and with each other. Sam walked between them, holding onto a hand of each. When he emitted SIRs the Es ignored them.

Experimental sessions were identical to the control sessions except that when Sam hit himself, Es jerked their hands free so that he had no physical contact with them. The time-out from physical contact lasted 3 sec following the last SIR. At the end of 3 sec, Es allowed him to grasp their hands and the walk resumed. No comments were made to Sam when a hit occurred — the only responses to the SIR were withdrawal of contact and cessation of talk if Es were talking at the time.

All sessions began when Sam left his room and entered the corridor leading outside the building. The same route around the campus was followed each day. Each session ended while he was outside the building, but the procedure for the particular session was continued until Sam was returned to his room, undressed, placed in bed, and restrained — usually about 12 additional min. Records were kept by one E who silently marked the SIRs on a piece of paper during the walks.

Results of Study I

Virtually all of the SIRs made during the sessions were chin-to-shoulder hits. On a few

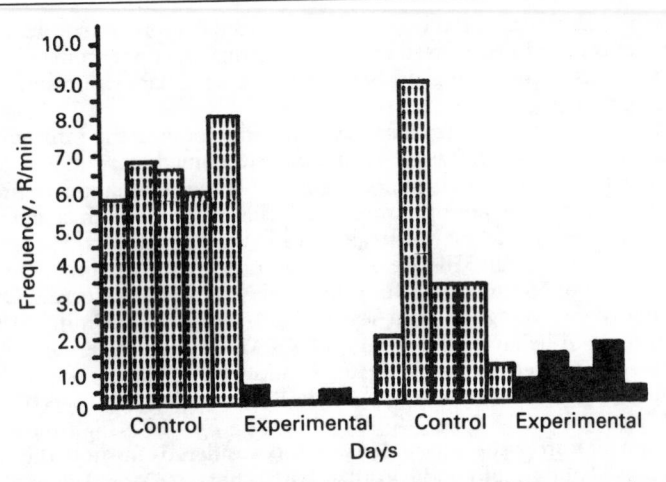

Fig. 1. Effect of the punishment procedure of Study I on the daily average frequency of SIRs. On experimental days SIRs were followed by withdrawal of human physical contact and reinstatement of contact after a minimum interval of 3 sec. On control days the SIRs were ignored.

occasions Sam would punch his head with his fist during punishment but he rarely withdrew his hand from an assistant and hit himself.

Figure 1 presents the average SIRs per min for each day of the study. The median average rate of SIRs for the first 5 control days was 6.6 responses per min and sharply declined to a median average of 0.1 responses per min for the following 5 experimental days. The response rate recovered somewhat (median average = 3.3) during the second 5 control days and decreased again during the second 5 experimental days (median average = 1.0). The unusually high rate of SIRs on the second day of the second control run was associated with a temper tantrum which lasted about 15 min.

On the experimental days an interesting change in Sam's behavior occurred which was noticed by both Es and the authors. On control days Sam typically whined, cried, hesitated often in his walk, and seemed unresponsive to the environment in general. His behavior on experimental days was completely different — he appeared to attend more to environmental stumuli, including the Es; there was no crying or whining, and he often smiled. A brief discussion of this change in behavior appears at the end of the paper.

The results of this study indicate that the relatively simple procedure of controlling the contingencies of this chronic SIB produced a dramatic reduction in its frequency. Of interest also are the relative effects of punishing the SIR and ignoring it. These results do not, of course, mean that long-term effects would be the same.

Study II: Control by electric shock

Although the SIB could be reduced by response-contingent withdrawal of physical contact, it was decided that the risk of completely destroying the right retina by further head-banging was great enough to preclude the long term use of this method. Parental permission was then obtained for the use of painful electric shock.

The shock apparatus was a stock prod (Sears & Roebuck Number 325971) similar to the one used by the Lovaas *et al.* (1964). The prod was a cylinder 58 cm long and 3 cm in diameter containing seven D cells and an induction coil. With fresh batteries approximately. 130 V were available at the two 0.48 cm diameter terminals, 1.24 cm apart, projecting from one end of the prod. Shock was administered by turning the induction coil on and touching the terminals to the bare skin of the patient.

Study II began 46 hr after the termination of Study I.

Procedure

For 24 min prior to the administration of electric shock, Sam was allowed a free-responding period. The authors, accompanied by a physician, entered Sam's room, talked to him pleasantly and freed his hands, leaving him lying in bed with both feet restrained. They remained close to his bed while an assistant in an adjoining room recorded each SIR. After 24 min of observing and recording the free-responding behavior, it was explained to Sam that if he continued to hit himself he would be shocked, and the shock would hurt. A shock of approximately 0.5 seconds duration then immediately followed each SIR. No more comments were made to Sam concerning the shock which was delivered to the lower right leg.

The contingent shock period was continued for 90 min. After the first two shocks were administered, Sam's feet were untied and he was placed in a sitting position in bed. The authors talked pleasantly to him and encouraged him to play with toys. Approximately 1 hr after the first shock he was placed in a rocking chair for 30 min. Sam was then returned to his bed and left alone unrestrained, while being observed for another 90 min over closed-circuit television. Contingent shock was continued, but there was a delay of 30-35 sec between the SIR and the administration of punishment (time required to reach Sam's room from the observation room).

Shock was continued on subsequent days and was sometimes delivered immediately and sometimes delayed 30 sec depending on whether the therapist was with Sam or observing him on television. At night he was restrained in bed at the wrists and ankles with cloth restraints.

Results of Study II

As soon as Sam's hands were released for the 24-min free-responding period he began hitting his face with his fists. The intensity of the SIRs immediately increased as a temper tantrum developed during which he screamed, flailed his arms about wildly, twisted his body about, hit his face and head with his fists, hit his shoulder with his chin, and banged his head with great force against the iron side rail of the bed. The head-banging was so forceful that it was necessary to cushion the blows by placing the authors' hands over the bed rail. The average rate of SIRs during the 6-min temper tantrum was 14.0 per min. During the next 18 min he became calmer and the average rate dropped to 2.0 responses per min.

During the first 90-min contingent shock period a total of only five SIRs were emitted (average rate=0.06 responses per min). The shocks produced a startle reaction Sam and avoidance movements, but no cries. The authors talked to him, praised virtually all non-injurious responses, and generally behaved pleasantly. When led from the bed to the rocking chair, he immediately began crying and flailing his arms. A SIR was promptly followed by a shock and he became calm. A few seconds later he was sitting in the chair and smiling with apparent pleasure. At the end of the 90-min period Sam was returned to his bed and left in it free while being observed over closed-circuit television. Throughout the second 90-min observation period he remained quietly in bed posturing with his hands. Four SIRs were emitted and were followed by delayed shocks. The SIR rate had decreased from 2.0/min in the last minutes of the free responding period to 0.04/min. At the end of the period a meal was offered which he refused. He was then restrained for the night.

The following day Sam was free from 9.00 a.m. until 2.30 p.m. All of this time was spent in bed with toys except for 1 hr in the afternoon during which the authors encouraged him to rock in a rocking chair and walk around his room. Twenty SIRs of light intensity occurred during the 5½-hr period (average rate=0.06 responses per min). Four of these were followed by immediate shock and the other sixteen by delayed shock.

On the second day following the commencement of shock Sam was free from 8.00 a.m. until 4.30 p.m. There were only fifteen SIRs during the entire day (average rate=0.03/min) but most of these occurred during one brief period of agitation at noon. He was out of bed about 3 hr being rocked, walked, and entertained with toys.

In the ensuing days Sam's daily activities were gradually increased until he remained out of bed 9 hr a day. He was still restrained at night because of limited personnel available to check him. He began attending physical therapy classes for the severely retarded 3 hr a day where he was encouraged to play with a variety of toys. He now apparently enjoys walks, playground equipment, and playing "games" involving following directions and making discriminations, for example, various objects (ball, book, music box, etc.) are put on a table across the room and he is asked to bring a specific one to E. He is more spontaneous in his activities than he was when he arrived and he is now capable of walking and running alone without clinging to people.

Punishment of SIRs with shock was continued and the decline in rate progressed. Since the beginning of shock 167 days have elapsed. The last observed SIR was emitted on day 147.

Other changes in behavior

Sam's intake of food and liquids had undergone an overall decrease since his admission although there were wide day-to-day fluctuations. Three months after his admission (5 days before the use of shock), his weight had decreased by 14 lb (20 per cent). On days when he ate nothing he usually held great quantities of saliva in his mouth for hours — emptying his mouth only by accident or when forced to. In the 36 hr preceding the commencement of shock, Sam ate only a small portion of one meal and drank only 400ml of liquids. Supper was refused on the day shock was first administered. The following day he drank a small quantity of milk and ate some cereal for breakfast, but all other liquids and food were refused during the day — he had started saving saliva again. In addition he was posturing with his hands most of the day (posturing had been observed before any treatment began).

On the second day following the commencement of shock he refused all food during the morning. At 2.00 p.m., he was again offered juice which he refused. He was then told firmly to drink but he would not open his mouth. It was then discovered that a firm command followed by the buzz of the stock prod (but no shock delivered), would cause him to open his mouth and take the juice, but he then held it in his mouth without swallowing. Again, a command and a buzz produced swallowing. The sequence of "Drink," and "Swallow," was repeated until he had consumed all of the juice. Verbal praise and affectionate pats were used to reinforce each desirable response. With this procedure, command-buzz-reinforcement, he also drank a glass of milk and ate some ice cream. This was the most food he had consumed in 4 days. Only one shock was actually administered — buzzing of the prod was sufficient the other times. This procedure was continued for the evening meal and the following day. On the third day he began eating spontaneously and has continued, although there are still occasions when he has to be prompted. In the following 15 days he gained 10lb and his weight continues to increase, but at a normal rate.

The posturing was stopped in similar fashion. When, for example, Sam held his hands up instead of down by his sides, he was told firmly to put his hands down, and if he did not, the buzzing of the prod was presented. The act of holding saliva in his mouth was stopped by telling him firmly to swallow and sounding the prod if he did not obey. The same procedure was effective in reducing his clinging to people.

Discussion

Both punishment procedures effectively reduced SIB in this psychotic boy. Aversive control by withdrawal of physical contact was immediately effective both times it was used.

Aversive control by painful electric shock also reduced the SIB immediately and has remained effective over a 6-month period. In addition, it was found that eating behavior could be reinstated, posturing could be stopped, and saliva-saving and clinging could be terminated by firm commands followed by the sound of the shock apparatus if there was no compliance, and followed by social reinforcement if compliance occurred. Over the 6-month period since the inception of shock, its use has decreased. Part of the beneficial effects of punishment by shock obviously were derived from the more stimulating environment provided him following the initial treatment — an environment which could not have been provided had the SIR rate not been suppressed to avoid injury. A secondary gain was probably derived from the marked positive change in behavior of attendants and nurses toward Sam. It should also be noted that punishment by electric shock prevented accidental reinforcement of SIRs. Before any treatment began it was sometimes necessary to interfere with SIRs by holding Sam's arms, a procedure which may have been reinforcing to him. No deleterious effects of the shock were observed.

An intriguing area of speculation is how to account for the complete change in behavior observed on experimental days of Study I and observed often after shock was delivered in Study II. One plausible explanation for the difference in behavior is that the whining, crying and SIB belong to the same response class and the suppression of SIB also suppresses these other behaviors. Once the undesirable behaviors are suppressed the more desirable ones, e.g. smiling, listening, attending to the environment, and co-operating with others can occur.

Another conjecture is that both types of punishment produce a general arousal in the central nervous system which results in increased attention (Hebb, 1955). Attention to the external environment could account for the co-operative behavior, smiling and apparent listening. This idea is further supported by the immediacy of the punishment effect — not only did SIB, whining, crying, and negativistic behavior cease abruptly, but within seconds the more desirable behaviors emerged.

Acknowledgements — The authors would like to thank Mrs. Beth Maxwell and Mrs. Gail Spruill for their invaluable assistance in carrying out these studies, and Mrs. Rose Boyd for typing the manuscript.

References

Ball, T. S. Personal communication, 1965.

Cain, A. C. The presuperego turning inward of aggression. *Psychoanal. Q.* 1961; **30**, 171-208.

Dollard, J., Doob, L. W., Miller, N. E., Mowrer, O. H., Sears, R. R. *Frustration and Aggression*. New Haven: Yale University Press, 1939.

Freud, A. Problems of infantile neurosis: a discussion. *In The Psychoanalytic Study of the Child*. (Vol. IX.) New York: International Universities Press, 1954.

Goldfarb, W. Psychological privation in infancy. *Am. J. Orthopsychiat.*, 1945; **15**, 247-255.

Greenacre, P. Problems of infantile neurosis: a discussion. *In The Psychoanalytic Study of the Child*. (Vol. IX) New York: International Universities Press, 1954.

Hartmann, H., Kris E., Loewenstein, R. M. Notes on the theory of aggression. *In The Psychoanalytic Study of the Child*. (Vols. III-IV) New York: International Universities Press, 1949.

Hebb, D. O. Drives and the C.N.S. (conceptual nervous system). *Psychol. Rev.*, 1955; **62**, 243-254.

Lovaas, O. I., Freitag, G., Kinder, M. I., Rubenstein, D. B., Schaeffer, B., Simmons, J. B. *Experimental Studies in Childhood Schizophrenia. Developing Social Behavior Using Electric Shock*. Paper read at American Psychological Association Annual Convention, Los Angeles, California, 1964.

Sandler, J. Masochism: an empirical analysis. *Psychol. Bull.*, 1964; **62**, 197-204.

CASE REPORT: AVOIDANCE CONDITIONING THERAPY OF AN INFANT WITH CHRONIC RUMINATIVE VOMITING[1]

Peter J. Lang, Barbara G. Melamed[2]

University of Wisconsin

Summary

This paper reports the treatment of a 9-month-old male infant whose life was seriously endangered by persistent vomiting and chronic rumination. An aversive conditioning paradigm, employing electric shock, significantly reduced the frequency of this maladaptive response pattern in a few, brief treatment sessions. Electromyographic records were used in assessing response characteristics of the emesis, and in determining the shock contingencies used in therapy. Cessation of vomiting and rumination was accompanied by weight gains, increased activity level, and general responsiveness to people.

A variety of techniques have been used in the treatment of persistent vomiting in infants and children. In general these therapies are tailored to the known or hypothesized causes of the disorder. Thus, the presence of functional disturbance in the intestinal tract would encourage the use of pharmacologic agents — "tranquilizers," antinauseants, or antiemetics. If gastric, anatomical anomalies can be diagnosed, their surgical removal often proves to be the most effective treatment. Animal studies suggest that surgical manipulation of the central nervous system may also become a vehicle for emesis control (Borison, 1959).

When diagnosis excludes obvious, organic antecedents, both the etiology and treatment of the disorder appear less certain. However, clinical workers have described an apparently "psychosomatic" vomiting in children which is generally accompanied by a ruminative rechewing of the vomitus. In reviewing the syndrome, Richmond, Eddy, and Green (1958) adhere to the widely held psychoanalytic hypothesis that it results from a disruption in the mother-infant relationship. They suggest that the condition is brought about by the inability of the mother to fulfill an adult psychosexual role which is reflected in marital inadequacy. She is unable to give up her own dependent needs and is incapable of providing warm, comfortable, and intimate physical care for the infant. This lack of comfort from without causes the infant to seek and recreate such gratification from within. Thus, in attempting to regain some satisfaction from the feeding situation, he regurgitates his food and retains it in his mouth. The recommended treatment is the interruption in the mother-infant relationship by hospitalization and the provision of a stimulating, warm environment with a substitute mother figure. This method achieved success in the four cases reviewed. Berlin, McCullough, Lisha, and Szurek (1957) offer a similar psychoanalytic interpretation in reporting a case study of a 4-yr.-old child hospitalized for 8 mo. at Langley-Porter Clinic. Psychotherapy, involving concomitant counselling to improve the relationship between the parents, led to an alleviation of the child's vomiting reaction.

From the point of view espoused by learning theorists, emesis and rumination may be learned habits. In point of fact, vomiting has been clearly demonstrated as a conditioned

1 This study was supported in part by a grant (MH-10993) from the National Institute of Mental Health, United States Public Health Service.

2 The authors wish to thank David Kass, the physician in immediate charge of the present case, for giving the authors the opportunity to explore this treatment method and for his assistance during its application. The authors are also indebted to Charles Lobeck, Chairman of the Department of Pediatrics of University Hospitals, Madison, Wisconsin, who made facilities available for use, and to the assigned nursing staff without whose help and co-operation the present result could not have been accomplished. The authors also express their appreciation to Norman Greenfield and Richard Sternbach of the Department of Psychiatry, University of Wisconsin, for the loan of a polygraph, and to Karl G. Stoedefalke of Physical Education for providing additional EMG preamplifiers.

response in at least three independent studies (Collins & Tatum, 1925; Kleitman & Crisler, 1927; Pavlov, 1927). This prompts the corollary hypothesis that such behavior could be eliminated directly by counterconditioning procedures.

A number of case reports indicate that considerable success may be achieved in modifying alimentary habits in the clinic setting. Both Bachrach, Erwin, and Mohr (1965) and Meyer[3] successfully treated adult anorexic patients by making various social and physical reinforcers contingent on eating behavior or weight gain. Lang (1965) described the therapy of a young adult patient who became nauseous and vomited under social stress. In this case, counterconditioning methods increased the patient's tolerance of formerly aversive social situations, and thus markedly reduced the frequency of nausea and emesis.

The only study reviewed, attempting to apply conditioning methods specifically in the treatment of ruminative vomiting was reported by White and Taylor (1967). Electric shock was applied to two mentally retarded patients (23-yr.-old female, 14-yr.-old male) whenever throat, eye, or coughing gestures signaled rumination. They suggest that the shock served to distract the patient and he engaged in other activities rather than ruminating. Significant improvement occurred after 1 wk. of treatment, and gains were maintained at a 1-mo. follow-up.

The following case report illustrates the efficacy of aversive conditioning in reversing the vomiting and rumination of a 9-mo.-old infant whose life was endangered by this behavior. The case is of general interest because of the extreme youth of the patient, the speed of treatment, and the fact that conditioning procedures were undertaken only after other treatments had been either ruled out by diagnostic procedures, or had been given a reasonable trial without success. These data also have further implications for the understanding of aversive conditioning procedures in clinical practice.

History of problem and family

A. T. at the age of 9 mo. was admitted to the University Hospital for failure to retain food and chronic rumination. This infant had undergone three prior hospitalizations for his persistent vomiting after eating and failure to gain weight. Born in an eastern state after an uneventful 39-wk. pregnancy, the patient was bottle fed and gained steadily from a birth weight of 9 lb. 4 oz. to 17 lb. at 6 mo. of age. Vomiting was first noted during the fifth month, and increased in severity to the point where the patient vomited 10-15 min. after each meal. This activity was often associated with vigorous thumbsucking, placing fingers in his mouth, blotchiness of the face, and ruminating behavior. The mother remarked that the start of vomiting may have coincided with her indisposition due to a broken ankle which forced the family to live with maternal grand-parents for several weeks. Some friction was reported between the patient's mother and her own adoptive mother concerning care of the child. The patient's father is a part-time college student and the family received financial assistance from the paternal grandfather, a successful dentist. At the time of the most recent hospitalization, the social worker's report suggested that the parents were making a marginal marital adjustment.

Three brief periods of hospitalization which included medical tests (gastrointestinal fluoroscopy, EEG, and neuropsychological testing) failed to find an organic basis for this persistent regurgitation. An exploratory operation was performed and a cyst on the right kidney removed, with no discernible effect on his condition. The patient had no history of head trauma. One previous incident of persistent vomiting in a paternal uncle was noted to be of very short duration. The paternal grandfather and two uncles are reported to suffer ulcers.

Several treatment approaches were applied without success. Dietary changes (Pro-Sobee, skim milk), the administration of antinauseants, and various mechanical maneuvers to improve the feeding situation (different positions, small amounts at each feeding, burping) gave short-lived, if any, relief. As thumb sucking often preceded the response, restraints were tried. However, this did little to reduce the frequency of emesis. An attempt had been made to initiate intensive nursing care "to establish and maintain a one-to-one relationship and to provide the child with warm, friendly, and secure feelings [nurse's chart]." This had

3 Meyer, V. Personal communication, 1964.

to be abandoned because it was not inhibiting the vomiting and some observers felt that it increased the child's anxiety and restlessness.

At the time the present investigators were called in, the infant was in critical condition, down to a weight of 12 lb., and being fed through a nasogastric pump. The attending physician's clinical notes attest that conditioning procedures were applied as a last attempt, "in view of the fact that therapy until now has been unsuccessful and the life of the child is threatened by continuation of this behavior."

Therapeutic procedure and results

The patient was given a private room, continuous nursing care, and assigned a special graduate nurse to assist in the conditioning procedures. The authors closely observed the infant for 2 days during and after normal feeding periods. He reliably regurgitated most of his food intake within 10 min. of each feeding and continued to bring up small amounts throughout the day. Observers on the hospital staff suggested that vomiting was originally induced by thumb pressure at the back of the throat. However, at this stage thumb manipulations were not a necessary part of the vomiting sequence. He did protest, however, if hand restraint was enforced. His frail appearance and general unresponsiveness, made him a pathetic looking child as seen from a photograph taken just prior to treatment (Figure 1).

In an attempt to obtain a clearer picture of the patterning of his response, electromyograph (EMG) activity at three sites was monitored on a Gilson Polygraph. Responses leading up to and into the vomiting sequence reliably coincided with the nurse's concurrent description of the sequence of behavior. Figure 2 illustrates the typical response pattern. The uppermost channel of information represents muscle potentials recorded just under the chin, and shows the sucking behavior which usually preceded vomiting; the lowest channel is an integrated record taken from the throat muscles of the neck; the center channel which monitors the upper chest region is largely EKG artifact. It can be noted from this segment that the onset of vomiting is clearly accompanied by vigorous throat

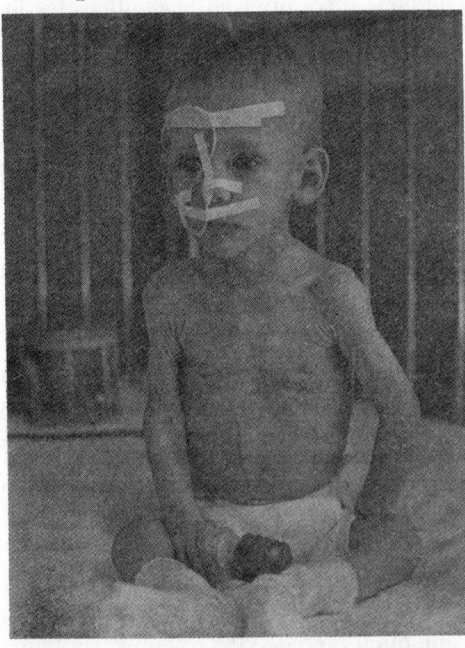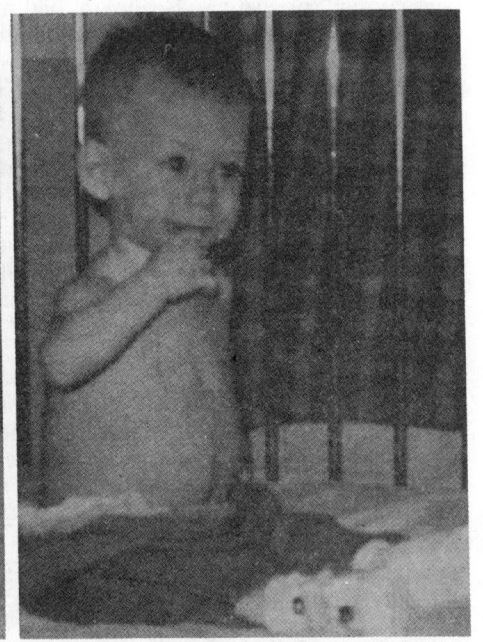

Fig. 1. The photograph at the left was taken during the observation period just prior to treatment. (It clearly illustrates the patient's debilitated condition — the lack of body fat, skin hanging in loose folds. The tape around the face holds tubing for the nasogastric pump. The photograph at the right was taken on the day of discharge from the hospital, 13 days after the first photo. The 26% increase in body weight already attained is easily seen in the full, more infantlike face, the rounded arms, and more substantial trunk.)

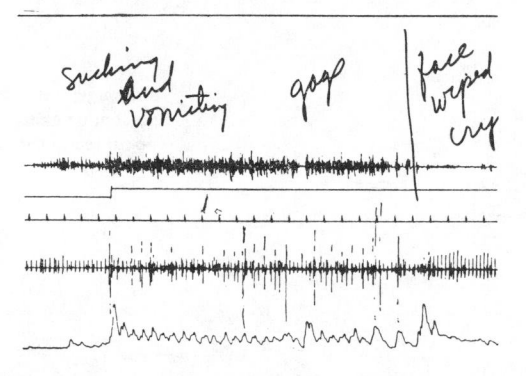

Fig. 2. Three channels of EMG activity are presented. (The nurse observer's comments are written just above the first channel. The intense muscle activity on this line is associated with sucking behavior, recorded from electrodes on the underside of the chin. The second channel is just below the one pulse per second, timing line, and was taken from electrodes on the upper chest, at the base of the throat. The EKG dominates this channel, with some local muscle activity. Electrodes straddling the esophagus yielded the lowest line, which in this integrated record clearly shows the rhythmic pulsing of the vomiting response.)

movements indicated by rhythmic, high-frequency, high-amplitude activity, in contrast with quiescent periods and periods where crying predominated.

The authors were concerned with eliminating the inappropriate vomiting, without causing any fundamental disturbance in the feeding behavior of the child. Fortunately, the child did not vomit during feeding, and the sucking and vomiting could be distinguished readily on the EMG. After 2 days of monitoring, conditioning procedures were initiated. The aversive conditioning paradigm called for brief and repeated shock (approximately 1 sec. long with a 1-sec. interpulse interval) as soon as vomiting occurred, continuing until the response was terminated. An effort was made to initiate shock at the first sign of reverse peristalsis, but not during preceding sucking behavior. The contingent was determined from the nurse's observation of the patient and the concurrent EMG records. In general, the nurse would signal as soon as she thought an emesis was beginning. If EMG confirmed the judgment, shock was delivered. Occasionally, the EMG would initiate this sequence, with the observations judgment following.[4] Shock was delivered by means of a Harvard Inductorium to electrodes placed on the calf of the patient's leg. A 3,000-cps tone was temporally coincided with each shock presentation.[5] Sessions were chosen following feeding to insure some frequency of response. Each session lasted less than 1 hour.

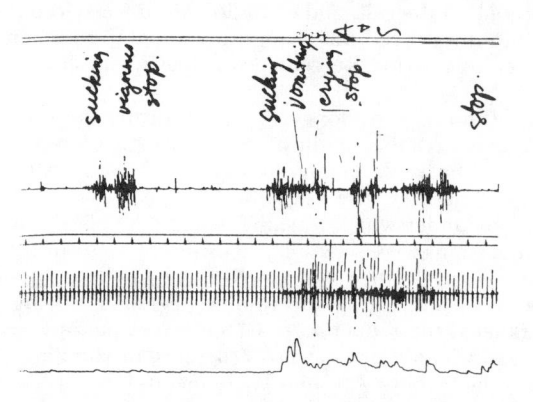

Fig. 3. The electrode positions are the same as in Figure 2. (The top line shows the point at which two brief shocks were administered. It may be noted that they follow closely on the first pulse of the vomiting response and that the rhythmic' regurgitation observed in Figure 2 never gets underway.)

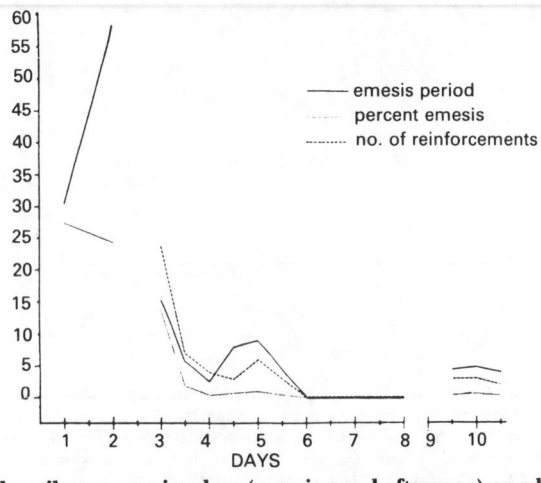

Fig. 4. The abscissa describes successive days (morning and afternoon) on which observation or treatment was accomplished. ("Emesis period" is the length of any continuous period of vomiting. "Percentage of emesis" is the total time spent vomiting divided by the time observed. Sessions varied from 16 min. to 60 min. Treatment began on Day 3 which included two unshocked emesis periods. In Session 10 tone alone was presented on one trial. It is of interest to note that following therapy, nursing staff reported that they could now block the very rare vomiting periods with a sharp handclap.)

After two sessions shock was rarely required. The infant would react to the shock by crying and cessation of vomiting. By the third session only one or two brief presentations of shock were necessary to cause cessation of any vomiting sequence. Figure 3 illustrates the typical sequence of a conditioning trial.

The course of therapy is indicated in Figure 4. Few shocks were administered after the first day of treatment, and both the time spent vomiting and the average length of each vomiting period were abruptly reduced. After only two sessions it seemed that the infant was anticipating the unpleasant consequences of his behavior. He would begin to suck vigorously using his thumb, and then he would remove his thumb and cry loudly.

The data graphed (Figure 4) for the second treatment session represent those reinforcers that the authors are certain were delivered. Early in this session, it became obvious that the infant was not receiving the majority of the administered shocks. The electrodes were at that time attached to the plantar surface of the foot. Observation suggested that the patient had learned to curl his foot, either coincident with emesis or at the first sensation of shock, so as to lift the electrodes off the skin and thus avoid the painful stimulus. At this point, the electrodes were relocated on the calf, and conditioning proceeded normally. If the shock administrations prior to this procedural change are added to those on the graph, Day 3, afternoon figures for emesis period, percentage of emesis, and shock, respectively, are 11 sec., 21.6% and 77.

By the sixth session the infant no longer vomited during the testing procedures. He would usually fall asleep toward the middle of the hour. Figure 5 indicates the sequence of response demonstrating the replacement of vigorous sucking with what the nursing observers described as a "pacifier" use of the thumb.

To vary the conditions under which learning would take place, thereby providing for transfer of effects, the sessions were scheduled at different hours of the day, and while the infant was being held, playing on the floor, as well as lying in bed. Nursing staff reported a progressive decrease in his ruminating and vomiting behavior during the rest of the day and night, which paralleled the reduction observed across therapy sessions.

After three sessions in which there was no occurrence of vomiting, the procedure was discontinued. Two days later there was some spontaneous recovery, which included some vigorous sucking, with a little vomiting and rumination. Three additional sessions were initiated to maintain the reduced frequency of the response (see Figure 4). Except for a brief slackening prior to these trials, there was a steady, monotonic increase in his weight as

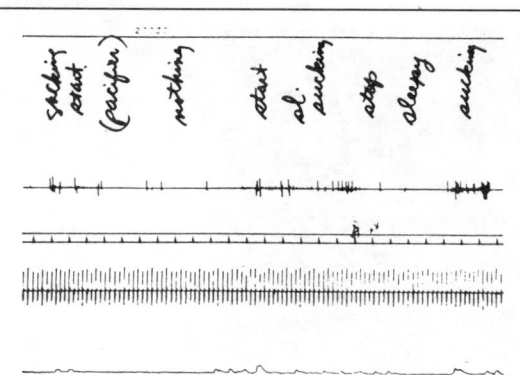

Fig. 5. The above segment is representative of behavior near the end of a conditioning session. (Only mild sucking activity is apparent in the upper EMG channel. The electrode positions are the same as in Figure 2.)

shown in Figure 6. In general, his activity level increased, he became more interested in his environment, enjoyed playroom experience, and smiled and reached out to be held by the nurse and other visitors.

The mother was reintroduced the day following the last conditioning trial. She took over some of the patient's caretaking needs, including feedings. There was no marked change in his ruminating behavior at this time. The mother responded well and her child reciprocated her attention. He was discharged from the hospital 5 days later, after exhibiting almost no ruminating behavior. The remarkable contrast in his physical appearance is noted in a photograph taken on the day of discharge (Figure 1).

Follow-up

Correspondence with the mother indicated that there was no further need for treatment. A. T. was eating well and gaining weight regularly. She reported that any thumbsucking or rumination was easily arrested by providing him with other forms of stimulation. He was beginning to seek attention from other people and enjoyed the company of other children.

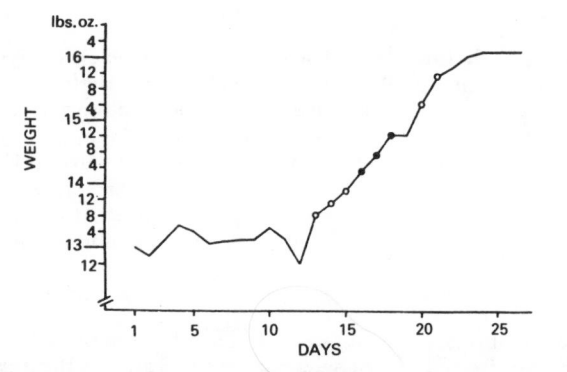

Fig. 6. The infant's body weight as determined from the nursing notes is plotted over time, from well before conditioning therapy was instituted to the day of discharge from the hospital. (Days on which conditioning sessions occurred are marked by circles on the curve. Reinforcers were delivered only on days marked by open circles. The decline in body weight in the few days just prior to therapy was probably occasioned by the discontinuance of the nasogastric pump, in favour of normal feeding procedures. The marked weight gain from Day 13 to 18 is coincident with the first 6 days of therapy. The temporary reduction in weight increase, associated with a resumption of emesis, is apparent at Day 19. The additional conditioning trials appear to have acted immediately to reinstate weight gain.)

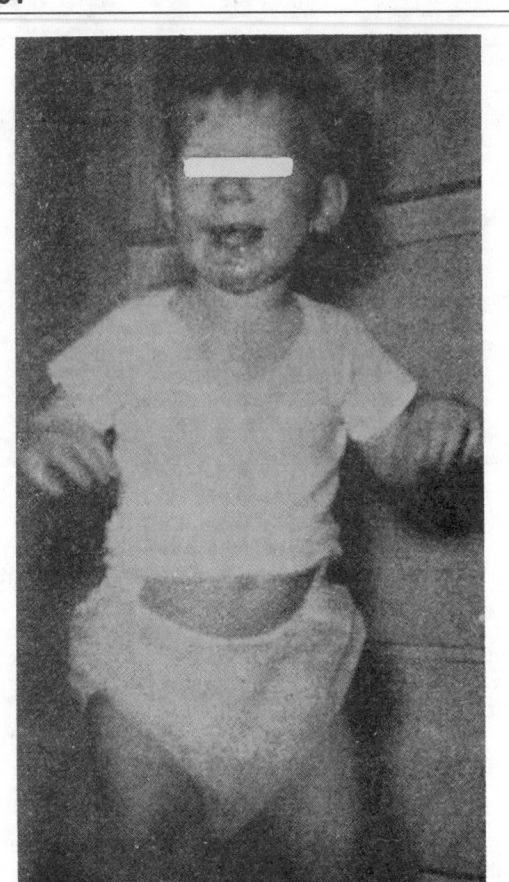

Fig. 7. The patient 5 mo. after treatment.

One month following discharge from the hospital, he was seen for a physical check-up. He appeared as a healthy looking 21-lb. child and, aside from a slight anemic condition, was found fully recovered by the attending physician. His local physician reported on a visit 5 mo. later when his weight was 26 lb., 1 oz. "His examinations were negative for any problems . . . He was eating quite well . . . no vomiting had recurred. He was alert, active and attentive. A snapshot taken by the mother a few weeks before this examination is reproduced in Figure 7. One year after treatment he continues to thrive. Mother and father are both pleased with his development, and no further treatment is indicated.

Discussion

The rapid recovery of this 9-mo.-old male infant following brief aversive conditioning therapy, argues for the effectiveness of behavioral modification in the treatment of this type of psychosomatic disorder. The vomiting and ruminating were treated as maladaptive behavior patterns, and electric shock was used to inhibit a previously well-established response sequence. Elimination of the response was accompanied by increase in the infant's responsiveness to people, as well as substantial weight gains, and physiological improvement.

Treatment was undertaken without analysis of the disorder's antecedents. Nevertheless, the family history of the infant could be construed as consistent with other cases in the literature. One clinical worker suggested that a feeling of hostility dominated this infant's home. It is true that the parents' wedding was attended by difficulties and the subsequent birth of the patient occurred before the parents were fully prepared for this responsibility. Furthermore, the mother later expressed anxiety about her marriage and complained of the problem of balancing the separate demands of father and child. She also reported her feeling that her own step-mother had not provided a good maternal model. As a consequence she felt inadequate herself and uncertain in the role.

The caseworker's notes are thus rich in "dynamics," and while one is unable to establish the relative accuracy or significance of these statements, it is clear that this case is interpretable within traditional personality theories. Nevertheless, therapies generated by this orientation were not successful in the present case. In deference, it should also be noted that "one-to-one" care was not maintained as long or as consistently as in many cases reported in the literature, and despite evidence of some marital discord, no extensive counselling of the parents was undertaken. However, like many psychiatric treatments, the above are expensive of professional personnel and prolonged in duration. The aversive conditioning procedures used here achieved success in little more than a week, and considering the developing danger to the child's life, speed was of more than usual importance.

No evidence of "symptom substitution" was observed following treatment. On the other hand, positive social behavior increased coincident with the successful conditioning therapy. The infant became more responsive to adults, smiled more frequently, and seemed to be more interested in toys and games than he had been previously. An analogous improvement in social behavior was noticed in the defective adults treated by White and Taylor (1967). Lovaas, Freitag, Gold, and Kassorla (1965) and Lovaas, Schaeffer, and Simmons (1965) have cited similar effects following the avoidance conditioning of tantrum behavior in autistic children. The latter investigators suggest that the *Es* attained secondary reinforcing value because of their association with shock reduction. This provides the basis for training the children to exhibit affectionate patterns toward adults. In the present case this contingency was very imprecise, and it is not clear that the above mechanism mediated change. What could be called normal infant behavior increased regularly, as the emesis decreased. The social environment appeared simply to replace ruminating as the infant's focus of attention.

Aversive conditioning has been applied widely in adult therapy as well as with autistic children. Eysenck and Rachman (1965) and Feldman (1966) describe its use in treating alcoholic and sexual disorders. However, one hesitates to interpret these findings in a straightforward manner. Adult patients may submit to aversive conditioning procedures from a variety of motives, and cognitive factors may blunt the impact or distort the meaning of aversive stimuli. The present case is of particular interest because these procedures were successful in treating an apparently normal child. Furthermore, the absence of language and the limited cognitive development achieved at this age permit one to interpret this change as avoidance conditioning, unmitigated by the above factors.

Finally, it should be noted that the present case represents a productive use of psychophysiologic recording in therapy. Not only did the EMG provide extensive documentation of the response, but concurrent recording was of considerable help in guiding the treatment effort. Specifically, these records confirmed in an objective manner external observations of mouth and throat movements which seemed to precede emesis. Furthermore, they extended these observations, helping the authors to specify those aspects of the response which were unique to the vomiting sequence, thus assuring that shock was never delivered following noncontingent behavior. Finally, observation of the recordings during therapy probably reduced the latency of reinforcement, particularly during the early trials when the validity of external signs seemed less certain, and provided the clearest indicator of the end of the response when shock was promptly terminated. While the importance of this information to the results obtained cannot be unequivocally established, it certainly increased the confidence of the therapists in their method, and, in turn, the speed and precision with which they proceeded. The further exploration of physiological analysis in the therapeutic setting is encouraged.

References

Bachrach, A. J., Erwin, W. J., Mohr, J. P. The control of eating behavior in an anorexic by operant conditioning techniques. In L. P. Ullmann, L. Krasner (Eds.), *Case studies in behavior modification*. New York: Holt, Rinehart & Winston, 1965.

Berlin, I. N., McCullough, G., Lisha, E. S., Szurek, S. Intractable episodic vomiting in a three-year old child. *Psychiatric Quarterly*, 1957, **31**, 228-249.

Borison, H. L. Effect of ablation of medullaremetic chemoreceptor trigger zone on vomiting response to cerebral intra-ventricular injection with adrenaline, apomorphine and pilocarpine in the cat. *Journal of Physiology*, 1959, **147**, 172-177.

Collins, K. H., Tatum, A. L. A conditioned salivary reflex established by chronic morphine poisoning. *American Journal of Physiology*, 1925, **74**, 14-15.

Eysenck, H. J., Rachman, S. *The causes and cures of neurosis*. San Diego, Calif.: Knapp, 1965.

Feldman, M. P. Aversion therapy for sexual deviations: A criticl review. *Psychological Bulletin*, 1966, **65**, 65-79.

Kleitman, N., Crisler, G. A quantitative study of the conditioned salivary reflex. *American Journal of Physiology*, 1927, **79**, 571-614.

Lang, P. J. Behavior therapy with a case of nervous anorexia. In L. P. Ullmann & L. Krasner (Eds.) *Case studies in behavior modification*. New York: Holt, Rinehart & Winston, 1965.

Lovaas, O. I., Freitag, G., Gold, V., Kassorla, I. C. Experimental studies in childhood schizophrenia. Analysis of self-destructive behavior. *Journal of Experimental Child Psychology*, 1965, **2**, 67-84.

Lovaas, O. I., Schaeffer, B., Simmons, J. Building social behavior in autistic children by use of electric shock. *Journal of Experimental Research in Personality*, 1965, **1**, 99-109.

Pavlov, I. P. *Conditioned reflexes: An investigation of the physiological activity of the cerebral cortex*. Lecture III, Oxford, England; Oxford University Press, 1927.

Richmond, J. B., Eddy, E., Green, M. Rumination: A psychosomatic syndrome of infancy. *Pediatrics*, 1958, **22**, 49-55.

White, J. D., Taylor, D. Noxious conditioning as a treatment for rumination. *Mental Retardation*, 1967, **5**, 30-33.

Reprinted from *J. Abnorm. Psychol.*, 1969; **74**:1, 1-8 by kind permission of the authors and the publishers Plenum Publishing Corp., New York, NY 10013.

AN EXTINCTION PROCEDURE FOR ELIMINATING SELF-DESTRUCTIVE BEHAVIOR IN A 9-YEAR OLD AUTISTIC GIRL[1]

Fredric H. Jones[2]

University of Rochester

James Q. Simmons, Frederick Frankel

Neuropsychiatric Institute, UCLA Center for the Health Sciences

Summary

A 24-week program of 2 daily 2-hour sessions of noncontingent social isolation was successful in eliminating multiple self-destructive behaviors in a 9-year-old autistic child. A previous program of response-contingent shock met with failure, resulting in (1) increased self-destructive responding, (2) complete suppression of self-feeding, and (3) the necessity for constant physical restraint. Generalization of the extinction program to the ward was inferred on the basis of the subject's subsequent cessation of restraint-wearing, a decrease in self-destructive behavior in the dayroom and subsequently in other settings following the removal of restraints, and a renewed interest in food. A brief program based upon elements of the noncontingent social isolation program was sufficient to reinstitute self-feeding. The subject was gradually removed from social isolation sessions with no reappearance of self-destruction. However, during week 72, self-destructive behavior again appeared, at which time a reinstatement of the original program dramatically reduced its rate.

Self-destructive behavior has been described as reaching problem proportions in several types of psychiatrically institutionalized children (Green, 1967). Self-destructive behavior is common to autistic and psychotic children (Lovaas & Simmons, 1969) as well as to children in a state of anaclitic depression (Green, 1967). In many autistic and psychotic children acts of self-destruction constitute a major management problem for parents and ward attendants alike (Simmons & Lovaas, 1969; Bostow & Bailey, 1969; Tate, 1972).

Systematic approaches to treatment of self-destruction have been numerous. For purposes of discussion, they may be classified into three groups, depending upon their focus: (1) establishing *competing* behaviors (differential reinforcement of other behavior — DRO), (2) suppressing self-destructive behavior (punishment such as contingent social withdrawal, time-out, shock), or (3) extinguishing self-destructive behavior (removing all contingencies associated with self-destruction by either passively ignoring all self-destruction or by employing noncontingent social isolation). Each of the above treatments has been employed with some degree of success. For example, a DRO procedure which reinforced behaviors competing with self-destruction yielded complete suppression of self-destructive behavior (Allen & Harris, 1966). Contingent withdrawal of social and food reinforcement (Whitney, 1966) and time-out as brief as two minutes (Pendergrass, 1972) have also been effective in eliminating self-destruction, and as few as 12 response-contingent shocks have reduced a moderate rate of self-destruction to zero (Bucher & Lovaas, 1968). Finally, extinction procedures such as three months of passively ignoring self-destruction in addition to using a time-out program (Rubin, Griswald, Smith &

1 Without the aid of the nursing staff on Ward 5-West this study could not have been possible. Special credit is due to Ellen Masters, Jo Anderson, Jo Smaltz, Bonnie Nealy, Terry MacDowell, and David Kilian for carrying out the programs reported here. Other members of the nursing staff who participated to a lesser degree and/or carried on ward functions while this study was being administered are also deserving of credit. The authors would also like to thank Jo Anderson and Michael Ritz for recording and tabulating the follow-up data. This research was supported in part by Maternal and Child Health Grant Number 927.

2 Requests for reprints should be sent to Dr. Fredric H. Jones, Department of Psychiatry, University of Rochester Medical Center, 260 Crittenden Boulevard, Rochester, New York 14642.

DeLeonardo, 1972) and 12 1½-hour sessions of noncontingent social isolation (Lovaas & Simmons, 1969) have also eliminated self-destruction.

Since all of the above-mentioned treatment forms have met with some degree of success, treatment of an individual case may be dictated by the availability of manpower on a given treatment team, ethical considerations regarding the use of contingent aversive control (see Bucher & Lovaas, 1968, for a more detailed discussion), and/or the behavior repertoire of the subject. In regard to this last point, a high base rate of self-destructive behavior makes the administration of many of the above therapies difficult. A DRO procedure may be impractical in the face of high-rate self-destructive behavior since appropriate behavior may rarely occur in such circumstances (Smolev, 1971). Extinction in the form of passively ignoring self-destructive behavior tends to be difficult in most settings due to accidental reinforcement by attending adults. The use of response-contingent time-out may be difficult also since the total time spent in seclusion for high-rate behavior may be so great as to render the procedure equivalent to noncontingent social isolation. Furthermore, time-out may involve a large degree of struggling by the staff in getting the child in and out of the isolation area which may function as reinforcement (Wolf, Risley, & Mees, 1964). Thus, only punishment or noncontingent social isolation may be practical in cases of extremely high-rate self-destructive behavior.

The present study is concerned with the elimination of multiple high-rate self-destructive behaviors in a 9-year-old girl for whom a contingent punishment program failed to fully suppress self-destruction. A program of noncontingent social isolation was therefore carried out.

Method
Subject

Elaina is a 9-year-old girl who early in life displayed a severe degree of retardation in addition to the autistic features of preference for sameness, a high rate of stereotypic behavior, and echolalic speech. High-rate self-destructive behavior began in her fifth year coincident with the efforts of a speech therapist to build appropriate speech and of her father to enforce self-feeding behavior. The self-destructive behavior consisted of forcefully thrusting the back of her hand or wrist into her upper front teeth (hereafter referred to as *hitting*). Elaina was referred to the Neuropsychiatric Institute by her pediatrician in 1967, shortly after the onset of the severe self-destructive behavior. In only a few weeks Elaina had opened large lesions on the backs of both wrists.

Details of the initial treament procedures have been presented elsewhere (Reed, 1968; Simmons & Reed, 1969). Briefly, the first inpatient treatment program at age 5 consisted of punishment (electroshock) as a consequence of hitting. Although a near-zero rate was established and maintained during the child's first hospitalization of one year, self-destructive behavior was never totally eliminated. After nine months in the home, the subject was rehospitalized due to self-destructive behavior, and the electroshock program was reinstituted. The results of this program, however, were less satisfactory than the results of the previous program. The baseline rate of hitting did not decline until week 20 of the shock program and did not reach zero until week 32, and during this period Elaina's repertoire of self-destructive behavior expanded. Early in the program she extended the area of hitting from the back of her wrists to her palms, fingers, forearms, shoulders, and knees. At about week 22 her repertoire included pinching and jabbing with her fingers of sufficient intensity to open lesions on her sides, stomach, thighs, and the back of her neck. Thus, when hitting was completely suppressed in week 32, the increasing rate of jabbing represented a net increase in self-destruction. Finally, 6 weeks after the emergence of jabbing, the shock program was extended to this new response. This extended shock program lasted 1½ weeks before being discontinued for several very distressing reasons: (1) jabbing increased; (2) hitting reappeared and increased; and (3) Elaina completely stopped eating; resisted entering the dining area, and hit and kicked at the presentation of food. As a result she was restrained in order to be given tube feedings twice a day. For two months before the beginning of the program to be described here, Elaina was almost continually restrained with a neck collar and arm tubes.

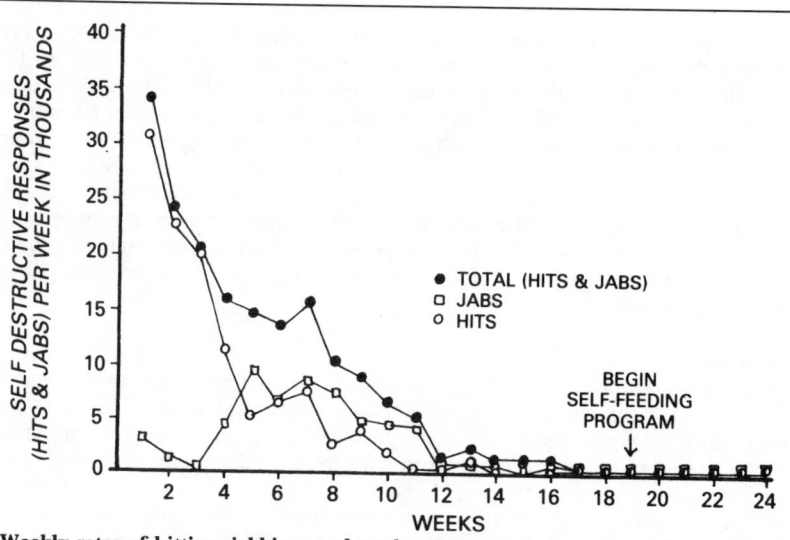

Fig. 1. Weekly rates of hitting, jabbing, and total self-destructive responses during the course of noncontingent social isolation (weeks 1—24).

Procedure

An extinction paradigm utilizing noncontingent social isolation was chosen subsequent to the failure of the electroshock program. Elaina was placed in an 8 × 10-foot isolation room situated off the ward, equipped with a one-way mirror and a supply of toys. Two-hour sessions were held in the isolation room twice daily, once in the morning and once in the afternoon.

During the initial stages the program was integrated into Elaina's ward life in the following way: Removal of restraints occurred immediately before she was placed in the isolation room. Immediately after each social isolation session she was taken back to the ward and placed in another isolation room for an additional five minutes. She was then taken to her bedroom, where her arms and neck were washed, bandaged, and placed in tube restraints. This procedure was carried out to obscure contingency relationships between removal from the isolation room and bandaging her or placing her in restraints. She was then allowed freedom of movement on the ward and access to the ward playroom.

Two types of behaviors were scored by the ward staff observing Elaina in the isolation room through the one-way mirror. These were (1) hitting, any discrete gouging of the body by the teeth, and (2) jabbing, forceful contact between the fingers with any other part of the body. Hitting and jabbing were scored using a simple frequency count throughout each session. The reliability index used was the percentage of agreement between the criterion scorer (Dr. Jones) and nursing staff across a half-hour of recording (dividing the smaller total by the larger total). Inter-rater reliability was established with each member of the ward staff before their participation in the project, with the requirement that 95% agreement be reached with the criterion rater. All staff members exceeded this, and monthly spot checks on each staff member revealed no instance of reliability below .95.

In addition, monthly probes were made during isolation sessions in which a staff member entered the isolation room during the second hour of the morning session and passively interacted with Elaina for 15 minutes and then, after leaving the room for 15 minutes, reentered the room to actively interact and attempt to play with Elaina for another 15 minutes.

Results

Figure 1 shows the course of response extinction during this initial program, collapsed by weeks. Separate curves represent total self-destructive responding, hitting, and jabbing. The extinction of the total number of self-destructive responses proceeded in a lawful fashion. Hitting, the response with the greater reinforcement history, was emitted more often at the beginning of social isolation and its rate decreased relatively rapidly. As the rate of self-hitting decreased, the rate of jabbing increased and then decreased to form an inverted U-shaped curve, finally approaching zero by week 12 of social isolation. Data from days in which both hitting and jabbing occurred during a single session show an almost perfect negative covariation between the rates of the two behaviours across time, indicating that they were alternate and interchangeable forms of self-destructive behavior.

Gross observations indicated that the intensity of Elaina's self-destructive behavior decreased during the course of extinction. By week 5, hitting had become a mere tap, and by week 7, the lesions on the backs of her wrists were healed. An inspection of the cumulative frequency of self-destructive behavior during the monthly probes showed the presence of an adult to have no effect.

Generalization

Changes in Elaina's behavior during ward activities occurred spontaneously and quite unexpectedly beginning in week 7 of the extinction program. Records of this behavior were kept systematically by the ward staff, but the lack of rigorous baseline and reliability assessment and independence of measure render these findings anecdotal and suggestive in nature.

Previous to extinction, Elaina had worn her restraints continuously for two months and had exhibited protestation, hyperventilation, a contorted facial expression, and rapid hitting whenever the ward staff attempted to remove them. Elaina began to resist having restraints applied during week 7 of extinction. Restraints were applied as long as Elaina did not physically fight having them applied. When she resisted by fighting, however, she was not forced. Surprisingly, when not forced, Elaina carried her restraints around with her for several weeks, during which time she became increasingly lax. By week 15 of extinction she was completely free of restraints.

When Elaina had worn restraints in the dayroom, she had typically stood or sat motionlessly at the edge of the room, not interacting with the other children. Freedom from her restraints allowed her to become more active and to interact sporadically with other children. Since self-destructive behavior now became a possibility in a setting other than the isolation room, instances of hitting and jabbing were recorded beginning in week 15 during one hour in the morning before isolation and one hour in the evening following dinner. Reliability spot checks were made on attending staff weekly, and reliability based upon percentage of agreement of hourly totals exceeded 85% in all cases. The rate of self-destructive behavior in the dayroom decreased from 20 hits or jabs per hour during week 15 to 0 by week 21 and remained at that level until the termination of the formal intervention in week 24.

During week 16, Elaina began for the first time to voluntarily enter the dining room during mealtimes and to touch food on other children's plates. This was in marked contrast to her eating behavior previous to the extinction program. An initial feeding program consisted of seating Elaina at a table with food and reinforcing her approximations of self-feeding. This, however, ended in Elaina's learning to throw food for peer attention. Consequently, a new program was devised in week 19 consisting of the following steps. First, tube feedings were reduced to one per day (at bedtime). This produced a progressively increasing degree of deprivation with each day in which her diet was not supplemented with self-feeding. In addition, she was placed alone in a small room on the ward for 20 minutes at each mealtime with a table, chair, and a plate of food. Eating sessions were observed through a one-way mirror. After one week of this program, playing with food decreased and Elaina ate an average of one full meal per day. By the end of the second week, Elaina was eating all three of her daily meals, and tube feedings could be discontinued. Follow-up data indicated that this pattern remained stable for nine months, at which time Elaina was integrated into the ward dining room for all of her meals.

Follow-up and reversal

Starting with week 25 of extinction, the total amount of time Elaina spent in the isolation room was decreased gradually and replaced with other structured activities such as school, outings, and recreation. Total time in isolation was reduced to 20 hours by week 36, 10

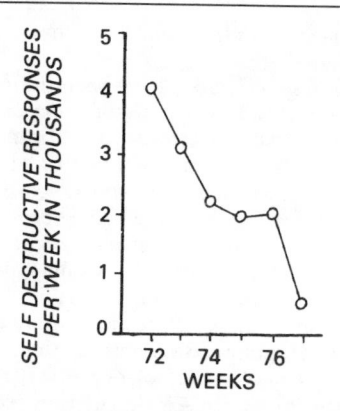

Fig. 2. Weekly rate of self-destructive behavior during the reinstatement of noncontingent social isolation following relapse (weeks 72-77).

hours by week 41, 5 hours by week 47, and 0 hours by week 59. This reduction in time spent in isolation was not accompanied by the reappearance of hitting or jabbing. Peer aggression, however, was occasionally observed in school and in the dayroom as Elaina rejoined various group activities. Instances of palm-biting in response to staff demands averaging three per week were also noted.

A reversal of the gains made during the intervention occurred for no identifiable reason during week 72. Elaina suddenly began jabbing on the ward and in the school at a rate of 350 per hour. At that time the initial isolation program was reinstated, with the exception that at no time was Elaina placed in restraints. The rate of self-destructive behavior during the following 6 weeks (measured during isolation sessions as before) is presented in Figure 2. As before, Elaina's rate of self-destructive behavior followed a lawful extinction curve but started at a lower frequency and approached zero more rapidly than it had during the first program. Follow-up data beyond week 77 was confounded by a separate drug program. In general, her frequency of self-destructive behavior has remained low, and she is once again being phased out of sessions in the isolation room.

Discussion and conclusions

The results show that noncontingent social isolation may be an effective procedure for eliminating multiple classes of high-rate self-destructive behavior. In general, other researchers have found the noncontingent social isolation procedure to be successful in eliminating self-destructive behavior (Ferster, 1961; Lovaas, 1967; Lovaas & Simmons, 1969; Simmons & Lovaas, 1969; Ullman & Krasner, 1965). Reports of failure in the use of this procedure (Bucher & Lovaas, 1968; Corte, Wolf, & Locke, 1971) may be attributed to session lengths of under 1½ hours per day administered for less than 12 days (a total of less than 15 hours of noncontingent social isolation). This total time in isolation would be roughly equivalent to a 4-day period of the initial isolation program reported here. It was evident from the results that no great changes in response rate occurred until week 2.

The reasons for the effectiveness of noncontingent social isolation in eliminating self-destructive behavior are not clear from this study or from the literature. Elaina's case offers some suggestions in this regard, however. The monthly probes showed that, for Elaina, self-destructive behavior was not noticeably under social control by the time the program was begun. If Elaina's self-destructive behavior were maintained by secondary reinforcement dispensed by adults such as the ward staff, an immediate change in rate should have been evident when the adult entered the isolation room. This finding seems to be in contrast to other studies showing a definite influence of attending adults on self-destructive behavior (study number 3 in Lovaas, Freitag, Gold, & Kassorla, 1965; Gregg in Lovaas & Simmons, 1969). However, the lack of stimulus control of self-destructive behavior by social agents does not imply that the initial acquisition of self-destructive responses was not motivated by gaining adult attention or escaping adult demands. Elaina's history of previous therapeutic interventions may have masked the initial stimulus control of self-destruction.

Self-destructive responding may ultimately have been under partial stimulus control of Elaina's arm and neck restraints. Before the initial isolation program, self-destructive behavior rarely occurred while restraints were worn. Immediately prior to the initial program, Elaina was placed in the isolation room with restraints on and attempted no self-destruction for the duration of this probe. In contrast, when restraints were removed, arousal seemed to increase, self-destruction immediately began, and she would repeatedly ask for her restraints. Asking for restraints was also noted during the reinstatement of social isolation. A relationship between the wearing of restraints and self-destruction has been observed in some children (John in Bucher & Lovaas, 1968; Linda in Lovaas & Simmons, 1969), but it has not always been present in self-destructive children (Marilyn in Bucher and Lovaas, 1968; case number 3 in Hamilton, Stephens, & Allen, 1967; Tate & Baroff, 1966). It is possible that, during the course of social isolation, the stimulus control exerted by the presence of restraints was lost as the rate of self-destruction decreased, resulting in Elaina's eventually refusing to wear restraints.

Stimulus control of restraints could have been acquired as a result either of their application consequent to the termination of the unsuccessful shock program, their association with the termination of a large number of shocks and demands, or the absence of pain accompanying self-destructive behavior. Restraints may therefore have come to be "explicitly unpaired" with shock and other aversive events (Rescorla, 1967). It is well-established in the animal literature that stimuli explicitly *unpaired* with a painful stimulus inhibit operant responding in the presence of other stimuli explicitly associated with the painful stimulus (Grossen & Bolles, 1968; Rescorla, 1966, 1967, 1968, 1969). Restraints could have acquired this function (referred to as a *safety signal*) for the abovestated reasons. The safety signal function would be lost as a result of noncontingent social isolation during long periods in which restraints were removed.

This hypothesis might help explain the generalization to the ward which began as a refusal to wear restraints. However, the reduction in hitting on the ward following the removal of restraints and the resumption of approach behavior toward food is more difficult to explain. In any case, studies reporting a lack of generalization of noncontingent social isolation to other situations (Bucher & Lovaas, 1968; Lovaas & Simmons, 1969) were not supported by the present results. Furthermore, for Elaina, noncontingent social isolation did not lose its effectiveness after the first successful application, but rather retained its effectiveness upon the second application. The treatment effects also apparently generalized across behaviors. Noncontingent social isolation may therefore be more broadly applicable than has been realized thus far and may in fact sidestep many of the problems of poor generalization across place and therapist noted with contingent aversive control (Bucher & Lovaas, 1968; Corte, et al., 1971).

References
Allen, K. E., Harris, F. R. Elimination of a child's excessive scratching by training the mother in reinforcement procedures. *Behav. Res. & Ther.*, 1966; 4, 79-84.
Bostow, D. E., Bailey, J. B. Modification of severe disruptive and aggressive behavior using brief timeout and reinforcement procedures. *J. Appl. Behav. Anal.* 1969; 2, 31-37.
Bucher, B., Lovaas, O. I. Use of aversive stimulation in behavior modification. *In* Jones, M. R. (Ed.). *Miami symposium on the prediction of behavior, 1967; Aversive behavior.* Coral Gables, Florida: University of Miami Press, 1968.
Corte, H. E., Wolf, M. M., Locke, B. J. A comparison of procedures for eliminating self-injurious behavior of retarded adolescents. *J. Appl. Behav. Anal.*, 1971; 4, 201-213.
Ferster, C. B. Positive reinforcement and behavioral deficits of autistic children. *Child Dev.*, 1961; 32, 437-456.
Green, A. H. Self-mutilation in schizophrenic children. *Arch. Gen. Psychiat.*, 1967; 17, 234-244.
Grossen, N. E.; Bolles, R. C. Effects of a classical conditioned "fear signal" and "safety signal" on nondiscriminated avoidance behavior. *Psychonom. Sci.*, 1968; 11, 321-322.
Hamilton, J., Stephens, L., Allen, P. Controlling aggressive behavior in severely retarded institutionalized residents. *Am. J. Ment. Defic.*, 1967; 71, 852-856.

Lovaas, O. I. A behavior therapy approach to the treatment of childhood schizophrenia. *In* Hill, J. (Ed.). *Minnesota symposium on child development.* Minneapolis: University of Minnesota Press, 1967.

Lovaas, O. I., Freitag, G., Gold, V. J., Kassorla, I. C. Experimental studies in childhood schizophrenia: analysis of self-destructive behavior. *J. Experi. Child Psychol.,* 1965; **2,** 67-84.

Lovaas, O. I., Simmons, J. Q. Manipulation of self-destruction in three retarded children. *J. Appl. Behav. Anal.,* 1969; **2,** 143-157.

Pendergrass, V. E. Timeout from positive reinforcement following persistent, high-rate behavior in retardates. *J. Appl. Behav. Anal.,* 1972; **5,** 85-91.

Reed, B. J. The use of reinforcement principles to decrease negativism in an autistic child. (Unpublished master's thesis.) UCLA School of Nursing, 1968.

Rescorla, R. A. Predictability and number of pairings in Pavlovian fear conditioning. *Psychonom. Sci.,* 1966; **4,** 383-384.

Rescorla, R. A. Inhibition of delay in Pavlovian fear conditioning. *J. Comparative & Psycholog. Psychol.,* 1967; **64,** 114-120.

Rescorla, R. A. Probability of shock in the presence and absence of CS in fear conditioning. *J. Comparative & Psycholog. Psychol.,* 1968; **66,** 1-5.

Rescorla, R. A. Conditioned inhibition of fear. *In* McIntosh, J. N., Honig, W. K., (Eds.). *Fundamental Issues in Associative Learning.* Halifax, Nova Scotia Dalhousie University Press, 1969.

Rubin, G., Griswald, K., Smith, I., DeLeonardo, C. A case study in the remediation of severe self-destructive behavior in a 6-year-old mentally retarded girl. *J. Clin. Psychol.,* 1972; **28,** 424-426.

Simmons, J. Q., Lovaas, O. I. Use of pain and punishment as treatment techniques with childhood schizophrenics. *Am. J. Psychother.,* 1969; **23,** 23-26.

Simmons, J. Q., Reed, B. J. Therapeutic punishment in severely disturbed children. *Current Psychiat. Ther.,* 1969; **9,** 11-18.

Smolev, S. R. Use of operant techniques for the modification of self-injurious behavior. *Am. J. Ment. Defic.,* 1971; **76,** 295-305.

Tate, B. G. Case study: Control of chronic self-injurious behavior by conditioning procedures. *Behav. Ther.,* 1972; **3,** 72-83.

Tate, B. G., Baroff, G. S. Aversive control of self-injurious behaviour in a psychotic boy. *Behav. Res. & Ther.,* 1966; **4,** 281-287.

Ullman, L. P., Krasner, L. (Eds.). *Case Studies in Behavior Modification.* New York: Holt, Rinehart & Winston, 1965.

Whitney, L. R. The effects of operant conditioning on the self-destructive behavior of retarded children. *Exploring progress in maternal and child health nursing, Practice, ANA, 1965, regional conference #3.* New York: Appleton-Century-Crofts, 1966.

Wolf, M., Risley, T., Mees, H. Application of operant conditioning procedures to the behavior problems of an autistic child. *Behav. Res. & Ther.,* 1964; **1,** 305-312.

Reprinted from *J. Autism & Child. Schiz.,* 1974; **4**:3, 241-250 by kind permission of the publishers Plenum Publishing Corp., New York, NY 10013.

SEVERE SELF-INJURIOUS BEHAVIOR: THE PROBLEM OF CLINICAL CONTROL

Raymond G. Romanczyk, Elizabeth R. Goren

Rutgers — The State University

The long-term treatment program and follow-up of a case of chronic, severe, multiple self-injurious behavior is presented. The intensity, frequency, and multiplicity of self-injurious behavior is unparalleled in the literature. Treatment spanned 10 months and more than 1,000 therapy hours. Contingent electric shock and differential reinforcement of other behavior were the primary techniques utilized. The specifics of the punishment and reinforcement contingencies were modified throughout the program as a function of the behavior, thereby allowing for evaluation of the various components of the treatment procedures. Although initial results were only partially successful, total suppression was eventually achieved in the laboratory setting. The procedures described for extending this control to the natural environment proved only moderately successful. The technical, ethical, and theoretical issues concerning the treatment of severe self-injurious behavior are discussed. It is suggested that the extrapolation of laboratory evidence to the natural setting is premature in the case of severe self-injurious behavior. Suggested criteria for the assessment of successful clinical treatment of self-injurious behavior are offered.

Chronic self-injurious behavior severe enough to endanger survival is rarely observed, occurring in less than 5% of psychiatric populations (Bachman, 1972; Lester, 1972). With few exceptions (Allen & Harris, 1966; Merbaum, 1973; Risley, 1968), the majority of reported cases of self-injurious behavior are institutionalized females (Green, 1967; Lester, 1972) with the diagnosis of schizophrenia, infantile autism, or functional or organic retardation. Chronic self-injurious behavior has been observed in various forms: slapping, punching, hitting, pinching, scratching, biting, tearing, burning, and banging on all areas of the body, particularly the limbs and head. In some cases, self-injurious behavior occurs as one isolated behavior (Allen & Harris, 1966; Collins, 1965; Corte, Wolf, & Locke, 1971; Hamilton, Stephens, & Allen, 1967; Myers & Diebert, 1971; Risley, 1968; Ross, Meichenbaum, & Humphrey, 1971; Tate & Baroff, 1966). In other cases multiple self-injurious behavior, a combination of several individual behaviors, is the predominant pattern (Baroff & Tate, 1968; Corte et al., 1971; Hamilton et al., 1967; Peterson & Peterson, 1968; Tate, 1972; Hitzing & Risley, Note 1). Rates have ranged from as few as one per day to thousands per hour, with responding occurring in discrete unitary forms as well as continuously or in bursts. Although the necessity for partial restraint has been frequently reported (cf. Myers & Diebert, 1971; Tate & Baroff, 1966), the need for total restraint is only occasionally reported (Lane & Dormath, 1970; Tate, 1972).

Functional analyses of self-injurious behavior have revealed social variables — attention and social deprivation — as important in the establishment and maintenance of self-injurious behavior (Bachman, 1972). Reduction of self-injurious behavior with a variety of techniques has been attempted, but punishment of self-injurious behavior in combination with some schedule of positive reinforcement for incompatible behaviors has consistently proven to be the most effective procedure (Bachman, 1972). For cases in which the individual's mobility is not restricted, the use of contingent time-out and differential

This is a much abbreviated form of the original report. Due to space constraints, a great amount of case background and procedural detail has been omitted.

Copies of the full report and/or reprints of this article may be obtained from Raymond G. Romanczyk, who is now at the Department of Psychology, State University of New York, Binghamton, New York 13901.

reinforcement of non-self-injurious behavior (differential reinforcement of other behavior) has produced positive results (Baroff & Tate, 1968; Lane & Dormath, 1970; Myers & Diebert, 1971; Peterson & Peterson, 1968; Tate & Baroff, 1966), and complete *elimination* has been reported in a few cases in which the behavior was discrete and of low initial frequency (Allen & Harris, 1966; Hamilton et al., 1967). In contrast to time-out and differential reinforcement of other behavior procedures, contingent electric shock punishment has produced more immediate and dramatic results. Given the consistent and extreme reduction of severe, chronic self-injurious behavior by this procedure (Baroff & Tate, 1968; Corte et al., 1971; Merbaum, 1973; Lovaas, Freitag, Gold, & Kassorla, 1965; Lovaas, Schaeffer, & Simmons, 1965; Risley, 1968; Tate, 1972; Tate & Baroff, 1966), many behavior therapists consider the use of contingent electric shock both ethical and the treatment of choice in cases of severe self-injurious behavior (Miron, 1968).[1]

The present case study is a description of a long-term comprehensive treatment program to modify chronic, severe, multiple self-injurious behavior on an outpatient basis, unparalleled in the literature.[2] Intensive sessions were conducted with electric shock punishment of self-injurious behavior, primary reinforcement of non-self-injurious behavior, and training of the parents in the application of these procedures. All behavioral contingencies were extended to a special placement facility as well as at home under the close supervision of the therapists. The treatment period spanned 10 months and included four discrete phases. Both the unique and generalizable aspects of this case are described with an emphasis on the long-term clinical treatment of self-injurious behavior, the pitfalls to be anticipated in the treatment of similar cases, and the conceptual and ethical issues that must be considered.

Case history

Peter's birth was long and difficult; labor lasted 17 hours and culminated in a breech delivery. Although the parents were Rh incompatible, no transfusion was necessary.

Peter's behavior was "unusual" very early in his development. At about 2½, Peter began what the parents described as head "tapping." At 4½ Peter was diagnosed as having "infantile autism with functional retardation" and was described as having "a vacant stare, he withdraws by singing or saying meaningless phrases, bangs his head, scratches others, is echolalic, throws objects, and is unable to function unless he is held in some manner."

At 6½ Peter was referred to the Psychological Clinic at Rutgers University. His self-injurious behavior had worsened to the point where total restraint was required. His speech remained primarily echolalic and nonfunctional. In addition to hitting and scratching himself and others, various forms of self-stimulatory behavior comprised almost the entirety of Peter's response repertoire. He had no self-help skills. He spit out all food that was offered, and it was necessary to forcibly place and hold pureed food in Peter's mouth until he swallowed. Release of his legs immediately occasioned head banging with the knees. Release of his hands similarly resulted in face slapping, head knocking, or head banging with any available object. If let go while sitting or standing, Peter would immediately begin to bang his head with great force on the floor or against any nearby projection.

Responding often occurred in bursts, although single hits of varying interresponse latencies were frequently observed. Some hits seemed light, others, bone jarring or flesh tearing; self-injurious behavior varied in intensity even within the same burst of responding. Peter was observed to engage in self-injurious behavior in various contexts — while singing, smiling, laughing, watching television, when crying, alone, and with others present.

[1]The fact that nonbehavior therapists do not share this opinion was dramatically demonstrated to the authors. A psychiatrist attempted to bring legal charges against the first author and the Director of the Child Behavior Research and Learning Center through the State Attorney General after having learned indirectly of the treatment program. On the basis of the Attorney General's investigation, the charges were dropped.

[2]Special recognition is made to the invaluable assistance given the authors by the following people: Charles Diament, Wayne Kashinsky, Lynne Mofenson, Gert Sommer, and G. Terrence Wilson.

Phase 1

Primary focus was placed on counselling the parents. A pilot program was instituted for Peter in which an attempt was made to reinforce an incompatible response (differential reinforcement of other behavior) using food reinforcement. At the end of one particular session, although in the care of both the therapist and mother, Peter hit his head on the sink during preparation for bed. This single blow was of such magnitude as to require immediate hospitalisation. It was clear at this time that Peter was in severe physical danger from self-inflicted blows and that even constant adult attention did not sufficiently insure his safety. The situation was discussed with his parents, and it was decided that the use of response-contingent electric shock for self-injurious behavior was the treatment of choice.

Procedure

Sessions were conducted in Peter's home in a small room where he spent most of his waking hours. A hand-held inductorium (Hot Shot Products, Savage, Minnesota) delivered the electric shocks. It produced an extremely painful electric shock (average output 15 mA at 500 V)[3] that was localized to the point of contact. At first only the right arm was unrestrained, and shocks approximately .3 sec long were delivered to the forearm. Treatment sessions were 20 minutes long, preceded by two baseline sessions of shorter duration.

Results

As may be seen in Figure 1,[4] the initial rate of self-injurious behavior was approximately 5,400 hits per hour, or 1-2/sec. The intensity of these blows — again, only one hand was unrestrained — was sufficient that redness was apparent on the face after two or three blows, and bleeding was seen after 10-15 sec. Due to this intensity, frequency, and resulting physical injury, only two baseline sessions were conducted, each lasting for 1 min.

The delivery of shock for each response dramatically reduced the frequency of self-injurious behavior in the first session. However, the rate of self-injurious behavior was fairly constant at about 300 per hour for the six treatment sessions, an unacceptably high level.

Phase 2

In reevaluation of the initial treatment program, it was wondered whether the use of the shock prod permitted sufficient discrimination of the contingency between shock and self-injurious behavior due to the latency of shock onset; that is, there was a delay between self-injurious behavior and the therapist actually reaching over, making contact, and delivering the shock. As a result, alterations in the type of shock, method of delivery, and selection of target and alternative behaviors were made.

Setting

All sessions were conducted at the Psychological Clinic, Rutgers University. Peter was restrained by a body harness and air splints (Paul & Romanczyk, 1973) in a large relaxation chair.

Procedure 1: Response prevention and punishment

As in the initial sessions, it was decided to begin with the right hand. In Sessions 1-12, each self-injurious response was punished by a brief electric shock and followed by immediate restraint for 5 minutes. At the end of this 5-minute interval Peter was allowed to make one response that was punished. He was then immediately restrained again for 5 minutes, and the procedure was repeated for a total of seven trials per session. The original shock device was replaced by a unit (Scientific Prototype Model 108-2K) that allowed electrodes to be attached directly to the wrist of the free hand and permitted regulation of shock intensity. Shock intensity was set at 10 mA. During these 12 sessions differential reinforcement of other behavior programming was again attempted.

---

[3]The amount of current actually received was lower than the output current because of the client's skin resistance. For a complete discussion of this and related issues, see Butterfield (1975).

[4]All data have been converted to rate per hour to allow comparison across the various phases. Also, Roman numerals used along the abscissa of the graphs indicate points that coincide. Thus, while the times scales vary, corresponding Roman numerals represent identical chronological dates.

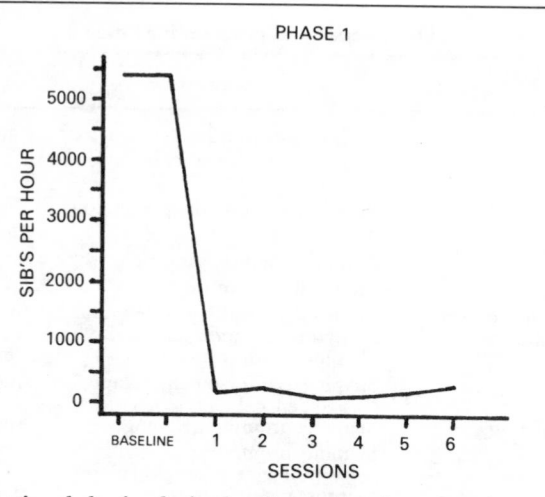

Fig. 1. Rate of self-injurious behavior during baseline and sessions of contingent electric shock with free responding.

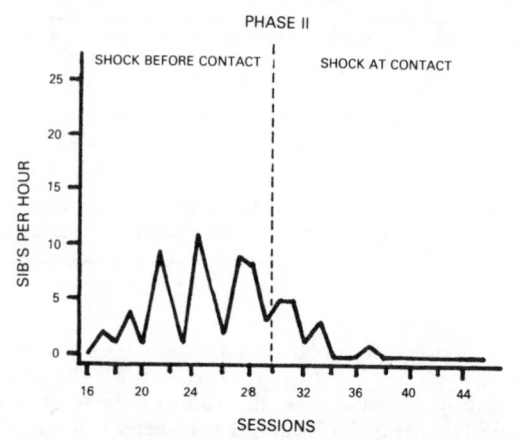

Fig. 2. Rate of self-injurious behavior during sessions of contingent electric shock with free responding and decreasing degree and number of limb restraints.

Results

During this phase the latency of hits from time of release gradually increased. More important, the topography of Peter's self-injurious behavior changed. Its intensity was noticeably reduced, and the speed of the hand movement from the area of the lap to the face was drastically reduced. By Session 12 Peter was eating semisolid foods.

Procedure 2: Free-responding punishment

Punishment contingencies were the same as in Procedure 1, except that responding was no longer prevented. Also, shock onset occurred as soon as Peter raised his hand, so that delivery took place prior to contact. As response suppression increased, restraints were gradually removed.

Results

Figure 2 shows that Peter emitted no self-injurious responses for the first session; the remaining sessions were also characterized by low frequencies of responding.

Procedure 3: Punishment of terminal behavior

Beginning with Session 30, electric shock was delivered only for hits making physical contact; that is, the terminal response was punished rather than the initial components as in

Table 1. Behavioral program for Phase 2

Behavior	Procedure	Results
Self-injurious	Punishment, differential reinforcement other behavior	Elimination
Spitting	Overcorrection	Elimination
Throwing	Punishment, response prevention	Elimination
Screaming, crying	Time-out	Elimination
Echolalia	Emphasis, fading, ignoring	Improvement
Fear of loud noises	Progressive exposure	Improvement
Tension increases in response to therapist's demands	Controlled breathing — deep and slow inhale and exhale	Improvement
Eye-contact	Shaping, reinforcement	Normative
Physical contact	Shaping, reinforcement, escape, avoidance	Adequate
Self-feeding, self-toileting	Shaping, prompting, fading	Adequate
Appropriate speech	Shaping, prompting, reinforcement, overlearning	Moderate improvement
Appropriate play	Reinforcement, avoidance	Moderate improvement
Folding hands, hands on lap	Shaping, reinforcement, avoidance	Excellent improvement

Note: Reinforcement consisted of food, physical contact, and verbal praise delivered under continuous reinforcement, variable interval, and variable ratio schedules.

Sessions 16-29. By Session 39 all restraints had been removed. The main target behaviors and treatment techniques are presented in Table 1.

Results

The dramatic success of the Phase 2 procedures is best evidenced by the contrast between Figures 1 and 2; in Figure 1 the *lowest* rate is 125 hits/hr — in Figure 2, the *highest* rates observed were only 11 hits/hr. During this phase, Peter learned to eat solid food and began to ask for certain foods.

Parent training

Concurrent with the above program, Peter's mother was given training and was gradually phased into the therapy session. At the end of Session 31, the original shock device was modified to include a strap that placed the electrodes on the wrist and a 20-foot (6-m) cable between the device and the strap. This was given to Peter's mother for home use between sessions and permitted the response contingencies to be in effect continuously. By Session 40, Peter was spending most of his waking hours at home unrestrained, playing or following his mother. The frequency of self-injurious behavior as recorded by Peter's mother at home is shown in Figure 3.

Discussion

Results during this phase of treatment were most impressive. It is important to note that the initial frequencies recorded reflect responding during total restraint, whereas later sessions both at the clinic and at home reflect self-injurious behavior under conditions of no restraint. This accounts for what appears to be variable suppression, since daily rate increases were usually a function of a further lessening of restraint.

On the negative side, at no time was it possible to remove the use of attached electrodes for more than a few minutes. As soon as the electrodes were removed, Peter appeared to panic and self-injurious behavior was immediately elicited.

Phase 3

Given the success of Phase 2, Peter was enrolled in the Child Behavior Research and Learning Center,[5] Rutgers University. The school is specifically designed for individual,

[5]Special thanks go to Sandra L. Harris, Director of the Center, without whose cooperation Peter's treatment could not have proceeded.

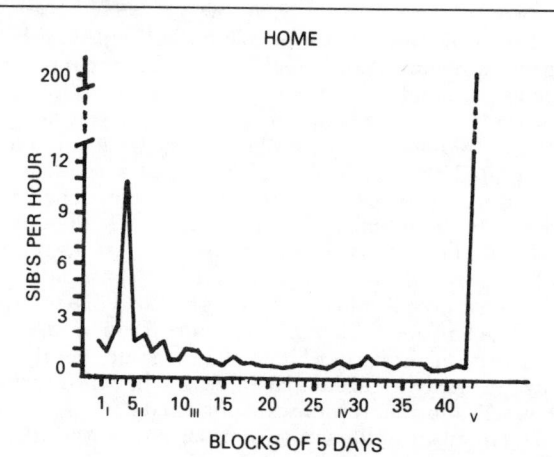

Fig. 3. Rate of self-injurious behavior recorded by mother at home during the entire treatment period.

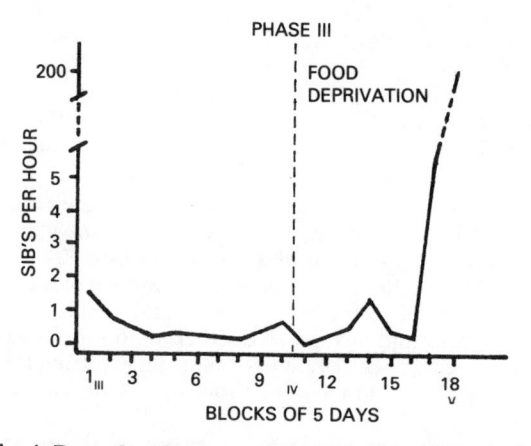

Fig. 4. Rate of self-injurious behavior during school sessions.

intensive behavior modification for severely impaired children. Because both authors worked and consulted at the school, this placement was seen as ideal.

School program

Undergraduate students[6] were recruited from the regular school staff on the basis of academic and practical experience to work with Peter. The authors trained these assistants to carry out the required programs.

Procedure

Peter initially spent much of his time in a large relaxation chair in a corner of the classroom, where preacademic skills were taught in small increments. As he became more adjusted to the school routine, he was given greater freedom of movement, increased academic training, and was encouraged to interact more with the other children.

Results

Figure 4 indicates that by Blocks 7 and 8 Peter's self-injurious behavior had been almost totally suppressed at school and at home (cf. Figure 3). The first 2 months of school were

[6]The authors wish to thank the following undergraduates who took a personal interest in Peter and were invaluable in conducting the school program: Ken Adams, Tom Braddock, Jim Fimiani, Jeff Kapust, Susan Plishker, Nick Romano, and Cheryl Weiss.

marked by complete or near complete suppression of self-injurious behavior, screaming, scratching, spitting and throwing. Additionally, Peter made rapid progress in appropriate speech, self-help, academic, and social skills.

As Figure 4 shows, Peter's deviant behaviors especially self-injurious behavior, began to increase in intensity and frequency at about Block 9. The frequency records of the various target behaviors indicated that each was increasing in a sequential fashion, that is, beginning with spitting, then throwing, then scratching, followed by screaming, and finally self-injurious behavior. In an attempt to regain control over these behaviors, Peter was deprived of his breakfast at home each morning so as to increase the reinforcing value of the food rewards at school for appropriate behavior. For 7 consecutive days following the initiation of this procedure, no self-injurious behavior occurred. As can be seen in Figure 4, however, self-injurious behavior gradually became more frequent, and other deviant target behaviors began to increase again at a quickly accelerating rate. The deterioration of Peter's behavior eventually resulted in substantial increases in self-injurious behavior, to a frequency of over 200 self-injurious repsonses in one day (cf. Point 5, Figure 4). During that day, the frequency and intensity of the self-injurious behavior was sufficient to cause some bleeding.

This sudden increase was most likely the result of an equipment failure at home the evening before (cf. Point 5, Figure 3). When Peter's parents attempted to deliver a shock contingent upon a self-injurious response, the prod apparently failed. Repeated attempts to deliver the electric shock resulted in intermittent application due to a defective part. The behavior increased to such an intensity and frequency that Peter was in danger of severely injuring himself, and the parents fully restrained him. A replacement unit was immediately brought to the home and the new device applied. Self-injurious behavior immediately ceased, and Peter prepared himself for bed without further difficulty. The next day at school, the rate of self-injurious behavior recovered to the high rate of the evening before.

Discussion

The sharp increase in Peter's self-injurious behavior over the course of a few hours is difficult to explain. A combination of factors — intermittent punishment, reinstatement of full restraints, inadvertent reapplication of a former punishment paradigm (cf. the full report, see footnote on P. 374), the extreme emotional reaction of the paradigm (cf. the full the reestablishment of the proper punishment contingency — all in the span of a few hours probably contributed to this rapid increase. Nonetheless, this is of secondary concern; the pattern of this deterioration had been evident for some time. Even if this unfortunate series of events had not occurred, it is doubtful that the final result could have been avoided, merely postponed.

At this point, a brief session was conducted in a controlled setting to determine what effect, if any, shock still had on self-injurious behavior. Peter was placed in a large relaxation chair with all limbs except his right hand restrained. After baseline determination of self-injurious behavior, the electrodes were attached. Figure 5 demonstrates that the attachment of the electrodes suppressed self-injurious behavior dramatically. Toys were then placed near Peter, efforts were made to encourage him to play with them, and self-injurious behavior immediately increased. Shock was then administered contingent on each response; and as can be seen in Figure 5, the effect was substantially reduced from its earlier level of suppression but not dissimilar to that observed in Phase 1.

Given these results and the occurrences of the previous few days, it was decided to discontinue electric shock punishment. The only available alternative was to attempt an extinction procedure. If the behavior could be reduced to manageable levels through extinction, differential reinforcement of other behavior would then be reattempted on a more intense level with the possibility of reinstituting punishment procedures.

Phase 4

The rationale for the use of extinction was that the use of shock always involved some social consequences, that is, the therapist observing the response and reacting to it by applying the punishment contingencies. Due to the multiple forms of self-injurious behavior, an automated method of punishment that would have eliminated this problem was not possible. Furthermore, through every phase of the treatment, self-injurious

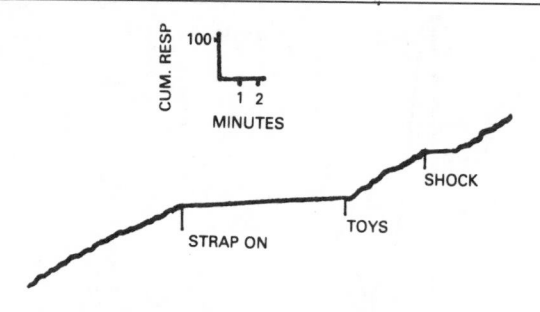

Fig. 5. Cumulative record of self-injurious behavior during the introduction of attached electrodes, toys, and response-contingent electric shock.

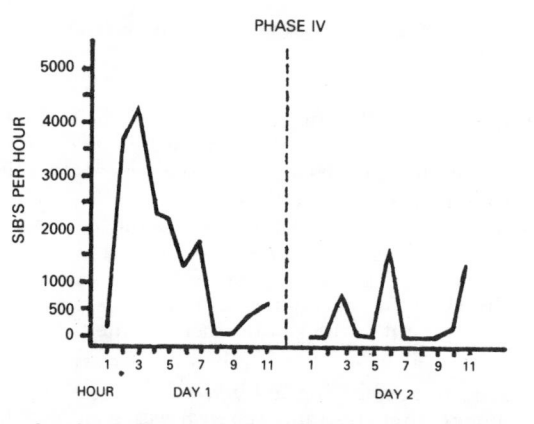

Fig. 6. Rate of self-injurious behavior during the first 2 days of extinction.

behavior of sufficient severity (e.g., a burst of knee hits) as to produce bleeding typically resulted in the approach of one or more adults. Because of the intensity of the behavior, the natural consequences of any severe burst of self-injurious behavior were always interdicted, thus intermittently chaining punishment and adult attention. An isolation room was constructed with extensive padding to minimize physical injury, and it was equipped with a two-camera videomonitoring and audio amplification system.

Procedure 1: Extinction

Each morning Peter was brought to the clinic by his parents for 12-hour extinction sessions. Peter was dressed in pajamas with the feet and hands sewn shut to prevent him from removing the clothes or tearing the foam rubber. His forehead was bandaged, padded, and air splints were placed over his knees.

Rate of self-injurious behavior was recorded by 10-minute time samples each hour, through observation over the TV monitoring system. Additionally, Peter was continuously monitored throughout the 12-hour period to insure that intervention could occur should he injure himself.

Results

The rate of self-injurious behavior for each hour of Days 1 and 2 of the extinction procedure is presented in Figure 6. The rate of self-injurious behavior was fairly low in the first hour, then dramatically increased to extremely high levels, and finally gradually decreased in frequency over the course of the first day. Day 2 produced an atypical extinction curve characterized by abrupt alterations in frequency. The large rises seen during Hours 6 and 11 occurred each day with regularity and appear to coincide with the times just prior to removal for feeding and toileting.

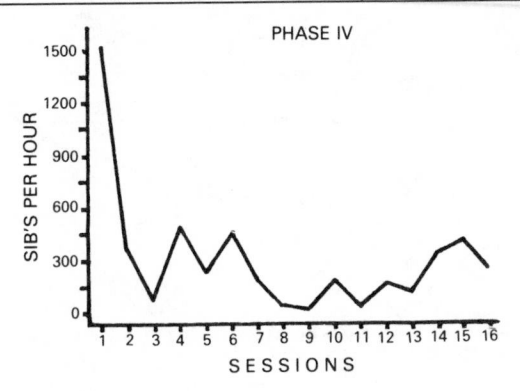

Fig. 7. Rate of self-injurious behavior during extinction period.

Figure 7 presents the rate of self-injurious behavior for the entire extinction procedure for each day. The initial results of the first three days were very encouraging. The rate then rose and became more variable during each period. It appears that this was due to Peter's extricating himself from the restraints and padding. Indeed, a number of times each day Peter managed to remove enough of the padding so that the therapists had to intervene and reapply the padding. Even with constant surveillance and padding the chamber bore blood stains to attest to Peter's speed in moving the restraints. Contrary to its purpose, the procedure failed to eliminate the social interaction patterns that were so dominant in all prior treatment procedures and in the contingencies in the natural environment.

Procedure 2: Increased protection from self-injury
Intervention contingent upon restraint removal was seen as a form of intermittent reinforcement for high-frequency and high-intensity self-injurious behavior. In an attempt to eliminate this, new protective padding was employed. The morning procedure of applying the new padding and restraints typically required three adults and took 45 minutes. In this phase, removal during the 12-hour period for feeding and toileting was done on a random basis to eliminate the peaks seen at the formerly scheduled removal times.

Results
As can be seen in Figure 7 when this new procedure was applied, the rate of self-injurious behavior declined immediately (on Days 7, 8, 9, 10, and 11). However, with these new restraints Peter was able at times to extricate himself so that intervention was required. Within days, the rate of self-injurious behavior became erratic and showed a general increase. Further increases in the amount or strength of the restraints were not feasible, since this would have essentially made Peter immobile and would have become a response prevention procedure rather than an extinction procedure.

Cumulative records demonstrate that the pattern of self-injurious behavior changed over the course of the extinction procedure. In Figure 8, a representative record indicates that self-injurious behavior was fairly constant on the second day (Record A); by the 13th day variations in slope occurred frequently, even with the same 10-minute interval (Records B and C). It can also be seen that in general the duration of the pauses seemed to extend while the responding continued to occur in short bursts. Temporal effects were evidenced in the consistently higher frequencies during evening hours and the hours around noon when Peter was being removed for lunch.

During Days 17-19, the standard procedure was modified to include half-hour periods of extinction with a therapist sitting in the room next to Peter and ignoring the self-injurious behavior. A sample of the responding in the 5 minutes before, during, and after the

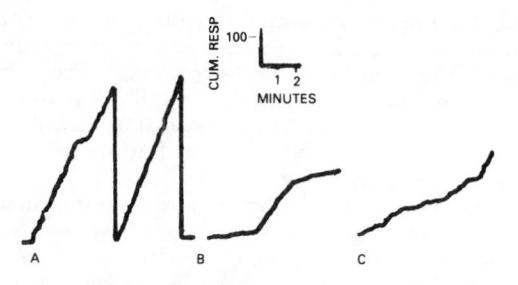

Fig. 8. Representative cumulative records of extinction sessions on Days 2 (Record A) and 13 (Records B and C).

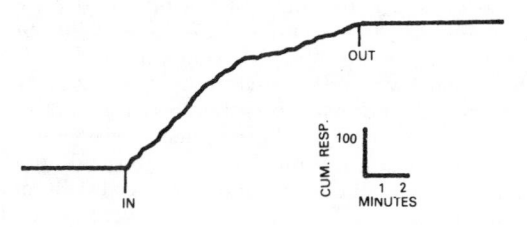

Fig. 9. Cumulative record of self-injurious behavior before, during, and after the presence of an adult in the extinction chamber.

therapist's presence is shown in Figure 9. The presence of the therapist markedly increased local responding. Anticipation of the therapist's entrance as well as his actual presence reliably produced a higher rate of self-injurious behavior lending support to the hypothesis that Peter's self-injurious behavior was reinforced by social stimuli. However, the daily variation, the failure to significantly reduce responding for even one day and the eventual rapprochement of self-injurious behavior to earlier levels, all suggest that unspecified variables were controlling self-injurious behavior. These were probably the same factors that had contributed to the eventual behavioral deterioration in all prior treatment procedures. For these reasons, the extinction procedure was terminated after 19 days.

Discussion

At this point both the frequency and intensity of self-injurious behavior were greatly reduced as compared to pretreatment. However, the use of the portable inductorium was no longer as effective as it had been in suppressing self-injurious behavior. When used for brief periods in relatively low-demand situations, a moderate degree of control was still possible. The results of all of the treatment procedures were reviewed with the parents, and they were advised that institutionalization should be considered. The parents reluctantly agreed with this assessment, and placement proceedings were started.

Follow-up

Peter was placed on a small children's ward of a state hospital[7] where there are sufficient staff to insure that he does not have to be kept in a state of constant restraint. The use of the portable inductorium at the institution is not permitted. Even without its use, however, Peter is able, with partial restraints, to attend school at the institution for approximately 5 hours a day and to participate in number of simple tasks.

[7]As part of standard admission procedures, Peter received full medical, neurological, and psychological examinations. The results were consistent with the findings mentioned earlier: No evidence of organic or neurological involvement was found.

Peter has been seen by both authors on a number of occasions during home visits, and the use of the inductorium is permitted during these relatively brief visits. Approximately 1 year after the cessation of the formal treatment program, during home visits, the use of attached electrodes has been eliminated, and the rate of self-injurious behavior during these periods has never been seen to exceed 15 per hour and is usually less than 5 per hour. More important, Peter has never administered a blow of sufficient intensity to cause injury or bleeding at any time during home visits.

In summary, the degree of suppression achieved was not sufficient to justify evaluating the outcome as clinically effective, as institutional care is required for Peter's continued well-being. Nevertheless, the dramatic reduction of self-injurious behavior in frequency and intensity has allowed Peter a less restricted existence than was possible before treatment.

Discussion

This article describes a treatment program that exceeded 1,000 therapy hours over a 10-month period. To the authors' knowledge, there is no reported case of self-injury that was as severe in terms of intensity, frequency, multiplicity, and chronicity. Nevertheless, it was possible with appropriate clinical and experimental rigor to completely suppress self-injurious behavior in highly controlled environments for short periods of time (e.g., during Phase 2). This degree of suppression corroborates earlier findings, and if this article had been written at that time, the case would have been considered a success. However, when treatment was continued beyond initial suppression and attempts were made to gradually expand Peter's environment, increase his prosocial skills, and at the same time maintain suppression of self-injurious behavior, the difficulty of extending the laboratory evidence to the natural environment becomes apparent.

The technical difficulties in applying punishment contingencies are of critical importance in explaining the lack of long-term success in controlling severe self-injurious behavior. The use of mechanical devices such as attached electrodes and a portable inductorium provide an efficient method of gaining initial control. However, a major disadvantage of these devices is their highly discriminative qualities, which complicate or preclude their eventual removal. Similarly, punishment delivered for each response is potentially a very discriminable contingency. A single response that is not punished signals the apparent termination of the contingency, a possibility discussed earlier in terms of equipment failure. Also, when using an intense punishment such as electric shock, the possibility of the client habituating to the shock is a problem not easily solved by increasing the intensity of the electric shock (Azrin & Holz, 1966).

The treatment of self-injurious behavior is one of the most serious problems confronting the clinician. A review of the literature seems to indicate that the contingent application of electric shock is the treatment of choice (Bachman, 1972, Corte et al. 1971, Smolev, 1971). A critical evaluation of the research and case reports, however, indicates that with moderate and severe levels of self-injurious behavior, there is no evidence that this behavior can be suppressed for more than short periods of time. It appears that the *experimental* control of self-injurious behavior has been extrapolated to lead to the conclusion that *clinical* control is possible. Within the clinical setting it is not sufficient to reduce severe self-injurious behavior to "very low levels." Complete suppression for extended periods is the only acceptable criterion.

At first blush the evidence for the efficacy of the use of contingent electric shock for the punishment of self-injurious behavior is most impressive; closer inspection reveals a less optimistic conclusion. The ethics of employing such a severe punishment will remain controversial and complicated until a more effective treatment strategy is devised. For low- and moderate-intensity self-injurious behavior, effective treatments exist. For severe self-injurious behavior, however, the clinician is left with the quandary of knowing that the use of electric shock as a punishment does not eliminate self-injurious behavior, and it is therefore difficult to justify its use, even though it is the most effective treatment strategy to date. For the present authors, the consequences of *not* employing such a treatment strategy, even given its limitations, are unacceptable.

Reference Note
1. Hitzing, E. W., Risley, T. *Elimination of self-destructive behavior in a retarded girl by noxious stimulation.* Paper presented at the meeting of the Southwestern Psychological Association, Houston, April 1967.

References
Allen, K. E., Harris, F. R. Elimination of a child's excessive scratching by training the mother in reinforcement procedures. *Behav. Res. & Ther.*, 1966; **4**, 79-84.
Azrin, N. H., Holz, W. C. Punishment. *In* Honig, W. K. (Ed.)*Operant behavior: areas of research and application.* New York: Appleton-Century-Crofts, 1966.
Bachman, J. A. Self-injurious behavior: a behavioral analysis. *J. Abnorm. Psychol.*, 1972; **80**, 211-224.
Baroff, G. S., Tate, B. G. The use of aversive stimulation in the treatment of chronic self-injurious behavior. *J. Am. Acad. Child Psychiat.*, 1968; **7**, 454-470.
Butterfield, W. H. Electric shock-safety factors when used for the aversive conditioning of humans. *Behav. Ther.*, 1975; **6**, 98-110.
Collins, D. T. Headbanging: the meaning and management in the severely retarded adult. *Bull. Menninger Clinic.*, 1965; **29**, 205-211.
Corte, H. E., Wolf, M. M., Locke, B. J. A comparison of procedures for eliminating self-injurious behavior of retarded adolescents. *J. Appl. Behav. Anal.*, 1971; **4**, 201-213.
Green, A. H. Self-mutilation in schizophrenic children. *Arch. Gen. Psychiat.*, 1967; **17**, 234-244.
Hamilton, J., Stephens, L., Allen, P. Controlling aggressive and destructive behavior in severely retarded institutionalized residents. *Am. J. Ment. Defic.*, 1967; **71**, 852-856.
Kanfer, F. H., Saslow, G. Behavioral diagnosis. *In* Franks, C. M. (Ed.). *Behavior Therapy: appraisal and status.* New York: McGraw-Hill, 1969.
Lane, R. G., Dormath, R. S. Behavior therapy: a case history. *Hosp. & Commun. Psychiat.*, 1970; **21**, 150-153.
Lester, D. Self-mutilating behavior. *Psychol. Bull.*, 1972; **78**, 119-128.
Lovaas, O. I., Freitag, G., Gold, V. J., Kassorla, I. C. Experimental studies in childhood schizophrenia. *J. Experi. Child Psychol.*, 1965; **2**, 67-84.
Lovaas, O. I., Schaeffer, B., Simmons, J. Q. Building social behavior in autistic children by use of electric shock. *J. Experi. Res. in Personal.*, 1965; **1**, 99-100.
Merbaum, M. Modification of self-destructive behavior by a mother-therapist using aversive stimuli. *Behav. Ther.*, 1973; **4**, 442-447.
Miron, N. B. The primary ethical consideration. *Hosp. & Commun. Psychiat.*, 1968; **19**, 226-228.
Myers, J. J., Deibert, A. N. Reduction of self-abusive behavior in a blind child by using a feeding response. *Behav. Res. & Experi. Psychiat.*, 1971; **2**, 141-144.
Paul, H. A., Romanczyk, R. G. Use of air-splints in the treatment of self-injurious behavior. *Behav. Ther.*, 1973; **4**, 320-321.
Peterson, R. F., Peterson, L. R. The use of positive reinforcement in the control of self-destructive behavior in a retarded boy. *J. Experi. Child Psychol.*, 1968; **6**, 351-360.
Risley, T. R. The effects and side effects of punishing the autistic behaviors of a deviant child. *J. Appl. Behav. Anal.*, 1968; **1**, 21-34.
Ross, R. R., Meichenbaum, D. H., Humphrey, C. Treatment of nocturnal headbanging by behavior modification techniques. *Behav. Res. & Ther.*, 1971; **9**, 151-154.
Smolev, S. R. Use of operant techniques for the modification of self-injurious behavior. *Am. J. Ment. Defic.*, 1971; **76**, 295-305.
Tate, B. G. Case study: Control of chronic self-injurious behavior by conditioning procedures. *Behav. Ther.*, 1972; **3**, 72-83.
Tate, B. G., & Baroff, G. S. Aversive control of self-injurious behavior in a psychotic boy. *Behav. Res. & Ther.*, 1966; **4**, 281-287.

BEHAVIOUR MODIFICATION WITH CHILDREN: MANNERISMS, MUTILATION AND MANAGEMENT

C. Williams, P. Surtees

Lea Hospital, Stourbridge Road, Bromsgrove, Worcs.

A changing sensory environment seems essential for human beings. Without it the brain ceases to function in an adequate way and abnormalities of behaviour develop.

HERON, 1957

The general conclusions to be drawn from work on experimentally induced sensory deprivation appear to suggest that an environment offering little or no stimulus change is an aversive state, and, as such, would tend to result in behaviours that serve to avoid such a state (Schults, 1965).

Apart from the deliberate restriction of sensory input as used in laboratory studies, there can also be naturally occurring sensory deprivation conditions of which probably the best exemplars are those conditions resulting from either: 1. congenital defects of the sense organs or 2. environments severely restricted in stimulus change.

In 1941 Gregg, an Australian opthalmologist, first reported an association between the infection of the mother with rubella virus, especially during the first trimester, and the subsequent congenital defects of the foetus. Cataracts, malformation of the heart and deafness are the most noticeable defects produced by congenital rubella, and they form the common symptom triad of the rubella syndrome. Defects of the nervous system, intellectual retardation and behavioural anomalies are now also recognized as belonging to this syndrome (Chess, et al., 1971). Hence, any individual suffering from such a syndrome can be viewed as a natural analogue of the experimental subject in a sensory deprivation study.

The first part of this paper describes work currently being carried out on such a group of children and presents some of the results of the effects of stimulation on the baseline repertoires of individuals from such a group when studied under stimulus controlled conditions.

The second naturally occuring sensory deprivation condition we identify is that present in many wards in hospitals for the severely subnormal where staff shortages produce conditions in which many individuals receive only minimal stimulation and where attention from staff is largely contingent on disruptive behaviour.

In the second part of this paper we present an experimental study on such a patient whose limited behavioural repertoire included bouts of very severe self-mutilation by repeated head-banging.

I. Study 1

In an earlier report (Williams, 1972) it was noted that observation of a group of retarded rubella syndrome children would show that much of their activity involves the performance of repetitive and stereotyped movement patterns involving rocking, arm-flapping, head-banging, finger-waving and eye-poking. A continuous taped commentary of samples of behaviour of an eight year old SSN rubella syndrome child indicated that the child spent some 40% of the total observation time eye-poking — that is, inserting the first finger of his right hand into his right eye socket and moving the eyeball itself up and down. Clearly eye-poking has reinforcing consequences, but without direct evidence it is difficult to identify precisely what these are. The child is probably experiencing similar visual phenomena to those experienced by sighted persons pressing on closed eyelids by pressure stimulation of the optic nerve endings. Since the optic defect of rubella children is largely restricted to the lens there is little reason to suppose that the retina, the optic nerve and the visual cortex are not at least physiologically reactive.

In this same subject, rocking occupied a further 25% of his free operant repertoire. He was free from any form of stereotyped self-stimulatory activity during only 11% of the observation period. However, when tactile stimulation was applied by using a vibration tube worn against his back, the percentage of time spent without stereotypy increased significantly to 26% (p=.001). Thus, the provision of a continuous tactile stimulation decreased self-stimulation markedly.

A further finding from preliminary observations of this group was that some of them, instead of physically poking their eyes, would wave their fingers back and forth in front of their eyes, especially in areas of particularly bright light. A common feature among this group was that some remnant of vision was present and that the lens was sufficiently transparent to allow at least light-dark discrimination.

The present study grew in part from that described above in an attempt to modify the tactile stimulus presentation so that it was subject-operated and hence analogous to a standard operant manipulandum through providing tactile feedback as a result of bar pressing.

Three major hypotheses were to be tested:

1. that rubella children who showed finger-waving in their free operant repertoire would be able to discriminate light stimuli and that they would approach such stimuli. In other words, given partial sight, but deafness, light stimuli would reinforce approach behaviour;

2. that the provision of subject-operated stimuli would compete with self-stimulation; and

3. that tactile stimulation would serve to reinforce bar-pressing activity.

The studies described below were done using two additional experimental subjects. Preliminary results are presented to show how such subjects can be investigated under control conditions and the contribution they can make to a theoretical formulation of stereotypy and self-mutilation.

II. Subjects

Subject 1, whose study has provided the results for testing the first hypothesis, is a 4½-year-old female whose mother contracted rubella at 6 weeks of pregnancy. She has the classical rubella symptom triad though her sensory defect is not total in that the cataracts have been needled and she is now light sensitive. She is also reactive to sounds above 80 decibels at all frequencies. She can walk and feed herself with a spoon. She has a Maxfield-Buchholtz adapted Vineland SQ of 43 and is currently on no regular medication. Baseline frequency counts of her behaviour in the observation area indicated a mean percentage of 55% visually oriented mannerisms (finger-wave and eye-poke).

Subject 2, used for testing the second and third hypotheses, is a young man of 8½ years, diagnosed as rubella syndrome, whose mother was affected at 3 weeks of pregnancy. He presently feeds himself but is not toilet trained. There is no speech present. He has only minimal light-dark discrimination following cataract needling. His Maxfield-Buchholtz adapted Vineland SQ is 38, and he is receiving 20 mg of Pemoline t.d.s. His free operant repertoire consists largely of finger-sucking, arm-flapping and eye-poking.

III. Apparatus

1. The observation area used for these studies was specially constructed inside a larger room. It consists of four 6' high wood walls enclosing a 9'×9' floor area. This floor area is marked off in 16 equal squares, each one numbered.

2. A stimulus box was made measuring 60 cm by 45 cm by 30 cm. The top has a sloping panel of translucent plastic mounted in a sponge rubber frame and is pressure sensitive. Pressing on the panel operates a micro-switch which activates a vibration unit mounted beneath the panel. The sensitivity of the micro-switch was adjusted to be sensitive to the lightest possible touch but to switch off when released.

A 150 watt electric light bulb giving a white light was fixed inside the box. Operation of either the vibration or light circuit is controlled by the experimenter, who uses over-ride switches.

IV. Method

Each child was observed from a vantage point outside the marked floor area using a time sampling technique. The observer wore a hearing aid ear piece through which was fed an auditory signal every ten seconds at which time the observer would write down in code those behaviours exhibited by the child. The coding of behaviours was determined previously using two independent observers, and the reliability of the procedure was established. This observation procedure was continued for 50 observations per experimental condition, the number of conditions for any one session being determined by the particular experimental design in use at the time. All observations were taken in dimmed light to enhance the light-dark contrast.

V. Results

1. The data from the study using *Subject 1* are presented in a classical graph form (Fig. 1).

   They indicate a clear situational preference in that in all three sessions she moved towards the box whenever the light came on and moved away when the light was switched off. The first hypothesis is therefore supported, and evidence for positive phototropism is provided.

2. The data from *Subject 2* are presented in the form of cumulative curves (Fig. 2) showing the results of two similar sessions run on different days. Each session consists of an ABA design — each part of which consists of 50 ten-second time samples of behaviour.

   The curves are drawn by recording observations of stereotypy along the abscissa and absence of stereotypy along the ordinate (the term 'gaze' has been adopted as the code for absence of stereotypy, though it is clear no gazing as such is possible).

It can be seen from the cumulative curves that:

1. in both sessions the baseline free operant rate of gaze is about 25% of the time;

2. when vibration-contingent panel-pressing is made available on a CRF schedule, the subject makes use of such a contingency indicating the reinforcing consequences of vibration (each hatch mark indicates a panel press response of sufficient strength to activate the vibrator);

3. the percentage gaze under the CRF-VIB condition is 100%, indicating a total suppression of stereotypy;

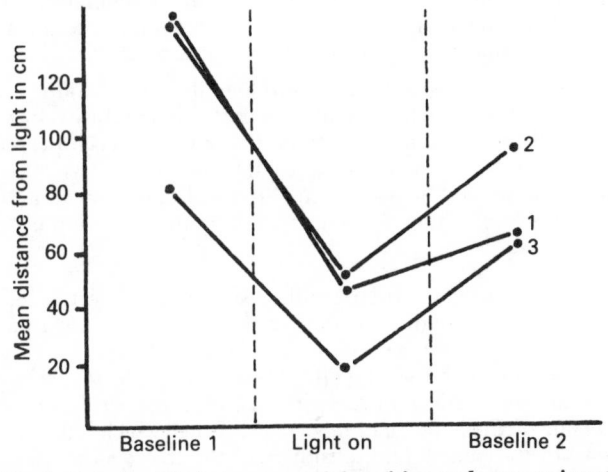

Fig. 1. Relationship between spatial position and sensory input.

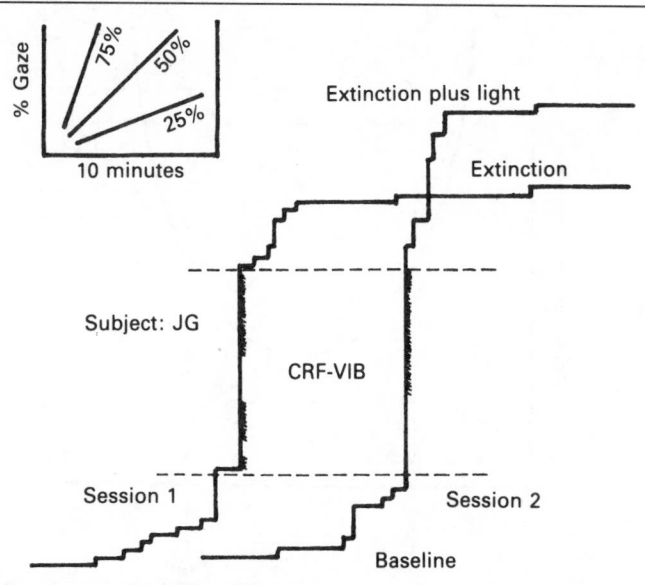

Fig. 2. Cumulative curves of 'gaze' against stereotypy under various conditions of contingent sensory reinforcement.

4. extinction is very rapid, and response contingent vibration produces no long-term behavioural effect when the contingencies are removed;

5. in the extinction period of session 2 the box light was left on, and the extinction of the 'gaze-suppression' effect was delayed until the light was switched off.

VI. Summary of results

These data support the three experimental hypotheses in that in rubella syndrome subjects, sensory stimulation reinforces approach behaviour, and tactile stimulation from a

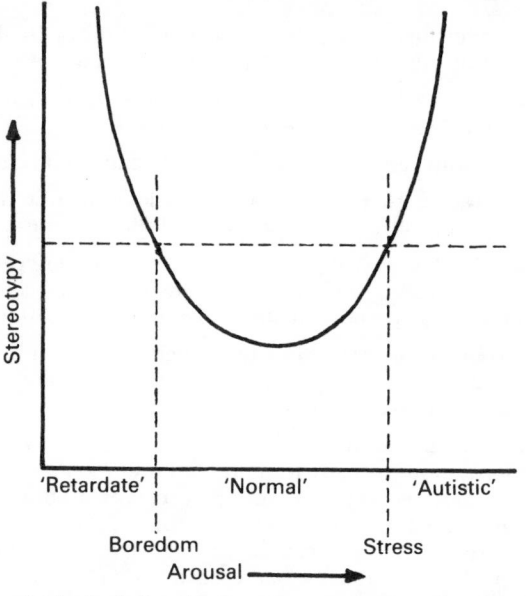

Fig. 3. Hypothetical relationship between stereotypy and arousal level.

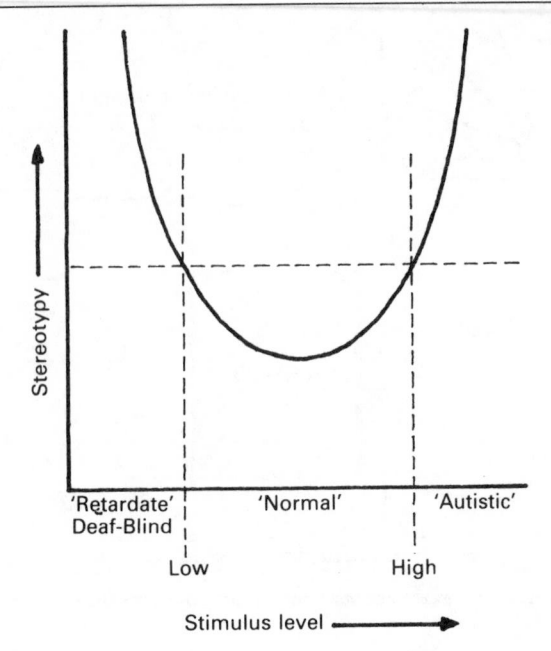

Fig. 4. Hypothetical relationship between stereotypy and stimulus level.

subject-operated manipulandum competes with self-generated stimulation, thereby reducing markedly stereotyped mannerisms.

VII. Discussion

Drawing on theoretical and experimental data published by other workers on various aspects of non-specific sensory stimulation, the present authors have noted particularly the following:

1. a hypothesis suggesting the existence of a mechanism in the brain mediating behavioural functions having to do with levels of alertness (Malmo, 1959);

2. that visual stimulation will reinforce operant behaviour in visually deprived animals (Fox, 1972; Sackett, *et al.,* 1963; Wendt, *et al.,* 1963);

3. a reported relationship between stimulus intensity and hedonic tone (Berlyne, 1969);

4. a relationship between high levels of arousal as indexed by EEG and the occurrence of stereotypy in autistic children (Hutt and Hutt, 1968);

5. a statement by the Hutts that 'whilst the autists' stereotyped behaviours occur significantly more frequently with increase in environmental complexity, those of the defectives seem to occur predominantly in the absence of stimulation;

6. heart rate data from a group of children diagnosed as autistic, indicating the possibility of a pathology in arousal control in such children (MacCulloch and Williams, 1971; MacCulloch and Sambrooks, 1972).

From such studies plus those extensively reviewed by Berlyne (1967), the authors have interpreted the present findings firstly using the arousal model shown in Fig. 3.

The proposed arousal-stereotypy relationship is seen as producing a U-shaped curve relating the two variables. As arousal level decreases through 'boredom' for normal subjects to conditions of environmental deprivation in 'retardates', the amount of stereotypy increases, and, conversely, as arousal level increases through 'stress' with normal subjects to over-arousal with 'autistics' then similarly, stereotypy again increases. The model implies that an optimal level of arousal could exist where stereotypy is at a minimum and that any divergence from this optimal level could serve as a drive cue in the Hullian sense to initiate stereotyped behaviour whose function was related to arousal regulation.

There is, however, a growing dissatisfaction amongst certain theorists over the use of such 'internal' concepts as arousal (Skinner, 1969; Blackman and Thomas, 1971). As a result, the present authors felt that a more parsimonious model for our data should relate, not to 'events taking place somewhere else, at some other level of observation, described in different terms and measured, if at all, in different dimensions' (Skinner, 1950), but to observable environmental events.

Accordingly the U-shaped model was used to plot the two variables stereotypy and stimulus level such that both extremes of stimulation, over-stimulation and under-stimulation, are directly related to increase in stereotypy (Fig. 4).

We feel that our present data fit well with the model when considering the retarded individual and the congenitally sensory-deprived individual at the lower end of the stimulus level continuum. There is, however, little data to support the placing of the autistic group at the higher end of such a continuum; the justification for doing so will depend upon demonstrating a behavioural counterpart to the concept of hyperarousal. The physiological model (MacCulloch and Sambrooks, 1972) provides a mechanism whereby one could suppose that the stimulus input in autistics is over-amplified by the ascending reticular activating system of the mid-brain which would support, in theory, such a placement on the model. Until further evidence is available we present this solely as a very tentative suggestion.

We would now like to introduce the second part of the study by reiterating a number of points:

1. Under conditions of sensory deprivation individuals are reinforced by events that provide non-specific stimulation.

2. Present staff shortages on hospital wards ensure that a state of social deprivation exists for many patients.

3. Staff attention is a reinforcing event and can serve to strengthen behaviour patterns upon which it is contingent (Gardner, 1971).

Given these factors we propose a model for the genesis of self-mutilation from initial self-stimulatory behaviours resulting from deprivation, developing to severe self-mutilation by a process of shaping, unwittingly carried out by staff, who intervene progressively later in the chain of mutilation responses. Since the opportunity for acquiring incompatible behaviours in some cases is lacking, we feel that self-mutilation can be viewed as an operant that becomes maintained by the resultant staff attention which such behaviour elicits. As such it was considered that an operant approach to the treatment of self-mutilation should be attempted in one particularly severe case.

The subject for this study was a 24-year-old female, institutionalised at the age of 6 years, when her parents felt they could no longer control her behaviour. Her early admission notes describe her as an "idiot" showing persistent head banging and biting. She is totally blind and has no executive speech. She can now feed herself but is not toilet trained. Her present drug regime consists of Phenobarbitone 60 mg t.d.s. and Pericyazine 30 mg t.d.s. Her head-banging is at present so severe that throughout the day she is seated on her ward with her hands in restraints to prevent the self-injury that would occur should she be released. This regime has been in existence for 15 years prior to the present study.

Most of the self-injurious behaviour consists of raising her left wrist and repeatedly striking her forehead with blows of increasing strength until it becomes necessary to intervene with attention to prevent serious damage. The result of this behaviour is that she has produced a number of prominent swellings on her head which need repeated nursing attention to prevent infection.

The problem as we saw it was, therefore, chronic, incompatible with ultimate rehabilitation and resistant to current treatment practices.

The following is an account of the procedures we adopted in an attempt to modify this behaviour.

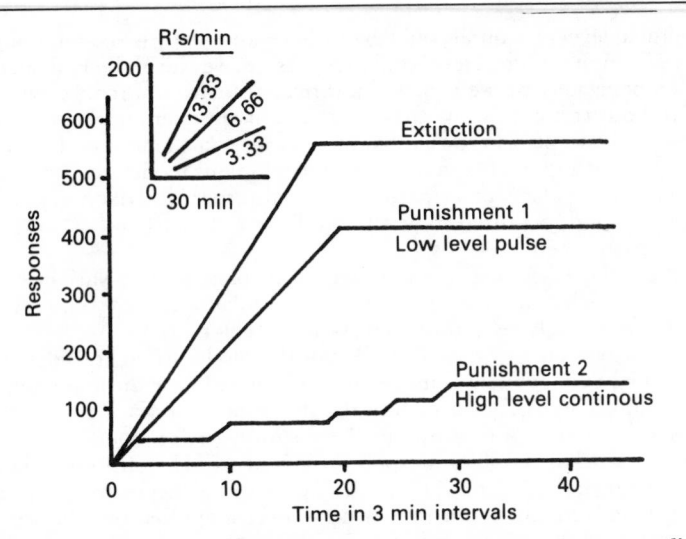

Fig. 5. Cumulative curves of head-banging responses under three treatment conditions.

VIII. Experimental and treatment procedures

Baseline measures

In view of the problem of allowing the head-banging to occur when unrestrained, the subject's forehead was protected with cotton wool and crepe bandage to prevent serious injury. This procedure would clearly alter quite drastically the stimulus situation under which the response was occurring. The authors, however, did not feel justified in allowing such injury to occur solely in order to establish 'good' baseline data.

This baseline period was essentially a series of extinction trials and appears as such in the graph of the cumulative curves (Fig. 5). The curve is made up of the total pre-treatment observation time of 110 three-minute periods taken over one month in 40 minute sessions. A steady state of head-banging of approximately 12 responses per minute was recorded up to the eighteenth three-minute observation period, when they ceased completely. This extinction was specific to the experimental room, as would be predicted (Lovaas and Simmons, 1969), and did not generalise to the ward where she would again be placed in the restraints. Clearly extinction is not an adequate procedure.

The second experimental study involved the presentation of response contingent negative reinforcement. A shock box designed to give a two millisecond pulse at 90 volts[+] across two electrodes placed on the calf of the left leg was used to present the aversive stimulation. The target response was defined as any hand-to-forehead contact that was similar to the early steps in the self-injury chain of behaviour.

The results of this period are shown as punishment 1 in Fig. 5 and indicate the cessation of head-banging responses after 400 shock contingent trials (it should be noted that this represents a total shock time of only 0.8 seconds). Not only was the response rate markedly reduced but the force with which the hand was moved to the forehead also dimished until during the final punishment trials what had been previously a severe head-bang became a light touch to the head.

The third experimental study involved the presentation of a relatively higher level of continuous shock at 125 volts. On each trial the shock was terminated upon cessation of head-banging. The effect of this procedure was to produce a markedly accelerated cessation curve, shown in the graph as punishment 2. This decrement in self-injury responses was produced even though it may have been predicted that an adaptation effect should have occurred following the previous use of low level shock (Azrin and Holz, 1966).

+ The maximum current possible from any of the shock boxes used in this study was measured at 8 milliamps through a direct short of nil resistance.

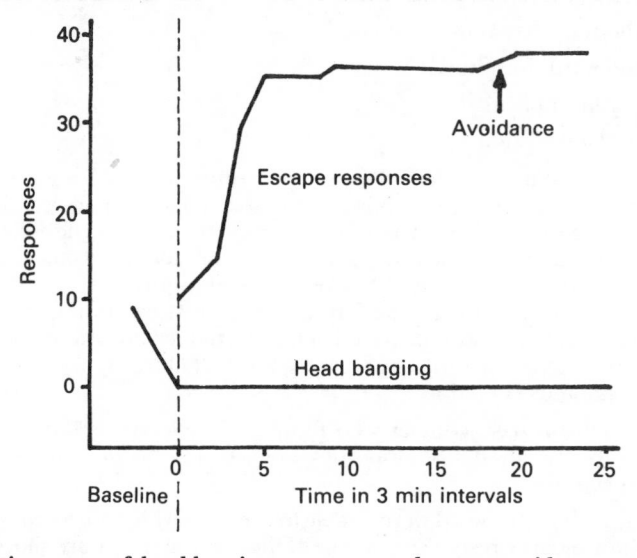

Fig. 6. Cumulative curve of head-banging responses and escape-avoidance responses during escape-avoidance training.

In view of the stituational specificity of the punishment procedures, we felt that a direct suppression of the self-injury responses by using high shock level was grossly unsatisfactory, particularly in this case where self-injury constituted the major component of the subject's behavioural repertoire. We therefore decided to teach a response incompatible with self-injury. Since previous attempts using food as a reinforcer on a DRO schedule had not proved very successful in producing a lasting effect, it was decided to attempt such training using escape-avoidance conditioning. The incompatible response to be trained was defined as having both hands holding a toy doll. The subject had been tested with the doll during the initial observation periods but with no effect on the self-injury frequency. The avoidance response of doll holding was shaped by using escape training in a procedure similar to that described by Whaley and Malott (1971, pp. 377-383). A loud buzzer was used as the CS, having been paired with shock as the UCS. The electrodes on these trials were attached to the subject's left arm where it was felt the point of punishment would be more clearly associated with the self-injury behaviour. The subject's right hand was placed on the doll whilst her left arm was raised by the second experimenter to the position adopted prior to each self-injury response. Both buzzer and shock were then switched on and the subject's left hand was taken down from its position and held to the doll when both buzzer and shock would be terminated. No protective head covering was used during these escape training trials.

During the first 15 minutes, 35 such training trials were completed, followed by 15 minutes of unrestrained doll holding, after which a further shaped escape trial was performed. Again, unrestrained doll holding occured, this time for a period of 45 minutes, after which time the first signalled avoidance responses were made when the subject raised her left hand to strike her forehead, the buzzer was sounded and she replaced her hand to the doll without shock being delivered. The doll holding continued for the remainder of the session. The progress of this phase of the treatment is shown in Fig. 6.

During the follow-up sessions the subject, when given the doll, ceased head-banging and actively resisted when the experimenters attempted to get her to raise her left hand to her head. The follow-up sessions were conducted over a further period of 1 hour 45 minutes observation time.

Since it was now felt that the self-injury response had been brought under control in the laboratory, it was decided to repeat additional shaped escape training trials in more realistic situations:

1. seated in the ward day room,

2. seated in the ward dormitory,

3. seated at the meal table,

4. lying on her bed at night.

In all of these situations the shaped escape procedure was used, and in a total training time of 2 hours, 14 shaped escape trials were used and 10 spontaneous avoidance responses occurred. Following these training trials it was possible to exchange the doll for a number of other toys with similar effects, and observation for a whole day using only the buzzer as a CS indicated a successful suppression of her previous self-injury.

Subsequent follow-up, however, has indicated that the suppression effect has not been permanent and that arm restraints have been re-introduced by the nursing staff.

We would like to suggest a number of reasons for this failure to control self-injury except under specific stimulus conditions.

1. Not only was the buzzer acting as a CS for avoidance learning, but the experimenters themselves also acquired CS properties associated with the sounds specific to the training procedures.

2. The nursing staff on the ward were unable to continue with the procedures necessary to maintain the avoidance response by virtue of the constraints of ward shortage and lack of available time for special treatment of an individual.

3. As a result of foregoing factors, the subject acquired a discriminated avoidance response, only restraining from self-injury when the experimenters were present. The staff were, therefore, obliged to react to her head-banging by attention to prevent injury and subsequently by arm restraints for more permanent control.

IX. Conclusion

Self-injury behaviour can be controlled effectively using an escape-avoidance training procedure. This procedure, however, is only recommended with extreme caution since, unless the established avoidance response can be maintained by, and in the presence of the permanent care staff of the ward, the self-injury responses will be reinstated. It is our belief that unless an incompatible response that is to some extent self-maintaining can be taught to such individuals, it will remain very difficult to deal with severe cases of self-injury, particularly when those individuals' behavioural repertoires are as limited as was the repertoire of the individual described in this paper.

References

Azrin, N. H., Holz, W. C. Punishment. *In* Honig, W. K. (Ed.). *Operant Behavior: areas of research and application.* New York: Appleton-Century-Crofts 1966.

Berlyne, D. E. Arousal and reinforcement. *In* Levine, D. (Ed.). *Nebraska Symposium on Motivation.* Nebraska: University of Nebraska Press 1967.

Berlyne, D. E. Arousal, reward and learning. *Ann. N.Y. Acad. Sci.,* 1969; **159**, 1059-1070.

Blackman, D. E., Thomas, G. V. Critical notice: reinforcement and information. *Br. J. Psychol.,* 1971; **62**, 403-407.

Chess, S., Korn, S. J., Fernandez, P. B. *Psychiatric Disorders of children with Congenital Rubella.* London: Butterworths, 1971.

Fox, S. S. Self-maintained sensory input and sensory deprivation in monkeys: a behavioural and neuropharmacological study. *J. Comp. Physiol. Psychol.,* 1972; **55**, 438-444.

Gardner, W. I. *Behaviour Modification in Mental Retardation.* London: University of London Press, 1971.

Gregg, N. M. Congenital cataract following German measles in mother. *Trans. Ophthal. Soc. Aust.,* 1941; **3**, 35-46.

Heron, W. The pathology of boredom. *Scientif. Am.,* 1957; **196**, 52-56.

Hutt. S. J., Hutt, C. Stereotypy, arousal and autism. *Hum. Develop.,* 1968; **11**, 277-286.

Lovaas, O. I., Simmons, J. Q. Manipulation of self-destruction in three retarded children. *J. Appl. Behav. Anal.,* 1969; **2**, 143-157.

MacCulloch, M. J., Sambrooks, J. E. *An aetiological theory of infantile autism.* Paper presented at the Second European Conference of Behaviour Modification, Wexford/Ireland, 1972.

MacCulloch, M. J., Williams, C. On the nature of infantile autism. *Acta Psychiat. Scand.*, 1971; **47**, 295-314.

Malmo, R. B. Activation: a neuropsychological dimension. *Psychol. Ref.,* 1959; **66**, 367-386.

Sackett, G. P., Keith-Lee, P., Treat, R. Food versus perceptual complexity as rewards for rats previously subjected to sensory deprivation. *Science,* 1963; **141**, 518-520.

Schultz, D. P. *Sensory Restriction: effects on behavior.* New York: Academic Press, 1965.

Skinner, B. F. Are theories of learning necessary? *Psychol. Rev.,* 1950; **57**,193-216.

Skinner, B. F. *Contingencies of Reinforcement.* New York: Appleton-Century-Crofts, 1969.

Wendt, R. H., Lindsley, D. F., Ross Adey, W., Fox, S. S. Self-maintained visual stimulation in monkeys after long-term visual deprivation. *Science,* 1963; **139**, 336-338.

Whaley, D. L., Malott, R. W. *Elementary Principles of Behavior.* New York: Appleton-Century-Crofts, 1971.

Williams, C. *A functional analysis of stereotypy in the rubella child. Conf. report No. 62.* The Southern Regional Association for the Blind, 1972.

Reprinted from Brengelmann, J. C. (Ed.)., *Therapy,* 1975 by kind permission of Chris Williams, Director of Psychological Services (Learning Disabilities), Exeter Health Authority, UK and the publishers Springer-Verlag, Heidelberg 1, Germany.

EMPLOYING ELECTRIC SHOCK WITH AUTISTIC CHILDREN
A Review of the Side Effects[1]

Kenneth L. Lichstein[2]
University of Tennessee

Laura Schreibman
Claremont Men's College, Claremont, California

The use of electric shock in a punishment paradigm has continued to be a highly controversial issue in the treatment of autistic children. While the experimental literature argues for the effectiveness of the procedure for reducing maladaptive behaviors, some clinicians and researchers have expressed fear of possible negative side effects. The reported side effects of contingent electric shock were reviewed in an attempt to evaluate the validity of these fears. The review indicated that the majority of reported side effects of shock were of a positive nature. These positive effects included response generalization, increases in social behavior, and positive emotional behavior. The few negative side effects reported included fear of the shock apparatus, negative emotional behavior, and increases in other maladaptive behavior. The implication of these findings for the use of the shock procedure are discussed in terms of correct usage of the shock, therapist reservations, and alternative procedures.

The use of electric shock in the treatment of autistic children has proven to be one of the most hotly debated issues facing the researcher or clinician concerned with the welfare of these children. On one hand, some point out that it is an extremely effective method of reducing behaviors which pose an immediate threat to the child's welfare (e.g., self-destruction) and on the other hand, some express concern over possible negative side effects of the shock.

Actually, there are two main issues to be addressed. The first concerns the use of punishment per se and the second concerns the use of electric shock as the aversive stimulus in the punishment paradigm. Punishment refers to the operant conditioning procedure whereby an aversive stimulus is presented contingent upon the occurrence of a specified behavior for the purpose of decreasing the probability of the recurrence of that behavior. A formidable body of research exists which argues for the beneficial use of punishment (e.g., Azrin & Holz, 1966; Solomon, 1964), while there have been cautions voiced by others regarding the undesirable emotional side effects which may accrue to the recipient of punishment (Adler, 1930/1970; Maurer, 1974; Skinner, 1953; Yates, 1962). Additionally, the operant researchers have emphasized the temporary nature of response suppression by punishment (e.g., Estes, 1944; Azrin & Holz, 1966) and those representing psychodynamic theory predict symptom substitution (Freud, 1926/1959; Freud, 1946). Regarding autistic children in particular, warnings predicting various noxious side effects including worsening of the autistic withdrawal and decrease in social behavior continue to be voiced (Bettelheim, 1967).

A more specific issue pertains to the use of shock as an aversive stimulus with autistic children. Unlike the use of punishment, this area does not have the benefits of decades of research to help us evaluate its effectiveness on target behaviors and potential positive and negative side effects. However, there has been a considerable amount of recent work in this area and the facts are accumulating. It is the purpose of this paper to review the use of

[1]The authors wish to thank Janis Costello, Ph.D. and Robert L. Koegel, Ph.D. for their helpful comments on an earlier draft.
[2]Requests for reprints should be sent to Kenneth L. Lichstein, Department of Psychology, Memphis State University, Memphis, Tennessee 38152.

electric shock with autistic children in an attempt to evaluate the nature of any side effects it may produce.

Electric shock has been applied to autistic children as a punisher to eliminate self-destructive behaviors (Baroff & Tate, 1968; Browning, 1971; Bucher & Lovaas, 1968; Lovaas & Simmons, 1969; Merbaum, 1973; Tate & Baroff, 1966), aggression toward others (Birnbrauer, 1968; Browning, 1971; Risley, 1968), playing with electrical equipment (Bucher & King, 1971), self-stimulation (Baroff & Tate, 1968; Lovaas, Freitag, Kinder, Rubenstein, Schaeffer, & Simmons, 1966; Lovaas, Schaeffer, & Simmons, 1965; Tate & Baroff, 1966), attempts to leave the experimental setting (Bucher & Lovaas, 1968; Lovaas, et al., 1965), climbing on furniture (Risley, 1968), whining and inattention (Simmons & Lovaas, 1969), destroying property and soiling pants (Birnbrauer, 1968), tantrum behavior (Lovaas, et al., 1966; Lovaas, et al., 1965), saliva holding (Baroff & Tate, 1968; Tate & Baroff, 1966), and clinging to people (Tate & Baroff, 1966).

This paper will survey those articles in which electric shock has been employed to promote the well-being of autistic children. The reported side effects of such treatments will be reviewed in order to evaluate the assertion that seriously undesirable, unintended effects result from the use of electric shock with these children. The selection of articles included in this review was somewhat arbitrary. This is due to the absence of general agreement regarding the definition of *autism*. Research with children labeled autistic, schizophrenic, or psychotic has been included while research with children identified as primarily mentally retarded has been omitted.

General considerations

There were 12 such articles. Almost all of these employed shock in a punishment paradigm. That is, shock was delivered contingent upon a specified undesirable response with the intention of suppressing the response. The shock was usually delivered by a hand-held inductorium which delivered a painful localized shock. The amperage usually employed with autistic children is in the 4- to 5-mA range. Although this is subjectively experienced as painful, this is a safe level of current. It is important to remember that the pain of the shock is localised and is terminated immediately when the shock is discontinued. Unlike electroconvulsive shock, there are no convulsions, no loss of consciousness, and no tissue damage (Craven, 1970).

One major point is that in *all* of these studies, electric shock proved to be a highly effective therapeutic agent with autistic children. In all cases the target undesirable behavior was reduced or eliminated using the shock procedure. This is not to say that this treatment approach is described as a panacea. On the contrary, it has shortcomings. Birnbrauer (1968) stated dissatisfaction with the lack of long-term durability of the shock contingency effects following 120 days of satisfactory treatment by punishment. Other authors have reported that setting specificity of such beneficial results proved to be a frequent obstacle to an overall satisfactory therapeutic effect (Merbaum, 1973; Ridley, 1968).

A few studies used shock in ways other than as a punisher. One article was devoted to the use of shock in an escape-avoidance paradigm. This was done with the intention of building social behaviors (Lovaas, et al., 1965). In this study the children could escape, and later avoid, a shock to the feet if they responded to the experimenter's request to "come here." The procedure was successful in that the children soon learned to come when called, a response they had not shown prior to treatment. The threatened use of shock was reported by Baroff and Tate (1968) and Tate and Baroff (1966) to reinstate eating behaviors in an avoidance paradigm.

Side effects

In two of the articles reviewed there was no mention of side effects (Browning, 1971; Lovaas, et al., 1966). Of the articles that do mention side effects, these observations were only tangential to the main point of the study, which was the elimination of the undesirable behavior. In most of these studies, side effects were not directly measured but were reported as post hoc observations. It is possible that many side effects were not reported, either because they were not detected or because their occurrence was unrelated to the main interest of the research. Nonetheless, it is interesting to note that those side effects that have been reported show rather clear patterns.

Positive side effects

Response generalization. Probably one of the most interesting and important of the reported positive side effects of shock was the occurrence of response generalization. The shock training apparently altered several behaviors which were not directly treated. In most cases these generalized responses led to reductions in other inappropriate behaviors.

In their treatment of self-destruction, Lovaas and Simmons (1969) reported that for one child, John, a decrease in self-abuse following shock was accompanied by a decrease in both whining and avoiding an attending adult. The authors speculated that self-destruction, whining, and avoiding might have been members of the same response class. Another child in the same study, Linda, also showed response generalization. There was a substantial decrease in both avoiding attending adults and whining. Lovaas, et al. (1965), in their study using shock in an escape-avoidance paradigm, found that nurses who rated the children following the experimental (shock) sessions noted that as whining and avoiding adults decreased in the sessions, other pathological behaviors decreased in a different interpersonal setting. Tate and Baroff (1966) reported increases in interest in the environment, such as playing with toys, and decreases in episodes of whining and crying following the treatment for self-destructive behavior.

Social behavior. Another side effect often reported is an increase in social behavior. Since one of the major characteristics of autistic children is their lack of social behavior, any approach that leads to an increase in such behavior is indeed worth study. In the Lovaas, et al. (1965) shock-avoidance study cited above, it was found that in addition to learning to approach the experimenter, the children became more affectionate and seeking of the adult's company. The attending nurses, after the experimental sessions, also noted increases in affection-seeking behaviors. In employing shock to eliminate severe head banging, Merbaum (1973) found that after shock, the child's reaction to the therapist was one of approach and desire for closeness. Also, the child responded warmly to the therapist's attention. Simmons and Lovaas (1969) reported the case of Stanley, who received shock contingent upon whining and inattention. Although he temporarily showed a marked aversion to the experimenters, he soon developed an extremely affectionate response to them, permitting physical contact and eye contact, and displaying smiling and hugging in their presence. Risley (1968) also reported an increase in eye contact between the child and the experimenter concomitant with the decrease in the target behavior (bookcase climbing). Birnbrauer (1968) applied shock to eliminate destruction of property, soiling of pants, and physical aggression toward others. He reported a decline in all offenses and a general increase in sociability and cooperation. Bucher and Lovaas (1968) reported the case of Kevin, to whom response-contingent shock was delivered for persistently covering his ears and attempting to leave his chair during language training. The investigators reported that Kevin immediately initiated very good eye contact with the attending adult. (Also of interest is that by the end of the first day he performed 100% correctly on the tasks where he had not improved during the preceding four months.) Increases in general sociability by the target child were also described by Tate and Baroff (1966) as self-destructiveness decreased.

Positive emotional behavior. In contrast to the predictions of severe emotional damage advanced by some clinicians, it appears that several positive emotional changes have occurred following the use of shock. In the Lovaas, et al. (1965) shock-avoidance study, the experimenters reported that, somewhat surprisingly, during successful shock avoidance the children seemed more alert, smiled, and appeared happy. Simmons and Lovaas (1969) found that Stanley (shocked for whining and inattention) smiled in their presence. In addition, Tate and Baroff (1966) described their work with a self-destructive child and reported that following the shock, the child became calm. Soon thereafter he was sitting in a chair and smiling with apparent pleasure. In the Merbaum (1973) study, the mother used shock to reduce self-abusive behaviors of her child. Once these were eliminated, the mother reported the child appeared quieter and happier.

Negative side effects

Fear of shock apparatus. Most of the negative side effects of shock reported in these studies appear to be direct emotional responses to the shock device itself. Baroff and Tate (1968) reported that the only deleterious effect observed in their successful use of shock was a phobic response to buzzing sounds. In the Simmons and Lovaas (1969) study, where a child was shocked contingent upon inattention and whining, the authors reported that while the target behaviors decreased, the child showed marked aversion to the sight of the hand-held shock stick, which soon had to be replaced with a remote-control device. Merbaum (1973) reported that after using shock to eliminate severe head banging, the child showed an immediate fear of the shock device. Similarly, a fear response by the child was noted by Bucher and King (1971) as the experimeter approached with the shock device, in their treatment to reduce hazardous play.

Negative emotional behaviors. In addition to fear responses to the shock apparatus itself, a few other negative emotional behaviors have been reported following the use of shock. Bucher and Lovaas (1968) reported that when Kevin was shocked for covering his ears and leaving his chair, he would cry and shiver. Bucher and King (1971) reported that their child became quiet and sullen. Similarly, Lovaas, *et al.* (1965) observed a decrease in happiness and contentment as reported by the attending nurses.

Increase in other undesirable behaviors. Some authors report that when response contingent shock was used to eliminate one undesirable behavior, another undesirable behavior increased in frequency. While psychodynamicists might interpret such increases as due to "symptom substitution," the available data indicate that increases in other undesirable behaviors might be attributed to an attempt on the child's part to reinstate the reinforcer previously available for the shocked behavior. Bucher and Lovaas (1968) reported that when one child was shocked for self-abuse, her aggression toward other children on the ward increased at a later time. The authors attributed this increase to the fact that the reinforcers which maintained the self-destruction were still operating in the child's environment (but now in favor of aggressive behaviors). Since she had not learned another, more acceptable, behavior she returned to a form of behavior which led to large quantities of attention. Risley (1968) used shock to elimate dangerous bookcase climbing in an autistic child. He noted a concomitant increase in chair climbing as the rate of bookcase climbing decreased. However, this too was subsequently eliminated by the contingent use of shock and no similar increase in undesirable behavior was noted. Lovaas, *et al.* (1965) reported increased dependency behaviors according to nurses' reports, following experimental sessions to increase social approach.

The positive and negative side effects described above are summarized in Table 1. A total of 25 positive and 13 negative side effects were described in the studies included in this review. As mentioned, of the 13 undesirable effects, 8 were basically fear reactions to the shock apparatus. To be effective, the shock had to be painful. Therefore, the whining, crying, and fearfulness which sometimes occurred evidenced the potency of the contingency and could be considered as the autistic child's ability to discriminate and respond appropriately to unpleasant stimuli. Consequently, these 8 changes might more appropriately be interpreted as direct responses to aversive stimulation rather than "side effects." With this interpretation of reported responses, the ratio of positive to negative side effects was 25:5.

Discussion

The reported side effects of shock with autistic children do not appear sufficient to rule out the use of this method of treatment. Although there is evidence to support the various contentions concerning temporary suppression, negative emotional effects, and increase in other undesirable behaviors, such evidence is minimal and does not characterize this treatment modality. The majority of unintended effects reported were of a positive nature. These included response generalization, increase in social behavior, and positive emotional behavior.

No evidence was found to support the fear that enduring or severe emotional damage occurred. On the contrary, as has been reported earlier in this paper, several authors report positive changes in the children including happiness, social behavior, affection, and calmness. This is consistent with Lovibond's (1970) conclusion in reviewing aversive techniques in therapy that "the danger of producing emotional disturbance, even with

Table 1. Positive and negative side effects of electric shock on autistic children reported in 10 studies

Study	Side effects	
	Positive	Negative
Baroff and Tate (1968)		1. fear of buzzing sounds (+)[a]
Birnbrauer (1968)	1. sociability (+) 2. cooperation (+)	
Bucher and King (1971)		1. fear of shock device (+) 2. quietness (+) 3. sullenness (+)
Bucher and Lovaas (1968)	1. eye-to-face contact (+) 2. imitation skills (+)	1. aggression (+) 2. crying (+) 3. shivering (+)
Lovaas, *et al.* (1965)	1. alertness (+) 2. affection (+) 3. sociability (+) 4. happiness (+) 5. pathological behaviors (−) 6. affection-seeking behaviors (+)	1. happiness-contentment (−)[b] 2. dependency (+)
Lovaas and Simmons (1969)	1. avoiding social contacts (−) 2. whining (−)	
Merbaum (1973)	1. sociability (+) 2. quietness (+) 3. happiness (+)	1. fear of shock device (+)
Risley (1968)	1. eye contact (+)	1. chair climbing (+)
Simmons and Lovaas (1969)	1. affection (+) 2. eye contact (+) 3. smiling (+) 4. hugging (+)	1. temporary aversion to experimenter (+) 2. aversion to shock stick (+)
Tate and Baroff (1966)	1. calmness (+) 2. smiling (+) 3. sociability (+) 4. playfulness (+) 5. whining and crying (−)	

[a] The + denotes an increase in the behavior.
[b] The − denotes a decrease in the behavior.

severe aversive stimulation, is quite remote" (p. 83). This opinion is shared in other review articles by Smolev (1971) and Tanner (1973). This is in direct contrast to the predictions of those speculating that severe emotional damage would result from the use of shock.

Thus, we have strong evidence indicating that response-contingent shock is a powerful, effective technique for suppressing undesirable behaviors and that the side effects of shock in these situations tend to be of a clinically desirable nature. However, just to say that the procedure works and does not typically produce negative side effects is not necessarily a blanket approval for its use. One must consider other factors. For example, one must remember that shock is a powerful treatment procedure but that it must be used correctly in order to be effective. That is, the shock must be delivered *immediately* after the target response. It also must be delivered *consistently* so that the child clearly discriminates the occasion for the punishment. Perhaps one should be more concerned about the *direct* effects of misapplication of such a powerful procedure, rather than worrying about fictitious negative side effects.

Also, as we have seen in our review, shock serves only to temporarily suppress the target behavior. In order to avoid reappearance of the behavior or an increase in another undesirable behavior, one must teach the child other more appropriate behaviors that will lead to reinforcement. In addition, we know that the effects of shock often do not generalize to other situations nor other therapists (cf. Lovaas & Simmons, 1969). Thus one may need to have other therapists deliver the response-contingent shock in other environments in order to provide for stimulus generalization. Thus the reported problems of temporary suppression, lack of stimulus generalization, and increases in other undesirable behaviors can be controlled for by the clinician. Given that the clinician is cautious and correct in the use of shock, he can expect positive results.

The fact that changes in behavior occur in addition to the expected change in the target behavior merits attention in its own right aside from the issue of positive and negative valence. The model of man in which a rigidly delineated, autonomous response is tied to a similarly defined stimulus is simplistic and questionable. It appears that classes of responses covary with the application of single or multiple stimuli. This notion has been experimentally demonstrated (Nordquist, 1971; Wahler, 1975; Wahler, Sperling, Thomas, Teeter, & Luper, 1970), and calls for the therapist to plan for multiple effects of any therapeutic intervention. Thus, an effect may be termed a *side effect* only as long as our ignorance delimits our ability to anticipate more than one direct effect (Willems, 1974). Such planning usually entails the teaching of alternative, appropriate behaviors.

Another factor which must be considered is that the use of shock itself is a powerful conditioned stimulus eliciting strong emotional behavior on the part of the therapist using the shock. That is, many people find it difficult or impossible to use shock because of their own strong adverse philosophies. Risley (1968) gives us some insight into this problem: "Observers of the sessions in which shock was applied reported that, on the basis of observable autonomic responses such as flushing, trembling, etc., the subject recovered from the shock episodes much faster than the experimenter" (p. 25). This points to a crucial issue. No matter how effective shock may be for suppressing undesirable behavior in autistic children, it is useless in those situations where people refuse to use it. Yet, punishment is the most effective procedure when one seeks the immediate reduction in a severely disruptive behavior. Thus, effective alternatives to shock as the aversive stimulus in the punishment paradigm would be desirable.

Although the area is still young, research employing other forms of aversive consequences in a punishment procedure have been shown to be effective in many instances where shock has previously been employed. A few examples will serve as illustrations. Overcorrection is a procedure by which the subject is required to engage in a long series of aversive behaviors (e.g., restoring a "disturbed" environment by cleaning, washing, sweeping, and repeatedly practicing correct behaviors by doing exercises or maintaining uncomfortable positions) contingent upon a target maladaptive behavior. This procedure has reportedly been effective in reducing self-stimulation (Azrin, Kaplan, & Foxx, 1973; Foxx & Azrin, 1973) and aggressive-disruptive behavior (Foxx & Azrin, 1972). Another alternative aversive stimulus was employed by Tanner and Zeiler (1975). They used aromatic ammonia in a punishment paradigm to successfully eliminate self-injurious behavior in an autistic woman.

To conclude, contingent electric shock has proven to be an effective treatment procedure for autistic children. Also, the reported side effects have proven to be of a generally positive nature. Treatment for autistic children, regardless of modality, is usually slow and difficult. We cannot afford to abandon any therapeutic approach with the population without a careful analysis of the costs and benefits. The decision to use electric shock as a therapeutic agent should be evaluated according to objective criteria including the child's needs, the feasibility of using the procedure in the child's environment, and available alternatives. The decision to use or to avoid the use of shock is often made on emotional grounds of the therapist rather than on any well-founded fears. It appears that the correct use of shock in a punishment paradigm leads to both positive direct effects and positive side effects.

References

Adler, A. *The education of children:* (E. Jensen & F. Jensen, Trans.). Chicago: Regnery, 1970. (Originally published, 1930).

Azrin, N. H., Holz, W. C. Punishment. *In* Honig, W. K. (Ed.). *Operant Behavior.* New York: Appleton-Century-Crofts, 1966.

Azrin, N. H., Kaplan, S. J., Foxx, R. M. Autism reversal: eliminating stereotyped self-stimulation of retarded individuals. *Am. J. Ment. Defic.*, 1973; **78**, 241-248.

Baroff, G. S., Tate, B. G. The use of aversive stimulation in the treatment of chronic self-injurious behavior. *J. Am. Acad. Child Psychiat.*, 1968; **7**, 454-470.

Bettelheim, B. *The Empty Fortress.* New York: Free Press, 1967.

Birnbrauer, J. S. Generalization of punishment effects — a case study. *J. Appl. Behav. Anal.*, 1968; **1**, 201-211.

Browning, R. M. Treatment effects of a total behavior modification program with five autistic children. *Behav. Res. & Ther.*, 1971; **9**, 319-327.

Bucher, B., King, L. Generalization of punishment effects in the deviant behavior of a psychotic child. *Behav. Ther.*, 1971; **2**, 68-77.

Bucher, B., Lovaas, O. I. Use of aversive stimulation in behavior modification. *In* Jones, M. R. (Ed.). *Miami symposium on the prediction of behavior, 1967: Aversive stimulation.* Coral Gables, Florida: University of Miami Press, 1968.

Craven, W. F. Protecting hospitalized patients from electrical hazards. *Hewlett-Packard J.*, 1970; **21**:7, 11-17.

Estes, W. K. An experimental study of punishment. *Psychol. Monogr.*, 1944; **57**:3, (Whole No. 263).

Foxx, R. M., Azrin, N. H. Restitution: a method for eliminating aggressive-disruptive behavior of retarded and brain damaged patients. *Behav. Res. & Ther.*, 1972; **10**, 15-27.

Foxx, R. M., Azrin, N. H. The elimination of autistic self-stimulatory behavior by overcorrection. *J. Appl. Behav. Anal.*, 1973; **6**, 1-14.

Freud, S. Inhibitions, symptoms and anxiety. *In* Strachey, J. (Ed. and trans.). *The standard edition of the complete psychological works of Sigmund Freud.* (Vol. 20). London: Hogarth, 1959. (Originally published, 1926).

Freud, A. *The ego and the mechanisms of defense.* New York: International Universities Press, 1946.

Lovaas, O. I., Freitag, G., Kinder, M. I., Rubenstein, B. D., Schaeffer, B., Simons, J. Q. Establishment of social reinforcers in two schizophrenic children on the basis of food. *J. Experi. Child Psychol.*, 1966; **4**, 109-125.

Lovaas, O. I., Schaeffer, B., Simmons, J. Q. Building social behavior in autistic children by use of electric shock. *J. Experi. Res. Personal.*, 1965; **1**, 99-109.

Lovaas, O. I., Simmons, J. Q. Manipulation of self-destruction in three retarded children. *J. Appl. Behav. Anal.*, 1969; **2**, 143-157.

Lovibond, S. H. Aversive control of behavior. *Behav. Ther.*, 1970; **1**, 80-91.

Maurer, A. Corporal punishment. *Am. Psychol.*, 1974; **29**, 614-626.

Merbaum, M. The modification of self-destructive behavior by a mother-therapist using aversive stimulation. *Behav. Ther.*, 1973; **4**, 442-447.

Nordquist, V. M. The modification of a child's enuresis: Some response-response relationships. *J. Appl. Behav. Anal.*, 1968; **1**, 241-247.

Risley, T. The effects and side effects of punishing the autistic behaviors of a deviant child. *J. Appl. Behav. Anal.*, 1968; **1**, 21-34.

Simmons, J. Q., Lovaas, O. I. Use of pain and punishment as treatment techniques with childhood schizophrenics. *Am. J. Psychother.*, 1969; **23**, 23-36.

Skinner, B. F. *Science and Human Behavior.* New York: The Free Press, 1953.

Smolev, S. R. Use of operant techniques for the modification of self-injurious behavior. *Am. J. Ment. Defic.*, 1971; **76**, 295-305.

Solomon, R. L. Punishment. *Am. Psychol.*, 1964; **19**, 239-253.

Tanner, B. A. Aversive shock issues: Physical danger, emotional harm, effectiveness, and "dehumanization". *J. Behav. Ther. & Experi. Psychiat.*, 1973; **4**, 113-115.

Tanner, B. A., Zeiler, M. Punishment of self-injurious behavior using aromatic ammonia as the aversive stimulus. *J. Appl. Behav. Anal.*, 1975; **8**, 53-57.

Tate, B. G., Baroff, G. S. Aversive control of self-injurious behavior in a psychotic boy. *Behav. Res. & Ther.*, 1966; **4**, 281-287.

Wahler, R. G. Some structural aspects of deviant child behavior. *J. Appl. Behav. Anal.*, 1975; **8**, 27-42.

Wahler, R. G., Sperling, K. A., Thomas, M. R., Teeter, N. C., Luper, H. L. The modification of childhood stuttering: some response-response relationships. *J. Experi. Child Psychol.*, 1970; **9**, 411-428.

Willems, E. P. Behavioral technology and behavioral ecology. *J. Appl. Behav. Anal.*, 1974; **7**, 151-165.

Yates, A. J. *Frustration and Conflict.* New York: Wiley, 1962.

Reprinted from *J. Autism & Child. Schiz.*, 1976; **6**:2, 163-173 by kind permission of the authors and the publishers Plenum Publishing Corp., New York, NY 10013.

LONG-TERM OUTCOME OF CONTINGENT SHOCK TREATMENT FOR SELF-INJURIOUS BEHAVIOR

G. H. Murphy, B. Wilson*

Institute of Psychiatry, University of London, and Hilda Lewis House, The Bethlem Royal Hospital, Croydon, CRO 8DR, England.

This study collected data (by means of questionnaires) on the long-term outcome of contingent shock treatment for self-injurious behavior. Despite the relatively small number of completed questionnaires, the results showed clearly that relapse after first treatment was very common: only 18% of patients showed no relapse over the 2 years after treatment ceased. The success of further contingent shock programs in the treatment of relapses was variable. The problem of interpreting retrospective data and the implications of the findings of the present study are briefly discussed.

The long-term outcome of contingent shock treatment for severe self-injurious behavior (SIB) is not a subject covered by many of the published reports in the area, simply because the majority of studies have involved only single subjects, usually with a relatively short follow-up period. Occasional reports of relapse after such programs have appeared, however (Kohlenberg, 1970; Jones, et al., 1974; Paton, personal communication, 1978). Moreover, although few of the expected negative side-effects of contingent shock treatment have been seen (Lichstein and Schreibman, 1976), there have been occasional reports of a sudden loss of behavioral control during a treatment program, with the rate of SIB suddenly increasing despite the continued use of shock (Jones, et al., 1974; Romanczyk and Goren, 1975). Thus it seems likely that the effects of contingent shock on SIB are not always as "immediate and highly durable" as has been recently suggested (Baumeister and Rollings, 1976).

This study therefore aimed to collect data on the long-term outcome of contingent shock treatment for self-injurious behavior. Two main hypotheses were set up, based on the effects of shock on lower animals (Azrin and Holz, 1966; Blackman, 1974): first, that cases in which the SIB had not been totally eliminated by the end of treatment would invariably relapse; and, second, that where the SIB had been totally eliminated there would be some cases with no subsequent relapse (within 2 years). Other factors that were thought to be of interest included the relationship between outcome and the use of positive reinforcement procedures, reliability of equipment, level of current used, and pretreatment SIB rates.

Method

A questionnaire[1] was constructed to elicit the necessary information. The areas covered were: patient characteristics (sex, age, mental age); target behavior (type and years duration of SIB); pretreatment SIB rates; treatment characteristics (method of generalization from sessions, length of treatment, number of shocks used, manner of terminating treatment); posttreatment SIB rates; type of equipment used (hand-held, automatic, or remote control; volts and current used); relapses (dates of relapses and methods of treatment); and use of positive reinforcement of other behaviors (during and after shock treatment).

The questionnaire was distributed in two ways. Authors of published studies of the use of contingent shock to suppress SIB were sent a questionnaire with a covering letter describing the purpose of the study. If no reply was obtained from the first author, a questionnaire and a letter were sent to other authors. In all, 22 studies[2] were discovered and questionnaires for

---

*Now at Rivermead Rehabilitation Centre, Oxford.

[1]A copy of the questionnaire can be obtained by writing to the authors.
[2]Only studies involving contingent shock for self-injuring behaviors were investigated. Such behaviors were considered to include severe self banging, biting, scratching, vomiting, dangerous climbing, or playing with electrical equipment. Studies of aggressive behaviors treated by shock were not followed up.

28 patients were sent out, the majority of studies having arisen from authors in the United States. Alternatively, the most senior clinical psychologist of every subnormality hospital with a psychology department in Britain was sent a letter describing the study and asking if any contingent shock programs had been carried out in that hospital. A positive answer resulted in a questionnaire being sent. In hospitals without a psychologist, the consultant psychiatrists were contacted instead.

Results

Of the 22 authors of published studies who were sent questionnaires, 12 replied (a response rate of 50% — one author replied that he had lost touch with the relevant patients and could provide no information). The remaining 11 authors all filled in the questionnaires, but could not always provide full information in every section. Because the questionnaires had mostly been sent far afield and often concerned studies published more than 5 years ago, it was felt that this response rate was relatively good.

Of the 51 psychologists working in British subnormality hospitals, 38 replied (a response rate of 75%). Only two (unpublished) programs of contingent shock for self-injurious behavior were discovered in this way, although several programs of contingent shock for other undesirable behaviors (such as aggressive behavior toward children and adults) were encountered (these are not discussed further here). No further programs were unearthed by contacting psychiatrists in subnormality hospitals without psychology departments.

Pretreatment behavior

Information supplied on the questionnaires indicated that in the majority of cases the self-injurious behavior had been a long-standing problem before the first contingent shock treatment (85% of the patients had shown the behavior for 3 years or more). The pretreatment rates of self-injurious behavior, the majority of cases of which were of the self-banging variety, ranged from less than five responses per hour to 5400 responses per hour, with 9 of the 13 patients (69%) showing more than 120 responses per hour.

Success of first period of contingent shock treatment

Treatments were classed as completely successful, partially successful, or not successful. "Complete success" was defined as a total absence of self-injurious behavior following cessation of treatment. "Partial success" was defined as a reduction of more than 50% in self-injurious behavior compared with pretreatment rates. "No success" was defined as a reduction of less than 50% or no change or an increase in the rates of self-injury. There were four complete successes, seven partial successes, and two unsuccessful treatments. Of the two unsuccessful treatments, one was successful in one setting but a planned generalization (from individual sessions to the ward) failed, largely for administrative reasons. The second unsuccessful treatment (Romanczyk and Goren, 1975) established control over the self-injury quite quickly, but a sudden increase in responses later occurred, despite continued use of shock, possibly because of a brief failure of the shock equipment on the previous day.

The success of the first treatment did not seem to be related to low initial rates of self-injury. Of the four complete successes, for example, 1 patient had an average pretreatment rate of 2700 responses per hour, 2 were over 120, and 1 was between 30 and 120 per hour. Nor was the success of the first treatment related to the number of shocks used; some completely successful programs needed very few shocks (less than 20) and others needed many shocks (over 200) before the self-injurious behavior had been eliminated.

Relapse rate

A relapse was defined as a marked increase in self-injurious behavior after treatment ended. Table 1 shows the length of time between the end of treatment and the number of patients showing relapse (the figures given are cumulative). In all, after an initial successful treatment, 64% of patients had relapsed within 2 years time, 18% showed no relapse, and, of the remaining 18%, insufficient information was available on one case and the other died before the 2 years were up. Treatments that resulted in partial success did not relapse

Table 1. Length of time between end of treatment and subjects' first relapses

Time	Relapse (N)	No relapse (N)	Not applicable[a] (N)	Not known (N)
Up to 5 months	2	8	2	1
Up to 12 months	6	2	3	2
Up to 2 years	6	2	3	2
Any relapses at all to date	7	2	3	1

[a] This category refers to subjects whose original treatment was unsuccessful (two cases) or who died during the follow-up period (one case).

Table 2. Degree of success of first treatment and length of time before first relapse

Degree of success of treatment	Relapse before 5 months	Relapse between 5 and 12 months	No relapse (up o 2 years)	Not known
Complete	2	1	1	0
Partial	0	3	2[a]	0

[a] This figure includes the 1 patient who died 6 months after the first treatment, without any relapse (death was unconnected with the SIB).

Table 3. Number of studies using planned positive reinforcement during and after treatment

	Planned positive reinforcement of other behaviors					
	During treatment			After treatment		
Outcome	Yes	No	Not known	Yes	No	Not known
Complete success	2	2	0	1	2	1
Partial success	4	2	1	3	2	2
No success (except in sessions)	2	0	0	2	0	0

earlier than those that resulted in complete success. Table 2 shows the degree of success and length of time before relapse.

Few relapses were treated by further shock. Only three studies are known in which the first relapse was treated by shock: two of these were completely successful and one was not successful. Only one case is known in which the second relapse was treated by shock, and in this case the subsequent third relapse was also treated in this way — both of these treatments resulted in complete success in that the SIB was totally absent at the end of each treatment (but a further relapse occurred on each occasion).

Positive reinforcement of other behaviors

Planned reinforcement of other behaviors both during and after treatment did not appear to influence degress of success or relapse rate. Table 3 shows the number of studies

Table 4. Reliability of equipment and treatment outcome

| | Treatment outcome | | |
Reliability of equipment	Complete success	Partial success	No success
Very reliable	3	2	1
Some breakdowns (1-10)	1	4	0
Many breakdowns (over 10)	0	1	0

using planned positive reinforcement during and after treatment together with the degree of success. There were only two cases with no relapse at all; one of these used planned positive reinforcement *during* treatment but did not say whether or not it was used after treatment. The second gave no information on positive reinforcement either during or after treatment.

Equipment characteristics

The voltage applied during contingent shock was not related to treatment outcome. Some unsuccessful studies used high voltage (over 150V), some completely successful ones (in terms of posttreatment SIB rates) used lower voltage (10 to 50V) and some medium voltage (50-100V), and some partially successful studies used lower and some higher (over 150V) voltage. Treatment outcome did not seem to be related to the current either; the studies used different levels of current and obtained various degrees of success.

It can be seen from Butterfield (1975) that the question of level of current provided by a piece of apparatus is a complicated one. The range of current that was reported from the various studies leads the present authors to feel that this information was not very reliable (in one study a current of 1000 mA was reportedly used, which should have proved fatal, but was clearly not so). Moreover, the amount of pain felt by the patient, which is presumably the important factor, depends also on electrode size and placement, according to Butterfield (1975), and information about this was not requested.

High equipment reliability did not appear to ensure a successful treatment outcome in terms of the posttreatment SIB rates, but, in the only two cases in which no relapse occurred (over 2 years), both reported using highly reliable equipment. Table 4 shows the equipment reliability and treatment outcome of the 13 cases.

Other factors

All the follow-up data obtained referred to mentally retarded patients. None of the variables investigated, such as patient characteristics (chronological age, sex, mental age), type of SIB, equipment type (hand-held, automatic), and treatment characteristics (method of generalisation) seem to be related either to immediate treatment outcome or to the occurrence of relapses.

Discussion

Information on the long-term outcome of contingent shock treatment was available for 13 patients. In considering the data provided by the follow-up questionnaires, the number of authors who did not provide long-term outcome data (11 of 22) must be kept in mind. Furthermore, because primarily published studies were followed up, it is not possible to estimate the overall *short-term* effectiveness of contingent shock treatment (only successful studies are usually published). Nevertheless, it is clear that contingent shock is *not* always successful even in the short-term in reducing self-injurious behavior (Jones, *et al.,* 1974; Romanczyk and Goren, 1975).

As regards the long-term outcome after a successful first treatment, it appears that the first hypothesis, that relapse would invariably occur if the SIB had not been totally eliminated by the end of treatment, was not confirmed by the data. One of the two cases with no relapse to date did reach a zero rate at the end of treatment, but the other was still showing some SIB when treatment ceased. This latter case is hard to explain in operant terms. Presumably it would have to be postulated that positive reinforcement of other behavior and/or reinforcement schedules responsible for maintaining the original level of SIB had changed during treatment. None of the information given on the questionnaire suggests that this was so, but it is of course possible that unplanned changes coincided with the contingent shock treatment.

Only four cases (30%) showed no self-injury at all when the first shock treatment terminated and only one of these four (a case mentioned above) did not relapse. The second prediction, therefore, that some cases showing zero rates would not relapse, had been met in one case. Interestingly enough, relapses did not occur earlier where self-injury was not completely eliminated. Indeed, the two earliest relapses occurred when self-injury *was* completely eliminated. Most relapses appear to occur between 5 and 12 months after the first treatment. If no relapse had occurred by 12 months, the chances of permanent relief from self-injury appeared to be increased.

Because of the very small number of cases in which relapse was treated by further shock treatment, few conclusions can be made about the efficacy of treating relapses. Three subjects received further shock after the first relapse; 1 showed no self-injury for 3 weeks before relapsing again, 1 relapsed 18 months later, and 1 increased the rate of self-injury before shock treatment was abandoned. Only in the second mentioned case was shock used again, this time followed by an injury-free period of 48 months, at which point a third relapse occurred (with the onset of puberty). Thus it seems that, although relapses often occur (usually within a year) after a first treatment by contingent shocks, further treatments are possible and are sometimes successful initially, but they may be followed by further relapses later.

There was no clear relationship among positive reinforcement procedures, outcome, and relapses. Both of the unsuccessful treatments made use of planned reinforcement during and after treatment; two of the completely successful cases did not plan for these either during or after treatment, and the case showing the earliest relapse after treatment did involve the use of positive reinforcement throughout. In contrast, the animal literature demonstrates that positive reinforcement of alternative responses produces, for a given shock intensity, a better suppression of the punished response (Azrin and Holz, 1966). It is possible that the same is true for retarded children whose self-injurious responses are shocked, the effect being obscured in the data obtained because different studies employed different shock intensities. It can be concluded, however, that the planned use of positive reinforcement does not guarantee a successful program.

As regards the other possible factors relating to successful outcome, it seems that nothing definite can be concluded. The length of time taken for the treatment to suppress the self-injurious behavior (as judged by the number of shocks used in the first treatment) does not seem to be related to outcome nor to the occurrence of relapses. High reliability of equipment did not seem to guarantee a successful program, with one completely successful program (i.e., one achieving a zero rate of self-injury at the end of the first treatment) using apparently unreliable (between 1 and 10 breakdowns during the program) equipment. The two cases in which no relapses occurred did use very reliable equipment, however, so it may be that reliable equipment protects patients from subsequent relapses, even though it may not aid suppression of responses during treatment. [Sudden absences of shock — "vacations from punishment" — during a treatment program have the surprising effect, in lower animals, of *not* producing an increase in the treated response (see Azrin and Holz, 1966).]

Predictions about the probability of a relapse do not seem to be possible, even at the end of first treatment. A complete elimination of the self-injurious behavior by the end of treatment by no means ensures a longer injury-free period than partial suppression of the behavior, according to the follow-up data obtained. Moreover, the use of planned positive reinforcement procedures during and/or after treatment did not seem to protect patients from relapses, nor did such procedures seem to ensure complete elimination of the SIB during treatment.

Examination of the two cases in which no relapses occurred over more than 2 years gives no clues as to the essential factors governing elimination of high rates of self-injurious behavior. In both cases highly reliable equipment was used, but the fact that other cases relapsed despite reliable equipment suggests that this is certainly not the only factor. Similarly, both studies involved hand-held equipment of over 150 volts and planned generalization of shock treatment. Again, however, other studies showed these features, but in them relapses did occur.

It is, of course, difficult to disentangle from retrospective data the possible factors determining long-term treatment outcome, particularly when few sets of follow-up data are available. It may be that a combination of several features is important for successful and durable treatment, something that perhaps would only become clear from a large number of studies. Alternatively, it may be that the beginnings of a relapse depend to some extent on chance (for instance, an accidental self-injury eliciting the old positive reinforcement and hence starting a chain of events leading to increased self-injury), in which case shock treatment factors may not be so important. Suffice it to say that, on the basis of the present follow-up data, those involved in planning contingent shock treatment for patients showing self-injurious behavior should not invariably expect fast treatment, successful treatment, or permanent treatment effects.

Acknowledgments
We are very grateful to Miss Valerie Barden of the British Psychological Society for providing us with a list of clinical psychologists in Britain for use in our survey of contingent shock programs.

References
Azrin, N. H., Holz, W. C. Punishment. *In* Honig, W. K. (Ed.). *Operant Behavior: areas of research and application.* New York: Appleton-Century-Crofts, 1966.
Baumeister, A. A., Rollings, J. P. Self-injurious behavior. *In* Ellis, N. R. (Ed.). *International Review of Research in Mental Retardation,* (Vol. 8.). New York: Academic Press, Inc., 1976.
Blackman, D. *Operant Conditioning: an experimental analysis of behavior.* London: Methuen, 1974.
Butterfield, W. H. Electric shock — safety factors when used for the aversive conditioning of humans. *Behav. Ther.,* 1975; **6**, 98.
Jones, F. H., Simmons, J. Q., Frankel, F. An extinction program for eliminating self-destructive behavior in a nine year old autistic girl. *J. Autism & Child. Schiz.,* 1974; **4**, 241.
Kohlenberg, R. J. The punishment of persistent vomiting: a case study. *J. Appl. Behav. Anal.,* 1970; **3**, 241.
Lichstein, K. L., Schriebman, L. Employing electric shock with autistic children: a review of the side effects. *J. Autism & Child. Schiz.,* 1976; **6**, 163.
Romanczyk, R. G., Goren, N. R. Severe self-injurious behavior: the problem of clinical control. *J. Consult. Clin. Psychol.,* 1975; **43**, 730.

SETTING EFFECTS, ADAPTIVE CLOTHING, AND THE MODIFICATION OF HEAD-BANGING AND SELF-RESTRAINT IN TWO PROFOUNDLY RETARDED ADULTS[1]

J. Rojahn
University of Vienna, Austria

J. A. Mulick
Eunice Kennedy Shriver Center, Waltham, Mass.

D. McCoy
Murdoch Center, Butner, N.C.

S. R. Schroeder[2]
University of North Carolina at Chapel Hill

Types of adaptive clothing were found to have a large effect on the self-injurious behavior (SIB) and severe self-restraint of two blind profoundly retarded men. In the first subject, wearing jackets with large pockets allowed appropriate self-restraint and decreased head and shoulder hitting by 90 percent. In the second subject a combination of adaptive clothing and time-out eliminated inappropriate self-restraint and SIB, and generalized beyond treatment sessions. The experiments show that many environmental stimuli set the occasion for SIB and often can be changed easily to reduce it.

Introduction

The literature on intervention with self-injurious behavior (SIB) is based almost exclusively on the premise that it is a learned social response subject to the laws of operant conditioning. Thus, the vast majority of treatments reported are based on the contingency management approach. The most often used procedures are *punishment* (e.g., restraint, Saposnek & Watson, 1974; and electrical stimulation, Tate & Baroff, 1966; Lovaas & Simmons, 1969), *time-out* from positive reinforcement (Hamilton, Stevens, & Allen, 1967), *positive reinforcement* for alternative behaviors (Lovaas, Freitag, Gold & Kassorla, 1966; Peterson & Peterson, 1968) and *overcorrection* (Foxx & Azrin, 1973). Recent views about therapeutic intervention with SIB in mentally retarded populations can be found in Bachman (1972) and Forehand and Baumeister (1976).

Little attention, however, has been given to the effect of noncontingent modifications of adaptive clothing on SIB or how such general environmental changes might lawfully interact with contingency management. Yet, a stimulus control analysis of SIB suggests that general environmental modifications and antecedent events must be taken into account in the treatment of SIB. For example, transitional periods of the day, from one activity to another, different teachers or ward staff, and situational demands during various program and non-program activities have all been shown to influence the rate and topography of SIB (Carr, Newsom, & Binkoff, 1976; Schroeder & Humphrey, 1977). Clothing might also be another important factor influencing behavioral change.

[1] This study was conducted at Murdoch Center while the senior Author was a Fulbright scholar at D.D.D.L.-B.S.R.C., the Child Development Research Institute, The University of North Carolina, Chapel Hill, N.C. 27514. It was supported by USPHS Grant No. HD-03110 to the CDRI and DDSA H.I.P. Grant No. 51-P-20521 to Stephen R. Schroeder. We thank Dorothy Currin and Narell Council for their cooperation and contribution to follow-up and arrangements for the subjects, and Bill Moore for data collection.
[2] Requests for reprints should be sent to: Stephen R. Schroeder, Division of Disorders of Development and Learning, Health Affairs Post Office, University of North Carolina, Chapel Hill, N.C. 27514, U.S.A.

The present study reports the findings of an applied behavioral analysis of two cases of severe SIB in which systematic variations of clothing were shown to be important factors in the outcome of therapeutic interventions. Both clients involved in the experiment showed a high probability of self-restraint and strong reactions when being prompted out of that position which eventually resulted in high rates of self-slapping and other SIBs. Both clients restrained themselves, i.e. wrapped their arms in their clothing. The object in Case I was to show the significant effect of adaptive clothing on the rate and pattern of a multiple SIB. The investigation of Case II emphasized the conjoint and/or separated implementation of a time-out procedure for head-slapping and for clothing which prevented self-restraint.

Method

Subjects

Subject 1 was a 30 year old, non-ambulatory and blind, profoundly retarded male adult. The client's SIB history dates back to the age of 4 years, the time he was first institutionalized. His SIB had been chronic. Early institutional records indicate extensive use of strait jackets as protective devices. The subject's SIB consisted of three high-rate head-injuring behaviors (head-slapping with the palm of his hand, hitting his forehead and eyebrows with the knuckles of his fist and whipping the head to one of his shoulders), and severe self-restraint. During the period of the present study his medication level was reduced three times from 150 mg Thorazine qid to 100 mg bid.

Subject 2 was a 26 year old blind ambulatory profoundly retarded male adult. Institutional records reveal a long history of SIB dating back to the age of 4 years. Early reports revealed continuously restrained arms and long periods of isolation. The client usually was dressed in a T-shirt in which he was allowed to wrap up his hands, since it was considered an "effective way to stopping head-banging", according to staff reports. At the time of this experiment the subject's head-slapping had recovered, although he was still provided with a T-shirt. The medication level during the experiment was 50 mg Thorazine tid and 5 mg Ritalin in the beginning and was cut down to 50 mg Thorazine bid only after 31 sessions.

Setting

The clients were brought from their home units to the SIB-unit every day from Monday to Friday from 9 a. m. to 11 a. m. A large room (10 m × 8 m) was set up as a simulated dayroom with controlled staff intervention particularly designed for contingency management and group activity with music and a variety of toys. There were usually eight other SIB clients and 1-3 teachers present at the same time. General interaction rules for the staff which were maintained throughout the whole study were to ignore or correct inappropriate behavior (e.g., SIB, aggression), to reinforce desirable pro-social behavior (e.g., initiation of social contacts,smiling) with social and edible reinforcers as specified in individual cases and to encourage appropriate play with toys and other stimulating materials.

Observational procedures

Observer stations and a video-camera were located behind a screened-in portion of the day room which provided an unobstructed view of all activities for as many as six observers. Two data collection systems were applied:

The first was a multi-category interval recording system (Repp, Roberts, Slack, Repp, & Berkler, 1976) for an *ecological assessment*. Each session lasted for 16 minutes and was divided into 48 alternating observation and recording intervals (10 sec. each). At the end of each observation interval, the observer recorded whether a behavior defined by one of the categories had occurred within the current interval. A tape recorder with ear phones instructed the observers either to observe or to record. The ecological coding system represented a modified form of the one developed by Wahler, House, and Stambough (1976). Thirty categories consisting of 21 response and 9 stimulus categories constituted the system. However, only 3 categories will be reported in the context of this study:

Tb = target behavior (any form of head-injuring behavior).

R — = self-injurious or inappropriate self-restraint (wrapping up arms and hands in clothing except keeping hands in the pockets, locking arms tightly under the arm rests of a chair, etc.).

R + = appropriate self-restraint (for Subject 1 – keeping hands in the pockets; for Subject 2 – clasping and folding arms in front of his chest, behind head or back).

The measures consisted of the total number of interval occurrences within each session, with a maximum score of 48 per category and session which were transduced into percentage scores (Lichstein & Wahler, 1976).

The second data collection system which was only used in Experiment I consisted of *frequency recording.* Parallel to the observation intervals of the ecological system, three observers recorded alternatively the frequency of three different head-injurious behaviors, response by response:

head to shoulders	= any occurrence of a whipping head movement toward the shoulder.
knuckles-to-head	= any occurrence of hitting the forehead with the knuckles of the fist.
head-slapping	= any occurrence of head slapping with the palm.

Using a 5-channel Lafayette Multicounter (Model No. 99-90318) frequency counts were collected beginning with the fourteenth experimental session. Thus, back-up validity measures for SIB categories between the two observational systems were provided.

Reliability

Each category code was examined by the total of code entries for both observations. Dividing the larger number of entries into the smaller then provides a percentage index of observer agreement for the entire observation session.

For the ecological data system about every thirteenth session of both subjects or experiments was video-taped and thereby preserved for a second observation at a later time (intra-observer reliability). Three inter-rater reliability checks were made additionally in Case II, to compare the results of the primary observer and two others.

The means of intra-observer reliabilities for Case I were:

Tb = 97 %, R + = 99 %, R — = 88 %; for Case II: Tb = 86 %, R + = 100 %, R — = 74 %.

The means of inter-observer reliability for Case II were:

R + = 100 %, R — = 100 % (Tb did not occur in those sessions).

For the interval frequency recording system reliability between two observers were estimated every 10th session:
head-to-shoulder = 89 %, head-slapping = 99 %; and knuckles-to-head = 92 %.

Clothing

The following garments were used as adaptive clothing for Subject 1:

What will be referred to as "jacket" subsequently:
– 3-piece linen suit with large side-pockets.
– 3/4 length denim jacket.
– 3/4 length nylon wind breaker.
– 3/4 length light cotton vest with large side pockets.

What will be referred to as "neckbrace" subsequently:
– 4 × 14 inches foam rubber band secured around client's neck with Velcro fasteners.

For Subject 2, a regular cover-all or jump-suit with or without sleeves was used as an adaptive device with the intention to prevent the subject's inappropriate self-restraint. It was impossible for the client to wrap up his hands in such a one-piece suit. The client's normal clothing consisted of a T-shirt and long pants.

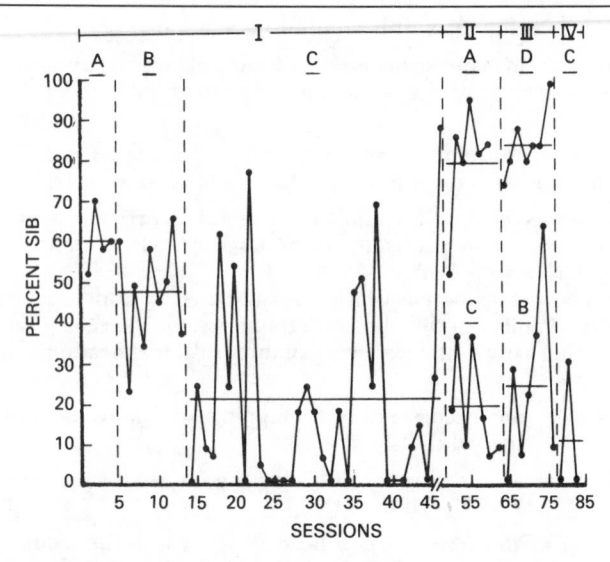

Figure 1. Percentages of occurrence (per session) of head-injuring behaviors for Subject 1 across the four experimental sections.

Treatment procedures (Case I)

The present study consisted of 83 16-minute sessions and was divided into three experimental sections with four phases and a short follow-up corresponding to the major clothing manipulations (see Fig. 1 legend).

Section I represented an ABC sequential design with one session per day and a total of 46 sessions.
Phase A — no jacket or neckbrace.
Phase B — the client was wearing a jacket.
Phase C — the client was wearing a jacket and a neckbrace simultaneously.

Section II was an AC multiple schedule design with random distribution of phases (Hersen & Barlow, 1976) on two succeeding sessions per day. There were six A and seven C sessions. The orders were: AC, AC, C, CC, AC, CA, AA.

Section III represented a multiple schedule BD design with random distribution of phases and one session per day. A new phase was introduced at this point:
Phase D — the client was wearing the neckbrace only. There were seven B and seven D sessions: DD, BD, DD, BB, BD, BB, DB.

Section IV represented three sessions with both adaptive devices simultaneously to provide a short follow-up period.

Results and discussion
Target behavior. The raw data (interval occurrence of behaviors in one session) are represented by the percentages of interval occurrence in Fig. 1.
It is clear that a successive decline in Tb (head-injuring) in the first three phases occurred as a result of the systematic addition of adaptive clothing. Though there is some overlap of rates between conditions, the means indicate a strong declining trend. The use of the jacket alone resulted in a slight decrease in Tb which then dropped even more when the neckbrace was added. The amount of variability and overlap in Section I made subsequent experimental analysis necessary to provide a more detailed interpretation of specific behavioral patterns and their dependencies. These considerations resulted in the design of two additional experimental sections.
Thus, when Phase A was simultaneously compared with Phase C in Section II, the reduction in Tb attributable to simply wearing the complete set of clothing, is confirmed

Table 1. Mean percentage of interval occurence (%) and frequency (F) per session of self-injurious behavior topographies in different treatment phases for Case I.

Section	Phase	Total SIB %	F	Head-to-Shoulder %	F	Head-Slapping %	F	Knuckles-to-Head %	F
I	A	59.9	—	—	—	—	—	—	—
	B	46.3	—	—	—	—	—	—	—
	C	19.9	52.2	3.7	3.2	4.0	6.1	13.1	37.6
II	A	76.7	203.8	7.7	8.3	55.2	96.2	15.2	94.8
	C	17.9	25.9	17.9	25.6	0.0	0.0	0.3	0.9
III	B	22.9	38.3	16.0	27.0	6.5	10.3	0.8	1.0
	D	81.2	253.1	2.9	1.4	62.7	138.0	31.9	113.7
IV	C	9.7	12.7	9.7	12.7	0.0	0.0	0.0	0.0

and much more obvious. A Mann-Whitney U-Test calculated with interval frequency measures for Tb shows a significant difference between the two conditions (Mann-Whitney $U = 0$, $p < 0.001$).

A comparison of the efficacy of the two devices in Section III displays the remarkably greater effect of the jacket on Tb (Mann-Whitney $U = 0$, $p = 0.000$). The final return to Phase C for three sessions proves the declining trend of Tb when the client was again wearing both adaptive devices. Table 1 also corroborates the effect on different SIB topographies of the combined application of the jacket and the neckbrace but also the jacket alone. The neckbrace by itself did not control the probability of head directed SIB.

Substitution. By breaking down Tb into three concurrent responses a substitution effect appears, so far mainly demonstrated with suppression (Rollings & Baumeister, 1977) or other contingency management procedures. Increased collateral whipping head to one shoulder accompanied the deceleration of head-slapping and hitting knuckles-to-forehead as a result of non-contigently applied and systematically varied adaptive devices. This substitution process becomes evident in Sections II, III and IV (see Fig. 2).

The U-tests reveal opposite effects of the adaptive devices on head-slapping and knuckles-to-head on the one hand and head-to-shoulder hitting on the other: whereas both devices combined led to an extremely significant decrease of the two head-hitting responses ($U_{\text{slapping and knuckles}} = 0$, $p < 0.001$); the rate of head-to-shoulder increased ($U_{\text{head-to-shoulder}} = 7$, $p < 0.026$). The same phenomenon becomes apparent in Section III, where the jacket was successfully used to control both head directed responses ($U_{\text{slapping}} = 2$, $p < 0.001$; $U_{\text{knuckles}} = 0$, $p = 0.000$), but permitted a significant increment of head-to-shoulder frequency ($U_{\text{head-to-shoulder}} = 6$, $p < 0.009$). The exclusive use of the neckbrace resulted in the very inverse proportion of Tb frequencies (see Fig. 2); while it reduced head-to-shoulder to a mean

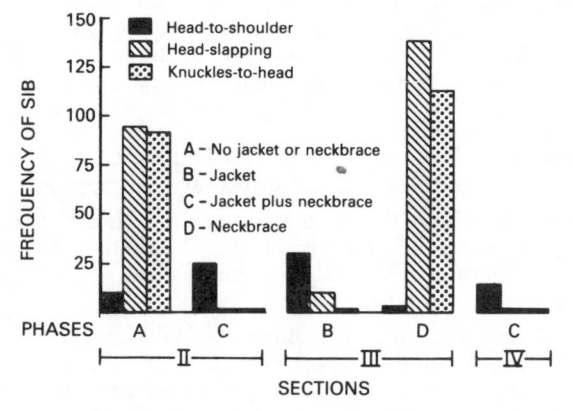

Figure 2. The substitution effect of the three concurrent head-injuring behaviors across sessions II, III, and IV for Subject 1.

session frequency of only 1.43 responses, head-slapping shot up to 138 and knuckles-to-head to 113.71 responses per session (see Table 1).

Pearson correlation coefficients between head-injurious SIBs calculated across settings were:

head-to-shoulder/head-slapping: $r = -0.30$
head-to-shoulder/knuckles-to-head: $r = -0.33$
head-slapping/knuckles-to-head: $r = -0.01$

These figures explain the internal relationship between the three responses. Both head-slapping and knuckles-to-head tended to fairly exclude head-to-shoulder but did not mutually influence their event probability. There was no functional interrelation between these two behaviors, although they were effectively controlled by the same stimuli (jacket and neckbrace). The mean of head-slapping and knuckles-to-head varied similarly across the experimental phases (see Fig. 2), but did not covary simultaneously within phases (exemplified by the correlation coefficients).

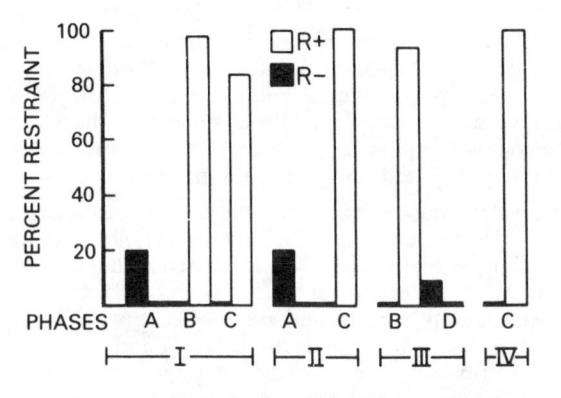

Figure 3. The percentage of appropriate and inappropriate self-restraint across sections I to IV in relationship to the subject's clothing (Subject 1).

Self restraint. The jacket was also used for the modification of inappropriate self-injurious self-restraint (R-) into appropriate "keeping hands in the pocket" (R +). Figure 3 shows the high probability of appropriate self-restraint, whenever the subject was dressed in his jacket with side pockets. R- only occurred when the subject did not wear the jacket. It seems obvious that there was a preference for R + which depended on the use of adaptive clothing. Moreover, the two types of self-restraint were mutually exclusive. This led to the consideration to use R + as an alternative treatment in a fading procedure to release hands and arms as the final goal in a positive behavior training program. Thus, the jacket proved to be a highly valuable device to reduce R- when used non-contingently.

Treatment procedures (Case II)

This study consisted of 76 16-minute sessions which were structured as a concurrent experimental design with shifted phases for two covarying responses (SIB, R-).

Baseline included 21 sessions of the normal dayroom routine in the SIB unit (see *Setting Conditions*). This phase represented the baseline for SIB, whereas self-restraint was only of secondary interest. Clothing was varied unsystematically; 17 T-shirt- and 4 jumpsuit-sessions were conducted.

Treatment I — A time-out procedure (Bostow & Bailey, 1969) was implemented to eliminate head-slapping. Contingent upon every SIB, the dayroom teacher said, "No hitting, you must lie on your stomach." He was then directed to lie on the floor, with his arms stretched out over his head for 30 sec. Since the client sometimes resisted lying on the floor in this position, he was held by staff members. (In the calculation of percentage of SIB,

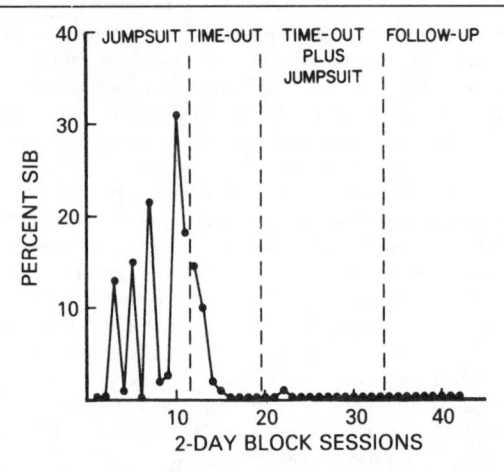

Figure 4. The mean percentage (per two sessions) of SIB occurrence for Subject 2.

those intervals were omitted in which the subject was lying on the floor.) Treatment I included 15 sessions of which T-shirts were used 14 times, the jumpsuit once after time-out had decreased the head-slapping.

Treatment II - While the time-out procedure was continued for SIB, an additional behavior analysis focused on the differential influence of clothing on self-restraint. T-shirt and jumpsuit were randomly distributed among 26 continuous sessions (10 jumpsuit-and 16 T-shirt-sessions) after SIB was under sufficient control of time-out contingencies.

The first three phases were conducted in the SIB dayroom only.

Follow-up. 47 days after the last experimental session, 14 observations were accomplished by a staff member in the client's home unit to provide follow-up and generalization data. The unit staff members were instructed to implement the time-out procedure contingent upon any occurrence of SIB.

Results and discussion

Head-slapping. Figure 4 shows the mean percentage of intervals in which SIB occurred per two-day blocks of sessions for the total 76 sessions. The increase in head-slapping during baseline was likely due to the introduction of the jumpsuit to prevent self-restraint in some of the sessions. SIB rate was 52% higher in jumpsuit sessions than in T-shirt sessions. When the jumpsuit was omitted and time-out was introduced in Treatment 1, SIB decreased and stayed at a low level in Treatment 2 when the jumpsuit was reintroduced. Follow-up data suggest that generalization and maintenance to extra-therapy settings were accomplished.

Self-Restraint. The subject's self-restraint in this first adaptive device (T-shirt) had become inappropriate because its SIB controlling value had extinguished and only kept him from engaging in manipulatory activity. Therefore, another adaptive device was implemented non-contingently (the jumpsuit) which focused on the type of self-restraint. As the jumpsuit prevented any R-, inappropriate restraint was eliminated by definition as soon as the client was dressed in this garment. The jumpsuit effectively eliminated inappropriate self-restraint, whereas the T-shirt did neither prevent R- (36,7% during the experiment; 42,9% during follow-up), nor maintained its earlier raison d'etre, the control of SIB.

General discussion

Although non-contingently applied adaptive devices are a very effective, practical and little time consuming means to control SIB and noxious self-restraint in the retarded, it is important to point out its disadvantages and limitations. A comparison of the two cases in the present study reveals an inherent relationship. Case II represents a theoretical continuation of Case I insofar as Client II already had had a history of adaptive devices before this experiment started. The first therapeutical clothing was used to control self-restraint, a behavior incompatible with SIB, in a manner comparable to the jacket and neckbrace in Case I. Since controlling SIB-related self-restraint by the use of particular clothing frequently results in other undesirable behavior patterns (e.g., inappropriate self-restraint), this strategy can only be of provisional relevance. Though self-hitting responses are considered to be a more serious behavior problem than self-restraint, being totally wrapped up in shirts and other garments still prevents the individual from engaging in many educational tasks of some importance. Since this new and less harmful response must not be perpetuated too long by contingency management, its SIB controlling power will extinguish sooner or later, as can be seen in the case history of Client II.

Thus the conclusion to be drawn is that the implementation of non-contingently applied adaptive devices is an important and helpful step in the design of treatment procedures - eventually in combination with contingency management techniques - for some forms of SIB with deliberately self-restraining retarded clients. Yet, it cannot be a final therapeutical goal, but rather should be faded out after a certain period of time and be replaced by an individually chosen positive behavior program.

References

Bachman, J. A. Self-injurious behavior — a behavioral analysis. *J. Abnorm. Psychol.*, 1972; **80**, 211-224.

Bostow, D. E., Bailey, J. B. Modification of severe disruptive and aggressive behavior using brief time out and reinforcement procedures. *J. Appl. Behav. Anal.*, 1969; **2**, 31-37.

Carr, E. G., Newsom, C. D., Binkoff, J. A. Stimulus control of self-destructive behavior in a Psychotic child. *J. Abnorm. Child Psychol.*, 1976; **4**, 139-153.

Forehand, R., Baumeister, A. A. Deceleration of aberrant behavior among retarded individuals. *In* Hersen, M., Eisler, R. M., Miller, P. M. (Eds.). *Progress in Behavior Modification.* (Vol. 2) New York: Academic Press, 1976.

Foxx, R. M., Azrin, N. H. The elimination of self-stimulatory behavior of autistic and retarded children by overcorrection. *J. Appl. Behav. Anal.*, 1973; **6**, 1-14.

Hamilton, H., Stevens, L., Allen, P. Controlling aggressive and destructive behavior in severely retarded institutionalized residents. *Am. J. Ment. Defic.*, 1967; **71**, 852-856.

Hersen, M., Barlow, D. M. *Single Case Experimental Designs.* New York: Pergamon Press, 1976.

Lichstein, K. L., Wahler, R. G. The ecological assessment of an autistic child. *J. Abnorm. Child Psychol.*, 1976; **4**, 31-54.

Lovaas, O. I., Freitag, G., Gold, V. J., Kassorla, I. C. Experimental studies in childhood schizophrenia: Analysis of self-destructive behavior. *J. Experi. Child Psychol.*, 1965; **2**, 67-84.

Lovaas, O. I., Simmons, J. Q. Manipulation of self-destruction in three retarded children. *J. Appl. Behav. Anal.*, 1969; **2**, 143-157.

Peterson, R. F., Peterson, L. R. The use of positive reinforcement in the control of self-destructive behavior in a retarded boy. *J. Experi. Child Psychol.*, 1968; **6**, 351-360.

Repp, A. C., Roberts, D. M., Slack, D. J., Repp, C. F., Berkler, M. S. A comparison of frequency, interval, and time sampling methods of data collection. *J. Appl.Behav. Anal.*, 1976; **9**, 501-508.

Rollings, J. P., Baumeister, A. A. The use of overcorrection procedures to eliminate the stereotyped behaviors of retarded individuals. *Behav. Modif.*, 1977; **1**, 29-46.

Saposnek, D. T., Watson, L. S. The elimination of the self-destructive behavior of a psychotic child; a case study. *Behav. Ther.*, 1974; **5**, 79-89.

Schroeder, S. R., Humphrey, R. H. *Environmental context effects and contingent restraint time-out of self-injurious behavior in a deaf-blind profoundly retarded woman.* Paper presented at the 101st Annual Meeting of the American Association of Mental Deficiency, New Orleans, La., 1977.

Tate, B. G., Baroff, G. S. Aversive control of self-injurious behavior in a psychotic boy. *Behav. Res. & Ther.*, 1966; **4**, 281-287.

Wahler, R. G., House, A. E., Stambaugh, E. E. *Ecological Assessment of Child Problem Behavior.* New York: Pergamon Press, 1976.

Reprinted from *Behav. Anal. & Modif.*, 1978; 2:3, 185-196 by kind permission of the authors and William Yule, Editor of the journal until its ceased publication in 1979, on behalf of the publishers. James A. Mulick is now Associate Professor of Pediatrics, The Ohio State University, Columbus, Ohio 43205.

PHYSICAL RESTRAINT AS POSITIVE REINFORCEMENT

Judith E. Favell, James F. McGimsey, Michael L. Jones, Preston R. Cannon
Western Carolina Center, Morganton, NC 28655

The reinforcing function of physical restraint was analyzed for three retarded individuals who had a history of restraint and appeared to enjoy it. Using a preference paradigm with one participant and a reversal design with two others, we found that an arbitrary response systematically increased for each participant when followed by brief periods of restraint. No comparable increases occurred in conditions in which responses were not consequated or were followed by stimuli designed to control for the nonrestraint components of the restraint consequence. Results were discussed in terms of three clinical issues: determining the possible role of restraint in maintaining behavior problems such as self-injury in natural settings, preventing or eliminating the reinforcing function of restraint, and using restraint reinforcement in treating behavior problems when this consequence is the only identifiable reinforcer for an individual.

Physical restraint with devices such as rigid arm splints, helmets, camisoles, beds or chairs is one of the most prevalent methods of controlling self-injury and sometimes other serious behavior problems of retarded and emotionally disturbed individuals (Schroeder, Note 1). Restraint is sometimes applied contingent on episodes of self-injury in an attempt to treat the problem (e.g., Hamilton, Stevens, & Allen, 1967), but more often it is not employed therapeutically, but simply to terminate or prevent the behavior (Tate, 1972). Although often the only readily available and practical method of protecting the individual or others in the environment, prolonged restraint has several widely recognized undesirable effects, including disruption of habilitative programming and muscular atrophy.

Recently, another apparent side-effect of the use of restraint has been informally noted. Some clients appear to enjoy being restrained. For example, these individuals may appear calm when restrained, but extremely agitated when released, and they often attempt to restrain themselves (e.g., Jones, Simmons, & Frankel, 1974; Lovaas & Simmons, 1969; Myers & Deibert, 1971; Tate & Baroff, 1966). Informal indications of this type suggest that restraint may be a positive reinforcer for these individuals. Such a possibility has received indirect support in research with self-injurers who appear to enjoy restraint (Favell, McGimsey, & Jones, 1978). In addition to the use of other procedures, when restraint was applied contingent on the nonoccurrence of self-injury, the behavior declined to near zero. In a more direct test of the reinforcing function of restraint, a further demonstration with one of these subjects indicated that when restraint was made contingent on an arbitrary (marble placement) response, that response systematically increased (Favell et al., 1978).

As an extension of these findings, the present study was conducted to delineate further the function of physical restraint as a behavioral consequence. To this end, in the present study we examined the function of restraint for three additional subjects who appeared to enjoy being restrained. These individuals had histories of varying forms of restraint for a variety of behavior problems. Further, the function of restraint was tested in isolation from other treatment components of which it is typically a part and in the context of a variety of tasks. In short, within the subpopulation of individuals who appear to enjoy restraint, we attempted to delineate the precise function of restraint and its generality as a reinforcer.

Portions of this paper were presented at the annual meeting of the American Psychological Association, San Francisco, 1977, and the annual meeting and conference of the National Society for Autistic Children, Dallas, 1978. This research was funded by a grant from the North Carolina Department of Human Resources, Division of Mental Health, Research Section. The authors thank Tom Shea, Gene Seals, and Jerry Merwin for their help and support with this research and Meda Smith for preparing the manuscript. Special thanks are due to Jim Favell and Todd Risley for their suggestions and encouragement and to the staff at Western Carolina Center and Caswell Center for their cooperation.

The clinical implications of such research are important, both for the possible role of restraint in maintaining behavior problems in natural settings and for its safe and effective use in remediating severe inappropriate behavior, such as self-injury and aggression.

Method

Subject Selection

Subjects were selected on the basis of two dimensions: exposure to restraint as a consequence for or control of some inappropriate behavior and informal indications that they appeared to enjoy being restrained.

Exposure to restraint was determined in one of two ways. For two residential units serving 85 residents at Western Carolina Center, cottage and individual records were reviewed for the previous 2 years, and a list was compiled of individuals who had either been restrained for a behavior problem such as self-injury at least 10 times within 2 weeks or had been restrained for medical purposes such as following surgery at least five times within a 1-week period. In a 120-client unit at another mental retardation facility, similar information was obtained by asking psychology, medical, and direct-care staff to list residents who met the same criteria.

For each of the 21 individuals who met the criteria for exposure to restraint, at least two staff members who were familiar with that individual independently completed a 5-item rating scale. The rating-scale items were selected from a list of common, informal indicators that restraint is pleasant to a client (Friedin, 1977). Each item was scored on a 5-point rating scale ranging from "always" to "never". The rating scale items were:

1. The client is visibly calm and relaxed while restrained.

2. The client is visibly aroused and disturbed during the release from restraint and/or while unrestrained.

3. When unrestrained, the client searches for restraints and may attempt to remove them from another resident.

4. While unrestrained the client exhibits behaviors suggestive of self-restraint such as placing arms under shirt or sitting on hands.

5. During replacement of restraints the client exhibits cooperative behaviors that facilitate the placement of restraints, such as placing arms in a position to be restrained, or seating self in the restraint chair.

Three of the four individuals who received scores of "always" or "usually" on at least 6 of the 10 rating scale items (5 items × 2 observers) were included in the study so that we could empirically assess the reinforcing function of restraint. One potential subject who met these criteria was excluded because her severe self-injury had been successfully treated and physical restraint discontinued (Favell et al., 1978), and we felt that reintroduction of restraint might increase the probability of self-injurious behavior. With the other participants, the test for the reinforcing function of restraint was designed to be as brief as possible in order to avoid risking increased rates of aggression and/or self-injury.

Parental and Human Rights Advocacy Committee approval were obtained for all participating subjects.

"Jane" (Subject 1)

Characteristics. Jane was 15 years old at the time of the study, a resident of Western Carolina Center, nonverbal, and profoundly retarded (Vineland Social Maturity Scale Age Equivalent = 2.2 years). Retardation was thought to be the result of premature birth. Jane had been institutionalized for 7 years prior to the study and had a long history of various types of inappropriate behavior. At the time of the study, Jane engaged in frequent aggression, self-injury, and pica.

Two years prior to the initiation of this study, Jane had been on a restraint program to suppress aggressive behavior. This program consisted of restraining her in a chair by securing her wrists and waist for 15 minutes, contingent upon each episode of aggression.

One year prior to this study, this program had been judged ineffective and was discontinued. From the time of the program's termination, staff members frequently reported that Jane enjoyed being restrained and consistently attempted to sit in the restraint chair.

Recording and reliability. For Jane, a correct response was defined as placement of a ring on a post within 5 seconds of being handed the item at the start of each trial. The experimenter (the third author) recorded whether a correct response occurred at the end of each trial.

Seven baseline and 11 experimental and control sessions were video taped so that interobserver agreements could be assessed. During sessions in which restraint was applied contingent on correct responses, the restraint consequence was not filmed, so that two naive observers viewing the tapes could not detect the differential characteristics of baseline and experimental conditions. Trial-by-trial agreement between the two observers and the experimenter was calculated by the following formula: number of trials scored the same by all observers divided by total number of trials per session and multiplied by 100. Reliability averaged 98.3 percent (range = 75 to 100 percent).

Procedure and design. Weekday sessions were conducted in an empty classroom, which included a small table, at which Jane and the experimenter sat on opposite sides. A wooden arm chair, that had been fitted with Velcro (registered trademark) fasteners for restraining the wrists and waist, was positioned approximately 3 m from the table, behind Jane's seat.

Each session consisted of 20 trials; during a trial, the experimenter said, "Jane," handed her a stack ring, timed the 5-second time limit, recorded either a correct or incorrect response, then timed a 10-second intertrial interval, and began a new trial. Only the consequence for correct ring placement differed across conditions. During baseline (A) both correct and incorrect responses were ignored. During experimental sessions (B), each correct response resulted in the following restraint procedure: Jane was escorted from the table to the restraint chair, where her wrists and waist were restrained for approximately 45 seconds. Aside from the physical contact involved in restraining Jane, the experimenter did not interact with her, i.e., did not talk to, smile at, or establish eye contact with her. During the first three experimental sessions only, contact with the restraint consequence was ensured by physically prompting Jane to place the ring on the post and restraining her

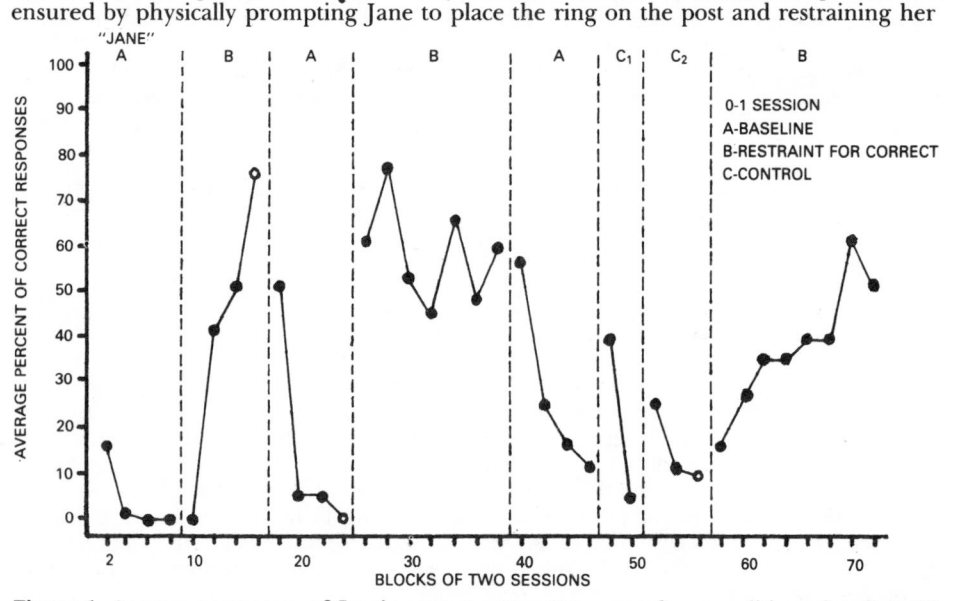

Figure 1. Average percentage of Jane's correct responses across three conditions: baseline (A) sessions in which correct responses were ignored, experimental (B) sessions in which each correct response resulted in restraint, and control (C) sessions in which correct responses were followed by the nonrestraint components of the restraint consequence.

briefly. These prompted trials were conducted after every fourth incorrect response and were not included in the data for these sessions.

Two control conditions were employed to determine whether characteristics of the restraint consequence, other than the restraint itself, might account for changes in performance. The first control condition (C1) was included to determine whether movement from the table where trials were conducted to a chair positioned away from the table (in place of the restraint chair) and the brief timeout from the task would affect Jane's performance. In C1, following each correct response, Jane was seated in a blue plastic arm chair for 45 seconds, and the experimenter manipulated her arms as if restraining her but did not actually apply the restraints.

The second control condition (C2) was included to determine whether some characteristic of the restraint chair itself could account for changes in performance. This condition was conducted in a manner identical to C1, except that the actual restraint chair was used.

A reversal design was employed, with a manipulation of conditions in the following sequence: A, B, A, B, A, C1, C2, B.

Results. Figure 1 shows the average percentage of correct ring placements for blocks of two sessions (open circles represent data from a single session) across baseline (A) and experimental (B) and control (C) conditions. (The average of two successive sessions was used where possible simply to condense and simplify the graph and accurately reflects performance within each session.) Results indicate that when correct responses were followed by restraint, they systematically increased over levels observed during either baseline or control conditions, when restraint was not employed.

"Don" (Subject 2)

Characteristics. Don was 29 years old at the time of the study, a resident of Western Carolina Center, a nonverbal, and profoundly retarded (Vineland Age Equivalent = 3.2 years). Prior to admission at Western Carolina, he had a 4-year history of being continuously restrained in rigid arm splints and in a camisole to prevent self-injurious head slapping and face scratching. During his 13 years at Western Carolina Center, Don's only encounter with physical restraint had been a 2-week period following a head injury, during which time he was required to wear a protective helmet.

At the time of the study, Don's self-injurious behavior was not considered to be a problem; however, there were frequent reports of Don attempting self-restraint. This usually involved wrapping his arms in whatever cloth was available (e.g., bed linen or his shirt).

Recording and reliability. A preference measure was employed. On each trial Don was allowed to select which of two chairs to sit in. A selection was defined as crossing a line that was 3 cm in front of each chair. The experimenter (the second author) recorded which chair Don selected on each trial.

During one of the four sessions, a naïve observer recorded this information simultaneously with but independently of the experimenter. Trial-by-trial agreement was 100 percent.

Procedure and design. The reinforcing function of restraint was assessed in four sessions ranging from 20 to 36 trials, by a discrete trial-preference procedure; in each trial Don was allowed to choose between sitting for 30 seconds while being physically restrained or sitting for 30 seconds unrestrained. Sessions were conducted in a room with two identical chairs, spaced approximately 2 m apart. An assistant stood behind each chair. Each assistant remained behind the same chair during all sessions. During the first three sessions, one held a white sheet, the other a patterned sheet. As an aid in discriminating in which chair (left or right) the restraint was available, the white sheet was used for restraining Don, the patterned sheet was not. During the fourth session, the patterned sheet was replaced by a white one to control for the possibility that material color rather than restraint itself controlled Don's preference.

At the start of each trial, the experimenter placed Don 2 m in front of and equidistant

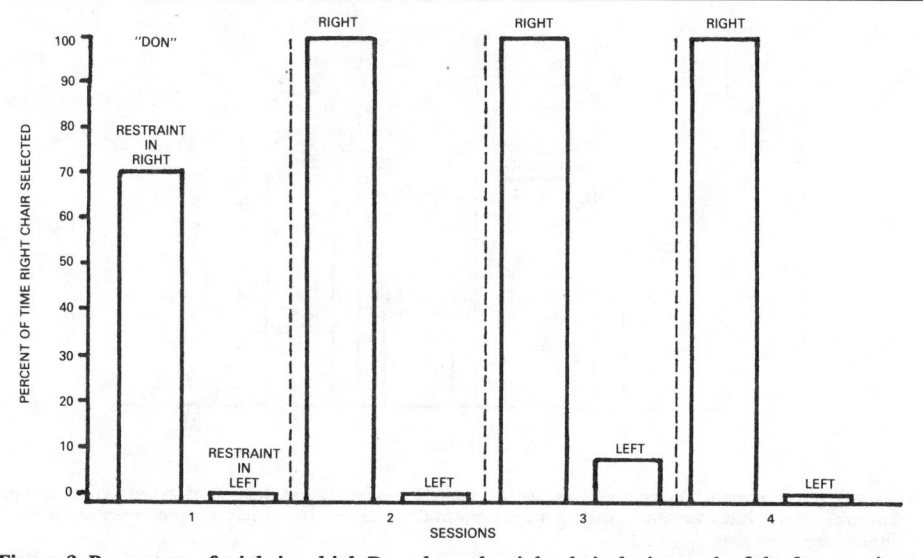

Figure 2. Percentage of trials in which Don chose the right chair during each of the four sessions, when it alternately served as the restraint chair (left bar in each session) and as the nonrestraint chair (right bar).

from the chairs and prompted him to select a chair by directing his head toward each in turn, then speaking his name, and touching his back. When Don selected a chair (i.e., crossed the line in front of it), he was seated in that chair by the assistant. If he selected the "restraint" chair, the sheet was wrapped tightly around his arms and shoulders for 30 seconds. If Don selected the "nonrestraint" chair, he was briefly touched on the arms and shoulders (to provide physical contact equal to that involved in applying the physical restraint), handed the sheet, and allowed to sit for 30 seconds. After 30 seconds in either chair, Don was returned to the point between the two chairs, and after a 30-second intertrial interval, another trial was begun.

The location of the restraint consequence was alternated between the left and right chairs to control for position and assistant preference. The position of restraint was alternated between the chairs after an average of every five trials in the first three sessions and after an average of two trials in Session 4. To ensure that Don came in contact with the consequences, several series of four "forced-choice" trials were given; i.e., during two trials the experimenter seated Don in the restraint chair and restrained him, and during two alternating trials, the experimenter seated him in the nonrestraint chair. (Forced choices were not counted in the preference data.) These forced-choice trials were conducted at the beginning of each of the first three sessions and before every switch in the position of the restraint consequence (i.e., after every two trials) in the fourth session.

Results. Figure 2 shows the percentage of trials Don chose the right chair during each of the four sessions when it alternately served as the restraint chair (left bar in each session) and as the nonrestraint chair (right bar). In Session 1, when restraint was available in the right chair, Don chose that chair 71 percent of the time. During that same session when the restraint consequence was alternately shifted to the left chair, he chose that chair 100 percent of the time, shown on the graph as 0 percent preference for the right chair. With all sessions combined, the overall preference for the chair in which restraint was available was 95 percent.

"Lee" (Subject 3)

Characteristics. Lee was 30 years old at the time of the study, a resident of Caswell Center, nonverbal, deaf, blind, and profoundly retarded (Stanford-Binet Intelligence Scale IQ = 30). He had a 9-year history of being continuously restrained in a variety of devices, including a camisole, arm splints, and a wrist-to-waist belt, to prevent self-injurious head

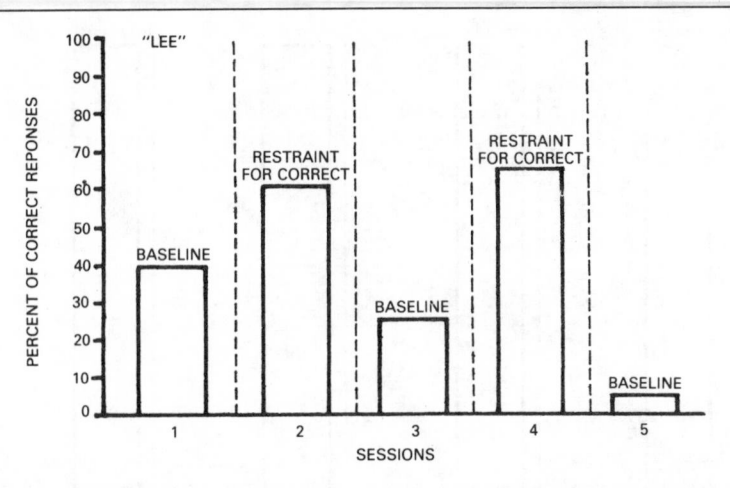

Figure 3. Percentage of correct sitting responses by Lee during baseline sessions in which correct responses were ignored and during experimental sessions in which correct responses were followed by restraint.

slapping. At the time of the study, Lee engaged in low-intensity headslapping at a rate of approximately three responses per minute and was almost continually restrained.

Recording and reliability. For Lee, a correct response was defined as sitting down in a chair within 5 seconds of a tactile cue. The experimenter (the second author) recorded whether a correct response occurred at the end of each trial.

One of the baseline sessions and one of the experimental sessions were video taped (with the restraint consequence deleted) so that interobserver reliability could be assessed. Trial-by-trial agreement between a naïve observer and the experimenter was 100 percent.

Procedure and design. Five 15-minute sessions, each consisting of 20 trials, were conducted during a one day period in Lee's living unit. During each trial, the experimenter cued Lee to sit by touching the back of his legs with a chair, timed a 5-second time limit, recorded a correct or incorrect response, then timed a 40-second intertrial interval, assisted Lee to stand, and began a new trial. During baseline, Lee wore wrist-to-waist belt restraints on his wrists, but these were not secured to his belt. Correct sitting responses during baseline were ignored. During experimental sessions, correct responses resulted in 30 seconds of restraint during the 40-second intertrial interval. Restraint consisted of bringing the wrists to the belt by shortening the strap connecting them. No personal contact was involved in this process. Baseline and experimental conditions were alternated in an ABAB reversal design.

Results. Figure 3 shows the percentage of correct sitting responses across baseline and experimental sessions. Results indicated that when physical restraint was applied contingent on correct responses, these systematically increased to an average of 62.5 percent in comparison to baseline levels of 23 percent when correct responses were ignored.

Discussion

Results indicated that physical restraint was a positive reinforcer for all of the three retarded individuals who had been exposed to physical restraint and had indicated informally that restraint was enjoyable.

In this demonstration we employed three different restraint devices and individuals who had been restrained for different behavior problems, i.e., self-injury and aggression. The type and duration of history with restraint also differed; e.g., Jane had been on a 6-month program of contingent restraint for her behavior problem, and Don and Lee had been subjected to prolonged, noncontingent restraint. Thus, the generality of restraint as a reinforcer was established across a variety of parameters for the population selected.

Although the durability of the reinforcing effects of restraint were only examined with Subject 1, results indicated that the effects were maintained over the 70 sessions of the investigation with that subject.

The present study provides information on the function of restraint and the generality of its effects as a reinforcer for the subpopulation of individuals who appear to enjoy restraint. It does not address the generality of restraint as a reinforcer for all developmentally disabled persons who have been exposed to restraint. Further research is needed to determine the prevalence of the effect across this broader population.

In the absence of such actuarial data, it appears reasonable to assume that the number of clients for whom restraint is a reinforcer is relatively small (3 of 21 clients in the present study); however, the management and treatment of these clients is inordinately difficult. Often they are the most severely self-injurious or aggressive and in many cases are chronically restrained. For such individuals, the present findings have several implications. First, restraint itself may be at least partially reponsible for increasing and maintaining their self-injury or aggression, since it is consistently used to terminate episodes of such behavior. Further, as the behavior problem is reinforced and increases, the need for restraining the individual increases. Thus, individuals gradually evolve into chronic restraint. Second, the reinforcing power of restraint may be responsible for the relative lack of success of nonaversive treatment procedures (such as differential reinforcement of other behavior), since these are often employed in conjunction with continued use of physical restraint to terminate severe problem behavior. Thus, the therapeutic effects of treatment may be competing with the continued reinforcement of the problem.

For all clients, the present research underlines the importance of analyzing the function of any generally applied technique prior to, or very early in treatment, instead of assuming that a given technique has similar functions with all individuals. Physical restraint specifically may be neutral or punishing (Hamilton et al., 1967) or may instead be a positive reinforcer; its function must be empirically determined in each instance.

The need for an individual empirical validation of the effects of a procedure before employing it in treatment suggests the need for economical and valid diagnostic and prescriptive tools. In the present study, although no formal effort was undertaken to establish the predictive validity of the rating scale, it is of interest that for all the clients rated as enjoying restraint, restraint was indeed established as a reinforcer in subsequent empirical tests. Such a finding raises the prospect that a formally validated rating scale could be used prior to treatment to predict the function of restraint and, thus, how it might be used in treatment. The ease of administration of a rating scale over the more arduous process of actually applying the restraint as a consequence for an arbitrary response supports the importance of proceeding with validation efforts.

When confronted with an individual for whom restraint is reinforcing, it is probably difficult, if not impossible, to identify what factors in that individual's history account for such an effect. Such was the case with the subjects in the present research, whose records documented exposure to restraint but provided no information on contingencies or conditions possibly responsible for establishing restraint as a reinforcer. In research now ongoing, however, we are experimentally analyzing what environmental conditions may establish restraint as a reinforcer, for purposes of either preventing it from becoming one or eliminating its reinforcing function with individuals for whom it is already a reinforcer. The two most likely hypotheses are that restraint is paired with positive reinforcement (such as caretaker attention) or with escape or avoidance of aversive situations (such as training demands or crowded, noisy environments). Our ongoing research suggests that when either positive reinforcement or escape from aversive conditions (negative reinforcement) is paired with a benign analogue to restraint (such as cloth sleeves substituted for rigid arm splints), individuals will respond to obtain the "restraint" (sleeves). The clinical point is that physical restraint should not be differentially associated with increased positive reinforcement such as attention or removal of aversive situations. Thus, practitioners should ensure that there are relatively higher rates of positive reinforcement out of restraint than in. Similarly, demands and other aversive environmental aspects should be equalized in and out of restraint or, indeed, be increased under restraint conditions. Procedures such as these may be useful in preventing restraint from becoming a reinforcer or reversing its reinforcing function, so that individuals will not engage in self-injury or aggression to obtain physical restraint.

A third strategy may apply to the group of individuals referred to previously, who perhaps represent the greatest challenge to our present technology and resources: those who engage in extremely dangerous behavior and who, through the failure of many therapeutic attempts, are now maintained in near chronic restraint. For members of this group for whom restraint is already a reinforcer, the reinforcing function may be used to treat self-injury in a nonaversive way, by applying it contingent upon gradually increasing periods of noninjury (or nonaggression). In a study cited previously, Favell et al. (1978) demonstrated the effectiveness of just such an approach in reducing severe self-injury. We stress, however, that the use of physical restraint as a consequence for either noninjury (or nonaggression) or more appropriate behavior would only be indicated when more conventional reinforcers are ineffective and probably only when the client is presently maintained (at least partially) on a restraint regime. The present results and proper ethical practice do not support the use of restraint as a reinforcer when other "less aberrant" reinforcers can be identified or with individuals whose problems do not also include a dependency on restraint.

Reference Note

1. Schroeder, S. *The analysis of self-injurious behavior: Pathogenesis and treatment* (Final Grant Report). DDSA H.I.P. Grant No. 51-P-20521, 1977.

References

Favell, J., McGimsey, J., Jones, M. The use of physical restraint in the treatment of self-injury and as positive reinforcement. *J. Appl. Behav. Anal.*, 1978; **11**, 225-241.

Friedin, B. Clinical issues on the physical restraint experience with self-injurious children. *Res. & Retard.*, 1977; **4**, 1-6.

Hamilton, H., Stevens, L., Allen, P. Controlling aggressive and destructive behavior in severely retarded institutionalized residents. *Am. J. Ment. Defic.*, 1967; **71**, 852-856.

Jones, F., Simmons, J., Frankel, F. An extinction procedure for eliminating self-destructive behavior in a nine-year-old autistic girl. *J. Autism & Child. Schiz.*, 1974; **4**, 241-250.

Lovaas, O. I., Simmons, J. Q. Manipulation of self-destruction in three retarded children. *J. Appl. Behav. Anal.*, 1969; **2**, 143-157.

Myers, J., Deibert, A. Reduction of self-abusive behavior in a blind child by using a feeding response. *J. Behav. Ther. & Experi. Psychiat.*, 1971; **2**, 141-144.

Tate, B. G. Case study: Control of chronic self-injurious behavior by conditioning procedures. *Behav. Ther.*, 1972; **3**, 72-83.

Tate, B. G., Baroff, G. S. Aversive control of self-injurious behavior in a psychotic boy. *Behav. Res. & Ther.*, 1966; **4**, 281-287.

Reprinted from *Am. J. Ment. Defic.*, 1981; **85**:4, 425-432 by kind permission of the authors and the publishers American Association on Mental Deficiency, Washington DC 20009.

PROTECTIVE EQUIPMENT: CONTINUOUS AND CONTINGENT APPLICATION IN THE TREATMENT OF SELF-INJURIOUS BEHAVIOR

Michael F. Dorsey, Brian A. Iwata, Dennis H. Reid, Patricia A. Davis

Temple University — Woodhaven Program, The John F. Kennedy Institute and the Johns Hopkins University School of Medicine, and Northern Indiana State Hospital and Developmental Disabilities Center

This study evaluated the use of protective equipment in treating self-injurious behavior (SIB) exhibited by three retarded persons. In experiment 1, the equipment was first applied continuously during 20-min sessions in individual multiple baseline designs across settings. Results showed substantial reductions in head hitting, eye gouging, and hand biting. Brief periods of time-out with the protective equipment were later made contingent on SIB and combined with a differential reinforcement procedure. Reduced levels of SIB was maintained with all subjects. Additionally, the amount of time during which the equipment was applied decreased as the SIB diminished. Experiment 2 evaluated the use of contingent protective equipment (the final condition in Experiment 1) when applied directly in the subjects' living units during the day. During Experiment 2, SIB remained at or below the levels found at the termination of Experiment 1. Finally, in an effort to assess the long-term effectiveness of the procedure responsibility for implementation was given to the staff who were typically assigned to provide therapy to the subjects. Follow-up probe observations conducted up to 104 days after termination of the final experimental condition showed continued low levels of both SIB and equipment usage. Results of these experiments suggest that contingent protective equipment and differential reinforcement may be effective in reducing chronic self-injury.

DESCRIPTORS: retardation, self-injurious behavior, protective equipment, restraint, time-out.

The reduction and maintenance of self-injurious behavior present major problems, both in terms of habilitative programming as well as protecting individuals from self-inflicted harm. The use of mechanical restraint devices has become the most prevalent method of control and protection of self-injurious persons clients (Schroeder, Note 1). Unfortunately, many forms of restraint have been noted to cause long-term negative side effects such as demineralization of bones, shortening of tendons, and arrested motor development, secondary to disuse of the restrained individual's limbs (Lovaas & Simmons, 1969). The restraint of physical movement may also interfere with other client training goals (Rojahn, Schroeder, & Mulick, 1980). Problems such as these have become the basis for a number of legal and regulatory controls limiting the use of restraint (Joint Commission on Accreditation of Hospitals, 1975).

Despite the attention paid to restraint devices in applied settings, research regarding their use in programs designed to eliminate self-injury has been relatively limited. A review of this literature suggests a variety of therapeutic uses for restraint, including applications as consequence (Favell, McGimsey, & Jones, 1978; Favell, McGimsey, Jones, & Cannon,

This study was approved by both university and institutional human subjects committees, as well as the administrative staff of the institution and local school district. We thank Robert Crow for his continued administrative support, Marilyn Bezeredy, Steve Coleman, and Thomas Pritzel for their assistance in conducting the study, and Arthur Snapper, Paul Weiner, and Wayne Fuqua for their assistance in preparing an earlier dissertation version of the manuscript. Reprints may be obtained from either Michael F. Dorsey, Temple University, Woodhaven Program, 2900 Southampton Road, Philadelphia, Pennsylvania 19154; or Brian A. Iwata, Division of Behavioral Psychology, The John F. Kennedy Institute, 707 North Broadway, Baltimore, Maryland 21205.

1981; Hamilton, Stephens, & Allen, 1967; Rapoff, Altman, & Christophersen, 1980) as well as antecedent events (Parrish, Aguerrevere, Dorsey, & Iwata, 1980; Rojahn, Mulick, McCoy, & Schroeder, 1978), and both as punishing (Hamilton et al., 1967; Rapoff, et al., 1980) as well as reinforcing stimuli (Favell et al., 1978, 1981). Hamilton et al. (1967) reported the use of a time-out procedure involving a padded restraint chair for periods ranging from 30 min to 2 hrs, with five individuals who engaged in self-injurious and aggressive behaviors. Rapoff et al. (1980) presented a case study of a 7-yr-old blind child who engaged in self hitting. A 30-sec period of physical restraint was used successfully in the elimination of her self-injury. Favell et al. (1978), on the other hand, described the successful use of restraint, contingent upon the *absence* of self-injury, for three profoundly retarded persons. Because their results suggested that restraint functioned as a reinforcer, Favell et al. (1981) conducted a subsequent experiment in which contingent restraint was found to increase appropriate toy play.

Two studies have examined the antecedent effects of restraint upon self-injury. Rojahn et al. (1978) reported the successful use of adaptive jackets with large pockets, designed to allow appropriate "self-restraint," in the reduction of self-injury. Parrish et al. (1980) investigated the effects of a padded football helmet on rates of head hitting in a profoundly retarded client. During a series of brief reversal periods, an average of 60 responses per min occurred during non-helmet periods as compared with 5 responses per min during periods with the helmet on.

The results of the Parrish et al. (1980) study lend some support to the position that many forms of behavior, which appear to provide no external consequence, may be maintained by their sensory-stimulating properties (Carr, 1977). Research by Rincover, Cook, Peoples, and Packard (1979) and Rincover (1978) with children exhibiting self-stimuatory behavior suggests that an apparatus designed to attenuate or mask sensory stimulation derived from a specific response may create an extinction effect, causing a reduction in retarded children's self-stimulatory behavior. This analysis seemingly may be applied to self-injury. Clearly, many forms of self-injury are topographically similar to self-stimulatory behavior, and may occur in the absence of identifiable reinforcement contingencies. For example, in assessing the differential effects of environment on the self-injurious behavior of nine subjects, Iwata, Dorsey, Slifer, Bauman, and Richman (1982) found that four exhibited higher levels of self-injury in a situation where opportunities for social stimulation and reinforcement were absent, and external sources of physical stimulation were minimized (i.e., toys and other manipulable items were unavailable). The major difference between self-injury and self-stimulatory behavior is that the immediate or long-term effect of self-injury is some form of physical trauma. Thus, a procedure that either attenuates or masks the self-stimulatory components of self-injury and, at the same time, protects the client from the deleterious results of the behavior, might prove to be both clinically effective and medically safe.

The initial focus of the present research was to extend previous work by Dorsey, Iwata, Ong, and McSween (1980), in assessing the effects of a punishing stimulus — a water mist applied to the face — across time and settings. This procedure was found ineffective in reducing self-injury during the initial stages of treatment with one subject. Rather than using more intrusive measures (e.g., electric shock), the purpose of the research was altered to evaluate the effects of equipment designed to protect the individual from self-inflicted harm, and potentially attenuate the sensory stimulation which occurred as a result of the self-injurious behaviors. Additionally, the study investigated the maintenance of reduced levels of self-injury via the use of response-contingent application of the apparatus combined with a differential reinforcement procedure.

EXPERIMENT 1

Method

Participants

Three retarded clients of a state residential facility participated in this study. Selection was based upon a display of a high rate of behaviors considered to be self-injurious. Each resident was considered to be a chronic self-abuser whose behavior resulted in some form of tissue damage. Previous unsuccessful attempts at eliminating these behaviors included differential reinforcement, overcorrection, restraint, time-out, and various drugs.

Ron was a 16-yr-old male, institutionalized since the age of 2. His primary diagnosis was profound mental retardation due to encephalopathy, secondary to a prenatal injury that caused anoxia. He had impaired hearing and vision and was nonambulatory. His medical records indicated a history and variety of SIBs, with head hitting and hand biting being predominant. Physical damage, consisting of scalp nodules (i.e., subdural hematomas) and abrasions of the skin resulted from his SIB.

Marjie was a 16-yr-old female, institutionalized since the age of 6. Her primary diagnosis was severe mental retardation of undetermined causes, combined with congenital glaucoma. She was ambulatory and seemed to have normal hearing. Medical records indicated a long history of self-injurious behaviors, including inserting her fingers into her eye sockets, hand biting, and head hitting. Superficial cuts, calluses, and scar tissue resulted from the hand biting behavior while reddened areas and scar tissue around her face and eyes occurred as a result of the other behaviors.

James was a 14-yr-old male, institutionalized since the age of 4. His primary diagnosis was severe mental retardation secondary to rubella during pregnancy, combined with a severe loss of vision. He was ambulatory and had a hearing impairment. His target behavior was eye gouging — inserting his index finger into the eye socket between the eye ball and eye lid to approximately the second knuckle. This resulted in swelling to both the eyeball and the tissue within the eye socket. Medical records indicated that James had fractured a cataract as a result of this behavior.

Setting

Two daily sessions were conducted individually with each client. Afternoon sessions were held in the day area of the institution's living unit, while morning sessions were conducted in the day area for Ron and James, and in a special education classroom at a local public school for Marjie. The day areas measured approximately 5.8 × 5.8 m, and were used as activity areas in which residents spent time while not engaged in other structured activities. Sessions were conducted by both institution psychology staff and paraprofessionals hired through the Comprehensive Employment and Training Act (CETA) program. Immediate supervision was provided by the first author.

Observation

Response definitions were as follows:

1. Head Hitting. Striking the head with any portion of the hand, or (during treatment sessions) contact of a glove with the helmet (Ron and Marjie).

2. Hand Biting. Insertion of the hand into the mouth, or (during treatment sessions) contact of a glove with the face mask (Ron and Marjie).

3. Eye Gouging. Contact of the fingers with the skin within the orbit of the eye, or insertion of the fingers into the eye socket; or (during treatment sessions) contact of a glove with the face mask (Marjie and James).

4. Toy Play. Physical contact with available toys in which a toy was elevated manually from the floor or table by the participant a minimum of 1 in (Ron).

Occurrences of these behaviors and the use of protective equipment were recorded during non-continuous intervals in which the observer recorded the behavior for five consecutive 10-sec intervals and rested during the sixth, using a partial interval observation procedure (Powell, Martindale, & Kulp, 1975). A cassette tape containing prerecorded prompts was used to indicate the beginning of each interval. The percentage of intervals during which the target responses and/or use of the equipment occurred was obtained by dividing the positively scored intervals by the total number of intervals and multiplying by 100. All sessions were of a constant 20-min length for each participant.

Observations were conducted by the trainer assigned to the session. Observers were trained through instructions and modeling, and each achieved a minimum criterion of 90% reliability with the first author prior to formal data collection.

Reliability

Interobserver agreement on the target behaviors and protective equipment usage was assessed during 23% of the total sessions, distributed across all participants and conditions.

During sessions in which reliability was assessed, data were collected by both the trainer assigned to that session and an independent observer. Agreement percentages were calculated on an interval by interval basis by dividing the number of agreements on the occurrence or nonoccurrence of the behavior and/or equipment usage by the number of agreements plus disagreements and multiplying by 100. Scores ranged from 87% to 100% (mean = 90%) for agreements of occurrence and 80% to 100% (mean = 95%) for agreements of nonoccurrence for Marjie; 68% to 100% (mean = 91%) for agreements of occurrence and 33% to 100% (mean = 97%) for agreements for nonoccurrence for Ron; and 88% to 100% (mean = 99%) for agreements of occurrence and 66% to 100% (mean = 99%) for agreements of nonoccurrence for James. Lower occurrence agreement scores were obtained during sessions in which relatively few occurrences of the target behaviors were recorded (e.g., 68% occurrence reliability for Ron in session 61 [unit] with SIB = 28%).

Procedure

Baseline. Target behaviors were observed and recorded during individual sessions for each participant. No contingencies were applied to the target responses. Clients were not involved in educational or recreational activities at this time, with the exception of Marjie during school sessions, and the observers did not interact with the clients. Marjie's teacher was instructed to treat her as she had in the past relative to the target behaviors, as well as all academic tasks.

Reinforced toy play plus verbal reprimand. Four to five toys, selected from those available on the clients' living units, were placed within reach of each participant during this condition. Social praise and edibles (e.g., cookies, M&Ms) were provided on a 30-sec schedule contingent upon toy play, and the absence of SIB. Each occurrence of self-injurious behavior was followed by a verbal "no" from the trainer in a forceful but normal speaking voice (American Sign Language was used with James).

Reinforced toy play plus verbal reprimand plus mist. Social and edible reinforcement were provided contingent on contact with toys in a manner identical to that described previously. In addition, the verbal reprimand provided in the previous condition was paired with a fine mist of water directed toward the client's face contingent upon the occurrence of a target SIB. The mist was delivered from a standard plant sprayer and the method of application was identical to that described by Dorsey et al. (1980).

Continuous protective equipment. At the beginning of each session, an apparatus was placed on the client designed to prevent injury and possibly attenuate the tactile stimulation received as a result of the SIB. Due to the topographical similarities of the behaviors, a combination of foam padded gloves and a football helmet lined with additional foam padding was used for all participants. The equipment did not fully prevent participants from engaging in the target responses, but did prevent injury from resulting. For example, Ron could continue to engage in a head hitting and/or hand biting response with the apparatus on by striking the football helmet with the foam-padded gloves, or biting the gloves. The apparatus remained in place throughout each session during this condition.

Two-minute protective time-out plus sensory stimulating toy play. Contingent upon the occurrence of a target SIB, the protective equipment was applied for a period of 2 min, and the toys provided were removed. The contingent use of the protective equipment was based on results obtained during the continuous protective equipment condition and the hypothesis that if antecedent application suppressed SIB, consequent application might also be effective. The equipment was left in place until 30 sec had elapsed with no SIB. Due to the fact that the clients were physically restrained from responding during the application and removal of the apparatus, data were not collected during these periods and the session length was increased to compensate for this lost time. In the absence of SIB, continuous access was provided to toys designed to provide sensory stimulation within the same sensory modality as their SIB. Again, due to the topographical similarities of Ron and Marjie's SIBs, the same types of toys were provided to both participants (e.g., a hand puppet with a battery operated vibrator enclosed, Busy Box), while James was provided with visually stimulating toys (e.g., a flashlight, mirrors).

Experimental Designs

Multiple baseline designs (Baer, Wolf, & Risley, 1968) across settings were used for each client. Following initial baselines in both morning and afternoon sessions, the reinforced toy play and verbal reprimand condition was introduced simultaneously in both sessions for Ron. Next, the verbal reprimand was combined with the water mist during afternoon sessions while a return to baseline was introduced in the morning sessions. These conditions were implemented for two reasons: (a) to establish the verbal reprimand as a conditioned punisher (first setting) and (b) to allow for a functional relationship between the treatment and behavior to be demonstrated later. Next, the continuous protective equipment condition was implemented, first in the afternoon and later in the morning sessions. This was done to evaluate the effects of the protective equipment prior to beginning the sensory stimulating toy-play condition. Finally, the two minute protective time-out plus sensory stimulating toy play condition was introduced in a multiple baseline fashion across sessions.

Two deviations from this basic design were made for Marjie. The reinforced toy play plus verbal reprimand plus mist condition was not conducted. Additionally the continuous protective equipment condition was implemented only in the first setting. These changes were made for two reasons . First, the water mist procedure was dropped because Marjie had a history of aggressive reactions to water. Second, the *continuous protective equipment* condition was withheld from the second setting to control for possible sequence effects between this and the final condition.

Finally, one additional deviation from the original design was made for James. Prior to the use of the protective equipment, access to sensory stimulating toys was made available to James throughout the session as long as no SIB occurred. The toys were removed contingent upon the occurrence of SIB, plus an additional 30 sec change over delay. This change was implemented to control for the possibility that the sensory stimulating toys alone would act to control SIB, without the need for protective equipment.

Results and discussions

Data for Ron, Marjie and James, expressed as percent intervals of total SIB, are presented in Figures 1, 2, and 3, respectively. Participants typically exhibited high rates of SIB during baseline. Ron's SIB was highly variable throughout baseline, and no particular events could be identified to account for either high or low levels of responding. Inconsistent changes in responding were noted during the initial treatment conditions. The mean changes in behavior were as follows: Ron's SIB increased from 33.8% and 34.4% in the afternoon and morning baseline sessions to 81.8% and 60% upon implementation of the verbal reprimand and reinforced toy play condition. Marjie's SIB, however, decreased from 87.7% to 79.1% with the introduction of the same procedure. Use of the water mist procedure reduced Ron's SIB from 81.8% to 34.6%. Finally, the use of contingent access to sensory stimulating toys reduced James' SIB from 92% to 73%. Similar changes were noted in other conditions, in that none of the initial attempts at eliminating the clients' SIB resulted in clinically significant reductions.

Upon implementation of the continuous protective equipment conditions, SIB decreased noticeably for all three participants. For example, Ron's SIB was reduced from 34.6% to 8.3% in the afternoon sessions and from 90% to 3.6% in the morning sessions. Marjie's SIB decreased from a mean of 79.1% to 18%, and James' from 73% to 4%. Across all participants, SIB was reduced from the mean of the prior conditions of 69.4% to a treatment mean of 8.5%. During the last five days of treatment, SIB across all participants averaged 1.25% with a range of 0.0% to 6%.

The final change in treatment to the two minute protective time-out plus sensory stimulating toy play condition was effective in maintaining low levels of SIB, and reduced the percentage of time which clients were exposed to the protective equipment. SIB for this condition averaged 11.7% in the afternoon sessions and 18.6% in the morning sessions for Ron, 14.7% on the unit and 12% in school for Marjie, and 1.2% in the afternoon and 0.7% in the morning for James. The last five days of treatment for Ron showed SIB averaging 2.6% in the afternoon sessions and 9.4% in the morning sessions, while Marjie had a mean of 11.2% SIB for the last five days of treatment on the unit and 7.8% in school, while James remained at 0.0% during both a.m. and p.m. sessions over the last five days of treatment.

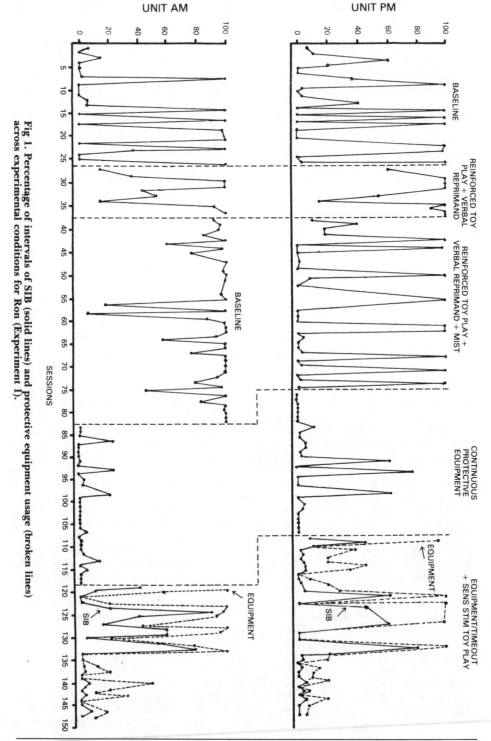

PERCENT 10 SEC. INTERVALS

Fig 1. Percentage of intervals of SIB (solid lines) and protective equipment usage (broken lines) across experimental conditions for Ron (Experiment 1).

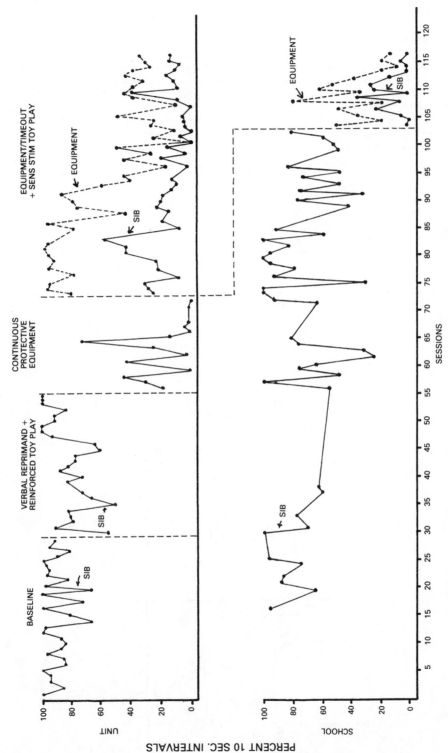

Fig 2. Percentage of intervals of SIB (solid lines) and protective equipment usage (broken lines) across experimental conditions for Marjie (Experiment 1).

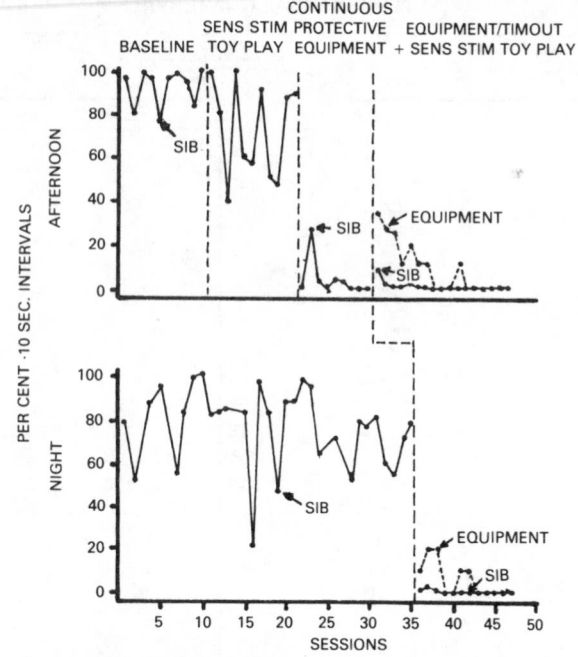

Fig 3. Percentage of intervals of SIB (solid lines) and protective equipment usage (broken lines) across experimental conditions for James (Experiment 1).

Similar results can be noted for the percentage of time the participants were exposed to the protective equipment. The mean percentage of time that clients spent wearing the equipment during this condition was: 29.9% in the afternoon sessions and 39.7% in the morning sessions for Ron, 50.9% on the unit and 35.4% at school for Marjie, and 9.7% in the afternoon and 6.0% in the morning for James. As with the SIB data, these means do not accurately reflect descending trends noted for all three participants. For example, the means for the last five days of treatment for Ron were 9.4% in the afternoon sessions and 13.6% in the morning sessions.

One possible explanation for the procedure's suppressive effect on behavior is that the weight of the gloves may have increased the "response effort" of SIB. Alternatively, the wearing and/or corresponded to reductions in SIB. Ron was in striking of the helmet alone may have had punishing properties. In order to evaluate these confounding variables, several pre- and posttreatment probes were conducted with Ron, on session days 113, 114, and 115, in which only the gloves or only the helmet was applied. In all cases, Ron engaged in this particular SIB at rates comparable to those observed during the initial baseline, averaging 73% SIB with the helmet alone and 92% with the gloves alone across three sessions.

Within the present experiment little data can be provided to demonstrate the establishment of behavioral alternatives to SIB (i.e., toy play). Although this was an initial goal of the present research, final use of the data collected toward this end was not possible due to a particular flaw in the observation procedure. Specifically, "toy play" was initially defined as "physical contact with available toys involving their manual elevation from the floor or wheelchair table a minimum of 1 in." The purpose of this particular definition was to exclude instances in which participants merely rested an arm or hand upon the toy. However, such a definition precluded the recording of many appropriate "toy play" responses in subsequent sensory stimulating toy play conditions. That is, when presented with a toy that provided the client with the same stimulation regardless of the topography of his or her interactions with it, the highest probability response would be the one with the least effort (i.e., resting an arm or hand on the toy). In order to prevent confounding the

Table 1. Mean percentage of toy play and self-injurious behavior by condition for Ron.

Condition	Afternoon Sessions	
	Toy Play	SIB
Baseline	No Toys Available	
Reinforced Toy Play + Verbal Reprimand	2	81.8
Reinforced Toy Play + Verbal Reprimand + Mist	14	34.6
Continuous Protective Equipment	No Toys Available	
Two Minute Protective Time-out + Sensory Stimulating Toy Play	19	11.7

Condition	Morning Sessions	
	Toy Play	SIB
Baseline	No Toys Available	
Reinforced Toy Play + Verbal Reprimand	3	91
Baseline	No Toys Available	
Continuous Protective Equipment	No Toys Available	
Two Minute Protective Time-out + Sensory Stimulating Toy Play	12	18.6

data by changing definitions across conditions, this particular response was eliminated from the observational system at the conclusion of treatment for Ron (both Marjie and James were involved at some earlier point in the study at the time the definitional problem was discovered, eliminating the possibility of correcting the problem for either of them). Data using this definition of "toy play" for Ron are presented on Table 1, expressed as the mean percentage of intervals across conditions. As the table shows, Ron engaged in the highest levels of toy play during the final protective time-out plus sensory stimulating toy play condition during both morning and afternoon sessions. Although problems do exist with these data, it is interesting to note that SIB and toy play appeared to be inversively related. Finally, subjective observations of all three participants suggested that interactions with the various toys did increase as a function of the introduction of sensory stimulating toys in the final condition.

Results of Experiment 1 indicate that protective equipment may be a useful treatment for SIB. However, the results are limited because of the short duration of experimental sessions, as well as the specialized training of the staff who implemented the procedure. Experiment 2 was designed to assess the effects of the treatment implemented in more naturalistic settings across a longer period of the day by staff normally employed on institutional wards.

EXPERIMENT 2

Method

Participants and Settings

Ron, Marjie, and James also participated in this study. Daily sessions were conducted individually within their day area, bedroom, and dining room, beginning approximately 1 mo after the conclusion of Experiment 1. Sessions were run Monday through Friday, from the time each client returned to the center from school (3:00 p.m.) until bedtime (8:00 p.m.). No attempt was made to isolate the participants from environmental distractions or to restrict their normal daily schedule. Therapists were three CETA/grant employees, one assigned to each participant. During follow-up observations, procedures were conducted by direct care staff of the institution.

Observation

Response definitions were identical to those used in Experiment 1. The occurrence of these behaviors and the application of the protective equipment were recorded using a partial interval observation procedure (Powell et al., 1975). Observations were conducted daily, with behavior sampled for six continuous 10-sec intervals every 15 min.

Reliability

Reliability on the occurrence of the target behaviors and the use of the protective equipment was assessed during all conditions by assigning two observers to record independent observations a minimum of four days per week, overlapping 2-3 observation periods per participant. Results were calculated as described previously. Scores ranged from 91% to 97% (mean = 94%) for occurrence and 80% to 100% (mean = 97%) for nonoccurrence.

Procedure

Baseline. Target behaviors were recorded daily for each participant during regularly scheduled activities. Examples included games, crafts, outside play, and involvement with nursing or rehabilitation staff in various therapies. No experimenter-controlled contingencies were in effect for the target responses during this condition. Staff were informed that data were being collected and were instructed to interact with the clients as they had previously. Examples of contingencies currently in effect were: nonsystematic differential reinforcement procedures, response interruption, verbal reprimands, and physical prompting of other behaviors.

Two minute protection time-out plus contingent sensory stimulating toy play. Contingent upon the occurrence of SIB, the apparatuses used in Experiment 1 were placed on the clients for a period of 2 min, as described previously. Contingent upon the absence of a target SIB, sensory-stimulating toys were made available in the same manner as described previously. Implementation of these procedures was accomplished by the CETA staff member assigned to each participant.

Follow-up. During follow-up sessions, contingencies remained essentially the same as in the previous condition. However, implementation of the treatment program was turned over exclusively to the direct care staff assigned to the clients' living unit. Feedback was given to the staff regarding the application of the procedure via the unit program supervisor (fourth author) in a manner similar to that concerning other programs conducted on the living unit.

Experimental Design

Following the collection of baseline data for all three participants, the two minute protective time-out plus sensory stimulating toy play condition was implemented in a multiple baseline design across Ron and Marjie, and in an A-B fashion for James. The follow-up condition was implemented for Marjie and James to provide an assessment of the procedure when run completely by direct care staff on a long-term basis (i.e., over a period of 104 and 100 calendar days, respectively). Follow-up was not possible for Ron, due to his transfer to a nursing home during the final experimental condition.

Results and discussion

Data for Ron and Marjie are presented in Figure 4, and data for James are presented in Figure 5. All three clients typically exhibited rates of SIB during baseline equivalent to those seen at the onset of Experiment 1. Upon implementation of treatment, rapid reductions were noted for all three participants. Mean changes from baseline to treatment were as follows: Ron, 48% to 7.2%; Marjie, 47% to 6.4%; James, 63.2% to 1.9%. Additionally, the percentage of time each client wore the equipment also decreased throughout the treatment condition and corresponded to reductions in SIB. Ron was in protective equipment an average of 13.1% of his days, Marjie 33.6%, and James 4.2%. Means for the final five days of treatment showed further reductions in equipment usage. During this period, Ron was in the protective equipment 6%, Marjie 13.8%, and James 0.0%. Thus, both the reductions in SIB as well as the percentage of time in protective equipment were very close to the results found in Experiment 1.

A major goal of Experiment 2 was to evaluate the procedure when implemented by nonprofessional staff. This was accomplished during the follow-up phase of treatment with Marjie and James. Although Ron was discharged to a nursing home, his discharge was contingent upon the development of a procedure that would successfully control his SIB. Several visits to the nursing home conducted by the institution's social service staff over a period of 6 mo suggested that the procedure was being carried out and that Ron's level of

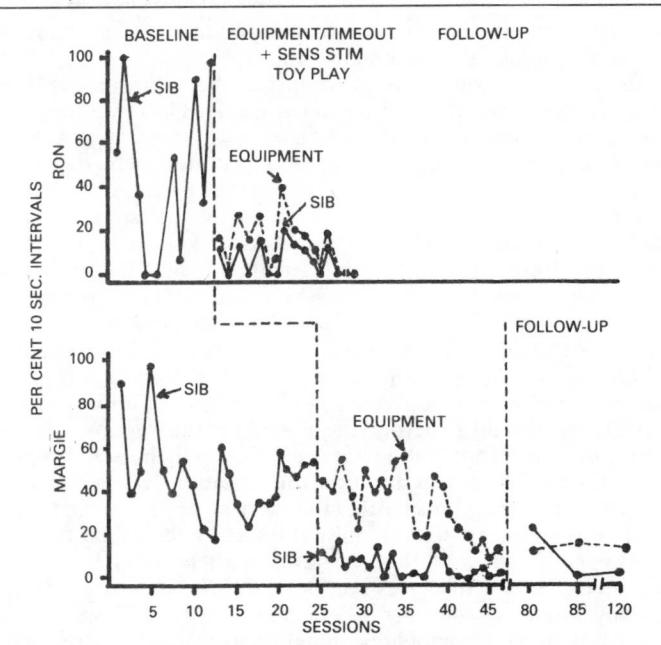

Fig. 4 Percentage of intervals of SIB (solid lines) and protective equipment (broken lines) across experimental conditions for Ron and Marjie (Experiment 2).

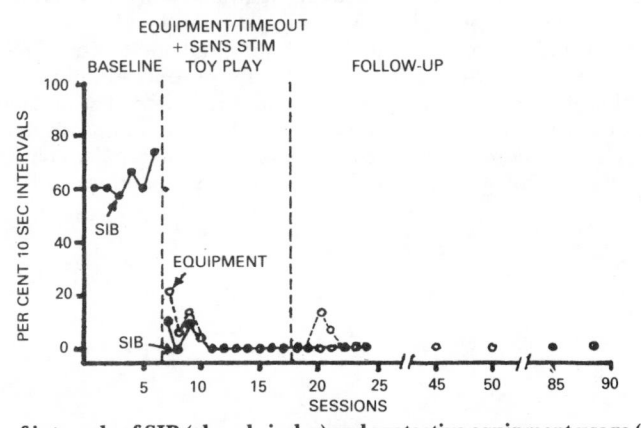

Fig. 5. Percentage of intervals of SIB (closed circles) and protective equipment usage (open circles) across experimental conditions for James (Experiment 1).

SIB was being maintained at acceptably low levels.

Follow-up data for Marjie and James indicated that the direct care staff assigned to work with them were able to implement the procedure successfully. Results of the first probe conducted with Marjie 48 calendar days after the termination of the treatment condition showed an increase in SIB, while data for the second and third probes conducted 55 and 104 calendar days post-treatment were comparable to those found at the termination of experimenter-implemented treatment. Similar results were noted for James, with these use of the equipment observed during only one of the follow-up probes over a period of 100 calendar days following the termination of experimenter-implemented treatment.

General discussion

Results suggest that the use of protective equipment may affect both rapid and substantial decreases in SIB. In addition, the data from Experiment 2 suggest that the combination of contingent protective equipment and access to sensory-stimulating toys may support the maintenance of treatment gains.

The use of the protective equipment procedure in the reduction of SIB seems justified relative to many aversive procedures currently available. The development of a hierarchy of techniques, based upon the model of "less restrictive" procedures (May, Risley, Twardosz, Friedman, Bijou, Wexler et al., 1975) would seem to include contingent protective equipment as a more desirable procedure than even "mild" aversive stimulation. The technique does not require that the client be exposed to stimuli which, subjectively, cause pain to the individual. In addition, the procedure affords the client some degree of protection from self-inflicted injury during treatment, but does not include many of deleterious components of common forms of restraint (e.g., arm splints, camisoles). However, two issues should be considered prior to its general use.

First, precautions should be taken to ensure the safety of the client, as well as others within his or her environment when the procedure is used. Care should be taken to protect the client from extreme bursts of responding which may occur initially as a function of the procedure. That is, one should go beyond the intensity of the response as it exists in baseline when considering the type of apparatus to be used. Although this aspect may be critical for a small segment of the total treatment duration, the final effectiveness of the procedure may rest upon this specific issue. It is possible that the use of an apparatus that does not attenuate severe levels of responding may serve only to intensify the initial level of responding. Additionally, physical features of the apparatus must be considered in relation to its potential use as an instrument of aggression. Devices such as helmets or faceguards may be potentially used by the client to increase the effectiveness of aggressive behavior. Whenever possible, the apparatus selected should be designed so as to take these potential problems into consideration.

Second, learning principles from which this treatment is derived may be important when considering its use. The procedure was originally designed, based upon the work of Rincover (1978) and Rincover et al. (1979) with self-stimulatory behaviors. Rincover suggested that certain classes of behavior directly produce reinforcement of a sensory nature, and that if one could mask or attenuate this source of stimulation, the response would decrease as a function of extinction. Although the present study did not provide data to support such a position, clearly, the behaviors had many similar characteristics to those behaviors studied by Rincover, in that they were highly repetitive and seemed to occur in

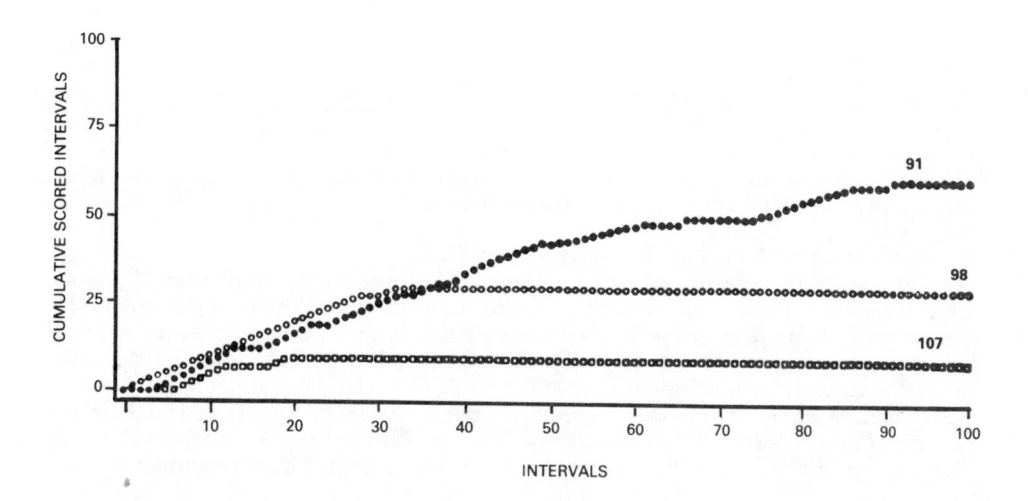

Fig. 6. Cumulative number of intervals in which Ron engaged in SIB during sessions 91, 98, and 107 (Experiment 1).

the absence of any external consequences. Because of the risk of physical injury these behaviors posed to the participants, however, manipulations such as those conducted by Rincover were not attempted. In the absence of such data, one can only speculate as to the actual conceptual basis of the procedure. However, one means of empirical support can be seen through a within-session analysis of responding during treatment. Skinner (1938) described a typical extinction curve as having "a high rate of elicitation maintained for a short time" subsequent to the termination of the delivery of reinforcement contingent upon responding, a fluctuating response rate later within the session, and a smooth flattened curve finally developing. Continued reexposure to such a situation, as was created in this experiment, should have caused progressively flatter curves each time the client came in contact with the protective equipment. That is, a discrimination would be established between the within-session equipment condition and the between-session reinforcement condition. The records presented in Figure 6 show cumulative, within-session responding for Ron during sessions 91, 98, and 107 within the continuous protective equipment condition of Experiment 1. The data appear to match the typical pattern of responding described by Skinner and add some support to the position that the phenomenon observed in this experiment was an extinction effect. If, in fact, such a conceptual basis is a correct assumption, the procedure would provide an alternative whose focus is directly in line with those variables responsible for the maintenance of some forms of SIB. Such an approach in the selection of a treatment technique would seem to have a higher probability of success than an attempt to reduce SIB through the manipulation of contingencies irrespective of the variables responsible for the behavior.

An alternative explanation for the procedure's effectiveness is that the placement of equipment on the client and removal of access to toys combined with systematic ignoring is simply a time-out procedure in which the client is protected from physical injury. The reduction in SIB would then be attributed to the contingent removal of social attention and/or preferred activities. A third position that must be considered is that the application of the apparatus acts as an aversive stimulus, causing a decrease in responding simply as a function of punishment. The determination of which, if any, of these three potential variables are responsible for the procedure's effectiveness seems to be an important issue and one that should be resolved through future research. Th results of such an analysis should not detract from the procedure's technical or ethical significance. In fact, if those results tended to support either the time-out or punishment paradigms, as opposed to the sensory extinction model, the technique's generalized applicability would seem enhanced.

Finally, the results of the present study should be considered in relation to other research findings on the use of restraint procedures. As noted previously, restraint may have reinforcing as well as punishing properties. Although the present study adds yet another example of the punishing effects, it should be noted that the devices used were different from those described by Favell et al. (1978, 1981), in that they did not restrict the subjects' movement during treatment. Rather, they served only to protect the individuals from self-inflicted harm. Although this difference may have contributed to a divergence in the results of the two studies, a number of other variables may function to establish restraint as either a reinforcing or punishing event, including increased adult attention and/or increased physical comfort during periods of restraint (Favell et al., 1978), the opportunity to escape from a more aversive environment (Carr, 1977), or the discriminative properties of restraint as a "safety signal" from response requirements or aversive events (Jones, Simmons, & Frankel, 1974). Nevertheless, it is apparent that restraint can have similar effects on the occurrence of a common target behavior when used in different ways. This observation underscores the importance of improving our understanding of the motivational variables responsible for a client's behavior prior to attempting to treat the client (e.g., Iwata et al., 1982), while taking advantage of the idiosyncratic nature of reinforcers and punishers.

Reference Note
1. Schroeder, S. The analysis of self injurious behavior: Pathogenesis and treatment (DDSA H.I.P. Grant No. 51-P-2051). Chapel Hill: University of North Carolina, 1977.

References

Baer, D. M., Wolf, M. M., Risley, T. R. Some current dimensions of applied behavior analysis. *J. Appl. Behav. Anal.*, 1968; **1**, 91-97.

Carr, E. G. The motivation of self-injurious behavior: a review of some hypotheses. *Psychol. Bull.*, 1977; **84**, 800-816.

Dorsey, M. F., Iwata, B. A., Ong, P., McSween, T. E. Treatment of self-injurious behavior using a water mist: Initial response suppression and generalization. *J. Appl. Behav. Anal.*, 1980; **13**, 343-354.

Favell, J. E., McGimsey, J. F., Jones, M. L. The use of physical restraint in the treatment of self-injury and as positive reinforcement. *J. Appl. Behav. Anal.*, 1978; **11**, 225-242.

Favell, J. E., McGimsey, J. F., Jones, M. L., Cannon, P. R. Physical restraint as positive reinforcement. *Am. J. Ment. Defic.*, 1981; **85**, 425-432.

Hamilton, J., Stephens, L., Allen, P. Controlling aggressive and destructive behavior in severely retarded institutionalized residents. *Am. J. Ment. Defic.*, 1967; **71**, 852-856.

Iwata, B. A., Dorsey, M. F., Slifer, K. J., Bauman, K. E., Richman, G. S. Toward a functional analysis of self-injury. *Anal. & Intervent. Development. Disabil.*, 1982; **2**, 3-20.

Joint Commission on Accreditation of Hospitals. *Standards for Residential Facilities for the Mentally Retarded.* Chicago: Accreditation Council for Facilities for the Mentally Retarded, 1975.

Jones, F. H., Simmons, J. Q., Frankel, F. An extinction procedure for eliminating self-destructive behavior in a nine-year-old autistic girl. *J. Autism & Child. Schiz.*, 1974; **4**, 241-250.

Lovaas, I. O., Simmons, J. Manipulation of self-destruction in three retarded children. *J. Appl. Behav. Anal.*, 1969; **2**, 143-157.

May, J. G., Risley, T. R., Twardosz, S., Friedman, P., Bijou, S. W., Wexler, D., *et al.* Guidelines for the use of behavioral procedures in state programs for retarded persons. *MR Research*, 1975: **1**.

Parrish, J. M., Aguerrevere, L., Dorsey, M. F., Iwata, B. A. The effects of protective equipment on self-injurious behavior. *Behav. Ther.*, 1980; **3**, 28-29.

Powell, J., Martindale, A., Kulp, S. An evaluation of time-sampling measures of behavior. *J. Appl. Behav. Anal.*, 1975; **8**, 463-469.

Rapoff, M. A., Altman, K., Christophersen, E. R. Elimination of a blind child's self-hitting by response-contingent brief restraint. *Educ. & Treat. Child.*, 1980; **3**, 231-236.

Rincover, A. Sensory extinction: a procedure for eliminating self-stimulatory behavior in developmentally disabled children. *J. Abnorm. Child Psychol.*, 1978; **6**, 299-310.

Rincover, A., Cook, R., Peoples, A., Packard, D. Sensory extinction and sensory reinforcement principles for programming multiple adaptive behavior change. *J. Appl. Behav. Anal.*, 1979; **12**, 221-234.

Rojahn, J., Mulick, J. A., McCoy, D., Schroeder, S. R. Setting effects, adaptive clothing, and the modification of head banging and self-restraint in two, profoundly retarded adults. *Behav. Anal. & Modif.*, 1978; **2**, 185-196.

Rojahn, J., Schroeder, S. R., Mulick, J. A. Ecological assessment of self-protective devices in three profoundly retarded adults. *J. Autism & Dev. Disord.*, 1980; **10**, 59-66.

Skinner, B. F. *The Behavior of Organisms.* Englewood Cliffs, N.J.: Prentice-Hall, 1938.

Reprinted from *J. Appl. Behav. Anal.*, 1982; **15**:2, 217-230 by kind permission of the authors and the publishers JABA, University of Kansas, Lawrence, Kansas 66045.

A BEHAVIORAL/PHARMACOLOGICAL INTERVENTION FOR THE TREATMENT OF SEVERE SELF-INJURIOUS BEHAVIOR[1]

V. Mark Durand[2]

State University of New York at Stony Brook

The effects of haloperidol and a mild punishment on the severe self-injurious behavior and several collateral behaviors of a 17-year-old profoundly retarded male were assessed. A 12-month analysis using a withdrawal design suggested that neither the medication nor the behavioral intervention alone was effective in significantly reducing the frequency of self-injurious behavior. When combined, however, these interventions produced dramatic reductions in the subject's self-injurious behavior. The haloperidol may have acted as a "setting event" for the successful use of the punishment. Suppression of this behavior was maintained at six months and 1 year following the end of the analysis. The collateral behaviors were differentially affected by the behavioral and pharmacological interventions. Time spent in bed and the appearance of drooling increased with the introduction of the haloperidol, while percent correct on a fine motor-task increased only when the interventions were applied simultaneously. The results point out the importance of a careful behavioral analysis for both pharmacological and behavioral interventions and their possible combined actions.

Perhaps the most disruptive and disturbing behavior pattern exhibited by developmentally disabled individuals is severe self-injury. While self-injurious behavior frequently interferes with most habilitative efforts in more extreme cases these behaviors can be life-threatening and/or can lead to permanent physical damage. Research on the function of self-injurious behavior has suggested that it may be multiply motivated (Carr, 1977). Implicated in the maintenance of self-injury has been social attention (Lovaas & Simmons, 1969), escape from aversive situations (Carr, Newsom, & Binkoff, 1976), sensory consequences (Durand, Note 1), and possible operant/organic interactions (Carr & McDowell, 1980).

Due to the serious nature of these behaviors, the interventions used most frequently include physical restraints (Favell, McGimsey, Jones, & Cannon, 1981) and pharmacological treatments (Campbell, 1973). Although noncontingent physical and chemical restraints are the most frequently used interventions, most systematic research on the treatment of self-injurious behavior has involved response-contingent procedures (Russo, Carr, & Lovaas, 1979). While interventions that do not involve aversive consequences have been well documented (e.g., Repp & Deitz, 1974), for more chronic and severe cases, the treatment of choice has been contingent aversive stimulation in combination with the reinforcement of alternative behaviors (Bachman, 1972; Smolev, 1971). Even this type of intrusive intervention has not always produced durable clinical control (e.g., Romanczyk & Goren, 1975).

The present study decribes one of the first systematic attempts to analyze the combined effects of a behavioral and pharmacological intervention in the treatment of self-injury. The unexpected results of the successful interaction of the two treatments are presented.

[1]The author wishes to thank Deborah Herriford, James Mikesell, Gil Langley, Joseph Higgins, Jim's parents, and the staff of Unit 3C of the Northern Virginia Training Center for their continued faith and efforts. The author gratefully acknowledges Paul Dores and Edward G. Carr for their invaluable comments on the manuscript. Special thanks go to Wendy Spiewak Durand for her editorial assistance and inspiration.
[2]Address all correspondence to V. Mark Durand, Department of Psychology, SUNY at Stony Brook, Stony Brook, New York 11794.

Method

Subject

The subject (Jim) was a 17-year-old profoundly retarded male who had been institutionalized since the age of 4. Self-injurious behavior appears to have begun at approximately 7 years of age. Two years prior to the present analysis, hits to his face, neck, and legs had become increasingly severe, requiring medical attention. In order to prevent further injury, various restraint devices and intensive behavioral programs were attempted in order to suppress Jim's self-injury (including differential reinforcement and overcorrection). Following these unsuccessful attempts at behavioral control, Jim was administered 4 mg of haloperidol per day for 6 months prior to the present analysis. No significant improvement in self-injury was observed.

Setting

All observations and therapy sessions were conducted either in Jim's residential unit or in the adjacent cafeteria. The unit consisted of one large dayroom surrounded by five bedrooms. Down the hall from the unit was the cafeteria. Two therapists took turns observing and working with Jim for a total of 5 hours per day, 5 days per week. Once or twice per week a third person was assigned to covertly observe Jim in order to check on the reliability of the observations.

A fine-motor program conducted in the dayroom and a mealtime program in the cafeteria were used to record the frequency of Jim's self-injury. These two programs allowed for the reinforcement of behaviors incompatible with the self-injury (placing blocks in a box and appropriate self-feeding, respectively). During all nonprogram times (approximately 3 hours per day), the therapist checked Jim every 5 minutes to record if (1) he was in bed and/or (2) if there was saliva on his chin. These two behaviors were selected for monitoring since the unit staff reported that increased time in bed and drooling appeared to be side effects of the haloperidol. Previous attempts to control drooling with anticholinergics (e.g., Artane) were unsuccessful.

Dependent variables

Self-injury was defined as the frequency of hits (or attempted hits) by the fingertips to the face, head, or legs. Percent correct on the fine motor-task was calculated by counting the number of shapes Jim placed in the box and dividing that number by the total number of possible correct responses (45 per session). Observer agreements for self-injury and the fine-motor task were obtained by dividing the lowest frequency/percentage into the highest for each session.

Data on drooling and time spent in bed were recorded as their presence or absence for each 5-minute interval. Drooling was defined as any moisture on Jim's chin. Time spent in bed was defined as any time Jim was sitting or lying on any bed in the unit. Observer agreement was obtained by dividing the number of intervals of agreement by the number of agreements plus disagreements.

Procedure

This investigation employed a withdrawal design (Hersen & Barlow, 1976). All changes in the interventions were approved prior to their implementation by Jim's parents, unit staff, and the institutions' human rights committee.

Medication Alone 1. This phase lasted 2 weeks and served as a preintervention baseline. Jim continued to receive 4 mg of haloperidol per day. A therapist recorded self-injury data during meals and observed Jim on the unit from 3:oo p.m. to 7:oo p.m., 5 days per week. During mealtimes, Jim's restraints were removed and the therapist would stand behind him, physically preventing Jim's attempts to make contact with his face. This "shadowing procedure" was necessitated by the extensive lacerations already on Jim's face. The therapist recorded the frequency of these attempted hits and verbally reinforced eating with a fork.

Twice per day the therapist conducted a 15-minute session of a fine motor-task with Jim in the dayroom. Using a wooden form box (Childcraft, No. 75M413), the therapist handed a wooden ball or cube to Jim every 20 seconds and said, "In." If after 10 seconds no response was made, Jim was physically and verbally prompted to bring his hand up to the box. Each correct, unprompted response was reinforced with praise and edibles. The therapist recorded percent correct and the number of attempted hits. During all nontasks and nonmealtimes, the therapist would check Jim every 5 minutes to record time in bed and drooling. Jim's restraints remained on during these times.

Medication and Punishment 1. Anecdotal reports from the staff indicated that Jim avoided contact with his hands (e.g., he avoided fingernail clipping and hand washing). This sensitivity appeared to have begun following the initial administration of the haloperidol. It was decided that contingent pressure to his hands could serve as a punisher that carried little risk of producing injury. The medication and procedures for this phase were identical to the previous phase, with the addition of this consequence for Jim's self-injury (during the fine motor-task and mealtimes). Contingent upon each hit, the therapist would lightly squeeze Jim' hand for 1 second and say, "No hitting." For the final 10 weeks of the phase (weeks 8-17) and during subsequent conditions, Jim's arm restraints were removed and he was consequated in all settings.

Punishment Alone. This phase was an attempt to withdraw the haloperidol from the treatment regime. Jim's physical therapist and his physician observed him closely during the postneuroleptic withdrawal phase for any behavioral changes. All procedures remained the same. The therapists and reliability checker were not informed of the medication change until 4 weeks following the complete withdrawal. The titration schedule for the haloperidol proceeded as follows: (a) 3mg/day at week 18, (b) 2 mg at week 20, (c) 1 mg at week 22, and (d) 0 mg at weeks 24-34. No additional side effects (e.g., dyskinetic movements, behavioral deterioration) were observed.

Medication and Punishment II. Haloperidol was reintroduced due to the failure of the punishment alone to suppress the self-injury. The haloperidol was reintroduced as follows: (a) 2 mg/day at week 36 and (b) 4 mg at week 38. Again the therapists and reliability checker were not informed of the medication changes. All previous procedures remained the same.

Medication Alone II. A 3-day withdrawal of the behavioral intervention occurred during week 49. This was a planned attempt to assess the function of the punishment almost 1 year following its initial implementation. All procedures were identical to the Medication Alone I phase.

Medication and Punishment III. This last phase consisted of all of the same procedures of Medication and Punishment I and II. During weeks 50-54, the therapists trained the unit staff in the punishment technique as well as the fine-motor task and mealtime program. At 6 and 12 months following this training, the therapists observed the staff working with Jim and collected data on Jim's self-injury and collateral behaviors.

Results

Observer agreement data for self-injury averaged 82% (range = 68-100%). Observer agreement for percent time in bed and drooling averaged 98% and 89.3%, respectively. Agreement on the fine-motor task equalled 100%.

The frequencies of Jim's self-injurious hits are presented in Fig. 1, collapsed across settings (i.e., cafeteria and dayroom) since no significant differences were observed. The baseline produced frequencies averaging 310.4 hits/hr. The addition of the punishment

Table 1. Collateral effects

Experimental phase	% correct fine-motor	% of intervals in bed	% of intervals drooling
Medication alone I	32.0	95	78
Medication and punishment I	74.3	91	83
Punishment alone	11.5	12	9
Medication and punishment II	79.8	90	73
Medication alone II[a]	17.3	100	85
Medication and punishment III	85.1	94	81
6-month follow-up	95.4	93	77
12-month follow-up	94.9	90	92

[a] This phase lasted 3 days.

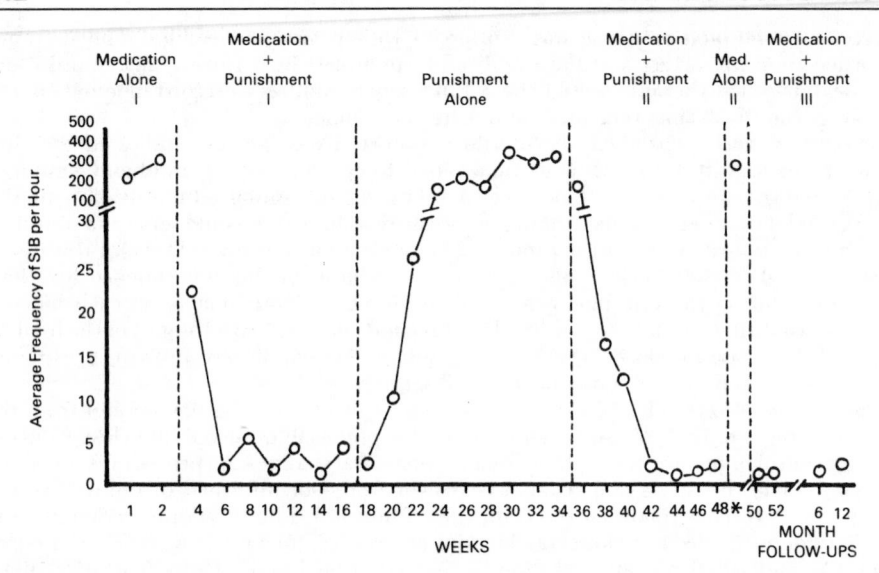

Fig. 1. Average frequencies of Jim's self-injurious hits per hour as a function of experimental conditions. The asterisk (*) indicates the 3-day withdrawal of the punishment contingency during week 49.

along with the drug resulted in a rapid decrease in the frequency of hits (means = 5.8 hits/hr. Withdrawal of medication (Punishment Alone) produced a concomitant increase in the frequency of self-injury (mean = 241.0 hits/hr). The reintroduction of the haloperidol (Medication and Punishment II) again resulted in a reduction of self-injury (mean = 33.7 hits/hr). The 3-day withdrawal of punishment (Medication Alone II) produced a rapid increase in self-injury (mean = 352.0 hits/hr), and was again suppressed following the reintroduction of the punishment (Medication and Punishment III, mean = 2.1 hits/hr). This suppression was maintained at 6 (mean = 1.2 hits/hr) and 12 months (mean = 2.5 hits/hr) following the end of the analysis.

Performance on the fine-motor task was lowest (mean = 13.7%) during those phases where the frequency of self-injury was highest (Medication Alone I and II and Punishment Alone), and highest (mean = 78.2%) when self-injury was lowest (Medication and Punishment I, II, and III). Significant reductions in Jim's drooling were seen only with the absence of the medication (Punishment Alone, mean = 9%). Similarly, the only time Jim spent less than 90% of his free time in bed was when the haloperidol was withdrawn (Punishment Alone, mean = 12%).

Discussion

This investigation appears to be the first systematically documented case of the successful treatment of severe self-injurious behavior using both behavioral and pharmacological interventions. The 12-month analysis suggested that the combined effects of the punishment and medication produced the first successful suppression of Jim's self-injury, improved his task performance, but also resulted in increased drooling and social isolation. Increased time in bed and drooling appeared to be side effects of the drug, while Jim's fine-motor performance seems to have been a function of the presence of a physically incompatible behavior, self-injury. The combination of treatments was so effective in reducing Jim's self-injury that his restraints could be removed during most of day and lacerations on his face healed completely for the first time in years. Maintenance of treatment gains were observed at 6 and 12 months following the end of the analysis.

Clinical and ethical exigencies resulted in several design concessions (e.g., a no-treatment baseline was not attempted due to concerns that Jim's behavior would worsen). Because of these and other limitations (e.g., only one subject), generalization of these results to other individuals would be premature and must await replication. These findings, however, should provide impetus to clinicians to closely evaluate the combined actions of behavioral and pharmacological interventions.

Interpretation of the interactive effects of the interventions is difficult. One could hypothesize that the unit staff, who knew of the drug manipulations, could possibly have influenced Jim's behavior. However, the fact that the therapists and the reliability checker were unaware of the drug changes would cast serious doubt on this interpretation. One additional explanation is that the haloperidol may have made Jim's hands and fingers more sensitive to pressure, thereby increasing the aversiveness of the hand squeeze. In support of this hypothesis, staff did report that when no drug was administered, Jim did not avoid contact with his hands. This avoidance reappeared with the reintroduction of the haloperidol. This interpretation suggests that the haloperidol may have acted as a "setting event" (Bijou & Baer, 1961); that is, the haloperidol produced an antecedent condition (hand sensitivity), which interacted with the consequating function of the hand squeeze. This case study should provide a valuable heuristic for future research efforts in the area of setting events and self-injury (Lazarus & Davison, 1971).

This case is not presented as an endorsement of the use of either punishment or pharmacological interventions for self-injurious behavior. Punishment remains a controversial issue, especially when used with children (Romanczyk, Colletti, & Plotkin, 1980). In addition, pharmacological treatments await convincing demonstrations of their effectiveness (Sprague & Baxley, 1978). What is advocated is the careful analysis of the full range of possible controlling variables influencing the behavior of the client. While it is sometimes the case that a clinician is prevented from performing an appropriate functional analysis prior to treatment (as was the case for Jim's severe self-injury), all possible environmental and organic influences should be explored experimentally. This expanded functional analysis, including medical-behavioral interactions (Thomson & Boren, 1977), should lead to more effective individualized treatments for the more persistent cases of self-injurious behavior.

Reference note
1. Durand, V. M. *Assessment of self-injurious behavior in a retarded male: a case of multiple motivations.* Paper presented at the 13th Annual Convention of the Association for Advancement of Behavior Therapy, San Francisco, 1979.

References
Bachman, J. A. Self-injurious behavior: a behavioral analysis. *J. Abnorm. Psychol.*, 1972; **80**, 211-224.
Bijou, S. W., Baer, D. M. *Child development I: A systematic and empirical theory.* Englewood Cliffs, New Jersey: Prentice-Hall, 1961.
Campbell, M. Biological interventions in psychoses of childhood. *J. Autism & Child. Schiz.*, 1973; **3**, 347-373.
Carr, E. G. The motivation of self-injurious behavior: a review of some hypotheses. *Psychol. Bull.*, 1977; **84**, 800-816.
Carr, E. G., McDowell, J.J. Social control of self-injurious behavior of organic etiology. *Behav. Ther.*, 1980; **11**, 402-409.
Carr, E. G., Newsom, C. D., Binkoff, J. A. Stimulus control of self-destructive behavior in a psychotic child. *J. Abnorm. Child Psychol.*, 1976; **4**, 139-153.
Favell, J. E., McGimsey, J. F., Jones, M. L., Cannon, P. R. Physical restraint as positive reinforcement. *Am. J. Ment. Defic.*, 1981; **35**, 425-432.
Hersen, M., Barlow, D. H. *Single Case Experimental Designs: strategies for studying behavior change.* New York: Pergamon, 1976.
Lazarus, A. A., Davison, G. C. Clinical innovation in research and practice. *In* Bergin, A. E., Garfield, S. L. (Eds.). *Handbook of Psychotherapy and Behavior Change.* New York: Wiley, 1971.
Lovaas, O. I., Simmons, J. Q. Manipulation of self-destruction in three retarded children. *J. Appl. Behav. Anal.*, 1969; **2**, 143-157.
Repp, A. C., Deitz, S. M. Reducing aggressive and self-injurious behavior of institutionalized retarded children through reinforcement of other behavior. *J. Appl. Behav. Anal.*, 1974; **7**, 313-325.
Romanczyk, R. G., Colletti, G., Plotkin, R. Punishment of self-injurious behavior: issues of behavior analysis, generalization, and the right to treatment. *Child. Behav. Ther.*, 1980; **2**, 37-54.

Romanczyk, R. G., Goren, E. R. Severe self-injurious behavior: the problem of clinical control. *J. Consult. & Clin. Psychol.*, 1975; **43**, 730-739.

Russo, D. C., Carr, E. G., Lovaas, O. I. Self-injury in pediatric populations. *In* Ferguson, J., Taylor, C. B. (Eds.). *Advances in Behavioral Medicine.* Holliswood, New York: Spectrum, 1979.

Smolev, S. R. Use of operant techniques for the modification of self-injurious behavior. *Am. J. Ment. Defic.*, 1971; **76**, 295-305.

Sprague, R. L., Baxley, G. B. Drugs for behavior management, with comments on some legal aspects. *In* Wortis, J. (Ed.). *Mental Retardation and Developmental Disabilities: an annual review.* New York: Brunner/Mazel, 1978.

Thomson, T., Boren, J. J. Operant behavioral pharmacology. *In* Honig, W. K., Staddon, J. E. R. (Eds.). *Handbook of Operant Behavior.* Englewood Cliffs, New Jersey: Prentice-Hall, 1977.

Reprinted from *J. Autism & Dev. Disord.,* 1982; **12**:3, 243-251 by kind permission of V. Mark Durand and the publishers Plenum Publishing Corp., New York, NY 10013.

Reviews of the literature

There are several excellent brief reviews of the literature pertaining to self-injurious behaviour. We have deliberately not included them in the book but, for readers who are interested, we have listed the recent ones here.

Baumeister, A. A., Rollings, J. P. Self-injurious behavior. *In* Ellis, N. R. (Ed.). *International Review of Research in Mental Retardation (Vol. 8).* New York: Academic Press, 1976.

Carr, E. G. The motivation of self-injurious behaviour: a review of some hypotheses. *Psychol. Bull.,* 1977; **84,** 800-816.

Corbett, J. Aversion for the treatment of self-injurious behaviour. *J. Ment. Defic. Res.,* 1975; **19,** 79.

*Hollis, J. H., Meyers, C. E. *Life-threating Behavior: analysis and intervention.* Washington DC: American Association on Mental Deficiency, 1982.

Favell, J. E. (Ed.). Self-injurious behaviour. *Analysis and Intervention in Developmental Disabilities,* 1982; **2.** A special issue of the journal, containing a series of excellent articles on recent research in SIB.

Frankel, F., Simmons, J. Q. Self-injurious behavior in schizophrenic and retarded children. *Am. J. Ment. Defic.,* 1976; **80,** 512-522.

Russo, D. C., Carr, E. G., Lovaas, O. I. Self-injury in pediatric populations. *In* Ferguson, J. M., Taylor, C. B. (Eds.). *The Comprehensive Handbook of Behavioral Medicine (Vol. 3).* New York: Spectrum, 1980.

Schroeder, S. R., Mulick, J. A., Rojahn, J. The definition, taxonomy, epidemiology and ecology of self-injurious behavior. *J. Autism and Dev. Disorders,* 1980; **10,** 417-432.

Singh, N. N. Current trends in the treatment of self-injurious behavior. *Advances in Pediatrics,* 1981; **28,** 377-440.

*This is a full-length book with chapters on various kinds of life-threatening behaviour.

References

Altman, K., Haavik, S., Higgins, S. T. Modifying the self-injurious behavior of an infant with spina bifida and diminished pain sensitivity. *J. Behav. Ther. & Exp. Psychiat.,* 1983; **14**, 165-168.

Anderson, L. T., Dancis, J., Alpert, M., Herrmann, L. Punishment learning and self-mutilation in Lesch-Nyhan syndrome. *Nature,* 1977; **265**, 461-463.

Axelrod, B., Nachtigal, R., Dancis, J. Familial dysautonomia: diagnosis, pathogenesis, and management. *Adv. in Pediat.,* 1974; **21**, 75-96.

Azrin, N. H., Gottlieb, L., Hughart, L., Wesolowski, M. D., Rahn, T. Eliminating self-injurious behavior by educative procedures. *Behav. Res. & Ther.,* 1975; **13**, 101-111.

Bailey, J., Meyerson, L. Effect of vibratory stimulation on a retardate's self-injurious behavior. *Psychol. Aspects of Disabil.,* 1970; **17**, 340-344.

Ball, T. S., Sibbach, L., Jones, R., Steele, B., Frazier, L. An accelerometer activated device to control assaulting and self-destructive behaviors in retardates. *J. Behav. Ther. & Exper. Psychiat.,* 1975; **6**, 223-228.

Ballinger, B. R. Minor self-injury. *Br. J. Psychiat.,* 1971; **118**, 535-538.

Bandura, A. *Principles of Behavior Modification,* (Ch. 3). New York: Holt, Rinehart & Winston, 1969.

Bartak, L., Rutter, M. Differences between mentally retarded and normally intelligent autistic children. *J. Autism & Child. Schiz.,* 1976; **6**, 109-120.

Baumeister, A. A. Origins and control of stereotyped movements. *In* Meyer, C. E. (Ed.). *Quality of Life in Severely and Profoundly Mentally Retarded People: Research Foundations for Improvement.* Washington DC: Am. Assoc. on Ment. Defic., 1978.

Baumeister, A. A., Forehand, R. Stereotyped acts. *In* Ellis, N. R. (Ed.). *International Review of Research in Mental Retardation (Vol. 6).* New York: Academic Press, 1973.

Baumeister, A. A., Rollings, J. P., Self-injurious behavior. *In* Ellis, N. R. (Ed.). *International Review of Research in Mental Retardation (Vol. 8).* New York: Academic Press, 1976.

Berkson, G. Abnormal stereotyped motor acts. *In* Zubin, J., Hunt, H. F. (Eds.). *Comparative psychopathology: Animal and Human.* New York: Grune & Stratton, 1967.

Berkson, G., Mason, W. A. Stereotyped movements of mental defectives: IV — the effects of toys and the character of the acts. *Am. J. Ment. Defic.,* 1964; **68**, 511-524.

Blackman, D. *Operant Conditioning: an experimental analysis of behaviour.* London: Methuen, 1974.

Blakemore, C. Maturation and modification in the developing visual system. *In* Held, R., Leibowitz, H. W., Teuber, H. L. (Eds.). *Perception: Handbook of Sensory Physiology (Vol. 8.).* Berlin: Springer Verlag, 1978.

Borreson, P. M. The elimination of a self-injurious avoidance response through a forced running consequence. *Ment. Retard.,* 1980; **18**, 73-77.

Boyd, E. M., Dolman, M., Knight, L. M., Sheppard, E. P. The chronic oral toxicity of caffeine. *Can. J. Physiol. & Pharmacol.,* 1965; **43**, 995-1007.

Bryson, Y., Sakati, N., Nyhan, W. L., Fish, C. H. Self-mutilative behavior in the Cornelia de Lange syndrome. *Am. J. Ment. Defic.*, 1971; **76**, 319-324.

Bull, M., La Vecchio, F. Behavior therapy for a child with Lesch-Nyhan syndrome. *Develop. Med. & Child Neurol.*, 1978; **20**, 368-375.

Butterfield, W. H. Electric shock — safety factors when used for the aversive conditioning of humans. *Behav. Ther.*, 1975; **6**, 98-110.

Bychowski, G. Problems of infantile neurosis: discussion. *In* Eisler, R. S., *et al.* (Eds.). *The Psychoanalytic Study of the Child. (Vol. IX).* London: Imago, 1954.

Carr, E. G. The motivation of self-injurious behaviour: a review of some hypotheses. *Psychol. Bull.*, 1977; **84**, 800-816.

Carr, E. G., McDowell, J. J. Social control of self-injurious behavior of organic etiology. *Behav. Ther.*, 1980; **11**, 402-409.

Carr, E. G., Newsom, C. D., Binkoff, J. A. Escape as a factor in the aggressive behavior of two retarded children. *J. Appl. Behav. Anal.*, 1980; **13**, 101-107.

Carr, E. G., Newsom, C. D., Binkoff, J. A. Stimulus control of self-destructive behavior in a psychotic child. *J. Abnorm. Child Psychol.* 1976; **4**, 139-153.

Carr, J. Imitation, generalisation, and discrimination. *In* Yule, W., Carr, J. (Eds.). *Behaviour Modification for the Mentally Handicapped.* London: Croom Helm, 1980(a).

Carr, J. *Helping Your Handicapped Child.* Harmondsworth: Penguin, 1980(b).

Christie, R., Bay, C., Kaufman, I. A., Bakay, B., Borden, M., Nyhan, W. L. Lesch-Nyhan disease: clinical experience with nineteen patients. *Develop. Med. & Child Neurol.*, 1982; **24**, 293-306.

Corbett, J. Aversion for the treatment of self-injurious behaviour. *J. Ment. Defic. Res.*, 1975; **19**, 79.

Corbett, J. A., Campbell, H. J. Causes of severe self-injurious behavior. *In* Mittler, P. (Ed.). *Frontiers of Knowledge in Mental Retardation (Vol. II).* Baltimore: University Park Press, 1981.

Corbett, J. A. Mental Retardation: psychiatric aspects. *In* Rutter, M., Hersov, L. (Eds.). *Child Psychiatry: Modern Approaches.* London: Blackwell Scientific, 1977.

Davenport, R. K., Berkson, G. Stereotyped movements of mental defectives: II — Effects of novel objects. *Am. J. Ment. Defic.*, 1963; **67**, 879-882.

Davenport, R. K., Menzel, E. W. Stereotyped behavior of the infant chimpanzee. *Archiv. Gen. Psychiat.*, 1963; **8**, 99-104.

Davies, C. A., Katz, H. B. The separate and combined effects of early undernutrition and environmental complexity at different ages on cerebral measures in rats. *Develop. Psychobiol.*, 1983; **16**, 47-58.

De Catanzaro, D. A., Baldwin, G. Effective treatment of self-injurious behavior through a forced arm exercise. *Am. J. Ment. Defic.*, 1978; **83**, 433-439.

De Lissovoy, V. Head banging in early childhood: a study of incidence. *Pediatrics*, 1961; **58**, 803-805.

De Lissovoy, V. Head banging in early childhood: *Child Dev.*, 1962; **33**, 43-56.

De Lissovoy, V. Head banging in early childhood: a suggested cause. *J. Genet. Psychol.*, 1963; **102**, 109-114.

Dorsey, M. F., Iwata, B. A., Reid, D. H., Davis, P. A. Protective equipment: continuous and contingent application in the treatment of self-injurious behavior. *J. Appl. Behav. Anal.*, 1982; **15**, 217-230.

Duker, P. C., Seys, D. M. Elimination of vomiting in a retarded female using restitutional over-correction. *Behav. Ther.*, 1977; **8**, 255-257.

Durand, V. M. A behavioral/pharmacological intervention for the treatment of severe self-injurious behavior. *J. Autism & Dev. Disord.,* 1982(a); **12**, 243-251.

Durand, V. M. Analysis and intervention of self-injurious behavior. *J. Assoc. Severely Disabled,* 1982(b); **7**, 44-53.

Durand, V. M., Crimmins, D. B. *The motivation assessment scale.* Personal communication, 1984.

Edelson, S. M., Taubman, M. T., Lovaas, O. I. Some social contexts of self-destructive behavior. *J. Abnorm. Child Psychol.,* 1983; **II**, 299-312.

Epstein, L. H., Doke, L. A., Sajwaj, T. E., Sorrell, S., Rimmer, B. Generality of side-effect of overcorrection. *J. Appl. Behav. Anal.,* 1974; **7**, 385-390.

Favell, J. E., McGimsey, J. F., Jones, M. L., Cannon, P. R. Physical restraint as positive reinforcement. *Am. J. Ment. Defic.,* 1981; **4**, 425-432.

Favell, J. E., McGimsey, J. F., Schell, R. M. Treatment of self-injury by providing alternate sensory activities. *Anal. & Intervention in Dev. Disabil.,* 1982; **2**, 83-104.

Fleming, A., Nolley, D. A comparison of techniques for the elimination of self-injurious behavior in a mildly retarded woman. *J. Behav. Ther. & Exp. Psychiat.,* 1981; **12**, 81-85.

Frankel, F., Simmons, J. Q. Self-injurious behavior in schizophrenic and retarded children. *Am. J. Ment. Defic.,* 1976; **80**, 512-522.

Frith, C. D., Johnstone, E. C., Joseph, M. H., Powell, R. J., Watts, R. W. E. Double-blind clinical trial of 5-hydroxytryptophan in a case of Lesch-Nyhan syndrome. *J. Neurol., Neurosurg. & Psychiat.,* 1976; **39**, 656-662.

Freud, A. Problems of infantile neurosis: discussion. *In* Eissler, R. S., *et al.* (Eds.) *The Psychoanalytic Study of the Child (Vol. IX).* London: Imago, 1954.

Goldfarb, W. Pain reactions in a group of institutionalised schizophrenic children. *Am. J. Orthopsychiat.,* 1958; **28**, 777-785.

Goodall, E., Corbett, J. Relationships between sensory stimulation and stereotyped behaviour in severely retarded children. *J. Ment. Defic. Res.,* 1982; **26**, 163-175.

Green, A. H. Self-mutilation in schizophrenic children. *Arch. Gen. Psychiat.,* 1967; **17**, 234-244.

Greenacre, P. Problems of infantile neurosis: discussion. *In* Eissler, R. S., *et al.* (Eds.). *The Psychoanalytic Study of the Child (Vol.IX).* London: Imago, 1954.

Harkness, J. E., Wagner, J. E. Self-mutilation in mice associated with otitis media. *Laboratory Animal Science,* 1975; **25**, 315-318.

Harlow, H. F., Harlow, M. K. Psychopathology in monkeys. *In* Kimmel, H. D. (Ed.). *Experimental Psychopathology.* New York: Academic Press, 1971.

Harris, S. L., Ersner-Hershfield, R. Behavioral suppression of seriously disruptive behavior in psychotic and retarded patients: a review of punishment and its alternatives. *Psychol. Bull.* 1978; **85**, 1352-1375.

Hollis, J. H., Meyers, C. E. *Life-threatening Behavior: analysis and intervention.* Washington, DC: American Association on Mental Deficiency, 1982.

Iwata, B. A., Dorsey, M. F., Slifer, K. J., Bauman, K. E., Richman, G. S. Towards a functional analysis of self-injury. *Anal. & Intervention in Dev. Disabil.,* 1982; **2**, 3-20.

Iwata, B. A., Pace, G. M., Cataldo, M. F., Kashler, M. J., Edwards, G. L. A center for the study and treatment of self-injury. *In* Griffin, *et al.* (Eds.). *Advances in the Treatment of Self-Injurious Behavior.* Austin, Texas: Dept. of Health & Human Services, Texas Planning, Council for Developmental Disabilities, 1984.

Jones, F. H., Simmons, J. Q., Frankel, F. An extinction procedure for eliminating self-destructive behavior in a 9-year-old autistic girl. *J. Autism & Child. Schiz.,* 1974; **4**,

241-250.

Kazdin, A. E. *Behavior Modification in Applied Settings* (p.192) Homewood, Ill.: Dorsey, 1975.

Kiloh, L. G., Gye, R. S., Rushworth, R. G., Bell, D. S., White, R. T. Stereotactic amygdaloidotomy for aggressive behaviour. *J. Neurol. Neurosurg. & Psychiat.*, 1974; **37**, 437-444.

Kish, G. B. Sensory reinforcement. *In* Honig, W. K. (Ed.). *Operant Behavior: areas of research and application*. New York: Appleton Century Crofts, 1966.

Kravitz, H., Boehm, J. J. Rhythmic habit patterns in infancy: their sequence, age of onset, and frequency. *Child Develop.*, 1971; **42**, 399-413.

Kravitz, H., Rosenthal, V., Teplitz, Z., Murphy, J. B., Lesser, R. E. A study of head-banging in infants and children. *Dis. Nerv. Syst.*, 1960; **21**, 203-208.

Lang, P. J., Melamed, B. G. Case report: Avoidance conditioning therapy of an infant with chronic ruminative vomiting. *J. Abnorm. Psychol.*, 1969; **7**, 1-8.

Leitenberg, H. Is time-out from positive reinforcement an aversive event? A review of the experimental evidence. *Psychol. Bull.*, 1965; **64**, 428-441.

Lesch, M., Nyhan, W. L. A familial disorder of uric acid metabolism and central nervous system function. *Am. J. Medicine*, 1964; **36**, 561-570.

Levison, C. A. The development of head-banging in a young rhesus monkey. *Am. J. Ment. Defic.*, 1970; **75**, 323-328.

Lichstein, K. L., Schreibman, L. Employing electric shock with autistic children: a review of the side effects. *J. Autism & Child. Schiz.*, 1976; **6**, 163-173.

Lloyd, K. G., Hornykiewicz, O., Davidson, L., Shannak, K., Farley, I., Goldstein, M., Shibuya, M., Kelley, W. N., Fox, I. H. Biochemical evidence of dysfunction of brain-neurotransmitters in the Lesch-Nyhan syndrome. *New England J. Medicine*, 1981; **305**, 1106-1111.

Lourie, R. S. The role of rhythmic patterns in childhood. *Am. J. Psychiat.*, 1949; **105**, 653-660.

Lovaas, O. I., Simmons, J. Q. Manipulation of self-destruction in three retarded children. *J. Appl. Behav. Anal.*, 1969; **2**, 143-157.

Lutzker, J. R. Reducing self-injurious behavior by facial screening. *Am. J. Ment. Defic.*, 1978; **82**, 510-513.

Maisto, C. R., Baumeister, A. A., Maisto, A. A. An analysis of variables related to self-injurious behaviour among institutionalised retarded patients. *J. Ment. Defic. Res.*, 1978; **22**, 27-36.

Marholin, D., Luiselli, J. K., Robinson, M., Lott, I. T. Response contingent taste aversion in treating chronic ruminative vomiting of institutionalised profoundly retarded children. *J. Ment. Defic. Res.*, 1980; **24**, 47-56.

Mason, W. A. Early social deprivation in the non-human primates: implications for human behavior. *In* Glass, D. C. (Ed.). *Environmental Influences*. New York: Rockefeller University Press and Russell Sage Foundation, 1968.

Mason, W. A., Green, P. C. The effects of social restriction on the behavior of Rhesus monkeys: IV — Responses to a novel environment and to an alien species. *J. Comparat. & Physiolog. Psychol.*, 1962; **55**, 363-368.

Mason W. A., Sponholz, R. R. Behavior of rhesus monkeys raised in isolation. *J. Psychiat. Res.*, 1963; **1**, 299-306.

Matson, J. L., Stephens, R. M., Smith, C. Treatment of self injurious behaviour with over-correction. *J. Ment. Defic. Res.*, 1978; **22**, 175-178.

McCoull, G. *Report on the Newcastle-on-Tyne Regional Aetiological Survey of Mental Retardation 1966-1971.* (Mimeographed Research Report.). 1971.

Measel, C. J., Alfieri, P. A. Treatment of self-injurious behavior by a combination of positive reinforcement for incompatible behavior and overcorrection. *Am. J. Ment. Defic.,* 1976, **81**, 147-153.

Meyerson, L., Kerr, N., Michael, J. L. Behaviour modification in rehabilitation. *In* Bijou, S. W., Baer, D. M. (Eds.). *Child Development: Readings in Experimental Analysis.* New York: Appleton Century Crofts, 1967.

Mizuno, T., Yugari, Y. Self-mutilation in Lesch-Nyhan syndrome. (Letter). *The Lancet,* 1974; **1**, 761.

Morgan, H. *Death wishes? The Understanding and Management of Deliberate Self-harm.* Chichester: John Wiley, 1979.

Morgan, L. L. Schneiderman, N., Nyhan, W. L. Theophylline: induction of self-biting in rabbits. *Psychonomic Science,* 1970; **19**, 37-38.

Murphy, G., Carr, J., Callias, M. Increasing simple toy play in the profoundly mentally handicapped: II — Designing special toys. *J. Autism & Develop. Discord.,* 1985; **15**.

Murphy G. Decreasing undesirable behaviours. *In* Yule, W., Carr, J. (Eds.). *Behaviour Modification for the Mentally Handicapped.* London: Croom Helm, 1980.

Murphy G. Overcorrection: a critique. *J. Ment. Defic. Res.,* 1978; **22**, 161-173.

Murphy, G. Self-injurious behaviour in the mentally handicapped: an update. *Assoc. Child Psychol. & Psychiat. Newsletter,* 1985; **7**, 2-11.

Murphy, G. Sensory reinforcement in the mentally handicapped and autistic child: a review. *J. Autism & Develop. Disord.,* 1982; **12**, 265-278.

Murphy, G. *Ways of increasing simple toy play in the profoundly mentally handicapped child.* (Unpublished Ph.D. thesis.). London: University of London, 1983.

Murphy, G., Wilson, B. Long term outcome of contingent shock treatment for self-injurious behavior. *In* Mittler, P. (Ed.). *Frontiers of Knowledge in Mental Retardation (Vol. 2).* Baltimore: University Park Press, 1981.

Nyhan, W. L. Behavior in the Lesch-Nyhan Syndrome. *J. Autism & Child Schiz.,* 1976; **6**, 235-252.

Nyhan, W. L. The Lesch-Nyhan Syndrome. *Dev. Med. Child Neurol.,* 1978; **20**, 376.

Nyhan, W. L., Johnson, H. G., Kaufman, I. A., Jones, K. L. Serotonergic approaches to the modification of behavior in the Lesch-Nyhan syndrome. *Appl. Res. Ment. Retard.,* 1980; **1**, 25-40.

Paul, H. A., Romanczyk, R. G. The use of air splints in the treatment of self-injurious behavior. *Behav. Ther.,* 1973; **4**, 320-321.

Primrose, D. A. Treatment of self-injurious behaviour with a GABA (gamma-aminobutyric acid) analogue. *J. Ment. Defic. Res.,* 1979; **23**, 163-173.

Rapoff, M. A., Altman, K., Christophersen, E. R. Suppression of self-injurious behaviour: determining the least restrictive alternative. *J. Ment. Defic. Res.,* 1980; **24**, 37-46.

Richardson, J. S., Zaleski, W. A. Naloxone and self-mutilation. *Biolog. Psychiat.,* 1983; **18**, 99-101.

Richmond, J. B., Eddy, E., Green, M. Rumination: a psychosomatic syndrome of infancy. *Pediatrics,* 1958; **12**, 49-55.

Rincover, A. Sensory extinction: a procedure for eliminating self-stimulatory behavior in developmentally disabled children. *J. Abnorm. Child Psychol.,* 1978; **6**, 299-310.

Rincover, A., Cook, R., Peoples, A., Packard, D. Sensory extinction and sensory reinforcement principles for programing multiple adaptive behavior change. *J. Appl. Behav. Anal.,* 1979; **12**, 221-233.

Rincover, A., Devaney, J. The application of sensory extinction procedures to self-injury. *Anal. & Intervention in Develop. Disabilities,* 1982; **2**, 67-81.

Rincover, A., Newson, C. D., Lovaas, O. I., Koegel, R. L. Some motivational properties of sensory reinforcement with psychotic children. *J. Experi. Child Psychol.,* 1977; **24**, 312-323.

Risley, T. R. The effects and side-effects of punishing the autistic behaviors of an autistic child. *J. Appl. Behav. Anal.,* 1968; **1**, 21-34.

Rojahn, J., Mulick, J. A., McCoy, D., Schroeder, S. R. Setting effects, adaptive clothing, and the modification of head-banging and self-restraint in two profoundly retarded adults. *Behav. Anal. & Modif.,* 1978; **2**, 185-196.

Romanczyk, R. G., Goren, E. R. Severe self-injurious behavior: the problem of clinical control. *J. Consult. & Clin. Psychol.,* 1975; **43**, 730-739.

Russo, D. C., Carr, E. G., Lovaas, O. I. Self-injury in pediatric populations. *In* Ferguson, J. M., Taylor, C. (Eds.). *The Comprehensive Handbook of Behavioral Medicine (Vol. 3).* New York: Spectrum, 1980.

Sajwaj, T., Libet, J., Agras, S. Lemon-juice therapy: the control of life-threatening rumination in a six-month-old infant. *J. Appl. Behav. Anal.,* 1974; **7**, 557-563.

Sallustro, F., Atwell, C. W. Bodyrocking, head-banging, and head-rolling in normal children. *Pediatrics,* 1978; **93**, 704-708.

Schaefer, H. H. Self-injurious behavior: shaping "head-banging" in monkeys. *J. Appl. Behav. Anal.,* 1970; **3**, 111-116.

Schroeder, S. R., Mulick, J. A., Rojahn, J. The definition, taxonomy, epidemiology, and ecology of self-injurious behavior. *J. Autism & Develop. Disorders,* 1980; **10**, 417-432.

Schroeder, S. R., Schroeder, C. S., Smith, B., Dalldorf, J. Prevalence of self-injurious behaviors in a large State facility for the retarded: a three-year follow-up study. *J. Autism & Child. Schiz.,* 1978; **8**, 261-269.

Singh, N. N. Current trends in the treatment of self-injurious behavior. *Adv. in Pediatrics,* 1981; **28**, 377-440.

Singh, N. N., Beale, I. L., Dawson, M. J. Duration of facial screening and suppression of self-injurious behavior: analysis using an alternating treatments design. *Behav. Assess.,* 1981; **3**, 411-420.

Singh, N. N., Gregory, P. R., Pulman, R. M. Treatment of self-injurious behaviour: a three year follow-up. *New Zealand Psychologist,* 1980; **9**, 65-67.

Singh, N. N., Pulman, R. M. Self-injury in the De Lange syndrome. *J. Ment. Defic. Res.,* 1979; **23**, 79-84.

Slawson, P. F., Davidson, P. W. Hysterical self-mutilation of the tongue. *Arch. Gen. Psychiat.,* 1964; **11**, 581-588.

Spain, B., Hart, S. A., Corbett, J. The use of appliances in the treatment of severe self-injurious behaviour.

Spitz, R. H. Problems of infantile neurosis: discussion. *In* Eissler, E. R., *et al.* (Eds.). *The Psychoanalytic Study of the Child. (Vol. IX).* London: Imago, 1954.

Steen, P. L., Zuriff, G. E. The use of relaxation in the treatment of self-injurious behavior. *J. Behav. Ther. & Exp. Psychiat.,* 1977; **8**, 447-448.

Tanner, B. A., Zeiler, M. Punishment of self-injurious behavior using aromatic ammonia as the aversive stimulus. *J. Appl. Behav. Anal.,* 1975; **8**, 53-57.

Tate, B. G., Baroff, G. S. Aversive control of self-injurious behavior in a psychotic boy. *Behav. Res. & Ther.,* 1966; **4**, 281-287.

Wells, M. E., Smith, D. W. Reduction of self-injurious behavior of mentally retarded persons using sensory-integration techniques. *Am. J. Ment. Defic.,* 1983; **87**, 664-666.

Williams, C. *Strategies of intervention with the profoundly retarded visually-handicapped child: a brief report of a study of stereotypy. Occasional Papers II, No. II,* (pp.68-72). British Psychological Society (Division of Education and Child Psychology). Leicester: BPS, 1978.

Williams, C., Surtees, P. Behaviour modification with children: mannerisms, mutilation and management. *In* Brengelmann, J. C. (Ed.). *Behaviour Therapy.* Berlin: Springer-Verlag, 1975.

Young, J. A., Wincze, J. P. The effects of the reinforcement of compatible and incompatible alternative behaviors on the self-injurious and related behaviors of a profoundly retarded female adult. *Behav. Ther.,* 1974; **5**, 614-623.

Yule, W., Carr, J. *Behaviour Modification for the Mentally Handicapped.* London: Croom Helm, 1980.

Zuk, G. H. Psychodynamic implications of self-injury in defective children and adults. *J. Clin. Psychol.,* 1960; **16**, 58-60.

Index